I0446064

RUTH ASAWA AND THE ARTIST-MOTHER AT MIDCENTURY

RUTH ASAWA AND THE ARTIST-MOTHER AT MIDCENTURY

JORDAN TROELLER

THE MIT PRESS   Cambridge, Massachusetts   London, England

© 2025 Massachusetts Institute of Technology

All rights reserved. No part of this book may be used to train artificial intelligence systems or reproduced in any form by any electronic or mechanical means (including photocopying, recording, or information storage and retrieval) without permission in writing from the publisher.

This book was supported with funding from the The Andy Warhol Foundation Arts Writers Grant and the Freigeist Fellowship of the Volkswagen Foundation.

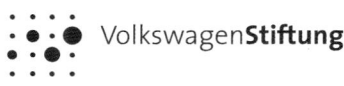

The Andy Warhol
Foundation
Arts Writers
Grant

The MIT Press would like to thank the anonymous peer reviewers who provided comments on drafts of this book. The generous work of academic experts is essential for establishing the authority and quality of our publications. We acknowledge with gratitude the contributions of these otherwise uncredited readers.

This book was set in Nimbus and Minion by the MIT Press. Printed and bound in China.

Library of Congress Cataloging-in-Publication Data is available.

ISBN: 978-0-262-04949-8

10   9   8   7   6   5   4   3   2

To Bruno, Ramona, Jack, and Ruby for showing the way,
and to Immanuel for making it possible

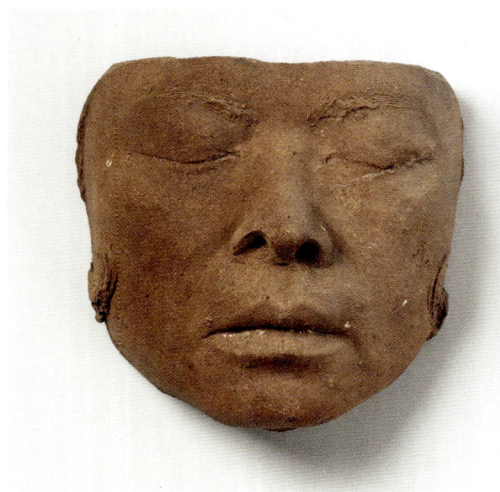

Taking us by and large, we're a queer lot
We women who write poetry. And when you think
How few of us there've been, it's queerer still.
I wonder what it is that makes us do it,
Singles us out to scribble down, man-wise,
The fragments of ourselves. Why are we
Already mother-creatures, double-bearing,
With matrices in body and in brain?
—Amy Lowell, "The Sisters" (1925)

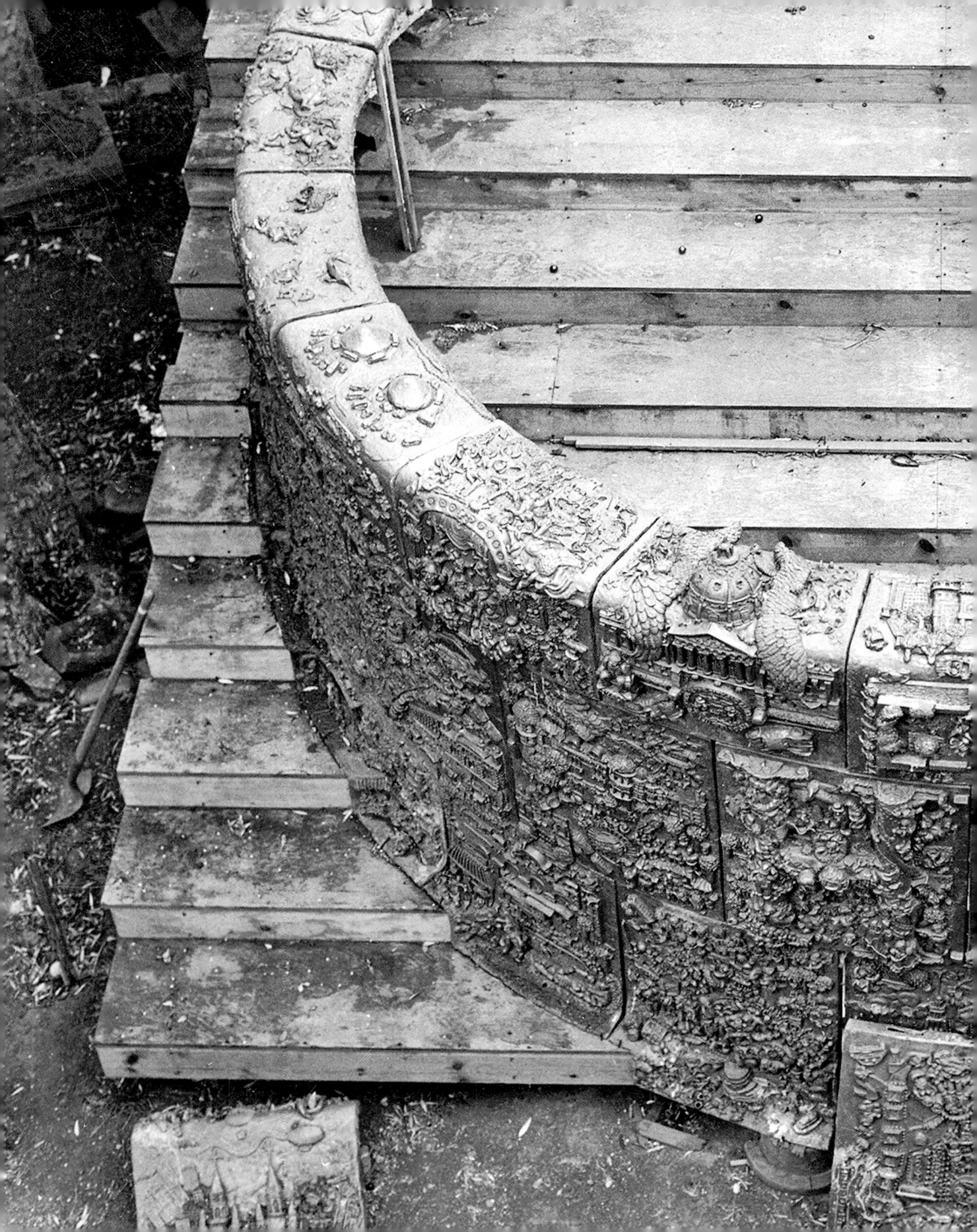

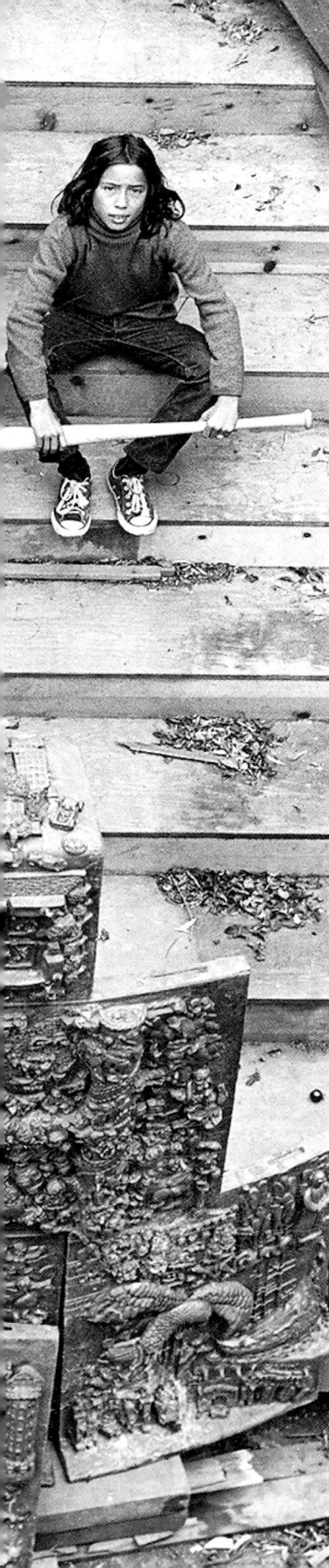

CONTENTS

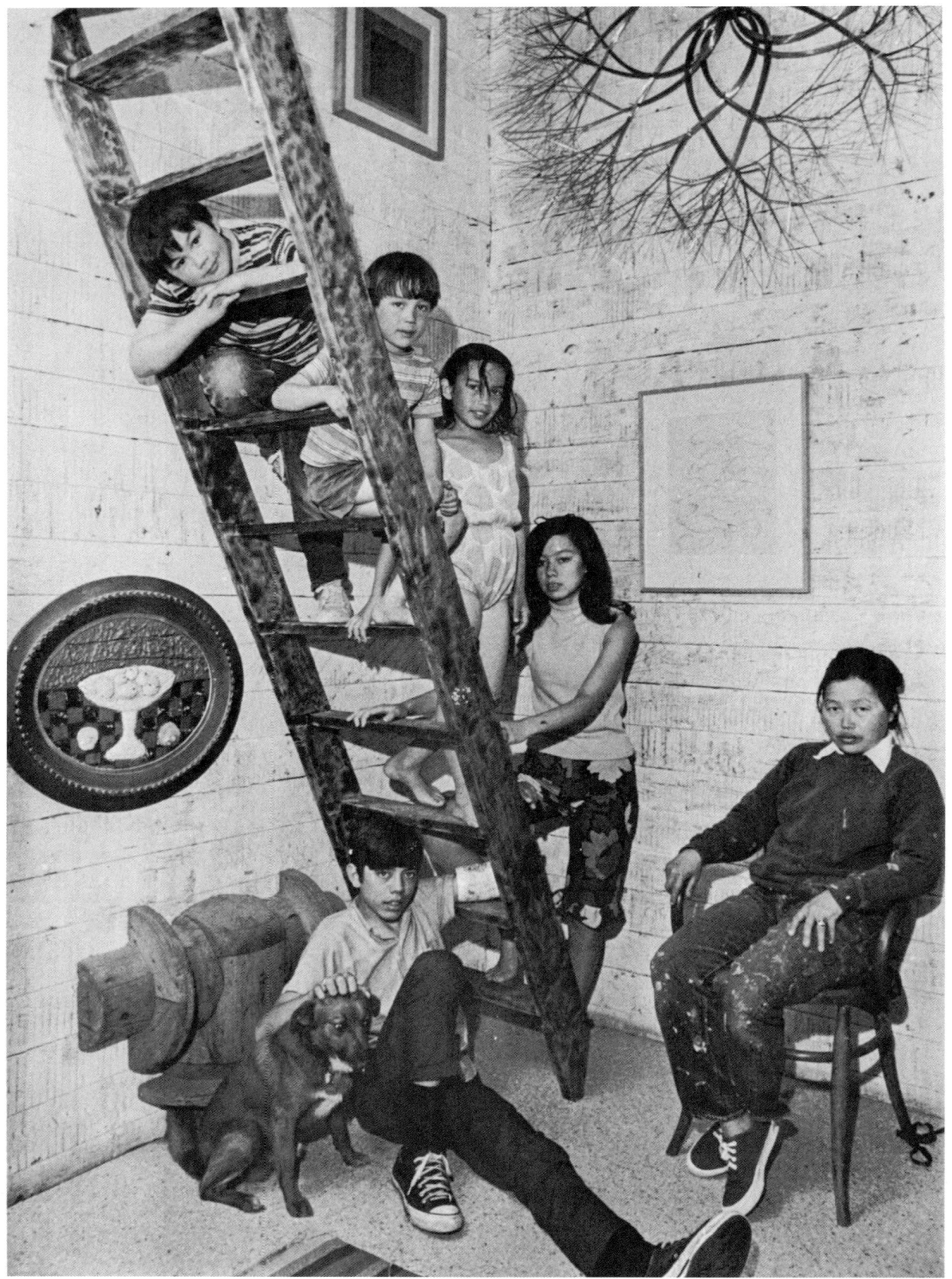

INTRODUCTION: ART AND MOTHERHOOD

Open the book *Portraits of Artists* by photographer John Waggaman, and you will find an unfamiliar portrayal of the artist in the mid-twentieth century: there she is with plaster-spattered jeans, a dark sweatshirt, and sneakers, sitting patiently for Waggaman's camera with an unamused expression that suggests she would rather be working (fig. 0.1). The caption, "Ruth Asawa, Sculptor, San Francisco," declares her to be a solitary artist; the domestic scene itself, though, tells another story, one of relationality, dependence, and community, narrated through multiple figures, both present and absent. An *Homage to the Square* by her mentor, the German painter and pedagogue Josef Albers, hovers above them, while a framed drawing of yellow squashes by Asawa's friend Georgia Guback, an artist and children's book illustrator, hangs on the wall behind her. Nearby is a still life, thick with encaustic, by Peggy Tolk-Watkins, whom Asawa and her husband the architect Albert Lanier had met while all three were studying at Black Mountain College and who, like Asawa and Lanier, had also moved to the San Francisco Bay Area in the late 1940s. These artworks attest to important social bonds, and they echo the most consequential aspect of the photograph: the presence of Asawa's children. Several perch on the ladder that led up to one of the bedrooms in the house, while another lounges on the floor, petting the family dog. All stare confidently at the photographer, as if the portrait of their artist-mother constituted a portrait of them, too.

This photograph is remarkable because it pictures the artist as a mother. Asawa is one of four women who appear in Waggaman's book of fifty-seven photographs of painters and sculptors. The publication accompanied an exhibition of the same name, which toured California in the late 1960s, making its way from San Diego up through the Central Valley into the San Francisco Bay Area and back down to Los Angeles. All of the artists were living and working in the state, and some of the names are by now well-known outside of that context, like John Baldessari and Sam Francis. Waggaman

0.1 "Ruth Asawa, Sculptor, San Francisco," from *Portraits of Artists: Photographs by John Waggaman* (San Diego: La Jolla Museum of Art, 1967).

pictures all of these artists, except Asawa, alone, and often in studios alongside their work. Joan Brown bears a cropped haircut and a striped T-shirt and holds a cigarette in her hand, while Karen Kozlow poses in a flower-print dress and knee-high boots next to a groovy wall painting. Such attributes—cigarette, Twiggy bob, stylish clothes—meet expectations of what a woman artist looks like and how she should be pictured. It is predictable, too, that Brown's son is absent, even if imagery related to him shaped her paintings after his birth in 1962.

What is astonishing in Asawa's portrait is how decidedly it departs from this script. Against these prototypical images of artistic femininity, Asawa foregrounds her status as a mother working from home. Her portrait as an artist is coextensive with her portrait as a mother in the sense that we cannot say where her artistic persona stops and her maternal identity begins. Asawa, her children, and the close friends represented by the artworks hanging on the wall all figure artistic identity as a series of meaningful relationships. Behold the maker of the metal branching sculpture mounted to the wall in this photograph, and you behold a woman raising six children and an artist serving her community, soon to be a leading force in the public schools and in the city's Art Commission. "My need to be an artist," she wrote definitively, "does not exceed my desire to be a parent, and also [to be] part of a community."[1]

To portray an artist's identity as not simply coincident with her motherhood but dependent upon it was utterly unheard of in midcentury America. This was an era when the solitary male artist—pervasive in Waggaman's photos—dominated public perception. Although many women who made art also indeed had children, few allowed themselves to be identified with this role. As feminist critic Lucy Lippard wrote in 1973, looking back on these decades, "the few women artists making it in the 1950s and 1960s were rarely housewives, and anybody who was took care to hide it when showing her work in the serious art world. (Because women were considered 'part-time artists' if they worked for a living outside of art, or were married, or had a child, they didn't have to be taken seriously.)"[2] Lippard's use of the parenthetical aside gestures to how such an observation was simply taken for granted. Every woman knew that the consequences of collapsing these two personas—mother and artist—were severe, resulting in ostracism and invisibility. To borrow from the Bay Area writer Ursula K. Le Guin, who belonged to Asawa's generation, this "received wisdom" stipulated "that any attempt to combine art work with housework and family responsibilities is impossible, unnatural. And the punishment for unnatural acts, among the critics and the Canoneers, is death."[3]

This book tells the story of life after death. Spanning the 1950s into the early 1970s, it argues for the difference that motherhood made to midcentury art, with a focus on Ruth Asawa and the San Francisco Bay Area. Originally from southern California, where she was born in 1926, Asawa moved to the city in 1949 after studying at the Milwaukee State Teachers College and at Black Mountain College in North Carolina, and she resided in San Francisco until her death in 2013. It was in her neighborhood on Saturn Street in the 1950s and then, from 1961 onward, in the nearby Noe Valley district that she established a vital community of other women artists, many of whom were also mothers. Often working collaboratively and with children, she generated an immense body of work that encompasses paintings and watercolors; ink, pencil, and stamped drawings; looped- and tied-wire sculptures; elaborate paperfolds; life casts in plaster, concrete, and bronze; and almost a dozen monumental public sculptures. Employing a visual idiom that spanned design, craft, and fine art, Asawa began to gain recognition in the mid-1950s, while caring for a growing family with Lanier. Despite offers of childcare, she made the pivotal decision against pursuing a career as an artist in New York—then the center of the commercial art world in the United States—seeing a career there as too precarious to warrant uprooting her family.[4] Instead she reinvented being both a mother and an artist, defining these roles on her own terms, terms under which both pursuits thrived. She chose nontoxic materials, like wire and paper, and methods that allowed her to work from home without a child-free, dedicated studio. Once her youngest child had started school, she shifted her attention to art in public space, establishing in 1968, with fellow artist-mother and art historian Sally Woodbridge, the first artist-led arts program in the city's schools. The Alvarado School Arts Workshop become a pioneering endeavor, even applauded by the National Endowment for the Arts.

As the Waggaman photo suggests, Asawa's home was full to the brim with work that she, her children, and a community of artist-mothers had made. This proliferation was a crucial component of her artistic commitment to motherhood. Artworks were often created with gift-giving in mind and subsequently bestowed on neighbors, friends, relatives, and colleagues. In the 1970s, Asawa enlisted her photographer son-in-law Laurence Cuneo to locate and photograph these works in an effort to record her prolific production. A few decades later, she and Lanier hired an assistant and began the Sisyphean task of cataloguing her sculptural production, almost all of which had the generic title of *Untitled*. Roughly a decade before her death, she admitted that while the sculptures could feasibly be catalogued, inventorying the drawings would be virtually impossible.[5] This abundance characterized not only the amount of work but its formal character as well, in which repetition was often employed as a technique. She began casting, for instance, in the early 1960s. First experimenting with casting the faces of friends and family members, Asawa soon began casting her own sculptures. When she became a grandmother in 1975, the situation accelerated. Drawings and casts of tiny hands and feet proliferated, at three weeks, at five months, at half a year, and on it went (figs. 0.2, 0.3). She titled these works accordingly: "Ken's Hands and Feet, 3 Weeks Old" reads one entry on the checklist for an exhibition at Capricorn Asunder, the municipal art gallery. This replicatory logic is so pervasive that it is not known how many such casts Asawa made. In her hands, the making of art becomes a potentially endless process. The brilliance of this gesture is in having outpaced the mechanisms we have for distinguishing art from non-art, original from copy, an Asawa life cast from just anybody's life cast. If, as stipulated by institutions like the art market and catalogue raisonné, an artwork conventionally entails some degree of uniqueness, then objects such as these are not properly artworks at all. On the one hand, they are utterly original, in that they capture a unique individual's features at a specific moment in time; on the other hand, their logic of repetition generalizes this individuality indefinitely. These are casts of little Ken's hands and feet, but in principle any infant hand or foot could do, thereby rendering originality generic.

Whether Asawa intended it or not, her predilection for generating work upon work, in close dialogue with family and friends and with little regard for the work's afterlife on the art market or in collections, challenged one of art's untouchable axioms: that art is an object set aside from life, to be had at a high price—which Asawa's work now commands—and above all, not to be touched. (The casts of little Ken's hands and feet, for instance, live in a home in which they are indeed picked up, held, passed from one beholder to another, as I experienced on a visit as part of writing this book.) Asawa herself had little interest in building a "career," much less an oeuvre. She rarely titled works, and when she made prints or casts, she did not keep strict records of editions. The life casts are a case in point: there is seemingly no end to the number of body and body part casts she made during her lifetime. Until very recently, a decade since her death, her children were still stumbling upon casts in the basement of the house that she had lived in since 1961. As part of her work in the public schools, she made hundreds of casts of students' faces over the decades. Many of the projects in this context also revolved around repetition—replicating tried-and-true techniques like paperfolding and what she called "baker's clay," a homemade mix of flour, water, and salt, which could be air-dried or baked in the oven and cast into elaborate figurative compositions.

It is the way that such replications escape the explanatory categories of art history that particularly interests me. For I propose it has much to do with Asawa's artistic persona as a mother. She not only chose materials and methods compatible with mothering; as someone in constant dialogue with fragility, dependence, and vulnerability, she also rejected reigning definitions of the artwork as an autonomous and self-sufficient entity—as well as the reigning definition of the artist as a solitary figure toiling away in a disheveled studio. Such definitions, according to the art historian Whitney Davis, are less fact than the "imaginative, ideal condition" posited by the discipline of art history. Art history construes the existence of what he calls "nonreplicatoriness"—being utterly original, first, and unique—at the same time as it relies on replication—on citation, influence, contextualization, and the like—to make sense of such objects.[6] This is a function of the artwork's "mythology of divine creation," to borrow from Linda Nochlin, with the "divine" here coded as godlike: parthenogenic and thus unmaternal.[7] If the Mother, according to the biological script, creates bodies for the here and now, the hallowed Artist, as far as history is concerned, creates *works* for posterity.

This book argues that such "received wisdom," to invoke Le Guin again, was briefly suspended in the San Francisco that belonged to Asawa and her fellow artist-mothers. In this maternal space of making, to which few from the official art world seemed to be paying attention, arose an entirely unfamiliar brand of both art and artist. I trace the unfolding of this process in Asawa's own production, examining a range of works, from the lesser-known drawings and undervalued public sculptures to the

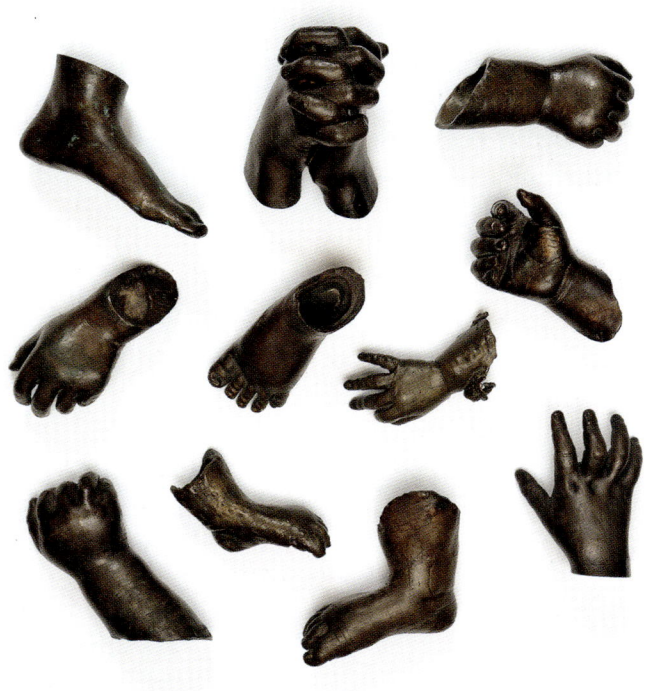

0.2 Ruth Asawa's casts of grandson Ken Cuneo's hands and feet, at various ages (three weeks to four years old), 1975–1979. Cast bronze, various sizes. Private collection.

0.3 Ruth Asawa, *Untitled* (FF.333, Baby Hands and Feet), 1978. Black ink on technical paper, 11½ × 13¾ in. Private collection.

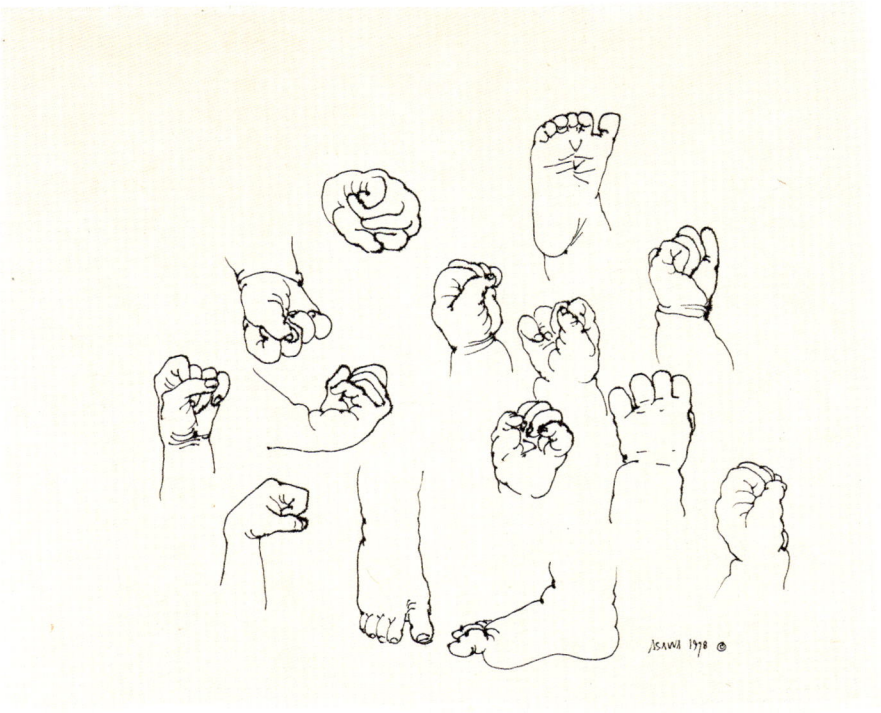

now-canonical looped- and tied-wire abstractions, to make the argument that all of this bears out a replicative logic that rejected the masterpiece by embracing motherhood. To understand this unusual moment in art's history, we have to understand such works as unfolding within a larger community of other artist-mothers—a context that has been all but erased from Asawa's reception. Barring a few exceptions, Asawa has been explained as a singular figure best represented through the monographic exhibition.[8] This book, however, situates her repetitive mode of working in a community of other artist-mothers, including Merry Renk, Sally Woodbridge, Nancy Thompson, and Imogen Cunningham. In each instance, the work produced is characterized by replication in the strong sense of the word, as used by Davis: by the embrace of the unoriginal, the mundane, the laborious, the *maternal*—of, above all, the "non-artist," as Asawa put it, citing those, including children, who have been systematically excluded from artmaking.[9] Unoriginal, though, *in the eyes of art history*. For, indeed, one could point to this or that original aspect of individual works—Asawa, for instance, was the first to use baker's clay in bronze casting. But this is beside the point; from the perspective of a discipline that deems artmaking and mothering incompatible pursuits, these women were a priori barred from the designation of Artist by virtue of their status as Mother. What that condition made possible, however, is what I explore in this study.

ARTIST-MOTHERS

A central term in the book is "artist-mother." The phrase comes from the curator of Asawa's retrospective in 1973 and condenses a longer chain of identities with which she was associated during her lifetime: "housewife-mother-artist-civic leader" names the four main ones, as the catalogue reads (with "artist" notably coming in at third place).[10] But the phrase has value beyond the specific context of Asawa's reception. Meredith A. Brown, for instance, has recently invoked this phrase "artist-mother" to describe Alice Neel, whose painted portraits negotiate "an important ambivalence between her gendered, embodied familial work, especially motherhood, and her artistic ambitions."[11] The phrase also appears in Lisa Tickner's call for a form of art history predicated on reciprocity instead of competition, a theme that I return to in chapter 3. An account of the artist-mother offers the beginnings of how we might distinguish the all-too-familiar story of the blurring of art and life endemic to American mid-twentieth-century art. Asawa's "non-artist," for instance, could be compared to Allan Kaprow's "Un-artist" and his similar effort to upend art history's ideal of autonomy.[12] But the project of the artist-mother was more specific and subversively critical than the better-known narrative embodied in Kaprow's work, for it intervened not in the gap between art and life but where the two terms became indistinguishable. These are aspects beyond the scope of this book, but they gesture to the potential of this category as an emergent object of study for art history.

My reconstruction of the artist-mother as an analytical category is much more modest: it is an attempt to lend a historical specificity and rigor to a term that has, until now, been used intermittently and in a self-evident sort of way. "Artist-mother," this book argues, does not just name a personal identity; it encodes a deep and abiding dilemma regarding how art, broadly construed, is identified and discussed. Coextensive with the era under discussion in this book, the literary scholar and fiction writer Tillie Olsen (also a Bay Area resident) coined "writer-mother" in her study of literary "silences"—literary works that, for a variety of reasons, never came to be or came to be only in an incomplete, fragmented form or that mark extended pauses in a writer's life, like Herman Melville's thirty-year break from prose. Olsen first wrote about this idea of literary silences in 1962, and her inquiry relies on her own experience as a writing mother with a full-time day job; by 1971, in a talk developing these ideas, it becomes the silenced *women* that matter most in Olsen's research, with motherhood shaping the conditions of that creative labor. Such deferrals and interruptions, Olsen argues, enable entirely new kinds of literature: the childless woman writer may have penned marvels, she writes, but had she allowed motherhood to appear in her writing, "might there not have been other marvels as well, or other dimensions to these marvels? Might there not have been present profound aspects and understandings of human life as yet largely absent in literature?"[13] These are the questions to be asked of the visual arts (and why they have not been asked until recently is a conundrum; for various reasons, literary studies came to think this problem long before art history could).

"Artist" comes first in my terminology with intention. This distinguishes the book from other efforts to assess motherhood's impact on the conditions of artistic creation by Rachel Epp Buller, Andrea Liss, Andrea O'Reilly, and Julie Phillips, among others. Phillips's study of the "mother-artist," for instance, investigates "what mothering plus creativity looks like, not just in the first few years but as part of a life story."[14] While Phillips examines the *lives* of writers and artists, including Alice Neel, in her study of "creative motherhood," my focus is not on biography. Though biography plays a role, my primary concern is tracking motherhood as a revision of authorship, grasping the multiple ways in which identifying and disidentifying as a mother shaped what art looked like and who would make it. At stake is motherhood not as a biographical horizon but as a relationship to artistic materials, a feature of artistic self-fashioning, and a condition of reception. In this respect, this study owes much to Anne M. Wagner's many insights into the sculpture of Barbara Hepworth—an artist-mother of an earlier generation than Asawa—as well as artist-mother Moyra Davey's anthology *The Mother Reader*, both of which first rendered visible for me many of the avenues of inquiry I develop in the chapters that follow.

In an attempt to employ a nonessentializing definition of motherhood, I rely on a body of writing that has dislodged this concept from the female reproductive body and biological motherhood. In recent decades, writers and theorists have pointed to the intellectual field opened up when we shift from speaking of motherhood as a noun to approaching it as a verb, as *mothering*. Angela Garbes writes, "The terrain of mothering is not limited to the people who give birth to children; it is not defined by gender," even if it may intersect with gender. It is more useful, argues Garbes, "to consider the work of raising children as mothering, an action that includes people of all genders and nonparents alike."[15] Less an identity, motherhood has become a practice, "the practice of creating, nurturing, affirming, and supporting life," argue Alexis Pauline Gumbs, China Martens, and Mai'a Williams in *Revolutionary Mothering*.[16] Such a redefinition is a result of how the term "mother" has become increasingly malleable: as Yasmine Ergas, Jane Jenson, and Sonya Michel point out, it has conventionally referred to "a woman who both bears and cares for a child. Today, however, as a consequence of transformations in reproductive technologies, social norms, and family constellations, the status of mother may be conferred on a person who fulfills only one or even neither of these roles."[17]

Although many of the women discussed in this book did have children, their status as artist-mothers is anchored less in their personal circumstances than in their having confronted, rather than turned away from, the antimaternal condition that structured artmaking at midcentury. Instead of dutifully conforming to a career without children, they embraced what poet Amy Lowell describes in the epigraph to this book as the "double-bearing" character of the artist. This is the artist who rejects art history's fantasy of the autonomous, self-sufficient work of art, embracing instead the logic of reproduction; not the artist with children per se but the artist who admits "double-bearing" as a condition of making, the artist with "matrices in body and brain"—the figure, not the literal person, of Lowell's "mother-creature." Making art, for these artist-mothers, involved dialogue with one another, with their community, and with art's responsibility to future generations. They understood their production to be enriched rather than inhibited by that exchange—and saw their double-bearing condition as enabling rather than limiting. Of course, dialogue is true of any instance of making art, but art history, especially art history in the mid-twentieth century, sublimated this fact to an ideal of individual authorship—of artistic vision so encompassing that it disallowed any other social bonds. Helen Molesworth, one of Asawa's most astute observers, illuminates this masculinist position in her comparison of photographs of Asawa working alongside her children to those depicting Jackson Pollock flinging paint onto monumental canvases on the floor of his studio.[18] Tortured expression rather than domestic maintenance guarantees the Artwork, canonical narratives of art history tell us. And this work is sequestered from daily reproduction. Once completed, it belongs to *him* as a singular achievement. To substitute *her* into this equation is to deform this ideal by introducing interruption and responsiveness as the condition of the artist-mother. It is, in the eyes of received wisdom, to become nonhuman or less than human, to become Lowell's mother-creature.

Embracing this alterity, Asawa forged close friendships with other artist-mothers who pursued practices that escaped the usual binaries of painter versus sculptor, artist versus craftsperson, writer versus practitioner. Merry Renk (1921–2012) worked in metals as a jeweler and sculptor. A portrait by the printmaker Beth Van Hoesen depicts Renk wearing her sterling silver and pearl necklace *White Clouds* (1972; fig. 0.4). She had two daughters who played with Asawa's three youngest children, and had bought a house next door on Saturn Street during the 1950s. In allowing herself to be publicly associated with motherhood, Asawa provided a powerful model

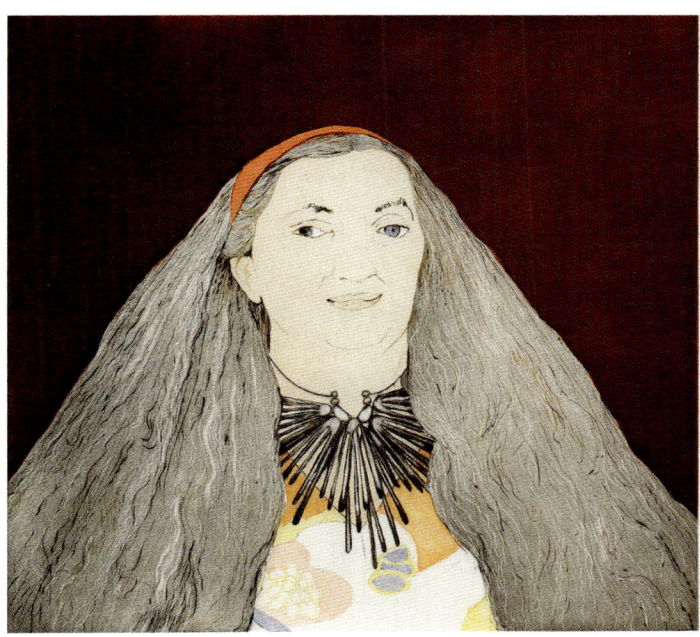

0.4 Beth Van Hoesen, *Merry*, 1973. Color aquatint and drypoint with roulette, hand colored with watercolor printed on moderately thick, moderately textured cream wove paper, plate: 9⅝ × 10½ in. Photo: M. Lee Fatherree.

0.5 Imogen Cunningham, *Sally and John Woodbridge and Their Children*, 1966. Gelatin silver print, 9½ × 9½ in. Collection of the Imogen Cunningham Trust.

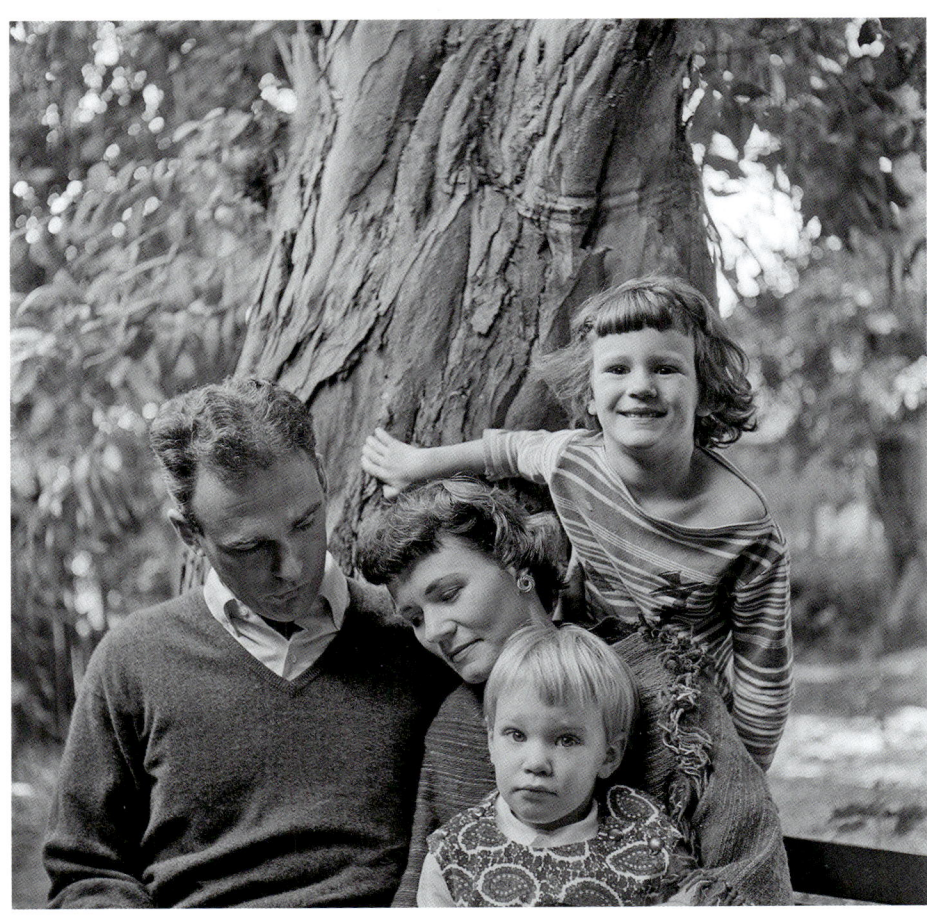

for the feasibility of having children as an artist: for Renk, it was nothing less than inspiring. As she recalled decades later, "You know what's interesting is that she could start getting recognition for her work, and be a mother of children. It was a time that wasn't so open for women, no matter what you did. You really weren't taken seriously. You're not going to stay with it. I will admit that the fact that Ruth had her children and did her work and did both gave me courage to go ahead and have children."[19] Asawa's friendship with Renk is also how we explain why Renk suddenly began creating drawings on plates made by her husband, the potter Earle Curtis. Around 1972, Joan Pearson Watkins relays, Renk had begun drawing portraits and dreams with oxide pencils on Curtis's porcelain platters.[20] It is also how we account for Renk's use of paperfolding, which she had learned from Asawa and adapted to jewelry.

Another protagonist in the book is Sally Byrne Woodbridge (1930–2020), a writer, editor, and architectural historian by training who also made ceramics and painted (fig. 0.5). Woodbridge had three small children in the 1960s, and she and Asawa were neighbors in the city's Noe Valley district, where they both sent their children to the neighborhood school. Their husbands had met while working as draftsmen in an architectural firm. With Asawa and several other mothers, Woodbridge helped to found the Alvarado School Arts Workshop and wrote a slim book on Asawa's early monumental public sculpture, the *San Francisco Fountain* (1970–1973), while Renk, Curtis, and Nancy Thompson were resident artists in that program. These were women who shared a common project as artist-mothers; they provided mutual support, swapped childcare, painted and drew in groups, worked out problems of form and technique together, and even exhibited alongside one another.

Once we grasp *mothering* as an action existing outside of a biological relationship to children, we recognize that this condition also included artists such as Beth Van Hoesen (1926–2010), whom I count as another member of this unofficial group, even if she did not have children. Sharing Asawa's birth year, Van Hoesen studied in Paris and in the Bay Area, before moving into a restored firehouse a few blocks away from Asawa and Woodbridge. Her work contributes to this alternative paradigm of motherhood in the arts, for Van Hoesen expanded printmaking's materials, while also pushing the medium to a degree of verisimilitude not seen since Albrecht Dürer. She, like her fellow artist-mothers, participated in a common language of plants, flowers, animals, and people, embracing a representational idiom at a time in the history of American art when it was very much in the minority. Citing "flowers, portraits, plants, trees," these "natural objects," as Asawa wrote home during a residency at the Tamarind Lithography Workshop in Los Angeles, represented a commitment to figuration during an era dominated by abstraction and minimalism: "it is not very stylish to make a picture recognizable nowadays," she put it bluntly.[21]

Asawa, Woodbridge, Renk, and Van Hoesen also shared a generational commitment to European modernism. They were all born in the 1920s and had studied either in Europe or with European artists, designers, and architects who had emigrated to the United States as a consequence of World War II. They understood art as a practice inseparable from architecture, craft, and design, sited within a trajectory from the

British arts and crafts to the Bauhaus to the adaptation of international modernism into the regional context of California. In this, they stood at a distance from more dominant strands of modernism in midcentury America, including that articulated by art critic Clement Greenberg, who strongly advocated for abstract expressionist painting—whereas Asawa repeatedly stressed not expression but experimentation as art's goal. Greenberg's account of modernism coincided with decades in which the mythology of the housewife reigned and motherhood was rigorously policed as a social role, affecting women both with and without children, as Rebecca Jo Plant has argued in tracing the shifting meanings of motherhood in America.[22] It seemed, however, that both dominant midcentury narratives—the artist and the mother—found little resonance in the circle of women I discuss.

At the same time, their work and artistic positions cannot be explained through second-wave feminism—a movement that brought motherhood into a critical framework. Asawa and her circle belonged to a "prefeminist generation" of women artists, to borrow from Norma Broude and Mary D. Garrard, who did not thematize their gender, much less their motherhood, in their work, as became typical in a younger generation, exemplified by Mary Kelly and Mierle Laderman Ukeles, who explicitly reflect on their positions as both artists and mothers in critical language.[23] By the time the women's movement gained momentum, Asawa and the others had homes to maintain, were married (or divorced), and many had school-aged children to care for; none were involved in feminism as a political movement. Adrienne Rich's distinction between the individual experiences of women in a "*potential relationship*" to one's "powers of reproduction"—experiences as multiple and complex as mothers themselves, on the one hand, and, on the other hand, motherhood as an institution, "which aims at ensuring that that potential—and all women—shall remain under male control," was still a long way off.[24] And yet, as this book tries to show, what we count as feminist can be expanded to include makers who did not embrace that discourse themselves, but created work that is best explained by it. Even if distinct from explicitly feminist engagements with motherhood, their work makes most sense when seen as anticipating that politics by living feminist lives—a point to which I return in the book's conclusion.

Another important figure in this constellation of artist-mothers is the photographer Imogen Cunningham (1883–1976). Although four decades their senior, Cunningham had ties to a generation in which pictorialism, sentimentalism, and Victoriana ruled—dimensions that the reader will encounter throughout this study. But she also regularly taught at the San Francisco Art Institute, supported antinuclear protests, and was one of the first to photograph a younger hippie generation laying claim to the city's Haight-Ashbury neighborhood. With a perennial peace sign around her neck, Cunningham saw herself as an antiwar hippie *avant la lettre*. She had been in the city the longest, having moved to the area with a small child and pregnant with twins in 1917. She had studied photography in Seattle and platinum chemical processes in Germany, and would become one of the most accomplished of the group in terms of exhibitions, publications, and professional associations (with the f64 group, Ansel Adams, and Edward Weston, to name only a few).

0.6 Ruth Asawa, *Imogen*, 1972. Glazed ceramic, 22 × 22 × 2 in. Private collection.

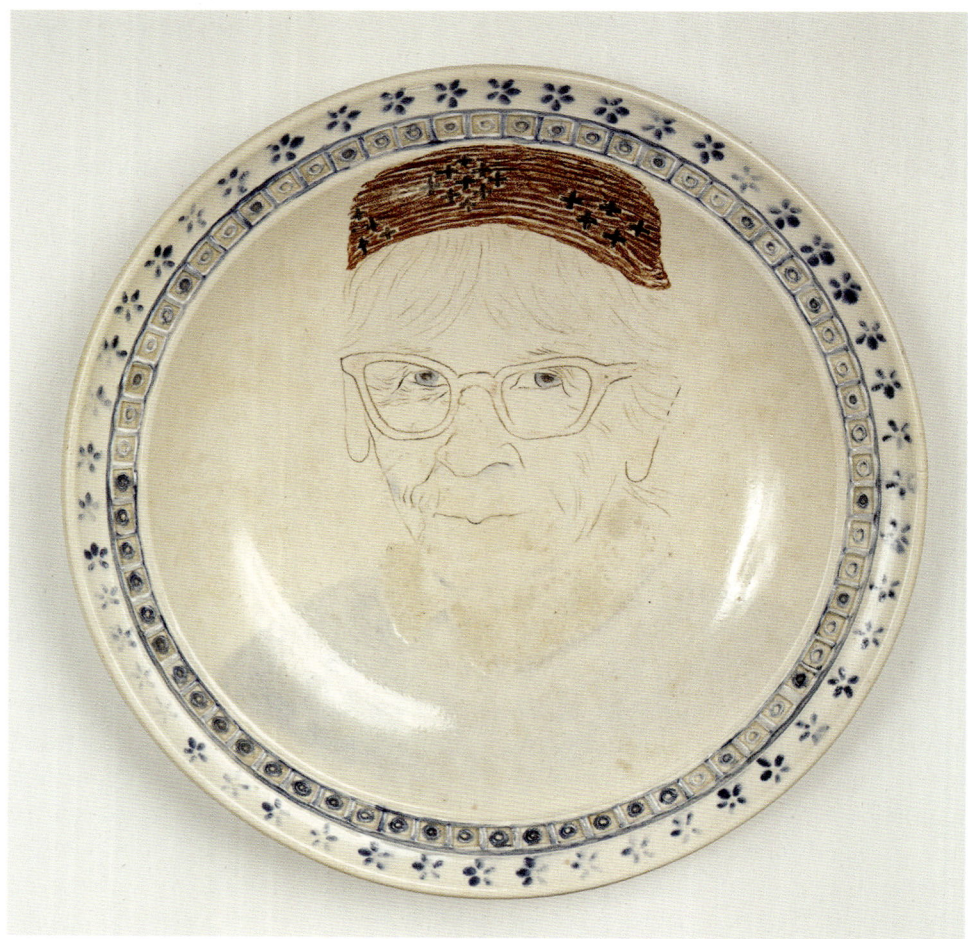

The reader will notice that Cunningham's work plays a substantial role in the book as compared to the other artist-mothers in Asawa's circle. This is because Cunningham represents an early, complex, and ambivalent example of an artist-mother, bringing to the fore some of the contradictions around this role. She was also the one to give many of these relationships explicit pictorial form, taking remarkable portraits of Renk, Woodbridge, Van Hoesen, and Asawa, as well as the latter's sculpture and children—as if all three terms (self, work, family) were part of a continuous exploration. Asawa and Cunningham, furthermore, pursued one of the most important dialogues between photographic and sculptural media of the twentieth century. This dialogue unfolded not only as a matter of shared subject matter—of children, aging parents, plants, and flowers; it also encompassed shared formal investigations into light and shadow across two and three dimensions.

All of these women had varying degrees of support from their artist-husbands: Cunningham divorced the etcher Roi Partridge after he forbade her to travel to New York for an exhibition opening. Woodbridge, too, eventually divorced a husband who frequently traveled, though the two continued to coauthor books of architectural history. Renk was married to the potter Earle Curtis, who helped Asawa make a series of drawn ceramic plates, including one with Cunningham's portrait (fig. 0.6). Asawa seems to have had the most support. Her husband, Albert Lanier, an architect, not only encouraged her work but actively facilitated it, lending his hand to exhibition designs, building studio models and bases, editing her correspondence, and ensuring that she was credited.

One of the conditions that sustained these women as they worked together was a shared geographic proximity. All had chosen, at one point or another, to move to San Francisco, which at the time was not the obvious choice. If you were a serious artist in 1949, you made your way to New York, not San Francisco, and if you were not in New York already, you tried to get there. It was virtually unheard of to be invited and decide not to go, as Asawa had done. During the 1950s, she had exhibited three times at the reputable Peridot Gallery, then showing formidable artists including Louise Bourgeois, but declined further ties to the city. Like Asawa, Renk also identified in the late 1940s as a designer. She had opened one of the first fine art and design galleries in the country, 750 Studio, in Chicago where she had studied at the Institute of Design, shortly before moving to San Francisco with an eye to the city's burgeoning architecture and design scene. It was similar with Woodbridge: after she received a degree in art history and a Fulbright to go to France, where she met her husband, the two went to Princeton. But because the university did not accept female students, she could not officially enroll and instead worked at the library; she nevertheless actively participated in this intellectual milieu, and twenty years later pursued a PhD in architectural history at the University of California, Berkeley (only to have her dissertation on Julia Morgan rejected by the one female committee member, who was also a Morgan specialist). By the 1950s, these women had all made San Francisco their home. They shared a neighborhood, an investment in the arts in the city, and for all but Cunningham, a sustained involvement in the public school system which their children attended. It was this common experience that would lead them all to extend their maternal practice into the public realm, which I explore in the last third of the book.

THE "AWFUL DICHOTOMY"

Even more than shared circumstances and geographical proximity, what holds these women together is that they all, to varying degrees, rejected the dominant narrative of motherhood and artmaking at midcentury. This is what painter Alice Neel called the "awful dichotomy" that pits artmaking and caretaking at odds with one another, as two opposing and irreconcilable terms.[25] We see this dichotomy invoked repeatedly in accounts of midcentury women artists, especially painters; it is often the mechanism through which art historical discourse judges a woman artist's legitimacy. Take, for instance, this recent account of Grace Hartigan, who in April 1951, the author relays, "had long before concluded that she could not be both a serious artist and a mother and had given [her son] Jeff to his grandparents to be raised in New Jersey. Now she saw her son only during emotionally charged weekends. The rest of her time was spent painting, or struggling to find the money to buy the materials to paint. The relationships she valued most were those that enabled or inspired her—with painters or poets, or lovers who were content to remain as such. Anything else (especially that cumbersome attachment called a husband) was a distraction she could not afford and would not tolerate."[26] The message here is clear: children amount to "distractions" from the serious business of artmaking, and those relationships that matter "most" had nothing to do with family, friendships, or neighbors. Anyone—or rather, any *woman*—wholly committed to her art had to make the difficult but necessary choice.

If this sounds old-fashioned, keep in mind that this passage was taken from the pages of a recent *New York Times* bestseller. It is powerful stuff, this mythology that the work of making art is so engrossing, so monumental in scope and feeling, that it would even drive a mother to abandon her son. It persists even in those accounts that attempt to be on the right side of history, telling the stories of women who had long been marginalized from the record. But even in the 1950s, it was not true that children were intolerable for the artist-mother—what was intolerable was motherhood itself from the perspective of an art world that compelled women to make a difficult choice. And just when we think this mythologizing is confined to the mass market, consider a recent scholarly book on Helen Frankenthaler, which frames the topic of motherhood as a litany of suicides, depression, dead infants, and miscarriages, all of which, we are told, Frankenthaler blithely rejected.[27] To describe such claims as pervasive is an understatement; they voice an institution, to invoke Rich again, deeply internalized in our conceptions of midcentury art history. We find it even reinforced by some of these women themselves, as in the case of Emily Mason when she told the painter Janice Biala that she was two months pregnant, to which Biala responded, "Oh good. There is still time for an abortion."[28] Or Louise Bourgeois, who describes a watercolor that she made in the early 1940s as portraying herself as a mother "stuffing my face with [the child] . . . Medea killed her children as an act of revenge. I want to abolish them because they are a fact, because they are such a huge burden."[29] The "burden" here, though, is not the fact of having a child, but the punishment imposed for wanting to be an artist at the same time.

The notion that "creation and femininity are incompatible," to borrow from Anaïs Nin, is not exclusive to the decades that this book addresses, but it is one of the period's overriding attributes: it is "the agony—particularly mid-century, escaped by their sisters of pre-Freudian, pre-Jungian times," as Tillie Olsen writes.[30] Which is to say that although this dichotomy tends to be cast as universal, it is historically specific, and relies on a theory of culture that gains traction in the wake of Freud. That theory of culture casts all artistic production as originating in the repression of erotic life, in a rejection of the Mother. Without going into the technical language of this theory, one can grasp its message in the words of sculptor Reg Butler, addressing a group of art students in 1962: "I am quite sure that the vitality of many female students derives from frustrated maternity, and most of these, on finding the opportunity to settle down and produce children, will no longer experience the passionate discontent sufficient to drive them constantly towards the labors of creation in other ways. Can a woman become a vital creative artist without ceasing to be a woman except for the purposes of a census?"[31] According to this script, the "vitality" of the artwork emerges only in the absence of vitality in its most literal form—as the generation of new life. When one is invoked, the other becomes superfluous. Literary scholar Susan Rubin Suleiman spells out how this tenet shifted from a moral obligation to "a psychological 'law'" for psychoanalysts like Helene Deutsch, who equated "the creative impulse with the procreative one and decree[d] that she who has a child feels no need to write books."[32] It is, as Suleiman suggests, what we might call "the menopausal theory of artistic creation."[33]

What is significant here is that statements like Reg Butler's cannot be explained away through recourse to misogyny. We are speaking here of a much more systematic problem, one that had less to do with gender bias than it did with a foundational paradigm of artistic making based on a Freudian model of subjectivity. One criterion of that paradigm was that art must stand in a relation of difference to life, to embody that vitality but also distinguish itself from it. Woman had to be "the antithesis of *cultural* creativity," because she was the epitome of biological creativity.[34] It is a narrative that bolstered the Romantic notion of the artist as tortured genius, which in turn informed the Freudian paradigm. As Sarah Kofman summarizes it: "Society takes the artist to be the father of his creation, and the artist, wishing to believe himself the father of his works, wants to be his own father. Society therefore grants full license to the artist to show that he is subject to no external constraints, that he is free and fully his own master, that like God, he is self-sufficient."[35] Fathers, even as women, make art, but Mothers cannot.

Another coordinate in sketching out the relationship of art to motherhood at mid-century is a 1954 *Life* magazine feature on the sculptor Isabel Case Borgatta. Here the situation is reversed: the artist's work is not opposed to her identity as mother but rather reduced to it. Photographs by Andreas Feininger depict the artist at work in her studio: Borgatta carving her wooden figure is mirrored in her daughters' dabbing at an easel nearby, as if mother is merely playing at making art (fig. 0.7). The *Life* feature not only collapses Child and Woman, it subtly invokes metaphors of artmaking which analogize it to pregnancy and birth, metaphors that historically have been invoked by men (an aspect I explore in part II). These are metaphors in which the action of artistic production is spoken of as if it were the action of mothering: Tillie Olsen points us to the example of Balzac's self-professed "unwearying maternal love, this habit of creation."[36] *Life* magazine casts Borgatta's pregnancy in the terms of this metaphorized maternity. Her rounded belly faces the pregnant statue in a kind of maternal revision of the Pygmalion myth, in which the male artist falls in love with his creation and thus brings her to life. "Now about to produce her third child," readers are told, "she has succeeded in completing her latest sculpture [*Expectation*] in just nine months."[37]

0.7 Isabel Case Borgatta with her two eldest children and *Maternity* (previously *Expectation*; 1955). Photo: Andreas Feininger.

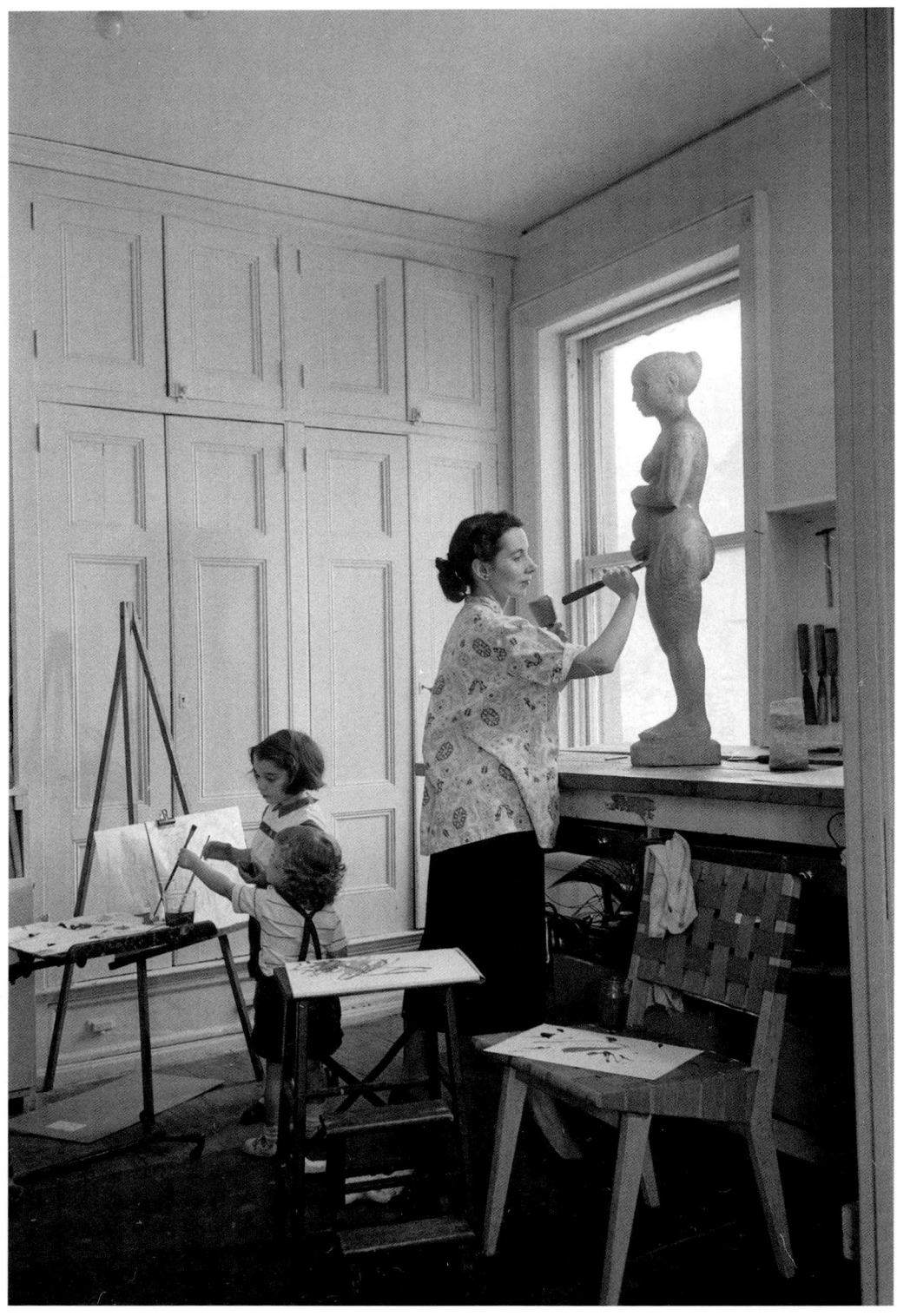

Behind the two expecting mothers, one animate and the other inanimate, two children play. True to the article's subtitle—"Wife Coordinates Her Statues with Her Babies"—*Life* went to some length to make certain for the reader that, whatever kind of artmaking this was, it was compatible with the duties of motherhood; there would be no possibility of neglect here. A carved alabaster child, the caption states, "was [a] subject suggested to Mrs. Borgatta by her 4-year-old daughter," while the figure of a mother and child "was made to express the intense protective love that [the] sculptor felt toward her own new baby"; and, finally, *First Born* "was actually made after [the] second Borgatta baby arrived," and it will serve as a "model for a large work which the sculptor will make after her next child is born."[38] No need for further explanation; motherhood encompasses art's subject, meaning, choice of title, and even deadline.

An elucidation of the mythology underlying the Borgatta feature is furnished by Roland Barthes in his essay "Novels and Children," which appeared in 1957. This is the same year that Cunningham took powerful photographs of Asawa working at home around her children, which I discuss at the end of chapter 1. Here the myth at issue is the inversion of Neel's awful dichotomy: it is only *because* the artist is a mother that her work is allowed to qualify as art. Let me explain. Barthes's topic is an issue of *Elle* magazine that profiles some seventy women writers. Each photograph, he tells us, is accompanied by captions such as these: "Jacqueline Lenoir (two daughters, one novel)"; "Marina Grey (one son, one novel)"; "Nicole Dutreil (two sons, four novels)"—the list goes on. This is the woman writer's "double parturition," he proposes; "children and novels alike seem to come by themselves, and to belong to the mother alone." What does it all mean, he asks? This:

Women are on the earth to give children to men; let them write as much as they like, let them decorate their condition, but above all, let them not depart from it: let their Biblical fate not be disturbed by the promotion which is conceded to them, and let them pay immediately, by the tribute of their motherhood, for this bohemianism which has a natural link with a writer's life.

Women, be therefore courageous, free; play at being men, write like them; but never get far from them; live under their gaze, compensate for your books by your children; enjoy a free rein for a while, but quickly come back to your condition.[39]

Determining and limiting this condition is the absent male figure, "nowhere and everywhere." It is his presence that undergirds the litany of children and novels, "the miraculous products of an ideal parthenogenesis able to give at once to women, apparently, the Balzacian joys of creation and the tender joys of motherhood." This is the other side of the dichotomy: instead of disallowing a woman's ability to create, motherhood guarantees it. Allow women "the Balzacian joys of creation," but let their work always be determined by "their Biblical fate." In this way, the creative power of the female sex is contained and controlled. Both *Elle* and *Life* stage "a Molièresque scene, say[ing] yes on one side and no on the other," and thus "displeasing no one."[40] This is so powerful a myth in Western culture that its components can be reversed and still hold true. To cite the poet Alicia Ostriker: "That women should have babies rather than books is the considered opinion of Western civilization. That women should have books rather than babies is a variation on that theme."[41]

This book argues that both of these narratives—motherhood in opposition to artistic creation and motherhood as its sole horizon of meaning—are insufficient. These binary terms fail to capture the full range of the artist-mother's experience. Take Jill Johnston, for instance, the lesbian dance critic, who became a mother in the late 1950s. By the early 1960s, she had left her husband and moved with her two small children to downtown Manhattan, where she found a group of other artists with children who "were, like myself, not willing to sacrifice ambition for motherhood."[42] In her memoir *Mother Bound*, Johnston names in particular three other mothers who were, in her estimation, also "successful artists": the painter and performance artist Marcia Marcus, sculptor and painter Mary Frank, and painter and writer Rosalyn Drexler. Marilyn Wood is another example whom Johnston names: she was an early dancer to join the Merce Cunningham Company, in 1958. Teaching dance classes at her children's elementary school led to a friendship with Elaine Summers, with whom she established an improvisational group that included Trisha Brown and Steve Paxton; Wood also participated in Anna and Lawrence Halprin's San Francisco-based workshops, bringing her into close orbit with the story I tell in this book. "Marilyn was my first model mother, the first mother, in fact, besides my own with whom I had ever spent real time while she was functioning as Mother." Johnston also names Mark di Suvero among these maternal figures, describing him as "one of my Jewish mothers at that time. His loft on Fulton Street was one of the four hangouts I frequented, with or without my children. With my children, it was better than the park or any playground."[43]

Even just in these few pages from Johnston's *Mother Bound*, we have the beginnings of a maternal counternarrative to Neel's dichotomy. Here motherhood is not an existential crisis, threatening the creative powers of what Johnston calls the long-accepted phenomenon of "the antisocial male artist." Instead, motherhood renders artmaking reciprocal, and, like all demands on one's time and energy, it is a matter of pragmatic concern: we learn, for instance, that Wood had an incredible knack for time management and that Drexler's husband, Sherman, had "put his wife's career (as artist) before his own." Moreover, we learn from Johnston that motherhood offers the potential for correcting the historical record, showing what the artistic past might look like as a succession of women *and* men. "I tended to think of the modern dance tradition in matriarchal terms," she writes, citing José Limón as a protégé of Doris Humphrey, of Cunningham as a student of Martha Graham, of Yvonne Rainer as "inheriting the mantle of Graham," and of both Graham and Humphrey as having danced with Ruth St. Denis.[44]

In other words, we learn from Johnston a paradigm of what queering motherhood in art might look like. The era under discussion here saw the demise of the heteronormative family as a dominant formation, giving way to an expansion of discourse and practices around queer kinship, pregnancy, and adoption. These discourses and practices approach queerness as a category that extends beyond identity—beyond parents who identify as queer or trans—in order to consider how normative practices of kinship and care are disrupted. This is especially true in the instance of adoption, the feminist philosopher Shelley Park argues, which is relevant to this study because two of Asawa's six children were adopted. Drawing on discourses that dislodge the term "queer" from sexual orientation, Park argues for "the queerness of the adoptive maternal body": insofar as a "pronatalist" perspective defines motherhood as "a natural, biological phenomenon," then "there is something queer about any adoptive maternal body—a body that presupposes, yet is defined in opposition to, procreative activity; a body that is marked as defective yet chosen as capable." This "impossible status," she suggests, furnishes "a unique position from which to examine and resist normative conceptions and practices of mothering."[45]

"Queering motherhood," Margaret F. Gibson writes, "can therefore start where any of the central gendered, sexual, relational, political, and/or symbolic components of 'expected' motherhood are challenged."[46] What was expected of Asawa and her fellow artist-mothers was to subordinate artistic practice to the demands of a husband, children, and the maintenance of a home—following Barthes's reading of women with children being allowed to "play at being men"—or disavow domesticity altogether, creating the "agony" that Tillie Olsen identifies. Asawa, by contrast, did not see this as an either/or decision, but rather integrated the labor of mothering into her work as an artist, and her work as an artist into her labor as a mother. In doing so, she was in good company. The designer Jean Maurice Rochin was another neighbor, one whom Asawa knew from studying at Black Mountain College in the late 1940s; she and Asawa had daughters of the same age who played together. In 1963, Rochin moved to France but regularly corresponded with Asawa, sending her scarfs, which Rochin had made to be sold at the upscale I. Magnin store. Her letters to Asawa reflect on being a mother, wife, and artist; on periods when she was able to get work done in the studio, wanting to get more done, or needing to help her husband in the office, all the while inflected by moments of determination: "My health is good now so that I have no excuse not to get back to work and to hell with the housework."[47]

Queering normative expectations of the artist-mother also involves shifting the focus from the mother-child dyad to relationships that mothers have with one another. Park proposes as much when she broaches the notion of expanding queer mothering to include affective mother-mother relationships:

To queer mothering is, in one sense, to understand lesbian mothering as a prototype for other forms of mothering (rather than viewing it as an odd or deviant form of mothering). What would happen if we viewed (and lived) mother-mother relationships as (at least) equal in importance to the affective bonds between mothers and children? What would happen if maternal love was configured not only (or even primarily) as a putatively unconditional bond between a woman and her offspring, but also as an affectionate—and perhaps even erotic—relationship between mothers?[48]

Mother-mother relationships certainly defined Asawa and her peers: strong social bonds held these women together, even if they themselves would never have described those bonds as "erotic," much less "queer." Their queerness was not at the level of sexual orientation but at the level of disrupting normative expectations, and the protagonists I discuss here are only a handful of a much larger cast of characters. Although they exceed the scope of this book, their stories are waiting to be told.

Consider these thoughts in relationship to a photograph that Asawa's son-in-law Laurence Cuneo took of two looped-wire sculptures staged as if lying in bed (fig. 0.8). Instead of hung, as they usually were displayed, they lie horizontally, with the bed foregrounding their human-like dimensions. Shot in the bedroom that Asawa shared with her husband, the photograph suggests that the sculptures can be seen as surrogate bodies for the absent couple and, depending on your perspective, a comical stand-in for the missing inhabitants. This staging could be read in a number of ways—as a gorgeous composition, as unexpected in its dramaturgy, as sentimental in its use of the bed, or as slapstick in its posing of abstract sculptures as people; in any case, Albert Lanier, who shared that bed, never liked the image much, Cuneo recalled.[49] He may have seen its polyvalence as straying too far from his directive that Cuneo track down and document all of the works by Asawa that had been given to friends and neighbors throughout the years. The photograph marks how these works traversed relationships between mothers, and how those relationships generated affective bonds in which both children and artworks played vital roles.

Never before published, this photograph exemplifies the kind of archival discoveries that ground my inquiry. When I began writing this book, I was struck by the discrepancy between the prominence of motherhood in the archive, particularly in Asawa's papers and in photographs of her work taken by Cunningham, Cuneo, Paul Hassel, and others, and its absence in art historical assessments of her work. The many photographs I found featuring Asawa as both artist and mother simultaneously— many of which were never even printed—were especially instructive. Those select photos of her that were published and thus became widely circulated often represent the artist alone and thus misrepresent this visual archive. But without having encountered the archive, one is not even aware that this is a misrepresentation. In such unknown views, a maternal register comes into focus in ways that are otherwise invisible. My intention in this book is to restore this largely unseen perspective at a pivotal moment in Asawa's reception, with the artist now enjoying an unprecedented visibility, and to show the difference it makes when we recognize that such celebrated work simultaneously challenges long-standing ideas about who the artist is and what the artwork should do.

In identifying the challenge that the artist-mother poses to how we define both art and artist at midcentury, I am thus excluding whole groups of artworks by Asawa and her peers. Readers will find little discussion here of Asawa's engagement with the history of Japanese Americans during and after World War II, such as in her *Japanese American Internment Memorial* (1990–1994) in San Jose, California, and her *Garden of Remembrance* (2000–2002), installed on the campus of San Francisco State University. Nor do I spend much time on her artistic training—her years as a high school student, when she first began practicing art, while imprisoned in a Japanese internment camp; likewise the three formative years that she spent at Black Mountain College receive hardly any attention. Finally, what Asawa proposed as arguably even

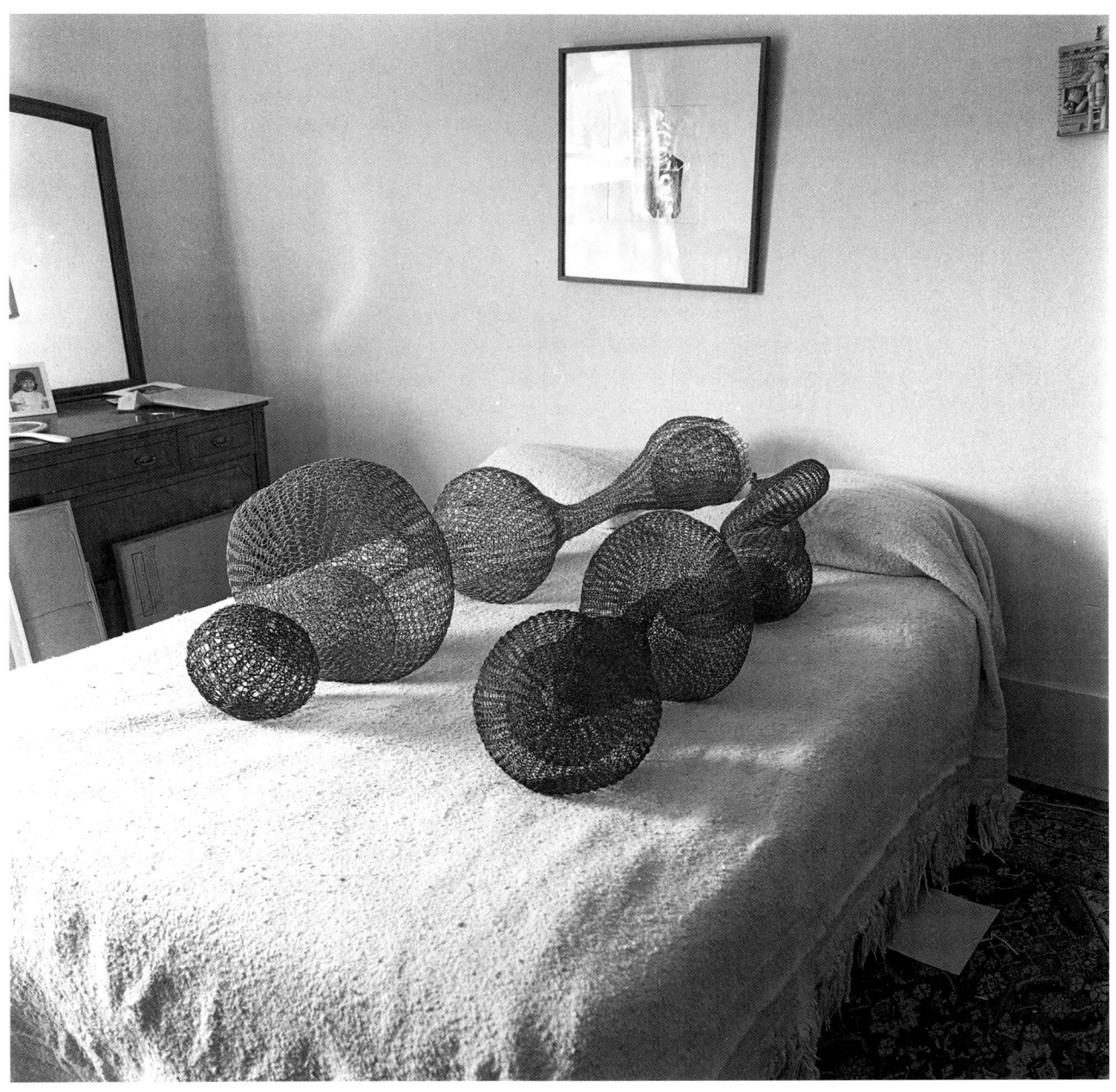

0.8 Laurence Cuneo, *Reclining*, 1972. Gelatin
silver print, 7½ × 7½ in. Private collection.

more important than art—her work with schoolchildren in general and the gardening program in particular—is woefully curtailed.[50] Comprising this book's last two chapters, the Alvarado School Arts Workshop as a mother-led initiative merits its own book (or books). My hope is that this study in part serves as impulse for future scholarship in these directions.

Instead of an exhaustive account of Asawa's work, I focus on concentrated episodes in which she and her fellow artist-mothers willfully betrayed the prohibition on motherhood, which I take to be distinctly modernist in its form. And here I have built upon literary scholar Ann Douglas, who argues that "maternal rebuke and filial revolt" constituted a key strategy of modernist innovation, with the paradigm of the nineteenth-century Victorian matriarch the central figure that must be hunted down.[51] Writers now regarded as pioneers of modernist literature, including Ernest Hemingway and Hart Crane, emerged from the world wars of the twentieth century strongly disavowing their own mothers and any debt to the maternal body or mother tongue. This "theme of the matricidal wish," Douglas claims, can "be found everywhere in the lives and works" of these modernist American writers.[52]

Challenging modernism's matricidal script, the work of the artist-mother at midcentury foregrounded collaboration and care. This figure forged bonds along personal and professional lines, and made art that was better for it. In Cuneo's photograph, for instance, not coincidentally made by a son-in-law, we see evidence of such shared affective bonds. The drawing above the bed is a watercolor that Asawa had made, in multiple versions, of "Mae's vase": Mae Lee was a close personal friend, active herself in various creative pursuits, and there are many drawings in which flowers grace her ceramic vessel (figs. 0.9, 0.10). Lee herself could be described as an origami artist, but was consistently self-effacing and little interested in publicizing her work. A longtime next-door neighbor, she devoted much of her time to supporting Asawa's practice, contributing to *Andrea* (1968), Asawa's first public sculpture, created from casting the postpartum body of their neighbor Andrea Jepson; to the *San Francisco Fountain* (1970–1973) as a baker's clay portrait of the city with the participation of over 250 adults and children; and to origami and milk carton workshops as part of the Alvarado School Arts Workshop.

Foundational for these artist-mothers was the practice that art stands in an ethical responsibility to other life forms; indeed, it presumes that it is within the realm of art that we work out our various imaginings to those life forms. Very concretely: all of these women were invested in making work as part of sustaining a family, a community, a city, an environment. All, as mothers, implicated their own children in their work, and the work even at times calls forth its viewer as a child, as an ever-growing being, in the sense that we can speak of both literal processes of generation—on the level of material transformation—and figurative processes of generation—on the level of considering what art owes to future generations. Such practices further erode that opposition between abstraction and figuration, as art historian David Getsy has urged us to recognize, which has long failed to grasp the ways that the human body persists, exceeding those binaries set out for it by posterity.[53] Adding to that

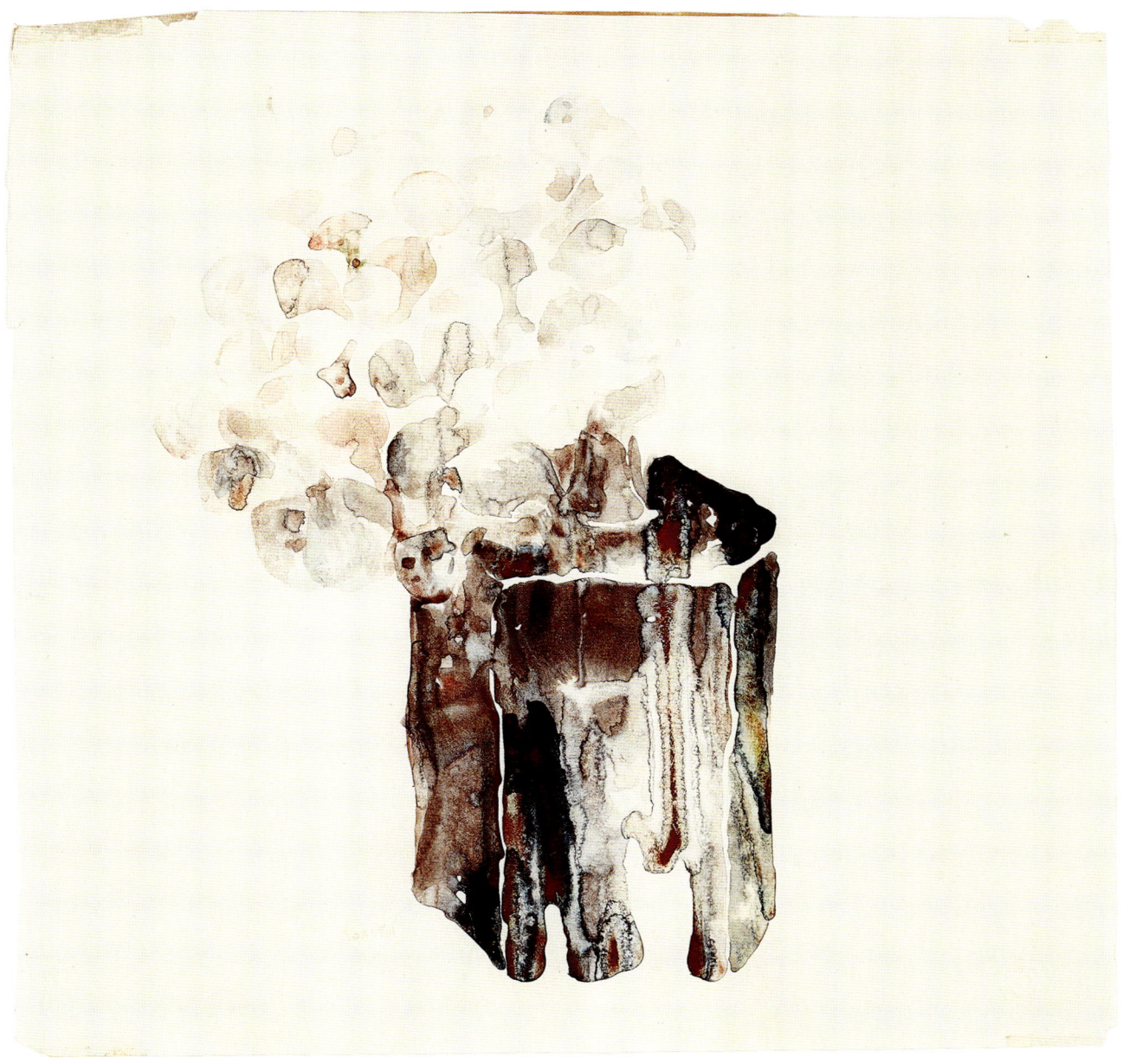

0.9 Ruth Asawa, *Untitled* (WC.034, Purple Hydrangea
in Mae Lee's Vase), 1964. Watercolor paint on coated
paper, 12¼ × 12½ in. Private collection.

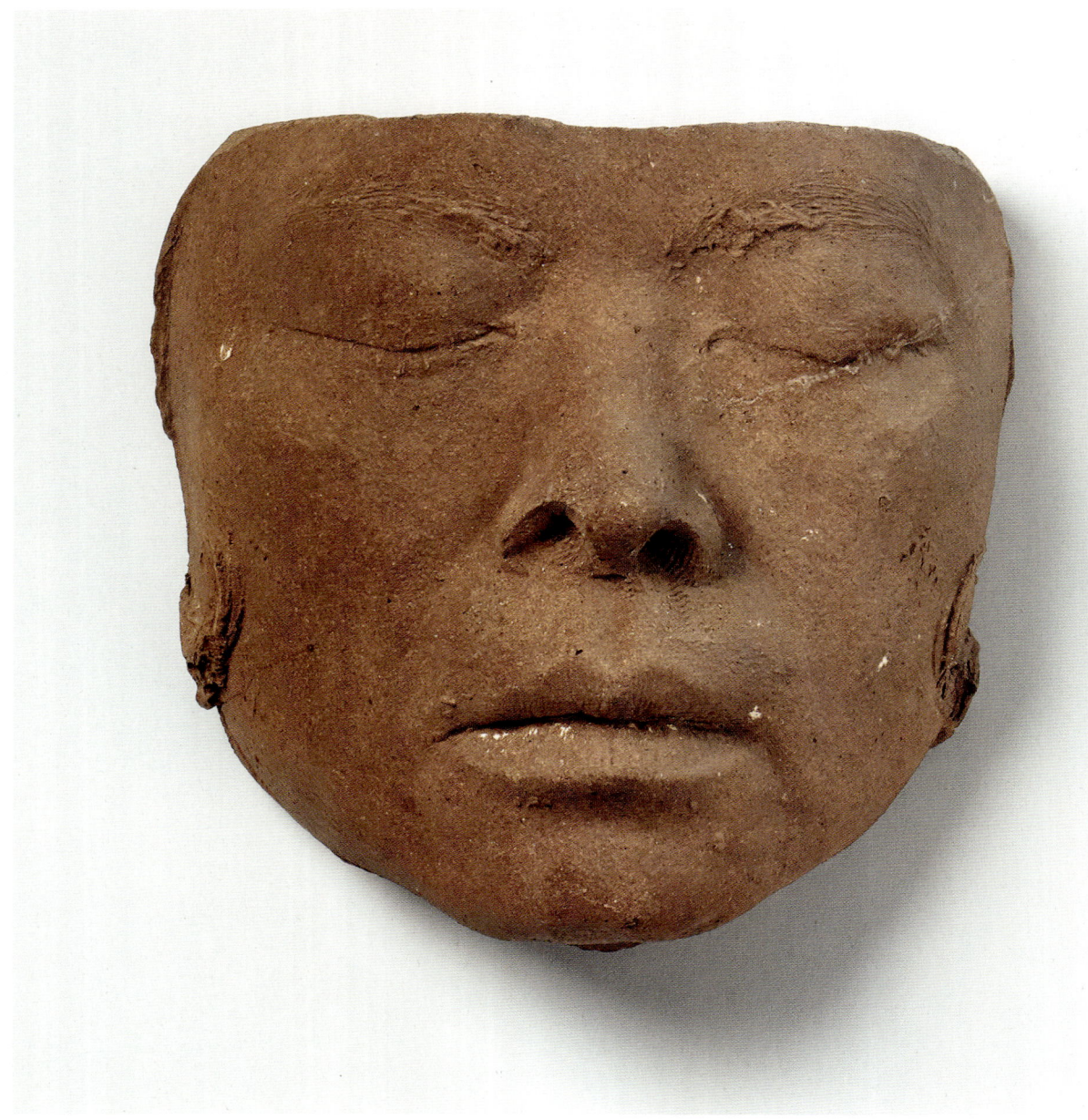

0.10 Ruth Asawa, *Untitled* (Mae Lee), detail of *Untitled* (LC.012, Wall of Masks), c. 1966–2000. Ceramic, bisque-fired clay, 4⅞ × 4⅞ × 2¾ in. Cantor Arts Center at Stanford University; William Alden Campbell and Martha Campbell Art Acquisition Fund. Conservation made possible by the Robert Mondavi Family Fund at the Cantor Arts Center and the Asian American Art Initiative Fund.

discussion of how sex and gender complicate our narratives of sculpture's ambition, let us now add maternity, in both its queer and straight forms, as further expanding the parameters of this inherently bodily medium.

Asawa included the watercolor of the hydrangea in Mae's vase in her 1976 exhibition at the city-run Capricorn Asunder Gallery in San Francisco. In the brochure, she described the work on view as "a diary of those years" spent in the city: "I have reared my own family here and have tried to integrate that undertaking with 'being an artist.'"[54] On view was a wide range of her work up until that date: ceramic plates and cast bronze paperfolds; a carved redwood door that she had made with her children; drawings of flowers and friends; lithographs depicting her father, eldest daughter, chairs, and plants, which she had completed during her residency at the Tamarind Lithography Workshop in 1965; as well as tied-wire and "woven wire sculpture," the checklists consistently read, made from steel, iron, copper, and brass wire. Only some of these she considered "finished works"; many more, she wrote in the exhibition brochure, were "works in progress," "first attempts," and evocations of ideas "first encountered thirty years ago [that] still require more study." This is an attitude toward art as an ongoing endeavor continuous with everyday life, but one that at the same time, Asawa argued, requires a "total commitment" to being an artist. Modernism may have viewed that commitment as irreconcilable with motherhood, but Asawa did not; the two for her and her peers were mutually enabling.

San Francisco as a city may have had something to do with the consolidation of the artist-mother. Certainly the city had one of the most progressive museum directors in the country, Grace McCann Morley, who frequently showed the work of the women I discuss.[55] All of the protagonists in this study—including its guiding theorists, Olsen and Le Guin—were Bay Area residents. Far from New York as the symbolic center of the fine arts in midcentury America, the West Coast belonged to the "well-furnished margins" of the country's artistic production, part of the "untidy continental diversity of American culture," as Tara McDowell argues in relation to Jess and Robert Duncan, two artists who also lived and worked there at that time. McDowell calls for historical accounts "that fully admit this capaciousness as a salutary fact and free themselves of the model of 'center-and-periphery,' or at least build in a continual sense of the fragility of the U.S. center (in terms of cultural hegemony) and the advantages of the wide, well-furnished margins."[56] Unlike Jess and Duncan, however, who traveled often during the 1960s and 1970s, the artist-mothers in my study were committed to the region. Duncan "saw absolutely no meaning at all to being in something called San Francisco," whereas Asawa was deeply committed to the city, served on its public arts committees, and reshaped its school system.[57] Looking back in 2001, she described it as the place where she began her "career as an artist, wife, and mother."[58] Her work even became identified with the city, given the frequency and prominence of her public sculpture in "Ruth Asawa's San Francisco," as local journalist Mildred Hamilton put it.[59]

It was in her house in San Francisco that the daily incorporation of art into life first took form: "As a mother and grandmother," Asawa wrote toward the end of her life, "I expected my six children and ten grandchildren to participate in the making of art as well as washing the dishes, taking the garbage out, weeding the garden, and building things." She treated her children as co-makers and often recruited their help in the production of work, as in a set of carved redwood doors for their house in Noe Valley. Asawa even designated authorship of a bronze full-body life cast as "Ruth Asawa and Family."[60] Subtle statements like these, evident in an exhibition brochure, are easy to overlook. But their appearance in photographic form makes the point more overtly. Joan Pearson Watkins, an accomplished potter who led the ceramics department at the California School of Fine Arts in San Francisco from 1951 to 1957, and who had a weekly television program on KQED interviewing local designers, took several photographs of Asawa, her sculptures, and her children. One portrays her son Paul in his mother's studio, posed among the many sculptures, prints, and drawings in various stages of completion, as if he were one more ongoing process of creation among many others (fig. 0.11).

The modernist alignment of the artist with childhood also takes on a new connotation in the work of these artist-mothers, as Watkins's photograph suggests. Typically romanticized as the embodiment of so-called naive, unfettered creative forces, the child has long stood as the desired ideal of the modern artist, who aspires to unlearn everything she or he has been taught by society. As art historian Jonathan Fineberg has explored, modern art dreams of the unmediated image, and the child is the vehicle for that typically modernist conceit.[61] Although we find children and childhood throughout the work of Asawa and her peers, this fantasy is absent. What we have instead is a turn to the child as a turn toward considering the responsibility of art to thinking futurity. If the history of the avant-garde has been the history of negation, could a maternal avant-garde potentially be a form of critical affirmation? How would art history's categories of criticality, of negation, of seriousness, need to change in order to justly accommodate this kind of contribution?

In mounting a challenge to modernism's prohibition on motherhood, these artist-mothers took up discarded tropes and references, including sentimentality and Victoriana. One of the subcurrents of this book is the place of such long-ridiculed tropes in midcentury American art. To return to objects I have mentioned already, the casts of infant hands and feet furnish a good example. A format that can be traced to mid-nineteenth-century Britain, casts were made of Queen Victoria's infant children at her request by the otherwise unknown artist Abraham Kent, who carved marble versions on the basis of these casts. As was true of Asawa's use of this practice, making the casts was easiest while the children were sleeping, still enough for him to capture an adequate likeness.

Such objects are often explained with reference to sentimentality—an attempt to halt fleeting time and to remember the child who is ever disappearing into the adult.[62] This same sentimentality reappears in the reception of Asawa's use of the format. Helen Molesworth has described the casts as "remembrances in sculptural form of the growth and regeneration of her family line."[63] Another paradigm for understanding these objects is proposed by Katherine Fein in writing about Victorian-era life casts. The indexical quality of the cast, with the resulting object denoting a physical relationship

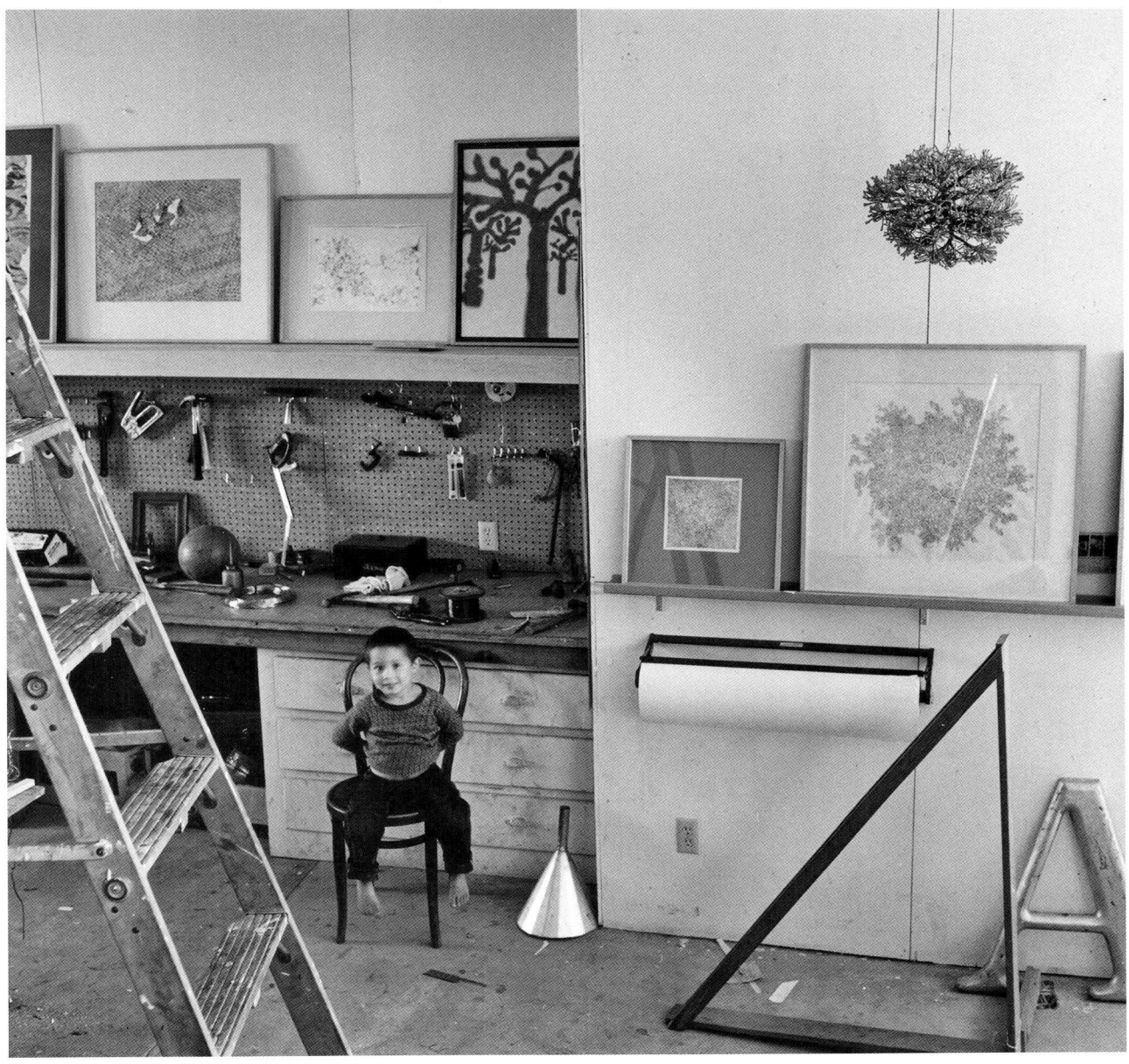

0.11 Joan Pearson Watkins, *Untitled* (Ruth Asawa's studio), c. 1965. Gelatin silver print, 7½ × 7½ in. Special Collections, Stanford University.

of reference to the absent object that shaped its form, is typically marshaled to grasp such objects. But Fein proposes that we consider instead "the intimacy between object and representation," looking especially at the relationships at play in the creation of these works.[64] My study follows this attempt to explore other models, beyond dichotomies of Victorian sentiment and (post)modern indexicality, to understand the significance of life casting for a discipline predicated on the originality of artifice.

This tendency to embrace terms typically opposed—such as modernist and Victorian—qualifies the artist-mother's work as boundary-defying, and this may be one reason it has proven difficult to assess with these normative models. In addition to hybridizing styles typically held apart, Asawa and her peers often worked across two- and three-dimensional form. It was not uncommon for Asawa, for instance, to submit a single material, like paper, to a number of permutations that resulted in varying degrees of material permanence: paper as drawn upon, as stamped, as folded, as cast in plastic, as cast in bronze. She was especially excited when these permutations could be at once enacted and then retracted: paper as flat surface transformed into an elaborate three-dimensional folded object, and then flattened again to become just as it was. This transformation also played out in life casting, including full-body casts in cement, plaster, and bronze. Several exist of the bodies of her own children at various ages, and these often headless casts deflect attention away from the sitter's identity and toward the astonishing quality of a growing body—a body suspended between childhood and adulthood (fig. 0.12). Life casting formed the two female figures of *Andrea*, but otherwise many of these casts remained as plaster or concrete objects piling up in Asawa's basement, only to be found decades later by those same children now grown and helping to reconstruct their mother's oeuvre.

These boundary-defying themes of childhood, Victorian sentimentality, and material metamorphosis are entwined throughout this book. Part I focuses on how the artist-mother reclaimed the domestic interior: long a coveted site of modernism, the domestic interior had become an incubator for universalist fantasies and archetypal manifestations of Man, Woman, and Universe. To reclaim this space as one of clutter and childrearing was to render it particular again, thus proposing a radical reorientation in where art is made and seen. Part II turns to an examination of how motherhood inflected normative discourses around art. I focus here on metaphors that invoke the maternal while at the same time disavowing mothers—as in the example of Picasso calling Georges Braque "ma femme" (my wife) and in descriptions of the artwork as "grow[ing] under the power of the artist as a child in the mother's womb."[65] In calling upon pregnancy, birth, and the female reproductive body, such metaphorical language rendered the artwork more powerful than the inert object that it was. What happened to such metaphors, I ask, when they were appropriated by the artist-mother, a figure who played out this drama of proliferation not only figuratively but literally as well? The third part of the book examines how motherhood mounted a challenge to reigning notions of art's social purpose: here I account for how these artist-mothers displaced the artwork from the gallery and museum and resited it in the public school classroom—a space historically opposed to aesthetic experience.

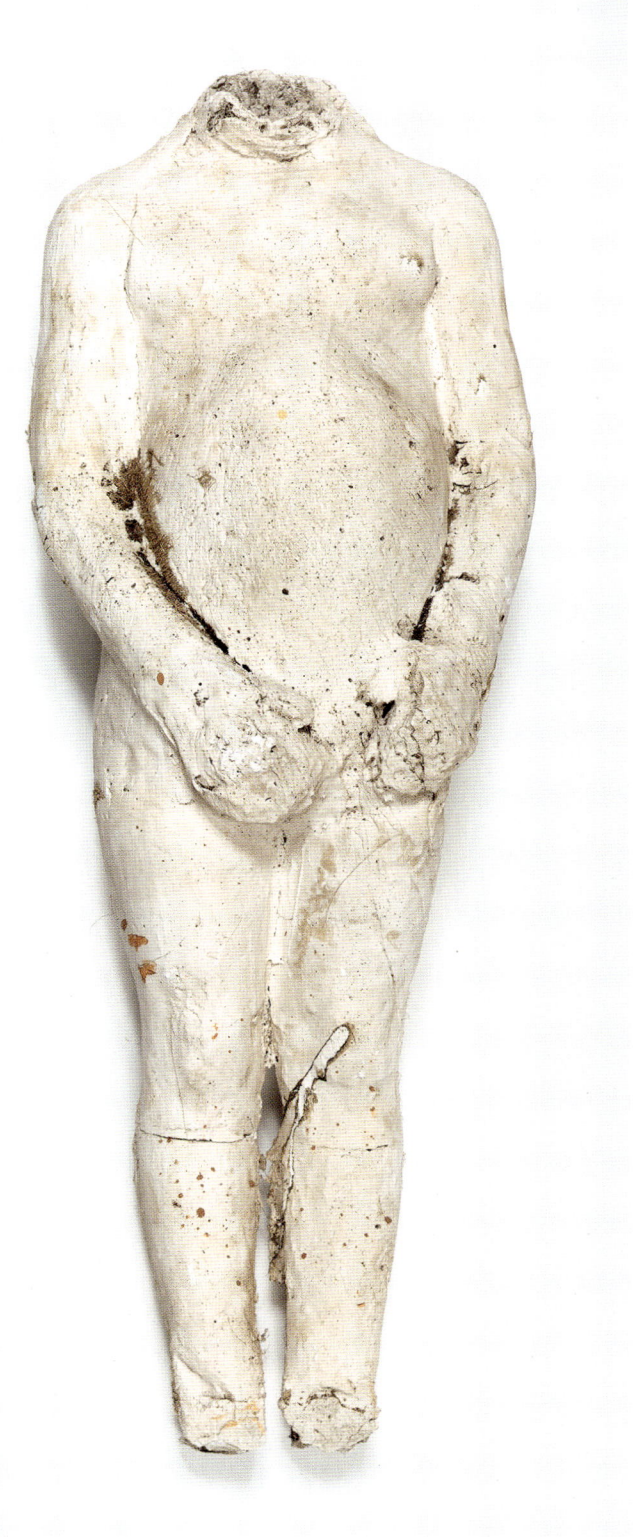

0.12 Ruth Asawa, *Untitled* (LC.024, Child's Full-Length Body—Front), no date. Cast plaster, 38½ × 13 × 9 in. Private collection.

Reading this book requires a willingness to take seriously a topic long regarded as banal, even embarrassing ("no subject offers a greater opportunity for terrible writing than motherhood," observed the *New York Times Book Review*). It requires setting aside long-standing assumptions about motherhood "as the reactionary choice, the choice made because it's what's socially expected," and to see it instead "as something hard won, intellectually demanding, a form of creative labor," as has been the case in an emergent "countercanon" of writing on motherhood by thinkers like Jacqueline Rose, Maggie Nelson, and Rachel Cusk.[66] To see this as possible requires that one separate the "artist-mother" from the discourses that have determined this figure's meaning—discourses summed up by Neel's "awful dichotomy." This is a request I borrow, as have these other writers, from Adrienne Rich, who, as a lesbian mother in the mid-1970s, denaturalizes motherhood's normative discourses. Rich argues that the history of motherhood has been its history as an institution, which is to say, a structure built and maintained by forces seeking to control its meaning. In reality, Rich says, whatever we call motherhood is no more natural a part of the "human condition" than "rape, prostitution, and slavery are"—the provocation of that assertion is itself telling—and "those that speak largely of the human condition are usually those most exempt from its oppressions—whether of sex, race, or servitude."[67] In the same way, those who create representations of motherhood, as one of the oldest subjects in the history of art, have been predominantly those largely exempt from a direct experience of it. "*Mothers*," as Susan Suleiman argues, drawing on Julia Kristeva, "*don't write, they are written*."[68]

Add Rich's observations to those made by Johnston and Barthes—all queer theorists taking up the topic of motherhood—and we begin to get closer to that term's definition as I am using it in this study. I have written elsewhere of what it might look like to conceptualize a nonnormative, nonbinary paradigm of maternal artistic creation.[69] The artists at stake in this book practiced the queering of motherhood by devising forms that resist normative structures around how art history defines its objects. The task is to understand how for a brief moment a group of artist-mothers wrote their own understanding of the work of art. To do so, we must suspend what we take to be so-called "natural" about art's relationship to procreation and instead look at individuals and circumstances, at particular relationships of desire and dialogue, collaboration and conflict, which shaped art and motherhood at midcentury.

▌ HOUSEHOLD OBJECTS

In the 1950s and 1960s, a studio visit with Ruth Asawa meant a visit to the artist's San Francisco house. Visitors often described in wonderment the scene that they encountered upon arrival:

Hugging the side of Saturn Str. as it cascades down Twin Peaks is an unpretentious two-story house, home of the Albert Laniers. Nothing unusual about it from the outside, but open the lower door and your attention is locked to a giant bauble of wire dropped from the high white ceiling. Watch it for a minute. When the sun catches the pattern intricate shadows—a dozen of them in black and grey—are traced on the nearby living room walls. But this is merely an introduction. To the right in a studio room, against a background montage of paintings and a blackboard of youngsters' scribbles, lies a remarkable world of wire. Here are 10 or 12 more of the sculptures in black, brass, copper, gold and silver wire hung at varied heights between floor and ceiling. Some are shaped like Byzantine spires or complex doodles or gourds, with one form growing out of another.[1]

This observation comes from the pages of the local newspaper, and Asawa's papers are filled with such descriptions, in which viewers marvel at how the work shaped the appearance of the interior. With titles including "World of Wire: Sculpture Comes from Crocheting" and "Making an Art of Living," these articles routinely sited Asawa and her art in the space of her own home. In the 1950s, that home was the two-story Victorian house on Saturn Street mentioned here; beginning in 1961, it was a much larger craftsman-style home in the adjacent neighborhood of Noe Valley, where Asawa lived until her death in 2013. In both instances, Asawa's home was the primary place in which her sculptures were seen, a "world of wire" created by dozens of looped-wire sculptures populating the interior.

The following two chapters address the significance of domestic space for the production and reception of the artist-mother's work, with a focus on Asawa and her next-door neighbor Merry Renk. Rather than painting representational scenes of interior domesticity, as Meredith A. Brown has pointed out in reference to fellow

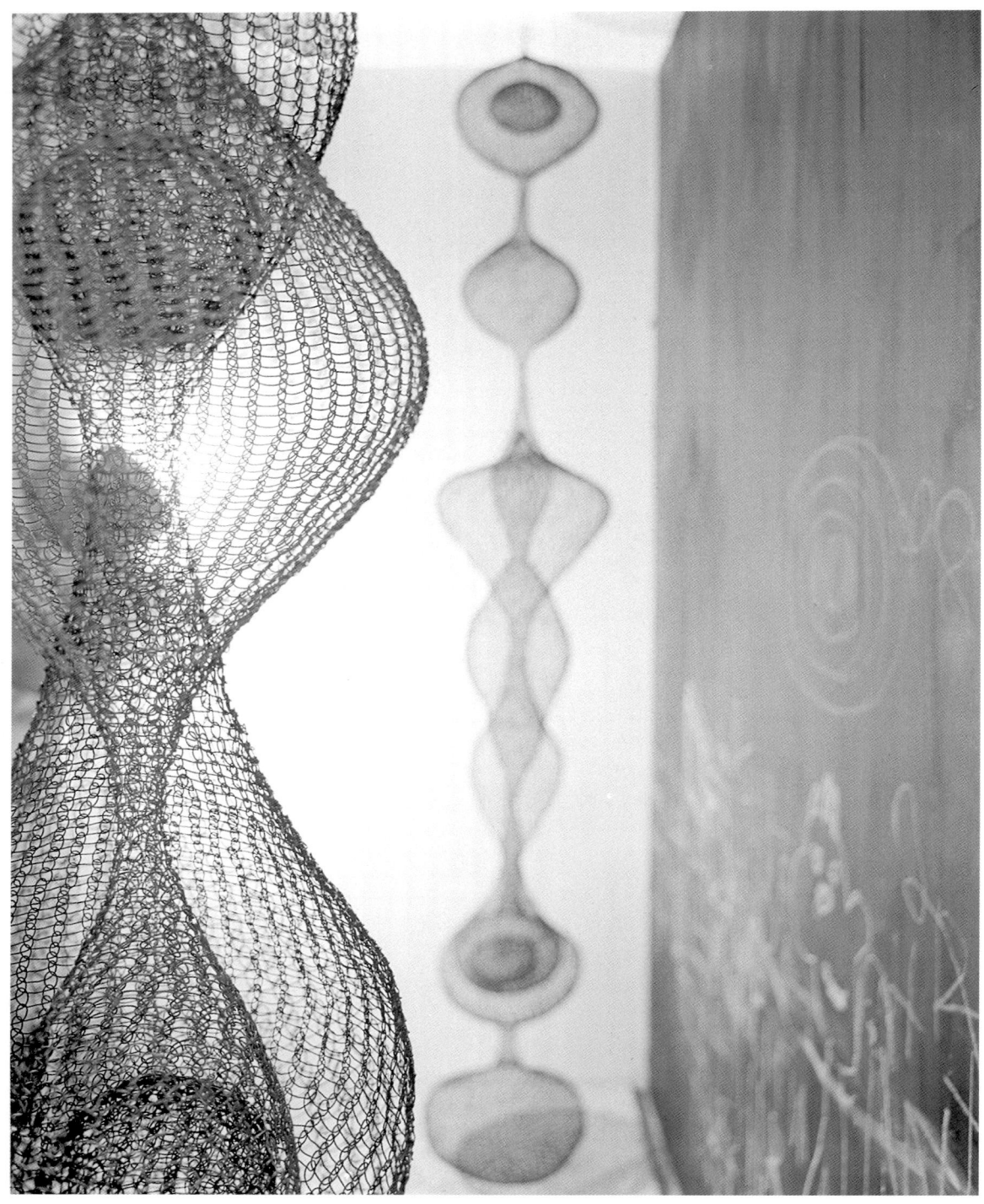

I.1 Paul Hassel, *Chalkboard and Looped-Wire Sculptures in Ruth Asawa's Saturn Street Home*, 1956. Gelatin silver print, 10 × 8 in. Private collection.

artist-mother Alice Neel, Asawa created abstract work that intervened in this space.[2] That space of domesticity in turn became the primary frame of reference for her works' significance, even when they were encountered outside of the home. I explore how this domesticity unfolded on two levels simultaneously. On the one hand, Asawa's domesticity was coded as a feminized space of childrearing and family, a space of knitting and "crocheting," as this particular journalist stressed, framed by "a blackboard of youngsters' scribbles." On the occasion of her retrospective at the San Francisco Museum of Art in 1973, this version of domesticity persisted, announcing Asawa's open embrace of her home and family: "She believes it is a normal and responsible part of an artist-mother's life to produce her art at home, even asking [for] help from her children, and not in a pristine studio elsewhere."[3]

Accompanying this model of the domestic as maternal was another, fairly incompatible version of the domestic as a space of modernist design. During the 1950s and 1960s, Asawa's sculptures were regularly featured in the showrooms of Laverne Originals and Design Research Inc.—pioneering sites of midcentury interior decoration, characterized by an ornament-free space of sleek design, the integration of indoor and outdoor spaces, and light-flooded rooms. The play of light that Asawa's sculptures orchestrated in their semitransparency, with the looped-wire surfaces nearly dissolving at the brightest point in a photograph by Paul Hassel, rendered them compatible with an emergent taste for natural light and glass walls (fig. I.1).[4] The context of modernist design also welcomed her rejection of a sculptural base, exposing the sculptural object to the contingency of lived space, including the movement of air and play of light. Very often, art critics picked up on this warm reception in the field of modernist design and went to some length to iterate just how much Asawa's sculptures actually belonged to this space of interior decoration—indeed, to the modernist *home*, rather than to the modernist museum. "These are 'domestic' sculptures in a feminine, handiwork mode," observed one critic in 1956, "small and light and unobtrusive for home decoration, not meant as is much contemporary sculpture, to be hoisted by cranes, carted by vans and installed on mountainsides."[5]

It was often the case that both versions of domesticity—as "feminine, handiwork" and as "home decoration"—had to be erased for Asawa to be received as an artist, as a practitioner of "contemporary sculpture." And we can see an exemplary instance of this selective history when we compare Hassel's photograph to its cropped version— the version that appeared on the exhibition announcement for Asawa's first solo show at Peridot Gallery in New York: notice how the chalkboard is conspicuously missing from the scene (fig. I.2). As a visual testament to the presence of children and to the Asawa-Lanier home, this object was excised from the picture. Once observed, other instances of the chalkboard's disappearance also come into view, such as in a more widely reproduced photograph by Hassel taken in the same corner of the house, in which Asawa sits on a stool, surrounded by her hanging creations, while behind her the chalkboard, once full of scribbles, has been conspicuously wiped clean. The topic of motherhood—indexed by the child's chalk drawings—is censored, literally erased, to fit a model of artistic meaning supposedly antithetical to that experience.

I.2 Peridot exhibition
announcement, 1958,
with photograph by
Paul Hassel. Private
collection.

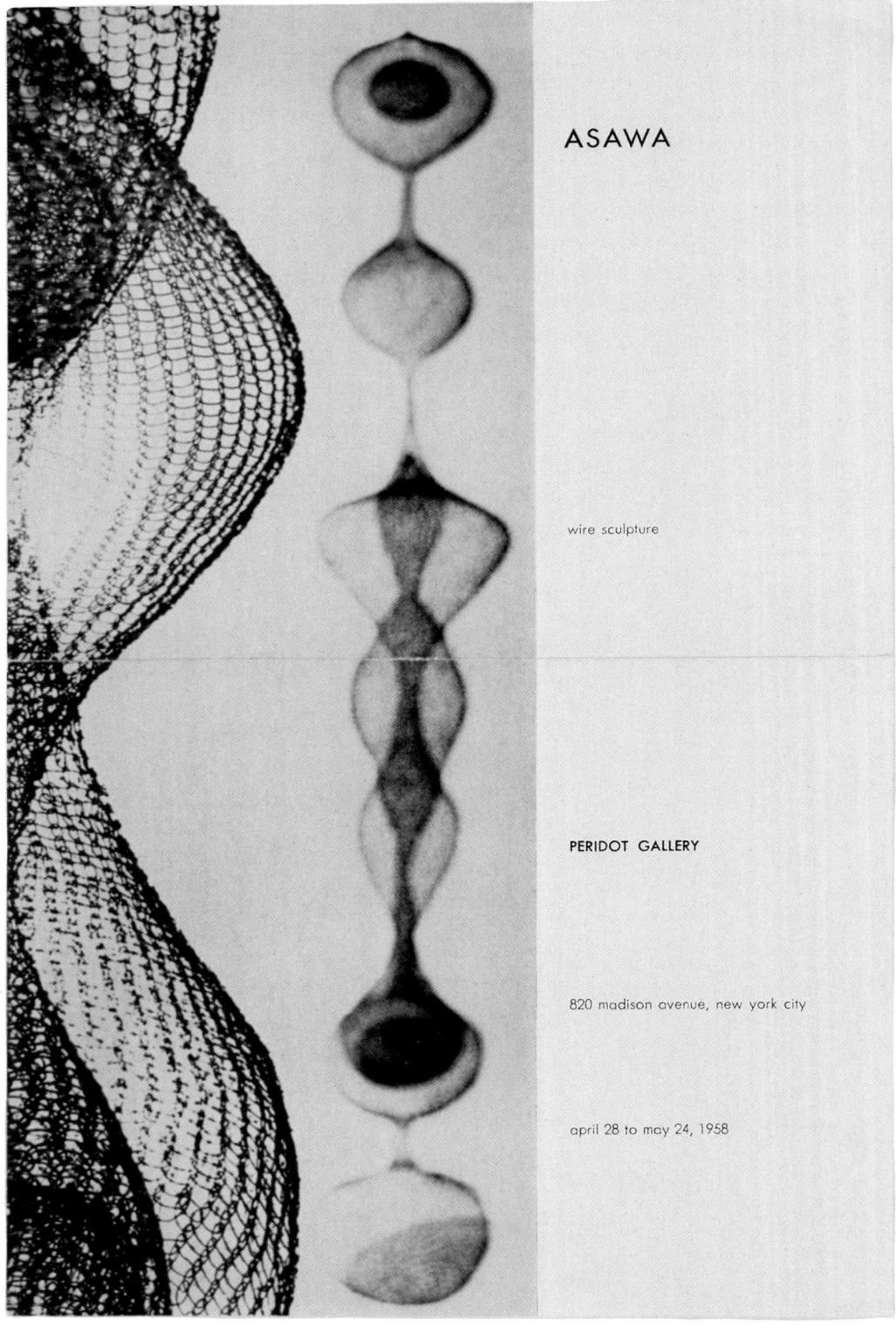

ASAWA

wire sculpture

PERIDOT GALLERY

820 madison avenue, new york city

april 28 to may 24, 1958

This is, in other words, the image of a profound disappearing act, not unlike that which Freud observed in his own toddler-aged grandchild, who used the terms *fort* (gone) and *da* (there) when playing. Freud was concerned with the role of repetition in childhood development; we are concerned with the compulsions of history writing. Page through the many exhibition catalogues on the artist that have appeared in the last few decades, and one immediately sees the emerging trope that her sculptures are meaningful beyond and apart from their maker's biography. Writers invested in admitting Asawa into the canon of American modernist sculpture have tended to claim that her reception should not be limited by her identity as a wife, mother, and second-generation Japanese American; that her work did not "directly correspond to her Japanese heritage or her role as a mother and wife."[6] The strength of her work lies in its mediation of light, space, and movement and its appearance of weightlessness—attributes that can be traced to sculpture's transformation in the early twentieth century from a medium of weight, mass, and memorialization to one of suspension, dynamism, and volume—which includes sculpture becoming, for the first time, an element of the domestic interior. If her biography plays any role at all in this modernist narrative, it is on the level of metaphor: in one account, transparency and opacity stage the visibility/invisibility of Asawa's racial background as an incarcerated Japanese American.[7]

In excising what Asawa often underscored—the imbrication of her art with motherhood, broadly defined—the assumption seems to be that her achievement as an artist could be made legible by suspending this aspect of her artistic persona or, alternatively, by sublimating biography to metaphor. But, as Helen Molesworth first asked, in the only critical reflection to date on Asawa's motherhood, "What if instead of insisting that women artists be judged by the same formal parameters as their male counterparts we instead ask what the terms 'mother'—or even the more scandalous, and typically pejorative 'housewife'—might have to teach us about being an artist?"[8] This is a question that could only be asked in the aftermath of second-wave feminism, when women artists began to stage the figure of the housewife as the producer of art. In the context of England in 1975, women "confined by childcare and domestic responsibility" sent one another images via post, which were then exhibited as a "postal art event" called Feministo and on view in the exhibition *Portrait of the Artist as a Housewife*, reviewed by Rozsika Parker.[9] Molesworth's question is informed by this feminist past, but it also revalorizes a space—of childcare and domesticity—historically regarded with contempt, even by feminists. Asawa differed from these feminist practitioners by embracing the conditions of childcare and domestic responsibility as—to invoke her retrospective catalogue once again—"a normal and responsible part of an artist-mother's life."

The task in what follows is to restore the cropped areas of Hassel's photograph. Such a task entails digging up those photographs that were never published, never even printed—I found another example, of Asawa holding her son, as a negative in the archives of the *San Francisco Examiner* (fig. I.3). It stages the artist-mother at home, sandwiched between a hanging looped-wire sculpture on one side and a toddler on her hip on the other, with the chalkboard and its marks of childhood in the background. Compare this to the cropped Hassel photograph as the more typical image employed to represent Asawa, and one immediately sees the contrast between two very different contexts of midcentury domesticity: the maternal and the modernist. In the 1950s and 1960s, Asawa occupied both spaces simultaneously—she was received as both a mother of six and a modernist designer. That we have difficulty today accounting for these multiple roles tells us less about history than it does about the machinations of the contemporary art market, as Sarah Archer astutely observes.[10] Hassel's photograph and its cropped version in the gallery exhibition announcement foreshadow this problematic. The erasure was made in an effort, no doubt, to ensure that this young, Asian American woman artist would be taken seriously in the male-dominated art world of 1950s New York. It is a seemingly innocuous gesture, surely made to focus the attention of potential visitors, but it speaks volumes now, given that Asawa was for so long written out of art history. The difference between the scribbled board and the board wiped clean tracks the profundity of that erasure.

To restore the domestic in Asawa's sculpture, I argue, is thus to take seriously both the journalists who pointed to Asawa's motherhood and the early critics with their pejorative dismissals of "domestic" sculptures. Neither should be explained away by pointing to originality and innovation elsewhere in the work, as if these voices somehow got it wrong. Nor do I think such a reception should be critiqued, if "critique" means simply reinscribing the opposition, but this time privileging "sculpture" over the "decoration" that her earlier critics dismissed.[11] Rather, we need to recognize how enduring this theme was in the first three decades of her production—at times to such a degree that children and sculpture, family and house, recursively stood for one another, as in the words of one *San Francisco Examiner* journalist describing "her Twin Peaks studio home, which colorfully mirrors her creativity, and that of her children and architect husband, Albert Lanier."[12] If this equation is not an isolated occurrence, then we need a context for why it proved so resilient. And we need to know more about that context—why it allowed for a coexistence of these terms in ways that other contexts did not. Why were modernist design and later craft, as we shall see, realms in which this alignment could unfold, whereas Asawa was repeatedly turned down by the Guggenheim Foundation for grants to support her work? Why the difference in tone between the local *Examiner*—generally enthusiastic about her work—and the *New York Times*, put off by the artmaking housewife from the Bay Area? Why does the art press have so little to say on the matter, while Asawa appears repeatedly in magazines geared toward the "housewife market," like *Ladies' Home Journal*?[13] What role, moreover, did photography play in mediating this context, given the hundreds of photographs by Imogen Cunningham, Paul Hassel, the ceramicist Joan Watkins Pearson, and others, which portray the making of sculpture—including its public forms—as a maternal act?

I address these questions by distinguishing between two domestic contexts in Asawa's reception: in chapter 1, Asawa's own home; and in chapter 2, the many other domestic sites in which her work appeared. Asawa's own home shaped the materials she would use and the way her sculpture would be viewed. This home was characterized

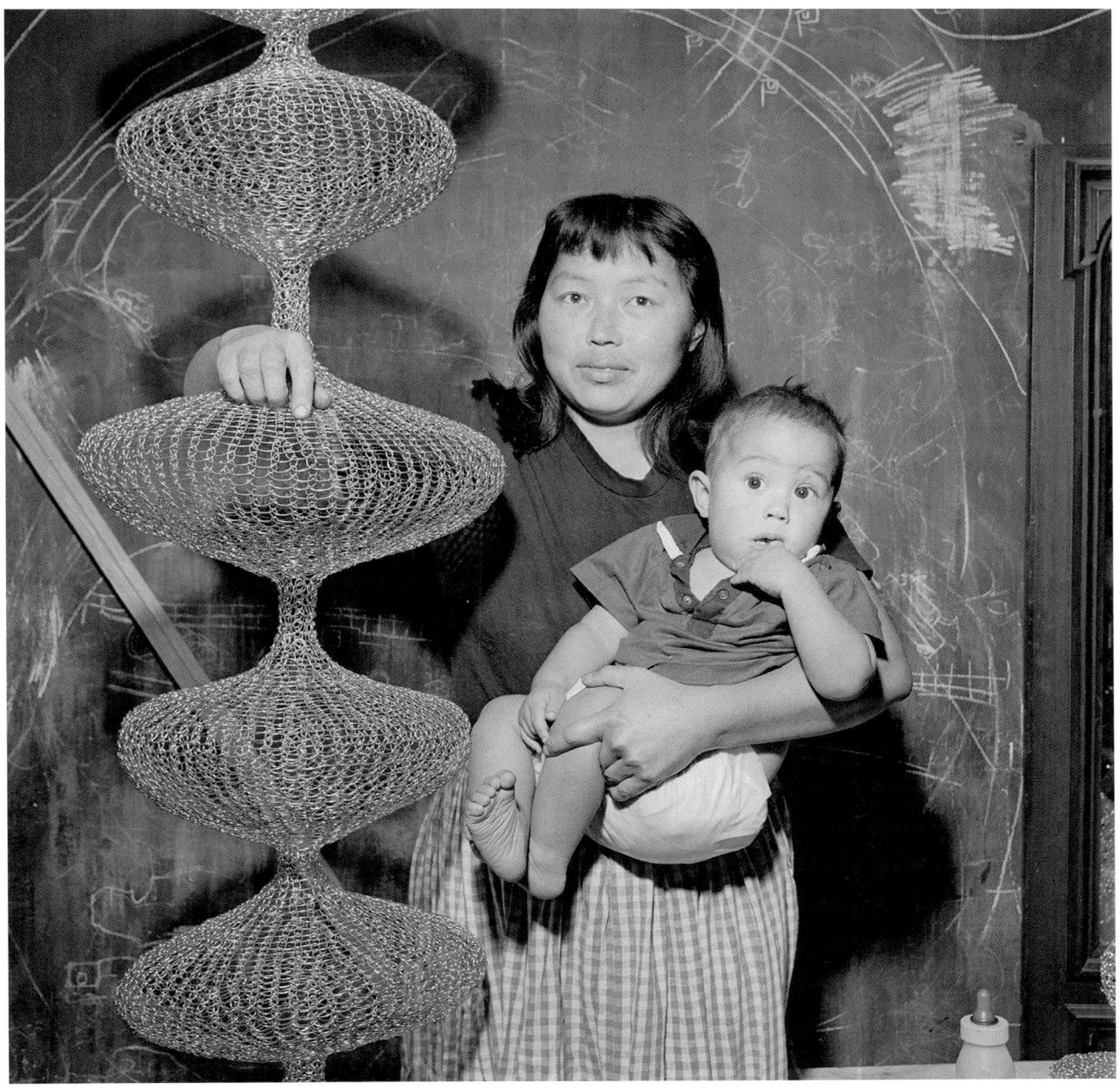

I.3 Ruth Asawa with son Paul in their Saturn Street home,
November 22, 1960. Photo: John Gorman. Fang family
San Francisco Examiner photograph archive negative files,
BANC PIC 2006.029—NEG, The Bancroft Library, University
of California, Berkeley.

by a confrontation between Victorian architecture and Bay region modernism. Photographs taken by Hassel as well as those by Nat Farbman for *Life* magazine place Asawa's sculptures in direct dialogue with the Victorian houses characteristic of the neighborhood, symbolic as they are of Victorian domesticity itself, whose rigid gender roles "call[ed] for a clear choice—either books or babies for a woman, not both," as Ursula K. Le Guin observed.[14] Asawa's close friend Sally Woodbridge was one of the first to historicize San Francisco's Victorian architecture, while Imogen Cunningham's photographs contributed to its visual sensibility; in both instances, Victorianism stood at odds with modernism. As I explore, the queer couple and the artist-mother unexpectedly converge around the recovery of Victorian architecture for alternative familial constellations, particularly because of its rejection by the modern aesthetic and social regimes that had become so dominant. This is architecture, as Woodbridge writes of Victorianism, "which seemed to successfully straddle all sorts of ideological fences."[15] The studio-home, I propose, furnished a place in which to foreground and at the same time *reclaim*, through a Victorian idiom, the modern interior as a space of maternal labor—a proposal utterly unconventional at the time. And in this Asawa was not alone. Renk, Cunningham, and Woodbridge, too, carried out their work in dialogue with the home as both a modernist and a maternal space. For all four, the "home" was decidedly not a space of oppression and exclusion, but a space in which another version of aesthetic production could be claimed. To be artist-mother sculptor, photographer, writer, and jewelry maker was to claim the generative status of maternal domesticity.

Chapter 2 moves away from Asawa's studio-home to consider her sculpture's traffic through the ideological contexts of design and craft—two other "interiors" that her sculptures inhabited in the 1950s and 1960s. I first consider Asawa's early work as a designer and how this shaped the direction of her sculptural practice as one in dialogue with the traditionally nonsculptural media of textiles, ceramics, and jewelry, leading to the important self-organized exhibition *Four Artist-Craftsmen* with Asawa, Merry Renk, Marguerite Wildenhain, and Ida Dean in 1954. Here the stakes were the so-called "female techniques" of this era, as Lucy Lippard described the sexual coding of "sewing, weaving, knitting, ceramics, even the use of pastel colors (pink!) and delicate lines."[16] This was a form of labor explicitly aligned with the domestic and feminine, which Asawa and Renk had adopted willingly, most specifically in a call-and-response exchange that unfolded over years of living and working in proximity to one another. These were also the terms by which Asawa's sculpture was repeatedly described—as "knit" and "crocheted"—even when the speaker knew that the words mischaracterized the technique (which was actually a form of looping). Examining this association with domesticity, we begin to see how Asawa's work was never at home in any of these modernist domestic spaces—given that "gender" and especially "motherhood" were often the suppressed terms. A closer look at how Asawa's work disturbed boundaries between craft and art, between the functional and the aesthetic, allows us to resolve this incoherency into a maternal genealogy of modernist design and craft.

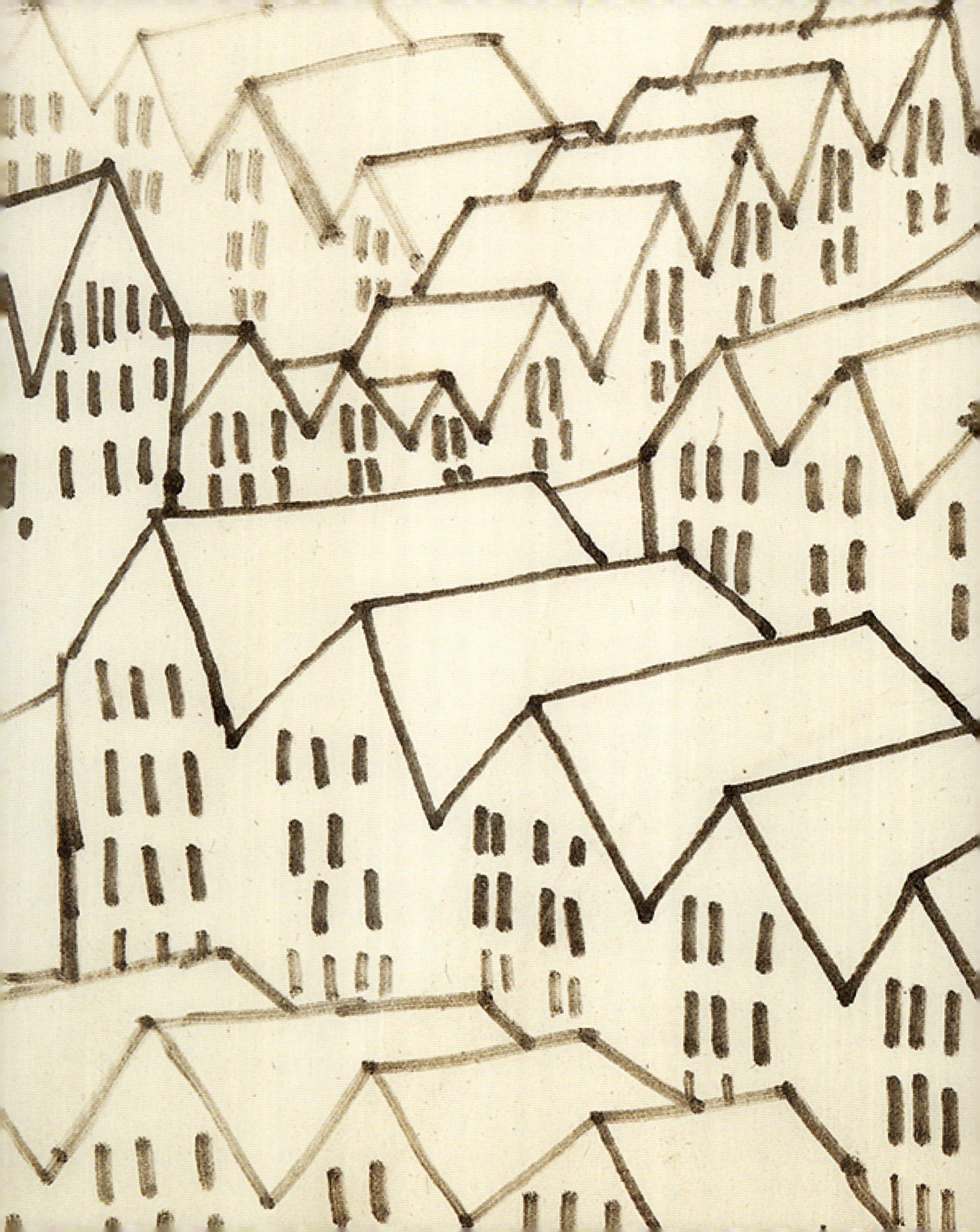

1 THE VIEW FROM SATURN STREET

In August 1954, Asawa wrote to family friend Celia Sieverts, "We have bought a sixty-year-old house and have moved to 21 Saturn Street, San Francisco 14, and [are] still tearing the house apart to make rooms larger to let sunlight in."[1] The house in question was a two-story Victorian built in the 1890s as part of a building boom in which this imported style, adapted to local needs, came to define the city's residential architecture. By the mid-twentieth century, as tract housing and suburbanization took hold, many of San Francisco's Victorians had been abandoned—and were to be had at affordable prices, especially by those capable of renovating this outmoded architecture. "We've been busy," Asawa continues in her letter. "Albert has just planned a house for his parents, is remodeling a friend's house while trying to fix the plumbing in ours." "Still in a mess," the renovations to the house were plagued by "interruptions": "Last week a friend called us up to gather cobblestones from a street that the city was tearing up to put new paving on, so instead of working on the house we spent the whole day gathering cobblestones. The next day we were completely worn out, but we are so happy with the stones. When we have time next spring, we'll work in the garden using them to build a wall around the edge of the property line," with the intention of adding soil in order to level out the ground.

Salvaging and repair characterize Asawa's orientation toward the making of her domestic space, as well as the making of her art. In addition to cobblestones, she gathered colored wire from slot machines that were being thrown away because of new city ordinances, incorporating these colored wires into her early sculptures. Anticipating their first child, she made a Japanese bamboo suitcase into a bassinet and sewed a mattress cover and sheet for it from discarded bedding and a Navy blanket.[2] This was an ethos of domestic repurposing that Asawa shared with other Bay Area artists with whom she otherwise had no contact—Jay DeFeo who made elaborate Christmas tree assemblages in lieu of a Douglas fir tree, and Jess who transformed the Victorian that he shared with poet Robert Duncan into a *Gesamtkunstwerk*-like "kitchen-painting," according to Tara McDowell in her study of how their "alternative household" as a gay couple challenged the postwar studio.[3] Sally Woodbridge, too, undertook elaborate wall paintings in her Berkeley kitchen. Even beyond these domestic sites, recycling shaped an approach to art's relationship to the domestic, emblematized in the founding of the SCRAP program in 1976 by Anne Marie Theilen, a leading force in the Alvarado School Arts Workshop. SCRAP rerouted surplus and discarded materials from local businesses to the schools, where art projects became an extension of experiments Asawa had long practiced at home with her children. Such initiatives, both private and public, were part of an overarching sensibility in which art and architecture were "cobbled from local and imported pieces of the past," Woodbridge wrote in her history of Bay Area houses.[4]

Asawa's studio-home existed within a broader landscape of Bay Area artist homes in which the domestic, "so often maligned as a site of conservatism and conformity, could be appropriated in radical and innovative ways," to borrow again from McDowell (fig. 1.1).[5] It was largely California's lack of a robust public infrastructure for the arts and its indifference toward the art market that prepared the ground for these "domestic utopias."[6] In such a landscape, as Elizabeth Ferrell argues in relation to Jay DeFeo, the domestic offered "a protective space within which to create alternative identities, communities, and artistic practices—a belief that held up a dark mirror to mainstream America's conformist and materialistic cult of domesticity."[7] It also offered a space in which aspects of bourgeois homemaking, including Victorian sentimentality, could be salvaged and repurposed—such as Jess pointing not to Dada or surrealism as the origins of his turn to collage, but rather to flowers cut out of 1950s women's magazines which a friend's mother had shown him.[8]

What distinguishes Asawa from these other Bay Area alternative households is her relationship to the "anarchist bohemian tradition" out of which they grew.[9] Typically opposed to bourgeois domesticity, the bohemian lifestyle rejects its institutions—marriage, heterosexual monogamy, salaried labor, a tidy household, consumerism, and—as I explore in this chapter—children. Jay DeFeo may have been married but she otherwise fit the bill; in their rejection of heteronormativity, Jess and Duncan entirely fulfilled these expectations. Barred from the bohemian tradition, however, were artist-mothers like Asawa, who willingly embraced the labor of the 1950s housewife, raising six children and maintaining a home, even if her paint-splattered jeans and tennis shoes reject this figure's apron-clad attire. Similarly, her relationship to Albert Lanier took the form of a marriage, but one regarded as controversial at a time in which anti-miscegenation laws in the state had just been repealed.[10] We can extend this complexity to the sculptures, which can be read simultaneously as engaging an outmoded Victorian sensibility—Ray Johnson's friend May Wilson memorably called one of her looped-wire pieces a "Victorian string holder"—and as belonging to the emergent Bay region modernist interior—homes that, as Sally Woodbridge wrote, rejected the "Victorian penchant for gaudy ornament" and embraced "the ideal of the indoor-outdoor house" native to California, with its mild climate and

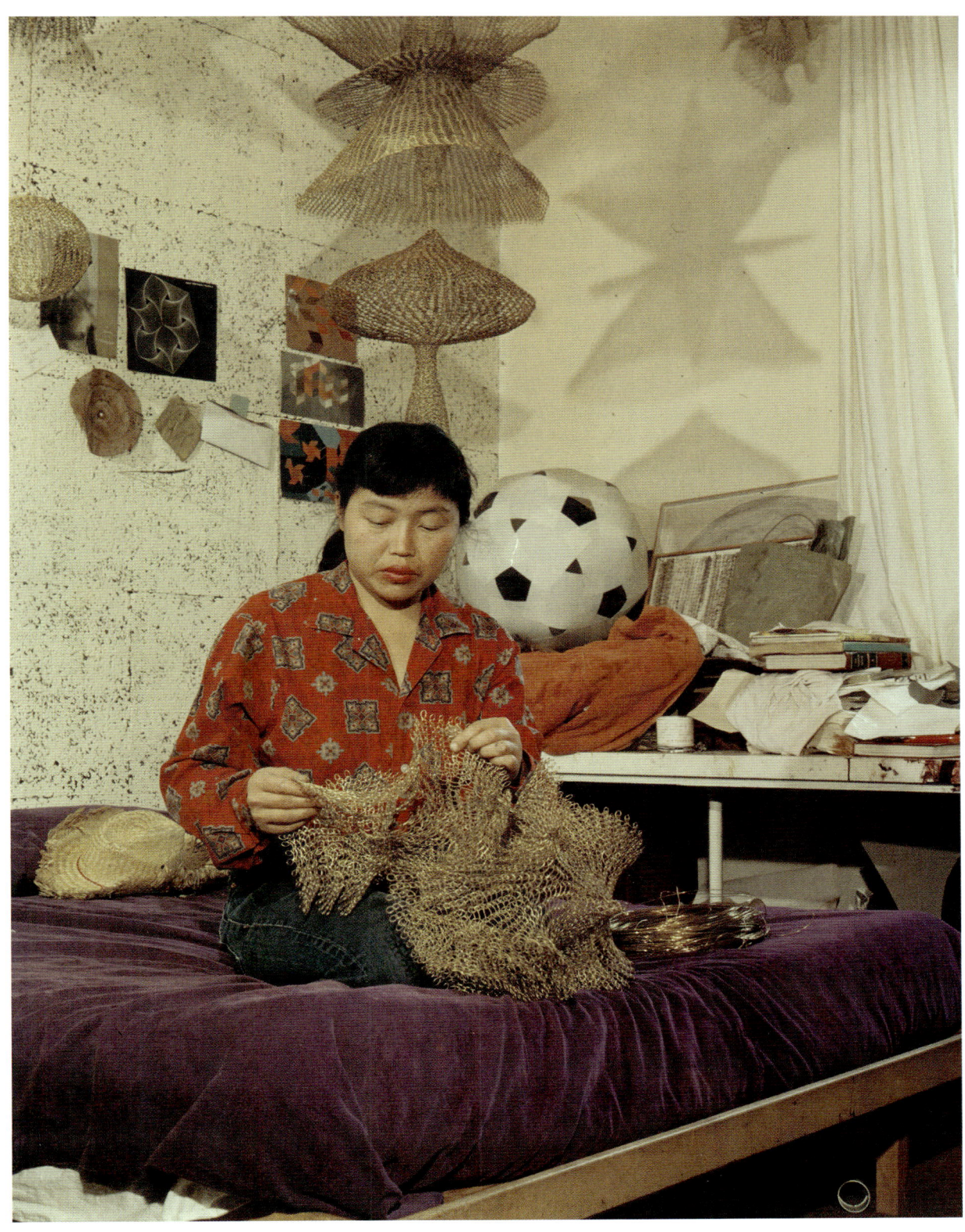

1.1 Ruth Asawa Lanier, February 12, 1961. Unknown photographer. Fang family *San Francisco Examiner* photograph archive negative files, BANC PIC 2006.029—NEG, The Bancroft Library, University of California, Berkeley.

lush landscape.[11] Bohemia, Victorianism, and modernism called forth very different models of alternative domestic space, and yet they were spaces that Asawa and her peers treated as compatible.

MATERNAL AMBIVALENCE

While studying at Black Mountain College in North Carolina, Asawa had already been confronted with both the expectations of postwar domesticity and its challengers. The confrontation came in the form of a brochure the artist Peggy Tolk-Watkins had sent her in January 1949—six months before Asawa's move to San Francisco. Tolk-Watkins and her partner, Ragland ("Rags") Watkins, had moved to the city the previous fall, making the cross-country drive with Lanier. San Francisco was an unusual choice for the time. "An artistic wilderness," as Lanier once described it, the city had none of the arts infrastructure that New York offered.[12] And for that reason it likely proved attractive to the alternative-thinking, architecture-and-design-oriented Black Mountain crowd. An instructor in weaving there, Trude Guermonprez, joined the fledgling crafts-based school Pond Farm near Guerneville, seventy miles north of San Francisco, which counted Marguerite Wildenhain among its faculty. Lured by cheap rents and the affordable cost of living—Tolk-Watkins boasted of a five-course Italian dinner and a bottle of red wine in North Beach for seventy-five cents—Lanier was also attracted to the area's booming architecture. A city experiencing a population growth at a time when many inner cities were witnessing an exodus to the suburbs, San Francisco offered opportunities in the building trades: "perhaps no place offers stiffer competition for architects than California which possibly makes it true that no better work is being done, or more uniformly demanded, than here," Lanier wrote to his parents on April 13, 1949.

The brochure that Tolk-Watkins sent to Asawa portrays this expansion of the area's housing in the form of an advertisement to buy a house in Sausalito, a sleepy hamlet just north of the city, which was billed as a "city of homes [and] gateway to the redwood empire" (fig. 1.2). Inscribing the depicted aerial photograph, Tolk-Watkins showed Asawa exactly where she had opened her nightclub-cum-gallery, the Tin Angel, one of the city's earliest gay bars, which also had an attached cottage where the couple lived.[13] With her sarcastic "ha!" scrawled next to the cover's cheery use of the word "homes," Tolk-Watkins undercut the brochure's fantasy of domestic belonging. This was domesticity to be bought, ready-made and en masse, with the "home" as a site of consumption and conformity, an ideology that Joan Ockman describes as "the mythological imagery of the house as a nest and haven presided over by a nurturing mother figure."[14]

Asawa would have agreed with Tolk-Watkins's dismissal of this mythical version of the postwar house "as nest and haven." In a letter to Lanier while visiting her parents' temporary housing in one room of the former Japanese language school in southern California, in which "six of us sleep in a room as big as Peggy's living room," she bemoans suburban sprawl. "We are surrounded by 1000s of American homes, and one can see so well how patterns of idle thinking develop. Every fifth house thinks the same

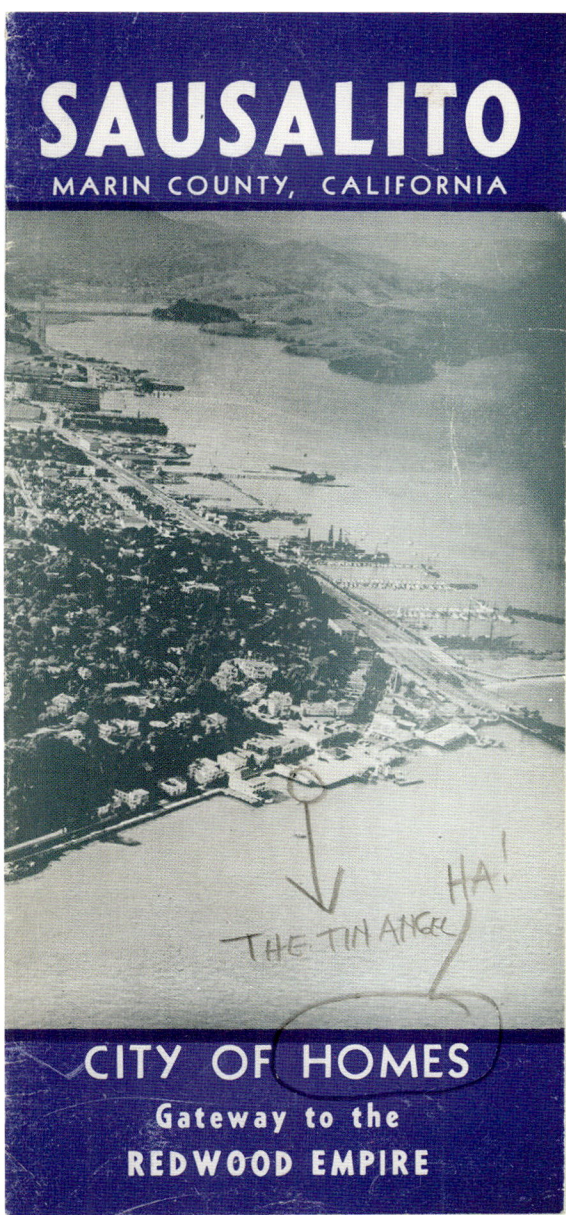

1.2 Brochure included in a letter from Peggy Tolk-Watkins to Ruth Asawa, January 28, 1949. Private collection.

because their houses are painted pink, etc. It is terrifying."[15] This was the monotony and conformity that Black Mountain resisted, generating instead creative, independent, self-determined individuals who worked collectively across disciplines. Home-making at Black Mountain was not consumed but constructed, from the school's work program—to which Asawa contributed by churning butter, cutting hair, and working in the laundry room—to the making of domestic possessions in the woodshop and on simple looms.[16] Black Mountain was a place where "if you wanted a chair they'd say, 'Go up there. There's a wood shop there. You can make your own chair.'"[17] A house was a work in progress, malleable to the needs of the inhabitant and open to change.

As a newly minted mother and housewife seeking to redefine those terms, Tolk-Watkins was having none of it. Though technically a nuclear family—the Watkinses had had a baby in October 1948—they were not exactly the brochure's intended audience. The couple's bisexuality was an open secret: a former Black Mountain colleague, Paul Williams, referred to their "unique methods" as a euphemism for their open relationship.[18] Lanier stayed with the couple when he first arrived in the city; he often joined them for dinner and helped out with the household chores, "minding the baby occasionally or rendering other services" in return for his keep.[19] One evening, he returned "to find half of the living room ceiling knocked out by Peggy and Rags while we were away. We cut out the rafters and now Peggy has a mezzanine doubling her floor area. This lasted until 2 A.M. and I was so exhausted I couldn't write what I had felt earlier," he relayed to Asawa.[20] Tolk-Watkins was especially fond of Asawa, and her interjections pepper Lanier's letters. "Ever since [arriving]," he wrote to Asawa, "our lives have been those of young men perpetually on the brink of 'big deals.' Peggy has inexhaustible numbers of leads and we have been going every minute. All of this has been accompanied by a private but persistent song in Praises of Ruth sung by Peggy to me."[21]

It was during these months, before her arrival in San Francisco, that Asawa collaborated with Tolk-Watkins on a collection of the latter's "poemstories." Tolk-Watkins requested from Asawa "simple line drawings in black ink on white paper," which would help to convey how "the poems are themselves pictures."[22] For a poem about a tiger with six stripes, Asawa came up with the idea of using vertical rows of postage stamps, with the wavy lines of the post office stamp cancellation serving as provisional paws (fig. 1.3). The canvas by Tolk-Watkins which later hung in the Asawa-Lanier home was likely part of this project, portraying a six-striped tiger—three stripes on each side—looking out at the viewer as it walks along the bottom edge of a blue and green landscape (fig. 1.4). As reviewers observed on the occasion of an exhibition of Tolk-Watkins's paintings in 1961, the paintings' surfaces were "sculpted into shape" through layers that sometimes reached two inches thick—"a fascinating three-dimensional effect" that, as one critic put it, "a child (and adult) is tempted to rub his hands over." *Tiger with Six Stripes* was part of a series of animal paintings that critics described as "primitive" due to their embrace of recognizable subject matter, lack of shadow, flat planes of color, and shallow landscapes. In the vein of Morris Hirshfield, whose *Tiger* (1940) was on view in *Modern Primitives: Artists of the People* at New York's Museum of Modern Art in the 1940s, Tolk-Watkins was categorized among the "self-taught" artists of the era—even though she had studied art at Black Mountain College—with critics suggesting that her canvases were "related to what a child might see and paint," and even were "perfect for decorating a nursery or child's bedroom," while at the same time admitting that "her 'primitivism' is that of a sophisticated adult."[23] Local art critic Alexander Fried was clearly disturbed by what he saw, writing, of the "housewife" artist who had written a children's book and taught as a settlement house worker, that her "primitive visions of crude animals and landscape give out a brassy, brash coloristic blast in which she plasters on the pigment as thick

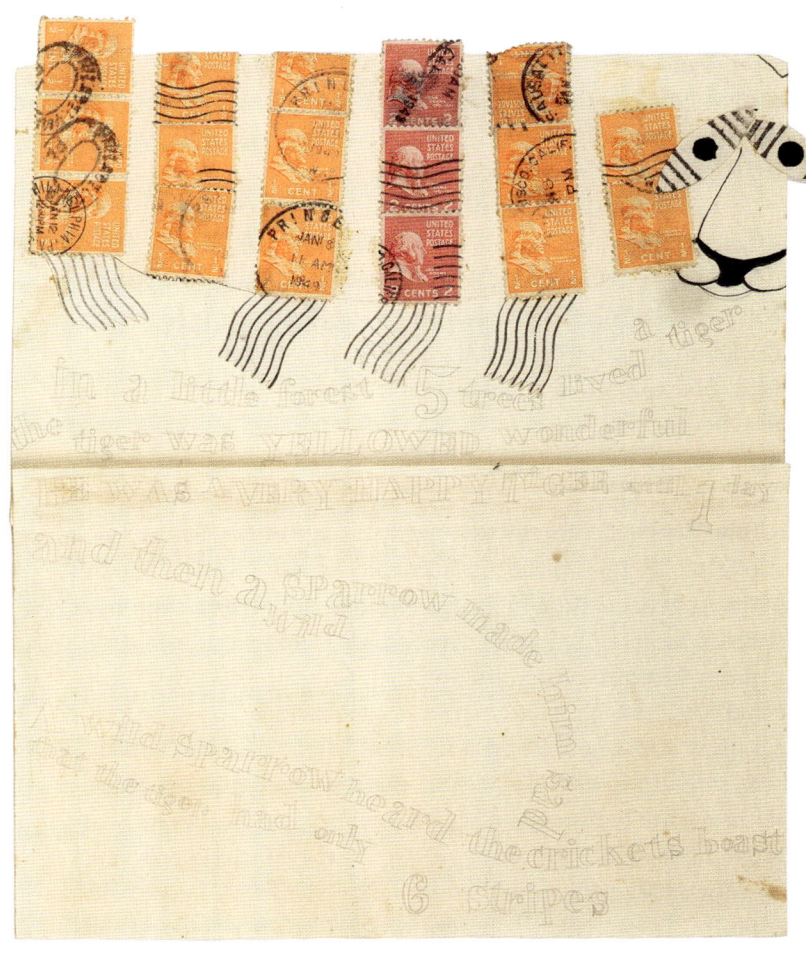

1.3 Ruth Asawa, drawing included in a letter to Peggy Tolk-Watkins, January 8, 1949. Private collection.

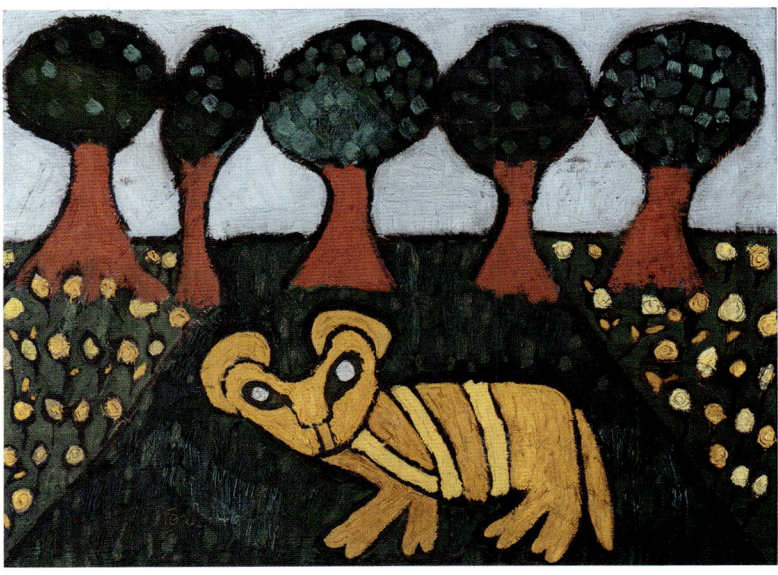

1.4 Peggy Tolk-Watkins, *Tiger with Six Stripes,* 1946. Oil on canvas on board, 17¾ × 24 in. Private collection.

as bas-relief. There's a childish nightmare aspect in the way she here and there makes an animal cast a Charles Addams sort of horrific eye at the viewer."[24]

The planned collaboration between the two artist-mothers presumably was never completed, and it would seem that Tolk-Watkins published the book, *Pigs Ate My Roses*, without Asawa's drawings.[25] But the collaboration furnished an opportunity for each to reflect on how they felt about the topic of motherhood. Tolk-Watkins wrote to Asawa on feeling conflicted about her new role as mother and artist: "To be really articulate one must give, and giving, really giving, is to be creative—I feel creative, but not outgoing in my creativity." She thanked Asawa for "a very green frog"—Asawa must have sent her an origami jumping frog, for Tolk-Watkins added, "he jumps beautifully."[26] Asawa responded to Tolk-Watkins's ambivalence by encouraging her to embrace her new role: "being a mother is far more than anything. Why not two years or four of just being a mother? I can think of nothing better. I could love nothing better."[27]

Another response to Tolk-Watkins's identity as a mother comes from Susan Sontag, who recorded her visit to "Peggy's place" in Sausalito in her journal. Sontag had been invited to the Tin Angel's opening by Harriet Sohmers Zwerling, who had known Tolk-Watkins at Black Mountain College, where they were lovers. We know that this "oppositional queer feminist" circle, as Stephen Duncan describes these women, directly intersected with Asawa's: a letter attests that Zwerling, Tolk-Watkins, and Asawa all attended a party at the house of the architect Mario Corbett (Lanier's boss at the time).[28] Sontag's description of the visit to the renovated cottage points to Tolk-Watkins's refusal to decide between her artistic identity and her identity as a mother. "When we walked back [in the house] I discovered two more girls plus Peggy's baby son. . . . The idea of Peggy's harem seemed very ridiculous—I especially wondered how Rags took it. . . . The three of them went to sleep in the other bed and Harriett and I went in to sleep on a narrow cot in the back of the Tin Angel."[29] This is a situation in which the queer expansion of erotic relationships intersects with relationships, such as that between mother and child, which have been typically excluded from such nonnormative forms of kinship, as Sontag's own biography demonstrates. A decade later, with a nine-year-old of her own, David, and an ex-husband suing her for custody on the basis of her relationship with a woman, the courts forced Sontag to choose between being a lesbian and a mother, an episode that Julie Phillips recounts in her book *The Baby on the Fire Escape: Creativity, Motherhood, and the Mind-Baby Problem*: "the price for keeping her son is a piece of herself, and she pays it. To the end of her life she will lie about her love for women."[30]

NOT BOHEMIA

Upon moving to San Francisco in summer 1949, Asawa intersected tangentially with these bohemian circles. When Tolk-Watkins closed the Sausalito location of the Tin Angel and reopened it on San Francisco's Embarcadero, one of the first events at the new location was an exhibition of Asawa's work alongside paintings by Black

Mountain College instructor Jean Varda, titled *Six of Asawa, a Dozen of Varda*, during the summer of 1953. It was through the Tin Angel that Asawa very likely met her longtime patron William Roth, who became one of her earliest collectors, buying a wire piece during a fundraiser that Tolk-Watkins had organized. Roth would later become owner of Ghirardelli Square and commission Asawa to contribute the public sculpture that became *Andrea*, which I discuss in chapter 5.

Lanier was even more involved in the Tin Angel than Asawa. Tolk-Watkins had tried to convince him to become a partner in the nightclub. He declined the offer, worried that such a project would interfere with his ability to establish himself as an architect. ("What would have happened to Bill de Kooning if he had taken a job as a jewelry salesman so that he could eventually retire to his painting?" he wrote to Asawa on September 25, 1948.) But he supported the venture in other ways: Tolk-Watkins's papers at the Sausalito Historical Society contain drawings with elaborate lettering done by Lanier for the restaurant's menus. He also appears to have drawn up in handwritten typography a cryptic excerpt from a 1900 women's cosmetic guide, entitled *How to Become Beautiful*, on the use of "paints and powders" in wearing makeup—undoubtedly at the request of Tolk-Watkins, who had likely found its Victorian obsession with over-the-top feminized self-presentation fitting the campy aesthetic she wanted to create in the bar.

Above all, with his expertise as an architect and with building, Lanier was recruited to help with the renovations to the former crab restaurant and the attached cottage at the Tin Angel's first location. The cottage renovations set out the direction that his and Asawa's homes would take over the next decade—knocking down walls, adding loft levels, maximizing light, using readily available materials. In letters to Asawa back in Asheville, North Carolina, Lanier details their progress: "cottage almost finished— beautiful, glowing white inside—bath wonderful—canvas shower stall—they did all the plumbing—at night while the tide was out from under the dock."[31] Drawing on an economy of materials that he had learned from Buckminster Fuller, Lanier knocked down the interior wall separating the "crab room" and the "rented area" in order to open up the main area into a living space–bedroom, with the two smaller tool rooms now adapted as the baby's room and the bathroom. The former restaurant which would house the Tin Angel, however, was decidedly at odds with this repurposed modernism. Described as "part Greenwich Village, part Paris" by local critic Ralph Gleason, the nightclub embodied the opposite of what Lanier was trying to accomplish in the cottage.[32] Its aesthetic "practically invented camp as interior decoration" and included Fuller-style global lights, Renaissance paintings, vintage circus posters, a carnivalesque stage set, and the club's trademark, a silhouetted tin angel, which Tolk-Watkins had acquired from a church by "hot-foot[ing] it to New York" while leaving "husband Rags to look after their new baby," reported the local newspaper.[33] When "mad painter" Jean Varda began "the decoration of the Tin Angel" with "wild colors," Lanier wrote to Asawa and an unknown recipient, "I kept thinking of work with Fuller, work on the model, and even work with the carpenters—I do not like Bohemia and do not want to live 'Bohemianly.'"[34]

This is an astonishing comment and offers multiple readings, which I will expand in the following section. For now, though, it is crucial to see that the term "bohemian" offers a clue to what Asawa's domesticity defined itself against. For the dominant understanding of this term is its opposition to heteronormative, bourgeois sociability. In addition to claiming a socialist politics, Tolk-Watkins moved in the area's anarchist-libertarian circles, "bringing together elements of jazz/bohemianism and the city's gay and lesbian community," Duncan points out.[35] Jay DeFeo's husband, the painter Wally Hedrick, summed up this opposition to bourgeois normativity when he relayed to an interviewer in 1985: "I decided a long time ago that I can't be a nice, middle-class American and do what I want to do. . . . You have to be really egocentric and think of yourself first. Kids, wives, mothers—all of that has to be set aside."[36] Bohemia is a child-free place, both literally—DeFeo and Hedrick did not have children—and figuratively: it was a place in which creative production unfolded autonomously, with collective authorship allowed only insofar as it did not infringe on creative autonomy. This was the "challenge, if not the impossibility," as Ferrell writes, of Bay Area bohemian domesticity at midcentury.[37]

Yet both Tolk-Watkins and Asawa insisted that creative autonomy and motherhood could be made compatible. And that insistence unfolded in large part through the remaking of their own domestic spaces—with the help of Lanier, of course. In this respect, it is instructive to examine briefly his approach to interior architecture, for the cottage did not belong to the bohemian aesthetic of the carnivalesque Tin Angel, and neither did it conform to the midcentury modernist interior.

Lanier's first steady job in San Francisco was employment with the architect Mario Corbett. Sally Woodbridge describes Corbett's office as "a kind of graduate school of design."[38] Many young architects worked with him and then went on to establish their own successful practices—including Lanier. Twenty years older than Lanier and trained in Europe, Corbett had been practicing in California since the 1930s and was regarded as one of the state's five leading architects.[39] He was also one of the most widely published California architects of the era, largely due, as Lanier recalled, to the efforts of his wife June who promoted his work to publications.[40] Personal letters indicate that Lanier had first met Corbett through former Black Mountain teacher Jean Varda, whose studio mate in California was the English surrealist painter Gordon Onslow Ford (the two men shared a ferryboat in the bay at Sausalito). Corbett regularly hosted dinners and parties with artists who had been at Black Mountain, including Asawa, Lanier, and Tolk-Watkins. Lanier had landed the job by bringing in photographs of the Minimum House, a Black Mountain project—Lanier excitedly relayed to Asawa Corbett's praise of her work on the garden wall, "thinking the stonework beautiful (!)."[41] Corbett also admired his drawings for "the Asawa house," which he was developing for her parents' farm in Norwalk, California, and which, if built, was to be "a masterpiece of low-cost housing."[42] Corbett took a liking to Lanier, and often invited him and his Black Mountain friends over for dinner at his house on Wolfback Ridge in Sausalito. He was impressed by Lanier's work ethic and innovative approaches, asking that Lanier forgo the "customary pencil sketches" for the Smith

House and instead "make line drawings like you did for the Black Mountain house" and a model, with the intention to send photographs to *Arts and Architecture* for publication.[43]

As a young architect in Corbett's practice, Lanier often intertwined his work with both his affection for Asawa and the home that they would build together. Referring to a house for "a young engineer—about 27—who has read all the popular magazines on 'modern California homes,'" he wrote to her, "at night my dreams are mixed with you and a difficult dimension of the house I plan now."[44] Lanier's engagement with modern architecture was also an expression of his love for Asawa. San Francisco's urban fabric embodied that romantic charge: "Last night and today I have been in love with everything—torn billboards, brick walls, my little room and most of all you," Lanier wrote in April.[45] He culled these romantic musings on the city from evening site visits he made to the hill in Sausalito, where he had bought a plot of land and wanted to build a house. In his letters, architectural features of the urban landscape became imbued with libidinal investments that are only superficially veiled: "Will think of you every time I cross Golden Gate bridge—it is at once religious, sculptural, sexual—the wire supported bridge spanning the beginnings of an ocean—from a nervous city to dumb, barren mountains."[46]

It was in Corbett's house in Sausalito in the summer of 1949 that Asawa and Lanier held their wedding reception. After Asawa's arrival in the city, the couple lived in their rented loft on Jackson Street, in the city's industrial district. The wedding was as unconventional as they come. Asawa wore a black dress made of fabric gifted by Anni Albers. Trude Guermonprez's mother, Johanna Jalowetz, sewed the fabric into a suit with a long skirt, designed in such a way that Asawa could shorten it after the wedding and wear it as part of her regular wardrobe.[47] The German-Jewish composer and music pedagogue Charlotte Schlesinger, who had taught at Black Mountain, played the piano. Apparently, Asawa had trouble reciting her vows. As Lanier recalled, "They all laughed and we cried and we laughed and we got through it. [Tolk-Watkins's] baby, Ragland, was crawling on the floor and it was a riot."[48] Buckminster Fuller had designed Asawa's wedding ring, which he described in the same terms as he did his architectural experiments: "a wedding ring for you and Albert is in process of design. It is dymaxion i.e.: 'unity is (at minimum) two fold.'"[49] The reception at Corbett's house, a humble affair of cold cuts and champagne among Black Mountain friends (including the Watkinses and their baby), was framed by "Corbett's hill with the most beautiful view of the ocean and bay on either side."[50]

VICTORIA'S LEGACY

The bohemian interior of the Tin Angel, on the one hand, and the Bay region modernism of Mario Corbett's Sausalito bungalow, on the other, are two moments in a broader history of what Elizabeth Ferrell calls, with direct reference to DeFeo's monumental household painting *The Rose* (1958–1966), "domesticated high modernism." With this term, Ferrell expounds an understanding of art's imbrication with the private sphere in which "the domestic environment principally protected (rather than liquidated) the possibility for autonomy and transcendence by providing a rare space of creative freedom."[51] This is an "alternative tradition of the avant-garde sublation of art and life," which can be traced back to Piet Mondrian's Paris apartment, which he painted as if a three-dimensional version of his gridded canvases, and to Kurt Schwitters's *Merzbau*—a form of domestic intervention that "posits the home as a site, perhaps the only site, where the grand ambitions of romanticism are still potentially achievable in the twentieth century."[52]

That last term—romanticism—is complex; here it functions as a catchall for a concept of art's autonomy. Whether it goes by the name "high modernism," the "avant-garde," "artistic Bohemia," or "romanticism," art as an autonomous sphere of engagement posits the artist as a self-made genius and his or her artworks as a condensation of that transcendence. This is a familiar story; it is one that feminist scholar Linda Nochlin pointed to in her now-canonical essay "Why Have There Been No Great Women Artists?" (1971) when she argued that the conditions underlying such conceptions must be investigated, rather than accepted as fact. And even though the myth of the Great Artist is by now well deconstructed, what remains untouched is how this orientation led to the kind of antimaternal comments articulated by Hedrick above. In this defense of autonomy, there is no space for a maternal figure in the position of creator; such a figure is far too relational and contingent to embody this autonomy—a self that, as Susan Griffin wrote in her essay "Feminism and Motherhood" (1974), is defined in Western culture as continually sacrificed for the benefit of the child.[53] A self, in other words, that does not properly exist at all.

This conscription of the maternal figure as selfless—as the relational figure at odds with the romantic vision of the autonomous artwork—is why one repeatedly encounters women artists hostile to being identified with this category. DeFeo, for instance, resented her prescribed role as housewife in her marriage with Hedrick, who expected her to perform the household chores.[54] A comparative example is Louise Bourgeois, who, despite employing an iconography that admits maternal imagery, regarded her dual identity as artist and mother with antipathy. In the 1940s, she made a series of works depicting the conflation of a female body and architectural structures, which she titled *Femme maison*, "housewife," or more literally, "woman house." In each of these works, the house seems to cannibalize the female figure and deform her torso. Julie Phillips relays how destabilizing Bourgeois's self-doubt became: "When a fellow artist referred to her as a 'housewife' she raged in her diary: 'I could twist the neck of the world.' At one point her son had to bar the door of her studio to keep her from destroying its contents. Though her husband tried taking charge of the children so she could work, anxiety attacks caused her to stop showing her art for nearly a decade. 'I had the feeling that the art scene belonged to the men, and that I was in some way invading their domain. Therefore my work was done but hidden away.'"[55] This ambivalence is the subject of Mignon Nixon's study on Louise Bourgeois, *Fantastic Reality: Louise Bourgeois and a Story of Modern Art*, in which she illuminates how a woman artist at midcentury posed a "challenge to the Oedipal narratives of late modernism."[56] Nixon's subject is close to my own: here were women making work that rejected the Freudian imperative that the mother be sublimated in order for the child to enter into culture. Nixon argues that a more relevant model is provided by the early twentieth-century psychoanalyst Melanie Klein. Klein's theory of object relations, in distinction to Freud's theory, assigns a prominent role to the interaction between mother and child, which is far more complex than a matter of sublimation. But even as Bourgeois's ambivalence toward motherhood—especially her engagement with aggression, depression, and mourning—may be explained by Klein's theory of infant development, that ambivalence remains, further reinforcing my claim that the prohibition on motherhood persisted even for those figures hostile to the romantic vision of the autonomous work.

Consider, however, another picture of domesticity, which we can distinguish from both the bohemian and the modernist interior, as spaces largely antithetical to motherhood. It is conveyed in an unpublished photograph taken by Nat Farbman, on assignment for *Life* magazine, during a visit to Asawa's Saturn Street house. He captures Asawa standing at a washbasin cleaning a soap-covered looped-wire sculpture, with three children observing their mother at work (fig. 1.5). Here the labor at issue is not the cleaning of dishes but the maintaining of art—the labor not of an artist, nor of a mother, but of someone who occupies both roles. A clue to this photograph can be found in the view framed by the window at the left: a vista looking out onto the city's rows of Victorian homes. This architecture housed a conception of motherhood that the romantic view of things—and its modernist inheritors—squarely rejected, namely, "an all-encompassing identity rooted in notions of self-sacrifice and infused with powerful social and political meaning," as Rebecca Jo Plant defines late-Victorian motherhood.[57]

Asawa and her fellow artist-mothers were careful observers of these Victorian structures. The house on Saturn Street, which Asawa and Lanier moved into as their family grew in size, was situated on a hillside with windows facing the rolling topography of the city's landscape. Furnishing a particular view of the city, the house motivated Asawa to create a series of drawings in pen, pencil, and marker, many of which conflate the flatness of the page with the city's steep topography: "this fantastic city built on seven hills," as Asawa put it, "Telegraph hill, Russian Hill, Nob Hill, Twin Peaks, Potrero Hill, Bernal Heights, Pacific Heights, all with a view of the bay or/and the Golden Gate Bridge."[58] With its inhabitants as "cliff dwellers," Twin Peaks offered a vista described by residents as "the best urban view in the world."[59] In Farbman's photograph, though, the view does not open up onto a horizon so much as onto visual pattern itself. The photographer Phiz Mozesson (née Mezey) had also depicted the same hillside, located behind the houses on Saturn Street, in photographs for the book *Our San Francisco*. Shot in her neighborhood, around the block from Asawa, one photograph depicts two children with a Victorian house in the background, while two others, including Mozesson's daughter, play on the backyard slope nicknamed "rocky hill."[60] The hill was a frequent site of play for the neighborhood children, and Mae Lee's daughter recalls going there often with her brother and the two eldest Asawa children (the Lee family lived just up the street).[61] It is likely this hill that is depicted in

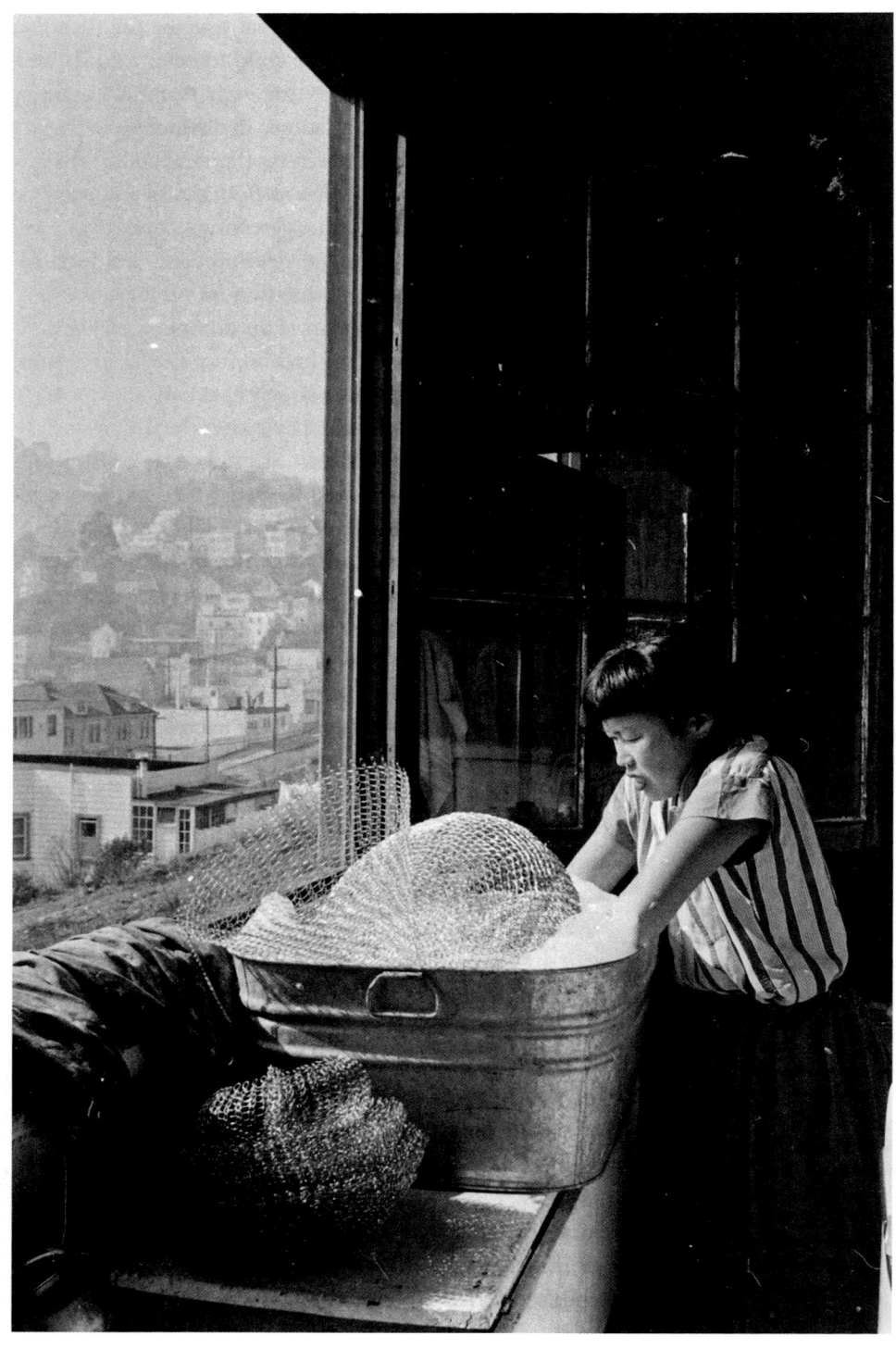

1.5 Ruth Asawa washing a wire sculpture, November 1954. Photo: Nat Farbman. The LIFE Picture Collection.

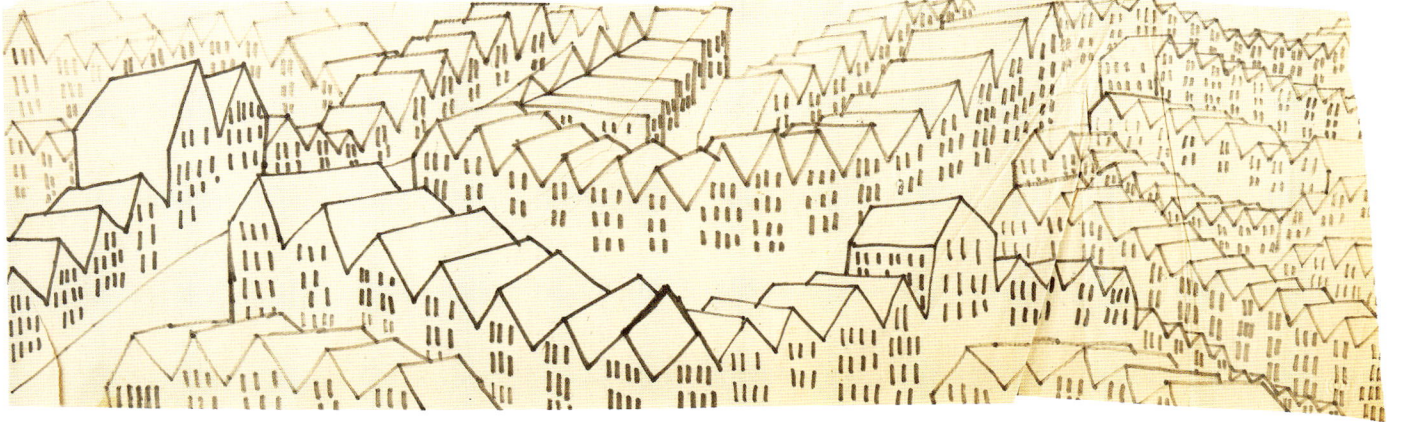

1.6 Ruth Asawa, *Untitled* (MI.107, Cityscape),
c. 1958. Black ink on newsprint, 9 × 30 in.
Private collection.

Asawa's *View from Saturn Street*, a marker drawing in which a prominent land mass in the foreground frames a vista of pitched roofs in the background.

That pattern of pitched roofs was the undulating seriality of the row-house Victorians that had come to define Twin Peaks and the surrounding area, a hilly terrain once thought unsuitable for building. The views of undulating triangles, interrupted only by pairs of vertical dashes to indicate the gabled windows characteristic of the Queen Annes, pepper Asawa's sketchbooks (fig. 1.6). Merry Renk recalls the significance of these vistas and how they would go to the nearby home of weaver and former Black Mountain College instructor Trude Guermonprez on Clipper Street "and paint the view from her window."[62] This pattern is echoed in Imogen Cunningham's study of the back staircase of the adjacent house, occupied by Merry Renk, and the shadows created by its banister—though this is a view onto that staircase that was very likely from the Asawa-Lanier house next door (fig. 1.7). Cunningham further revved up the patterned effect by doubling the staircase (which she accomplished by creating a copy of the negative, cutting out the staircase, and then affixing this to the first negative, thus getting the effect of "stairs and stairs"). Such examples are close studies of these discarded homes, gradually inhabited by a younger generation with little interest in the mass-market housing otherwise on offer. They are the unbroken, bay-windowed ribbons stretching along what was once a cable car line and along Dolores Heights' Liberty Street.

What was distinctive about this architecture was its sheer stylistic diversity combined with the regularity of the pattern created when these structures occupied an area en masse—as they did in the area around Saturn Street. Sally Woodbridge emphasizes this diversity in her 1978 book *Victoria's Legacy*, co-written with Judith Waldhorn, who drew the illustrations (fig. 1.8). (Waldhorn also participated in the Bicentennial celebrations organized by the Alvarado School Arts Workshop that year, with a talk

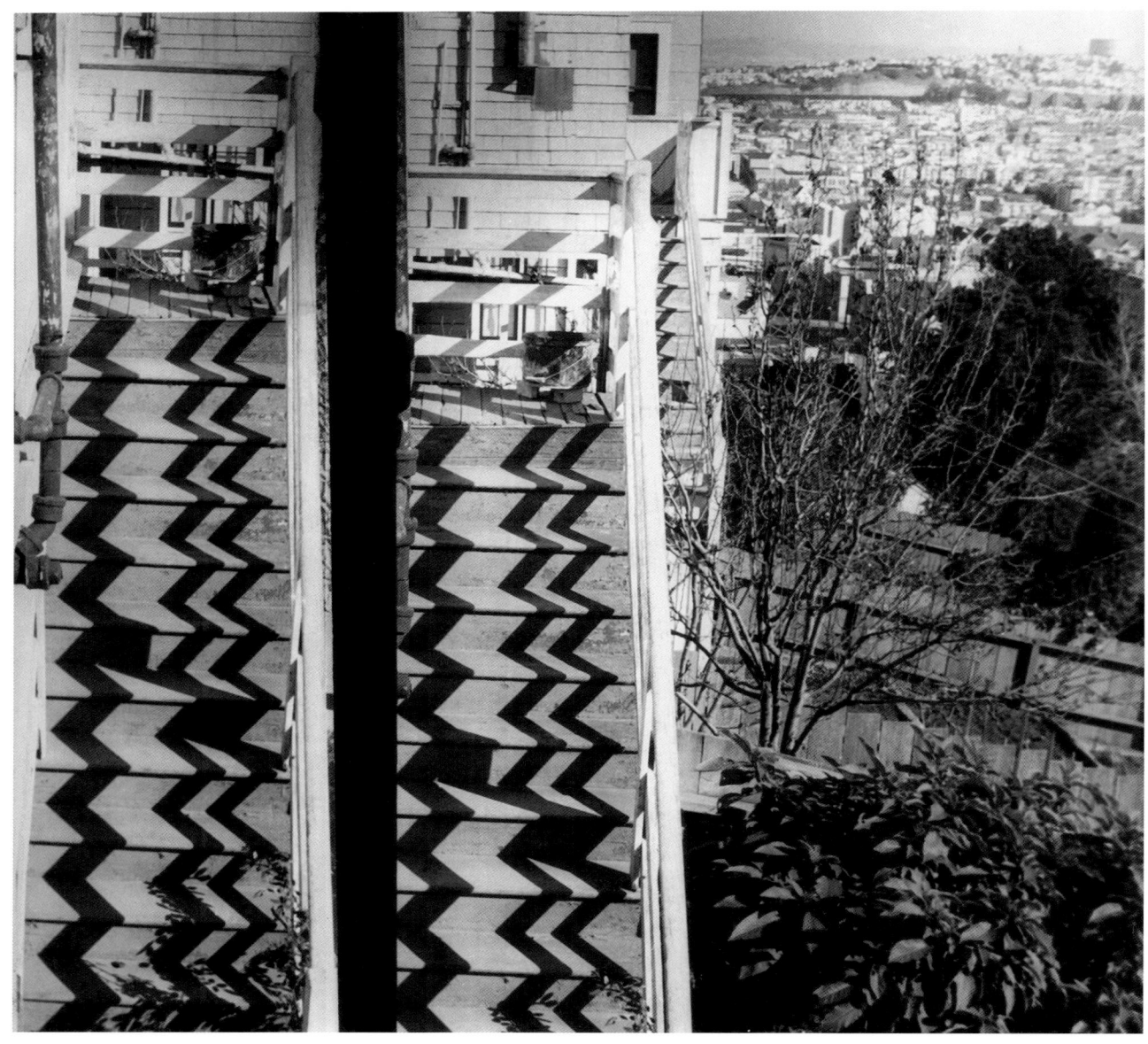

1.7 Imogen Cunningham, *Stairs and Stairs at Merry's*, 1959. Gelatin silver print, 10¾ × 10⅝ in. Seattle Art Museum, Gift of John H. Hauberg, 89.50.

on the area's Victorians.) The book is framed as a bird-watcher's guide to the city's Victorian architectural heritage, encouraging the reader to get up from her seat, walk the city blocks, and observe the seemingly "infinite variety" of detail as varied as the area's inhabitants.[63] The obsession with detail is evident in a range of building types, from the flat-roofed Italianate to the pitched-roof Queen Annes. The term "Victorian" thus does not designate a unified style, Woodbridge argues, but refers rather to a period whose reach extended well into the twentieth century.

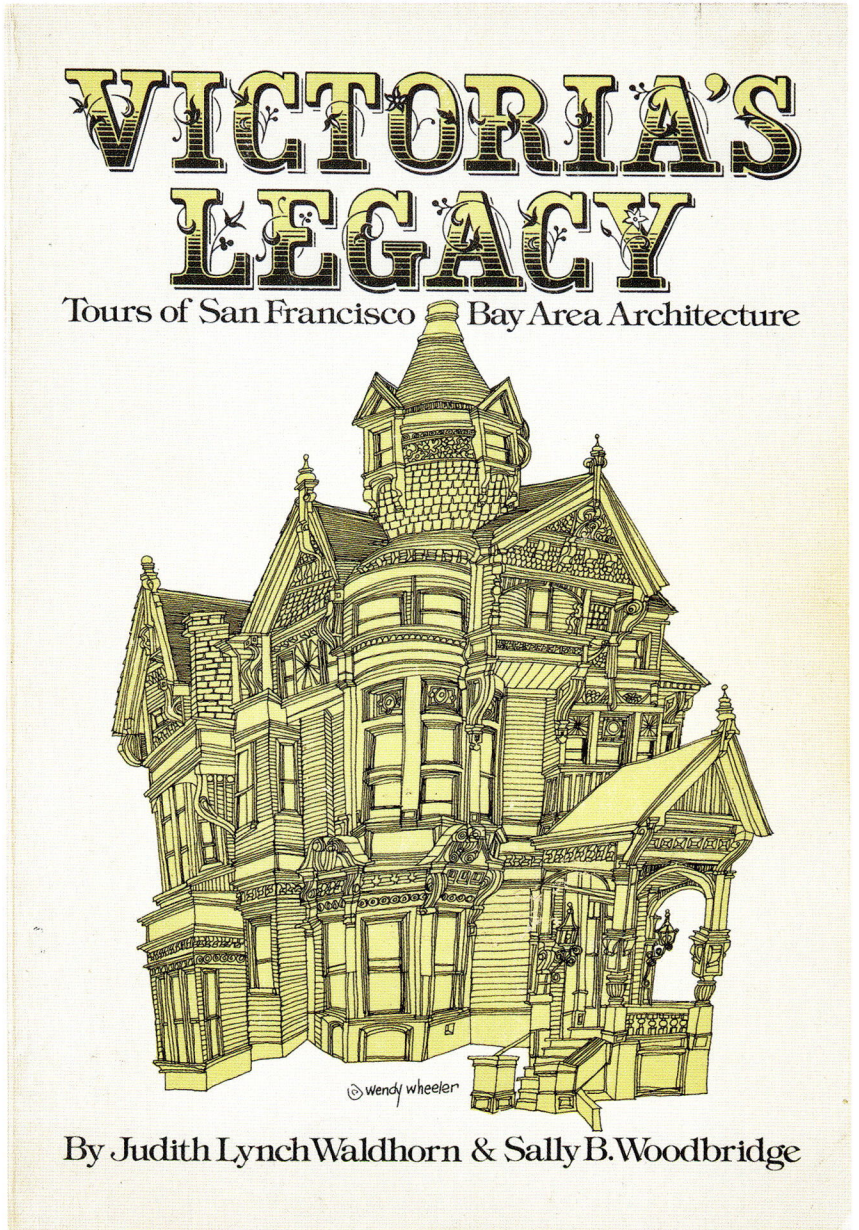

1.8 Cover of Sally B. Woodbridge and Judith Lynch Waldhorn, *Victoria's Legacy* (San Francisco: 101 Productions, 1978).

Woodbridge and Waldhorn's survey responded to the recent rehabilitation of these outmoded structures, which had been virtually abandoned with the shift in taste toward a European-imported modern architecture of ornament-free structures. By 1939, a Works Progress Administration guide to California could lament the "epidemic of the Victorian pestilence" that had seized the state in those years and produced "thousands of Victorian horrors."[64] According to one observer, ornamentation had rendered San Francisco a "City of Sham": "For as the women seek to counterfeit the charms denied them, by the use of rouge and enamel, so the men daub and spatter redwood to imitate marble and granite, copy wood-carving by machinery, and carry the deceptions of concrete and cement to indecent limits."[65] Victorian ornamentation became feminized and, on that basis, dismissed as frivolous and misguided by proponents of an international modernism. *Victoria's Legacy* thus sought not only to salvage this architecture, but also to support the movement around its rehabilitation, as new communities inhabited the area and sought to save the Victorians as "a vital and active piece of the city and not museum pieces."[66] This movement played an implicit political role; defending these outmoded structures served as a retort to the emptying of the American inner city by policies like those of the Federal Housing Administration and the National Highway Act, which gave rise to the suburbs and to the ghettoization of social life in the form of the single-family unit. Woodbridge's intervention thus took its place alongside those by other women writers and feminists looking back to the Victorian era, including *Suffer and Be Still: Women in the Victorian Age* (1972), which includes an essay by Kate Millett triangulating an emergent feminist consciousness with the work of John Stuart Mill's *The Subjection of Women* (1869), on the one hand, and John Ruskin's lecture "Of Queen's Gardens" (1865), on the other.[67]

A sheet by Beth Van Hoesen portrays the spectrum of this architectural detail (fig. 1.9). It represents the view out of her own house, which she shared with tapestry artist Mark Adams—a renovated firehouse on Twenty-Second Street, around the corner from both Asawa and Woodbridge, when after 1961 all three women lived in Noe Valley; Woodbridge occupied a Queen Anne on Castro Street.[68] Excising all contextual information, including the many trees lining the street, Van Hoesen focuses solely on the variety of the detailed façades. Her close observation of this Victorian ornamentation parallels its embrace by the gay and queer communities in the area. In his account of the gay subcultures that began to take root in the Castro beginning in the late 1940s, Jim Duggins relays the importance of this abandoned architecture of the working class in creating spaces for communities otherwise denied participation in the normative family structures and its attendant tract housing.[69] Although these two identity positions—the heterosexual mother and the "queer household" of an artist pair like Jess and Robert Duncan—are typically held apart, in the rehabilitation of Victorian architecture they shared common ground. This identification with Victoriana, as McDowell writes, was one of a range of "domestic queering tactics" that made this domestic space "doubly different, at a remove from postwar American heteronormative, nuclear family models *and* from Beat bohemianism."[70]

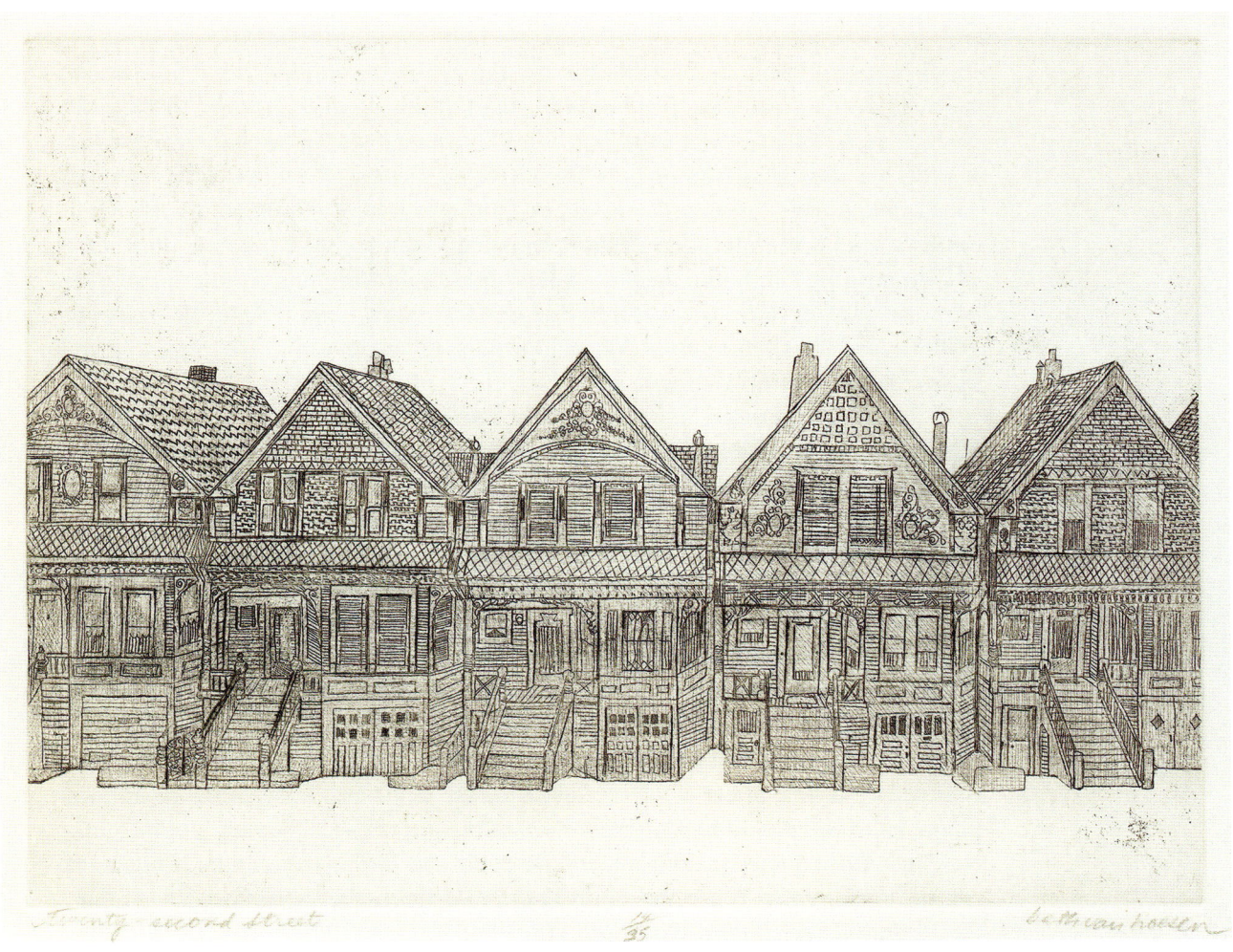

Twenty-second street   14/35   beth van hoesen

1.9 Beth Van Hoesen, *Twenty-Second Street*, 1960.
Drypoint with roulette, printer's ink on paper, 9 × 11¾ in.
(image). Photo: M. Lee Fatherree.

Inhabiting this outmoded architecture in the 1950s, Asawa and her fellow artist-mothers were a world away from bohemianism, at that point epitomized by the city's North Beach district, where Beat poet Allen Ginsberg lived.[71] They belonged instead to working-class neighborhoods of old Victorian houses, whose residents included Mexican and Irish Americans. Asawa and Lanier, too, were working full-time: while Lanier spent his workday at the architectural firm, Asawa spent it at home, taking care of their growing family and the household chores, and continuing to experiment with wire and drawing. Her sister came to live with the couple from 1950 to 1954, helping at home, and for a short period Asawa took a job to help pay bills, watching a neighbor's children several evenings a week.

It was in this house on Saturn Street that Asawa established a mode of working in which art was integrated into the daily rhythms of family life—an orientation that she would continue for the rest of her life. She worked primarily on the main, bottom level, where she installed a provisional divider of flat files and a bed on the floor. On the same level as the kitchen and eating area, this area allowed her to work and tend to domestic tasks without having to run up and down the stairs. Photographs by Imogen Cunningham portray Asawa kneeling on this bed, her head and torso encircled by one of her sculptures hanging from the ceiling rack, as well as lying on her back, so that she could work on the underside of another structure hanging from the ceiling. This area was her nominal "studio," but in practice her work unfolded throughout the house: she also worked at a table in an adjacent room or while sitting on the floor surrounded by several of her children. Following the modernist ethos of the open floor plan, Lanier and Asawa had adapted the small rooms of the Victorian interior to the airy, light-filled domestic environment one could also find in the case study homes of *Art and Architecture*. When the family began to outgrow the Saturn Street Victorian, they found a larger, Bernard Maybeck-style house in nearby Noe Valley, where Lanier excavated a split basement level so that Asawa could have her first dedicated studio space and there were sufficient bedrooms for the children. But, as Sally Woodbridge observed, Asawa's work still spilled over into the rest of the home. "Theoretically," Woodbridge wrote in the early 1970s of the home in Noe Valley, the studio "occupies a 20 × 40 foot room at ground level under the living room. Practically it often takes over the whole house."[72]

On a tip from Albert Lanier, Merry Renk had bought the adjacent Victorian on Saturn Street, using her part-time salary as a design instructor in the decorative arts department at the University of California, Berkeley. The interior was renovated by Lanier to make the most of the high, vaulted ceiling and included a large window in front of which hung one of Asawa's looped-wire sculptures, which is occasionally visible in photographs of Renk working. Lanier also created a dedicated workspace in a loft above her open-plan kitchen–living room. This loft studio is represented in a three-dimensional model that Renk made later in life, rendering the studio as if it were an entire house unto itself (fig. 1.10). In the model, one of Renk's interlocking

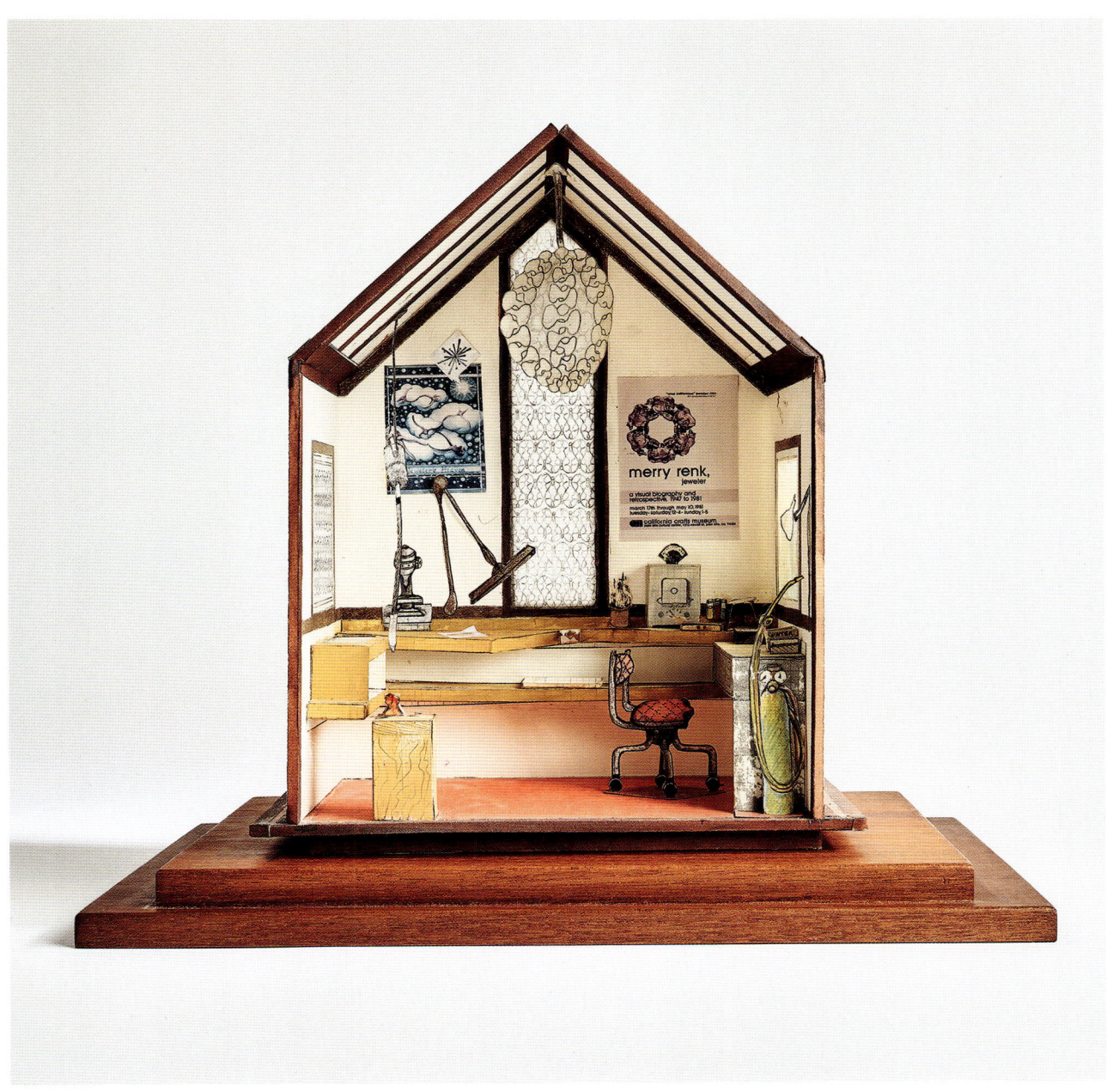

1.10 Merry Renk, *Untitled* (model of studio in Saturn Street home), c. 1990. Paper and wood, 12¼ x 10¼ x 6 in. Collection of Baunnie Sea. Photo: James Paonessa.

paper lamps hangs from the beams, echoing the Asawa sculpture that was also hanging in the open-plan interior. Knowing how necessary it was that her own workspace be physically separated from her children, Renk observed that Asawa in contrast had chosen materials that were especially conducive to having small children around. "She was able to carry her wire work and go out into the yard. . . . My work, it had to be protected from my children because of the dangerous acids and tools and stuff, so I couldn't do it that way with mine. She got the right medium to have children. It was nontoxic."[73] Wire and paper—Asawa's primary materials in the 1950s and early 1960s—were relatively harmless, unlike Renk's soldering iron and enamels. They allowed Asawa to create the hybrid space of a mid-twentieth-century Victorian sensibility, one in which maternal domestic space was still prominent while the ethos of separate spheres was challenged.[74]

The open-plan character of the Asawa-Lanier remodeled Victorian can already be found in the letters that the couple exchanged before Asawa had moved to San Francisco. "I have wonderful visions of a bare, clean space, all corners realized—to work and to love," Lanier wrote to Asawa.[75] It was essential that whatever home they made for themselves be a "playhouse," not unlike Varda's loft, that it be "the most active, thought-moving space in San Francisco," with "room for friends or a buzz saw or room to make a stage set."[76] Or elsewhere: "a workshop" with "space to dance."[77] It would not have walls but "screens," which would be "completely moveable so that we can change it often or throw the whole thing together on occasions."[78] In many ways, it was Lanier who played the role of homemaker, as the more pragmatic Asawa questioned whether San Francisco was the right place to begin a life together ("Darling—I think any place is the place to begin life together," he responded) and expressed doubt about "the *probability* of our marriage. It is so *vague*," to which Lanier responded, "You must know how this torments me."[79] She warmed to his enthusiasm, reminding him "that someday I would like you to design a house for me"; "I would have very few requests, only a simple place light and clean; noise does not bother me. A room with a love corner, work corner, and sunlight corner. The fourth corner is left up to you to plan."[80]

In addition to tearing down walls, the couple also allowed for a large empty room upstairs. This space accommodated six or seven people dancing, and Asawa often hosted dancing and drawing sessions with fellow artist-mothers in the neighborhood.[81] Other artists and friends nearby included Jean Rochin, N'aima Leventon, Mae Lee, and the dancer Miriam Kay. Many of these women were looking for provisional spaces in which to practice art with others, as none had a dedicated studio outside the home. The shared space offered an opportunity not only to practice art but to build community, and it was in the context of the dancing sessions that Asawa met Mae Lee, with whom she would work closely over the following decades.[82] While sharing childcare duties, these women were able to paint and sketch in what were effectively provisional art classes without any designated instructor. Sometimes these sessions would extend late into the evening: as Renk recalled, "kids would be put to sleep and told to be good kids, and our kids all seemed to behave beautifully the night we were drawing."[83]

This Victorian sensibility, I argue, mounted a challenge to the romantic picture of the artist working in an isolated studio—even if that studio was at home. "The topos of the isolated artist in his studio," Caroline Jones has written of the post-World War II studio, presented "a continuation of nineteenth-century romantic traditions" and constituted "a gendered construct excluding women."[84] Or, to be more precise, it could very well be available to women, as Jay DeFeo demonstrates, but what it absolutely excluded was the maternal figure. Increasingly identified with privacy and a hermetic family unit, the Mother as a mythic structure of the twentieth century had no place in the modernist studio. The few exceptions proved the rule: regarding Barbara Hepworth, Anne M. Wagner describes the ethos of the modernist studio as the space of "a new universalism that would leave nostalgia behind; the artist's dwelling was to serve as the place to model the visual means of psychic and social change."[85] Hepworth, a participant in that vision, may have integrated references to figures of mother and child into her carved stone sculpture, but her actual children—including four-year-old triplets during the time that Mondrian was working in a studio next door—had to stay out.

Children are antithetical to the traditional imagination of both bohemia and modernism as kid-free realms. The responsiveness involved in caretaking is cast as the opposite of the self-absorption required by aesthetic production: "While the images of both Artist and Mother are overly romanticized and revered in our culture," the artist Bailey Doogan wrote in response to a questionnaire on motherhood in the 1990s, "the Artist is construed as complex, sexually potent, and creative, the Mother as selfless, nonsexual, and nourishing. The Mother the boundless giver, the artist the deserving taker."[86] This is what Sontag drew our attention to in her description of Peggy Tolk-Watkins's "harem" as "ridiculous": the typical dichotomy between maternity and bohemianism. Tolk-Watkins's example demonstrates that this opposition is a highly circumscribed and limited model of the artistic author, and it in no way encompasses the much broader range of subject positions that did in fact grapple with caretaking combined with the production of art. In such instances, it was no longer a matter of bohemianism *or* motherhood, artmaking *or* familial constellations. The two could and did coexist. But art history's blindness to that possibility, at least until recently, goes some way in explaining why figures like Tolk-Watkins have so far remained invisible.

This understanding of the studio-home as an autonomous realm served to distinguish "artist" from other social roles, such as, for instance, "housewife." Such a dichotomy was so entrenched that even those aware of it and on the search for evidence to the contrary overlooked the glaring examples: for various reasons, Asawa remained a nonentity to the early feminist critics. Lucy Lippard recalls, "In the winter of 1970, I went to a great many women's studios and my preconceptions were jolted daily. I thought serious artists had to have big, professional-looking spaces. I found women in corners of men's studios, in bedrooms and children's rooms, even in kitchens, working away."[87] One of those women was Eva Hesse, who had a two-floor studio on the Bowery in New York, which she shared with her husband, fellow sculptor Tom

Doyle. The top level was used for storing materials, and it was where she made her latex and fiberglass pieces; the lower level was the apartment where she lived and worked on smaller things, as she relayed to Lippard. But as she told the art historian, "I only work downstairs. In my corner. It is really crowded with work and tools and all sorts of paraphernalia," with small latex pieces set out to dry "on the radiator or in a muffin tin in the oven. She washed out the rubber tubing in the bath. Every available surface was covered with the clutter of a working life."[88]

The same language of "clutter" characterizes Asawa's reception as an artist-mother: "Since she does all of her work at home, the pieces, as she herself says, 'clutter' the whole house. At the same time she can keep an eye on her three sons and two daughters, the oldest nine years, the youngest not quite a year old." This was an artistic practice made to be continuous with maternal labor, a space in which "coils of wire, childish drawings, and puppets are constantly underfoot," observed the journalist.[89] This continuum characterized not only the studio space but the making of the artwork itself, as Asawa recounted the construction of puppet theaters with her children alongside the making of her pieces for art exhibition, and her daughter Aiko experimenting with the same looped-wire technique that Asawa used to create her sculptures. Tacked up to a cork wall were drawings in which it is difficult to separate Asawa's mark from those of children; sketches of Sally Woodbridge's two kids exist comfortably next to other attempts by a much younger hand (figs. 1.11, 1.12). In this collapse of artistic and maternal identity, Asawa was not alone, and the same language of children working alongside their mother in an endlessly proliferating clutter characterizes a visitor's description of artist Mary Beth Edelson's home, where she worked and raised four young children: "the entire gang troops down stairs to her studio. It is a marvelous mess with a long trestle table filled with paints."[90]

By appropriating Victorian domesticity and transforming it into a space of modernist artistic exploration, Asawa devised yet another alternative in the many alternative domestic utopias on offer in mid-twentieth-century California. Just as the open floor plan deconstructed the rigidity of dedicated rooms that had separated gendered domestic space, Asawa rejected the Victorian notion of maternal self-sacrifice: *work got done*, even as the children continued to be cared for. In an evocation of the modernist studio's "public domesticity," to borrow again from Wagner, such an interior recast maternal labor as a sphere for artistic labor.[91] The distinction between private and public could be overcome in the act of making. Consider, for instance, the similarity between how Woodbridge memorably ends her history of California's endlessly evolving domestic architecture and how Asawa described the labor of both artmaking and living. Woodbridge quotes "one of California's most illustrious natives," Gertrude Stein, in her book on the state's architecture: "The composition is the thing seen by everyone living in the doing. They are the composing of the composition that at the time they are living is the composition of the time in which they are living. It is that that makes living a thing they are doing."[92] By the same token, Asawa maintained, "Doing is living. That is all that matters."[93]

1.11 Paul Hassel, *Sculptures and Drawings in Ruth Asawa's Saturn Street Home, San Francisco, CA*, c. 1955. Negative, 5 × 4 in. Private collection.

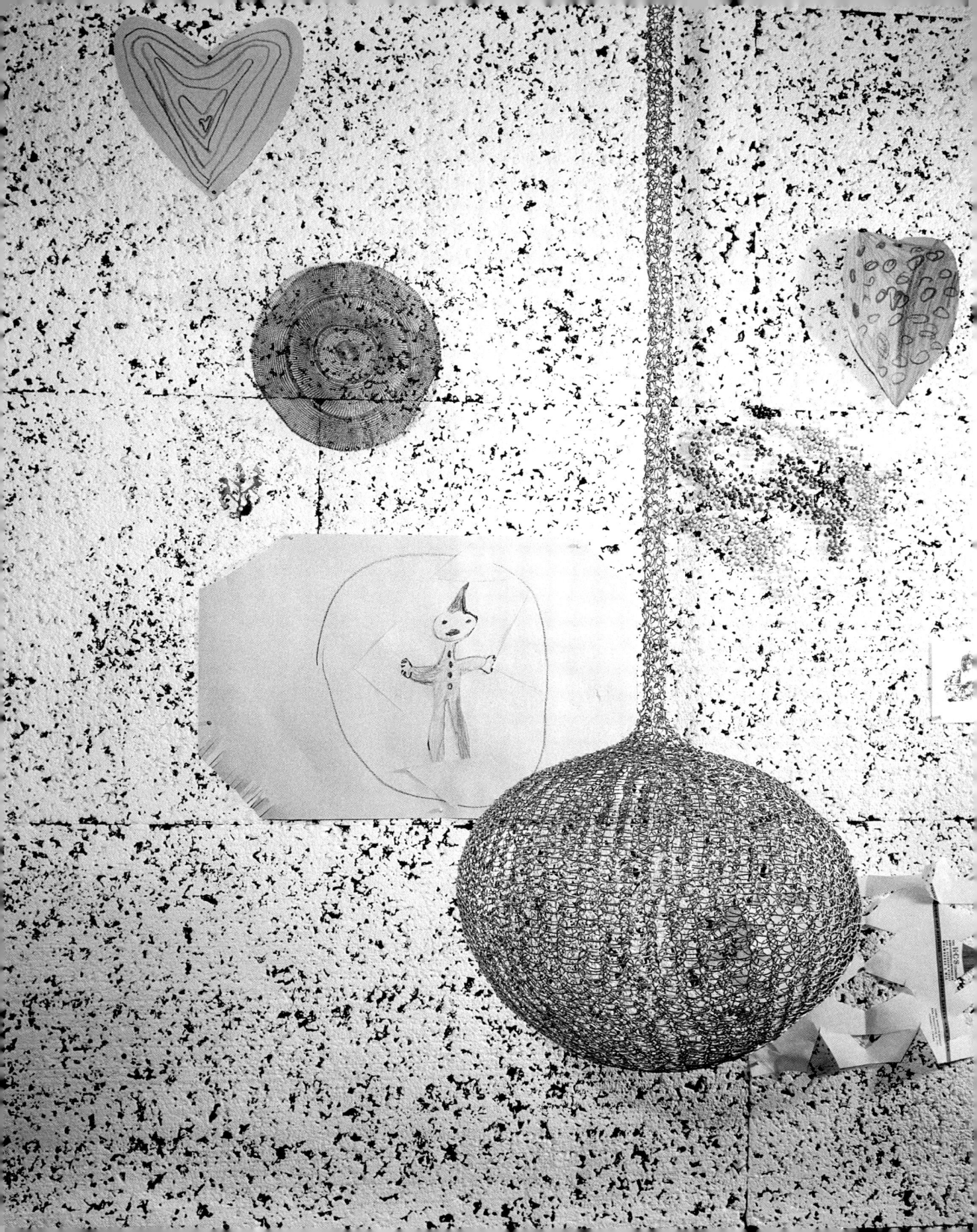

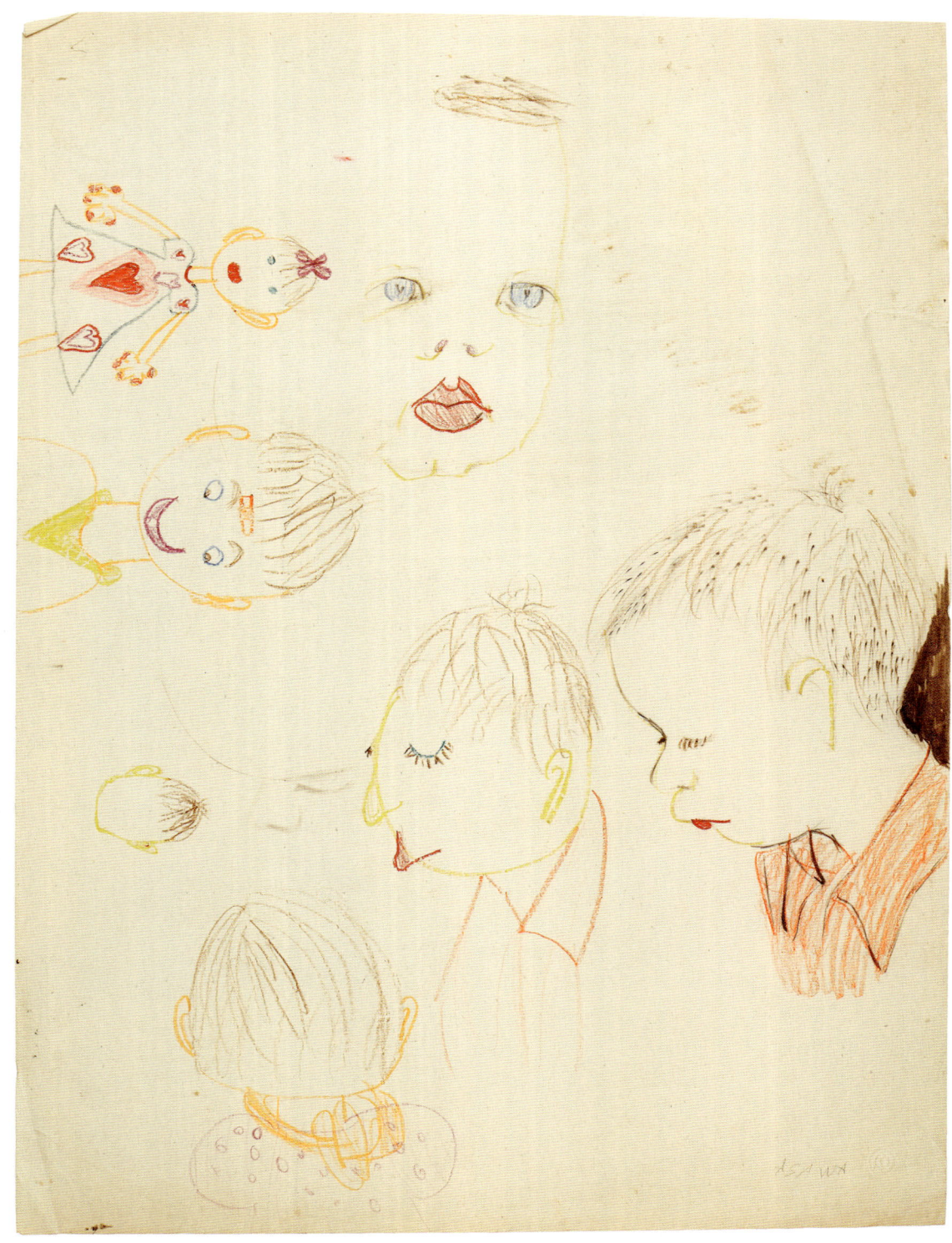

1.12 Ruth Asawa, *Untitled* (FF.915, Larry and Diana Woodbridge), c. 1963–1964. Crayon and brown ink on paper, 24 × 17¾ in. Private collection.

CODA: OUTLAWS FROM THE INSTITUTION OF MOTHERHOOD

Having identified the challenge that the artist-mother posed to the romantic conception of the isolated artist undergirding both bohemian and modernist conceptions of art, we can now look anew at one of the most compelling representations of Asawa in this role as artist-mother. It is a photograph that Imogen Cunningham took of Asawa working in her Saturn Street home in 1957, with several of her children nearby (fig. 1.13). Until the early 2000s, the photograph was little known. It was first shown in the 1957 annual exhibition of the San Francisco Women Artists and then published in the pages of *Aperture* magazine in 1964 as part of a special issue dedicated to Cunningham, with an introduction by Minor White.[94] In that publication, it appears toward the end of a series of twenty-five photographs that Cunningham had selected together with White. The series begins, importantly, with a self-portrait of the photographer and two of her grandchildren reflected in a distorting mirror; Cunningham's face is buried in the viewfinder of her camera. The self-portrait of a mother twice over, and the portrait of another artist-mother, half her age, can be seen as pendants, two views of the artist-mother at work, with the labor of mothering placed into dialogue with the labor of artmaking.

Cunningham clearly thought highly of the print, for she included it in portfolios submitted to museums interested in acquiring her work. The Museum of Modern Art in New York acquired a print in 1960—as far as I can tell, the first museum to have done so. At that point, it had the title *Ruth Asawa at Work with Children*, which would change in the *Aperture* issue to *Ruth Asawa, Family and Sculpture*; the copy in the George Eastman House, bought in 1977, offers another rendition, *Ruth Asawa, Sculptor and Her Children*. In one instance, her labor is specified; in another, the artist is juxtaposed with two seemingly opposing terms (family and sculpture); in the third, her identity as an artist is spelled out as doubly significant: "sculptor and her children." The slight shifts in wording mark an ambiguity regarding Asawa's status as an artist, for the photograph may have played a role in prompting Cunningham's later efforts to create a series engaging with prominent artists, writers, and intellectuals. Cunningham's photograph had long languished in Asawa's private files until it was published in an exhibition catalogue by the de Young Museum in 2006.[95] Since then, it has come to stand for the artist fully committed to the act of creating art. The exhibition's curator, Daniell Cornell, read the photograph as a testament "to the mental concentration and physical intention that creativity requires, underscoring the deliberate attention that preoccupies everyone in the scene."[96] Following Michael Fried's powerful account of modernism as an engagement with concentration, whose genealogy can be traced back to Jean Siméon Chardin with his beguiling soap bubbles, Cornell would seem to suggest that the image faithfully delivers absorption as the guarantee of serious art. And even if a new actor is inserted into this narrative, its basic proposition remains intact: concentration is essential to making good art. This may have been the reason that Cunningham selected this frame from the many shots that she took on that occasion. The others portray Asawa interrupted in her task, looking up at baby Adam,

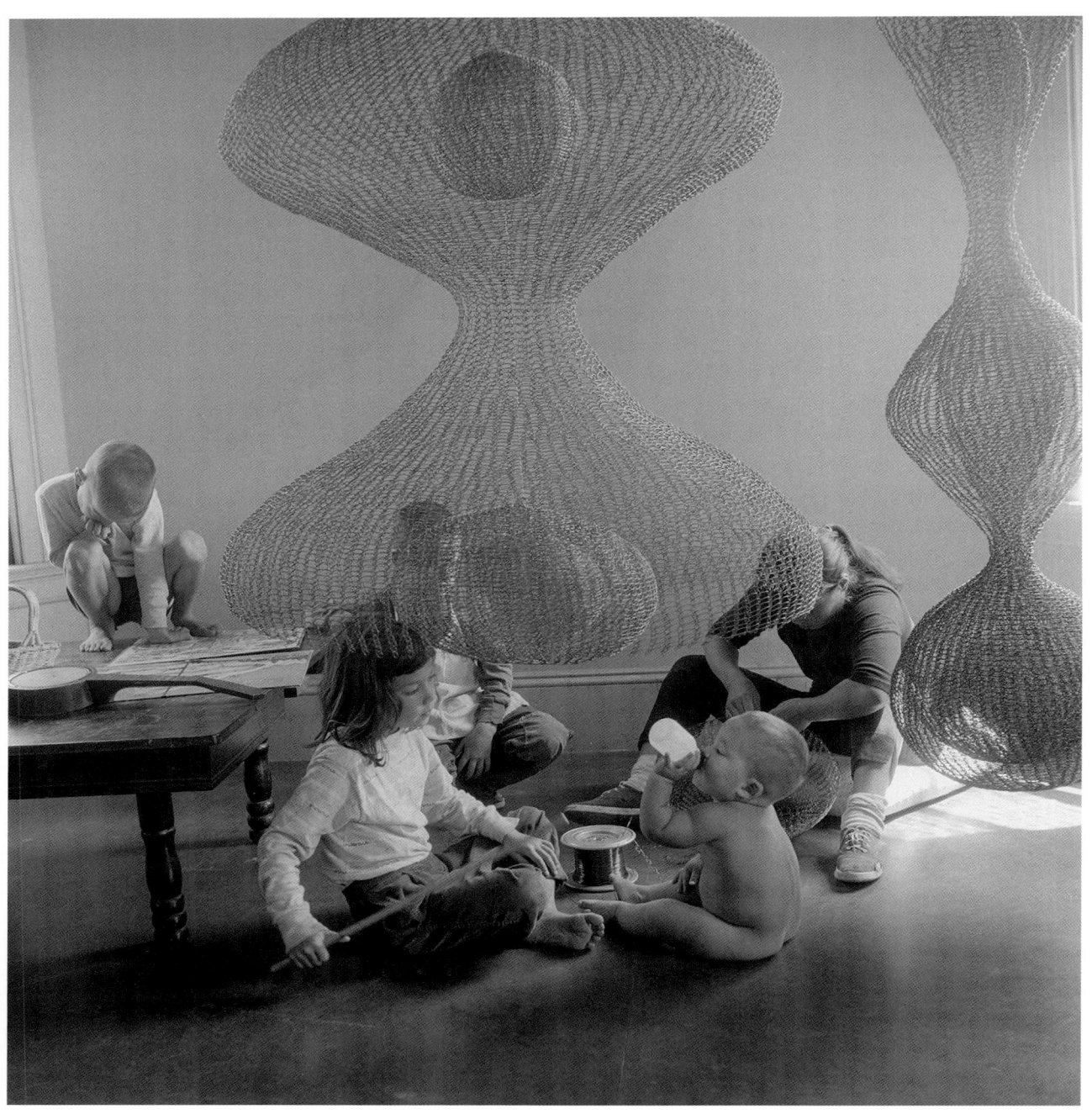

1.13 Imogen Cunningham, *Untitled* (Ruth Asawa with sculptures and children), 1957. Gelatin silver print, 9¾ × 10½ in. Fine Art Museums of San Francisco, Gift of Ruth Asawa and Albert Lanier, 2006. 114.10.

who totters toward the open window, or having to put down her wire because he has started to crawl into her lap and sit in the open wire form, at which point she seems, improbably, somehow able to keep working (fig. 1.14). Cunningham surely knew that the staging of absorption is a careful and orchestrated task, and to depict it required making a calculated selection.

This image is compelling, in other words, because it stages a reconciliation between the two very different paradigms of artistic labor that I have explored in this chapter—the studio as a space of autonomous, concentrated creativity, on the one hand, belonging to the bohemian and modernist interior, and the studio as a space of relational creativity, belonging to the artist-mother and subject to interruption. Cunningham's carefully selected photograph captures a fantasy that those two divergent spaces could be merged, made to be one and the same. It is the fantasy of a maternal bohemia, we might say, a fantasy in which modernism and motherhood have been reconciled. Mother, child, and art object coexist here in a kind of maternal pastoral, in which the labor of artmaking parallels the labor of mothering, undisturbed and unthreatened. Just as their mother is occupied, head bowed as she works, each child finds their own occupation, paging through picture books, waving a wooden dowel, or gulping down a bottle. This is why Helen Molesworth rightly recognizes the language of European allegory.[97] It is as much a wish-landscape as a portrayal of an artist-mother at work. One only need recall the various suppressed interruptions depicted in the other negatives from that occasion to feel the force of that Arcadian vision.

To borrow from Adrienne Rich, Cunningham's pastoral scene posits motherhood as having escaped its own institutionalization, controlled by discipline, schedules, routines, and authority. To leave all this behind, even if momentarily, is to figure Mother and Child as "outlaws from the institution of motherhood"—a scenario that Rich narrates in pastoral terms in her book *Of Woman Born* based on her own experience as a writing mother:

I remember one summer, living in a friend's house in Vermont. My husband was working abroad for several weeks, and my three sons—nine, seven, and five years old—and I dwelt for most of that time by ourselves. Without a male adult in the house, without any reason for schedules, naps, regular mealtimes, or early bedtimes so the two parents could talk, we fell into what I felt to be a delicious and sinful rhythm. It was a spell of unusually hot, clear weather, and we ate nearly all our meals outdoors, hand-to-mouth; we lived half-naked, stayed up to watch bats and stars and fireflies, read and told stories, slept late. I watched their slender little boys' bodies grow brown, we washed in water warm from the garden hose lying in the sun, we lived like castaways on some island of mothers and children. At night they fell asleep without murmur and I stayed up reading and writing as I had when a student, till the early morning hours. I remember thinking: This is what living with children could be—without school hours, fixed routines, naps, the conflict of being both mother and wife with no room for being, simply, myself.[98]

Rich's invocation of "castaways on some island of mothers" is the literary pendant to Cunningham's wish-landscape of the artist-mother at work—a space, if only even briefly won, in which mothers are allowed to be themselves, to pursue their writing and artmaking, while also providing for the well-being of three other lives.

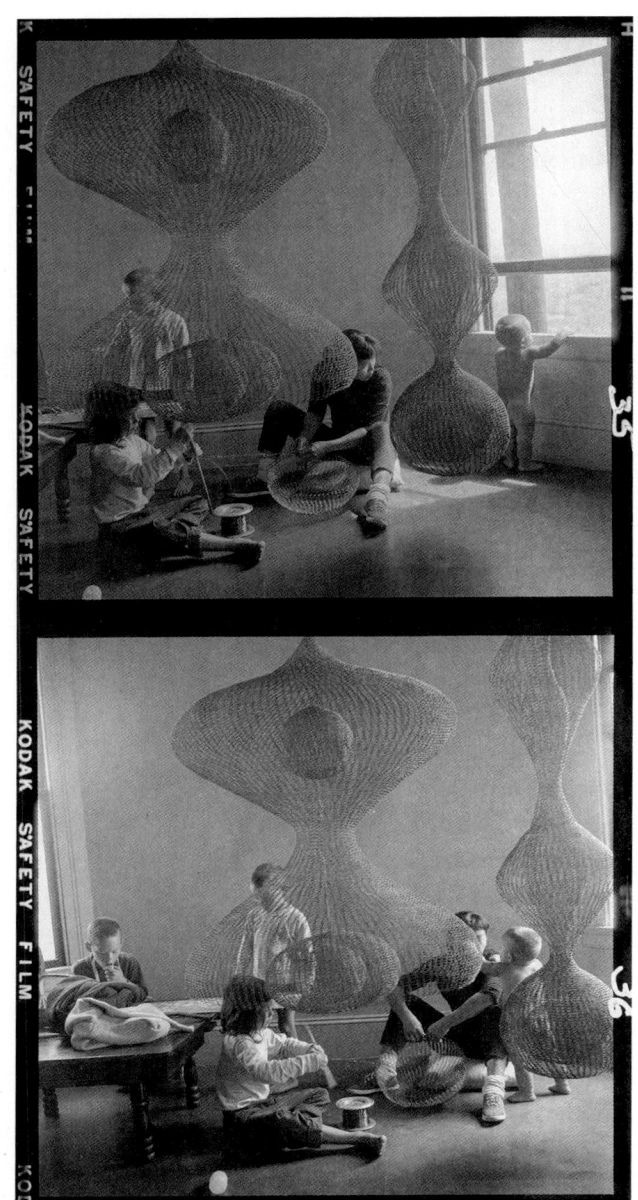
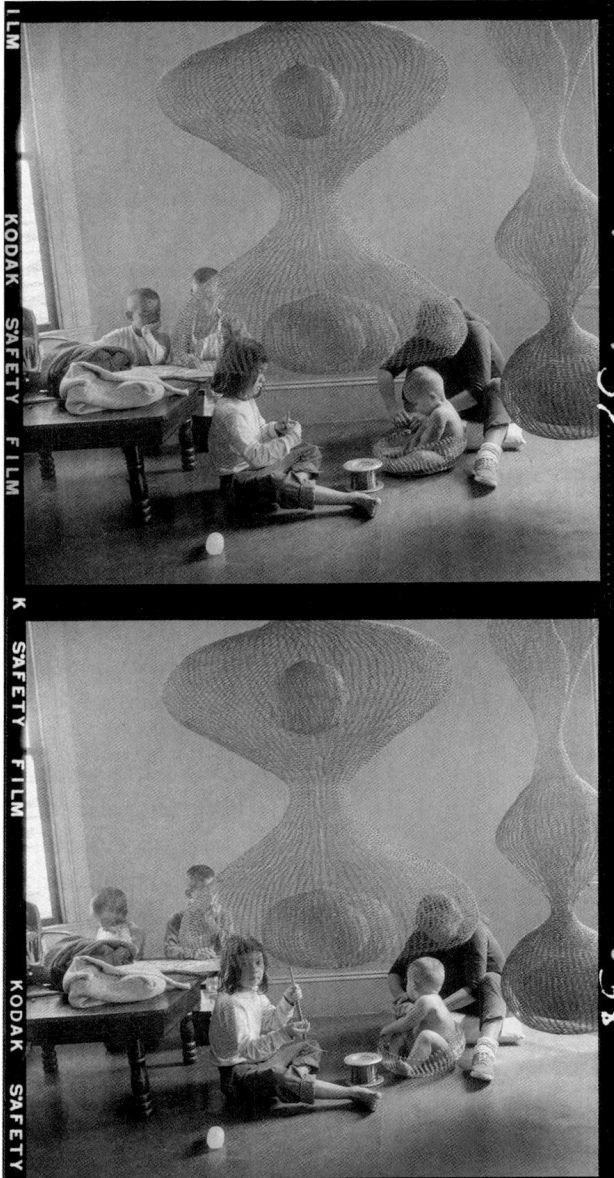

1.14 Contact sheet of film negatives taken by
Imogen Cunningham depicting Ruth Asawa with
sculptures and children, 1957. Collection of
Imogen Cunningham Trust.

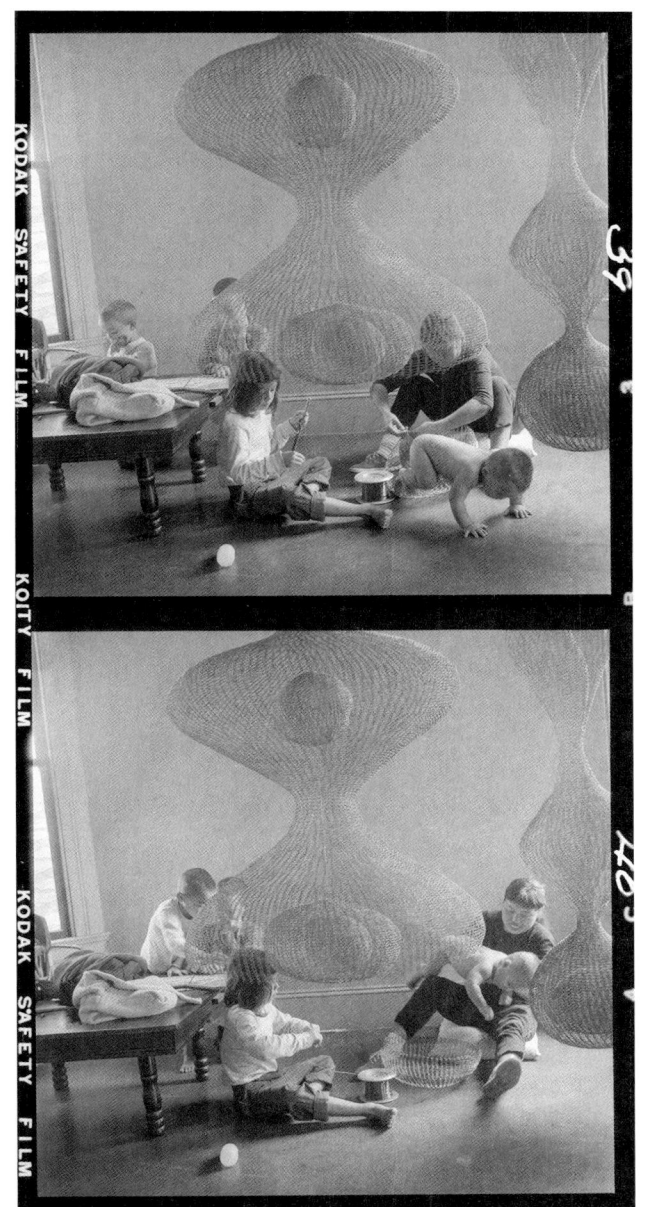
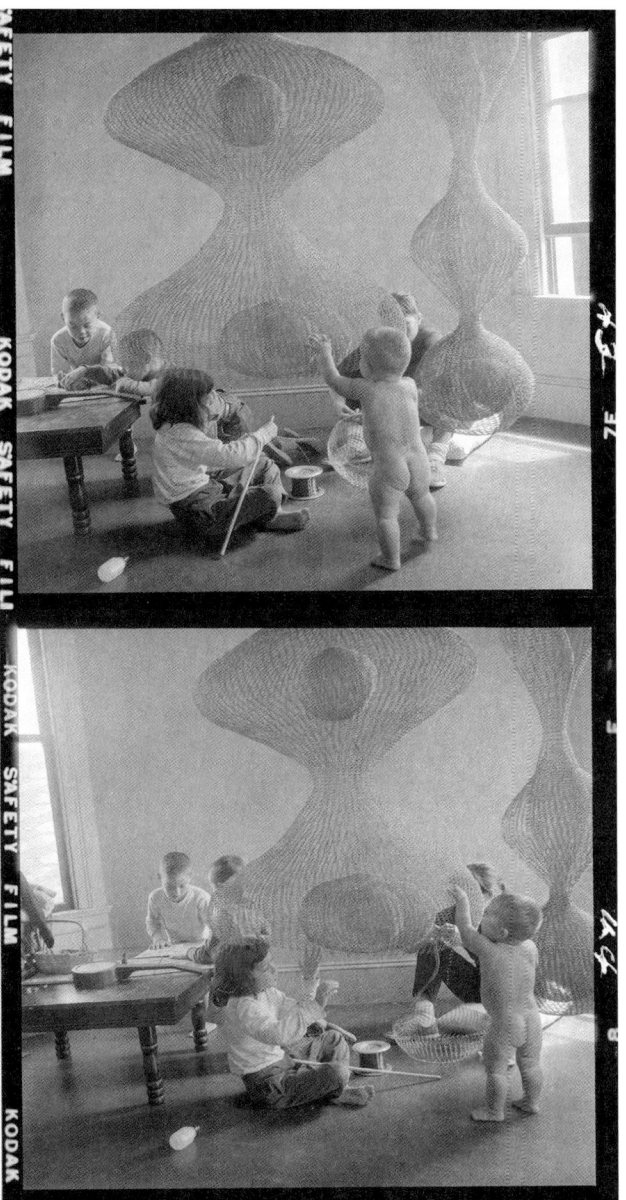

Cunningham's photograph captures this wish formation of modernism: a suspension of its own ruling institutions, including the prohibition on motherhood, in the creation of an all-encompassing autonomy that could even facilitate the labor of the artist-mother.

So it would seem that artifice is inescapable from absorption, just as "modernist notions of authenticity cannot be fully understood without reference to Victorian culture," Kenneth Ames argues in his study of Victorian America.[99] This, finally, is the version of domesticity on offer in Cunningham's image: a maternal utopia in which the contradictions of patriarchal norms no longer exist. The modernist-cum-Victorian interior would seem to have prepared the ground for that maternal utopia—the mother liberated from domestic chores, free to write and play and work with and among her family—in a house even built for it. Yet that utopia was not to be had, at least not in this idealized form: the older child grows bored with the baton, the turning of the book pages comes to an end, the toddler wanders away, all giving cause to look up from one's work and be carried by the rhythm of interruption.

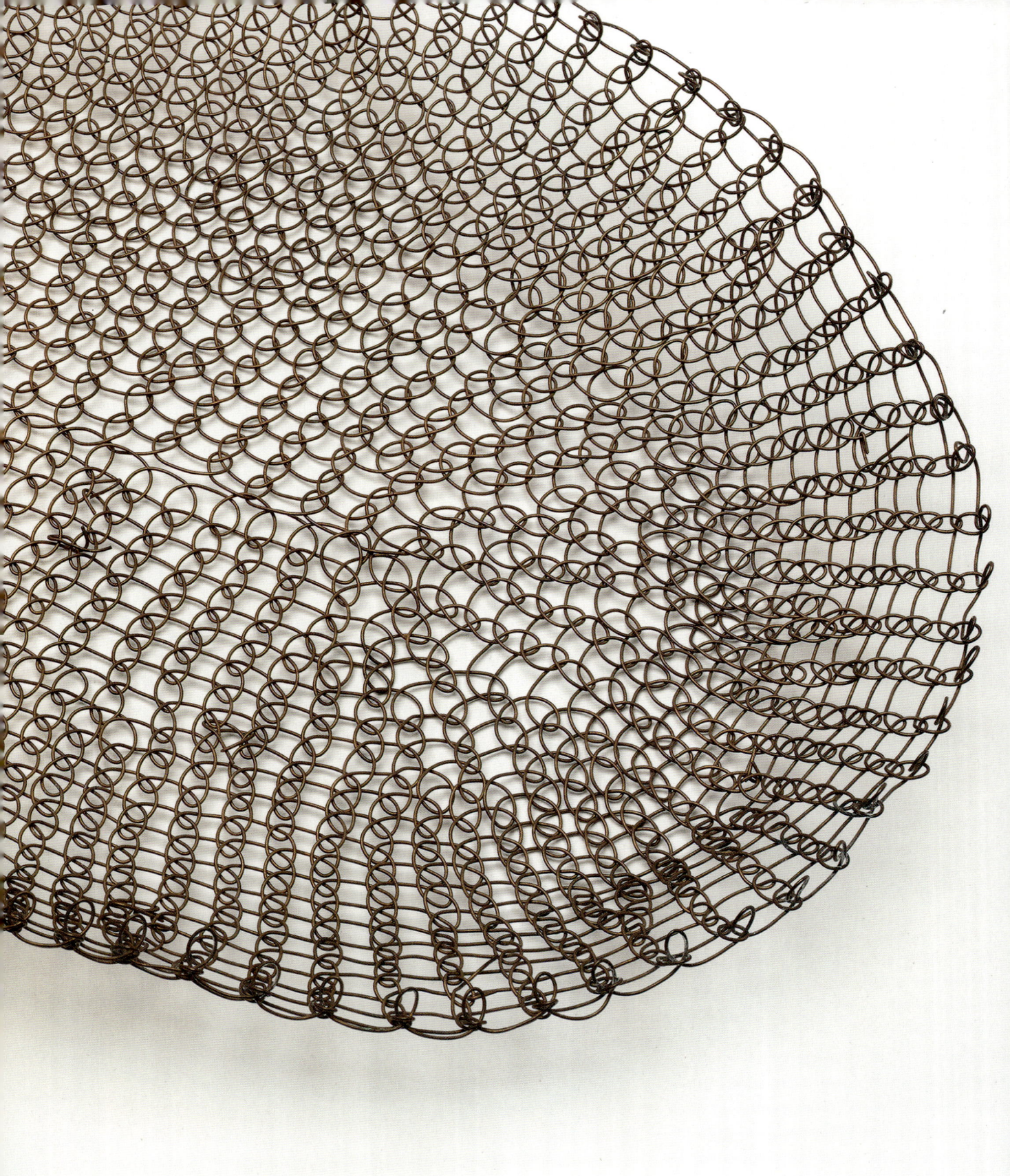

2 KNITTING WITH IRON

Woman, wife, thy name is weaving (Weib, weben).[1]

It is a fuller account of interruption, broached at the end of the previous chapter, that I turn to now, with a consideration of this temporality as a working method akin to knitting and crocheting. Just months before Asawa moved into the Victorian on Saturn Street in 1954, her looped-wire sculptures were included in the exhibition *Four Artist-Craftsmen* at the San Francisco Museum of Art. The gendered terminology of the exhibition's title belied the fact that on view was the work of four women: in addition to Asawa's looped-wire objects there were woven abstract textiles by Ida Dean, ceramic vessels by Marguerite Wildenhain, and metal jewelry by Merry Renk. What these other three women made was clear enough to observers, but Asawa's contribution prompted critics to ponder where exactly on the art-craft spectrum her "wire stuff" and "wire things" lay (fig. 2.1).[2] Were these objects to *use*, like pottery and jewelry, as Anni Albers did when she repurposed one of Asawa's baskets to hold her holiday cards? Or were they objects of decoration, to be suspended from the ceiling of a sparse interior? The critic Alfred Frankenstein, who visited the exhibition, was on the search for answers: "I have been told that the technique involved in producing things of this kind is a form of knitting with iron and copper and that it is very like the technique employed by medieval armorers for their suits of mail. At all events, some of Miss Asawa's sculptures are abstractions of trees, coral, and similar natural shapes, while others are completely without suggestion of things beyond themselves."[3]

Whereas I address the comparison to nature in chapter 4, here I consider Frankenstein's invocation of "knitting with iron." Frankenstein's substitution of hard metal in the place of pliable yarn emblematizes the recourse to craft generated around the work of the artist-mother. As the critic indicates, this discourse of craft came first and foremost from Asawa herself, who consistently located the origins of her looped-wire technique in a form of basket weaving that she had learned in Toluca, Mexico, in the summer of 1947 while on break from Black Mountain College. "I was teaching

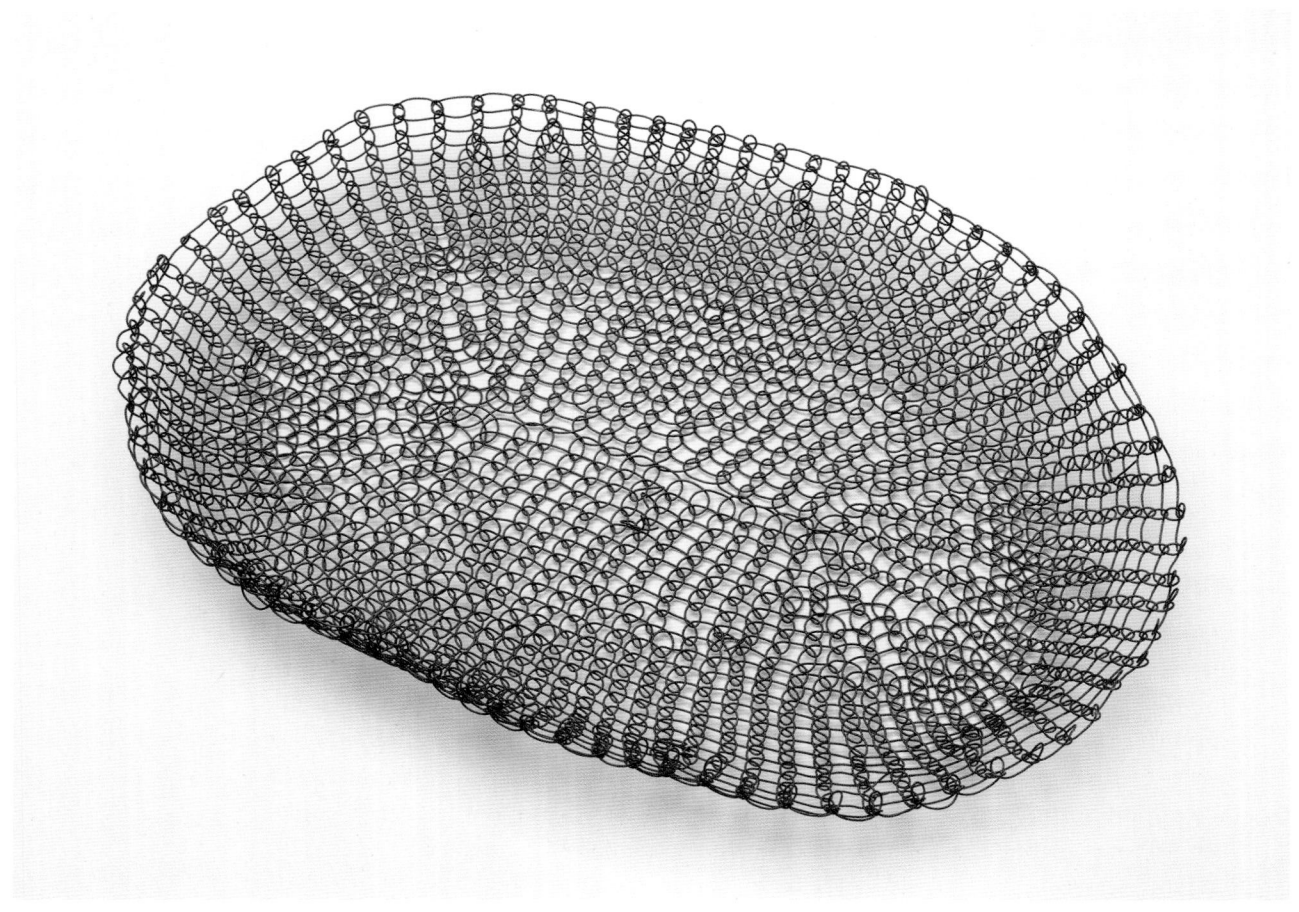

2.1 Ruth Asawa, *Untitled* (S.784), c. 1948–1949. Copper wire, 14 × 20 × 2½ in. The Josef and Anni Albers Foundation, 1976.30.3. Photo: Tim Nighswander/Imaging4Art.

children to weave palm leaves into baskets, then," she relayed to a journalist in 1957. "We used some wire in the process, and in playing around with this, I got the idea of crocheting it." Another journalist put the point even more succinctly, writing that she learned her art form from "Mexican kiddies": "'Crocheting', she says, 'bores me to death. But working with wire is fascinating.'"[4]

A close look at descriptions of her technique reveals that Frankenstein was not alone in associating Asawa's looped-wire objects with feminized craft. Critics regularly described these objects as "woven," "knitted," and "crocheted," even though the technique did not follow any of these methods, but was rather built up "loop by loop, then row upon row. The shape of the mesh is controlled by increasing or decreasing the number of loops. It works exactly as it would if it were yarn."[5] This speaks to a degree of incoherency in categorizing her work, and indeed the "wire stuff" moved through many different contexts, from craft to design to fine art. While in Mexico, Asawa had studied with the Cuban designer Clara Porset, who also drew on vernacular materials and techniques in her approach to modern furniture design. Asawa's training at Black Mountain College put this interest in the vernacular into dialogue with a modernist investment in transparency, the emptying of weight while maintaining volume, planar intersection, and the illusion of movement. As Ann Reynolds writes in an essay exploring Asawa's engagement with transparency, this debt both to vernacular craft and to European modernism has generated an ambiguity about how exactly to categorize Asawa's work, which resists easy classification as "drawing or crocheting, sculpture or craft, design object or architecture, Mexican or American modernism."[6]

What follows traces this resistance to classification and the role that craft played in it. During the 1950s and 1960s, the invocation of knitting and crocheting led to devaluations of her achievement by those invested in modernist art, with "the comparison to utilitarian objects effectively negat[ing] the ingenuity of Asawa's sculpture," as Emily Jennings observes.[7] The constructed hierarchy between art and craft within modern art, explored by art historian Elissa Auther, meant that "craft signified non-art."[8] To work in media coded as domestic and feminine was to work outside the sphere of the fine arts. As Lucy Lippard pointed out in 1973, this was less a description of reality than a discursive prohibition against feminized labor in modernist discourse: to be associated with "feminine techniques" disqualifies one from so-called serious techniques, so the logic went.[9] Whether knitting, crocheting, or embroidery, as Rozsika Parker argues in *The Subversive Stitch*, such techniques had not only a long association with women "but specifically mothers and daughters" in their invocation of maternal labor.[10] As a consequence, Asawa's reception as a practitioner in the sphere of "studio craft" has often been coded as maternal: "amazingly," notes Janet Koplos and Bruce Metcalf's recent *Makers: A History of American Studio Craft*, "she was most prolific when [her children] were small."[11] In the wake of the revaluation of feminist craft in the 1970s and 1980s by writers like Parker as well as artists including Faith Ringgold and Judy Chicago, a more recent reception of Asawa's work embraces this association with craft. Consider, for instance, Helen Molesworth making a comparison to weaving in order to describe the artist's total commitment to work and family: "Asawa's work pulls the threads of both art and life, fashioning an infinite gossamer weaving between the two extraordinary realms, a warp and weft, an inside and outside, a mobius strip of art and life in which there is no gap per se, only a perpetual doing, working, living."[12]

Whether dismissive or celebratory, such statements continually make recourse to the feminized crafts of weaving, knitting, and crocheting. Rather than take a side in this debate, I demonstrate how specific and pervasive that descriptive language was—and why it proved so resilient even when Asawa's viewers knew that her process of construction strictly followed none of these techniques. Asawa, too, continued to use this language when she very well knew the difference between her technique and weaving, knitting, and crocheting. This is a predicament articulated most vividly by Asawa's biographer when she described the artist's sculpture as "knitted without needles and woven without a loom."[13] I am less interested in resolving the contradictions of this language or taking a side in whether it is accurate or not than I am in contextualizing it within a broader history of the many domestic contexts in which Asawa's work moved, from modernist design to decoration to feminized craft to fiber art, with each positing a specific valuation of the artist-mother's labor.

INTERLOCKING FORMS, INTERRUPTED TIME

One way to understand the pervasive association with knitting is to grasp how this early work mobilized pattern and repetition: loop after loop came together to create a surface, which then extended into space, at times intersecting with itself, but otherwise repeating this technical orientation into ever more complex permutations. As a consequence, it takes some time to distinguish one looped-wire sculpture from another. What we have instead are broad categories of compositions: multilobed, single-layered forms; multilobed forms within forms; a continuous form within a form—and the list goes on, as Asawa took this basic technique and repeated it as far as it could go, creating remarkably intricate combinations of forms, all through pattern and repetition.[14] An exhibition brochure of the Oakland Art Museum's annual California sculpture exhibition describes these "suspended fantasies of woven wire" as comprising an utterly innovative "family of sculpture forms."[15]

Asawa explored repetitive pattern through line drawing, watercolor, and her so-called marker drawings. Begun in the late 1950s, the latter were drawings made from a Flo-Master marker, then typically used for commercial signage. Asawa carved grooves into its broad tip, which allowed her to create a regularized pattern of lines, not unlike a stamp, even though she used it as a tool for drawing. Its stamplike quality consisted in the reliable pattern of equally spaced lines when the marker was dragged across the page, and yet each use resulted in a slightly different application. Asawa's sketchbooks and loose-sheet drawings are filled with the varied possibilities of these equally spaced lines in varying widths. In addition to observing textures around the home, including knitted blankets, caning for bentwood chairs, and a wicker pull-cart for a doll, she could apply this technique with her Flo-Master marker to replicate the pattern of her wire objects, pushing the marker in at regular intervals to generate the effect of a bumpy, or looped, surface (fig. 2.2). Her interest here is not only in pattern, but how pattern, when marshaled alongside blankness, could produce volume—more volume than that generated through the depiction of the thing itself. "This way I use one line to define two forms—it's not what you put in, it's what you leave out that makes the picture what it is," she explained.[16]

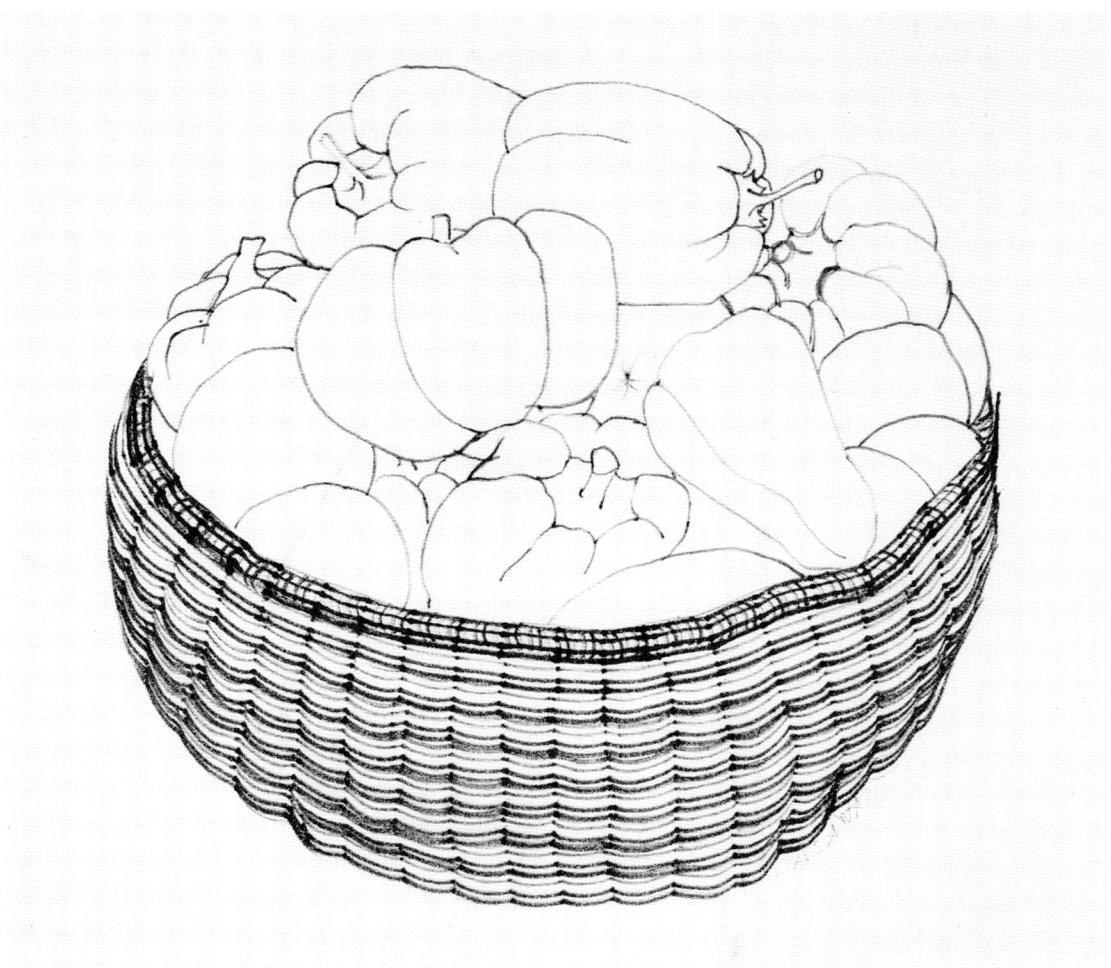

2.2 Ruth Asawa, *Untitled* (PF.335, Bell Peppers in Basket), no date. Pen and black ink on sketchbook paper, 9 × 12 in. Private collection.

This exploration of pattern in two dimensions fueled Asawa's understanding of pattern in three dimensions. In an application for funding to the Guggenheim Foundation, Asawa explained how she worked as often as "materials and family responsibilities have permitted," generating a proliferation of designs that she was anxious to execute: "I can make almost anything I am able to draw. The back-log of ideas is substantial and I am anxious to get them transferred to three dimensions."[17] Drawing served as a surface on which to work out the overall shape of her "wire stuff," but it also served as a medium through which Asawa could experiment with the play of negative and positive space. In the same way that she "misdescribed" her technique as crocheting, she "misdescribed" her three-dimensional wire sculptures as line drawings. This exemplifies her fundamental understanding of such categories as not different in kind but rather belonging to a single continuum of approach; such "mistakes" of course are not mistakes at all. Drawing also provided a means by which she could then study and reflect upon the patterned three-dimensional surfaces she had made, often drawing finished sculptures (instead of the more typical use of drawing as a preparation for sculptural making).[18]

As she began to extend her looped-wire surfaces into three-dimensional space, open forms were categorized as baskets, whereas closed forms became sculpture. Received as work that had "fundamental affinities with architecture and design rather than with more introspective, expressionistic statements," the two kinds of objects in the 1950s were exhibited alongside one another within modernist design sites that did not distinguish between the functional and the aesthetic object—sites like Design Research Inc., whose store in Cambridge, Massachusetts, held an exhibition in 1956 featuring "Japanese household objects" alongside "sculpture by Ruth Asawa."[19] The same mix of baskets (and even, as Erwine Laverne put it, "wastebaskets to go alongside our desks") and multilobed, hanging sculptures characterized Asawa's inclusion in the New York showroom of Laverne Originals in late 1951. After visiting the showroom, Asawa's friend Ray Johnson, whom she knew from Black Mountain College, described one multilayered, single-lobed hanging structure as enclosing "forms within forms within forms."[20] This exhibition of Asawa's wire objects alongside hanging mobiles by Alexander Calder and other artist-designers was the first major display of her work, and it included what had become her most complex piece to date, *Untitled* (S.535), a seven-and-a-quarter-foot-high, five-lobed interlocking looped-wire piece, whose photographic representation by Imogen Cunningham was featured on the cover of *Arts and Architecture* and in the Italian architectural magazine *Domus*.

It is important to recover this continuum between the category of "basket," ostensibly made for use, and the category of "sculpture," as representative of fine art. This was a distinction not of kind for Asawa but of degree, of differences in size and shape. It was according to such differences that she priced her wares and sold them to local and regional design stores, such as Miller-Pollard in Seattle, emphasizing their handcrafted nature.[21] Smaller pieces, typically the single-lobed forms, went for between $3.50 and $15 each; in comparison, she sold one of her early multilobed hanging pieces, *Untitled* (S.535), to Laverne Originals for $75—a significant sale and "the first

Ruth has ever had for a piece of the wire stuff," as Lanier pointed out in a letter to Erwine Laverne.[22] This continuum is also evident in what appears to be a mock-up for a publicity brochure: graphic representations of her sculptures as black and gray construction paper cutouts in hourglass shapes are displayed alongside her designs for paperfolded wall coverings and prints for textiles and wallpaper, with the capacious description "wire objects: basket, sculpture, candelabra."[23]

Received warmly within modern design circles, the same objects generated frustration when placed within fine art contexts. In 1951, for instance, she had submitted an eight-foot-high sculpture of copper, suspended from the ceiling and weighing twenty pounds, to the San Francisco Women Artists' annual exhibition of painting and sculpture. Although initially accepted, it was then rejected on the basis that the jurors doubted if it was sculpture at all: "It wasn't stone, it wasn't welded steel, it wasn't traditional sculpture. They thought it was craft, or something else, but not art. They couldn't define it in the early fifties when I was starting out."[24] A hanging iron-wire sculpture nearly ten feet tall, exhibited at the San Francisco Women Artists' annual exhibition in 1952, elicited a similar reaction: "people were fascinated—if somewhat mystified" by the work, which apparently "moved back and forth like the pendulum of a clock" when people walked by.[25] Even those visiting the Tin Angel, when her sculptures were on view in an exhibition alongside work by Jean Varda, expressed confusion. "People were interested but would ask, 'What is it? How do you make it? What do you use it for? Does it mean something? What does it represent? Etc.' At least they were curious."[26] A gift in 1958 from Ray Johnson to his friend May Wilson of four "wire ball shapes within one another," which were "made of coiled wire knitted," prompted this response when she opened the package: "I did not know what it was, except bulky. At the time I had a triangular 2x4 inch wood shape, open in the center, so I sat on the wire thing to flatten it, nailed it to the triangle, and painted it black."[27] Johnson relayed the episode in the mid-1970s, and it is unknown what became of Wilson's Asawa appropriation.

As a pendant to Asawa's use of repeated patterns, consider the jeweler-sculptor Merry Renk's use of what she described as "a repeating interlock design"—one that she had drawn for years before it materialized in her metalwork. The interlocking principle is illustrated in a watercolor in which Renk depicts herself as an artist-mother at her workbench; nearby stands a recipe box of 3 × 5 cards with tabs dividing the instructions for rings, bracelets, necklaces, and so on (fig. 2.3). Behind her, represented in magnified scale, are drawings of her interlocking wedding rings—one of which Renk, with infant in tow, is also sawing. These rings were likely intended as an engagement-wedding ring pair, with the engagement ring incorporating a stone or gem into its design, while the wedding band is solid gold. The rings did not simply sit next to one another on the finger; their design physically nestled the one into the other. This is best illustrated in the example at the top middle, where the wedding band wraps around the blue gem, and in the example at the top right, in which the band incorporates three grooves into which slide that part of the engagement ring that holds the three ruby stones.

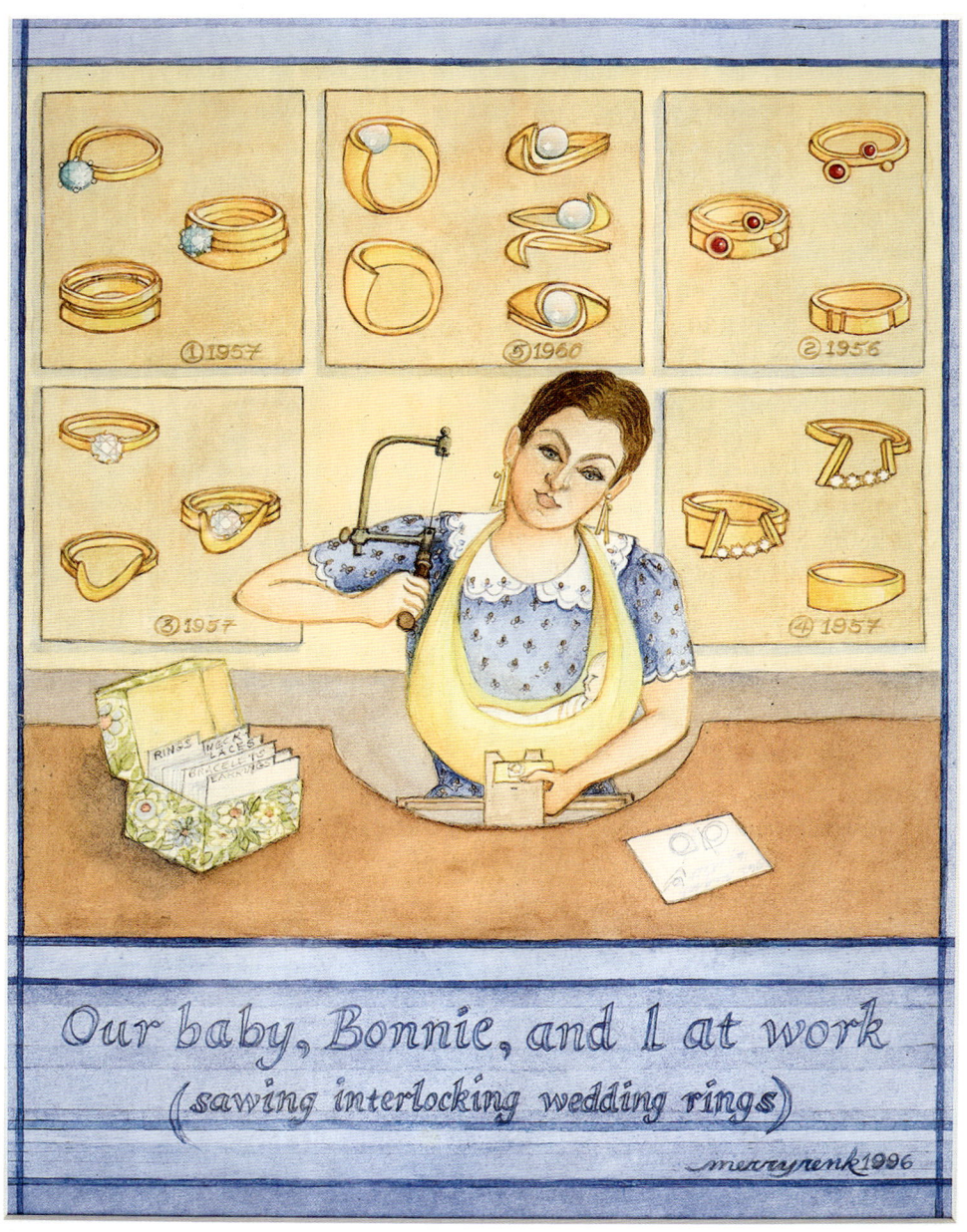

2.3 Merry Renk, *Our baby, Bonnie, and I at work (sawing interlocking wedding rings),* from the series "Memories for My Children's Children's Children's . . . ," 1989–1996. Watercolor, 14 × 11 in. Collection of Baunnie Sea.

Renk and Asawa turned to principles of design, like interlocking and looping, that were based on repetition, and thus could be stopped and started as needed. In this way, they took on a logic of interruption that a variety of scholars receptive to motherhood, including the social theorist Lisa Baraitser and the anthropologist Elizabeth Wayland Barber, have probed more deeply. Whereas Baraitser argues for interruption as fundamental to a maternal ethics of reciprocity, Barber concentrates on the historical association between women and textiles: in her book *Women's Work: The First 20,000 Years*, Barber asks why it is that for millennia textiles have been produced by women rather than men.[28] Her answer concerns the compatibility of spinning, weaving, and sewing with childcare. Here she draws on Judith Brown's research, twenty years earlier, on the sexual division of labor in food production. Brown discovered that those activities performed by women in any given social formation typically followed certain characteristics: they were repetitive and thus able to be easily put down and picked up again after interruptions, they were not dangerous for children, and they did not require being far from home. These observations were not a matter of essentializing labor; men could just as easily perform such tasks, and sometimes did. The issue, rather, was to identify those activities which a society could *rely* on women to do, which meant that whatever these activities were, they had to be compatible with other duties typically performed by women, such as breastfeeding. In returning to this argument to examine craft production, Barber realized that the making of textiles followed the same pattern of characteristics: "these are what societies worldwide have come to see as the core of women's work."[29]

This was the association invoked when a reviewer of the Laverne showroom described Asawa as "knitting like a woman Calder" in the pages of the modern architectural magazine *Domus*.[30] The reference was to the sculptor Alexander Calder, a paradigmatic modernist whose work could be informed by his own children but who remained an Artist; an artist-mother, however, marked a deviation, with maternal modernism fitting neatly into neither modern design nor women's work. If Asawa's work qualified as the former, this was in large part because it could be categorized as mobiles, sculpture that *moved*, with Erwine Laverne himself using this term to describe the sculptures.[31] Alongside views of the showroom in which Asawa's *Untitled* (S.535) was placed in visual dialogue with a Calder mobile, *Domus* included photographs of the work by Imogen Cunningham in her Russian Hill apartment just before it traveled to New York. The views of the work are far from the straightforward installation shots taken at Laverne and show the piece in unusual positions, curled onto itself on the floor and printed in negative. Cunningham had also titled one of her photographs *Aiko with Mobile* on submitting the work to the San Francisco Women Artists annual, placing Asawa's work within the category of the mobile and thus as contemporary sculpture. "Aiko" referred to Asawa's full name—Aiko Ruth Asawa—and thus to striking color portraits that Cunningham had taken of Asawa holding *Untitled* (S.535), which were also on display.[32] Cunningham had encouraged Asawa to use her Japanese name, just as she had encouraged her to exhibit under her maiden name—a suggestion that a credited "Ruth Lanier" had not yet implemented when she and Cunningham designed the cover of *Arts and Architecture* for its June 1952 issue with collaged photographs of *Untitled* (S.535).

Renk's status as a sculptor who worked with jewelry also relied on an engagement with the mobile form, adapting its size and format to the human body. In a photograph of Renk juxtaposed with Asawa's wire sculptures, she wears one of her so-called boomerang earrings (fig. 2.4). These consisted of two pieces of stacked bent metal attached by wire, instead of soldered, so that they were essentially an "iron mobile."[33] Taking on the discourse of mobile sculpture, exemplified by Calder's mobiles and László Moholy-Nagy's experiments in sculptural machines that moved of their own accord, these "mobile earrings," as Renk termed them, exemplified one of the central lessons that she had learned as a student at the Institute of Design (New Bauhaus): movement as a principle of three-dimensional form.[34] This principle, importantly, had a long history in the European and Soviet avant-gardes, first explored by practitioners like Aleksandr Rodchenko and transferred into the American context by European émigré artists, including Moholy-Nagy. Renk was one of the first to apply it to jewelry production, and in doing so, she was part of a growing group of jewelry makers who saw their métier as primarily sculptural. Traveling with fiber artist Lenore Tawney in the 1950s, Renk had spent time in Morocco, Spain, and France, which included a visit to Constantin Brancusi's studio, with the aging artist serving as a kind of oracle, as she later recalled.[35] In the same way that Brancusi dissolved the sculptural base, Renk released jewelry from the burden of representation: "i did not use realistic symbols. i designed rings that followed the contours of the finder. i worked with movement, rolling spheres, units that turn, interlock, interact or spin."[36]

As fellow Institute of Design student Margaret De Patta described the situation in 1955: "Problems common to sculpture and architecture are inherent in jewelry design—i.e.—space, form, tension, organic structure, scale, texture, interpenetration, superimposition and economy of means—each necessary element playing its role in a unified entity."[37] Such "design concepts," explored across wood, clay, plaster, plastics, and stone, sensitized De Patta, Renk, and Asawa to issues of volume and space, "and the line of demarcation between the fine arts, crafts, industrial design, dissolved before my eyes," De Patta recalled. Renk, the jeweler, produced sculptures, while Asawa, the sculptor, produced objects that could be worn. Both experimented with the format of the crown in its intimate relationship to the body. Asawa in turn also worked with the material of sterling silver in small formats, such as in her trio *Untitled* (S.6.33, 1956) of hanging looped forms ranging from fifteen to twenty-eight inches in length.

The photographic juxtaposition of Renk's jewelry and Asawa's sculpture makes this collapse across these spheres of craft, design, and fine art visible and emphasizes how movement served as their common basis. Employing the characteristic lowercase typography of Bauhaus writing, the young artist described her core design principles in the following terms: "i have suspended, overlapped, radiated, stacked, spiraled, fragmented, made inside forms and outside forms with this unit. the forms are light in weight and delicate in appearance but strong."[38] Renk's emphasis on verbs underscores

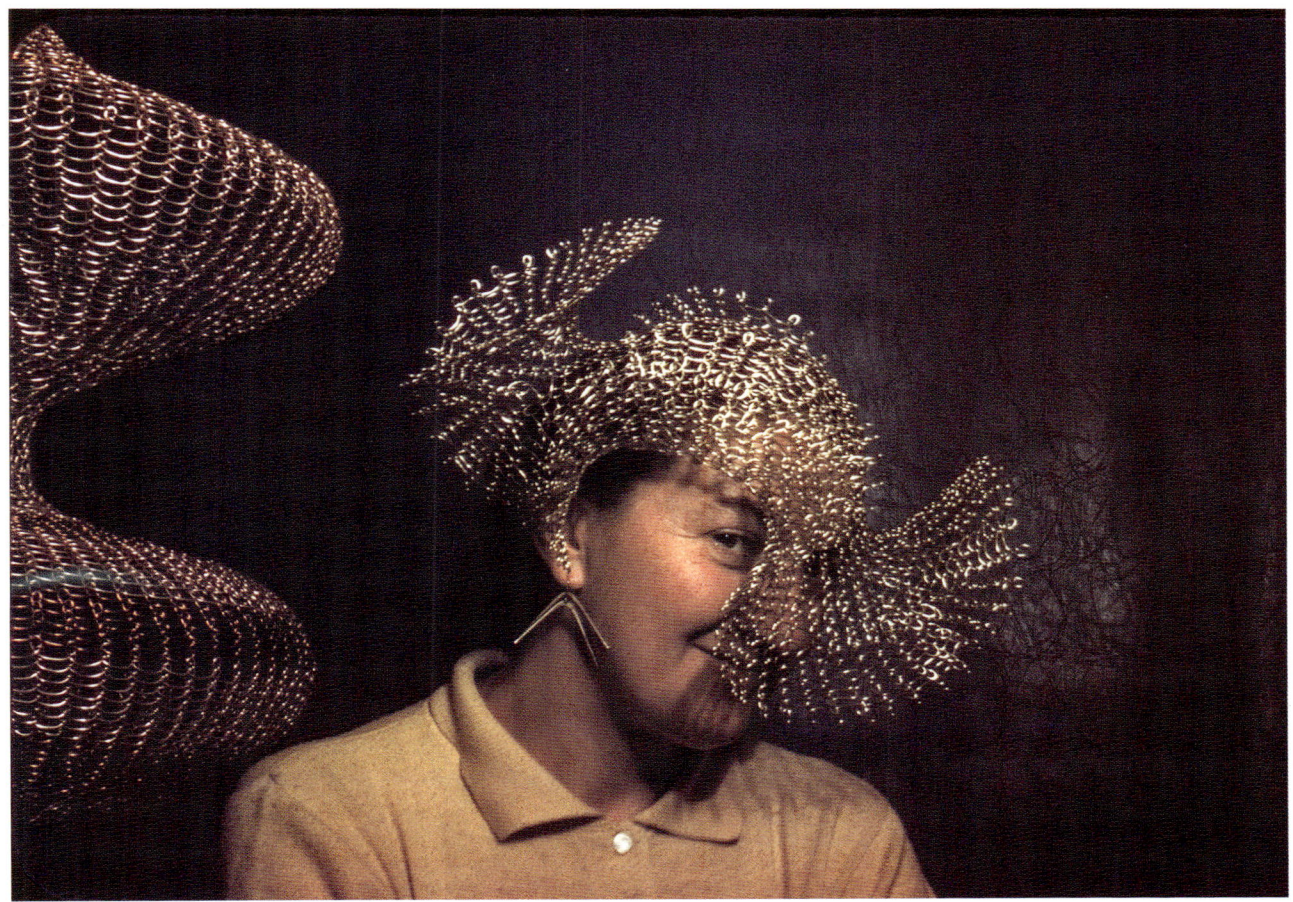

2.4 Merry Renk wearing her boomerang earrings with two of Ruth Asawa's looped-wire sculptures, c. 1958. Unknown photographer. Scanned color slide. Private collection.

movement as a central formal principle of her jewelry designs, which we can see in the photograph of a young Renk, head cocked and smiling, peeking out from beneath a wavy wire crown made by Asawa. Its curved edge frames her eye, cheek, and the ear on which hangs one of her own boomerang earrings. Both the earring and another Asawa sculpture beside Renk are caught by the exposure in a moment of spinning and turning. The two artists assembled and constructed these "mobiles," further distancing sculpture from its historical association with carving and bringing it into dialogue with architecture, design, and photography, where the shutter of the camera could now generate an image of sculpture as dynamic form. To borrow from Sarah Knott, this is mothering—sculpting—as *verb*, as a form acting in the world.[39] And we can see it in other frames from the same playful photo session, in which the movements of these blurred metal objects outpaced the camera's shutter.

That the interests of the two artists exceed boundaries of medium explains the astonishing episode in which Asawa's sculptures were confused as a work by sculptor-jeweler De Patta. Asawa and Cunningham had driven up to De Patta's house in Napa to deliver and install a looped-wire sculpture, *Untitled* (S.283), which Asawa had traded De Patta for a brooch. Once it was installed, Cunningham took a remarkable photograph of De Patta sitting next to the shadow-casting mesh form, with her husband Eugene Bielawski looking toward her from the opposite side. De Patta supplied the photograph to the journalist Bernice Stevens Decker, who wrote a feature on De Patta as part of the series "Handcrafts" for the *Christian Science Monitor*. The caption to the photograph stated that "sculptural designs are used not only for jewelry by [the] husband-wife team"; such "experimental craft also appears in decorative pieces, such as the one between them."[40] De Patta quickly corrected the mistake with Decker, prompting the journalist to write features on Asawa and Cunningham over the next year.[41] But that it was made in the first place is remarkable: the description of Asawa's looped-wire sculpture as a work by De Patta speaks to a profound fluidity between sculpture and jewelry as part of a broad field of "experimental craft" as "decoration."

FOUR ARTIST-CRAFTSMEN

Looking back on the field of design in the 1950s, Asawa told an interviewer, "that was a time when the decorators no longer wanted to be called decorators; they wanted to be called designers," and she cited San Francisco's Jackson Square, where Laverne had had Lanier design their West Coast showroom, as a site of this emergent idea.[42] Lanier and Asawa also submitted several designs for fabric and wallpaper to such firms, several of which were produced, including a pattern of letters that Asawa had first explored while still a student at Black Mountain College.[43] Advertised in the publication *Living for Young Homemakers* as part of a coordinated interior of patterned lampshades, curtains, upholstery fabric, and mattress ticking, such designs contributed to this paradigm shift away from the term "decoration" with its attendant sexual and gendered associations. Those associations, as design historian John Potvin writes, had to do with the stereotype of the decorator as "the female amateur and emotional effeminate male decorator," whose engagement with camp could be seen as akin to Oscar Wilde's "queer handing of the decorative arts as a mode of self-improvement and empowerment—a way of harnessing shame through decoration as agentic."[44]

In the 1950s, Asawa's "fantastic woven metal sculpture" moved between the queer-coded effeminate realm of interior "decoration," with its heterosexual pendant in the form of husband-and-housewife decorator couples like Elen and Hank Kluck, and its hypermasculine successor as interior "design."[45] Asawa's work belonged squarely to none of these categories and yet appeared frequently in all of them, and it is astonishing to see her work portrayed as often in the pages of *Ladies' Home Journal* as in *Arts and Architecture*. The contrast can also be detected in a juxtaposition of two designs for wallpapers—"baby footprints," on the one hand, and an untitled print made from inked potatoes on the other (figs. 2.5, 2.6). The first gestures to the spaces of feminized decoration, like the nursery, for which Asawa had made campy, cartoon-like drawings of plump infants with captions like "butterball" and "slumberbug"; the second gestures to abstraction as something that could be digested by this emergent, rationalized realm of interior design. And indeed it was well received: the curator Edgar Kaufmann of the Museum of Modern Art had asked Asawa for examples of her baskets for his *Good Design* exhibitions in 1952, and he described this term, "good design," as the response to "the wants of a new kind of public," one characterized by "needs and tastes molded by his status as a free individual in an industrialized world."[46] Asawa may have been received in this context, but it did not last long; there was little room in such formulations for "her" status as an artist-mother working at home.

In the decades after World War II, interior design stores mimicked modern art museums, and modern art museums featured design and craft. Lanier and Asawa had been introduced to Laverne Originals through John Entenza, chief editor at *Arts and Architecture*, who was enthusiastic about featuring Asawa's designs in his magazine.[47] Established in New York in the 1930s, Laverne Originals was one of the first interior design stores to introduce the concept of the interior space as an original work of art. The couple Estelle and Erwine Laverne had "rerouted two careers in painting to a joint one in applied design."[48] "Finding only dangling sculpture and a bench or two," read one article in *Interiors*, you might "conclude that you had wandered into a museum." This "museum-like quality" was generated through the rejection of mass production and a transference of the artwork's claim to originality and singularity into domestic space. The Lavernes were selling "not just designs (although nearly everything is Original, and for sale) but a concrete effort to relate fine and applied arts, business be darned."

That Laverne Originals had hired Lanier to design a showroom in San Francisco signaled the encroachment of "good design" on the West Coast. Good design's universalist aspirations in the form of the "free individual," unbound from nation and race, intersected with an existing language of the "designer-craftsman," which, by contrast, broached questions of national belonging. When Asawa and Renk arrived in San Francisco, in the late 1940s, California was quickly becoming a haven for

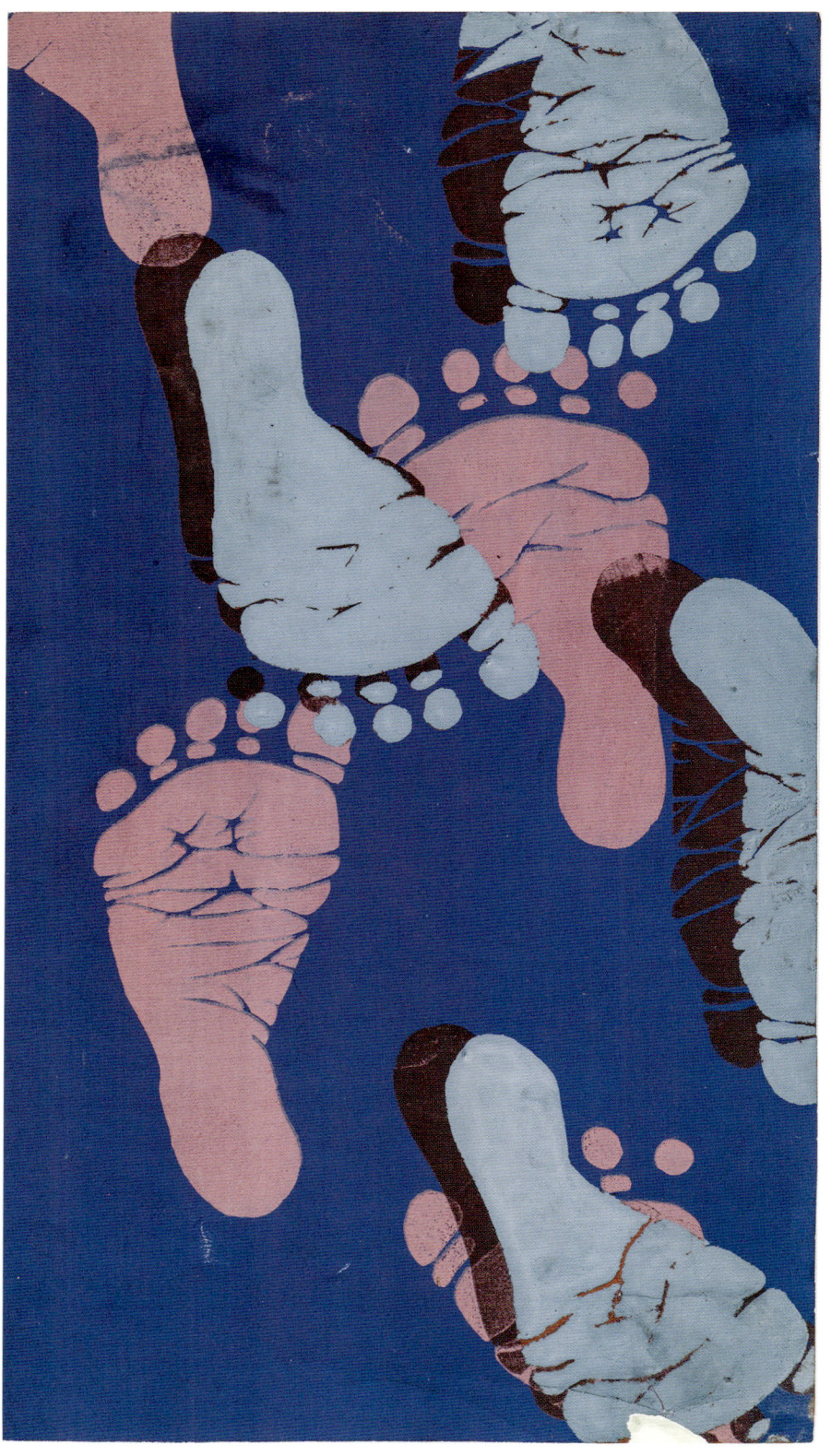

2.5 Ruth Asawa, *Untitled* (SF.012h, Baby Footprints), 1952. Pink, blue, and brown paint on coated paper, 10 × 5½ in. Private collection.

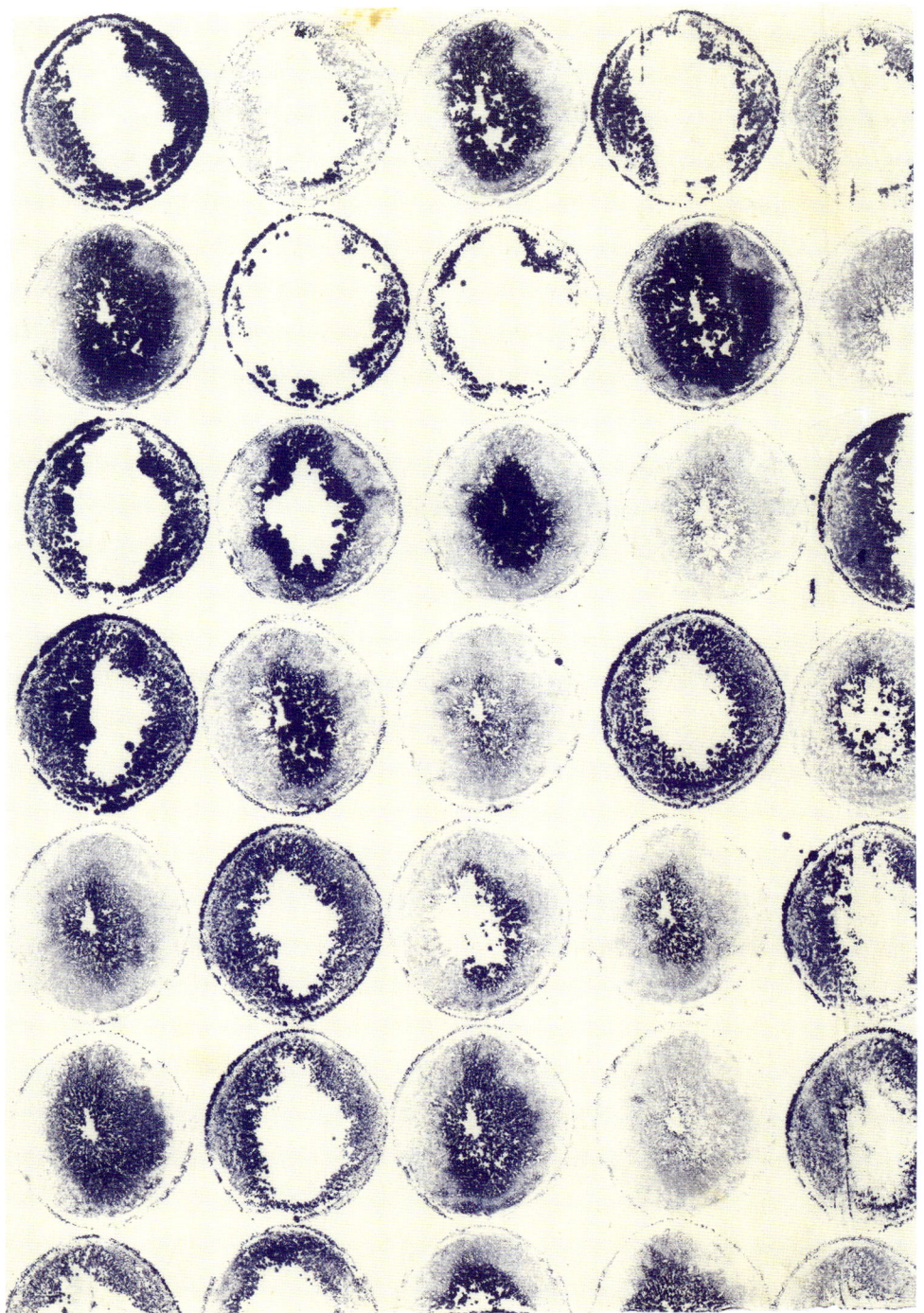

2.6 Ruth Asawa, *Untitled* (SF.046d, Potato Print, Blue Violet), c. 1951–1952. Blue violet ink on paper, 13¾ × 9 in. Private collection.

weaving, jewelry making, woodworking, metalsmithing, and bookbinding, with the publication *Craft Horizons* estimating that "some 150 full-time professional designer-craftsmen," of whom "as many are women as men," represented the core "of the California craft movement."[49] The gender of the term "craftsmen" did not reflect this diversity, but that was precisely the point: actual women were admitted into a field that was dominated by normative gender discourses. Despite this, women were leading the movement, and many of them were European émigrés. Craft, it seemed, could be coded as "ancient," such that "no race or nation can validly lay claim to them."[50] As Lippard writes, this realm of craft-design ran through "the taste gamut of the American lower-middle to upper-middle class," owing "as much stylistically to the 'primitive' or 'low' crafts—Mexican, Asian, American Colonial—as to the streamlining of the international design style."[51] In addition to Nanny Benderson, "the person who has done most for crafts in the burgeoning San Francisco Bay Area," *Craft Horizons* claimed, was the art historian and curator Elisabeth Moses, who had established a career in Cologne's applied arts museums and emigrated to California in 1934. Hired as a curator at the de Young Museum, she rose to prominence with exhibitions including *Design in '49* (1949), the *Contemporary Handweavers Exhibition* (1950, 1955), and *Designer Craftsmen of the West* (1957). The last of these included a booklet that Renk owned, with images of the so-called San Francisco Room, an interior in which craft objects were displayed as part of a modernist architectural ensemble. "California craftsmen," *Craft Horizons* definitively pronounced, were "leading the way in a movement to de-clinicalize the modern house."[52]

The architecture of the emerging Bay region movement, epitomized by Mario Corbett's house, where Lanier and Asawa were married, was a concrete example of such interiors.[53] The houses exhibited a preference for warm-textured redwood, open-plan layouts, sloping roofs, sun decks, porchlike interiors, lofted spaces, and radiant-heat concrete flooring. Sally Woodbridge would later describe this regional architectural style as aspiring to an integration of California's mild natural environment into domestic space.[54] This "Eden for everyman," to borrow her phrasing, was more than the modernist concern with functionality; it incorporated a relation to the natural environment that had become "synonymous with the American vision of the Good Life." This good life belonged to good design. Above all, such an architectural interior resisted the mass-produced tract house; "every good design" was "unique," a "dramatic and imaginative creation of wood, stone, trees, shrubs, and land"—and, of course, "interesting sculpture," as a feature on San Francisco houses in *Life* read, with Asawa's own sculpture regularly inhabiting such interiors.[55]

It was the spacious height of these interiors that led Asawa to begin lengthening the dimensions of her sculptures, at times creating site-specific commissions that responded to the interior dimensions of the space in which they would hang. One example is the sculpture in June Lane Christensen's dance studio, where children counted among her students (fig. 2.7). Christensen had studied with Asawa and Lanier at Black Mountain College, and the three had even pursued plans to open an artist residency on Treasure Island in San Francisco Bay, which never materialized.[56]

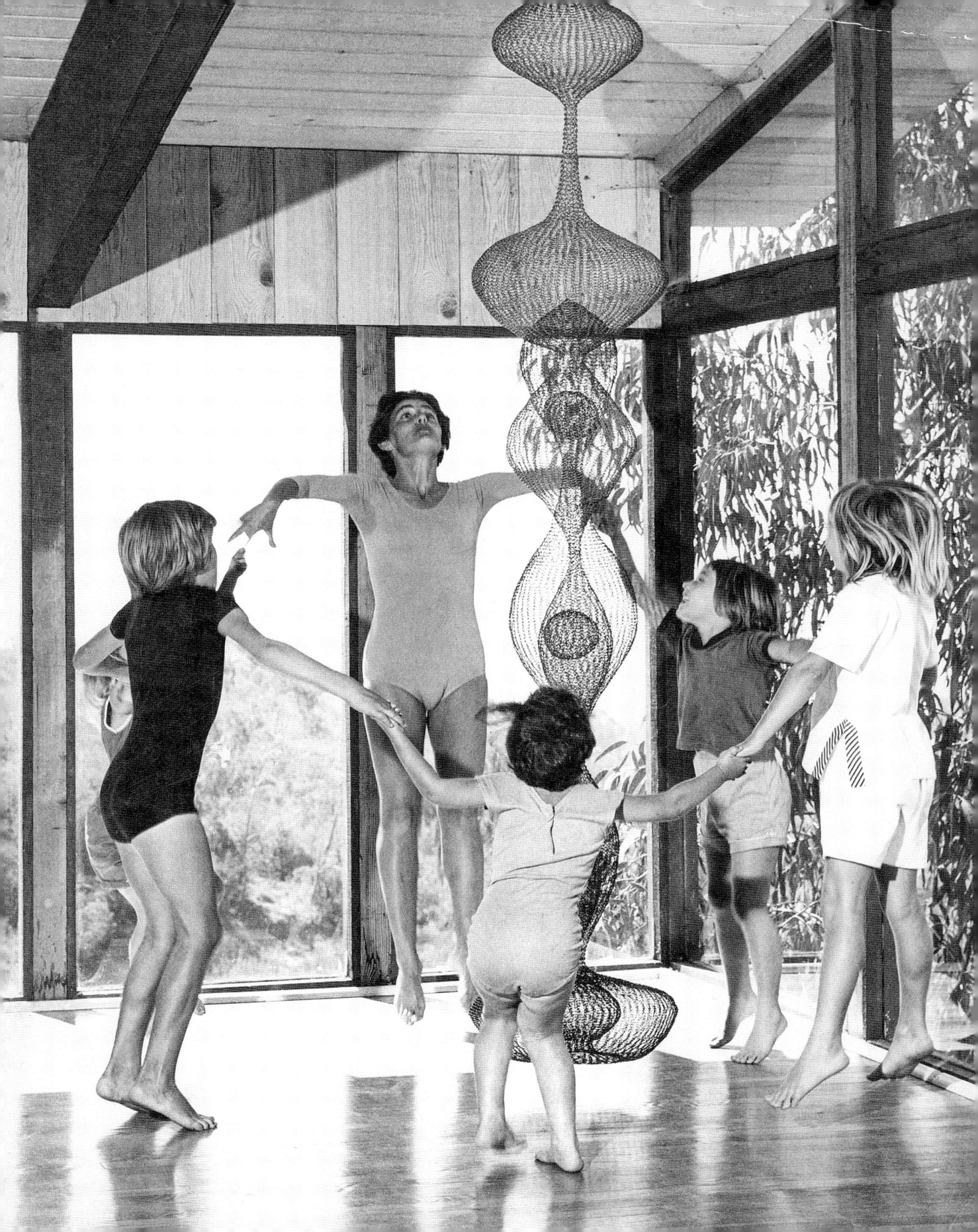

At some point, Christensen had commissioned a sculpture from Asawa for her dance studio, and it is very likely, as the curator and art historian Jenelle Porter claims, that the commission explains why this particular looped-wire sculpture matches the dimensions of the studio's interior height.[57] Once installed, the sculpture hung as a constant presence in the studio, with its semitransparent surfaces mediating dancing bodies of mothers and children, the modern glass architecture, and the California landscape of eucalyptus and rolling hills seen through the studio windows.

Asawa's interest in such experimentation in part led to the end of her brief affiliation with the Peridot Gallery in New York, whose eight-foot-high ceiling limited her exploration of larger-scale pieces (in 1955, she was making sculptures thirteen feet high and forty-two inches in diameter, and making full-size drawings to work out their designs).[58] She also earned the attention of designers like Charles Eames, who at an opening had "likened Ruth's wire unto the little pen and ink drawings one used to have to do in school but Imogen Cunningham close by reminded him 'but these are made of wire.'"[59] It was this dialogue with interior design that led Asawa to apply for a Guggenheim grant in 1955, in which her application states her intent "to work on a group of ideas to be used architecturally. These would be sculptures that could be used either in large spaces within buildings, spaces larger than the ordinary, or in outside spaces related to buildings," presenting technical challenges related to the prevention of rust, tarnishing, and discoloration. Well into the 1960s, Asawa would submit to sculpture competitions for new buildings, and in 1960, she designed a group of four looped-wire "decorative sculpture fixtures" to be used for lighting in the upscale Joseph Magnin store in downtown San Francisco.[60]

In what was perhaps a concerted effort to situate Asawa's work more precisely within this heterogeneous exhibition context of decoration, craft, and design, Albert Lanier proposed to organize an exhibition at the San Francisco Museum of Art (today the San Francisco Museum of Modern Art). The progressive director at the time, Grace L. McCann Morley, had spearheaded efforts to draw attention to West Coast craftsmen and designers, including by serving on the selection committee of *Designer Craftsmen U.S.A. 1953*, sponsored by the American Craftsmen's Educational Council, in which both Renk and Asawa entered objects (Asawa entered a "collapsible basket" and a "fruit basket" in the category of "home, garden or ecclesiastic accessories in any metals, decorated or undecorated").[61] Morley also participated in the selection committee for group exhibitions such as the *First Annual Pacific Coast Decorative Arts Competition* (November 4, 1949–January 8, 1950). This exhibition involved cooperation between local artists, sponsoring companies, and arts institutions in order to identify new talent that could then potentially be transferred into industry; part of the prize entailed a commission by the sponsoring firm. The participating artists included Asawa, who submitted five wallpaper designs, and the weaver and former instructor at Black Mountain College Trude Guermonprez, who was then teaching at the school of the Pond Farm Workshops, north of San Francisco, where Lanier and Asawa were regular visitors.[62]

In September 1953, Lanier wrote to Morley with the proposal to organize "a show of the work of four artist-craftsmen":

They are Marguerite Wildenhain, potter; Ida Dean, weaver; Merry Renk, jeweler; and Ruth Asawa, wire baskets and sculpture. If the show materializes my function will be designing the installation and assisting with it.

The idea behind the show is a mutual concern of the four artists which has grown out of the hodge-podge of the large group craft shows where the work of individual craftsmen is lost for lack of completeness and enough space to breathe in. Though none of these artists work in the same medium their approaches complement one another and each maintains a high degree of integrity in their work. In designing the show, I would try to preserve this separateness while relating them to make a worthwhile experience for the spectator.[63]

In describing these larger national exhibitions as a "hodge-podge," Lanier was taking a clear stance on the relationship between the object and its exhibition. It was not enough, in other words, to simply put such objects on display; they had to be displayed in a way that emphasized shared formal concerns, while maintaining the unique qualities of each approach.

This was the exhibition strategy that Lanier devised and what made the resulting exhibition at the San Francisco Museum of Art so unique for its time. For Lanier related these objects to one another in a carefully designed exhibition layout, in which all the objects occupied a single gallery (fig. 2.8). Several of Asawa's looped-wire sculptures hung from the skylit ceiling, illuminated by the natural light, while Wildenhain's pottery stood on raised platforms. Examples of Dean's textiles hung on the walls, and Renk's jewelry occupied recessed vitrines. One of these vitrines was built into an exhibition wall, while another was suspended by four cables, so that it floated in the exhibition space. It occupied a central place within the gallery, situated just behind the curved wall at the entrance upon which viewers encountered the artists' four last names in sans serif black font. Morley seems to have been especially pleased with Lanier's design choices, writing to him: "We believe craftsmen should be as concerned with presentation as painters are in framing their works or sculptors in providing bases for their pieces. This enterprise of yours is therefore most welcome."[64]

Marguerite Wildenhain, too, approved of Lanier's design approach and the concept of moving away from the usual craft exhibitions as "all over the place, scattered between mediocre or really bad objects," and even suggested it could be a chance to foreground Pond Farm, since Guermonprez taught there and "Ida nearly belongs to us too," floating the idea that Asawa come and give a class at some point as well.[65] Pond Farm served as a touchstone for Renk and Asawa during the early 1950s. It had been established by Gordon and Jane Herr in 1940 and expanded with the arrival of Guermonprez and Wildenhain, who would reestablish Pond Farm as a center for pottery in 1952 after the Herrs left. Lanier had learned originally of Wildenhain's pottery from the pages of *Arts and Architecture* while still a student. When he and Asawa moved to San Francisco, they made frequent visits to the artists' colony seventy miles north of the city, spending Thanksgivings and Christmases there. Renk often joined them. And each time they visited, they purchased Wildenhain's pots, eventually amassing a significant collection.[66] Lanier later designed the remodel of the Wildenhain house at Pond Farm, and in the early 1960s he and Asawa bought land in the adjacent town of Guerneville, which further strengthened their ties to the Pond Farm community.[67]

What is especially significant about *Four Artist-Craftsmen* was that it supplied a countermodel to the then-reigning identity of "designer-craftsman." That identity mobilized craft for industry, given the central role that sponsoring companies played in exhibitions such as *Designer Craftsmen U.S.A. 1953*. Such a functionalist orientation had the unintended effect of potentially limiting experiment and dialogue across media and formats—a dialogue that Lanier's careful selection and limited presentation sought to reinstate. "Good Taste," *Four Artist-Craftsmen* seemed to suggest, anticipating Lippard's insights some twenty years later, "will not be standardized in museums, but will vary from place to place, from home to home."[68] This investment in craft was an investment in overcoming the opposition between art and non-art. It was to advocate for what Anni Albers would describe as an identity that superseded the opposition implied in the term "artist-craftsmen": "These ancient craftsmen were artists, no hyphen needed."[69]

Four Artist-Craftsmen underscores how comparisons of Asawa's looped-wire technique to the so-called feminine techniques of knitting and weaving did not simply domesticate her artistic labor; the comparison also drew attention to the compatibility between weaving and architecture in this work. Asawa's understanding of weaving, as practiced by Ida Dean and Guermonprez, followed a conception of the medium derived from the Bauhaus, which, as she described, pursued the strategy of "building, instead of carving."[70] Trained by Bauhaus weavers, Guermonprez had taken over Anni Albers's courses during the several semesters when Albers was on leave from Black Mountain College. Guermonprez was an unofficial mentor to Asawa during the early 1950s, and she frequently taught weaving lessons to Asawa's, Lee's, and Renk's children at her nearby home, modeling approaches that the Alvarado School Arts Workshop would later use. As Bay Area fiber artist Kay Sekimachi recalls, the kind of weaving that Guermonprez introduced stood in stark contrast to the state of weaving in the early 1950s, when it was a field dominated by "all fairly well-to-do housewives who did it for a hobby."[71] In her courses, Guermonprez introduced weave drafts, explained the various kinds of weaves, discussed fibers, and emphasized hand weaving and its place in society. This was an approach closely related to Anni Albers's use of innovative exercises such as texture studies, in which pattern was explored through repetition of identical units like corn kernels.

Even if Asawa did not take any weaving classes while a student at Black Mountain, Guermonprez was an important interlocutor for her, and the two shared an exchange over questions of texture and structure across pliable materials. Their friendship seems to have developed toward the end of Asawa's time at the school, when she wrote to Peggy Tolk-Watkins about "understanding Trudi G. more and more."[72] Asawa had also seen firsthand the importance for Guermonprez of producing functional objects (a value also shared by Anni Albers at Black Mountain), and in the early 1950s she

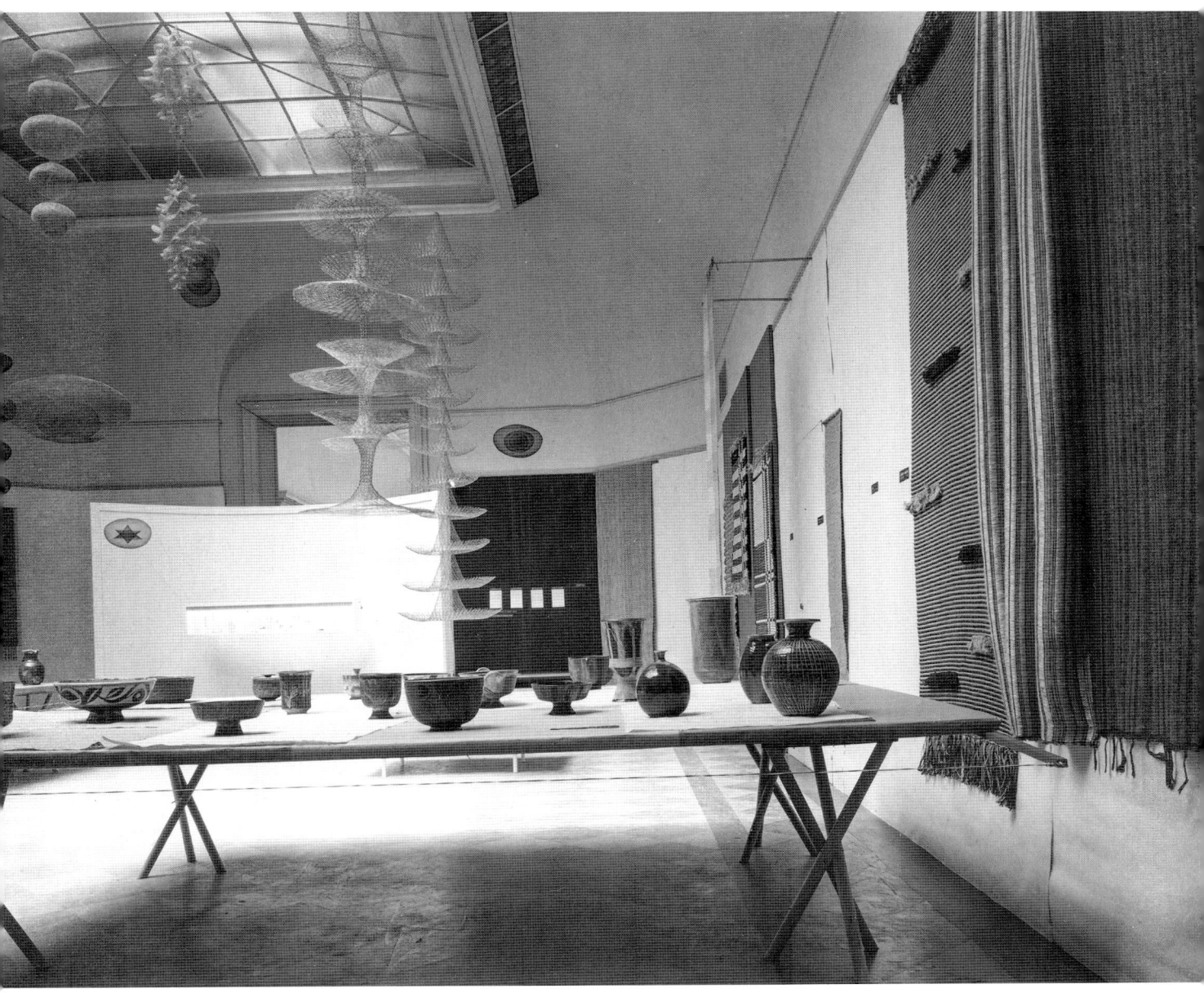

2.8 Installation view of *Four Artist-Craftsmen*, April 1–May 2, 1954, at the San Francisco Museum of Art, featuring Ruth Asawa, Marguerite Wildenhain, Ida Dean, and Merry Renk, with installation design by Albert Larier. Photo: Bob Hall. San Francisco Museum of Modern Art Archives.

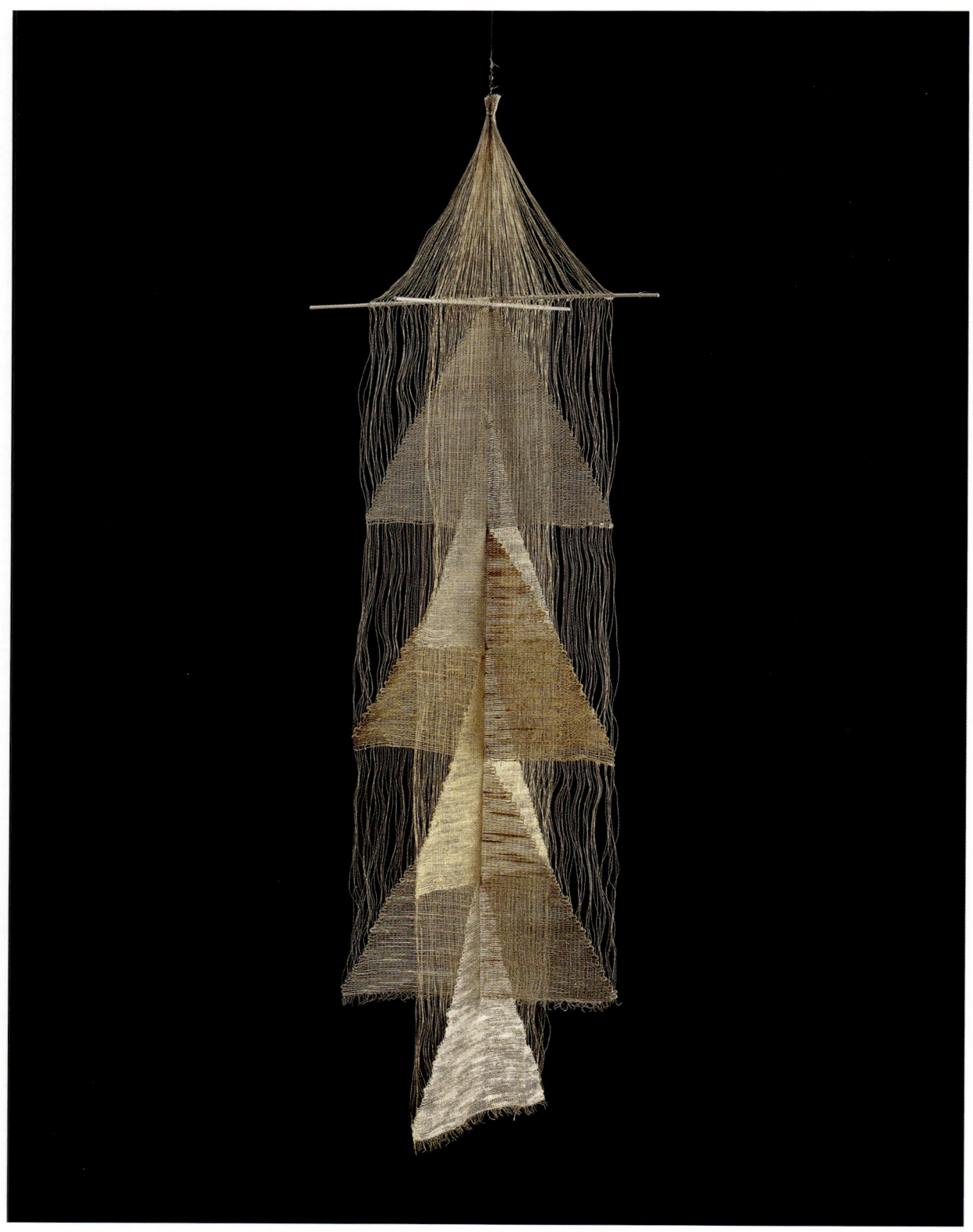

helped Guermonprez prepare seven demonstration panels for the San Francisco Museum of Art.[73] Although Guermonprez regarded weaving that was limited to artistic contexts as "not a professional thing to do," she was committed to aesthetic experimentation, seeing in the medium of weaving a concept of interrelationality, because "more than any other craft, weaving is related to something else."[74] Working on her series of "textile graphics"—Asawa would have known of the tapestry *Leaf Study* on view at the de Young's Pond Farm exhibition in 1950—Guermonprez painted directly onto warp threads, sometimes also using stencils. This was an explicitly anti-medium-specific definition of art, one that embraced an "imitation" of painting, Guermonprez states, "to achieve nuances just as the painter does with his pigments. At the same time, we also get a changing expression of texture which adds to the interest of design." Thus the structural variation of the weave and the architecture of threads—rather than the superimposition of "recipe books" or painter's cartoons—determined the structure's visual components.[75]

Both Guermonprez and Asawa employed the principle of "interpenetrating volumes" (a reviewer in *ArtNews* in the 1950s wrote of the "implied volumes—cones and spheres and flouncing flower shapes in grey, gold, or brown wire").[76] Just as Asawa structured her looped-wire surfaces so that they intersected with one another, often several times within a single work, so too did Guermonprez experiment with the crossing of planar shapes in her hanging fiber weavings, such as *Crystal* (1964; fig. 2.9). At the same time, Guermonprez introduced metallic gray weft threads and fine gold warp threads, drawing her pieces closer to the wire used by Asawa. As the hanging structures in *Four Artist-Craftsmen* demonstrate in their juxtaposition of weaving, pottery, and jewelry, many of the familiar dichotomies structuring midcentury modernism—including fine art and craft, decoration and design, the showroom and the museum gallery—do little to help us understand the heterogeneity of these works and their resistance to the era's normative aesthetic categories.

2.9 Trude Guermonprez, *Crystal*, 1964. Crossed warp three-dimensional hanging; warp: fine gold metallic thread; weft #1: gold color slub cotton; weft #2: natural slub cotton; weft #3: gray metallic; two gray metal bars, 42 × 15 × 15 in. Collection of Forrest L. Merrill. Photo: M. Lee Fatherree.

FOLDING

One of the most striking details of *Four Artist-Craftsmen* could be found inside one of Lanier's glass display cases. If the visitor looked closely, she would see a white, folded paper surface against which stood *Folded* (1953), one of Renk's folded pendants. This detail encapsulates one aspect of Renk and Asawa's working relationship: paperfolding. "When I was a student at the Institute of Design," Renk recalls, "there was a problem presented to us: Pretend you are a child and play with paper like a child, crush, rip, cut, puncture, roll, fold, etc. In this play you will make discoveries that will become your solution to this problem. Unfortunately, my discovery was, that I found no child and I discovered no solutions."[77] This frustration went unresolved until 1951, when Asawa began to work on a folded-paper wall covering (the same one displayed at the Laverne showroom in San Francisco).[78] Renk continues: "Ruth explained to me how [Josef] Albers had approached their 'Paper Fold' project. He directed the students to make a drawing of a folded paper rectangle that was placed on the table. Then on graph paper they would draw the angle which could be folded into a rectangle and fold it, then draw a six-sided form and fold it and draw an eight-sided form and fold it." The challenge was to limit oneself to paper and then see how one could fold a square, then a circle, then a hexagon. "After I did these exercises, I had learned the basic rules of the fold. I was inspired to attempt to draw and fold a shape similar to a paper egg carton. I spent two days and nights developing that solution."[79]

Paperfolding in Josef Albers's pedagogy constituted a crucial educational tool that had long been aimed at exercises in modeling and folding which mothers could do with their children.[80] These were exercises in how "to stretch a material," as Asawa described it, so that new qualities could be discovered in and through the material without destroying its inherent properties.[81] This is a good example of how Albers was interested not in medium specificity—the language dominant in the art criticism of the era—but in "a material's counterintuitive properties," explains art historian Jeffrey Saletnik in his book on Albers's pedagogy.[82] Instead of material purity, in which each medium strives toward a perfection of attributes unique to its own limits—such as flatness in painting—the goal here was a degree of promiscuity, of "paperfold metamorphosis," to borrow from the curator Gerald Nordland. Thrift and economy took precedence over inherent attributes, as students in Albers's courses were obliged to use careful planning and precise execution so that there was no waste. Instead of medium, at issue here were materials and *matter*.

Judith Butler has pointed to matter's historical association with femininity, founded in "a set of etymologies which link matter with *mater* and *matrix* (or the womb) and, hence, with the problematic of reproduction."[83] The association is not only a rhetorical one; it shapes how we now read the decision to focus on matter, instead of medium, by a group of artist-mothers working in an era in which the term "medium" and "medium specificity" bolstered a pervasive view of having children and making art as incompatible endeavors. Although Albers pointed the way, Renk and Asawa developed this approach to materials to such an extent that it far exceeded what the

German pedagogue could have imagined. The artists went on to experiment with paper and especially its folded and interlocking forms in a range of formats, including Asawa's "expanding construction" in the "Structures" section of the exhibition *Made with Paper* at the Museum of Contemporary Crafts in New York (November 18, 1967–January 7, 1968). In the exhibition, Renk was represented by her *Hanging Lamp* (1966), an eighteen-inch-diameter globe made from interlocking sections of vegetable parchment (a miniature example is visible in Renk's model of her studio illustrated in the previous chapter). The two artists also translated paperfolding into metal—in the case of Asawa, casting paperfolds in bronze as test pieces and later for public fountains, or having them fabricated in steel, whereas Renk opted for thirty-six-gauge silver sheet in order to take as much weight as possible out of the design; a heavier frame held the pendant together and protected the edges.[84] This was a decision in line with Renk's concern about the "wearability" of jewelry, the relationship between the object and the body on which it is displayed, as she explained to Joan Pearson Watkins in 1958, when interviewed on Watkins's television show *Design Workshop* (a weekly broadcast on KQED).

Renk later admitted that this requirement meant that pieces like the folded pendant were "too difficult to be economically practical for handmade jewelry."[85] They were first and foremost experimental: works of art as opposed to function. Indeed, this experimentation fueled both artists' interest in paperfolding. Consider a photograph taken by Laurence Cuneo of a paperfold held by one of Asawa's daughters (fig. 2.12). The photograph is more than a documentation of the folded object; it sets these folds in direct dialogue with the female body and with domestic space, signaled by the striking contrast between the vertical floral curtains along the image's edge and the curved linearity of the collapsed folded structure, as if crowning her head. This is a decorative object on multiple registers, but it far exceeds the terms of decoration—or rather, it is a form of decoration indivisible from softness and structure, expansion and collapse, figure and ground.

Even as Renk was labeled a jeweler and Asawa a sculptor, both were concerned with the same formal problems and explored these problems in parallel, across a shared language of materials. This shared terrain registered in surprising ways, such as that made visible in a comparison between Renk's folded hairband, scaled to the human body, and Asawa's *Aurora* (1984–1986), a monumental public sculpture (figs. 2.10, 2.11). The one is a scaled version of the other, and without this scale, the two objects would seem to be one and the same. This is not a case of appropriation; Renk and Asawa both freely credited one another for these developments in their work. Rather, in comparisons such as this, we have a model of recursive production: Asawa had introduced Renk to the fold, Renk developed it in relationship to metal and the human body, which Asawa then further developed into larger, expandable versions, which Cuneo then photographed in striking juxtapositions with her daughters, and which she then adapted to monumental public works cast in bronze—all in a process of call-and-response in relationship to one another's work.

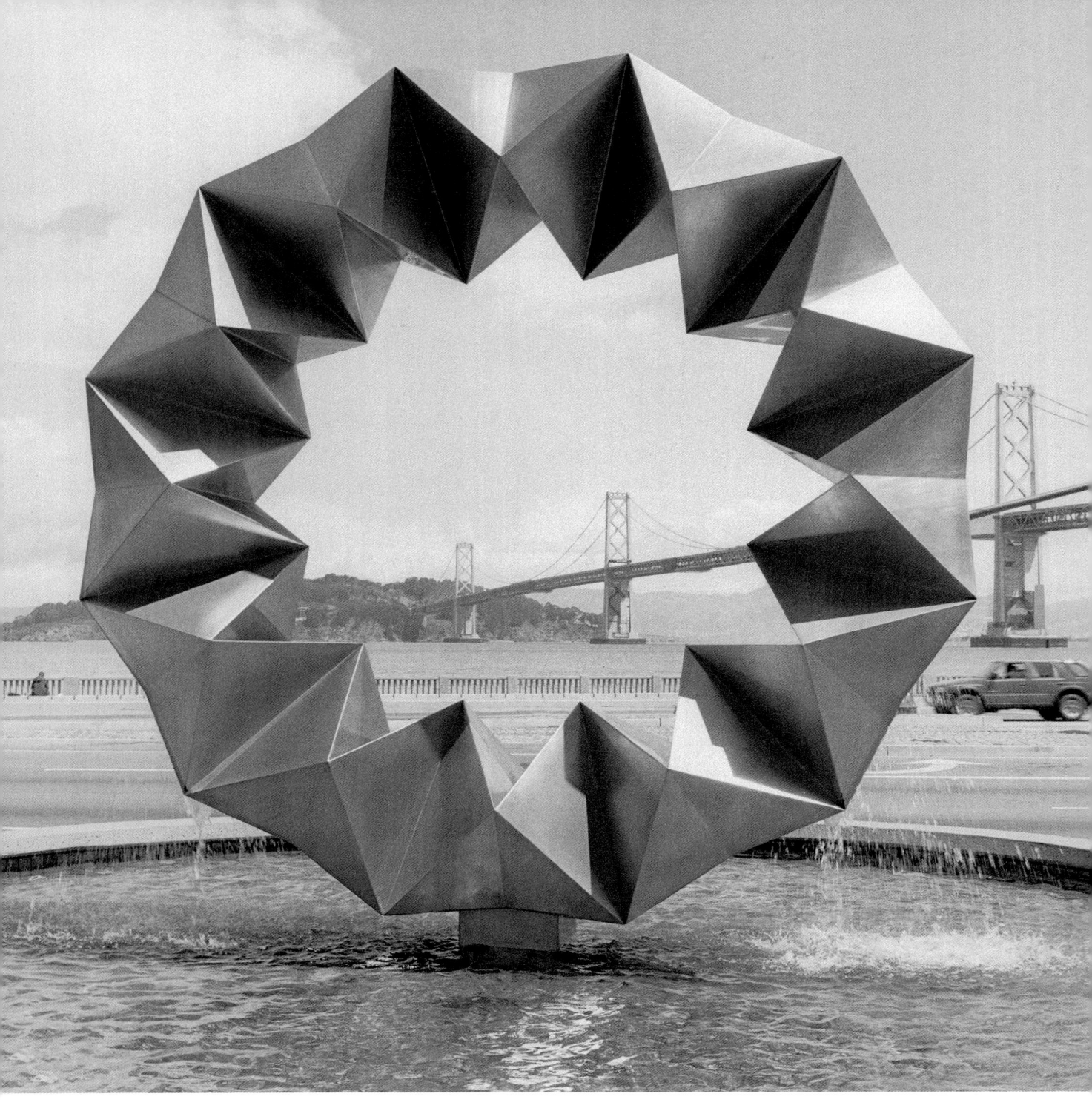

2.10 Ruth Asawa, *Aurora* (PC.009, Bayside Plaza, San Francisco), 1984–1986. Polished stainless steel, 156 × 156 × 39 in. Photo: Hudson Cuneo.

The recursive, process-based character of these paper experiments is legible in one final example, which also does the work of bringing us back to textiles. This example is a quilt fabricated on the basis of these paperfolds, except here it is fabric rather than paper which bears the folded structure. The quilt was shown in Asawa's 1976 exhibition at San Francisco's municipal art gallery Capricorn Asunder, and it was categorized in the checklist under the section "Ideas in Progress"—a designation that suggests we might not even be able to view such works as "works" at all, but rather as one stage on a continuum of material exploration (fig. 2.13). The same kind of doubt is introduced into the category of authorship, for the work is attributed not to Asawa but to her two daughters. It would seem that the investigation of two-dimensional

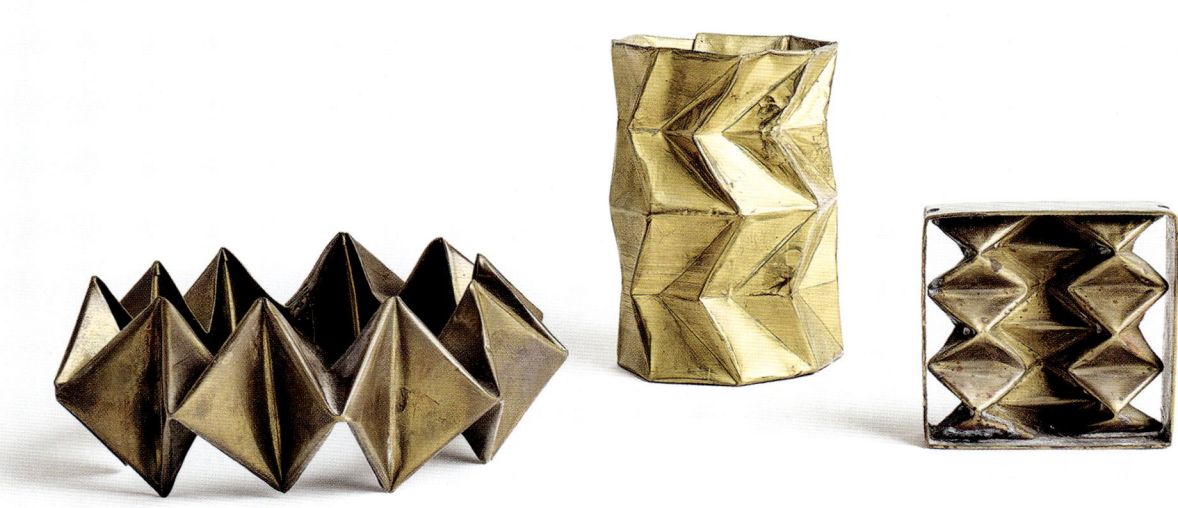

2.11 Merry Renk, *Folded Crown*, 1953, silver hairband, 2 × 6 × 6 in. (left); *Untitled*, c. 1954, curved and folded silver sheet with gold wash, 3¾ × 2½ × 2¼ in. (center); *Folded*, 1954, sterling silver pendant, 3½ × 2½ × 1 in. (right). Collection of Baunnie Sea.

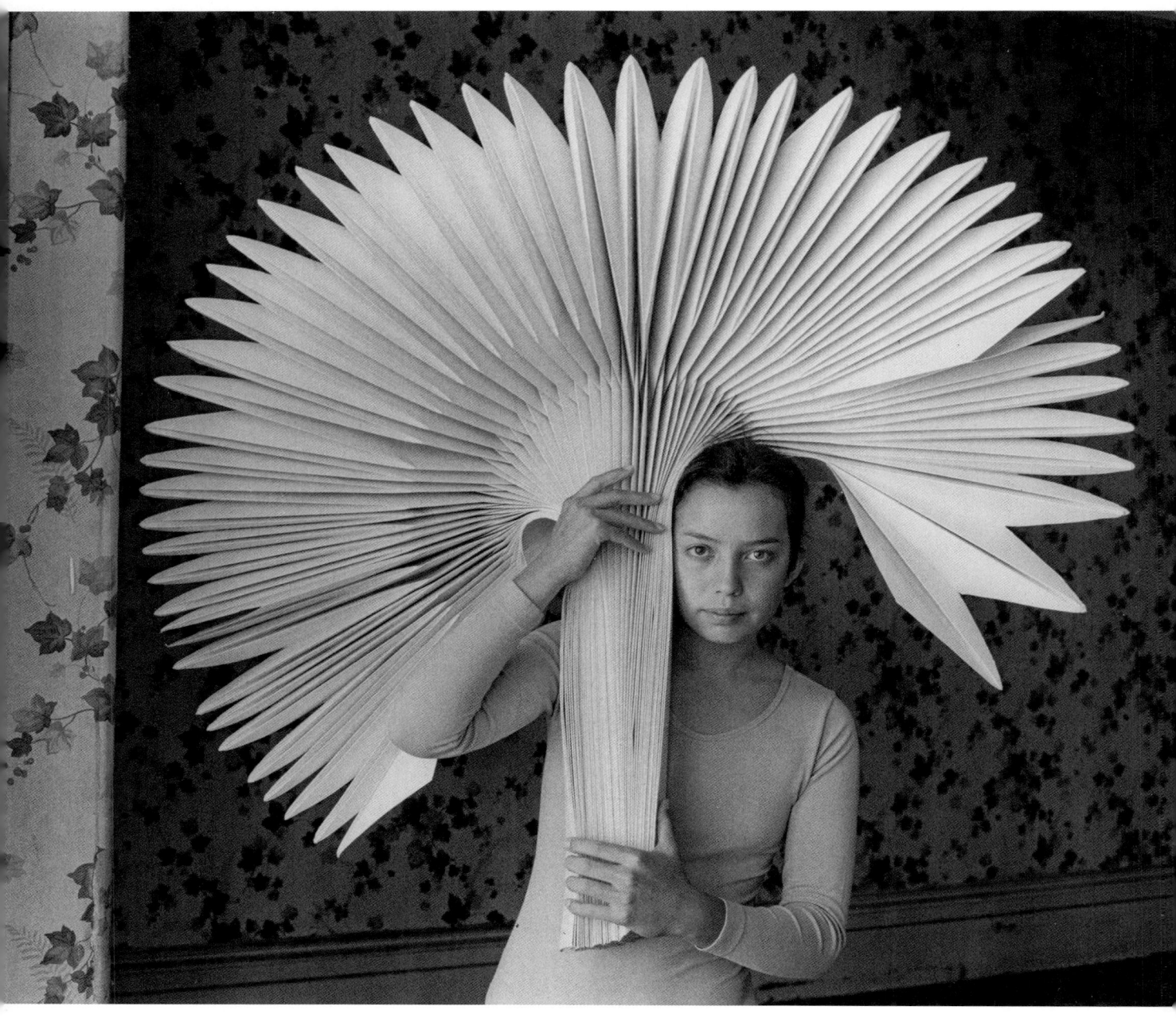

2.12 Ruth Asawa's daughter Addie Laurie
Lanier holding one of Asawa's paperfolds,
c. 1975. Photo: Laurence Cuneo.

materials in three-dimensional form and then back into two-dimensional surfaces in an altogether different material (fabric instead of paper) required an equally expanded (or at least malleable) conception of fabrication: at issue is not this or that individual as author in the way Kaufmann called for as part of "good design." Rather such designations seem to have been necessitated by the position of the artist-mother in the search for other modes of attribution and making better suited to her interests.

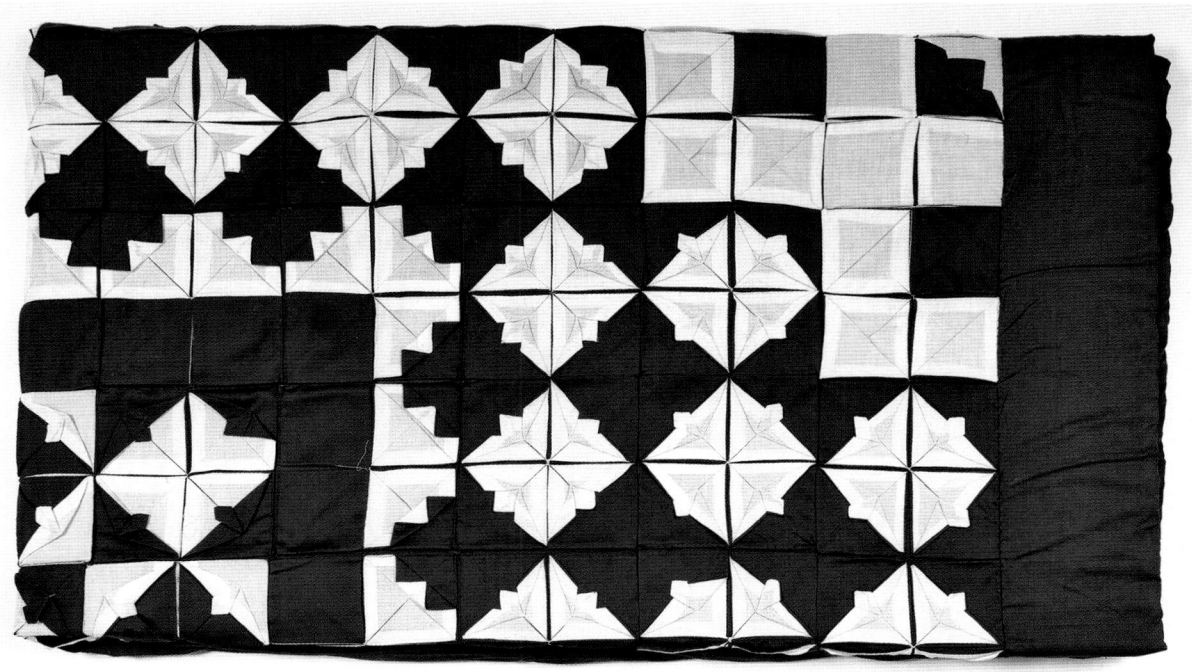

2.13 Quilt arranged and sewn by Ruth Asawa's daughters Aiko Cuneo and Addie Laurie Lanier (detail), c. 1970s. Private collection.

"There was a day in the not so distant past," a reviewer wrote in 1967, "when a sharp line of demarcation existed between what was considered art and what was considered craft. By conventional definition, an artist was considered an artist if he produced an oil painting or a piece of statuary. If tile trivets and woven pot holders were the artist's forte, he was considered a craftsman. This is no longer true. . . . Sculptors are dabbling in craft materials, craftsmen are experimenting with sculpture techniques—and out of it all has come new exciting work which diminishes the role of function, emphasizes imagery and says, in effect, anything goes."[86] The review reported on an exhibition organized by Dextra Frankel for the Laguna Beach Art Association, in which one of Asawa's tied-wire, wall-mounted sculptures was on display. Less than a year later, Frankel would include another of Asawa's sculptures, a looped-wire piece, in an exhibition she organized at California State Fullerton's art gallery, titled *The Intersection of Line*, which juxtaposed "ancient and primitive fabric construction techniques" with interpretations of these techniques by "contemporary craftsmen." Asawa's piece, titled *Sculptural Form* in that exhibition, is described as having been made with the technique of "knitting," defined in the catalogue as "the vertical interloping of a single element of yarn to construct a fabric."[87] Works by Ida Dean, Trude Guermonprez, Kay Sekimachi, and Lenore Tawney were also included in the exhibition. The photograph published in the *Los Angeles Times* places Asawa's work in dialogue with a building site, and pairs a hard-hat construction worker with the feminized rhetoric describing her technique. It is likely that the construction site was someplace other than the exhibition galleries, though exactly where is unclear.[88]

These instances anticipate the alignment of Asawa's looped-wire sculptures with the fiber arts movement, which would come to characterize her work's later reception. That alignment first appeared in the book *Beyond Craft: The Art Fabric* by Mildred Constantine and Jack Lenor Larsen, an inaugural effort to position fiber artists as "innovators of art rather than low laborers of craft."[89] Asawa is not one of the twenty-eight artists featured in the book's main text, but she is pointedly discussed in the introduction, which prefaces its discussion of her by noting Trude Guermonprez's significance at Pond Farm and the California College of Arts and Crafts. Reminding us of Elizabeth Wayland Barber's insight into the maternal reasons for textile's historical association with femininity, discussed at the beginning of this chapter, the authors point out that the University of California, Berkeley, had one of the great departments of physical anthropology, with strong collections of "American Indian and pre-Columbian basketry and fabrics," which influenced the direction of the university's Department of the Decorative Arts and its weaving program (offering the only master of arts degree in weaving in the country). And finally, the authors turn to the third significant fiber arts reference in the Bay Area: "There was in San Francisco a lone pioneer, Ruth Asawa, who much earlier utilized an Art Fabric medium without precedent and even today without peer. Her material was wire, her technique tubular knitting, often in layers, with one floating inside the other like a series of carved Chinese ivories. With this technique she was able to create large volumes of shadow-producing filigree in a material that is durable and soil-free. These, America's first monumental Art Fabrics, are an unequivocal success."[90] The statement appeared next to a full-page illustration of a nine-foot-tall, two-foot-wide "tubular knit" wire sculpture, *Untitled* (S.039, 1958–1959).

Typically construed as a divide along the axis of functional versus aesthetic, the art/craft divide can be productively recast as the difference between creative and pro-creative labor. As Lippard writes, turning to a feminist engagement with the margin-alized realm of "hobby art," it is a revaluation of "the ancient, sensuously repetitive, Penelopean rhythms of seeding, hoeing, gathering, weaving, spinning, as well as [of] modern domestic routines." With her looped- and tied-wire sculptures described as objets d'art, and her public sculptures later criticized for their sentimentality, Asawa checked all the boxes for a practitioner of what Lippard describes as "women's 'hobby art.'" Less a real category than a straw man by which to shore up the uniqueness of "fine art," Lippard argues, this spectrum of craft, both high and low, is associated with the amateur housewife-artist, who makes "'private' or 'closet' art (made for 'personal reasons' or 'just for myself'—as if most art was not)."[91] The so-called wire stuff was on a spectrum with art projects with Asawa's own children: her eldest son recalls wak-ing up on an Easter morning to discover sponge-painted bunny footprints hopping across the floor and disappearing into a heater.[92]

What would it look like for art history to take seriously this proposition that at the heart of the debates over art and craft is an ambivalence about the status of the mater-nal body? Such a proposition would go against what Christopher Reed has called a long-standing topos in Western art, "current at least since Odysseus, in which the domestic figures as the opposite of the heroic": "This has been the standard of mod-ern art: a heroic Odyssey on the high seas of consciousness, with no time to spare for the mundane details of home life and housekeeping."[93] Even the modernist category of "good design" followed this trajectory in that it sought to transform the mundane and domestic into an interior worthy of modern art. My interest in putting Asawa's work into dialogue with interior design is not to challenge her status as a modern-ist artist nor to deny her work this renown, but rather to provide a context for how complex these terms were at the time, a context that is specific to her work's polyva-lence during this decade, owing in large part, I suspect, to her ambiguous status as an artist-mother.

Just as Asawa inhabited the categories Artist and Mother, her "wire stuff" and "wire things" were categorized as both sculpture and non-sculpture, decoration and design, art and craft.[94] Consider, finally, their presence in *Ladies' Home Journal*, in an article titled "Art, Creativity, and the Home Fires," which profiles seven talented "artist-homemakers" (fig. 2.14). As one of these women, Asawa is busy with a tied-wire form, while surrounded by several of her children, with the chalkboard providing a background. The tied-wire sculpture on which she works would become a gift to the ceramicist and photographer Joan Pearson Watkins (and it is now in the collection of the Fuller Craft Museum). Watkins would also later teach as an artist in the public

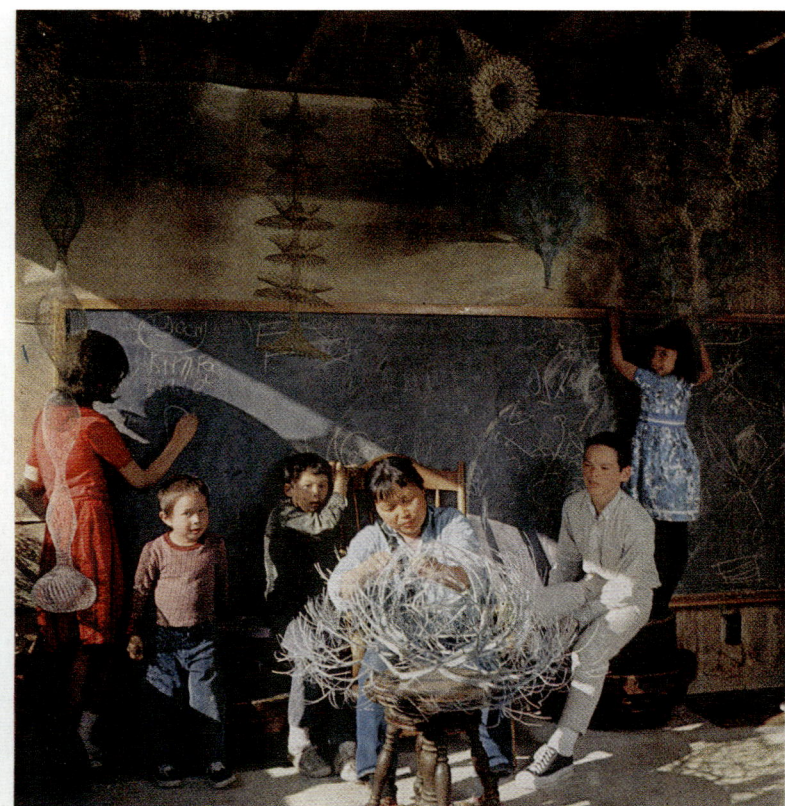

Everyone is creative in the San Francisco home of wire sculptress Ruth Asawa Lanier. Mrs. Lanier's husband, Albert, is a busy architect, and their six children participate avidly in myriad art projects. Mrs. Lanier, shown working amid her offspring Aiko, Paul, Adam, Xavier and Laurie, attended Milwaukee State Teachers College and Black Mountain College, N. C., learned the basket-weave technique of metal sculpture in Mexico. Her work is in the permanent collection of New York's distinguished Whitney Museum.

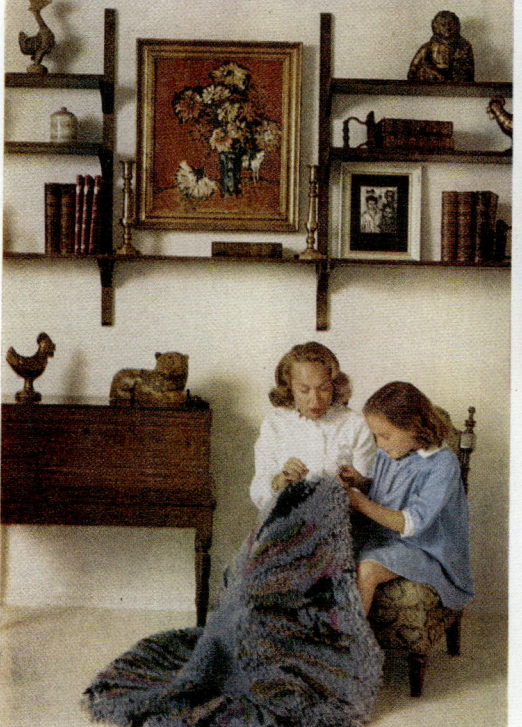

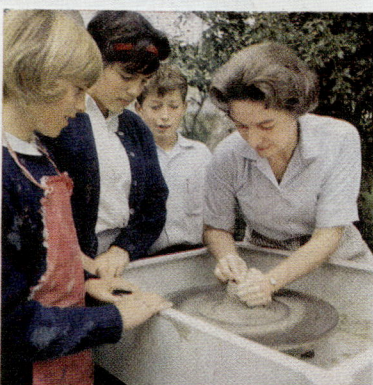

Roberta (Mrs. Frank) Treseder comes from an artistic family. She has four children, teaches art in a school near her home in Los Gatos, Calif., works mornings at her private passion, potting. Roberta makes her own dinnerware. The children in the photograph are pupils.

A representational painter who lives in Paradise Valley, Ariz., Lee Pickard has two children, Kim, 9, and Michael, 11. She and her husband, Gary, an insurance broker and journalist, lived in Mexico for 10 years, where Lee studied and became a serious painter. At left, she and Kim work at a hobby—hooking rugs.

68

schools, had embraced American folk art in her research on pottery traditions, and saw herself as making both "pottery and sculpture"; she, too, embodied the kind of artist-mother profiled in this *Ladies' Home Journal* article.[95] "All wives and mothers," we are told, these homemakers "are all creative on a professional basis," engaged in weaving, mural painting, stained-glass window design, pottery, and painting.[96]

Because Asawa's work was aligned with knitting, crocheting, and weaving—with maternal domesticity—its legibility as artistic production was always on the verge of eclipse, pushed back into the non-art terms of housework. It is because such female techniques have been so close to the maternal body that they have been devalued as forms of artistic labor. Perhaps this is why the association with weaving was so hard to shake from Asawa's practice, given that her own identity as a mother could never be untangled from her identity as an artist. It is also why, as I explore in the next three chapters, the issue of replication and reproduction became a central concern for the artist-mother, who took up figurative subjects like children, flowers, and the pregnant body in an era in which abstraction ruled.

2.14 Margaret White, "Art, Creativity, and the Home Fires," *Ladies' Home Journal*, June 1964, 68. Photo: Ernst Beadle. Special Collections, Stanford University.

II METAPHORS OF (PRO)CREATION

As you, the children of my body, have been
my tasks, so too are my other works.
—Käthe Kollwitz[1]

We know little about the image apart from what we see on its surface: four pregnant torsos arranged on the porch in Asawa's backyard (fig. II.1). Roughly hewn edges tell us that they are made of muslin gauze and plaster, and that what matters here is not finish but process: a developing fetus, out of our sight, re-forming the mother's body. Although we do not know who arranged these headless figures, we can imagine it may have been the artist herself, hauling them out of her workshop to take a look at them in the evening light, perhaps curious as to what impression they might make as a group rather than as isolated individuals, which is what they were when they were cast from the bodies of her daughters and daughters-in-law. Each woman was pregnant at a different time, over the course of several years, marking a transition from Asawa the mother to Asawa the grandmother. As an artist, having created these inanimate body doubles, she now looked at them with the eye of a sculptor, weighing their fullness of form, integrity of materials, and stability, having been propped up against the porch's architecture. "Could these be exhibited?" she likely asked herself. She may have even snapped the photo herself. But as someone with a familial relationship to the bodies from which they were cast, she also looked at these figures from the perspective of a grandmother, for each of these rounded bellies enclosed the grandson or granddaughter with whom she now also had a relationship.

It is, in other words, the particularity of these bodies that matters, and the work declares that specificity in calling upon us to contrast and compare. There, one breast is heavier than the other of the pair, whereas over here, the belly is pushed farther forward, carrying the baby out in front. As art historian Anne M. Wagner writes, only sculpture, with its capacity to register fullness of form, can register these particularities. And only in sculpture do we experience the doubleness of these figures: "sculpture env[ying] the body's aliveness and want[ing] nothing more than to realize some such quickening effect," Wagner suggests.[2] These are individuals caught in a

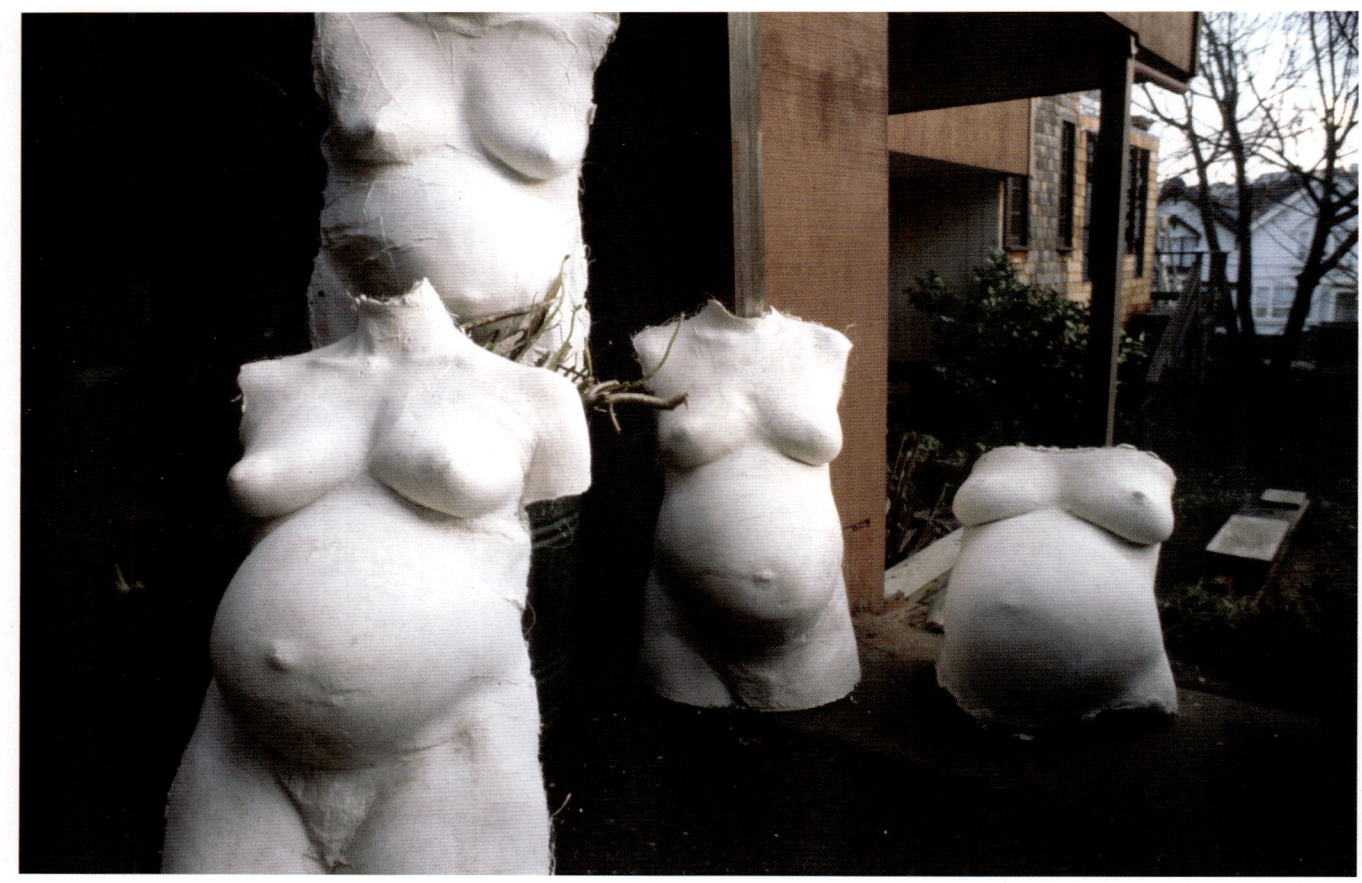

II.1 Four plaster life casts of pregnant bodies in the garden of Ruth Asawa's Noe Valley home, San Francisco, c. late 1970s. Unknown photographer.

moment of bodily transformation, but they are also surrogates for what is arguably the medium's greatest theme in the twentieth century: aliveness. This photograph holds us in suspension between these two tasks, between the cliché belly cast, made at countless baby showers, and the powerful claim of sculpture to far exceed the materials from which it is made.

These untitled objects point to the metaphorical force underlying the relationship between art and motherhood at midcentury—the subject of the following three chapters. Metaphor is typically something found most pronounced at the level of discourse, all that is said and attributed to this or that aesthetic object, whether by the artist herself or the many layers of reception that the object generates. We have already seen an example of metaphor in the tendency to describe Asawa's technique as knitted and crocheted; now I consider how metaphor functions beyond a specific word: how material transformation more broadly, in the process of making aesthetic objects, has drawn on the language of metamorphosis and vitality. Wagner gives us the necessary coordinates: Mesopotamian glassmakers who placed "embryo-gods" into the furnace chamber, and iron-smelters in central Africa who shaped their forge into female bodies that would then offer up as "children" the requisite iron objects.[3] Here the language of maternity is pervasive. But the point can be extended further to include the Greek sculptor Myron (fifth century BCE), who described his stones as not made but "born," and Michelangelo, who fashioned his own artistic prowess in terms of biological reproduction, rejecting the then-prevalent language of "ideas" for *concetti* (concepts), derived from the verb "to conceive," "as if the imagination were a matrix or womb," art historian David Summers suggests.[4] "Much of the metaphorical language—perhaps the fundamental metaphorical language—in which we discuss artistic invention is biological and, more specifically, sexual and reproductive in character," Summers writes in his study of the gendered dimensions of the terms "form" and "matter."[5]

This metaphor worked, Wagner points out, because "the place to look was clearly the body of the mother, although she herself, as a self, was not the key." She became a subterfuge of sorts, infinitely malleable to the task at hand, given the era's needs. For the Romantic poets, the sequence of chain reactions set off by the encounter of sperm and ovary—of first, proliferating cells, then blastocyst, then a mass large enough to be called an embryo, then fetus and placenta—all of this unfolding as if through some internal, unknowable force—became just the right terms to describe the gestation of the artwork: "A great statue or picture," Percy Bysshe Shelley states, in Wagner's account, "grows under the power of the artist as a child in the mother's womb; and the very mind which directs the hands in formation is incapable of accounting to itself for the origin, the gradations or the media of the process." If man is defined by directed action, "the poet," as Wagner sums up the Romantic position, "dreams like a mother as her womb works away."[6] The body of the mother could figure unconscious artistic forces, just as she could embody the opposite: the drudgery of caretaking and maintenance work. Tillie Olsen, citing Balzac, makes this metaphorical dimension visible for us: "To pass from conception to execution, to produce, to bring the idea to birth, to raise the child laboriously from infancy, to put it nightly to sleep surfeited, to kiss it in the mornings with the hungry heart of a mother, to clean it, to clothe it fifty times over in new garments which it tears and casts away, and yet not revolt against the trials of this agitated life—this unwearying maternal love, this habit of creation—this is execution and its toils."[7] How to explain the sheer detail in this monologue, which furnishes as good an account of the daily life of raising a child as it does of making art? Is there a difference anymore between the two? This is the logic of the metaphor of motherhood as a cipher of artistic labor, "that terrible law of the artist," to borrow from Henry James, which is "the law of fructification, of fertilization."[8]

Part of what was so powerful about the metaphor was that it existed apart from the identity of the artist. The "childbirth metaphor," as named by literary scholar Susan Stanford Friedman, "has yoked artistic creativity and human procreativity for centuries," across gender. While phallic metaphors like the pen and paintbrush excluded women from creativity, she writes, the childbirth metaphor could be appropriated by men and women alike, and as such could confirm female agency "by unifying their mental and physical labor into (pro)creativity."[9] The epigraph above from Käthe Kollwitz gives us one of the most succinct examples of this: here is the artist-mother appropriating one of art history's strongest metaphors, and thereby simultaneously scrambling its logic: I am an actual mother, but I am also an artist whose work is as powerful as the act of bringing new life into the world. Should we not see a similar logic at work in Imogen Cunningham's portrait of Merry Renk pregnant (fig. II.3)? Withholding the individuality of this pregnant woman by withholding her name from its generic title *It Is Spring*, Cunningham's photograph analogizes the making of art to the seasonal patterns of the natural world. In doing so, she repurposes a language that for so long belonged to male artists like Balzac and Shelley, reclaiming this language for the artist-mother. When we place this photograph alongside Asawa's *Spring*, with its abstract rupture of energy and splatter of ink, we witness a shift in these metaphorical terms—a disruptive introduction of the literal body of the artist as mother into metaphor's figural language of the artist as life-giving force (fig. II.2).

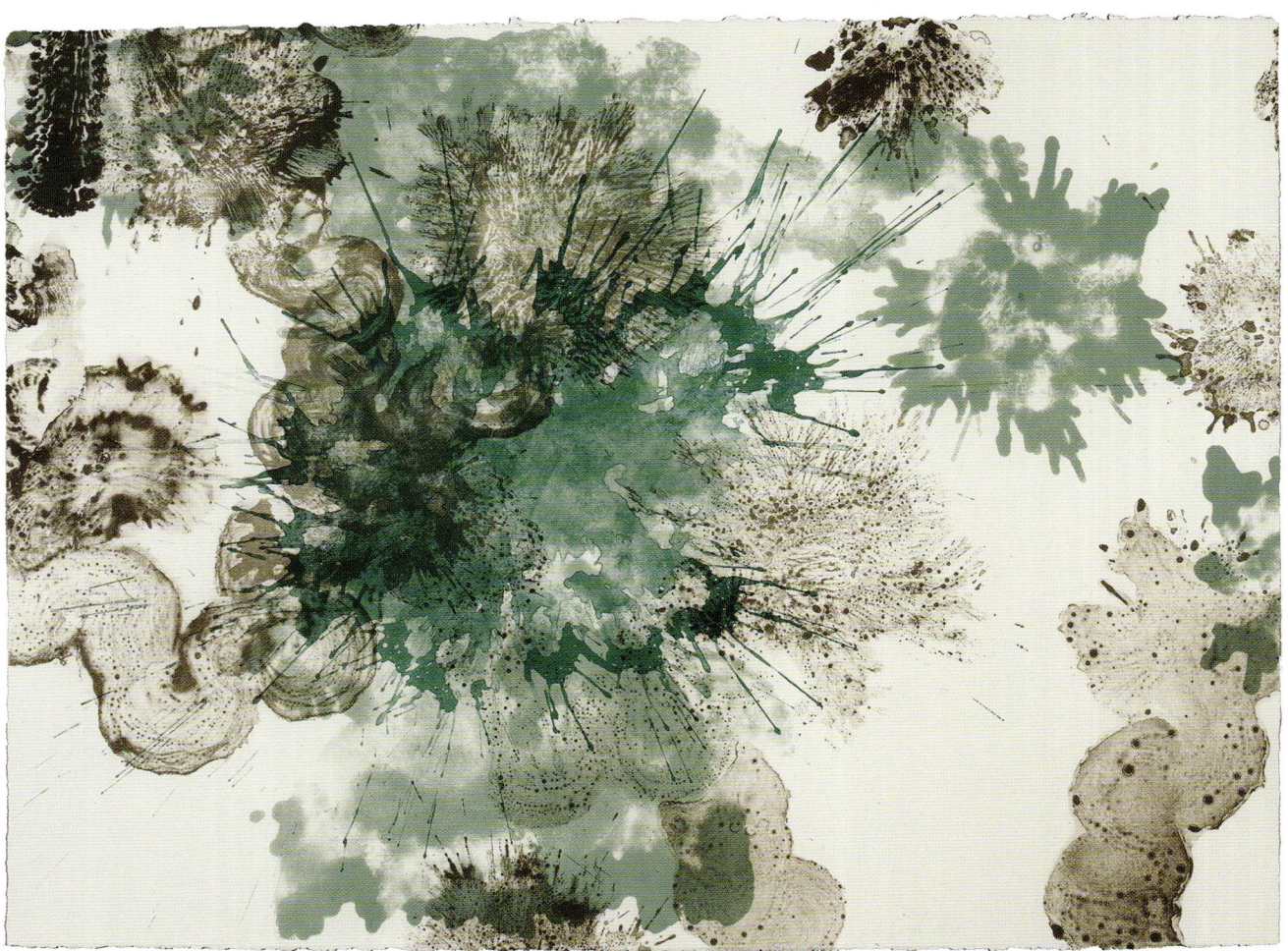

II.2 Ruth Asawa, *Spring* (TAM.1474), September 13–17, 1965. Lithograph, green and black ink on paper, 22⅛ × 30⅛ in. Private collection.

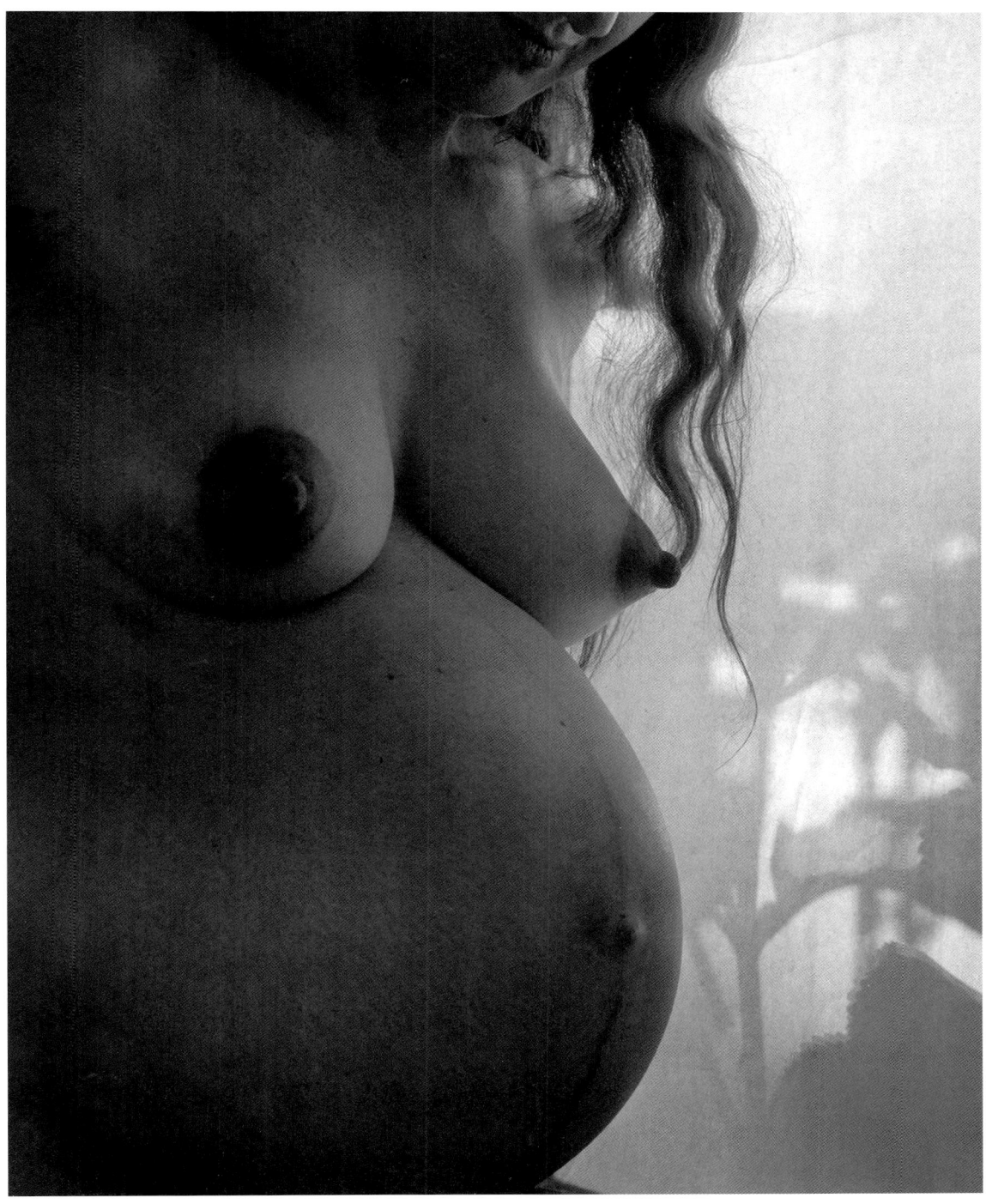

II.3 Imogen Cunningham, *It Is Spring*, 1959.
Gelatin silver print, 8½ × 7¾ in. Seattle Art
Museum, Gift of John H. Hauberg, 89.51.

II.4 Imogen Cunningham,
Eggs in Ruth Asawa's Basket,
1956. Gelatin silver print, 9½
× 7½ in. Collection of the
Imogen Cunningham Trust.

Writing about literature, Friedman poses the decisive question: does it *matter* that these are women who take up the childbirth metaphor? Friedman posed that question in 1987 in relationship to literary works of art; I pose it now in relationship to the visual arts, where it has long remained unasked, barring Wagner's magisterial study on modern British sculpture. In the three chapters that follow, I take up this question in the context of mid-twentieth-century American art. How does modernism's maternal metaphor change when appropriated by the artist-mother? How does a corporeal potential for biological and social reproduction on the part of the artist—a potential for childbirth but also for caretaking without childbirth—shift these terms? Does the metaphor only operate when that body is suppressed, or can the two be reconciled—operative body and metaphorical figure? Photographs by Cunningham especially beg this question, for her imagery routinely elicits such metaphorical references in complex and ambivalent ways. Compounded with representations of Asawa's sculpture, those references proliferate, as in Helen Molesworth's observation of a looped-wire sculpture, folded onto itself and printed in negative, as "ripe with metaphors about creation, be it human, cosmic, or aesthetic. . . . Eggs, uteri, seedpods, and ovaries all suggest various forms of fetal energy."[10] At the same time, to have filled one of Asawa's looped-wire baskets with eggs was to literalize Asawa's own descriptions of the egg-filled baskets that she saw in Toluca, Mexico, where she learned the technique (fig. II.4).

The following three chapters situate the artist-mother's work within this discursive field. I trace both the *representation* and the *metaphor* of procreation, distinguishing between these two registers while at the same time acknowledging how intertwined the two remained. In Cunningham's photographs we often have both components visible at once, with representations of pregnancy, childhood, and motherhood existing alongside one another and motivating visual metaphors for artistic creation. Chapter 3 focuses on this tension in Cunningham's photographs of Asawa's children. These portraits are often staged in a visual dialogue with Asawa's sculptures, suggesting that child and artwork can be compared—as if literalizing Balzac's metaphorical description of artmaking. In one instance, Cunningham situates both child and work of art in a landscape characteristic of northern California (fig. II.5). A looped-wire sculpture hangs from the branch of a California live oak tree, as if it were a seedpod about to fall. In the foreground, Asawa's eldest son, still small, crouches and holds what appears to be a globe. It is as if an entire world is constructed here in the equation child-art-nature, a world prefigured by the Mother, who is everywhere present but nowhere visible. Is this an instance of the childbirth metaphor as reductive and deterministic, as feminist critics from Simone de Beauvoir to Nina Auerbach have feared? This was a risk, in that photographs, drawings, and paintings of one's own children—when made by a mother—were often dismissed as sentimental, with sentimentality coded as the opposite of modernist innovation. Or should we see these as visual counterparts to Hélène Cixous's imperative that women, "never far from 'mother,'" write "in white ink"—that the artistic production by artists identifying as women can be empowered through the embodied knowledge of motherhood (with "white ink" here referencing breast milk)?[11] Whereas Cunningham oscillated between children as sitters for portraits and

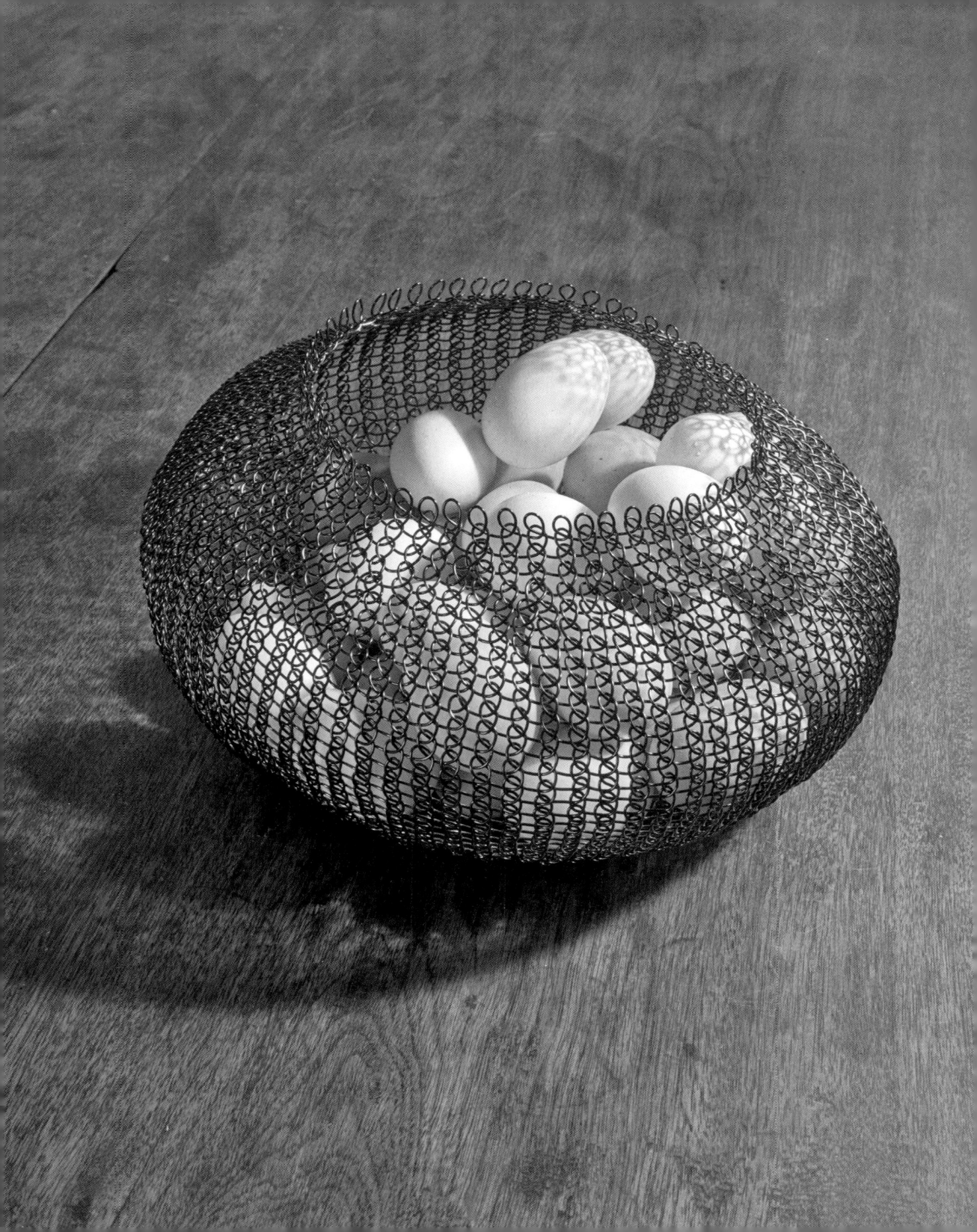

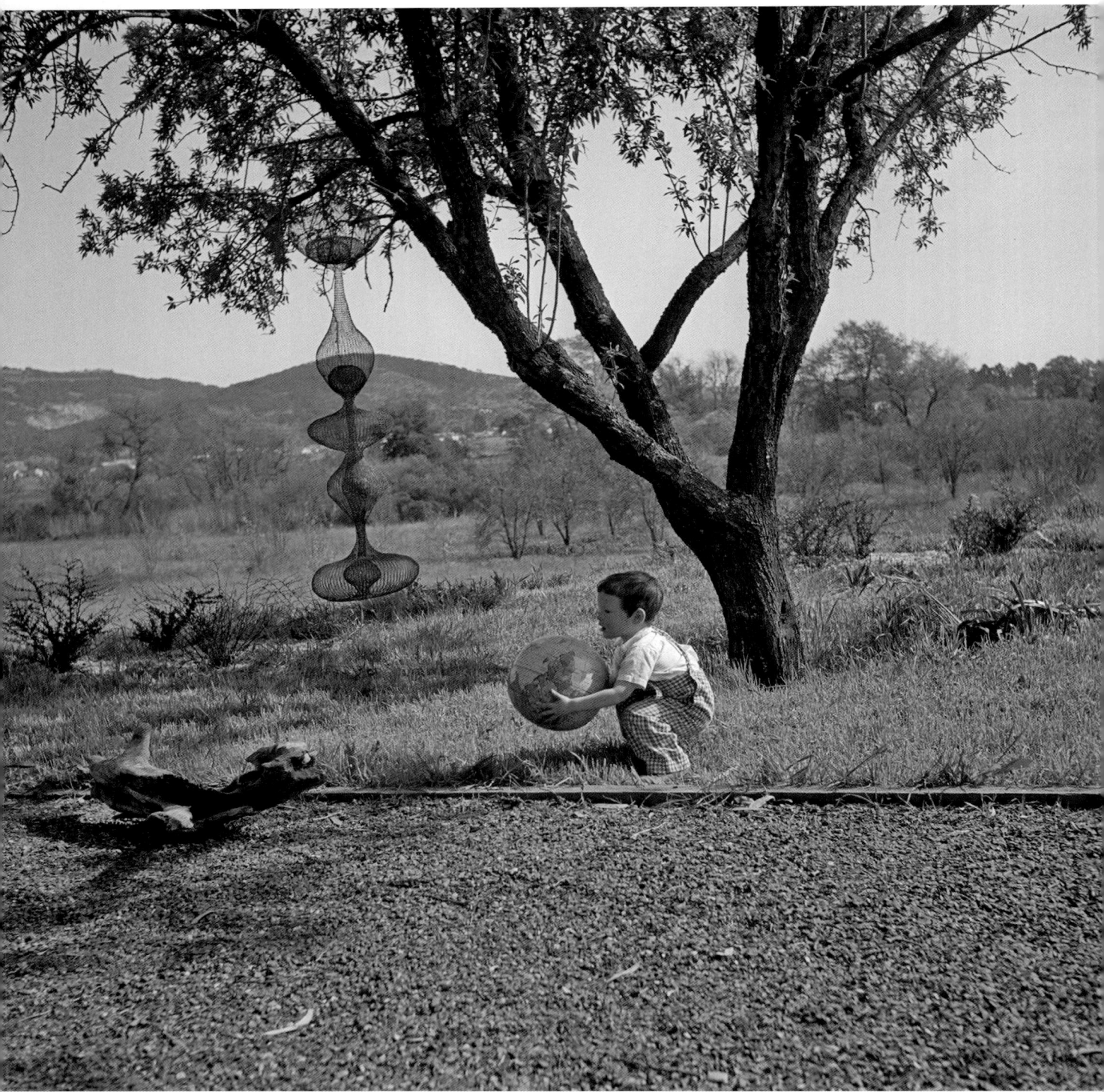

children as metaphors of artistic creation, Asawa seemed to leave metaphor behind altogether, taking an even greater risk that such works would be dismissed as the private musings of a mother rather than the serious work of an artist.

Chapter 4 delves further into Cunningham's tendency to site this metaphor in the natural world by looking at representations of floral imagery, both abstract and representational, in the work of the artist-mother. Here my focus is on the so-called vitalist metaphor at midcentury, the equation between the abstract work of art as exceeding representation and becoming like nature itself in its powers of creation. I look at how the artist-mother was often excluded from participating in the vitalist metaphor, reduced to her identity as a mother and thus confined to procreation. At the same time, Asawa and Cunningham engaged with nature as source material; both were acute observers of the natural world. Asawa, moreover, engaged with form and color from the perspective of Josef Albers's modernism, which mobilized metaphor in conveying the power of abstraction. "Just putting colors together is the excitement of it," he once told an interviewer. "The way green submits to blue, for instance, or vice versa. What interests me is the way they marry, interpenetrate and produce the baby, the color and that is their product together."[12] Asawa's own identity as a mother in turn inflected this metaphorical language: as she later recalled, Albers was against female students having children; his attitude was that "these paintings are your children," but if you do have children, "make sure they're yours," in the same way that he said, "you can paint flowers, but make sure they're Asawa flowers."[13]

Chapter 5 takes up the most overtly maternal of Asawa's sculptures: *Andrea* (1966–1968), installed as a fountain in a prominent public plaza by San Francisco's waterfront. The work was cast from the postpartum body of neighbor and fellow writer-mother Andrea Jepson, who would go on to publish an early history of the Alvarado School Arts Workshop, the subject of part III of this study. Asawa had drawn Jepson during her pregnancy and, shortly after the birth, asked to use her body as the figure for her first public commission. The resulting work doubled that already doubling body insofar as it represents two identical female figures, along with a baby, turtles, frogs, and lily pads. In addition to the maternal body, *Andrea* engages with fairy tale, for both female figures have been made into mermaids (the mer-baby, too). I consider not only how we are to understand the critical potential of a public sculpture that explicitly takes up the genre of the fairy tale (and was repeatedly viewed as "charming" and "enchanting"), but also how to make sense of the use of the term "camp" in critiques of Asawa's maternal imagery. This work brings together the central figures in the chapters that follow—children, plants, and animals—as analogies for the maternal body, and thus as figures for just how distant that body seemed to be from the heroic abstraction dominating the most visible forms of art at midcentury.

II.5 Imogen Cunningham, *Xavier Lanier Crouching in Front of a Sculpture by Ruth Asawa Hanging from a Tree*, 1953. Gelatin silver print, 9 × 9 in. Collection of the Imogen Cunningham Trust.

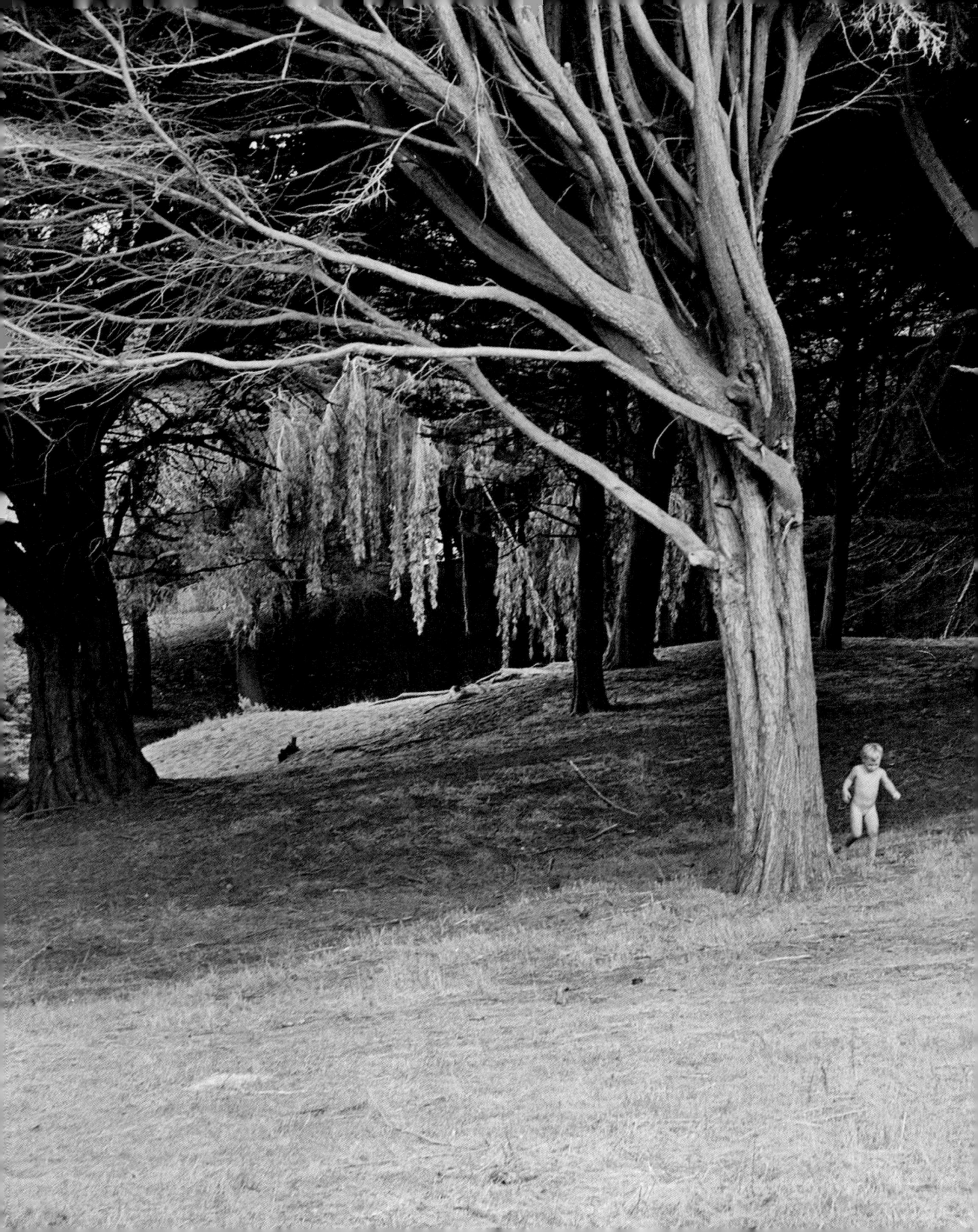

3 CUNNINGHAM'S CHILDREN

The cathexis between mother and daughter—essential,
distorted, misused—is the great unwritten story.
—Adrienne Rich[1]

A useful framework for staging the exchange between Imogen Cunningham and Ruth Asawa is offered by the relationship between mother and daughter. The two women were forty-three years apart in age and belonged to two very different generational formations, with Cunningham, born in 1883, introduced to photography during the heyday of pictorialism, while Asawa as a young painter came of age as an artist in the era of abstract expressionism. The two women first met one another in 1950, and over the course of twenty-six years—until Cunningham's death in 1976—Asawa herself, her children, and her sculpture repeatedly served as a subject for the older photographer. Many of these photographs are not adequately captured by the terms "portraiture" or "documentation" (genres which have been deployed to describe them). They are instead carefully composed views that place children and art into dialogue with one another. Consider, for instance, a print of Asawa's youngest son standing among towering stacks of wooden objects (fig. 3.1). These were patterns for municipal infrastructure, such as fire hydrants, which were used in the casting process. Asawa had salvaged these patterns when they were being discarded by the city and redeployed some of them as bases for her sculptures. Such patterns even made their way into Sally Woodbridge's diary: on a day in late February 1961, Woodbridge wrote with palpable excitement about how she and Asawa went "scavenging" for these wooden "forms that could make a Brancusi out of anyone."[2]

Asawa, in turn, repeatedly drew Cunningham. One sketch was singled out by the photographer for the frontispiece to her book *After Ninety*, which portrays the topic of aging through portraits of both notable and not so notable elderly sitters, including Asawa's own parents.[3] Asawa's delicate line drawing portrays the photographer in a rapid-fire sequence of poses, hunched over her large-format camera with her body engulfed in billowing fabric. She is accompanied by the wide shoreline of the beach at Fort Cronkhite in the Marin Headlands, just north of San Francisco, where

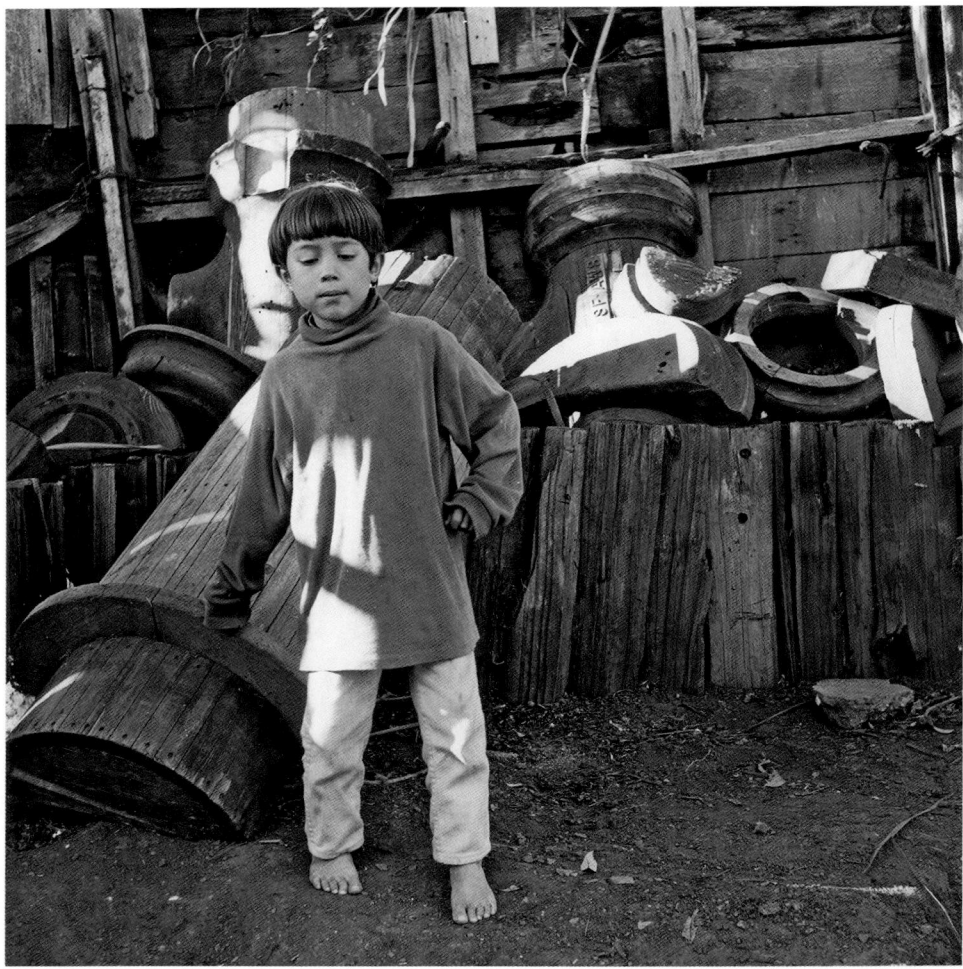

3.1 Imogen Cunningham, *Ruth Asawa's Son Paul Lanier with Wooden Patterns*, c. 1965. Gelatin silver print, 7 × 7 in. Private collection.

Cunningham took a stunning sequence of family portraits while Asawa sketched—in fact sketching Cunningham. Asawa had even ventured a looped-wire bust of Cunningham early on in their friendship. She mounted this portrait to an eight-by-eight-inch baking pan—a move that Susan Ehrens, in her account of the friendship between the two women, reads as "a witty nod to the competing demands of art and motherhood."[4]

The two women were clearly looking at—and looking *to*—one another, and it is the character of that gaze that interests me here. For it escapes the predictable coordinates for "creativity as an extraordinary (usually male) individual solitary struggle for artistic self-expression," as Whitney Chadwick and Isabelle de Courtivron write in their groundbreaking anthology on artist and writer couples in the twentieth century.[5] In examining creativity as a collaborative process, Chadwick and de Courtivron draw on literary scholars Ruth Perry and Martine Brownley, who wrote in the late 1980s of "mothering the mind": an exploration of those silent collaborators who generated the conditions of their partner's aesthetic achievement.[6] While this concept gets us closer to the subject at hand, it is also not quite fitting. Chadwick and de Courtivron are concerned with romantic collaborations; Asawa and Cunningham, by contrast, were close friends and not intimates. And yet the suggestion of artistic exchange as a generative relationship—rather than competitive one-upmanship—does describe the nature of their dialogue, and their story is the story of artistic creation as a maternal, rather than paternal, genealogy.

While art history offers multiple models for father-son relationships, we have virtually none for mothers and daughters—much less a theorization, as art historian Lisa Tickner argues, of how we might think creativity through this relationship. In her essay "Mediating Generation: The Mother-Daughter Plot," Tickner challenges the dominant understanding of artistic creation as a consequence of masculinized rivalry between established master and up-and-coming maverick, between proverbial fathers and sons. Drawing on Virginia Woolf, Tickner proposes that to be a woman artist is to "think through our mothers." By this, she means "elective rather than natural mothers": female precursors who, once identified, allow a younger generation to stake a claim "to a specifically matrilineal artistic heritage."[7] Thus, it is not enough to simply insert women artists into a model of artistic heritage predicated on rivalry; the entire model needs to change in order to properly acknowledge the contributions of women artists. It requires another orientation altogether toward those who have come before, to allow for the possibility of other modes of (dis)identification.

It is that task that concerns me here, with the very concrete example of two women in regular dialogue over the course of twenty-five years. In particular, I examine the trope of the child in both oeuvres, Cunningham's representations of the Asawa-Lanier children through photography but also Asawa's drawings of children. Numbering in the several dozens, Cunningham's photographs of Asawa's children seem to have been just as interesting a subject for her as were Asawa's sculpture and Asawa herself—the two other groups of imagery that Cunningham generated in relationship to the artist. This turn to the child is nothing new: from Wassily Kandinsky's and Gabriele Münter's collections of children's drawings to David Smith's monumental stainless steel *Becca* modeled after his daughter's paper horse, children and children's art have served as an embodiment of the avant-garde quest for authenticity, "as a reservoir of originating content."[8] In this respect, Cunningham and Asawa travel well-trodden ground.

But what I propose is that a particular problem emerges once the artist-mother takes up the representation of childhood, one that we can only adequately explain when we consider Tickner's gambit that creativity itself shifts with the matrilineal model. There is, in other words, a substantial difference between David Smith's use of his daughter's paper horse and Alice Neel's depiction of her own son, with robust, Fernand Léger-like proportions, in *Richard in High Chair* (c. 1940), or Sally Wood-bridge's *Untitled* (c. 1965), a portrait of her youngest daughter, Diana, painted onto a salvaged wooden high chair (figs. 3.4, 3.2). The life-size portrayal of its would-be sitter appears as if occupying the chair, even kicking one foot up, in the way that toddlers do, with a painted plate of green peas in between two pudgy hands. Here is the artist-mother indulging in sentimentality, proclaims the matricidal modernist script, a mother's attempt to relieve the dreary boredom of household chores, a

3.2 Sally B. Woodbridge, *Untitled*, c. 1965. Hand-painted wooden high chair, 39 × 16 × 22 in. Collection of Pamela Woodbridge. Photo: James Paonessa.

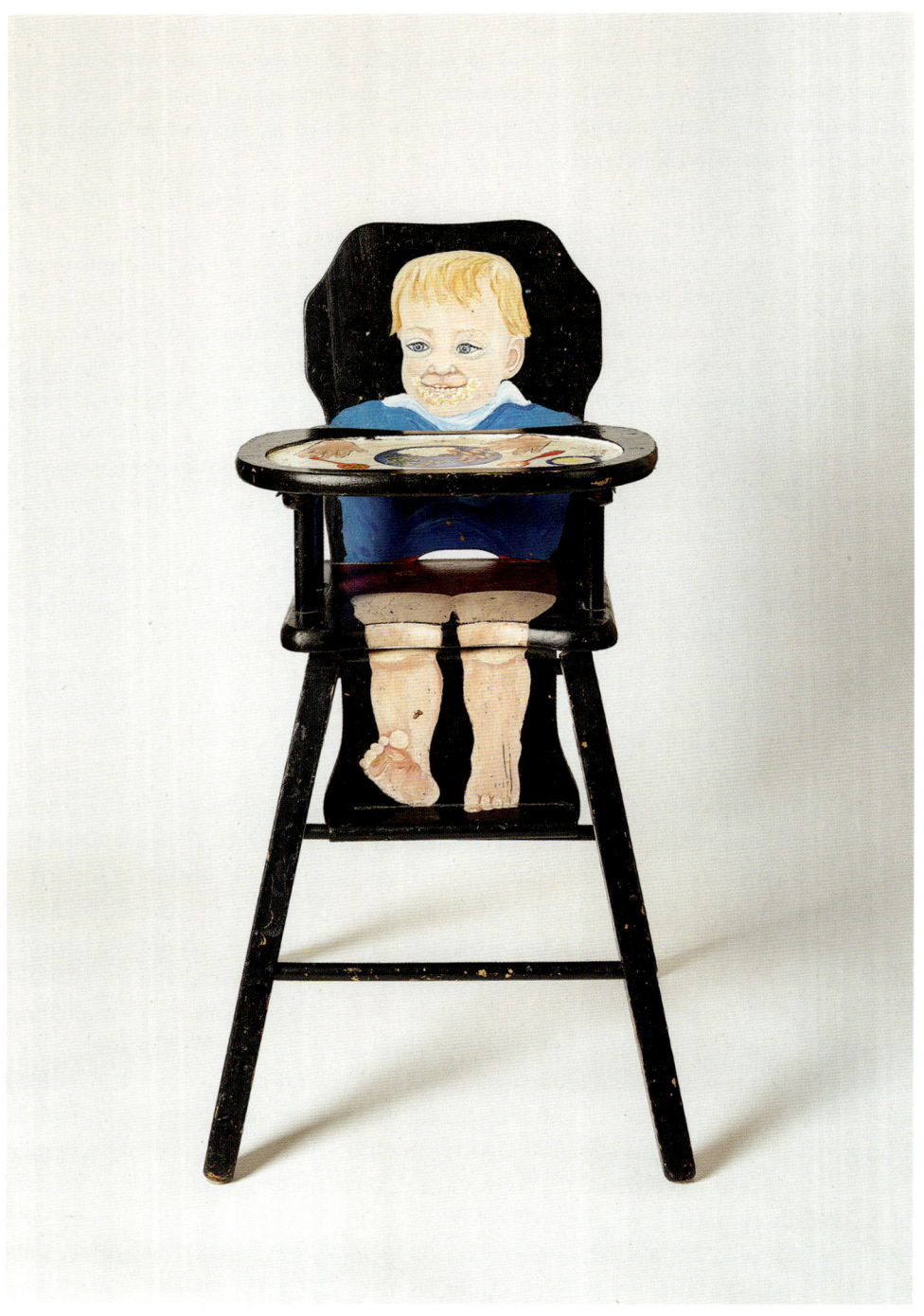

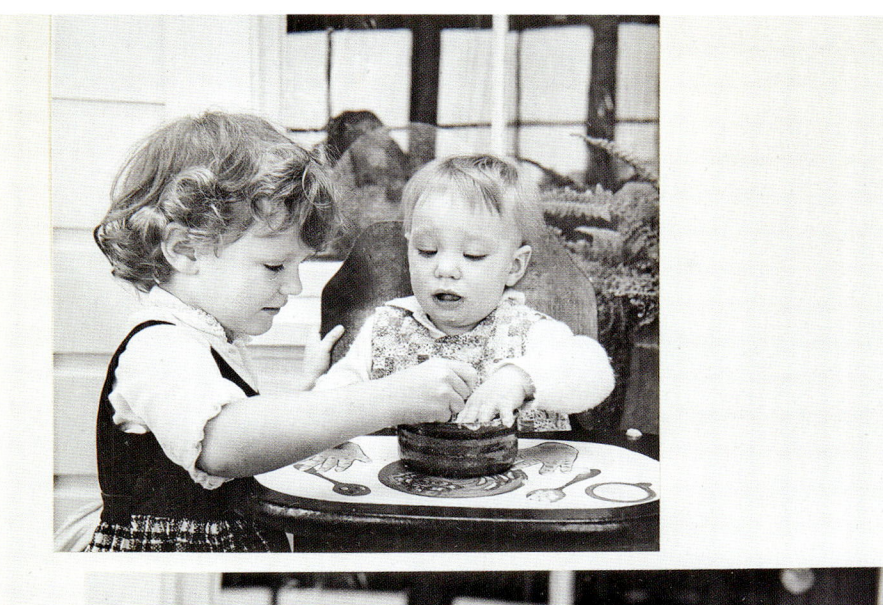

3.3 Imogen Cunningham,
Pamela and Diana Woodbridge,
c. 1965. Gelatin silver prints
mounted in album, 11 × 8.5 in.
Collection of Pamela Woodbridge.

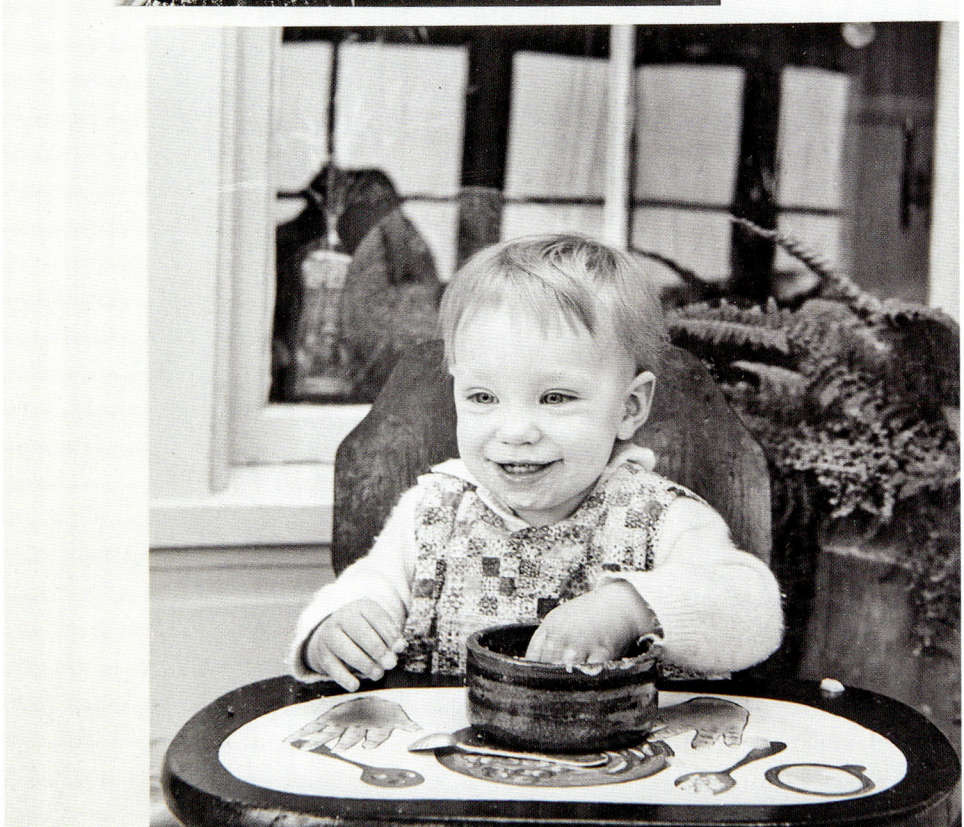

3.4 Alice Neel, *Richard in High Chair*, c. 1940. Oil on canvas, 23 × 19½ in. Private collection.

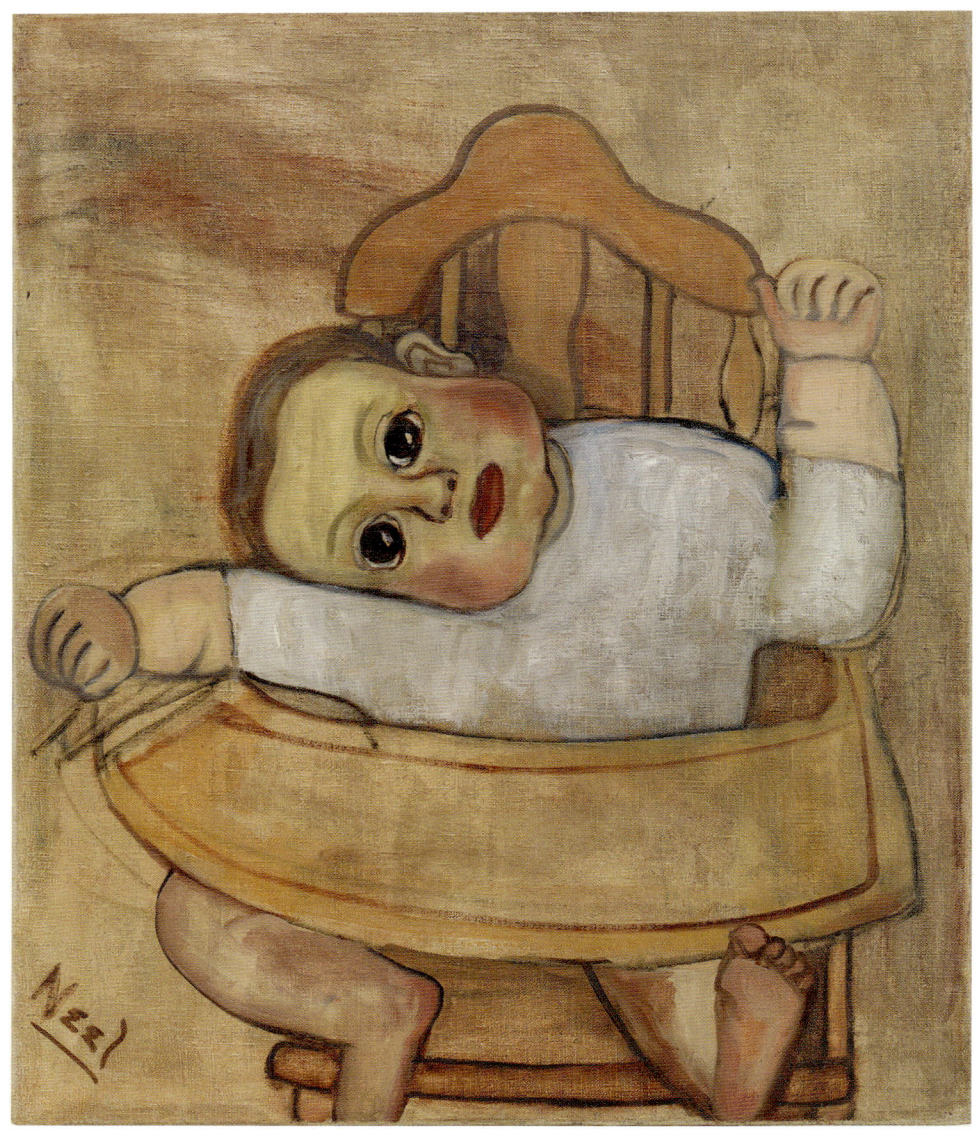

woman simply playing at making art. And Cunningham's snapshots of this object in action, which later entered an album of photographs gifted to Woodbridge and show Diana and her elder sister Pamela at mealtime in the backyard, would also seem to fall into this category—little more than mothers enthralled with their own creations, both artistic and biological (fig. 3.3).

But this way of viewing things has run its course; it is much more interesting to pause here on the strangeness of such objects: a crude depiction of the child that also sits in the same chair, and the sheer unlikelihood of turning that act of feeding, repeated at least four or five times a day—with all of the chaos and mess that it entails—into an opportunity for artmaking. Such works foreground a central paradox:

that the child could be a resounding trope of artistic creativity for avant-garde artists, while the depiction of actual children being fed and cleaned was to be avoided. Once we take seriously this paradox, the representation of children by the artist-mother operates in a very different way from the more canonical depictions of such subjects. I explore this proposition by first delving into Cunningham's representations of children, tracing how she mobilized both Victorian and modernist motifs, with a focus on her photographs of her own children as a young mother. I then consider Asawa's first contact with Cunningham in the latter's offer to photograph the Lanier children, out of which emerged baby albums, which have a hybrid status as both private family snapshots and significant works of art. Cunningham's influence can be seen in drawings by Asawa of her own children, which are just as ambivalent in their status. The chapter's third section takes up the mother-daughter relationship again, looking more closely at Asawa and Cunningham's shared indifference to reputation, which led to a coauthored work with Cunningham, *The Hair Skirt*, a photo-textile skirt mounted onto a life cast of Asawa's then ten-year-old daughter (see fig. 3.14). I end the chapter by returning to the difference that the mother-daughter relationship makes to the question of artistic influence and generational exchange.

DOUBLING

Looking back on her trajectory as an artist, Cunningham attributed her turn to photography to her encounter with the work of Gertrude Käsebier: "it was Käsebier whose work I saw in 1901 and who really started me with the camera," she told an interviewer in 1973.[9] "I can remember to this moment the things in one article in *The Craftsman*: [Käsebier's] daughter standing in a doorway, her hand on her child—mother and child—things like that."[10] As Carol Armstrong has argued, Käsebier's "pictorialist maternity scenes" embody the hybrid status of appearing both in the hallowed pages of Alfred Stieglitz's *Camera Work* and in private family albums—a dual status that Cunningham's own portraits of the Asawa-Lanier children would also have.[11] And while they may resemble scenes of motherhood in the work of Mary Cassatt or even Stieglitz's own *Journal of a Baby* (1899–1900), Armstrong argues, Käsebier's photographs depart from the tendency to depict mother and child as a closed circuit, mutually constitutive entities within the picture's frame. Käsebier, by contrast, stressed the fragility of this unit—with an emphasis on the child's independence, accompanied by a gaze out of the picture toward the beholder. This feature characterizes the photo Cunningham repeatedly pointed to as "the one that 'started her'"—Käsebier's *Blessed Art Thou among Women* (1899), with its demarcation of two worlds: one maternal, shared, protected, private; the other beyond the separating door frame and over the threshold into independence," writes the photo historian Judith Davidov.[12]

This was the example Cunningham would have had in mind as she continued to pursue photography after the birth of her first child, Gryffyd, in 1915. Letters to her husband during this time speak of hustling to complete "the necessary errands," filling orders, mailing off packages and sets of prints, and trying to execute some of her own ideas photographically, while, in a typically modernist voice, she bemoans the "sordidly domestic."[13] The birth of twins followed two years later, meaning that in the 1920s, as Cunningham began to be recognized internationally as a photographer—including having several prints in the prestigious *Film und Foto* exhibition in Germany in 1929—she had three young children to care for. It was a period of musing on these competing demands, with "one hand in the dishpan, the other in the darkroom," as her statement on artistic motherhood read.[14] A friend who visited the young mother recalled, "They [the three young boys] were just impossible, she had children, a husband, and a fairly large place to take care of . . . cooking, washing, ironing, shopping for clothes. At night, when her hellish big day was over, she'd go down in the laundry room where she had a little darkroom squeezed off in the corner and work at her photography. I've never known anyone with such will or such energy."[15]

Early on, Cunningham recognized the risks involved in taking up motherhood as a photographic subject. "I photographed Gryff with Miss Cann indoors and somewhat nude," she wrote to her husband in August 1916. "At best the proposition of

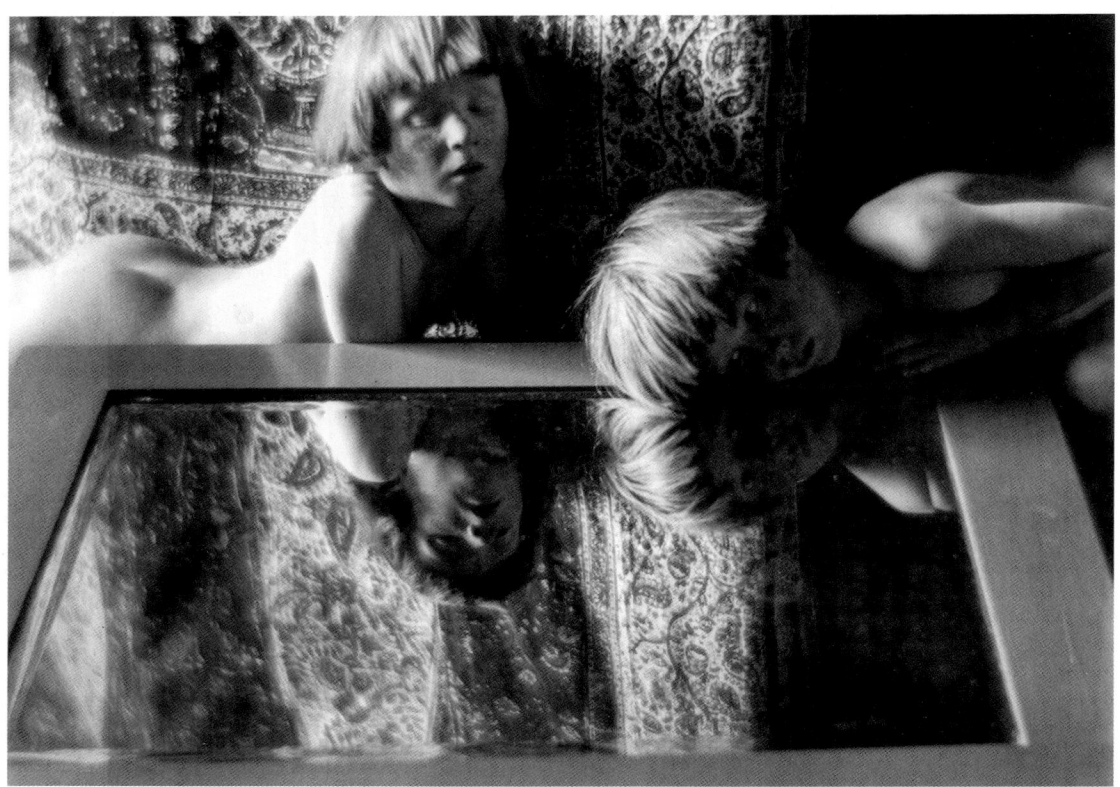

3.5 Imogen Cunningham, *Twins with Mirror 2*, 1923. Gelatin silver print, 9½ × 6¾ in. Collection of the Imogen Cunningham Trust.

photographing a mother and child is liable to be either sentimental or absolutely unpictorial but what I wanted to get today was a portrait of Gryff and something of him nude with a woman as background."[16] Photographs from this period fall into the genre of what Carol Armstrong calls maternal pictorialism, with staged familial dramas, soft focus, introspective gazes, and ambient lighting. One from 1923 depicts Cunningham's twin sons gazing into a mirror, a surface of representation brought down low and displayed for a child (fig. 3.5). Naked and reclining, contemplating their own reflections, these are iterations of the "come-hither children" that appear in representations from Julia Margaret Cameron to Sally Mann, as Armstrong has traced.[17] The addition of the mirror further complicates this genealogy by invoking the Narcissus myth of falling in love with one's own reflection. Here that story of selfhood is invoked in the figure of the young male gazing into a mirror, but it is also complicated, for selfhood in the case of twins is wonderfully doubled—one is both oneself and intimately bound to someone else. Cunningham invokes that doubling in the bodies of the twins themselves, and then intensifies it through their doubled reflection.

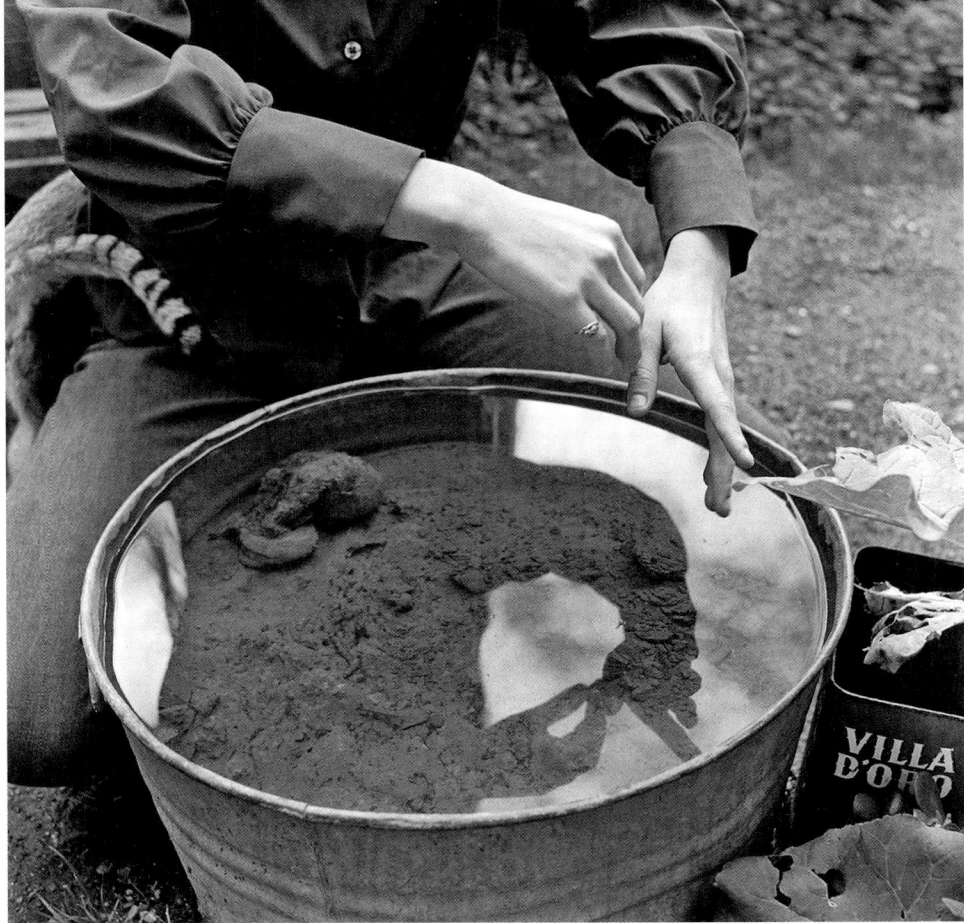

3.6 Imogen Cunningham, *Aiko's Hands*, 1971. Gelatin silver print, 9½ × 9¼ in. Collection of the Imogen Cunningham Trust.

Not exactly a mise-en-abyme structure of representations multiplied indefinitely, the photograph is nonetheless an image of proliferation. We have two figures sharing genetic code, and their reflections further multiply that point. The image gestures again—as so much of modernist photography does—back to the medium through which it has been formed: photography perennially framed as the ultimate mirror of the world. The camera doubles, just as the identical twin is doubled for the mother. "Everywhere she looked," Margery Mann observed of Cunningham, "there was a real-life double image."[18] Doubleness also became a feature of her own photographic production, from doubled exposures to multiplied bodies or plants within a single frame, to reflections, to superimposed negatives. This "seeing double," Judith Davidov observes, constituted a recurring theme in her work, "a sixty-year habit Cunningham later attributed to the birth of the twins."[19] Cunningham would return to this trope of reflection in later photographs of Asawa's eldest daughter, Aiko, whose hands dance above a still pool of water (fig. 3.6).

This staging of photography as a medium, within a realm coded as female, is what Armstrong describes, in relation to Julia Margaret Cameron's Victorian mothers and children, as photography "in the image of its own process, its own mode of production, rather than Photography ruled by the technical decrees of the established arts; Photography under the sway of the Mother, rather than the law of the Father."[20] Mobilizing such tropes in photographing her own children was one way in which Cunningham mitigated the risks of the artist-mother who takes up childhood as a theme. Those risks were repeatedly brought to her attention by friends and colleagues. In 1920, when as a young mother she expressed her frustration at trying to work while raising three small children, she was met by the response: "it is too brutal to say that of the two horns of the dilemma that pull you both ways at once—family and art—the youngsters are after all a finer contribution to the community than ever your photographs."[21] And yet Cunningham refused to have her life be determined by this dilemma. She not only continued photographing her children, she also wrote statements that staked out a claim for the artist-mother not having to grapple with this dilemma. Two years before she married, she wrote "Photography as a Profession for Women" (1913), arguing that taking photographs and raising children should be mutually beneficial:

An ideal profession for a woman is one which she does not necessarily have to lay down permanently in the care and rearing of children. The pursuit of any art brings women in contact with the larger interests of the world, and her excursions into broader fields even during the rearing of children is bound to have an enlarging effect upon the home. To deny a woman the right to extend her energies in the search for knowledge or to express herself through some individual work or art is hampering her usefulness in her highest sphere—motherhood.[22]

Defying the modernist prohibition against the compatibility of motherhood and artistic achievement, Cunningham argues that taking on this challenge makes one both a better artist, "in contact with the interests of the world," and a better caretaker.

Asawa and Cunningham first met through the photographer's son Rondal. From the age of five, Rondal had begun learning photography from his mother, initially through contact printing, where he would sandwich the negative and paper and let it develop in the sun. (He later passed his photographic knowledge on to his daughter Meg, who often worked with him, and sometimes with her grandmother, in the darkroom.)[23] In 1950, Rondal Partridge was hired by Albert Lanier's boss, the architect Mario Corbett, to document a house he had designed. Asawa joined Lanier and Rondal for the site visit, at which point Rondal suggested that Asawa should meet his mother. Soon after, Asawa recalls, Cunningham paid them a visit, bearing a jar of homemade Satsuma plum jam. Their friendship grew through shared interests: the young couple, and especially Lanier, were avid gardeners, while Cunningham had a horticulturalist's knowledge of plants (with many of their Latin names committed to memory). Lanier and Cunningham—as well as Sally Woodbridge's eldest daughter, Pamela—all shared a birthday (April 12) and regularly celebrated together in Golden Gate Park. Cunningham had also introduced Asawa to the association of San Francisco Women Artists, of which Asawa and Renk were briefly members.

In the immediate months after they met, Cunningham began to take stunning photographs of both Asawa's work and her children. In August 1951, referring to a proposal that Asawa and Lanier would do work on Cunningham's house on Greene Street, where she had lived since 1947, in exchange for photographs of their two toddlers, Cunningham wrote:

I keep thinking about the real earnestness of your offer and how inadequate my contribution is. . . . I did not give the best of my day to the record of the children, just tried to get something that would show how they are at the moment, but I would like to try to do a real record of their fetchings and carryings and make a continuous story of it—if that would interest you—let's talk about it. You do two of my rooms, bath and hall and I make a contract for three years coverage . . . I buy all the paint and all the photographic material. Call me sometime next week, if you have the impulse. Affectionately, Imogen.[24]

Cunningham went on to take several dozen photographs of the Asawa-Lanier children, long after the three years had passed. Her motivation exceeded the arranged exchange, and photographing children other than her own is evident in her practice at least as far back as *Brett Weston* (1922), a portrait of Edward Weston's son, posed with his arm propped up on the base of a miniature male nude sculpture. Weston was an artist who would soon leave his family for Mexico and for another woman, sacrificing family for art. Sally Woodbridge, Merry Renk, and Asawa, whose children Cunningham photographed in the 1950s and 60s, embodied another model of the artist, willfully refusing this cliché.

Many of these photographs went into albums that Cunningham made herself, printing the photographs one or two to a page and compiling them into spiral-bound volumes. One album portrays Woodbridge's youngest daughter, Diana, naked in the city's Golden Gate Park, running around in a cypress grove (fig. 3.7). Cunningham jokingly called this the "Babe in the Woods" series, invoking the fairy-tale trope of

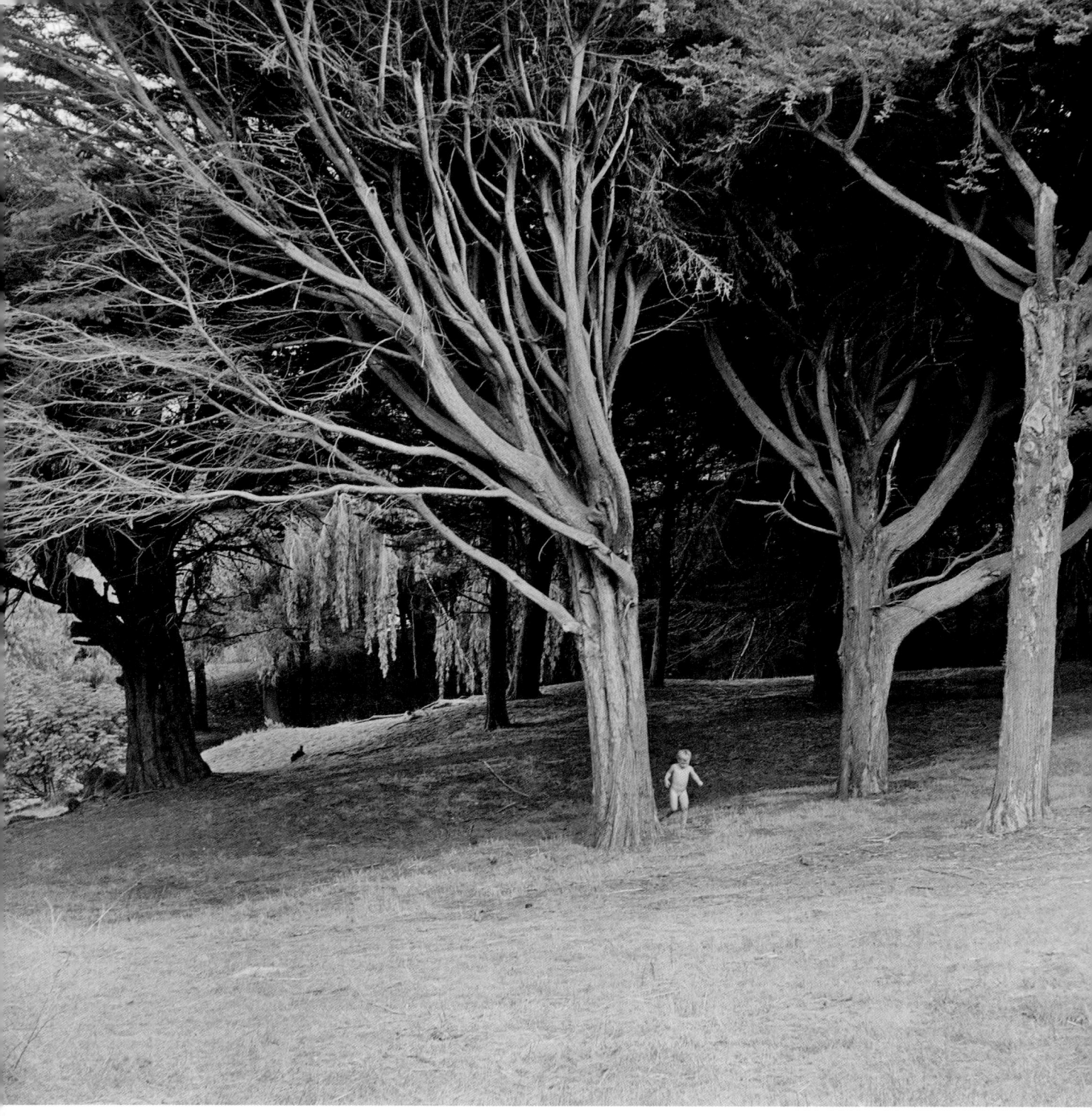

3.7 Imogen Cunningham, *Child in Landscape,*
1966. Gelatin silver print mounted in album,
8½ × 8½ in. Collection of Pamela Woodbridge.

children in the forest abandoned to wolves by their mothers or wicked stepmothers.[25] The remark was typical of Cunningham's legendary humor: here she calls upon the old English saying for someone innocent in a difficult situation, but she also literally describes what the photographs portray—a child in a grove of trees. The series also recalls one of her earliest successes as a photographer: a series of photographs of her husband Roi naked in a landscape (which caused an uproar when one was published), as well as the many iterations of her own sons, posed naked in rocky landscapes, smooth, supple forms against unyielding stone.

Many of the early photographs of the Lanier children portray them in a visual dialogue with Asawa's work, and can be categorized as neither personal nor public but somewhere in between. Certainly they were, as Cunningham promised, a record of the children in the form of imagery that would eventually fill baby albums, that well-known genre of family snapshots, often identified with motherhood, whose primary purpose is to document the impending loss of childhood.[26] But in many cases, such photographs far exceed this role and tell us something about the relationship of the artist-mother to both her work and her children. Take, for instance, a photograph in which Asawa's toddler Adam sits facing *Untitled* (AB.029, Continuous Form within a Form, 1956), casting the shadow of his raised arm as it reaches up to its mother's hand (figs. 3.8, 3.9). Both shadows bisect the radiating curvature of the painting. With the child sitting on the floor, it appears as if someone had taken the painting off the wall and repurposed it for this shadow play, subjecting the painted canvas to the discovery of light and dark facilitated by a mother for her child. As if made and displayed for this very purpose, the work of art becomes mere ground for another kind of formal experimentation taking place in its vicinity: the mind in the throes of its own perceptual development.

The painting pictured here is one of Asawa's untitled Masonite panels with acrylic paint—unusual materials for the time, which she knew from her training with Josef Albers. Albers's series *Homage to the Square*, begun in 1950, also employed acrylic (as well as oil) on Masonite. Blue and green curved bands radiate out from a central pink node, and grow in intensity as they approach and then exceed the edges of the canvas. In the same way that Asawa explored the potential of the whiteness of the page, surrounded by ink, to embody roundness, here she plays with the exchange between foreground and background: at the top of the panel, the blue serves as ground to the green bands, while at the bottom, the green bands stand as figure to the blue ground. In a funding application to the Guggenheim Foundation in the early 1950s, she describes this trope as the continuous exchange of interior and exterior spaces: "in the last year I have tried to make use of the space inside and find that what is an outer surface can become an inner surface and then an outer surface and so on to completion. This quality is similar to the moebius strip or the continuous tube which is turned inside-out and outside-in. This needs much more work to fully exploit for the ultimate excitement."[27] What she describes here is pervasive in her looped-wire sculptures of the 1950s: this exchange between outside and inside occurs as her wire surfaces create curved planes which intersect and swap roles, from being an outside

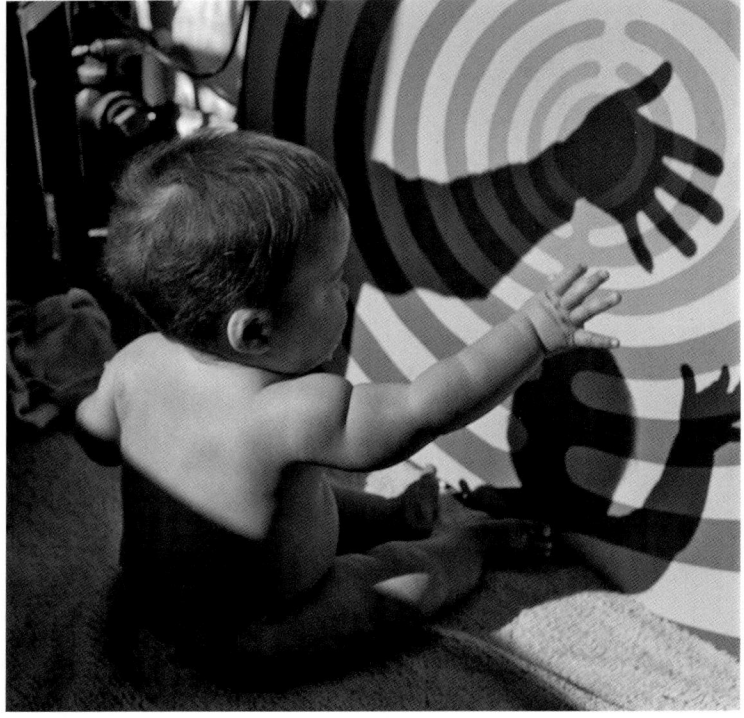

3.8 Imogen Cunningham, *Ruth Asawa and Adam Lanier Playing with Shadows on Untitled (AB.029, Continuous Form within a Form)*, 1957. Gelatin silver print, 9¼ × 9½ in. Collection of the Imogen Cunningham Trust.

surface of the work to being an inside one. It is also a moment in Asawa's formal interests that bears a striking resemblance to Cunningham's interest in the dialogue between negative and positive space.[28]

The operation is essentially that of a Möbius strip—another favorite visual tool in Albers's pedagogy—whose surfaces constitute a continuous plane that, just as Asawa's looped-wire surfaces do, exchange inside and outside contours. In her essay "The Inside Is the Outside," art historian Catherine de Zegher characterizes an "aesthetics of relation and reciprocity" that results "from the work of women artists, but also from that of some male artists often denied recognition precisely because of their 'feminine' approach to the world."[29] As instances of this reciprocity, she cites artists including Anna Maria Maiolino, Eva Hesse, and Lygia Clark—artists rarely brought into dialogue with Asawa's work. Clark and Hesse are especially relevant here as they shared pedagogical background: the Albersian interest in the exchange between background and foreground that was an enduring part of his classes. While Hesse and Asawa studied with him directly, Clark would have been exposed to these ideas through her reception of Max Bill in the neo-concrete artistic context of late 1940s São Paulo. The leap from San Francisco to São Paulo is not so far-fetched; Asawa did have a sculpture on display in the 1955 São Paulo Biennial. This is not to elide historical specificity across these two very different contexts, but to ask what it would mean if we understood such processes to have been unfolding simultaneously in the household of an artist-mother in San Francisco. If we saw Asawa's frequent invocation

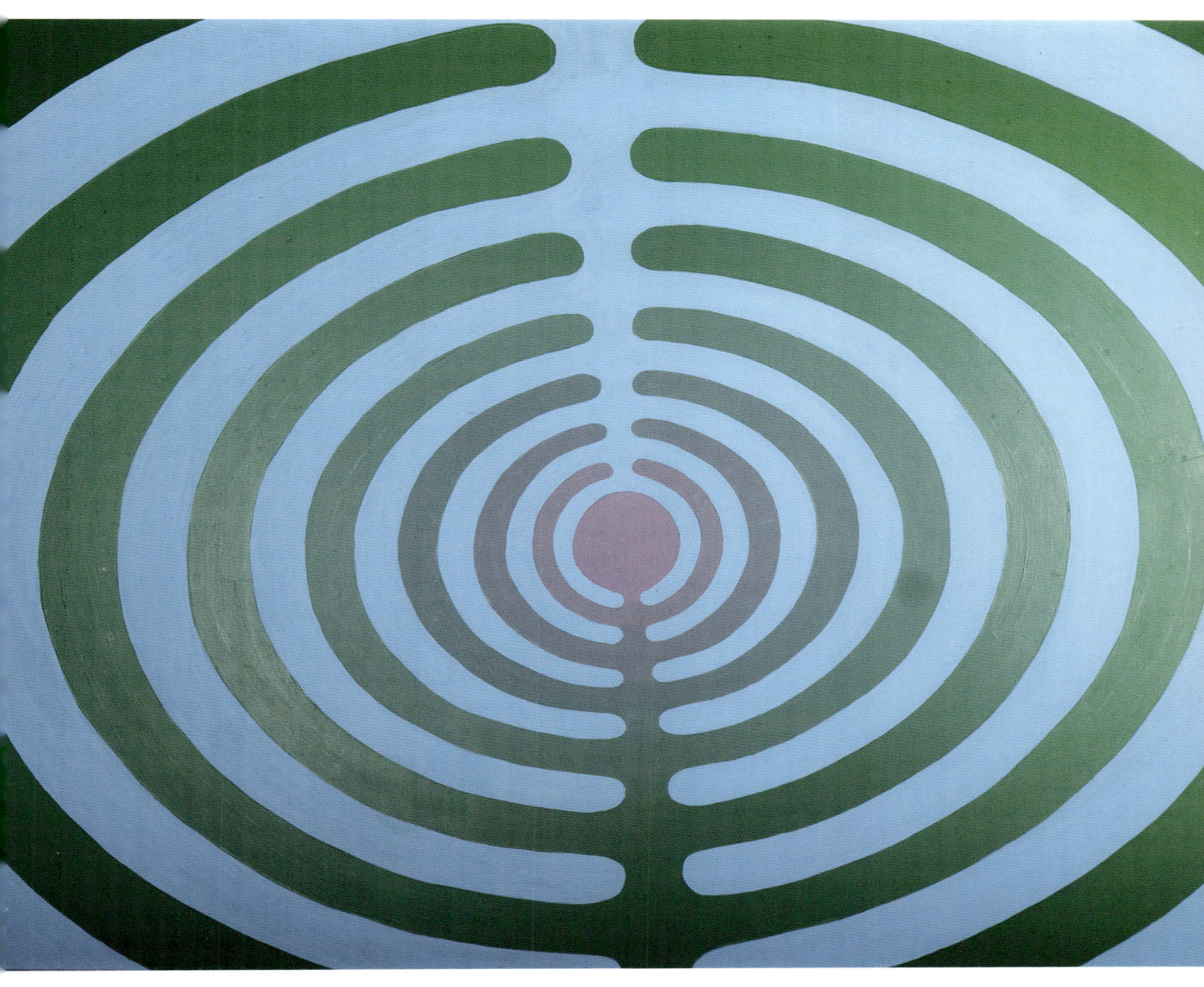

3.9 Ruth Asawa, *Untitled* (AB.029, Continuous Form within a Form), 1956. Acrylic on Masonite, 33 × 43 in. Private collection.

of the exchange between inside and outside not only as a modernist formal interest, as she often described it, but as an operation analogizing "the very gesture involved in the first separation (and exploration) when the child reaches out to the departing mother"?[30]

Inside-outside as a visual trope is extremely rich in metaphorical potential. One figural horizon is offered by Adrienne Rich, in her book *Of Woman Born*, suggesting that the terrain of "inside-outside" has at its core a maternal imaginary derived from the biological features of pregnancy. Essentially a metaphysical conundrum (not unlike the Möbius strip), pregnancy challenges basic definitions between inner and outer as a metaphor for self and other. While these challenges are now explored by the scientific and philosophical communities, they were first addressed in the fields of art and literature.[31] As Rich wrote, "The child that I carry for nine months can be defined *neither* as me nor as not-me. Far from existing in the mode of 'inner space,' women are powerfully and vulnerably attuned both to 'inner' and 'outer' because the two are continuous, not polar."[32] And while this attunement happens not only in pregnancy, Rich is quick to point out, pregnancy is one of its sites. It is one way in which we can argue for the polyvalent significance of Asawa's formal language: this was a language indebted to modernist explorations of pattern and pictorial space, but it was also a language of maternal embodiment from a nonheteronormative perspective; and importantly, Rich is writing her book from the perspective of a lesbian poet forging insights into subjectivity that go beyond binary structures. Diana Fuss, in her anthology of pioneering texts on gay and lesbian theory, published in 1991, points to the "figure inside/outside," best represented by "rings and matrices, loops and linkages," as necessarily "embodied, sexualized," and thus as demonstrating, like the Möbius strip, that "identity is founded relationally, constituted in reference to an exterior or outside that defines the subject's own interior boundaries and corporeal surfaces."[33]

Asawa and Cunningham's shared interest in the metaphorical potential of the inside/outside figure is joined, at the same time, by a tendency toward abstraction. As a consequence, these photographs cross genres of photography. In many instances, the title of the work signals this ambivalence: *Child in Landscape*, for instance, abstracts from the subject at hand—the portrait of a fellow artist-mother's daughter—while it also erases the reference to fairy tale in Cunningham's informal description of the work as the series "Babe in the Woods." Like Asawa's own boundary-defying artistic practice, Cunningham's images cannot be contained in rigid definitions of "straight photography" versus pictorialism, professional portraits as opposed to family snapshots, Victorian as opposed to modern. Instead, one often encounters both metaphor and portrait in a single, ambivalent image. A further instance of this hybrid status is *The Thonet Chair* (1959; fig. 3.10). According to its title, the photograph is a straightforward portrayal of a piece of iconic modern furniture: the undulating bentwood swirls of the rocking chair mass-marketed by the Thonet Company in the 1880s. However, the chair's swirling geometry enframes the photograph's unnamed sitter, Ruth Asawa, pregnant with what will be her last child. In her third term, her body is heavy and listless, its full weight supported by the chair. This is the embodied exhaustion of late pregnancy, buoyed by an icon of design history inextricably gendered as feminine in its vernacular function as rocking chair (or nursing chair), as Kenneth Ames writes in his study of Victorian material culture: "a challenge and an alternative to the European upper-class mode of formality." Rocking chairs were used by children, the aged, and the infirm, he writes, "not originally intended for adults at the height of their power."[34] What we are meant to see in this disjuncture between the photograph's title and subject is this core symmetry between its function and the maternal body. We are meant to notice, too, the way that the ample curves of the rocking chair multiply the curves of Asawa's expanding torso.

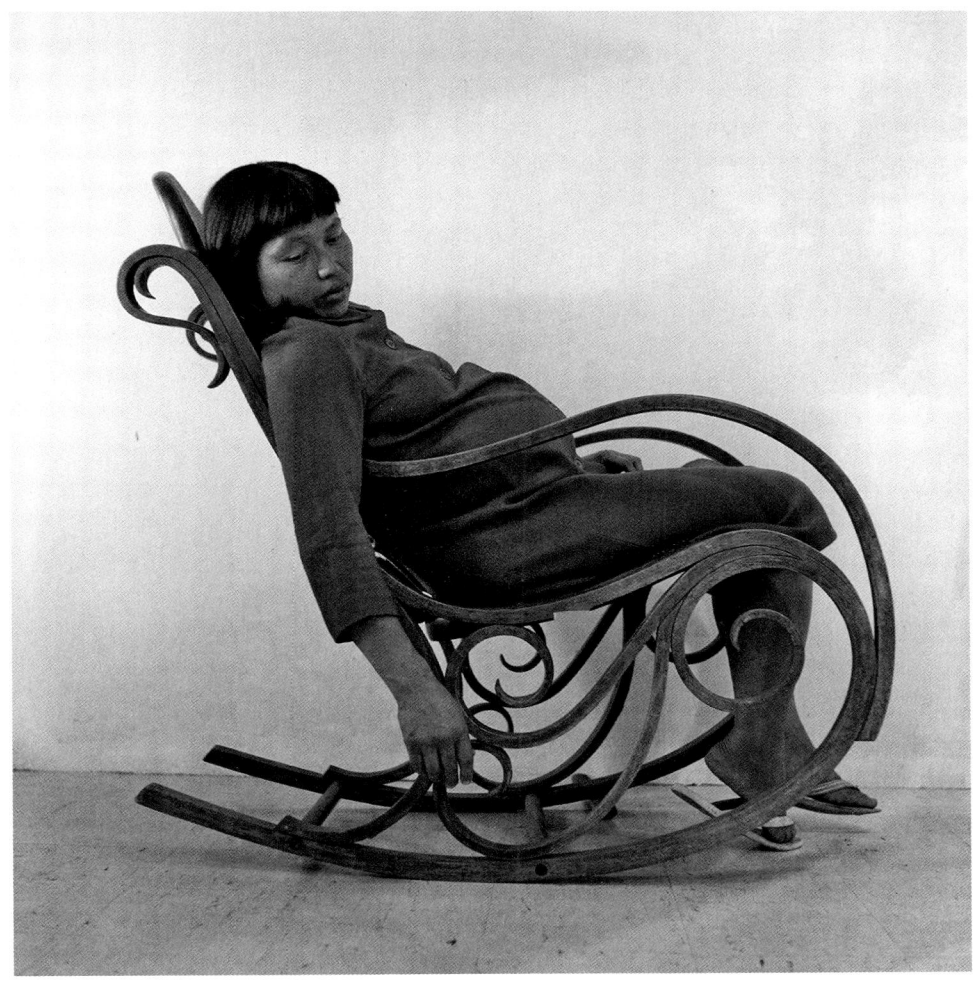

3.10 Imogen Cunningham, *The Thonet Chair*, 1959. Gelatin silver print, 7⅝ × 7⅝ in. Seattle Art Museum, Gift of John H. Hauberg, 89.57.

In the example of the rocking chair, we see how both artists took up the material world of motherhood. Asawa included the rocking chair in her drawing practice, where she used an incised marker to create a surface of radiating curves that explode from the center of the page. Here she was looking closely at the chair as part of her own furnishings as a mother. To have taken up such iconography was by no means neutral. In the 1950s the word "pregnant" was not even allowed to be spoken on television, as Cunningham's biographer Richard Lorenz points out.[35] Asawa's portrayal of the chair's radiating curves implicitly invokes the chair's purpose as a place for nursing, while in Cunningham's photograph they are explicitly tied to that subject. Cunningham did not reduce the pregnant body to an abstraction, but rather embraced its realism; "a refreshingly candid challenge to the societal taboos of the Eisenhower years," as Lorenz describes Cunningham's photographs of Renk pregnant, which I discuss above. Asawa, too, did not shy away from having her body depicted as pregnant and maternalized, with her identity as artist staged in close proximity to her identity as a mother through Cunningham's lens. She seems to have given Cunningham carte blanche in these portrait sessions, and the photographs that resulted stage the artist-mother as a challenge to dominant constructions of postwar artistic identity.

FROM INFANCY TO YOUNG ADULT

As is so often the case in parenting, where actions speak louder than words, Cunningham's example as an artist-mother spoke louder than her advice to Asawa that the younger artist not have any (more) children. Asawa may have also been emboldened by Cunningham's photographs of her own children to consider her own children as subjects for art. A remarkable series of drawings depicts her infant son Paul; one bears the inscription "Paul, 5 Days Old" in Asawa's handwriting (fig. 3.11). This is, without a doubt, a vulnerable body: only five days in the light of day and still uncurling its arms and legs, hands and feet—as Asawa faithfully renders on paper—from the folded, fetal position in which it spent some forty weeks. Asawa traces that smallness quickly, outlining the contours of cloth diaper and wrapped shirt, momentarily forgetting to add the edge of the tiny torso on the left just above the safety pin. This body just barely holds together. The hand that draws is vulnerable, too. Imagine, if you can, a body five days after giving birth—a body literally torn apart, from one into two, still assembling itself back into shape, in a daze of half-sleep, soreness, and exhaustion: of too much milk, of too little milk, of visitors coming and going. This is the unending experience of corporeality that is the postpartum condition, and it is astounding that in all of that Asawa mustered the concentration and energy to submit pen to paper, capturing even the details of the nappy pin and the tie of the newborn shirt, the wrinkles of the wrists and the tufts of hair. She beheld the body that had been growing inside her, which was now lying on the bed beside her, with the shrewdness of a cartographer, capturing contour and fold.

In the subsequent months and years, Asawa made several versions of this view, telescoping us above the scene. Sketches of infant Paul formed the basis of a stencil,

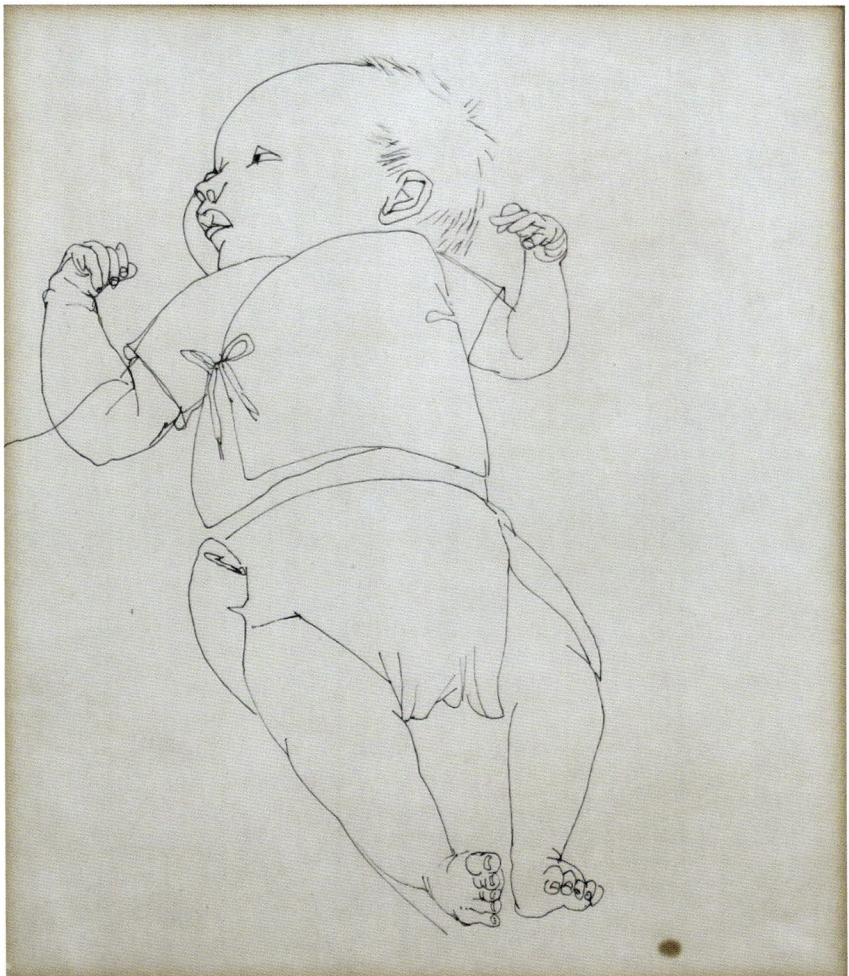

3.11 Ruth Asawa, *Untitled* (FF.1352, Paul Lanier at Five Days Old), November 1959. Black ink on paper, approx. 7 × 8½ in. Private collection.

which Asawa used to embed the body into a field of pattern. These marks were made by employing a method that she herself had invented: the incised felt tip of a broad ink marker, typically used for commercial signage, which I discuss in chapter 2. Asawa had cut into this felt tip to create ruts, which allowed her, once she put pen to paper, to leave three or four or five lines clustered together at regular intervals. This furnished her with a tool to generate cross-hatchings, which she oriented vertically and then horizontally, along a meandering path, creating a chain-link of pattern. She generated sheets of undulating folds that repeat as if extending endlessly, beyond the edge of the paper, all with the small figure of an infant lying in the middle of the scene (fig. 3.12). It must have fascinated her to see how such simple, two-dimensional marks could summon the billowing surface of a quilt or a patterned rug, a ground that didn't so much lie beneath the baby's body as envelop it, swirling around his small features and almost engulfing him, were it not for the bits of blank paper that Asawa had outlined and left alone, a blankness that, paradoxically, heightens our sense of undulating volume.

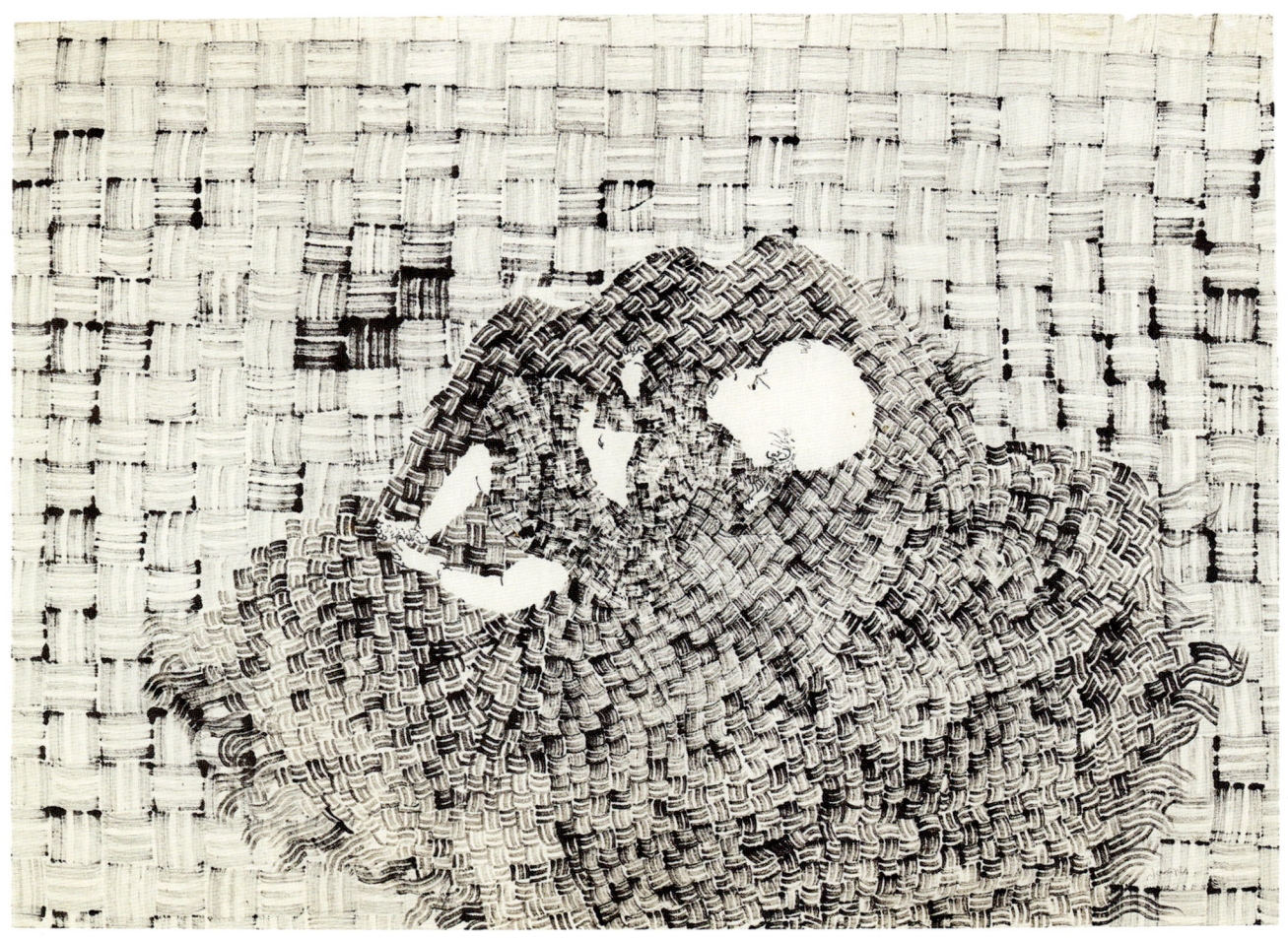

3.12 Ruth Asawa, *Untitled* (FF.075, Paul Lanier in Blanket on Woven Pattern), c. 1961–1963. Black ink on technical paper, 18 × 24¼ in. Private collection.

In her essay "Wide-Awake," curator and art historian Ruth Erickson describes the drawings Asawa made of her children, grandchildren, and husband sleeping (fig. 3.13). "While practical, her choice to study sleeping subjects enabled both the freedom and the caretaking that characterized her identity as an artist and a mother," Erickson writes.[36] Caretaking was a constant theme in Asawa's life, and friends and children remember her cooking meals, contributing to the schools, and tending to the garden. Drawing would seem to be unconnected to that reproductive work, but Erickson reads Asawa's practice of drawing as a continuation of her labor as a caretaker—as a form of self-care, "a conscious choice to carve time out of her busy days to practice looking and making in solitude, a kind of rest in and of itself."[37] It would thus seem that metaphor is no longer the operative term here, that instead of analogizing the unbridled creativity of the artist, as it did for so many male avant-garde artists, the child here evidences the labor of the artist-mother as a restorative practice. "For me," Adrienne Rich writes, "poetry was where I lived as no one's mother, where I existed as myself."[38]

Just as Asawa's interest in pattern as so-called knitted sculpture allowed her to work piecemeal, to pick up and put down the work as other demands necessitated, as I discuss in chapter 2, so too Erickson suggests that the crosshatch pattern of the marker drawings were, like the repetitive work in wire, a way to accommodate the interruptions that are so much a part of caring for children. Unlike a flowing line, one could stop in the middle of applying a hatch pattern to pick it up again a few hours later, without a noticeable interruption in the picture's composition. Interruption was thus built into Asawa's working methods—and interruption, as Tillie Olsen observed in 1968, is the state of mothering: "More than any other human relationship, overwhelmingly more, motherhood means being instantly interruptible, responsive, responsible. . . . It is distraction, not meditation, that becomes habitual; interruption, not continuity; spasmodic, not constant toil."[39] This insight, which Sarah Knott calls "interruption [as] the condition of caretaking," is an argument about the rhythms of maternal time, shaping diverse texts on motherhood from Knott as a historian, to the author Angela Garbes, to the psychologist Lisa Baraitser.[40] It is the temporality of interruption that emerges "whenever the archive gets closest to mothering," Knott writes.[41]

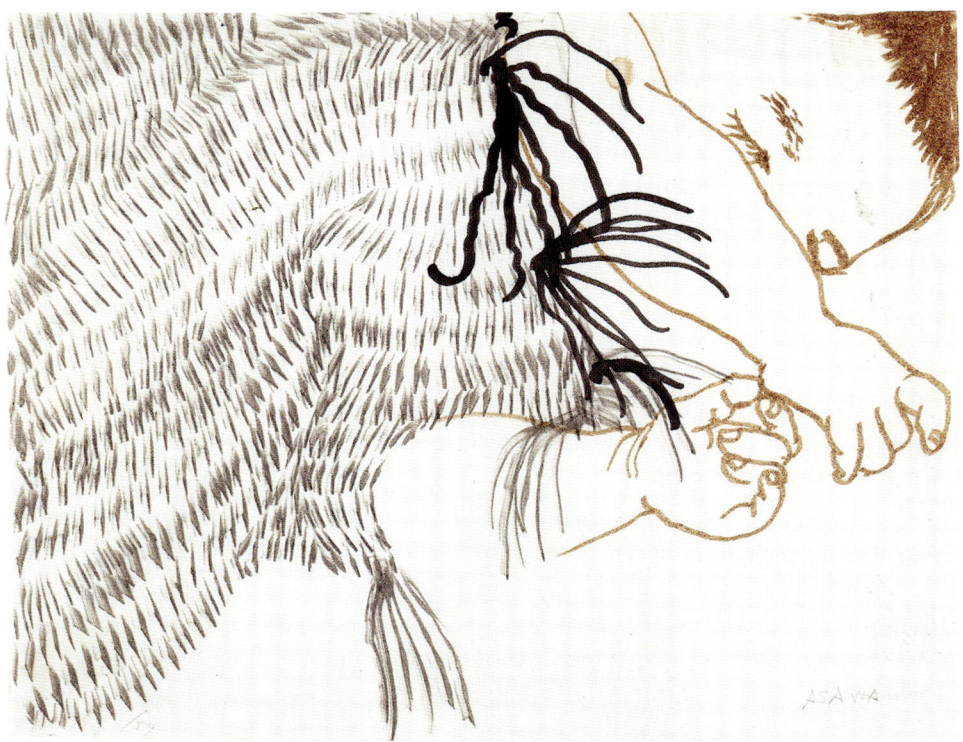

3.13 Ruth Asawa, *Untitled* (FF.385, Adam Lanier Sleeping in Patterned, Tasseled Blanket), 1959. Brown, gray, and black ink on tracing paper, 11 × 14 in. Private collection.

In addition to countless drawings of her growing children, Asawa collaborated with Cunningham on a sculpture cast from the body of her ten-year-old daughter (fig. 3.14). The work was on view in 1969, when Asawa and Cunningham participated in the exhibition *U.S.A. in Your Heart* at the San Francisco Art Institute. Curated by the photographer Jerry Burchard, the exhibition aimed to present a spectrum of work by both established photographers and a younger generation. Burchard had been newly appointed to the photography department and had taken classes with Cunningham, who regularly guest-lectured at the institute. Burchard had taken the exhibition title from the head sign at the Palace Theater, North Beach's popular movie house, and the photo of this head sign served as the poster for the exhibition. The photographs on display represented, as one reviewer put it, "a confrontation of work by established masters, new underground heroes and a cross-section of other photographers who have yet to achieve either status."[42]

The exhibition was a turning point in the transition from photography's status as an aestheticized picture to the medium's use in three-dimensional installations and as an addendum to sculptural practices. Alongside Burchard's work deploying filmstrips by Bruce Conner, which Burchard had printed onto abstractions of dancing bodies, was work by a younger generation to which Conner, Robert Heinecken, Ralph Gibson, Edmund Teske, Chris Enos, and Larry Clark belonged, as well as the output of established "masters" like Ansel Adams, Aaron Siskind, and Minor White. "One might add here the name of Imogen Cunningham, except that her 'Hair Skirt'—a pleated mini bearing the repeated image of a girl with flowing tresses and draped around a Degas-like standing figure by Ruth Asawa—is scarcely the kind of straight photography that formed her reputation."[43]

Upending "reputation" was precisely at issue. For this was a work about gender—and female generation—by the only two women participating in the exhibition, and as such it defied expectations. The work consisted, as the review describes, of a headless figure, which Asawa had cast from her daughter's prepubescent body. No longer child, not yet adult, the body's shape is suspended in that moment before it is constrained by the markers of gender identification. At the same time, posed in contrapposto, the body displays all the signs of sculpture's antiquity: arms and head are missing, the white plaster bears no trace of color. This is a classicized body, and yet it is a body whose gender can still be ambiguous, for although cast from a female-identifying sitter, it is a sitter suspended between childhood and womanhood. Muscular, firm legs support an androgynous chest, clothed, moreover, by a pleated miniskirt. On the surface of the skirt, which Asawa had sewed and pinned to the sculpture, barely visible through the folds, we see the flowing locks, printed on photosensitive cloth, of Cunningham's *Phoenix Recumbent* (1968), taken the year prior (fig. 3.15).

It is unclear whether Asawa had made the cast first and then the two women added the article of clothing, or the idea of adding a photographic skirt precipitated the cast figure. It is likely that the cast and the negative were made separately, and that the two women collaborated in putting them together to create a single, coauthored work. Asawa, though, seemed uninterested in claiming coauthorship, as the exhibition

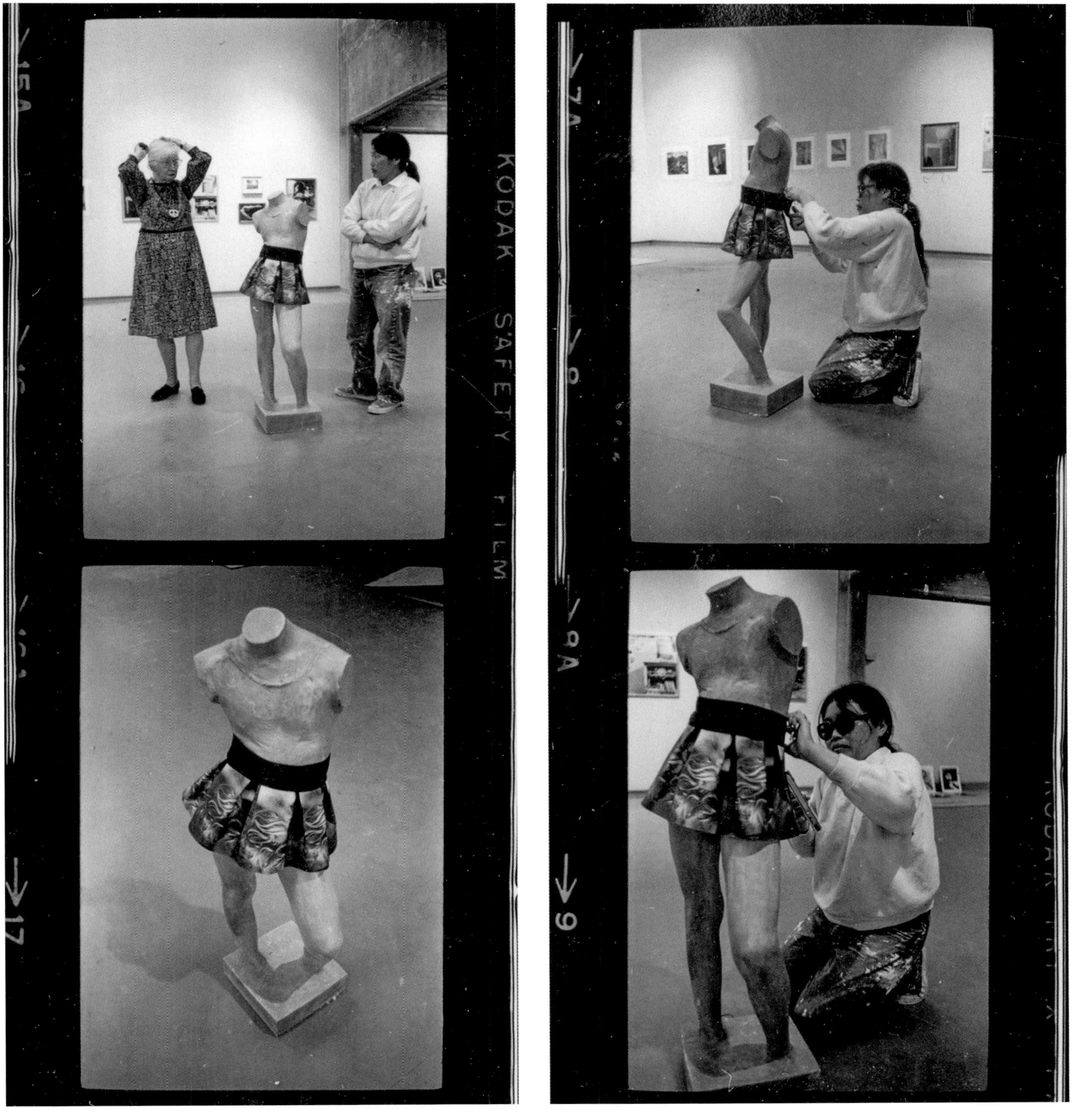

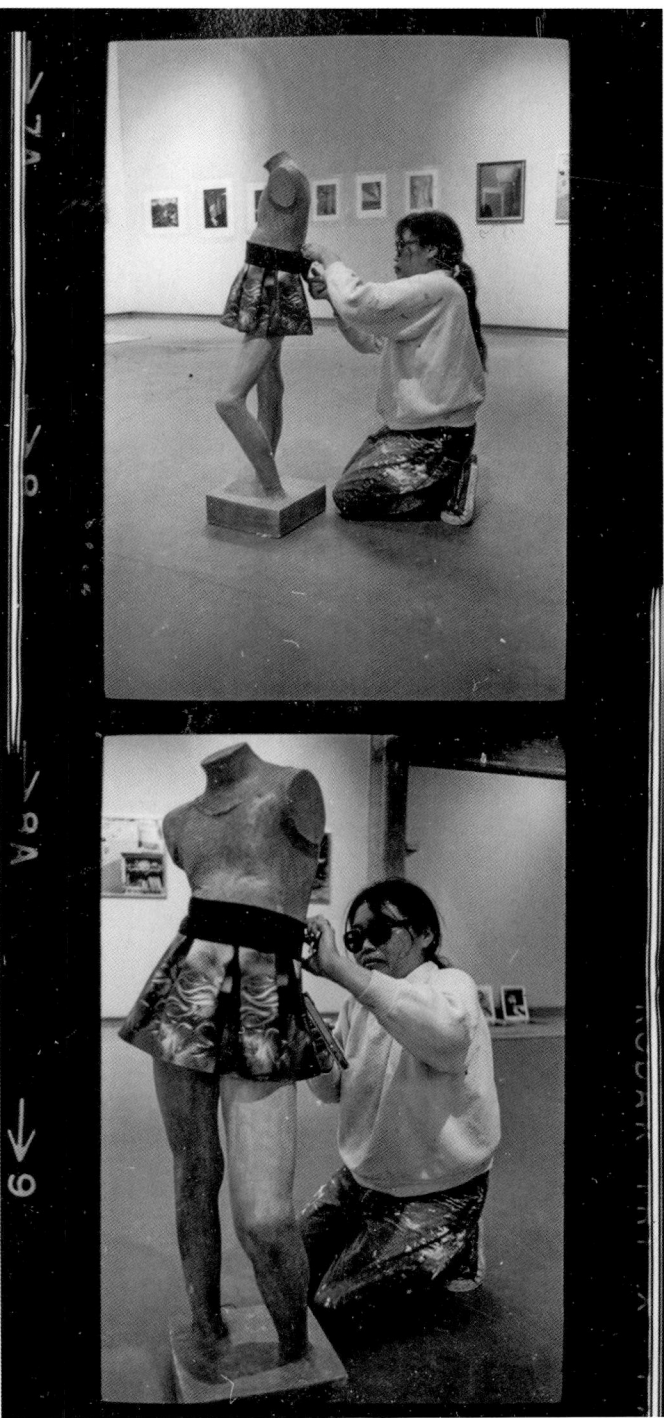

3.14 Imogen Cunningham and Ruth Asawa with *The Hair Skirt*, 1969. Detail of contact sheet with photos by Bill Young. San Francisco Art Institute Legacy Foundation + Archives.

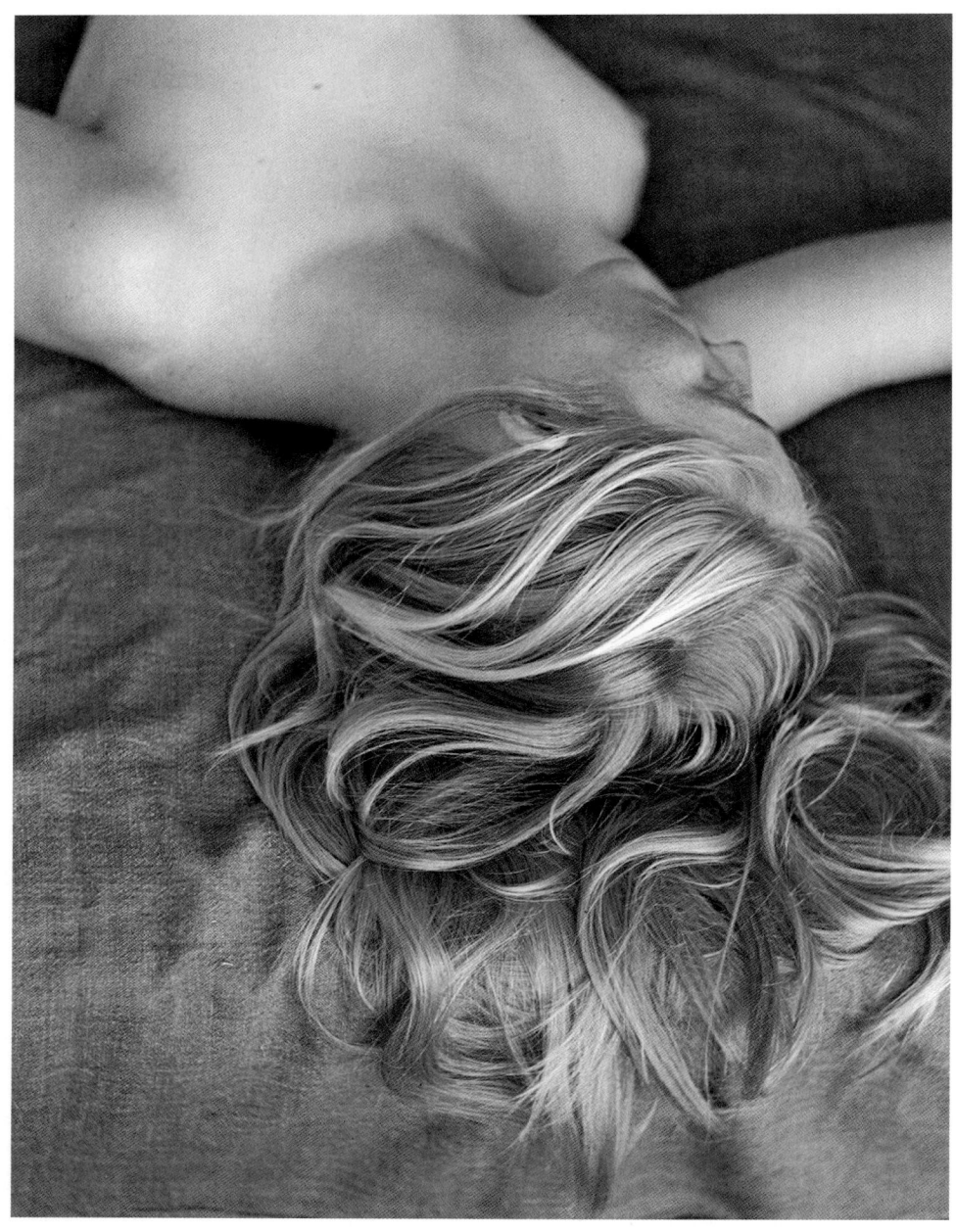

3.15 Imogen Cunningham, *Phoenix Recumbent*, 1968. Gelatin silver print, 13 × 10 in. Collection of the Imogen Cunningham Trust.

reviews cite only Cunningham as author of *The Hair Skirt*. This abdication of or disinterest in authorship goes against the persistent interest on the part of art history in the question of "where, in the case of a cast, originality might lie," as historian Marcia Pointon writes in her study of Victorian-era death masks.[44] Beginning with Rosalind Krauss's assertion that the body cast and the photograph structurally resemble one another in that both are indexes of an absent object, scholars have probed the shared terrain between these two media as both undermining originality.

Cunningham's sitter, Phoenix, was a frequent model for the photographer in the late 1960s and was likely a student at the San Francisco Art Institute. As part of her instruction at the Art Institute, Cunningham came into regular contact with a younger generation of artists (she also taught at the University of California Extension program, San Francisco State University, and Humboldt College, even rejecting the offer of a hotel during her summer course in order to room with the students in the dorms). The summer 1970 issue of *The Arrow*, the magazine of the fraternity Pi Beta Phi, featured Cunningham in its cover story "Famed Photographer, Octogenarian, Has Poetic Approach with Camera." The article opened with Cunningham's claim that she is "the world's oldest hippie . . . but a working hippie," and focused on the eighty-seven-year-old photographer's proximity to a younger generation, claiming that "her teen-aged grandchildren would rather have their parties at Imogen's modest cottage than at home."

"Imogen IS where it's at," says son Rondal. And no truer statement can be made. Only Imogen would wear such hippie-ish outfits as blanket-like capes and hair shirts. She was wearing such attire long before San Francisco's Haight Street turned on. Her beanie hat, perched atop a coil of snow-white hair, and her peace symbol are trademarks of Imogen, the woman. Her best friends are young people—most of them photography students. When asked why she prefers this age group, she says, "Have you noticed what my contemporaries are doing? Talking about their arthritis!"[45]

The Hair Skirt, as the photo-sculpture became titled, thus places into dialogue the bodies of two women from this younger generation: Asawa's own prepubescent daughter Addie Laurie, and college-aged Phoenix. And it does so through the format of the miniskirt, itself a symbol of liberated female sexuality in the late 1960s. The title *Hair Skirt* is a characteristic Cunningham play on words, riffing on the then-trending hair shirts among the hippie generation but also the fact that the photograph literally depicts flowing locks. That the reviewer above invokes Edgar Degas, whose reputation was made through sculptures of young ballet dancers, further demands that we read this work as a statement about gender. The reference to Degas is significant in his use of elements like tulle that were uncharacteristic for sculpture at the time and operated as signifiers of a world outside the aesthetic realm of art.

These were two women who were looking closely at what it meant to come of age as a woman in America circa 1968. The genre of portraiture began as the means in which to do so, but ultimately *The Hair Skirt* ended up not being a portrait: it was a deployment of portraiture that challenged conventions. Gone is the attempt to stabilize identity, for to come into one's own gender identity circa 1968 was to grapple with how radically this position had changed in comparison to the beginning of the decade. Already defying gender expectations in the 1950s—an era that Adrienne Rich describes as conformist and Freudian-dominated—Cunningham and Asawa were in a unique position to comment on what daughters, both biological and elected, would have to contend with.[46]

The Hair Skirt was typical of Cunningham's genre-defying approach to photography—it was likely why she was invited to participate in an exhibition that became a definitive moment in photography's increasing dialogue with sculpture. A premonition of that shift can be found in an unlikely site: the format of the wedding album, which Cunningham and her son Rondal Partridge made for Asawa's daughter Aiko and her husband, the photographer Laurence Cuneo, on the occasion of their wedding in 1971 (fig. 3.16). By then, wedding albums were old hat for Cunningham. She had had experience with the format as early as 1913, with her wedding album of ten platinum prints for Gertrude Walsh Coe (currently in the collection of the Getty Museum). With views of the bride and her bridesmaids in true Victorian pictorialism, the Walsh Coe wedding album is a far cry from the objects Cunningham and Partridge made in 1971.

The album takes the unconventional form of the contact sheet, with Cunningham's frames distinguished from her son's by their square format (not visible in the page illustrated here). Guests, including Andrea Jepson and Merry Renk, appear alongside artworks, including the life cast of a face, a five-pointed tied-wire star mounted to the wall, and a Nativity scene made from baker's clay—a material that featured in the wedding cake (a photograph of which graced the album's cover). These disjointed views are sutured together by the temporality of the camera: some frames have been left together, as they were taken on the roll of film, one after the other, while other frames have been cut up and reassembled for juxtaposition. This emphasis on the photographic medium creates a wedding album that is neither sentimental nor clichéd, but speaks to how intimate family events like these—the momentous occasion of one's eldest daughter's wedding—were also imbricated in the making of art. (Asawa would also later ask Aiko to sculpt her wedding scene for the *San Francisco Fountain*, the subject of this book's last chapter.) These were mothers committed to representing mother-daughter relationships, both real and elected, in ways that escaped the stereotypes of that genre—in ways that could also be extended to mother-son collaborations, as was the case in the album co-created by Imogen and Rondal.

3.16 Imogen Cunningham and Rondal Partridge's photographs in Aiko and Laurence Cuneo's wedding album (detail), 1971. Gelatin silver contact prints bound into an album, approx. 10 x 8 in. Private collection.

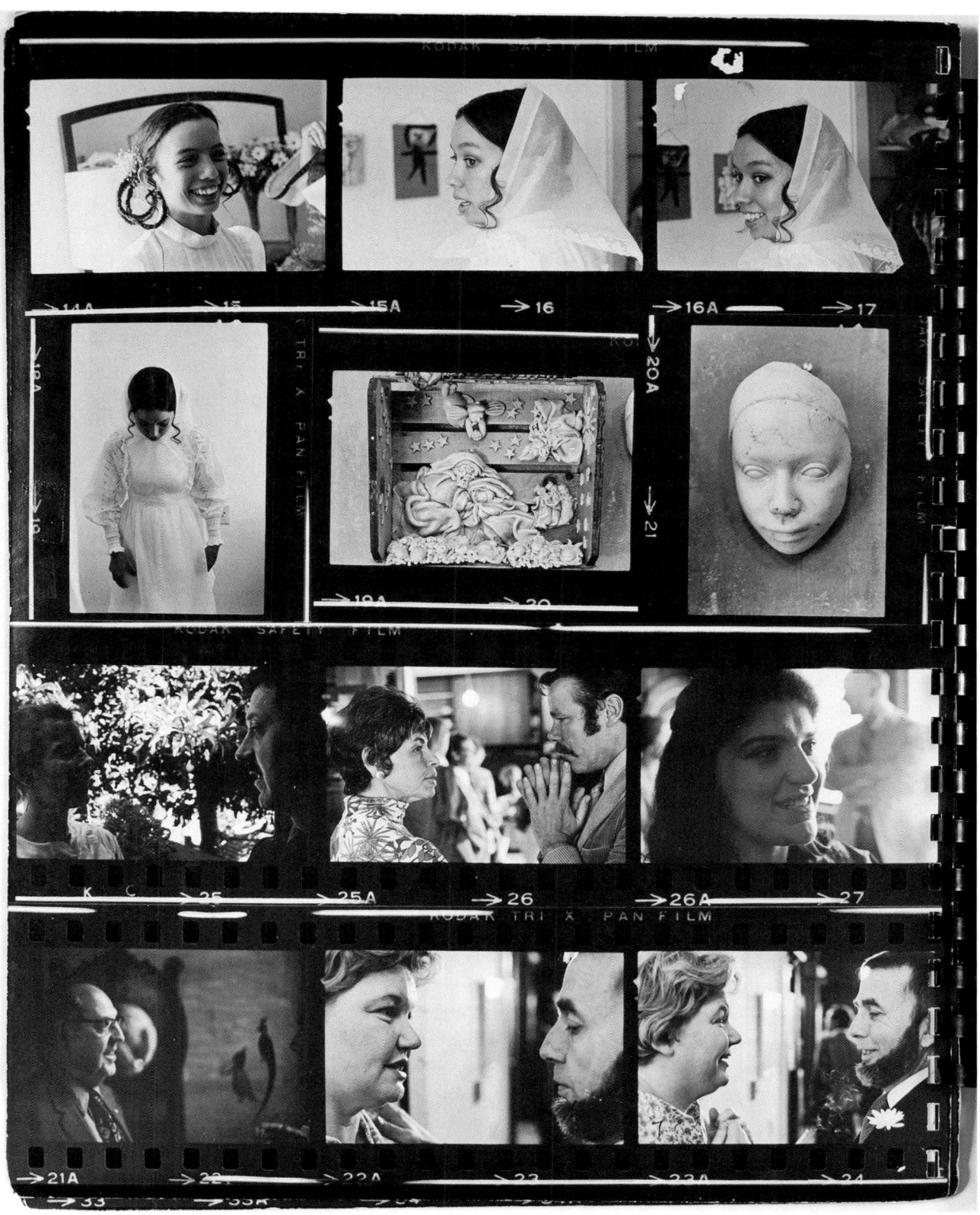

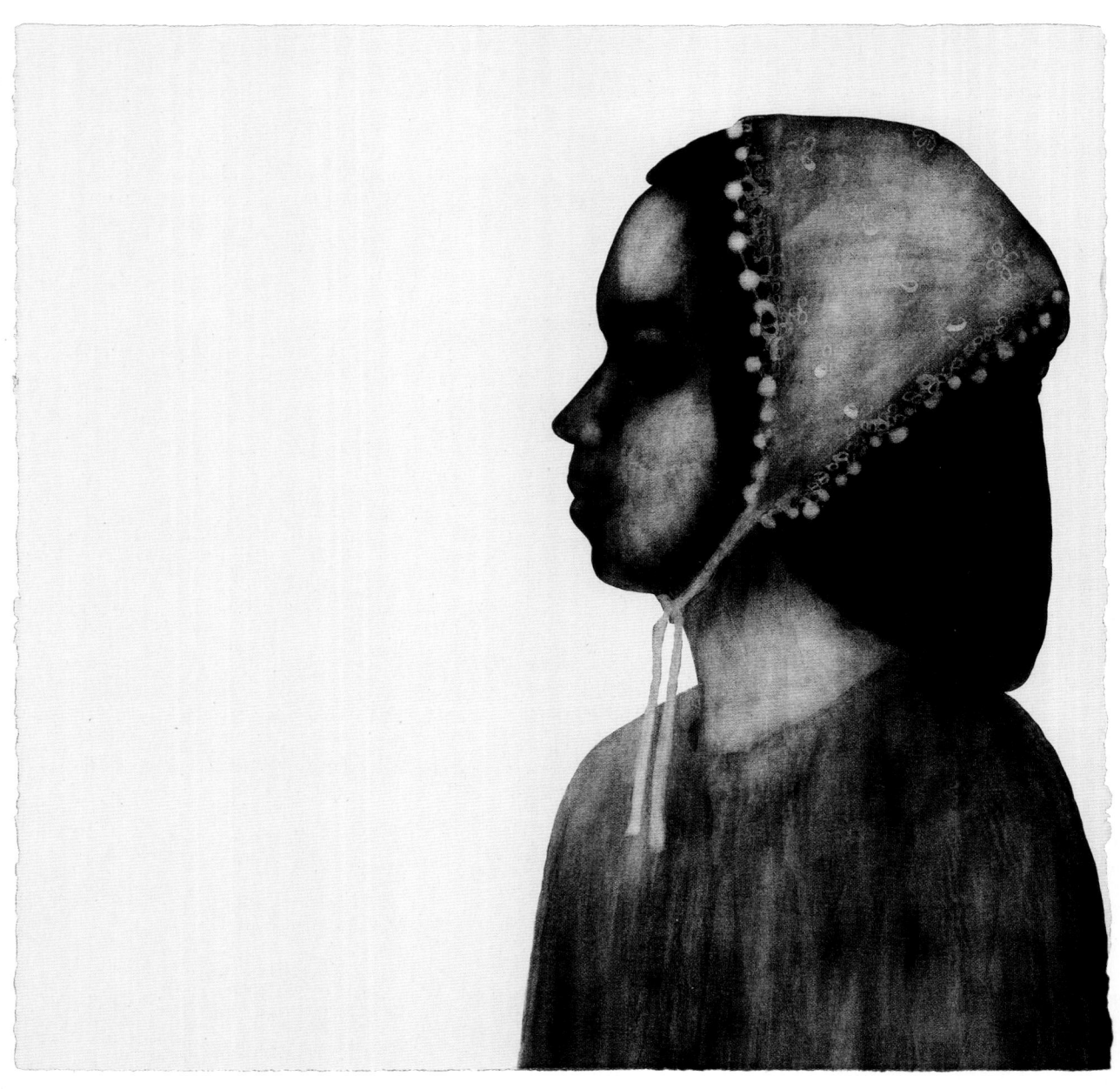

3.17 Ruth Asawa, *Aiko* (TAM.1473, Aiko Lanier), September 9–14, 1965. Lithograph, black ink on paper, 22 × 22 in. Private collection.

The breadth of this engagement with figures of childhood—of subjectivity in the process of formation—demonstrates how metaphor stands in tension with literal figuration. From the lyrical body of the reflected child in portraits of Cunningham's twins to the Möbius-like inside-outside figure of Asawa's abstracted paintings and sculptures, metaphor comes easily; such depictions are polyvalent reflections from the perspective of someone in close dialogue with subject formation. At the same time, an engagement with childhood takes on the diaristic character of the family album, with the artist-mother chronicling an era she knows will soon pass. Asawa drew her own children at moments of rest, which served as opportunities for studying them closely while also taking up the challenge of finding formal solutions for the scene at hand. This doubleness of childhood, as both a rich metaphorical terrain but also a mediation of intimate relationships, becomes especially apparent in the work of the artist-mother, whose identity allows for this multidimensional reading (fig. 3.17). What we can learn from this example is that such a duality is apparent elsewhere too, in the many engagements with childhood pursued by male artists, where it is often brushed aside as less significant than the subject's metaphorical register.

At the same time that Cunningham began taking photographs of Asawa's children, she was also taking photographs of Asawa's sculptures. Many such photographs depict the sculptures in what would appear to be unfinished states: as teardrop objects and open-ended lobes arranged against a plain white or dark ground (fig. 3.18). We can imagine Asawa hauling these over to the photographer's home, hoping she could make some decent pictures of them, and not yet herself knowing if they constituted completed works. At the time, in the 1950s and 1960s, Asawa was grateful for the stunning photographs that Cunningham had fashioned, redeploying them for applications to the Guggenheim Foundation and for exhibition brochures. Asawa and Lanier recognized early on that these photographs did double duty: many fulfilled their task of conveying the look and feel of Asawa's sculptures to those who could not see them in person, while others far exceeded this task, becoming "exciting photographically," as Albert Lanier put it.[47] Many such photographs abstract the sculptures beyond recognition, demonstrating their complex visual armature as a play of light, shadow, and texture. In one example Cunningham collapsed a wire object into foreshortened close-ups, whose reddish tones further estrange the object at hand and generate a fantastical image of multiple exposures. But Cunningham also staged Asawa's sculptures and paintings in dialogue with everyday objects; we have already seen baby Adam and his mother using the surface of a painting as a ground for shadow play. In another photograph, the beloved family doll Pitiful Pearl is propped up alongside one of Asawa's looped-wire objects (fig. 3.19). Here it is the material world of childhood that makes an appearance, with the sculptures populating this domestic landscape.

When the *Christian Science Monitor* reached out to Asawa with a request to feature the artist in its series "Women Today," Asawa responded with deflection, suggesting that the reporter do an article on Cunningham, "my photographer and friend." "Miss

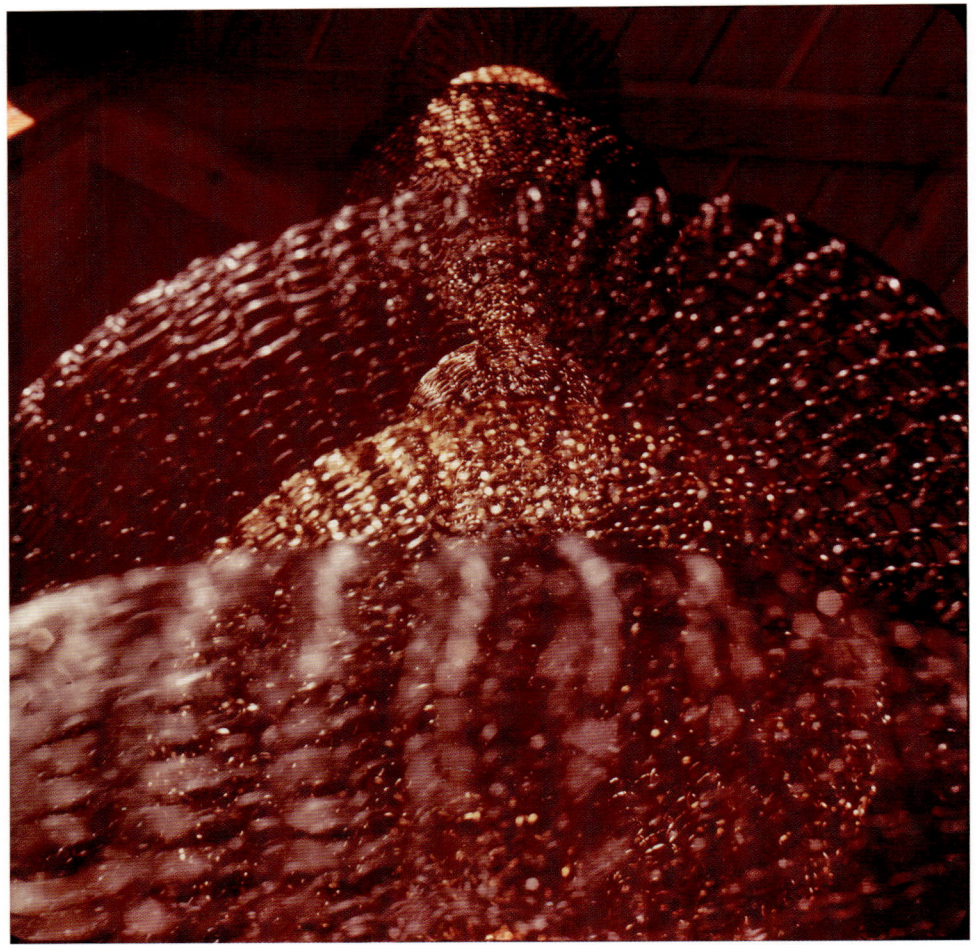

3.18 Imogen Cunningham, *Detail View of Ruth Asawa's Looped-Wire Sculpture*, no date. Gelatin silver print, 8¾ × 9 in. Collection of the Imogen Cunningham Trust.

3.19 Imogen Cunningham, *"Pitiful Pearl" with Looped-Wire Sculpture*, c. 1965. Gelatin silver print, 8¼ × 9 in. Private collection.

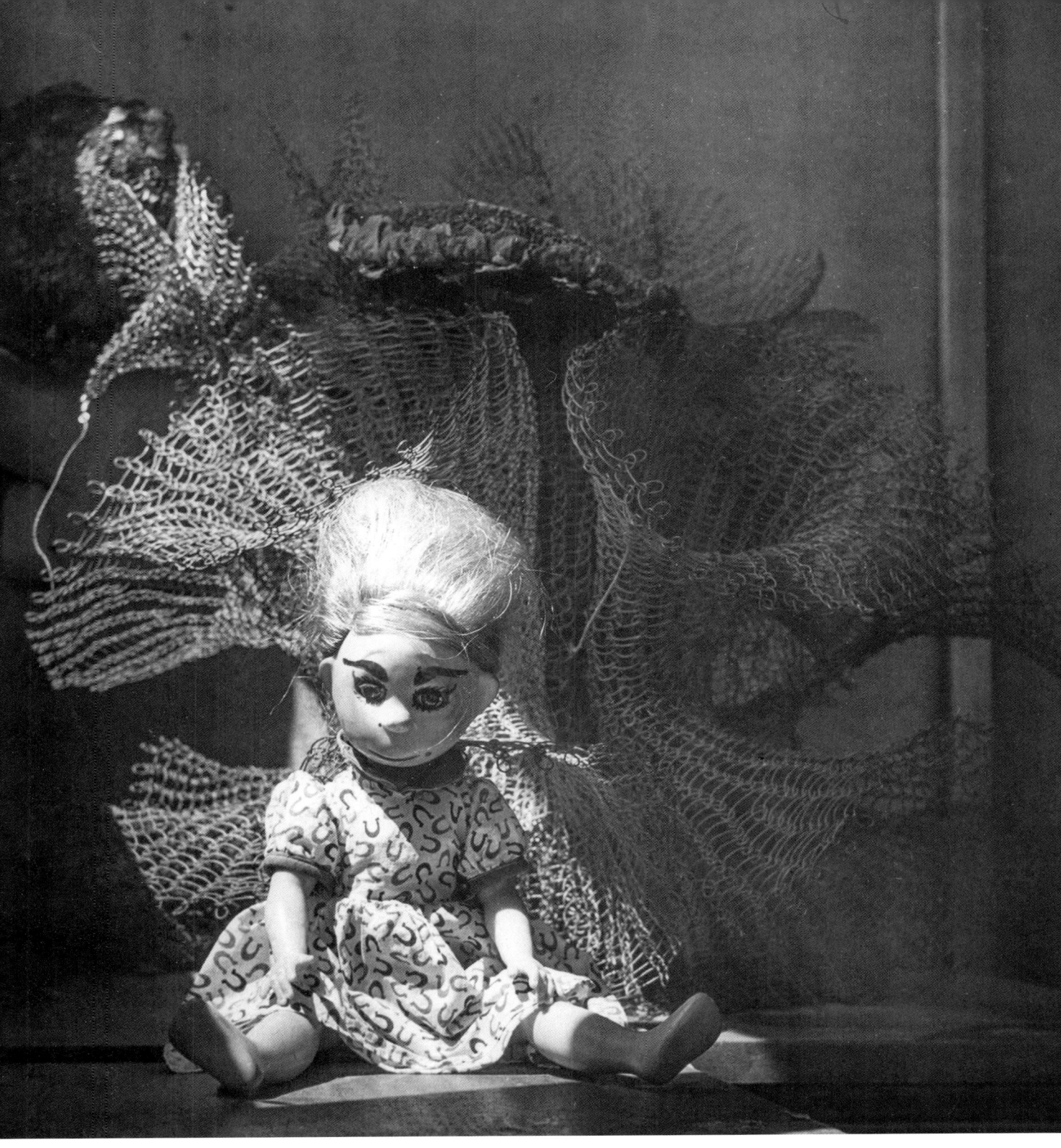

Cunningham has been photographing my work for years. She has been paid practically nothing for photographs reproduced with articles. If the Monitor pays a fee, I would appreciate her being paid, since her livelihood depends on it; also the photographers are the most needed and the least appreciated in the art field. I have come to realize how important a good picture is and how much it's worth to have a top notch photographer do the work."[48] The article that resulted thematized Cunningham's age with its title "Years Add Camera Skill," which would become a refrain in articles on Cunningham as her reputation grew in the 1960s and 70s, eventually becoming the "myth" of the photographer as the "living symbol of youth in old age," as Margaretta Mitchell put it in the introduction to Cunningham's own photographic reflection on aging, *After Ninety*.[49]

One of the photographs included in the article was an unidentified "Mother and Child," as the caption read—in actuality, a close-up of Asawa with a sleeping toddler. (Cunningham had included the photograph in Asawa's youngest daughter's baby album.) This is Cunningham engaging with an archetype—the age-old Madonna and Child imagery that constitutes the beginning of the Western art tradition. And yet at the same time, this is Cunningham claiming to be photographing simply what is, as the literal world before her lens. "She photographed Ruth Asawa because they were friends," Margery Mann wrote, paraphrasing the photographer, who described an image of Asawa at a door as "literal," "completely literal."[50] But the photographs that she made of the artist—just like the drawings and prints that Asawa made of her—are far from flat-footed realism (figs. 3.20, 3.21). They may have taken one another as subject matter, but just as often this subject matter becomes a ploy for an exploration of form, color, and light—of how little depiction could still constitute a portrait, as in Asawa's example, or in Cunningham's headless renditions of Asawa in her home on Greene Street, encircling the body by interior architecture, framed by a receding hallway, while in another instance refracting its form through a glass door.

In an interview with Asawa from 1983, we learn that she and Cunningham had discussed ideas for a book of Cunningham's photographs of Asawa, her family, and her sculptures, as well as Asawa's drawings of Cunningham.[51] The book was never made; had it been, it would have been the first instance of such a collaboration and a predecessor to the dual-authored texts that often characterize feminist scholarship. Surely, the sheer number of photographs that the two would have had to comb through for such a book was one reason for its unrealized state; we still do not know exactly how many photographs Cunningham took that are related to Asawa. It seems she had given many to the artist and did not keep the negatives. Many others lie dormant in an overflowing archive that still awaits an exhaustive catalogue raisonné. The two women shared this feature: they made work incessantly, with little care for its systematization. As Asawa herself later admitted, the drawings and works on paper presented an overwhelming task when it came to cataloguing her work. Cunningham, too, invested little energy in her own self-aggrandizement, delegating this task to posterity: "after I am gone, history will take care of everything."[52]

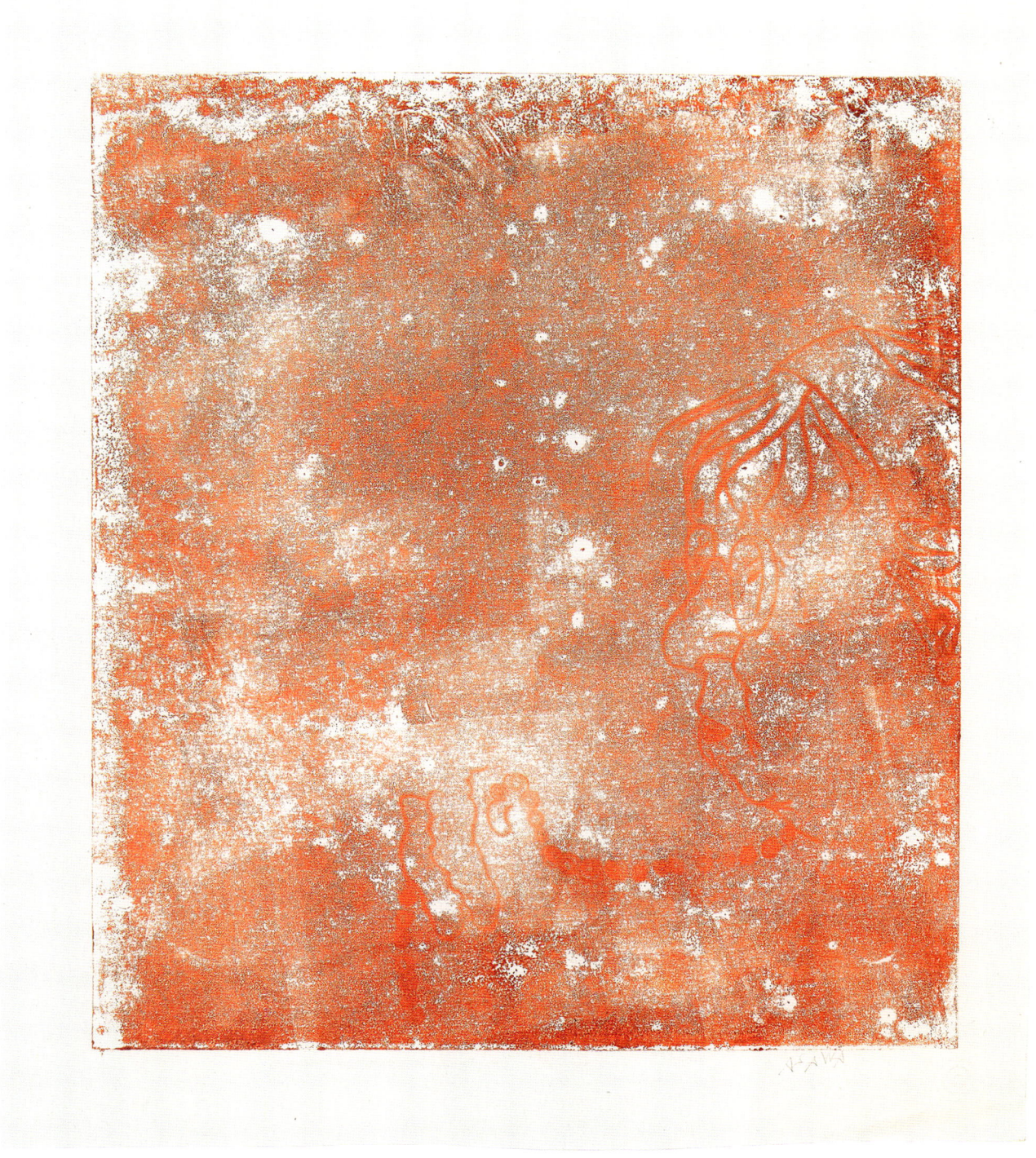

3.20 Ruth Asawa, *Untitled* (FF.567, Imogen
Cunningham with Beads), c. 1975 or after. Red
ink on paper, 15 × 13¼ in. Private collection.

3.21 Imogen Cunningham, *Ruth Asawa with Looped-Wire Sculpture*, c. 1960. Contact sheet with two negatives, each 9 × 8¾ in. Collection of the Imogen Cunningham Trust.

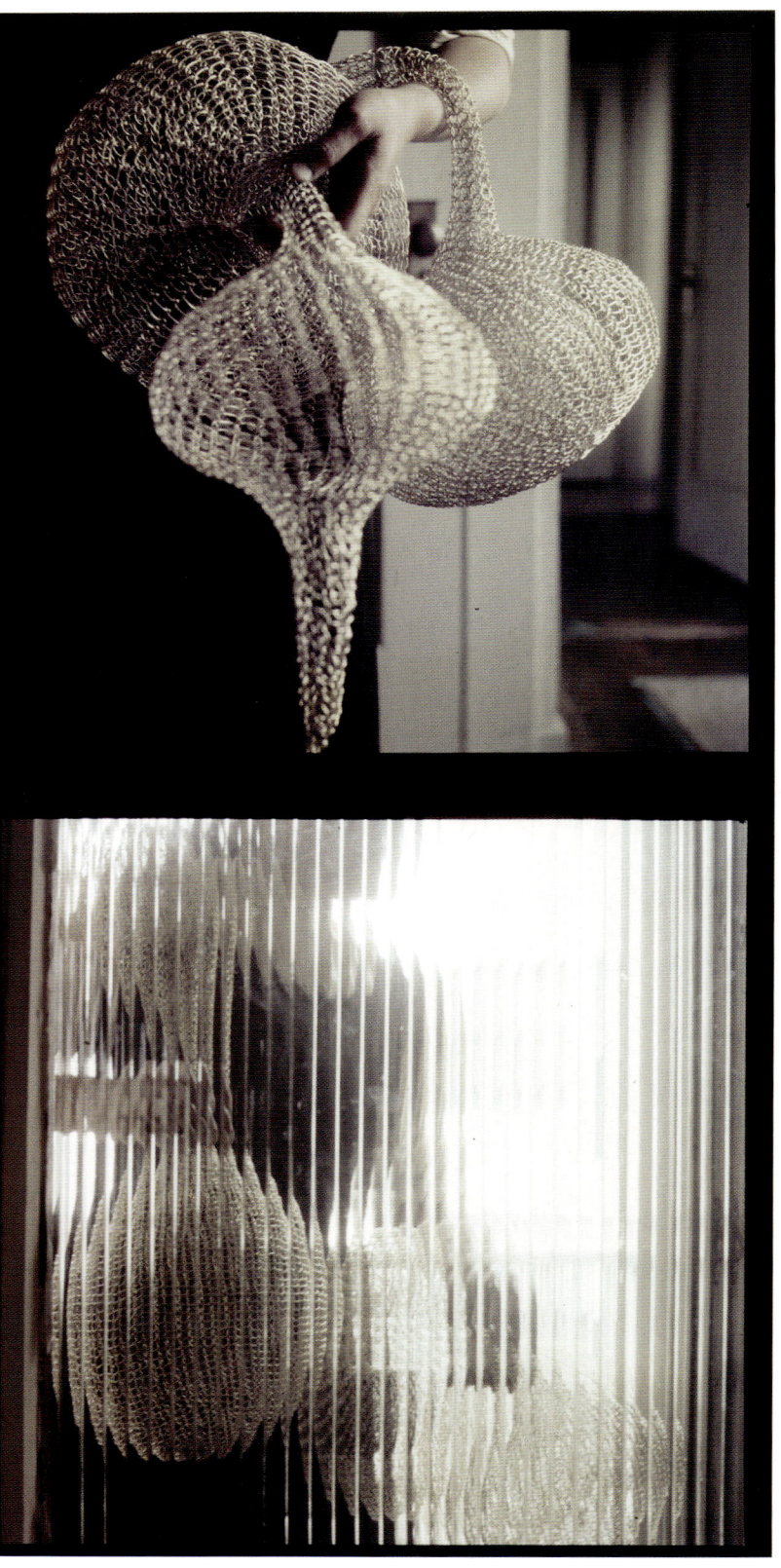

Many attributed whatever success Cunningham did receive to her "cult persona," as Lorenz put it, a larger-than-life personality that left many photo historians "still deliberating" as to the value of her work and hesitant to acquire more than one hundred images from a career that produced tens of thousands, effectively skeptical of the artist's "careless indifference to her reputation."[53] When asked in 1973 if the Virginia Slims Book of Days Engagement Calendar could include her as "Woman of the Week" with the description "Imogen Cunningham, called by many the mother of American photography," she replied, "I am definitely NOT the mother of photography but the mother of three sons. . . . If you really wanted to honor me you would give me the kind of job that I can still do—and that is photographing some of those female smokers."[54] It was this same "indifference to reputation" that Asawa saw as a commitment to artmaking, and one that had been hard-won. She described the camera, ever present on Cunningham, as her "most vital organ." In a speech on Cunningham, she acknowledged the photographer's tenacity in surviving in a male-dominated field, the difficult of getting paid as much as her male colleagues, the lack of recognition for many decades, the impact of divorce. She emphasized Cunningham's civic commitment, her protesting the plan to put a freeway through the Panhandle and testifying in support of a youth hostel against residents who thought it would attract "hippies to the Marina's background."[55]

For all they held in common in terms of a shared indifference to reputation in a field that categorically rejected the artist-mother, they also differed on many points. Cunningham was critical of Asawa's work in the schools, while Asawa saw it as vital to her sculptural development; though they were both civic-minded, Cunningham situated herself as an elder hippie, with her perennial peace pendant, supporting antiwar and environmental causes, while Asawa invested her energies not in political protest but in volunteer work. Asawa was soft-spoken; Cunningham said whatever was on her mind and often with a "salty humor," as Asawa later put it. And yet the two women nurtured a friendship of twenty-five years, beginning in 1950 and ending with Cunningham's death in 1976, a few months after her ninety-third birthday.

This was a mutual recognition, with Cunningham expressing her admiration of Asawa on several occasions. She described her as "an unfailingly creative person." In a letter to the Guggenheim Foundation, Cunningham wrote: "To me, Ruth Asawa Lanier as a person is phenomenal [sic]. She is young but with real maturity and a balance that few, either old or young, have these days. She is an indomitable worker. It seems as if the more she undertakes the more she accomplishes, both in work and real living. Her creative ability is not confined to wire sculpture, but she seems to think that this is her best expression. It is certainly the most original if that counts for anything in this era of trends."[56] This form of support coexisted with critique: Cunningham discouraged Asawa from having children and "was very critical of my volunteer work in the schools. She thought I was wasting my time, that I should be doing my own work."[57]

I end this chapter with a little-known portrait of an older Asawa, which Cunningham took in 1975. Departing from every other representation of the artist by

Cunningham, this is a portrait in what would appear to fit that conventional genre: Asawa sits, foregrounded against a dark backdrop, looking very serious (fig. 3.23). Forty years earlier, Cunningham had used the same conventions in a portrait of the writer Gertrude Stein (fig. 3.22). Both women are portrayed as titans, imposing figures at the height of their powers. I do not think it is a coincidence that Cunningham here cites herself, asking us to think about Asawa in relationship to Stein. For the two women have a remarkable number of parallels, which would have occurred only to someone as intelligent and experienced as Cunningham.

For one, Stein and Asawa both worked with repetition as their métier. Stein's texts reuse a limited number of words in all their permutations. Consider this extract from "Many Many Women": "In being married and feeling she was married and was conveying that thing that she was continuing. In having children and she had two children she was feeling what she feeling. She was feeling what she was feeling. She was

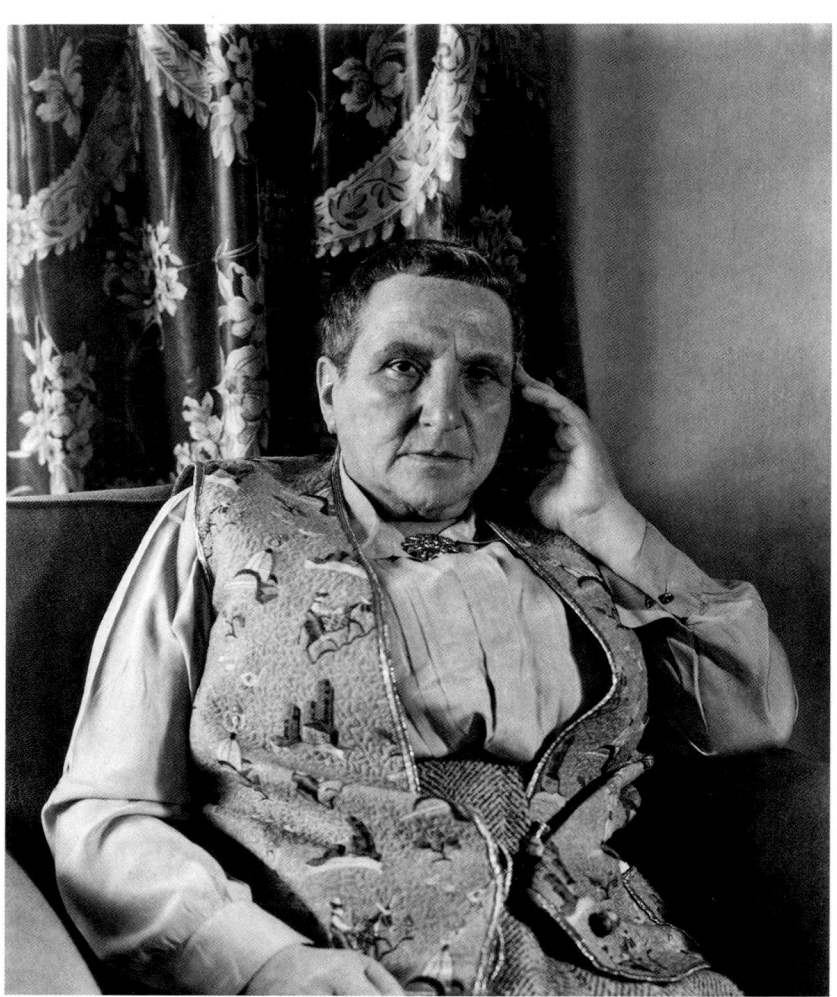

3.22 Imogen Cunningham, *Gertrude Stein, Writer*, 1935. Gelatin silver print, 9½ × 7¾ in. Collection of the Imogen Cunningham Trust.

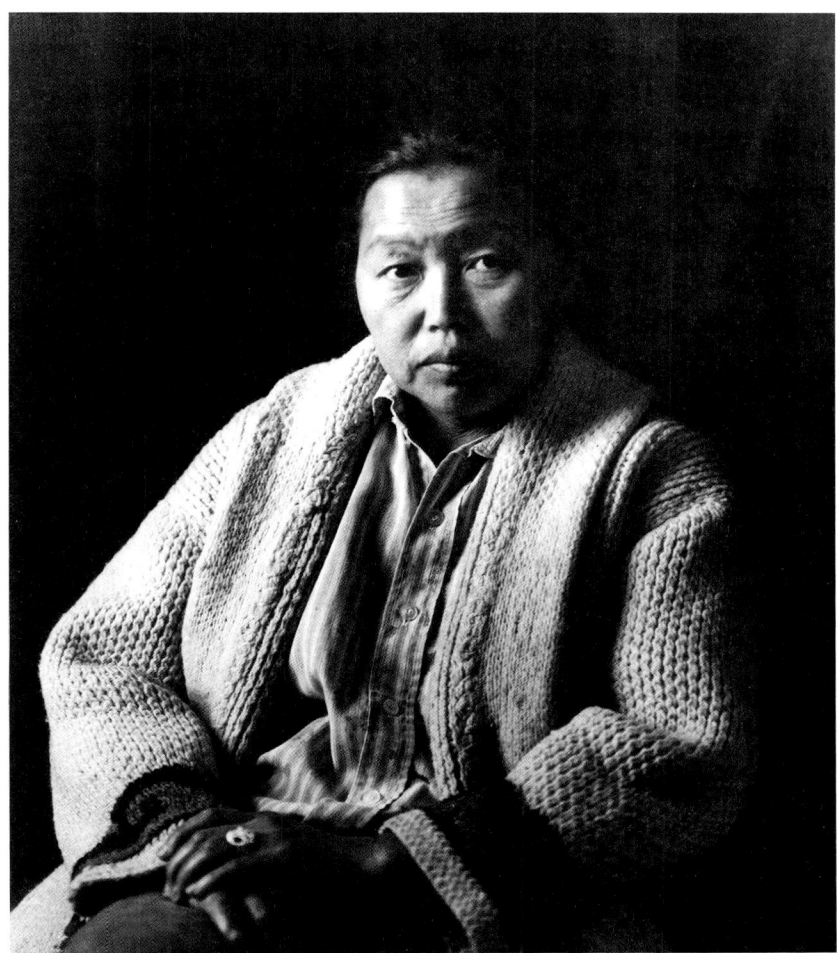

3.23 Imogen Cunningham, *Ruth Asawa*, 1975. Gelatin silver print, 9½ × 8 in. Collection of the Imogen Cunningham Trust.

feeling something."[58] Stein *works* language, twisting and turning words until they take on form and then another form and then a third form, and on it goes. Asawa did the same thing with wire, looping and twisting to create a surface that then extended into another surface intersecting with another surface, and so on. And then once she had exhausted the properties of wire, she went on to paper, then plaster, then concrete, etc. Both women severely limited their materials at any given moment in order to focus on what could be *done* with them.

Just as Stein exhaustively explored linguistic permutations, Asawa generated so many iterations that it is often difficult to tell one looped-wire sculpture from another—which is why her estate has had to affix elaborate descriptive titles in order to talk about specific works. This is an apparatus that attempts to rein in an artistic oeuvre that in fact outpaces those structures typically used to categorize and capture an artist's work for posterity. Delve into a catalogue of Asawa's work, and you will encounter "Untitled" ad infinitum. This is what one reader of Stein described as "a primary strategy of experimental art—doing the opposite of convention. If most writers strive for variety of expression, she would repeat certain words and phrases in numerous slightly differing clauses. ('It's not all repetition,' she once told a reporter. 'I always change the words a little.')"[59]

Cunningham, too, would have seen the direction of Asawa's reputation as paralleling what Stein experienced. For decades, Stein worked away while publisher after publisher refused her manuscripts. Asawa likewise went on making, even as her work rarely appeared in museums and galleries. While she received a short burst of nationwide recognition in the 1950s, once she determined to stay in San Francisco and be a mother as much as an artist, her shows were primarily local or regional. And, like Stein, this apparent marginalization was misleading, for both women continued to be highly visible within the specific context of the San Francisco Bay Area. Like Stein, Asawa called communities into being through the making of art, as she would go on to work tirelessly in the public sphere through the Alvarado School Arts Workshop and commissions such as the *San Francisco Fountain* with its hundreds of makers. Stein's impact on younger artists, both those whom she knew personally and those who read her work, was immense—an influence that has been cast in overessentializing maternal terms because of their status as women (with Stein called "the Totemic Mother of modern art," just as Imogen Cunningham has been called "the matriarch of American photography").[60] It is fitting that Cunningham cites her own work in drawing this parallel between two women separated by nearly fifty years in age. For citation is also a feminist strategy to wriggle out of those regimes of inheritance that exclude women artists. Mignon Nixon argues that Louise Bourgeois's challenge to "the Oedipal models of historical analysis" often deployed copying, turning to the invocation of "citation, mimicry, and parody to block the channel of influence"—all strategies that become overt in the twentieth century's later decades (Nixon cites the example of Sherrie Levine's appropriation of a photograph by Edward Weston of his nude son Neil from 1925).[61]

In this chapter, I have asked the reader to reconsider dominant models of artistic exchange and "influence" wherein artistic generation is "a matter of Oedipal rivalry and 'creative misreading,'" to cite again Lisa Tickner's summation of literary critic Harold Bloom. This is a picture of patrilineal genealogy, "a battle between strong equals, father and son as mighty opposites, Laius and Oedipus at the cross-roads," in which the Artist becomes nothing more than "an infantile idealization of the Oedipal Father."[62] The Asawa-Cunningham dialogue was not an instance of one-upmanship (à la Picasso and Braque), whose competitive terms are inevitably gendered. To recover the specificity of this exchange between two women and two mothers is to shift the terms from those of sexual difference to a paradigm of artistic exchange premised on an array of shared asymmetries—intergenerational, above all—that facilitated rather than stymied collaboration. It is to think through one's relationship to "elective" rather than "natural" mothers.[63] And although Asawa and Cunningham may have disagreed about what it meant to be an artist as a woman and a mother, they supported each other's work and reputations, generating one of the most important dialogues across sculpture and photography of the twentieth century.

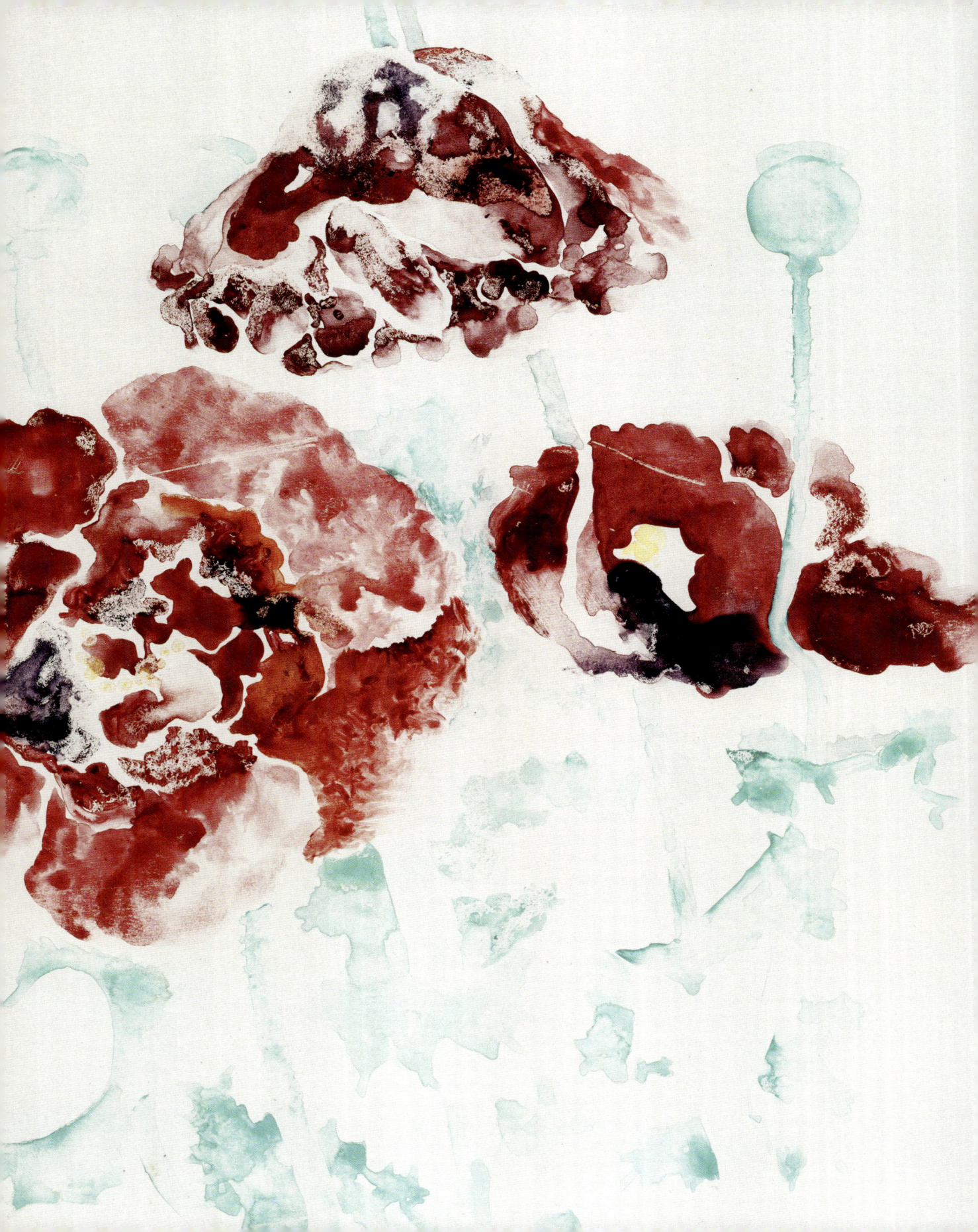

4 GROWTH

In Robert Snyder's film *Ruth Asawa: Of Forms and Growth* (1977), Asawa analogizes her own activity as an artist to the growth of plants: "When you put a seed in the ground, the ground doesn't say, well, in eight hours I'm going to stop growing. You put it in the soil and that bulb grows every second that it is attached to the earth. I think that every minute that we're attached to this earth, we should be doing something."[1] This was Asawa's understanding of artmaking: a continuous, ongoing endeavor that parallels the growth of a seed into a plant. And the artist often invoked farming, gardening, and plant life cycles as metaphors to describe her engagement as an artist. The comparison was not superficial: these insights drew on her own experience of having been raised on a farm in southern California, in which her parents worked twenty hours a day growing produce for sale, "stringing the bean pole for beans to climb up on and picking the beans and sorting the tomatoes, picking tomatoes, sowing and planting onions and gathering them," tasks that she also did while growing up. "All of these things make it very logical that I would select a way of work that would be very similar to that, only done in wire instead of plants."[2]

For Asawa, to create was to cultivate. This lifelong engagement was deeply invested in what Adrienne Rich would later describe as the mother's collective effort to place "the highest value on the development of human beings, on economic justice, on respect for racial, cultural, sexual, and ethnic diversity, on providing the material conditions for children to flower into responsible and creative women and men"—in short, mothering outside of both "the patriarchal State and the patriarchal family."[3] The growth of another human life and the growth of the natural world found common ground in the language of metaphor (which Rich also draws upon in describing this process of "flowering"). And yet this growth metaphor in the artist-mother's practice has gone untouched. Why? Because alignments of motherhood and nature historically have been deployed to neutralize and negate calls like Rich's and artistic activity like Asawa's. Even Robert Snyder, who had a deep and abiding respect for Asawa, fell prey to such reductions. His film effectively essentializes her as a child of Japanese immigrants, introducing her as a calligrapher and practitioner of tai chi (which she did do, but alongside many other things as well, which had nothing to do with her family background). As a result, her assigned identity in the film "as mother, teacher, woman of the earth" inadvertently reinscribes a long-standing collapse between femininity and nature.[4]

Produced under his company Masters and Masterworks and supported by his father-in-law, Buckminster Fuller, Snyder's "Ruth Asawa film" was to be a celebration of Asawa as a genius-like figure—in line with his other artist portraits (the most famous of which was his film on Michelangelo, whose title, *The Titan*, says it all).[5] Asawa, however, resisted this hagiography and had "insisted" that the film portray the Alvarado School Arts Workshop, which she and Sally Woodbridge had founded in 1968. Asawa saw Snyder's film and its distribution as an opportunity to make the Workshop available at a national level to other school districts considering forming similar programs that would bring together parents, artists, teachers, and children.[6] (In the end, the film devoted only eight out of twenty-eight minutes to the Workshop.) This is all to say that although Snyder understood the importance of nature for Asawa's understanding as an artist, he entirely missed the point. For Asawa looked to nature not as a universalizing force for the further mythologization of the artist, but as a model of how to put one's own ego aside; how, as she explains in the film, to "become background, just like a parent allows the child to express himself and the parent becomes supportive."

This chapter takes a long-overdue look at the complex and ambivalent alignment between the artist-mother and nature. In particular, it takes up an engagement with flowers and plants across the work of Asawa, Imogen Cunningham, Merry Renk, and the photographer Phiz Mezey, arguing that such imagery cannot be understood outside of an account of motherhood in midcentury art. In Asawa's work, she engaged with such organic subjects in detailed drawings—often committing gifted bouquets of flowers to paper—but also as intricate abstract structures both on paper and in wire. This engagement with plants and flowers circulated, moreover, in a broader discursive landscape where references to nature served as powerful metaphors to describe artistic practice. These were both self-ascribed metaphors, as in her use of the phrase "a way of growing" to describe her work's formation, but also a set of references brought to bear on the work as part of its reception.[7] In what follows, I consider how these references operated differently for the artist-mother than they did for her male counterparts, whose work was celebrated for its ability to transcend representation and become like nature itself. In addition, I discuss a more recent language of biology and botanicals in Asawa's reception, posing the question of how we are to understand this alignment with nature today. I conclude the chapter by returning to the circumstances of gift-giving and suggest some ways in which we can understand this imagery outside of metaphorical language.

MOTHER'S DAY FLOWERS

In the Western pictorial tradition, the representation of flowers in isolation has usually taken one of two forms: botanical illustrations and still lifes. Botanical illustration, the older of the two, dates at least to Pliny, who reflected on the accurate representation of the natural world, but it gained momentum in the early modern era, with its faith in the precept that all that can be seen can also be known. Sheets of opaque gouache and watercolor on vellum served up to the viewer fantastically detailed inventories of each specimen. The whole of the plant would typically be presented, including roots, stem, leaves, flowers, fruit, seeds, and even pests and diseases. Illustrators went to elaborate lengths to include the various phases of the plant at different seasons, at pollination versus budding and so on. The reproductive organs of the flower—the anther and filament of the stamen and the stigma, style, and ovary of the pistil—are clearly distinguished from the corolla of petals. All this is conveyed in true-to-life color and very often on a bare page, devoid of context, an effect that "paradoxically," as art historian Heather MacDonald writes, serves to underscore the illustration's claim of scientific objectivity, as it "seems to be almost a 'real' botanical specimen, freshly cut from the plant and presented to us on a clean, white sheet of paper."[8]

The still-life approach to representing flowers has less to do with empirical knowledge. Perfected by the Dutch and Netherlandish painters of the seventeenth century, floral still lifes offer a wide range of symbols and allegories. They reflect on the relationship of art to life and life to death through a cosmos of philosophical and religious references, and often serve to remind the viewer of his or her mortality. Historian Paul Taylor describes the association of floral imagery with the transience of existence as one of "the commonest metaphorical clichés of the [seventeenth] century."[9] A floral still life is an arrangement to be deciphered, and it renders the self-sufficiency of the botanical specimen reliant on a human interpreter. As such these pictures do not claim objectivity for their subjects. Even if individual flowers are depicted with the precision of a horticulturalist, the arrangements portray imagined bouquets of flowers that bloom in different seasons. In the history of art, moreover, floral imagery has long stood as proxy for the female body, as "the flower/woman metaphor," and often attends historical moments of social transformation, as evidenced by the transformation of women into floral landscapes in painting as part of an era that witnessed a shift from Victorian femininity to the New Woman of the early twentieth century.[10]

Enter Ruth Asawa, who closely observed flowers of all kinds, from bouquets to cuttings from the garden to potted plants. With sketchbooks filled with delicate line drawings as well as large sheets of watercolors depicting flowers, blossoms, their fruit—watermelons and persimmons—and leaves, Asawa keenly examined the natural world around her. Many of these drawings were made of flowers and plants from her spacious garden at the Noe Valley home that the family moved into in 1961, "a unique space—very mysterious—kind of a folk garden but with very sentimental plants, wisteria, roses, fuchsias, bleeding-heart, rosemary and columbine and iris," according to Albert Lanier.[11] This garden was as much hers as it was his, with cuttings and bouquets functioning both as portraits of individual species, but also portraits of relationships cultivated over the decades.

Asawa's approach to floral imagery, in other words, falls into neither of these two categories. The elaborate line drawings, almost always contour descriptions void of modeling and shadow, give us the plant in stark outline form at the moment of observation—that is to say without the convention of portraying multiple moments of its life cycle on a single sheet. They have an illustrative quality, with certain details faithfully recorded while many others are left out. Very often, leaves are rendered without their veins, showing only their outer edges and midrib. The repetition of certain shapes, found in the plant itself, is more interesting for her, it would seem, than any botanical information pointing to specificity and uniqueness. Void of chiaroscuro and very often void of color, these arrangements are a far cry from both botanical illustrations and allegorical flowers. Even on the rare occasion when an element that could be read as allegorical enters the frame, as is the case of a lone snail crawling up a stem in *Adam's Ranunculus* (P.F.1107; 1999), such elements function most strongly as compositional rather than allegorical elements, in this case extending a bottom arc suggested by the rest of the arrangement.

Such flower drawings would seem to suggest a third genre to the pairing introduced above, a genre of floral depictions that is dependent upon the ritual of gift-giving. An oft-overlooked aspect of these sheets is that they were often made after Asawa had received the flowers as a gift, bestowed by a family member or friend to commemorate a birthday or to mark Mother's Day. In one sketchbook, Asawa has depicted three bouquets that she received for Mother's Day in May 1995, alongside an arrangement of calendula, geranium, iris, and Greek oregano from Catherine Sneed and a potted orchid from Barbara Kowalcyk and Stephanie MacColl (gifted on March 2, but drawn on May 19, Asawa inscribes). As an acknowledgment of the gesture, it would appear that Asawa drew her gift and diligently recorded the gift-giver and the date in a simple inscription—an inscription that serves as this work's title: *Adam's Fox-glove Mother's Day* (fig. 4.1). Similarly, *Untitled* (P.F.293, Bouquet from Anni Albers; c. 1990s) marks the gift of an elaborate flower arrangement from the textile artist, while a sheet delineating dahlias and foxgloves in a pitcher was given to the art historians Karin Higa and Sally Stein as a thank-you for having brought the flowers during their visit to interview the artist in 2001. The visit would inform Higa's essay on Asawa, published a year later, which was the first attempt to reflect critically on the relationship between Asawa's multidimensional identity, including her status as an Asian American woman, and a body of work that spanned figuration and abstraction.[12]

These gift-giving rituals were not limited to flower drawings. The art historian Helen Molesworth points to a twice-over inscribed drawing of Asawa's eldest grandson, Ken, napping with her husband, Albert, his grandfather. Asawa had initially dated and inscribed that drawing with the names of both sitters. Six years later, she pulled it out again, but this time to give it as a gift to Ken's mother, Asawa's daughter Aiko: "Happy Mother's Day, Aiko. 5/12/1985." The sheet thus embodies a moment of intimate observation in 1978, with the artist beholding her sleeping husband and grandchild; in

4.1 Ruth Asawa, *Adam's Foxglove Mother's Day* (PF.846), May 9, 1993. Black ink on watercolor paper, 22¼ × 16 in. Private collection.

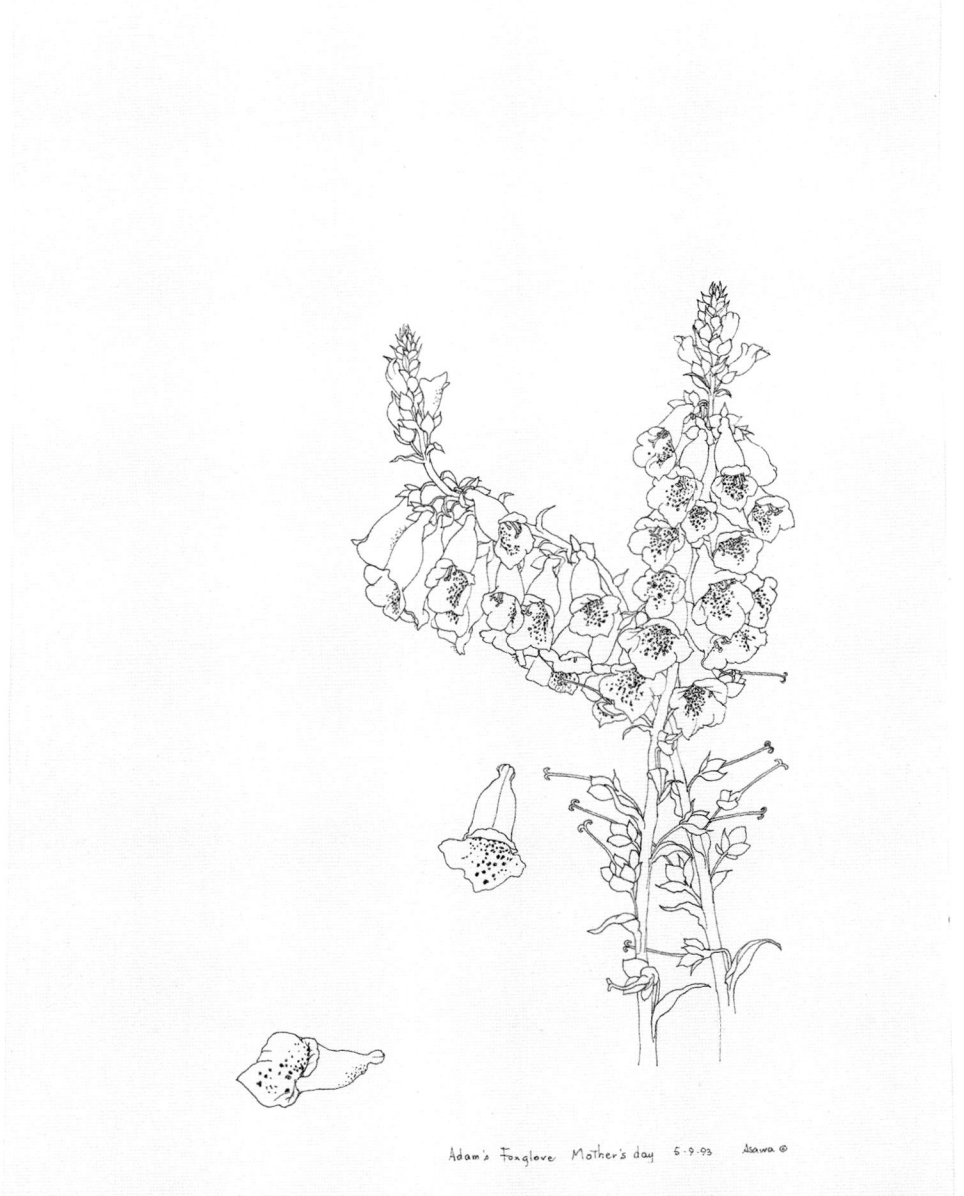

Adam's Foxglove Mother's day 5-9-93 Asawa ©

1985, the sheet encodes a gesture of love from mother to daughter—a gesture echoed in the daughter's father pictured in a tender moment with his daughter's child.[13] Gift-giving also marked the relationships of other artist-mothers with their children, family, and friends. In conversation with me, Merry Renk's daughter, Baunnie, pointed out how the giving of jewelry often served to mark momentous occasions, like getting a cast off and starting her period. Renk gave her daughter homemade dolls, while Baunnie had also received handmade storybooks from Asawa's children, with the giving of illustrated books constituting a tradition of sorts.[14]

These sheets are almost always inscribed—a profound departure from Asawa's practice of not titling her work—and were almost always made in the space of a single day or a few hours (thus having a temporality akin to sketching). In *Laurie Happy Birthday* (1991), Asawa marks her daughter's thirty-third birthday through the gift of a watercolor of red poppies (fig. 4.2). Many of these floral images are made either with ink on paper or watercolor on a coated paper, so that the color pools to create a terrain of its own, swathes of color that have little to do with mimesis. Just as Asawa approached line through the eye of design, she approached color as a former student of Josef Albers, interested above all in color's relativity, its visual relationships, and its interaction with other colors.

4.2 Ruth Asawa, *Laurie Happy Birthday* (WC.282, Four Red Opium Poppies and Pods), 1991. Watercolor paint on coated paper, 12 × 10½ in. Private collection.

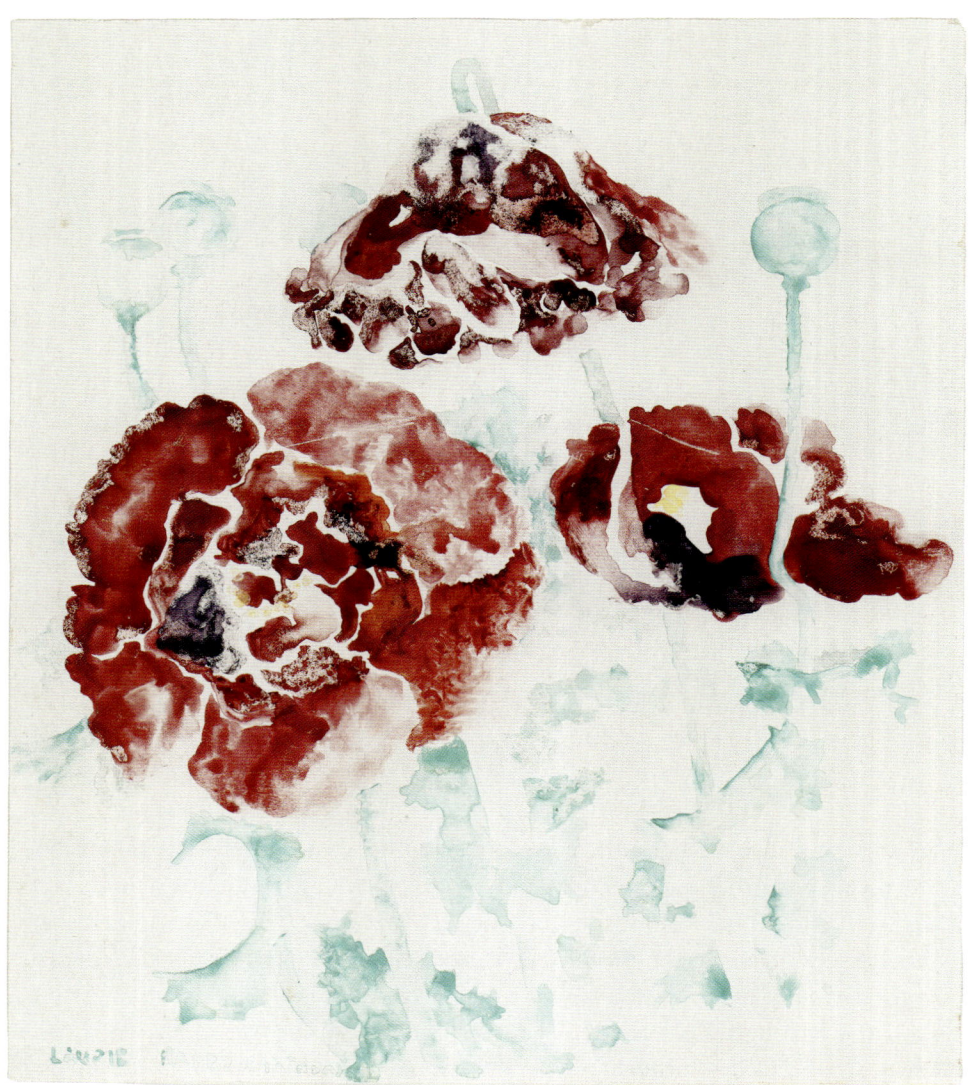

As concrete expressions of social bonds, these flower drawings and watercolors were answered in kind. Created the same year as this watercolor, Beth Van Hoesen's *Albert's Poppies* (1991) takes up the same subject (fig. 4.3). It is a vibrant aquatint etching that allowed her to create a gradated orange ground combined with the red and black of the corolla and spindly green stems. The flower is represented four times, each from a slightly different vantage point but all at the moment, it would seem, before the petals fall. "Albert" in this instance is very likely Asawa's husband, who had raised and cared for these poppies. The drawing is thus a reflection on care and friendship, with red poppies themselves standing for "cure," according to Kate Greenaway's Victorian-era classic *The Language of Flowers* (1884). Such an orientation is far from visually similar representations of flowers, such as the gridded blooms in Andy Warhol's iconic *Flowers* paintings of the 1960s. Whereas Warhol invokes flowers for their banal decorative character to reflect, in turn, on imagery of all kinds as potentially void of substantive meaning, *Albert's Poppies* and *Laurie Happy Birthday* stand much closer to something like an affirmative genre of flower imagery which nevertheless holds critical potential—a point to which I will return.

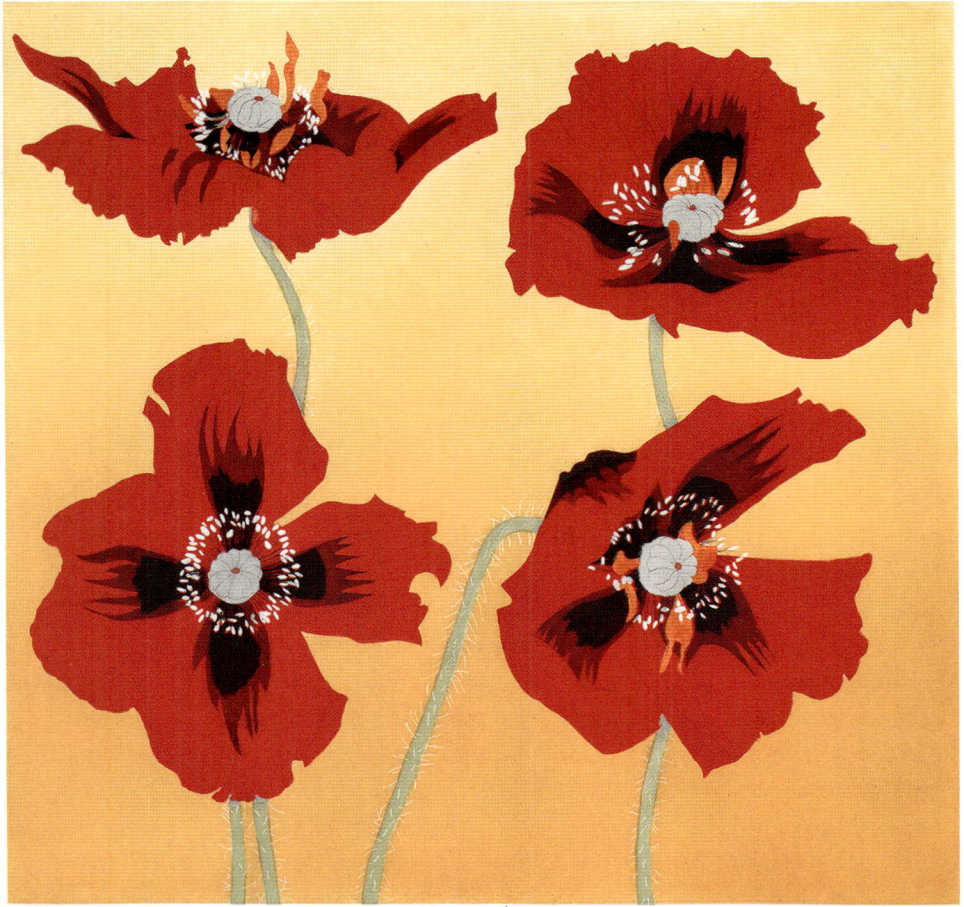

4.3 Beth Van Hoesen, *Albert's Poppies*, 1991. Color aquatint, etching, and drypoint, hand-colored with watercolor and gouache on moderately thick, moderately textured white wove paper, plate: 16 × 16⅝ in.; sheet: 23⅛ × 22¾ in. Photo: M. Lee Fatherree.

"POTS AND POTTIES"

I opened this chapter with the rituals of gift-giving through flower drawings in order to foreground how the artist-mother's engagement with seemingly neutral media was far more complex than we have thus far recognized. These artist-mothers took a detailed rendering of nature seriously at a moment in the history of modern art when Nature, writ large, meant metaphor, analogy, archetypes, and sublime landscapes—and very rarely observational drawing or as bound up with relations of gift-giving. Asawa recalled how Josef Albers only barely tolerated her preference for drawing flowers over abstract designs when she was his student at Black Mountain College, imploring her to "just make sure they are Asawa flowers"—making the same request when she expressed her intention to start a family: "you make babies, that is your art. Be sure to make them Asawas."[15]

This was the modernist injunction: to abstract from nature as a strategy of making the work of art more real, more *present*, than a simple collection of inert materials. At times, Asawa fulfilled this injunction, foregrounding plants and flowers as placeholders for a modernist engagement with one's materials and medium as an artist. *Laurie Happy Birthday* gestures to this interest, with a relationship between depiction and color that only barely suggests "poppy." In a series based on San Francisco's plane trees, she created modulated pools of ink and watercolor, abstracting these organic forms with the materials used to render them representational, and in doing so, she followed a familiar strategy of modernism. This was a strategy claimed, for instance, by Georgia O'Keeffe in her effort, as Anne M. Wagner writes, "to sever watercolor from simple bodily description," which "seems ultimately at least as powerful as the impulse toward embodiment, to make bodies that are vividly *there*."[16] Even in her effort to render natural forms with precision and resemblance, capturing the fracturing of light caused by the waterline in a vase of flowers, we have the sense that what matters is precisely this short-circuiting of depiction in order to elicit the viewer's attention to the rupture between line and form.

At the same time, Asawa, Cunningham, and their fellow artist-mothers admitted that the depiction of plants and flowers followed in large part from the conditions of their circumstances as homebound caretakers: "The reason during the '20s that I photographed plants was that I had three children under the age of four to take care of so I was cooped up. I had a garden available and I photographed them indoors," Cunningham reflected.[17] Teasing Ansel Adams for allowing the coffee company Hills Bros. to use one of his photographs of Yosemite Valley on its collectible coffee cans, Cunningham sent him one of the cans filled with dirt and a marijuana plant with the note: "Dear Ansel: With the idea that you might now begin collecting these pots, I am sending you one with a plant often mountain grown. As you must know, pots and potties have always been my specialty. Love, Imogen."[18] Cunningham's joke here points to the central difference in play when an artist like Ansel Adams takes up the representation of nature, in the form of vast, sublime vistas, as opposed to the artist-mother whose turn to plants and flowers is delimited by her circumstances, her identification with a domesticated nature in the form of potted plants, and a routine of caretaking ("potties" being shorthand for potty training).

The horticulturalist Mai Arbegast recalled how Cunningham first became interested in plants when she was at Mills College and met a professor who had done research on California and Pacific Coast trees. Arbegast would help Cunningham prune the clematis and brought plants over, including the Else Frye rhododendron, named after a childhood friend in Seattle, which "pleased her to have a plant named for someone she knew. Every plant was personal to her, and she cared very much where it was placed in the garden, and how it looked in every season of the year. The funny little plants on the porch, the bougainvillea that was held together with twistings from vegetables, the fig tree, that Mexican mock orange that was rather homely but had such a beautiful fragrance as you came up the steps—they were part of her."[19] Cunningham even had a geranium plant that she had brought over as a cutting from Virginia Woolf's garden in England.

Cunningham's approach to plants and flowers was to convey them in stunning detail, often foregrounded against a black ground (fig. 4.4). Arbegast described Cunningham's plant photographs as "terribly scientific, but at the same time, because they are so clear we really get to the heart of the plant, the gutsiness of the flower. She showed the general placement of the leaves in the cactus, or the relationship of the petals of a flower—that's scientific, but at the same time it's beautiful. The line, the way the flower is placed, the lights and darks—that goes beyond what a scientist would see."[20] The photographs are a form of botanical imagery, but one that is less devoted to narrating the species than to portraying its dramatic features at a single moment in its life cycle. The star of Persia in full bloom, for instance, bears six-part petals that remarkably resemble the formal language of both Asawa and Renk. Cunningham moreover chooses to depict the flower at the end of its life cycle, once its thin petals have fallen and it has begun to go to seed.

When invited to participate as a resident artist at the Tamarind Lithography Workshop in Los Angeles in September and October 1965—the first time she worked away from home since starting a family in 1950 (indeed she had never been away for more than four days)—Asawa took many of her flower sketches with her and experimented with how they might look when translated to the medium of lithography. During that residency, she transformed a number of her flower drawings in this other medium, transcribing their original ink or watercolor appearance in lithographic ink. This includes her magisterial stony blue and red *Poppy* (1965), whose petals are outlined by the absence of ink, but also chrysanthemums, succulents, Easter lilies, irises, hydrangeas, and marigolds. Ten of these compose the portfolio *Flowers* (1965), which Asawa had printed and bound in an edition of twenty, with the individual sheets at times abstracting dramatically from her subject, while others stay closer to a detailed rendering of contour and shape.

One of Asawa's most remarkable flower works in this series would seem to be no flower at all: its title reads *Desert Flower*, and yet a close inspection of its form reveals that its structure is far too regular and symmetrical to be a depiction of organic

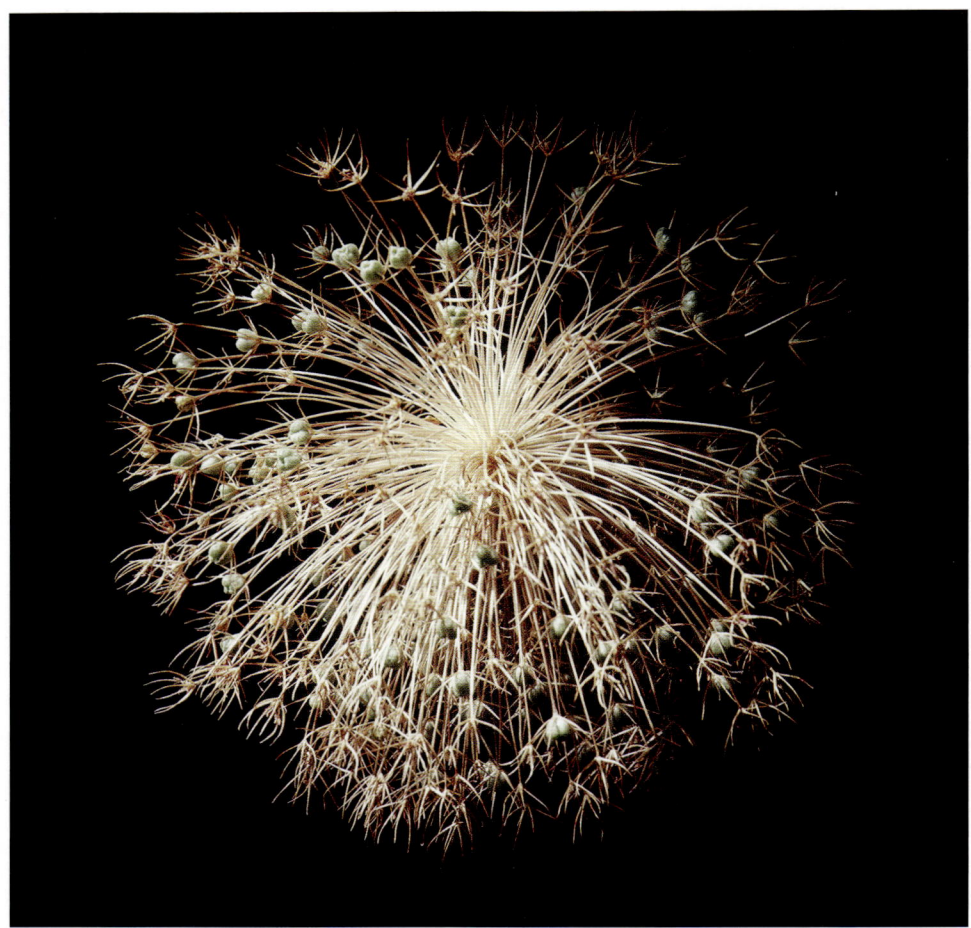

4.4 Imogen Cunningham, *Fireworks Plant*, 1965.
Gelatin silver print, 9½ × 9 in. Collection of the
Imogen Cunningham Trust.

matter (fig. 4.5). Her approach to *Desert Flower* extends visual interests that had long preoccupied the artist: transparency and reversibility. In one case, she additionally subjected the image to a reversal treatment, such that the linear elements become white against a black ground. In another, she printed on both sides of the thin paper, so that the transparency of the paper also plays a role in activating the linear elements. Asawa had proposed printing on both sides of the paper during her introductory talk at Tamarind, in which she presented drawings that she wanted to use in printmaking. June Wayne greeted the idea with enthusiasm, immediately recognizing Asawa's tendency to work with principles of reversibility in her drawing practice.[21]

Desert Flower is special because of the deliberately strange gulf in meaning opened up when we consider the work's title in dialogue with what we see, for the image resembles no recognizable plant. It is an abstract circular arrangement of branching lines radiating from a central point and becoming progressively smaller as they reach the edge of the paper. Indeed, this "flower" is no flower but rather a two-dimensional description of Asawa's tied-wire sculptural technique. This was a technique that she explored as much in two-dimensional form as she did in wire. Hundreds of drawing sheets bear these branching lines. These compositions typically begin with a thicker central intersection, or sometimes an open center comprising multiple adjacent bunches, which then become progressively thinner as they move from the center of the paper out toward its edges; almost all of these sheets portray marks that reach to these outer limits, as if they could continue to branch out in ever smaller dividing nodes.

This was a technique that Asawa introduced into her work beginning in 1962. In a letter to her former Black Mountain instructor Josef Albers, she recounted the process of gathering and dividing. Her enthusiasm around the "new sculpture" is palpable:

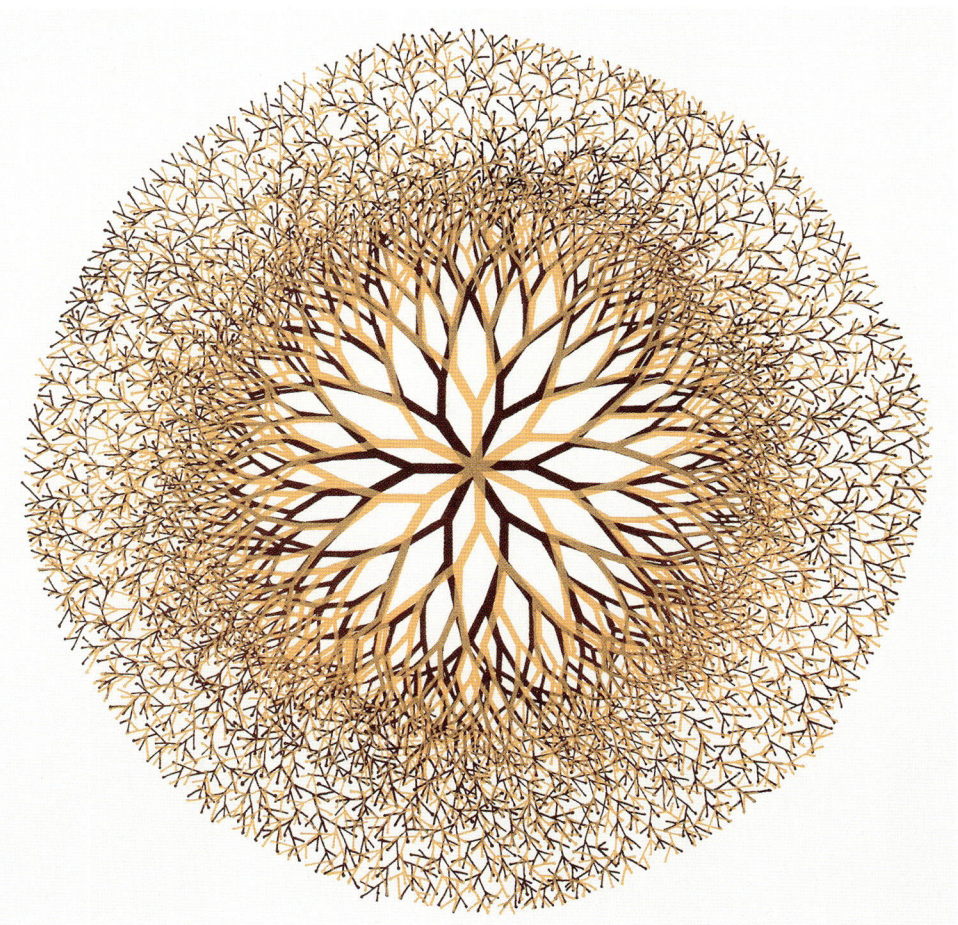

4.5 Ruth Asawa, *Desert Flower* (TAM.1460-II), October 21–22, 1965. Lithograph, brown and orange ink on paper, 18½ × 18½ in. Private collection.

4.6 Ruth Asawa, *Untitled* (S.052, Hanging Tied-Wire, Double-Sided, Center-Tied, Multi-Branched Form Based on Nature), 1965. Galvanized steel wire, 34 × 39 × 39 in. Private collection.

"It is very exciting, for example: I have 1000 strands of wire in a bundle; I divide them into 3 bunches of 333 strands. Each bunch is divided again and again until two strands are left. I tie each joint with the same wire, so there is no solder used. My tool is a pair of plyers that will cut and twist the wire. The variations are endless."[22] Variation as a principle of artmaking was an approach close to Albers's own. In his series *Homage to the Square*, the German artist essentially used the same procedure; instead of metal, he worked with color, and instead of dividing strands, he used the format of the square to organize these various color combinations. It was a mode of composition predicated not on epiphany or spontaneity—much less individual "expression"—but rather on rule-based tasks: in Asawa's case, mathematical division combined with the requirement that she introduce no new material into the composition, thus twisting the wire onto itself in order to secure groupings.

The principles of reversal and reflection played an important role in her formal development of this technique, as the tied-wire compositions evolved into ever more complex permutations. These could be bilaterally symmetrical or based on a cross or star form; at other times, she took a single form but then doubled it or mirrored its structure, so as to create interlocking centers, sometimes with multiple such centers in a single work. What was perceived later by observers and by the artist herself as

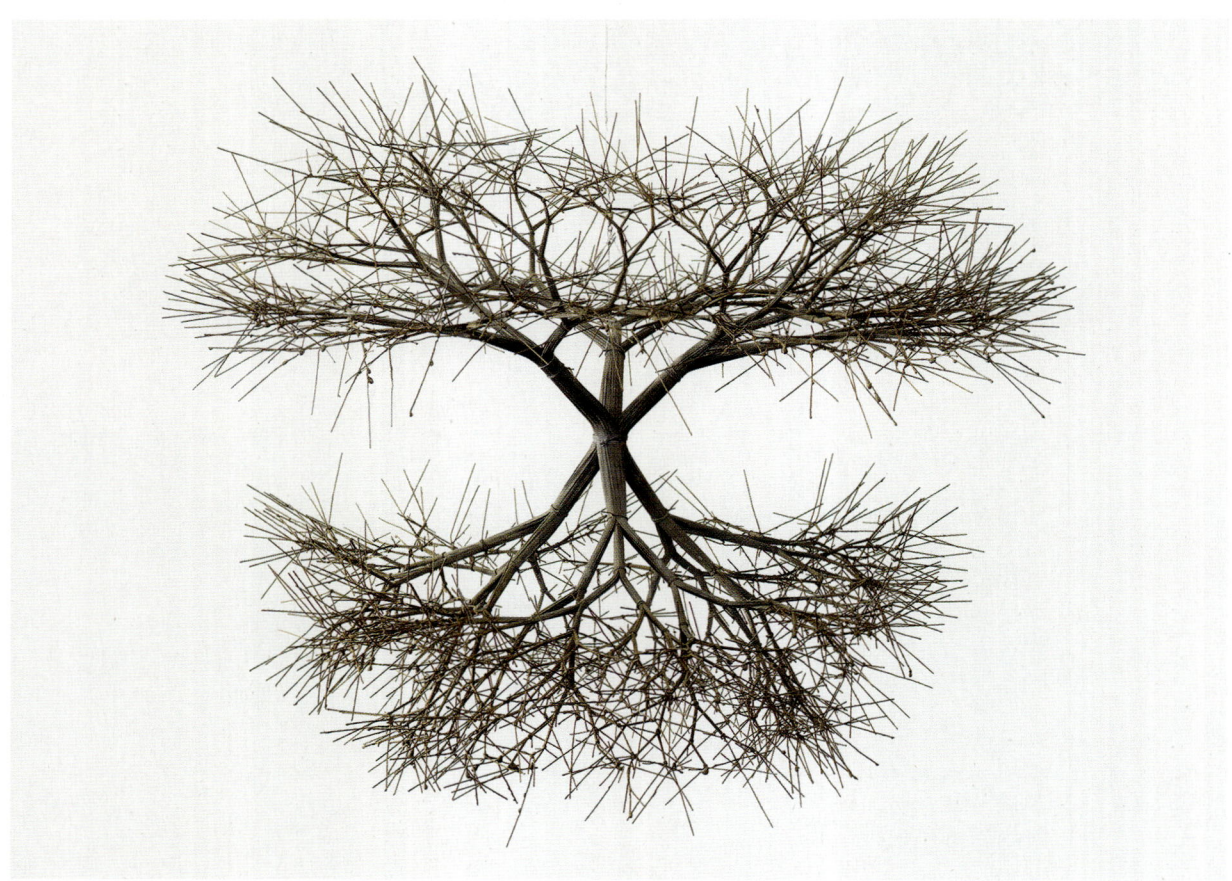

mimetic form (e.g., a branching tree or a root system) thus originated out of a concern with the abstract processes of division and replication. These permutations included examples doubled-sided, center-tied, and with an open center that could be either single- or double-sided. Additional changes involved how the sculptures were displayed, whether hung, wall-mounted, or stood upright on a base of driftwood or the salvaged wooden patterns that I mention at the beginning of chapter 3 (see also fig. 4.9). Asawa further developed the tied-wire forms by subjecting them to additional processes like casting, even at times flattening this three-dimensional form into relief.

Asawa consistently located her interest in this formal procedure in a close study of natural forms. Indeed, when late in life she began cataloguing her work, devising descriptive titles for her many untitled sculptures, she used the phrase "based on nature" to describe her tied-wire sculptures. A good example is the center-tied, double-sided *Untitled* (S.052; 1965): Asawa thought of the top part as branches and the bottom as roots, with the two mirroring one another (fig. 4.6).[23] Asawa nurtured this close association between artmaking and natural forms in her frequently told story of how she first arrived at the tied-wire forms: as a consequence of having been given a desert plant by the photographer Paul Hassel and his wife, Irene Hassel. As relayed by Gerald Nordland in the catalogue of the artist's first retrospective,

The gift of a desert plant to the Lanier family had the effect of influencing a whole new direction in Ruth Asawa's sculpture. She tried to draw the plant and found that somehow she couldn't understand how it worked and therefore she wasn't able to get her hand to describe the plant's structure. In an effort to understand the manner in which the plant had grown, Asawa took some wire, formed it into six bundles in parallel, tied the bundles into a root like a trunk and separated each discrete bundle into its own line of force, tracing the structure of the plant and its complex branchings. She then returned to the plant and found that she could draw its complex growth system.[24]

Just as she located the origins of this technique in her attempt to draw a desert plant, Asawa regarded these forms as resembling nature when she began to catalogue this vast collection of untitled objects. "Trees" were created from placement on wooden bases, while imagery of "trees" plus their "roots"—the two branching systems mirroring one another—emerge from those tied-wire works that extend both upward and downward.

Renk, too, drew on branching form as a structural pattern. Beginning in the early 1960s, around the same time that Asawa began exploring tied wire, Renk introduced clusters of six-pointed shapes into her formal language. This is one of the many structural developments that Joan Pearson Watkins identifies in Renk's work, a phase born of experimentation with specific technical and stylistic elements, but typically building on previous formal investigations (in this case, her "atomic" forms of the 1950s).[25] Renk explored these forms across jewelry, scaled to the human body, but also in both small- and large-scale sculptures, which she increasingly turned to when she lost sight in one eye in 1967. Working in larger formats—some of her sculptures are seven feet high—allowed her to keep producing.[26] In one example, *Sixes* (1976), about thirteen inches in diameter, she has soldered copper wire together to create a tangled, spiky form, whose internal coherence is difficult to parse (fig. 4.7).

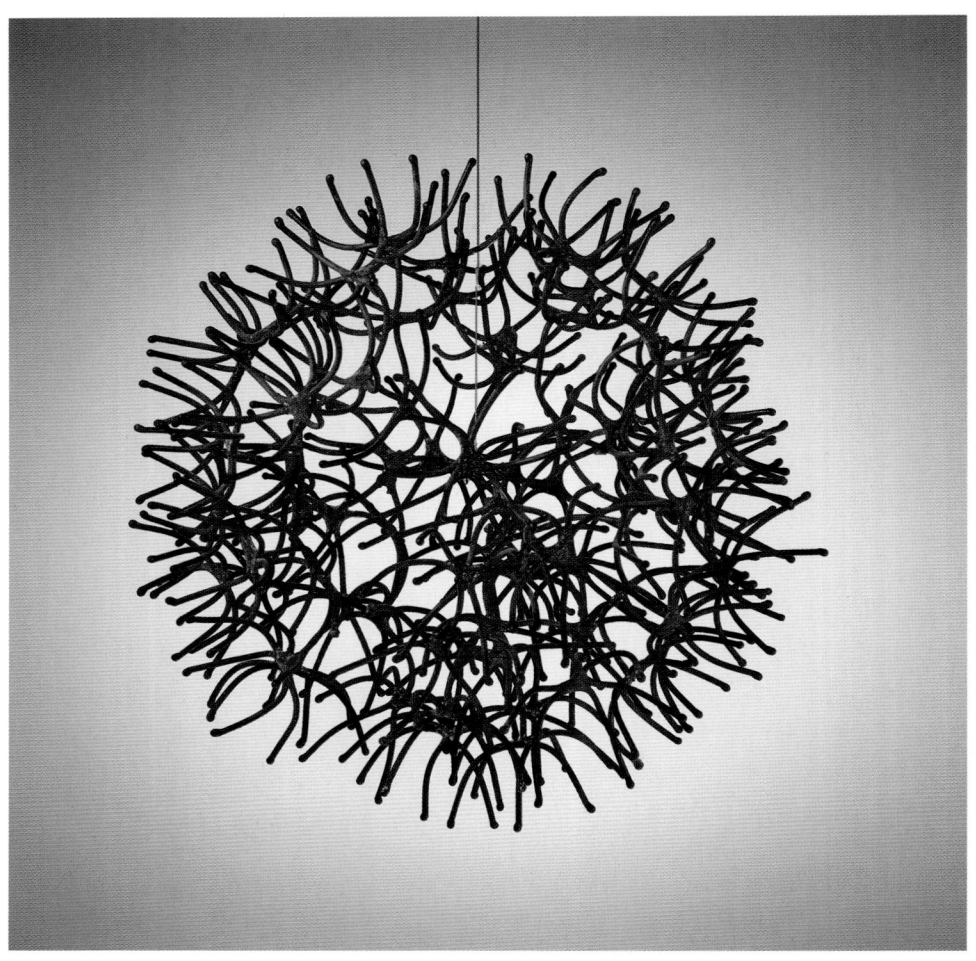

4.7 Merry Renk, *Sixes*, 1976. Soldered copper wire, diam. 13½ in. Collection of Forrest L. Merrill. Photo: M. Lee Fatherree.

According to Renk's visual inventory of her work, in which each piece is graphically depicted alongside a description of the kind of object ("ring," for instance), materials, date, title, and owner, we see how she adapted this branching form to her jewelry.[27] Both jewelry and tied wire structured themselves according to this principle of division and expansion. *Opal Branch* (1963), owned by Sally Woodbridge, is a pendant of gold and four opals, distributed in a way that upends the jeweler's convention of centering the stone (fig. 4.8). Asawa had a similar pendant, the sterling silver *Spark* (1963), which would appear to be a version of one of her hanging tied-wire sculptures in miniature. Renk titled these pieces of jewelry as if they were artworks: *Clover* (1963), a sterling silver earring, owned by Sally Woodbridge; *Starburst* (1960), an adaption of *Sixes* to sterling silver, owned by Beth Van Hoesen; and *Branching* (1967), a comb of sterling silver and pearls, owned by Joan Pearson Watkins.

Both Renk and Asawa repeatedly employed lines with small nodules at their tips; one sees this clearly in Asawa's drawings, as in *Desert Flower*, but also in the sculptures themselves. To create this effect, Asawa turned to electroplating, which she had first encountered as an industrial process deployed in auto repair. She quickly recognized its potential, when the process was reversed, for creating a new kind of surface quality on her wire. This involved coating the wire with a plastic resin, creating an encrusted surface or delicate droplets, depending on the treatment, which then reflected light. Asawa claimed that she drew on her observation of "garden droplets of water clinging to the tops of pine needles," according to Nordland, who described this comparison as "explod[ing] her mesh medium into a wire metaphor of natural growth from foliage and floral forms."[28]

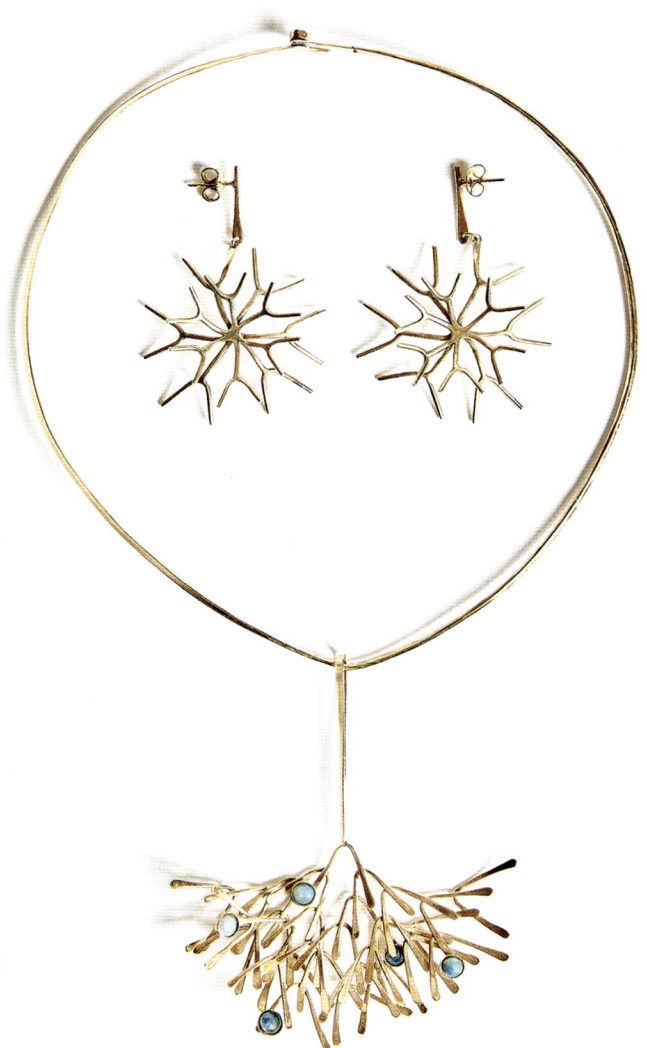

4.8 Merry Renk, *Opal Branch*, 1963. 14k gold with opals, 8 × 4¾ in. Shown with Renk, *Snowflake*, 1958. 14k gold, 1¾ × 1 in. Collection of Pamela Woodbridge. Photo: James Paonessa.

In Western art history, flower imagery and its genre—still life—rank the lowest in terms of respect and renown. "And in the institution of criticism, still life is to this day generally undiscussed," wrote Norman Bryson in 1990; "no theoretical body of work exists at a level of sophistication comparable to that found in contemporary discussions of history painting or landscape."[29] Bryson goes on to argue that encoded in this hierarchy is a gendered definition of the pictorial space generated by still life and genre scenes. Characterized by framing devices that posit the viewer as someone outside, looking *in*, onto these estranged interiors, such spaces are figured as feminized, alien to a male gaze. They are, as he describes them, spaces of the uncanny—spaces that would appear at first to be familiar but are, on closer examination, unnerving in their hyperrealism and vernacular detail.

Bryson marshals Freud's uncanny, and specifically his claim that in order to come into one's own subjectivity, one must turn away from the intimacy of the mother's body, from maternal nourishment and warmth, both literal and figurative. It is to move from total cohesion into "a space that is definitively and assuredly *outside*, behind a protective barrier, a space where the process of identification with the masculine can begin and can succeed."[30] Is that the space posited outside the frame of Imogen Cunningham's portrait of Asawa, kneeling among her sculptures (fig. 4.9)? A sign would point to the affirmative, insofar as Cunningham has mobilized here all the characteristic attributes of genre painting, especially its seventeenth-century Dutch iteration in which a female figure is sited in a domestic space. This figure is almost always accompanied by a window, whose light we can see, but whose vista we cannot. Patterned flooring marks off the gulf between looker and sitter, and all around the interior space we behold the attributes of a household. This is a space of attraction, offering up a wealth of detail, and yet it is also a space of alienation. Bryson writes: "The debt which the male painter of still life owes to the maternal enclosure is felt in an aesthetic practice which through and across secondary representation (the founding of signs, including the signs of painting) touches on the primal repression of the mother's body."[31]

It would seem that precisely because of this repression, Asawa, Renk, and Cunningham turned all the more decisively to the still life as a genre, and, more specifically, to floral imagery. The addition of bases—including a turned wooden object meant to evoke a vase in Renk's case and similarly rounded wooden patterns for molds which Asawa employed for her tied-wire "trees"—marks these works off from the space of the viewer (figs. 4.10, 4.11). What would seem to be a purposeful regression from the modernist abandonment of the sculptural base is here turned on its head to reassert these works as definitively not of the viewer's (masculinized) realm. In reinscribing this outside, the works partake explicitly of the "maternal enclosure" described by Bryson: they declaratively reassert "that cocoon and its fascinations"—"the mother as site of imaginary plenitude"—which Freud insisted must be abandoned.

4.9 Imogen Cunningham, *Ruth in Her Dining Room with Tied-Wire Sculptures*, 1963. Gelatin silver print, 9½ × 7¾ in. Collection of the Imogen Cunningham Trust.

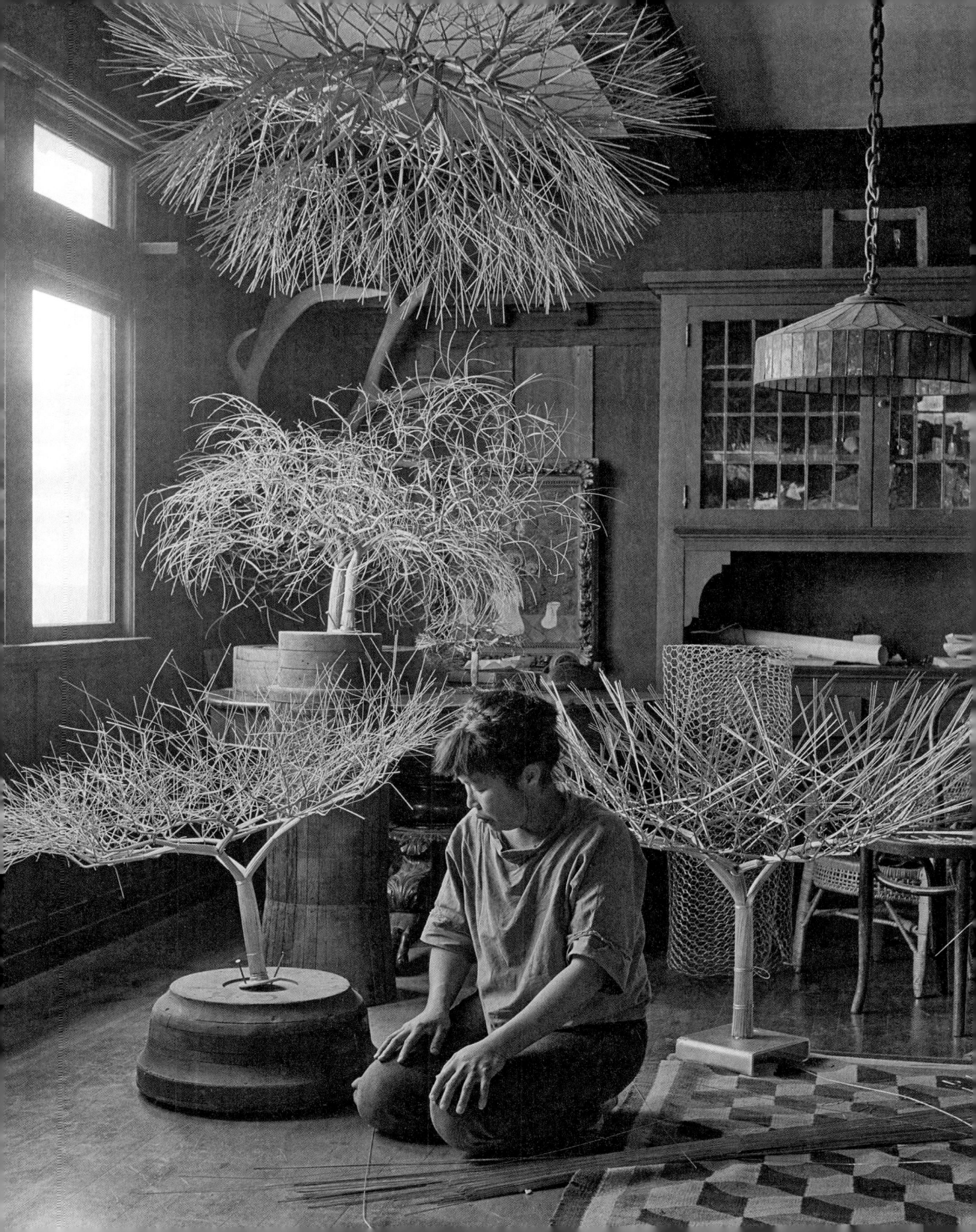

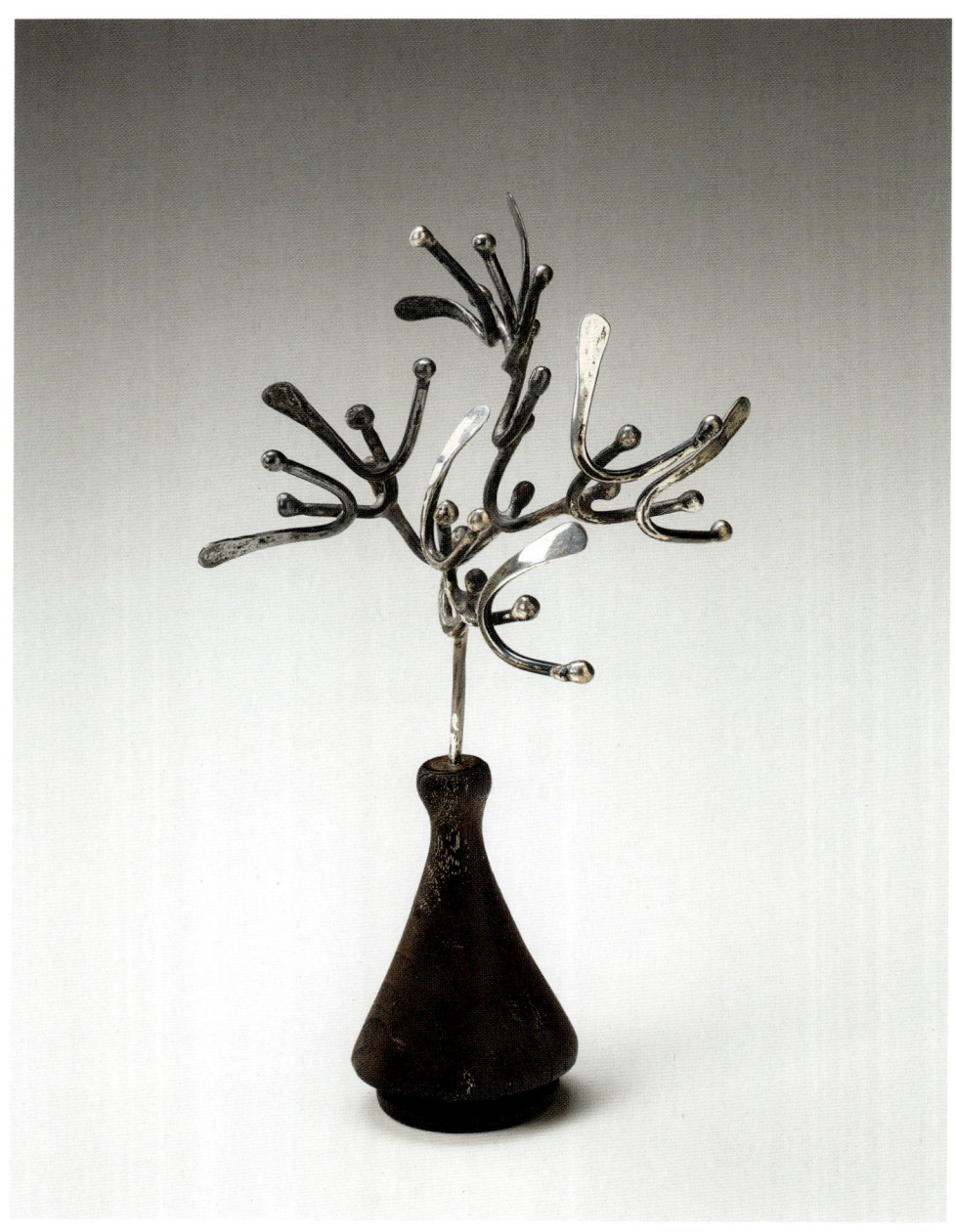

4.10 Merry Renk, *Untitled*, 1960. Soldered
silver and wood, 7 in. high. Collection of
Forrest L. Merrill. Photo: M. Lee Fatherree.

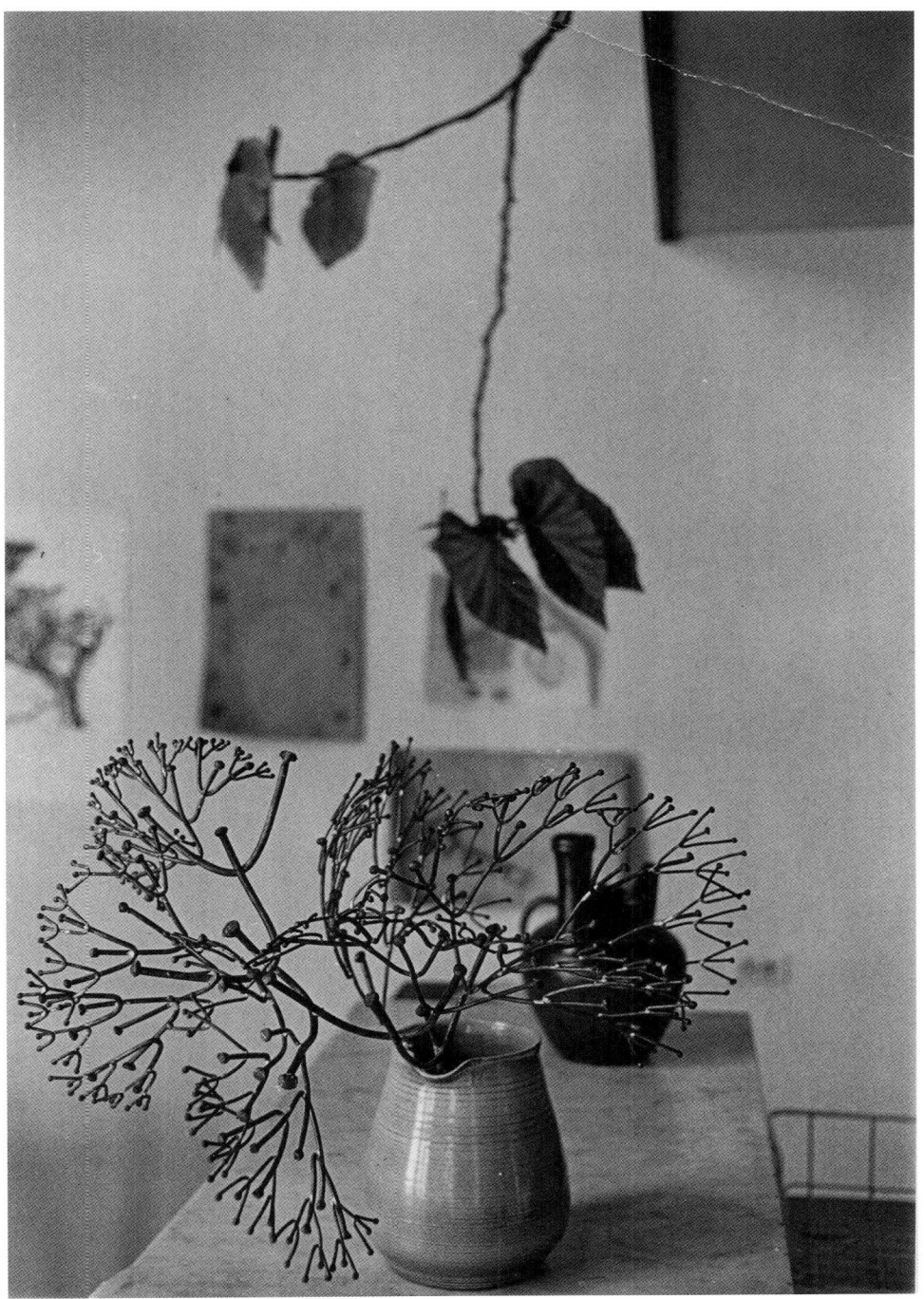

4.11 Phiz Mezey, *Sculpture by Merry Renk Curtis in Vase*, c. 1964. Gelatin silver print, 9½ × 6½ in. Phiz Mezey Photographs and Papers, San Francisco History Center, San Francisco Public Library.

In Asawa's case, this metaphorical plenitude consolidated through descriptions of nature abstracted. A review of her first exhibition of drawings in 1969 describes them as "a cross between nature and abstraction," suggesting that "her round ball of design"—called *Desert Plant*—is a potential "botanical first cousin to the dandelion," which Asawa develops in "interlocking stems and veins from a central core." These were sculptures that seemed "to live and breathe."[32] In similar terms, Nordland observed that "Asawa has taken a common wire and pushed it into a metamorphosis in which it is made magical, a transparent web of form that is in perpetual dialogue with itself, while sketching natural (fruit, gourd, bird's-nest-like) organic forms in space." Even more to the point, Martica Sawin saw them as pieces of nature itself, sculptures that were to be treated "as phenomena rather than art," adding, "her art is not merely decorative; it has expressive life."[33] The detailed veracity of Van Hoesen's prints and drawings was also described in such language—"drawing has been akin to breathing," as if completely integrated into the pulsating energy of life force itself.[34]

This language in part explains why certain photographs of Asawa's work are so successful, especially those that juxtapose her sculpture with two coordinates of this discourse: plant life and the female body. This is the case with a photograph taken by Asawa's son-in-law, Laurence Cuneo (fig. 4.12). One of her tied-wire sculptures was mounted onto redwood doors, which she had carved with her children—a project that itself took up these terms of abstracted nature, in that "bee holes," as Asawa's youngest child put it, comprised its central pattern. This was the Albersian meander, a figure of continual reversal between figure and ground, which Josef Albers had students explore in repeated drawing exercises.

Such critical claims about Asawa's work are understood in the context of a sculptural discourse that went by the name "vitalism." Delineating a body of work made primarily between the 1920s and 1960s, the vitalist aesthetic in sculpture amounted to treating inert material as though it were living. The sculptor's task, as Jack Burnham wrote in *Beyond Modern Sculpture* (1968)—one of the best accounts of this modernist tendency—was to "liberate the vital essence from the dormant heart of his material before he could call the result sculpture."[35] This was, of course, a myth—"the vitalist myth": such materials had no inherent living force in the sense typically assigned to organic matter, but they were treated as having such power. Sculpture was no longer limited to triumphal arches and memorialization of war generals; it now aspired to become as present for the viewer as the natural world. Burnham explained: "As concrete expression of the natural environment, vitalist sculpture contains certain common features. It copies nature through example and metaphor, not primarily through mimeticism. Whatever symbolism vitalism employs is related to the growth properties of materials, those at least which can be made visible. Vitalism generates an *intuition* that life is not literally, but plastically, present in a sculpted object. However, a viewer is never left to doubt that a vitalist sculpture is a man-made product rather than the result of natural forces."[36]

The pervasiveness of this rhetoric about sculpture in the first half of the twentieth century cannot be underestimated. It fueled some of the best writing we have on what sculpture is and does, precisely because of this fervent belief in metaphor: that

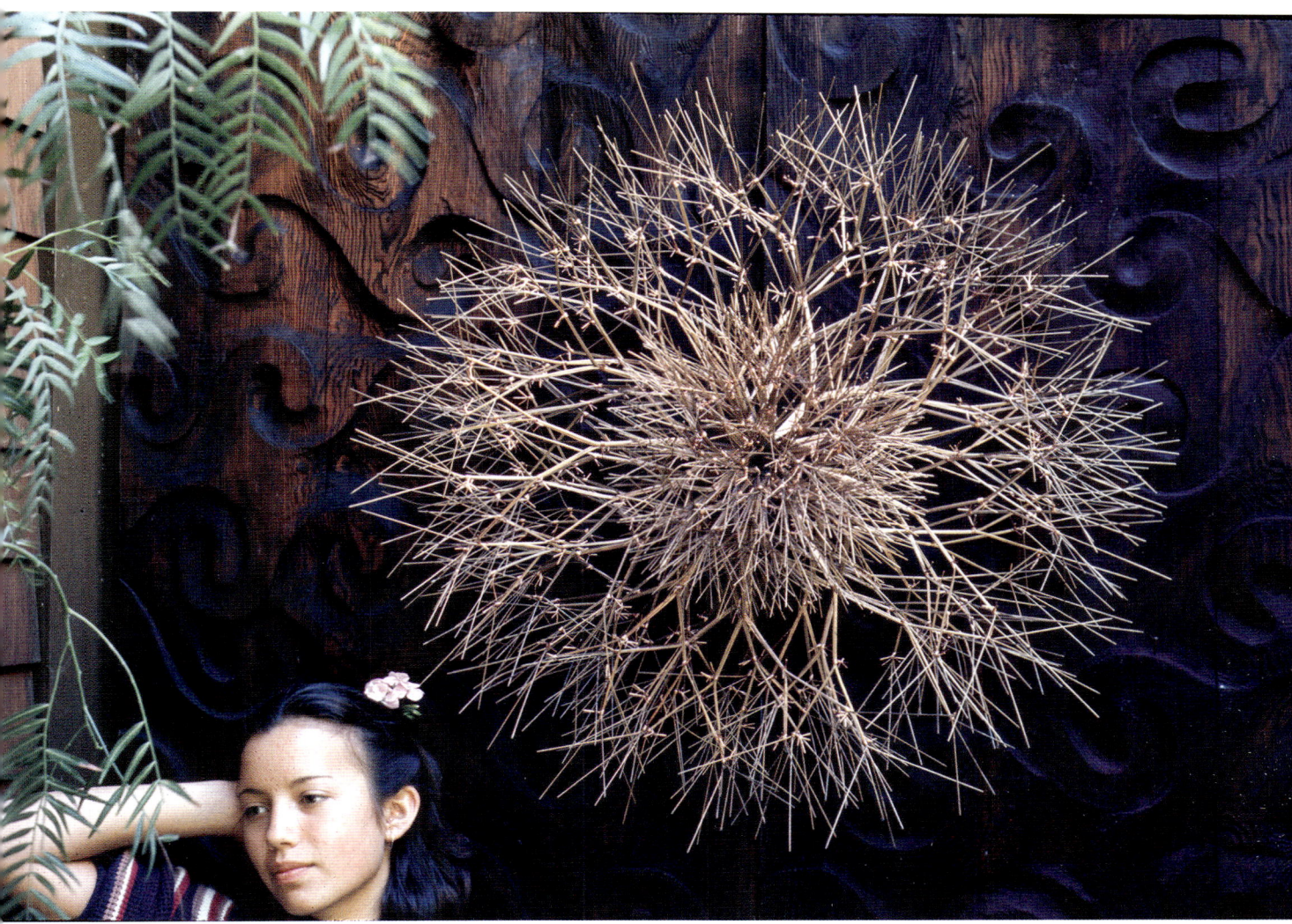

4.12 Addie Laurie Lanier in front of a tied-wire sculpture, *Untitled* (S. 226), and *Doors* (S.528), San Francisco, CA, c. 1974. Photo: Laurence Cuneo.

stone and steel could be so much more than they were. Consider George Bernard Shaw praising Rodin's portrait bust of the playwright, created through a process "that seemed to belong to the study of an embryologist and not an artist. The hand of Rodin worked, not as the hand of a sculptor works, but as the work of *Élan Vital*. . . . The hand of God is his own hand."[37] I use Burnham's summation of this discourse because it would have been the one most readily available to Asawa and, even more importantly, to those critics responding to her work. The 1960s was a moment when this language came into clarity as a discourse, when people like Burnham started to look back on what exactly was fueling this willful belief in sculpture's ability to create life. This was sculpture that, as Clement Greenberg wrote in his essay "The New Sculpture" (1949), had been "freed" from the task of imitation, "released from mass and solidity" to create a "self-evident physical reality, as palpable and independent and present as the houses we live in and the furniture we use."[38] Representatives of this new sculpture included David Smith, Theodore Roszac, Ibram Lassaw, and Richard Lippold, all "sculptor-constructors." Breaking away from the past and tradition, including above all figuration, this sculpture's lack of historical association "endows it with a virginality," Greenberg argued; "all [the sculptor] need remember of the past is cubist painting, all he need avoid is naturalism."[39]

This kind of language could lead, when applied to the (decisively not virginal) artist-mother, into strange territory. One of the most bizarre examples is found in a review of Asawa's exhibition at the de Young Museum in 1960, in which her sculpture was analogized to a bird's nest:

Now this particular piece of art is owned by Mr. and Mrs. William Roth of Sausalito, and was lent to the museum for the show. Most of the time it hangs near a customarily open window in a room of their house.

One day a bird flew in, spotted the wire work and apparently thought "now here's a nice bough in a sheltered location, an ideal place to raise a family." So she got out the blueprints for a traditional-type dwelling and started construction immediately.

The Roths, however, didn't feel that the production added anything to their décor. In fact, they thought it was for the birds.

But when they let it be known that the nest would have to go, their children set up a howl. How COULD their parents be so cruel and unfeeling!

The youngsters won out, of course, and the Roths were persuaded to cease and desist. So when the piece went to Golden Gate Park, Mrs. Bird's abode went with it.[40]

There is no other evidence of the sculptural nest beyond this newspaper column; it appears nowhere in the other reviews, installation photographs, or in the museum's exhibition files. One can only surmise that the article, written by the *Chronicle*'s "Society Editor," Millie Robbins, was meant less to report than to entertain, complete with parent-child drama and a happy ending—and above all, a clear analogy between homemaker-artist and nest-building bird.

The adaptation of Asawa's work to this logic of vitalism was evident in artistic responses to her work as well. Andrea Jepson's husband, the musician Warner Jepson, subjected Asawa's looped-wire sculptures and tied-wire drawings to the medium of video (fig. 4.13). He likely employed a video mixer then in use as part of his work with the National Center for Experiments in Television (NCET), a research lab for a multidisciplinary group of artists to experiment with the relatively new medium of television. A "video Bauhaus," the NCET was comprised of composers, musicians, filmmakers, dancers, and poets working across media.[41] The idea was to electronically manipulate video by subjecting the footage in real time to a synthesizer, whose processing mechanism created vibrant abstract, almost psychedelic colored patterns alongside sound. Mediated through this video synesthesia, Asawa's two- and three-dimensional structures transform into startling, unexpected compositions as if animated life forms. Such processes of electronic mediation enlivened her work in ways that were akin to photographers staging these objects as part of the natural, pulsating environment, as in Paul Hassel's photograph of a looped-wire work hung in Asawa's

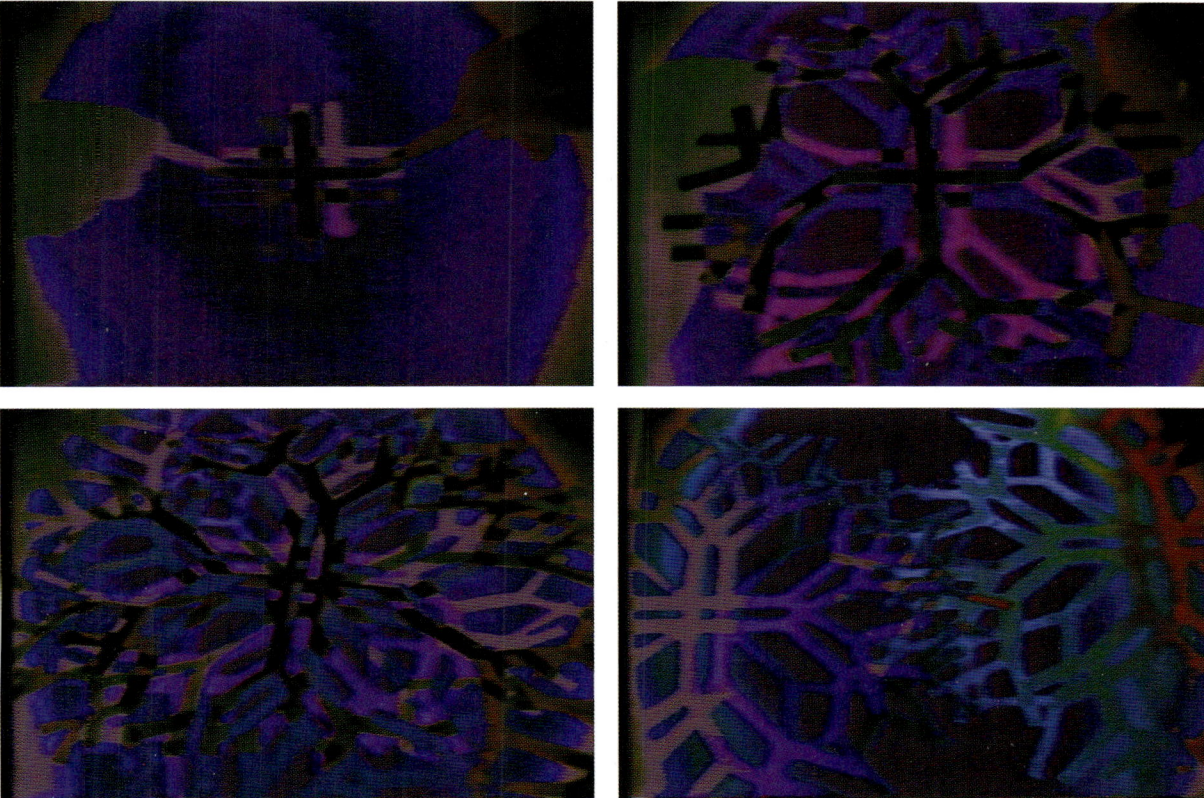

4.13 Film stills from Warner Jepson and Ruth Asawa, *Tape i21*, 1974. Video, 32:40. Berkeley Art Museum/ Pacific Film Archive.

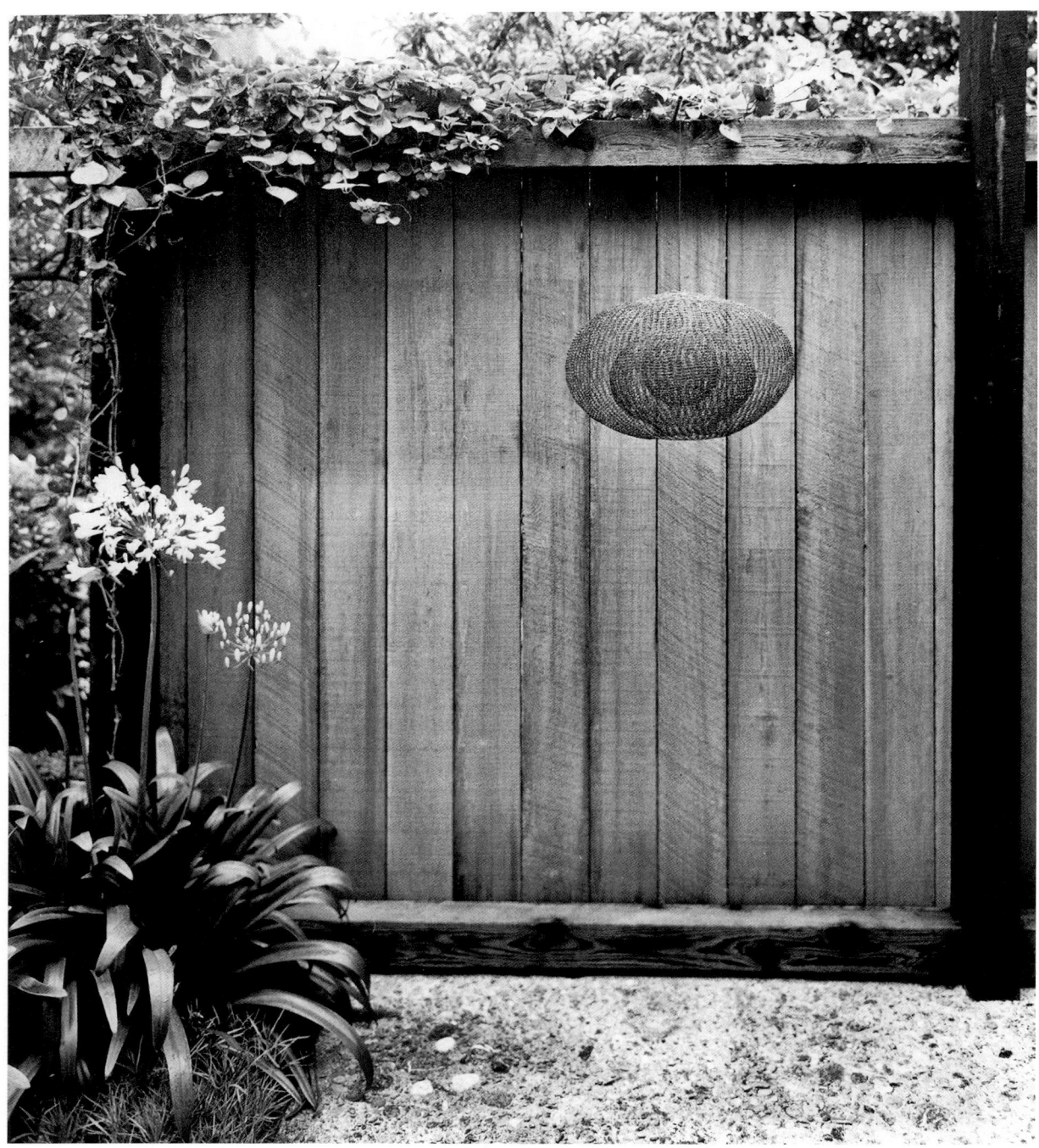

4.14 Paul Hassel, *Ruth Asawa's Untitled (S.393,
Hanging Single-Lobed, Three-Layered Continuous
Form within a Form) Hanging in a Garden*, c. 1960.
Gelatin silver print, 10 × 8 in. Private collection.

garden as if an extension of its plant life. And Asawa did indeed leave sculptures outside, where they became overgrown with ivy and brush (fig. 4.14).

These various receptions of Asawa's work as animated, either through technologically mediated video synthesis or staged as part of a landscape of organic forms, foreground the complexity of the vitalist imaginary when applied to objects made by the artist-mother. In her study of modern British sculpture, *Mother Stone*, Anne M. Wagner traces how this discourse in the 1920s and 1930s was already deeply imbricated with the maternal body. Her book addresses this body primarily in an iconographic register, examining the biomorphic carvings of Henry Moore, Jacob Epstein, and Barbara Hepworth. These sculptors committed themselves to countless renditions of Mother and Child, albeit often abstracted beyond recognition were it not for the work's title. "Hepworth's stone *is* a mother," Adrian Stokes claimed emphatically, with italics there to underscore, as Wagner elaborates, "the difference between simple representation and literal embodiment"; to italicize this verb thus "literalizes the metaphor and in so doing puts the brakes on the free play of its meanings. As a result, what William Empson calls the 'pregnancy' of metaphor is terminated, and its potential circuitry of meaning effectively closed down."[42]

By the 1960s, when applied to a mother of six making sculptures for architectural interiors, the vitalist aesthetic lost its explanatory potential. Remember, as Burnham instructs us, "it was imperative that the modern abstract vitalist create 'life' as Rodin had done—but in a radical form that would appear to be anything but a copy of life."[43] Asawa, however, was indeed copying life: creating open-ended series of life casts. Furthermore, in her "lifelong connection with growing things," as her 1973 retrospective catalogue read, mythologized comparisons to nature become impossible because they were already present in a *literal* way, inasmuch as Asawa's persona as an artist was imbricated in her identity as a mother.[44] In attempting to describe Asawa's achievement in this discourse—the reigning language for sculptural achievement—these observers found themselves making bizarre claims. Such comparisons ended up using language that reessentialized and naturalized her identity. Hers were "works of art that grew at home along with her six children"—a statement that equates artmaking with childrearing and trivializes both.[45]

AGING AND THE PASSAGE OF TIME

How then should we understand her sculpture's achievement if not in vitalist terms? Contemporary accounts would point, once again, to the work's capacity for moving between vitalism and metaphor. Art historian Jennifer Roberts has argued that Asawa's drawing and printmaking practice, of which *Desert Flower* is one example, engages the sheet of paper in such a way that it transforms that sheet into a structure akin to a leaf. Roberts focuses particularly on Asawa's interest in drawing and printing on both sides of her paper, as well as employing thin weights of paper in which the ink seeps through the fibers to the other side. In a reading of a chrysanthemum drawing, *Untitled* (PF.268; c. 1960–1969), Roberts suggests evocatively that "her inky flowers have pushed through to the other side, in reverse, just as beneath every plant you will find its inverted image in roots. Asawa, the farmer-calligrapher, planted this drawing." Enacting a form of radical openness, as suggested by contemporary writing on plants as organisms of connectivity and transversality, Asawa's works on paper can be read as "ultimately a form of botanical drawing."[46] Similarly, Jason Vartikar has argued recently for the resemblance of her tied- and looped-wire sculptures to cell diagrams, with which she was familiar from her training at the Milwaukee State Teachers College and at Black Mountain, where her courses included zoology. Vartikar claims that "the sculptures seem to be cells dividing or in the state of replication," and in this they "evoke biology—specifically the proliferation of cells, embryos, and invertebrates from early epochs—as a metaphor for racial equality."[47] The same argument was proposed by John Yau several years earlier in claiming that the sculptures are like "models for cells undergoing a transformation, generative forms giving birth to a similar being."[48]

Consider again Greenberg's complaint about work that would seem to resemble Asawa's output (work by Butler, Chadwick, Turnbull, and others), describing it as modernist sculpture that has "succumbed so epidemically to 'biomorphism' . . . after the fanciful and decorative improvisation of plant, bone, muscle, and other organic forms, there should have come a spinning of wires, twisting of cords, and general fashioning of cages and boxes—so that the most conspicuous result of the diffusion in the use of the welding torch among American sculptors has been a superior kind of garden statuary and a new, oversized kind of *objet d'art*."[49] The description could just as well have been of Asawa's 1958 exhibition at Peridot Gallery in New York—though at least Asawa was exempt from the bit about the welding torch. One can imagine with what contempt Greenberg would have railed against the "artiness" (another of sculpture's "afflictions") and decorative quality of the work on view there.

Haunting such condemnation of "biomorphic" sculpture was the specter of art nouveau—that ultimate example of the *objet d'art* whose singular goal was to decorate and ornament (the term "objet d'art" was also often imposed on Asawa's work). Figures like Greenberg and Josef Albers, typically at opposing sides of the American art divide, could finally agree on something: art nouveau was precisely what they were *not* interested in. In the 1960s, art nouveau stood for aesthetic decadence, for superficial detail, for whims and impulses, rather than structure, monumental form, and transhistorical universalisms. Art historian Rosalind Krauss put the matter bluntly when she described art nouveau as a style in which the art object would appear to have been shaped by external, organic forces: "they are executed in such a way that we feel we are looking at something that was shaped by the erosion of water over rock, or by the tracks of waves on sand, or by the ravages of wind; in short, by what we think of as the passage of natural forces over the surface of matter."[50]

The fact of the matter is that Asawa's work did aspire to this external shaping and thus to an effect of her having produced "works" that were not works at all, but rather consequences of a process of making in which she ceded intention (not to mention "genius"). These were works that were left in the garden to be reclaimed by unkept ivy; works that were subjected to accretions generated by the industrial process of electroplating, but whose form had nothing to do with industry, with its welding irons and massive sheets of Cor-Ten steel. These forms instead modeled themselves after incident—a wire bent this way or that—and contingency, in which the whole thing hardly even sits flat on the ground but rather is slightly off-kilter, its wire meanderings having a mind of their own (fig. 4.15).

It was this durational element that most interested Asawa in the process of electroplating. Sculptures took on the appearance of having been encrusted with matter over time, like barnacles growing on a piece of metal abandoned to the sea. But instead of reaching for the universal and heroic, Asawa worked in sites long marginalized from contemporary art, like botanical drawings. Several examples from a sketchbook dated to 1985 record the exact time that she began and ended the drawing: the inscribed caption "4:05 AM–3.16.85, hand unsteady, 3:20 PM–4:07 PM, 4:10–4:32 PM" accompanies three iris specimens, committed to ink during periods of sleeplessness (fig. 4.16). In other sheets, she notes down "Prednisone," the steroid medication that she was taking

4.15 Ruth Asawa, *Untitled* (S.534, Freestanding Electroplated Tied-Wire, Organic Form Based on Nature), 1963. Electroplated copper wire, 6¼ × 7¾ × 7¾ in. Private collection.

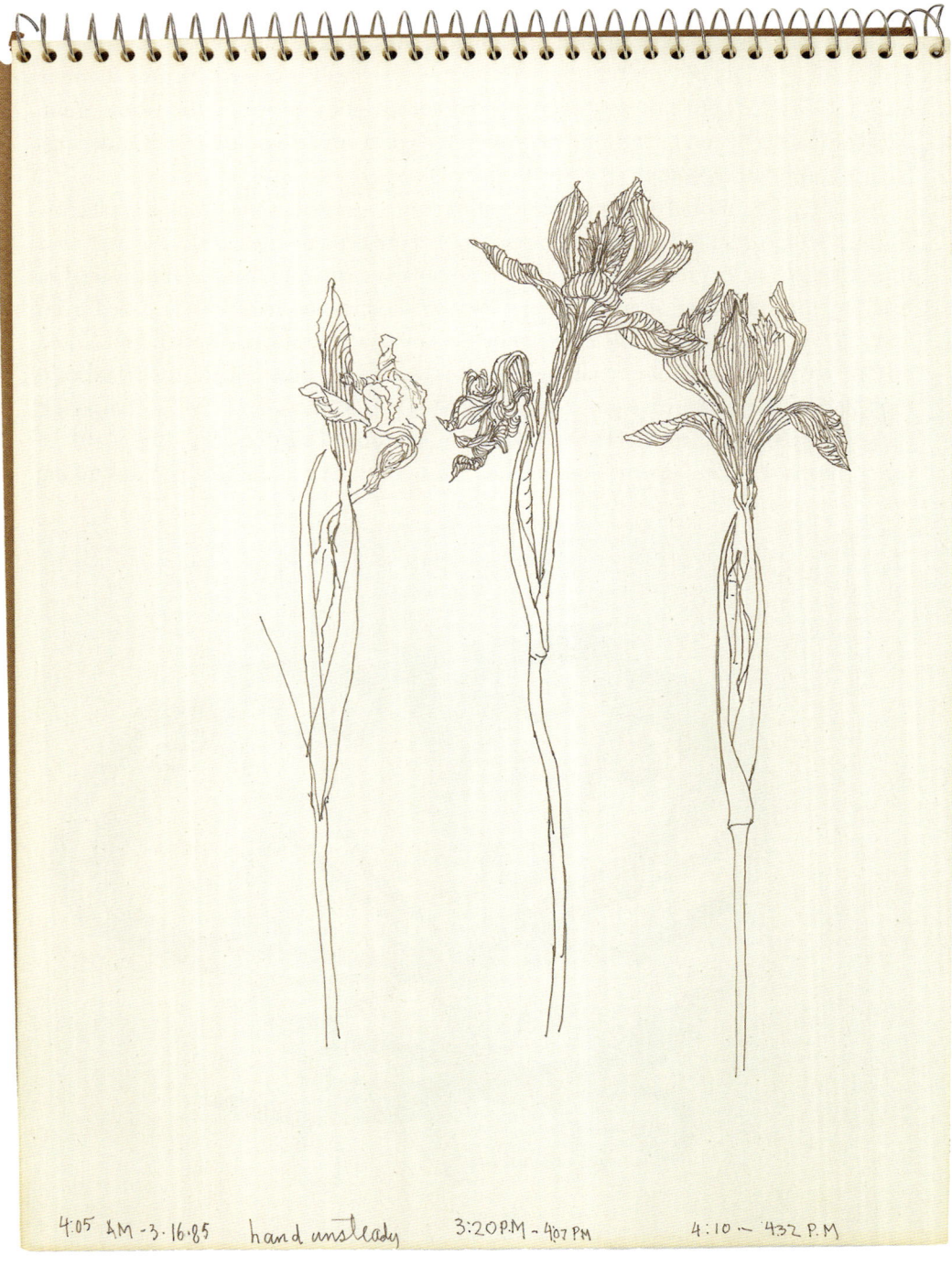

4.16 Ruth Asawa, *4:05 AM–3.16.85, hand unsteady, 3:20 PM–4:07 PM, 4:10–4:32 PM* (SB.157), 1985. Ink on paper in spiral-bound sketchbook, 12 × 9 in. Private collection.

to treat her lupus, but also the radio station that was on in the background and the song it was playing, further underscoring the mundane temporality governing these sheets.

Asawa also willingly engaged the theme of aging, alongside fellow artist-mother photographers Phiz Mezey and Imogen Cunningham; the latter's book *After Ninety* included portraits of Asawa's elderly parents (portraits that Asawa in turn used as source material to create lithographs during her Tamarind residency, placing her father against a background of chrysanthemums). One of Asawa's life casts depicts a mature female torso of an unnamed sitter, whose sagging breasts suggest the effects of time on that body (fig. 4.17). She also completed a tile mosaic mural for the entrance to the Bethany Senior Center in San Francisco, which depicts a vibrant orange, yellow, and blue tied-wire pattern, branching out from the middle toward the outer edges. *Growth* (1968–1969) upends old age's association with death, and points to aging as a process of metamorphosis and transformation, instead of aging as the undesired opposing term to contemporary society's obsession with youth. Such works parallel what Natania Meeker and Antónia Szabari have described, in their study of speculative fiction's imagery of plants, as a "pastoral vision," which "sees plants as restoring justice and order

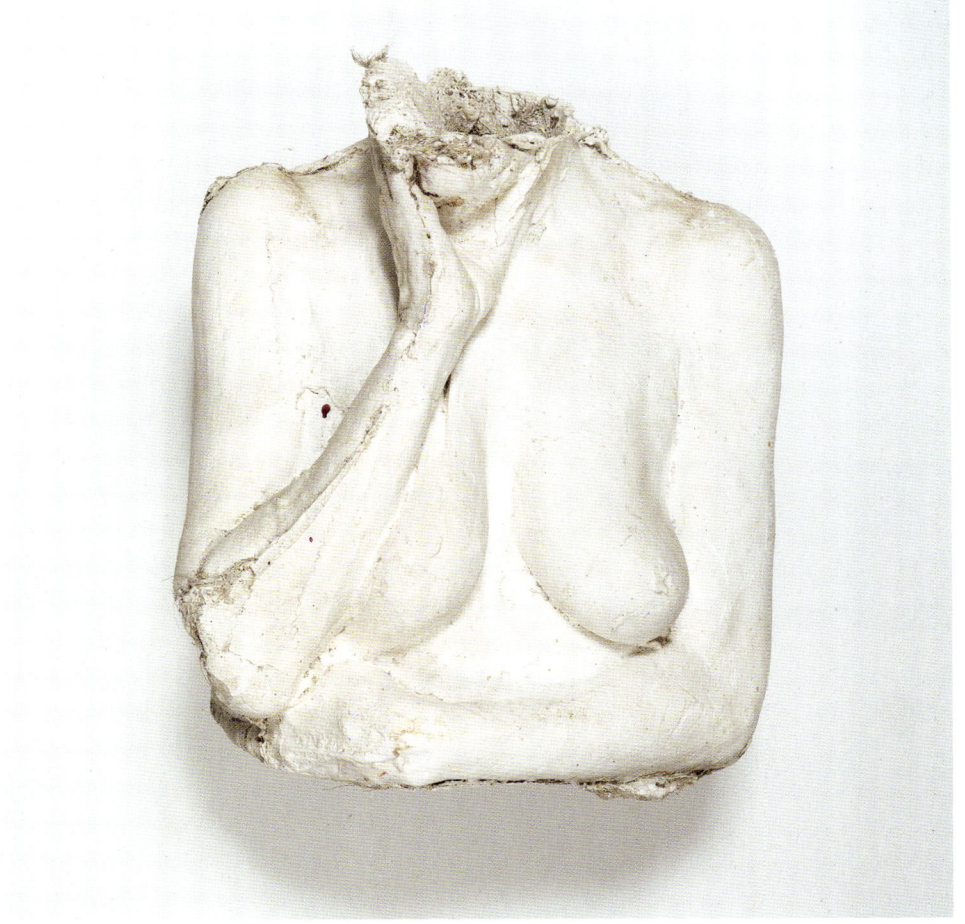

4.17 Ruth Asawa, *Untitled* (LC.031, Female Torso), no date. Cast plaster, 17 × 14½ × 12 in. Private collection.

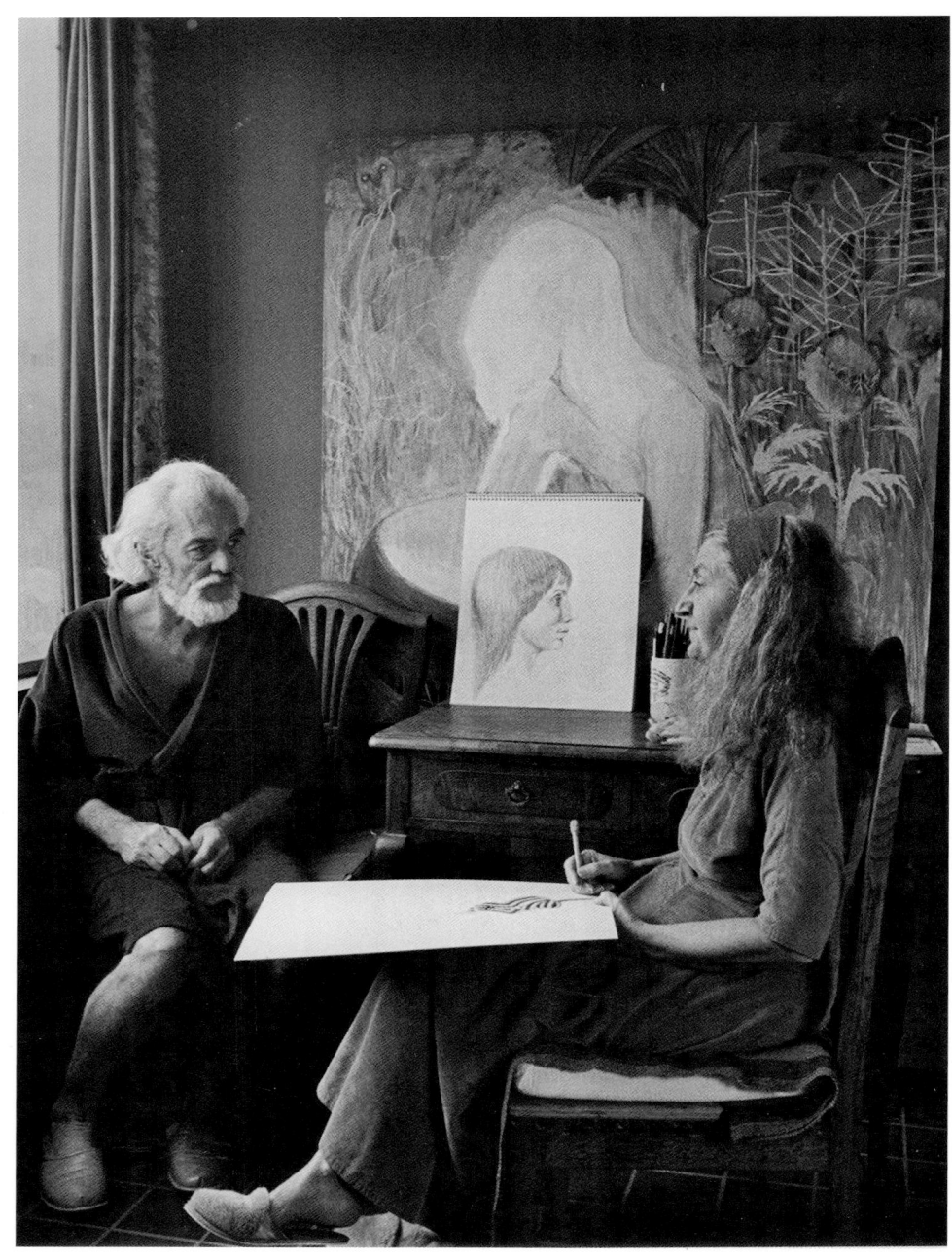

4.18 Phiz Mezey, *Merry Renk and Earle Curtis*, 1978. Gelatin silver print, 10 × 8 in. Phiz Mezey Photographs and Papers, San Francisco History Center, San Francisco Public Library.

to a pathological human world"; upending "pastoralism's insistence on the natural," such objects that take plants as primary "open up social norms and family structures."[51]

Those social structures appear in a series that Phiz Mezey took of floral imagery from an unexpected angle. One of her major unfinished projects was a book, illustrated with her photographs, of the plant known colloquially as a "pregnant onion" due to the way it grows a polyp on the side of the bulb. She also executed a series of photographs on marriage and age, which included portraits of Merry Renk and Earle Curtis in their Saturn Street home, with a chalkboard in the background that bears a floral pattern and a portrait (fig. 4.18). A photograph of Asawa and Lanier, taken in 1982, was also included in the series. This is a rare reflection on the intimacy and alienation that characterize the institution of marriage, especially over a long period of time. It is significant that Renk and Curtis's gazes do not meet, that the photograph encodes a closeness but also a distance between them. The floral, then, becomes a vehicle to explore this theme of relationality, a theme that, in its evocation of time, may have been a familiar one in depictions of flowers and plants across the arc of art's history. But such subject matter acquired a particular meaning when authorship lay with someone whose closeness to life and death, sickness and health, in her role as caretaker nevertheless excluded her from that history.

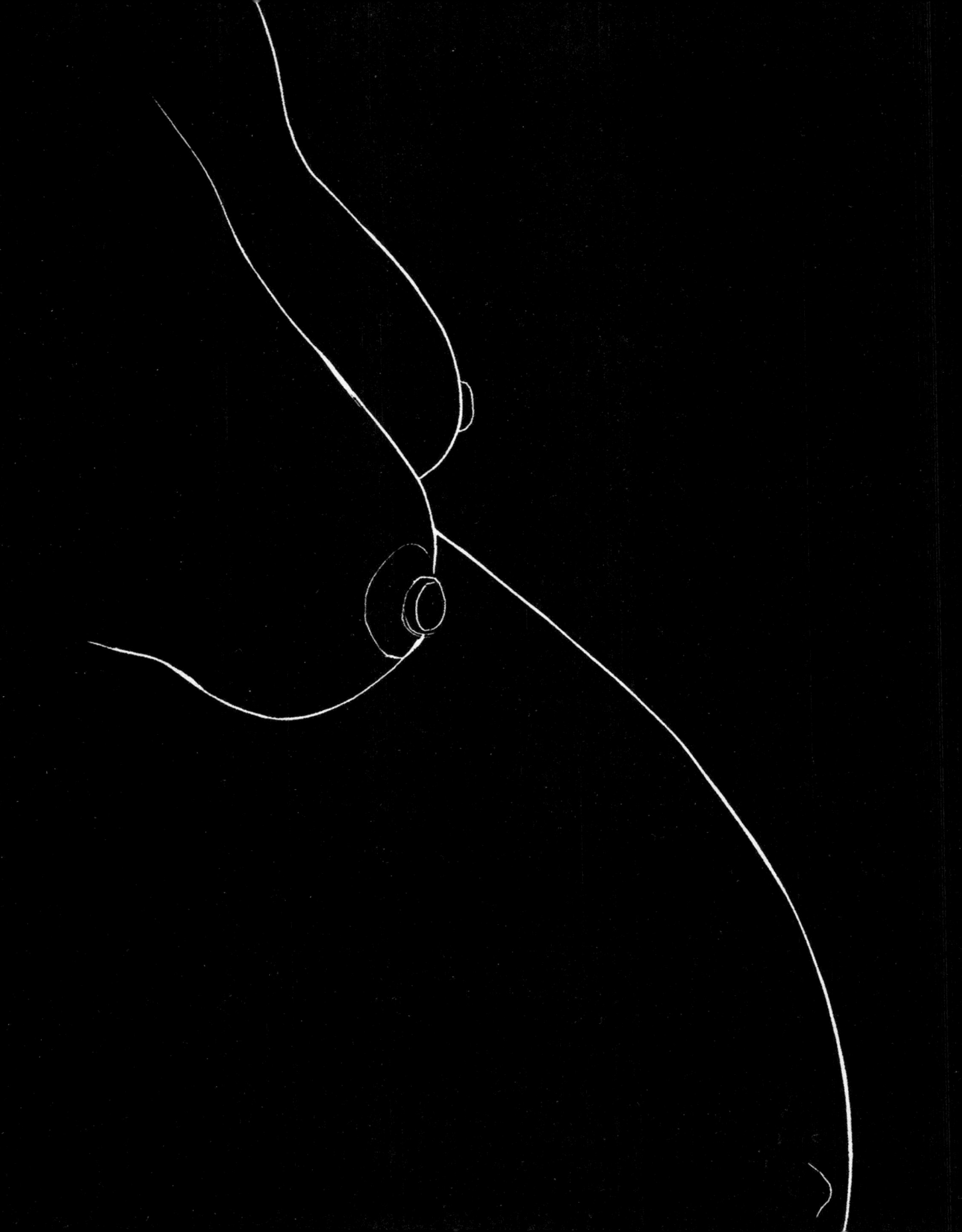

5 *ANDREA* AND MATERNAL CAMP

He says that woman speaks with nature. That she hears voices from under the earth. That wind blows in her ears and trees whisper to her. That the dead sing through her mouth and the cries of infants are clear to her. But for him this dialogue is over. He says he is not part of this world, that he was set on this world as a stranger. He sets himself apart from woman and nature.

And so it is Goldilocks who goes to the home of the three bears, Little Red Riding Hood who converses with the wolf, Dorothy who befriends a lion, Snow White who talks to the birds, Cinderella with mice as her allies, the Mermaid who is half fish, Thumbelina courted by a mole.

—Susan Griffin[1]

WOMAN, TURTLE, FROG

The artist-mother's alignment with plants, animals, and children culminates in what would become Ruth Asawa's first major public commission and what constitutes a turn to sculptural figuration after having worked for two decades as an abstract artist. Titled *Andrea* (1966–1968; see figs. 5.2, 5.12) and installed in San Francisco's Ghirardelli Square, where it can still be seen today, the bronze figural arrangement encompasses two female mermaids seated within an aquatic habitat of sea turtles, frogs, and lily pads. The mermaids are identical, having been created as life casts from the postpartum body of Asawa's neighbor and fellow writer-mother Andrea Jepson. The contours of that body register in a plaster cast created in the process of making the sculpture, which was photographed by Jepson's husband Warner. Breasts differently full with milk, a stomach still reassembling itself—these are the subtle markers of a body that had been rent in two (fig. 5.1). This doubleness is repeated in the number of female figures: in the final sculpture two mermaids face away from each other, with one holding a large leaf—perhaps in a send-up of this typical icon of modesty—while the other cradles a merbaby to her bare chest in a gesture that many at the time understood to be an act of breastfeeding, even if the infant was not latched.

The "bronze nursing mermaid fountain," as one journalist put it, has received little scholarly attention, even though it generated a controversy when it was installed in March 1968.[2] At the time it was read variously as an assault on good taste, a brash unveiling of the nude maternal body, an affront to public decency in its reference

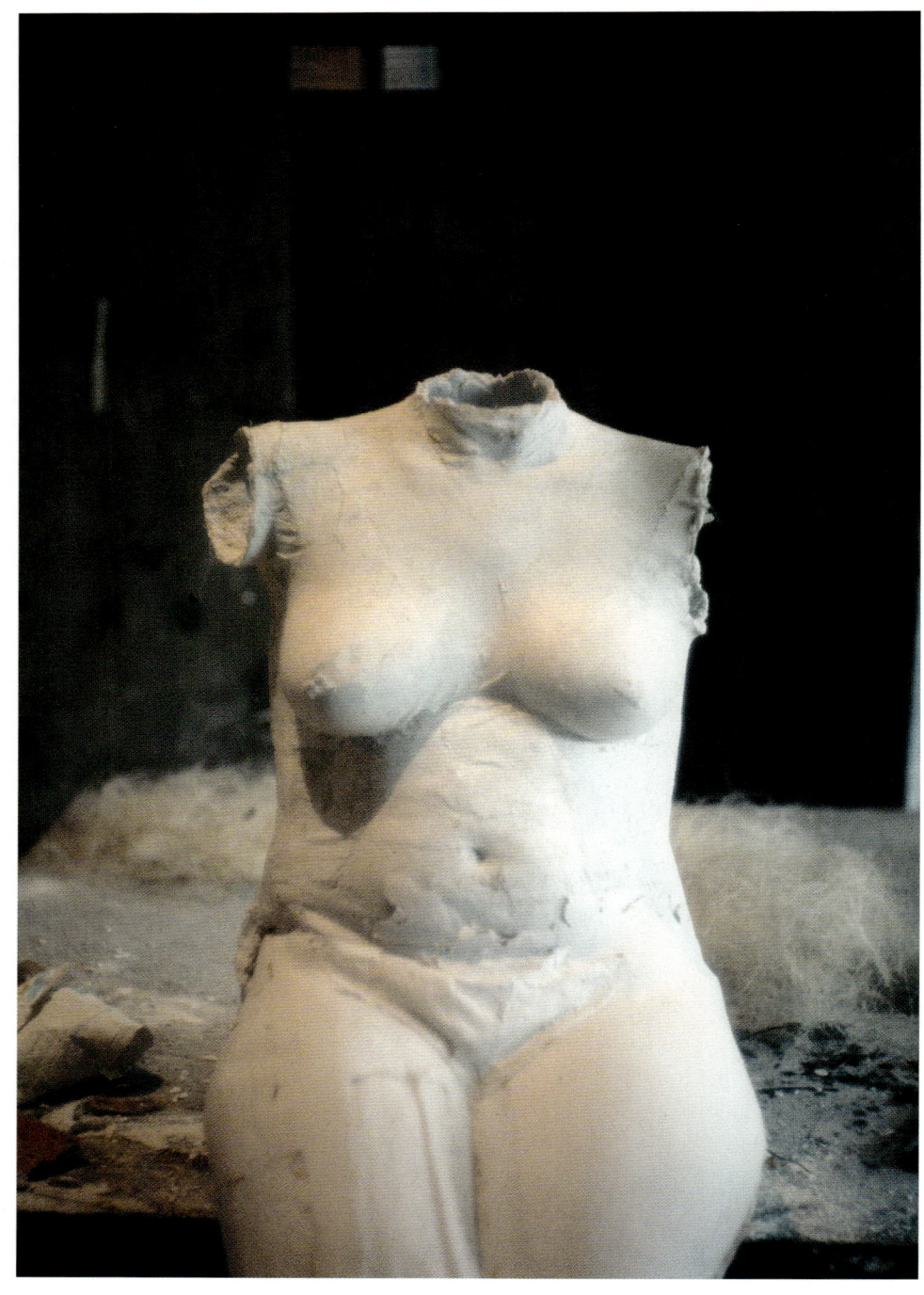

5.1 A plaster mold for Ruth Asawa's *Andrea*
(PC.002), c. 1966. Photo: Warner Jepson.

to breastfeeding, and a mockery of public art's civic responsibility. It was also, significantly, read as queer. Motivated by the doubleness of the sculpture's two identical bodies, a David Sawyer mailed Asawa the following poem in January 1969, describing the female couple as part of a nascent queer relationality:

soft bellied
mermaid a-
lone lesbian
created, knocked up
in a foundry
left pregnant
one day
in a fountain
to bathe a while
among the frogs.[3]

What is one to make of this semantic plurality, in which figurations of a mythical figure, half-human, half-fish, mediated conflicting responses ranging from straight to queer, and from the erotic to the maternal? These were "relatively unprecedented scenes," as urban design historian Alison Isenberg has argued, "breast-feeding, a lesbian family, an amphibian orgy, possibly mermaid vaginas."[4]

As a grouping of women, plants, and animals derived from the well-known fairy tale by Hans Christian Andersen, the sculpture represented the first time in twenty years that Asawa had worked figuratively. Although she had begun experimenting with life casting in plaster several years prior, she regarded these experiments as exploratory. When asked what motivated her decision to make this dramatic shift and to do so in such a public way—for a major commission in a highly visible area of the city—she wrote a response in her characteristically straightforward language:

What I had in mind was to make a sculpture that would relate to more than just the Plaza. The Square sits in a rich San Francisco environment, historically and aesthetically. You cannot ignore this fact. If I could make something related to the sea, the ocean would be included. I thought of all the children and maybe even some adults who would stand by the seashore waiting for a turtle or a mermaid to appear.

For six months I cast faces to find the right person. The original plan was to have a child's figure, but the scale was wrong, so I switched to a woman's figure. In switching I had to enlarge the turtles. Andrea Jepson happens to be appropriately Italian, and her figure was just perfect for the mermaid.

I wanted to make a sculpture that could be enjoyed by everyone. For the old it would bring back the fantasy of their childhood, and for the young it would give them something to remember when they grow old. The sculpture would be comfortable in a museum next to Larry [Halprin]'s 15 foot shaft sans water. I feel that by making a literal sculpture I do not water down my integrity as an artist, or limit the imagination of those who see it.

As you look at the sculpture you include rather than block out the ocean view which was saved for all of us, and you wonder what lies below that surface.

I am not interested in imitating man-made styles (Victorian, modern, etc.), because they do go out of style. I like to be inspired by those things that never change. I derive my pleasures from nature's tried and true patterns: woman, turtle, frog.[5]

There is a lot to explain here, not least of which is the reference to "Larry's shaft." The comment, along with her rejection of "man-made styles (Victorian, modern, etc.)," responds directly to the landscape architect Lawrence Halprin. Commissioned by William Roth, her longtime patron and the owner of Ghirardelli Square, the sculpture accompanied a major renovation designed and overseen by Halprin, who—essentially from the get-go—had been against Asawa's proposal of a figurative (or as she put it, "literal") sculpture, which he called "high camp." Days after it was installed, Halprin issued a two-page statement in which he called for the removal of *Andrea* and its replacement by a shaft of metal: "I had hoped for a grand scale of tallness and water dropping from heights," he lamented.[6] Asawa had long known of Halprin's disapproval; he had expressed it a year earlier to Roth as well as directly to the artist. (Halprin had also attempted, unsuccessfully, to select the commissioned artist himself.) From the start of the square's renovation, years before Asawa had been selected, Halprin had envisioned an abstract sculpture in accordance with a neo-Kantian vision of transcendent aesthetic experience: a nonrepresentational "event, where the materials of the fountain would come together forming the water, giving it shape. My conception was one in which the interplay of water and metal would give free play to the essential qualities of water—not formalized and constrained but organically evolved."

As if embodying the unnamed male protagonist invoked in this chapter's epigraph, who claims authority over both nature and woman, Halprin refused to hear Asawa's appeal to the sea; indeed, his complaints seem to have arisen because he held a very different conception of what nature was and where it could be found. Although neither Asawa nor Halprin states explicitly what that term "nature" means to them, I will argue in this chapter that their differing definitions of nature entail a debate about "appropriate" public art, a debate in which motherhood stood front and center. For Asawa, the public invoked by her intervention was simply "everyone," old and young, children and adults, whose "imagination" would be stimulated by her invocation of a mythical figure from the depths. Halprin's envisioned public was decidedly less familial: he wanted a viewer who was *engaged*, "a part of the event, giving them a sense and opportunity for participation. I did not think a static form appropriate—one which people would look at curiously and then leave—but of something open-ended, engaging their imagination, something one could come back to and each time derive something new from."[7]

Once Halprin's critique became public, *Andrea* received an overwhelming outpouring of support. The public response outweighed Halprin's complaints, and the sculpture stayed. Given that abstract, minimalist sculpture had "ascended to the status of an official style in the US art scene," the success of Asawa's figurative intervention is remarkable for this reason alone.[8] Surely it had something to do with Roth's trust in Asawa as an artist; he had been supporting her work since her first exhibition in San Francisco at the Tin Angel.[9] But the public defense of the sculpture was just as important, if not more so; Asawa reported receiving almost a hundred letters of support as a result of Halprin's criticism. When asked what sort of people wrote, Asawa responded: "Oh, a lot of women wrote to me. Some wrote me long letters on the meaning of the circle and about mythology and about motherhood and the significance or

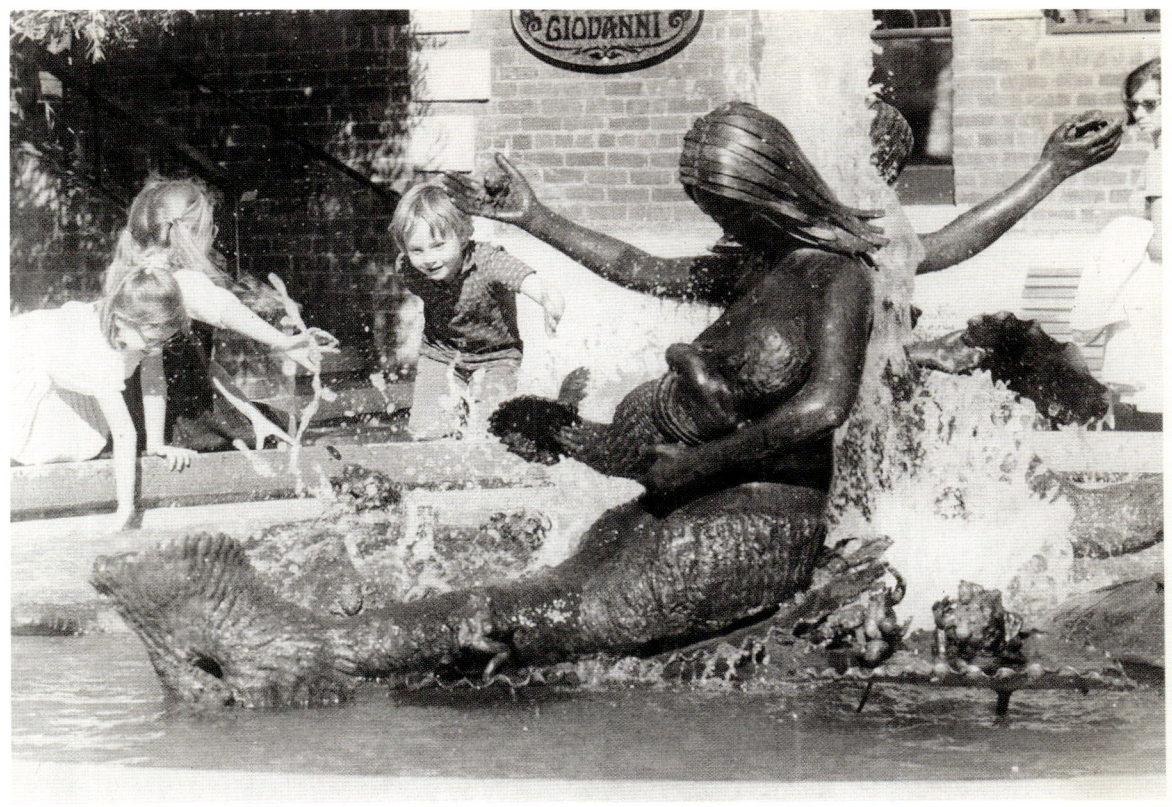

GHIRARDELLI FOUNTAIN · CAST BRONZE
LIFE SIZE   1966·68

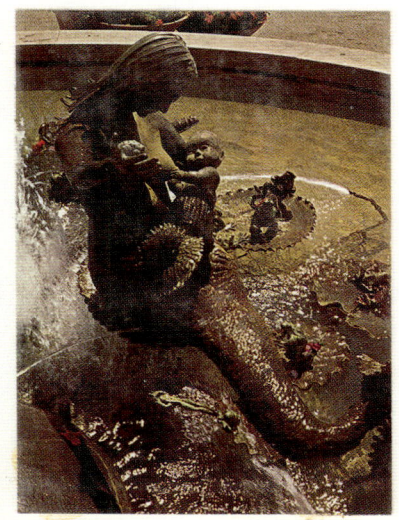

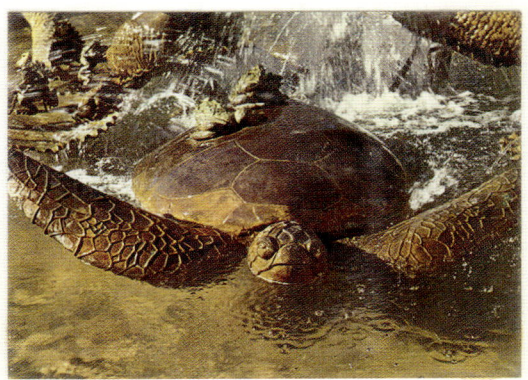

5.2 Views of *Andrea* (1966–1968) in a loose
album. Special Collections, Stanford University.

the symbolism of the mermaid and the frogs and the turtles."[10] One supporter even organized other women to form a protective circle around the fountain to prevent its removal. In addition to extended reflections on the sexual politics of the work, several writers expressed exasperation at the era's pervasive abstraction. One writer, who had stopped going to museums, was "sick of looking at circles, squares, hunks and spots deliriously designed to hood wink the American taste in arts"; by contrast, *Andrea* "gives you something to enjoy, to dream on, to smile, to revel in."[11]

This seemingly naive language, which also characterizes Asawa's own reflection on her sculpture—"nature's tried and true patterns: woman, turtle, frog"—has typically been taken at face value. *Andrea* is less than marginal in the canon of art history; it is entirely absent. This is because Halprin's account was tacitly accepted as the right one: of *Andrea* as a work of art appealing to the lowest common denominator of public taste. Thus, Asawa became a popular artist in the Bay Area, affectionately earning the nickname "fountain lady," while art history has remained virtually silent on the matter. Only Alison Isenberg has proposed that we look more closely at *Andrea*'s "feminist statements" in the form of a breastfeeding mermaid, statements that "were effective precisely because they were clothed in the guise of a charming sculpture for families."[12]

Building upon Isenberg's intervention, this chapter argues that we go even further in this direction: that we see *Andrea* as closer to a Warholian gesture, in which the deadpan indulgence of public taste, at first seemingly benign, morphs upon closer inspection into a scathing critique of prevailing norms around what constitutes "serious art." What if we were to take at face value Halprin's claims that Asawa had indeed created a work of camp? And, in turn, what if we define camp not in negative terms, as Halprin did, but as a form of critical humor, drawing on anthropologist Esther Newton who wrote in her study of female impersonators, published in 1972, that "camp humor ultimately grows out of the incongruities and absurdities of the patriarchal nuclear family; for example, the incongruity between the sacred, idealized Mother, and the profane, obscene Woman. If camp humor takes such problems as its special subject, then the drag queen is its natural exponent. He himself is a magical dream figure: the fusion of mother and son"?[13] What if Asawa's hybrid woman-fish is the analogue to the hybrid mother-son drag queen? Exploring this hypothesis, the chapter thus offers not only a rereading of *Andrea*'s maternal politics, but also a reflection on how a critical gesture is ever able to be read as such, and the challenges that arise when critique is spoken in an unfamiliar language—in this case, as fairy tale in drag.

THE PREGNANT NUDE

The model for the mermaids, as mentioned earlier, was the postpartum body of Andrea Jepson. A writer, political organizer, and neighbor, Jepson had been introduced to Asawa and Lanier shortly after moving in with their neighbor, Warner Jepson, whose videos of Asawa's sculptures and drawings I discuss in the previous chapter. Warner Jepson had introduced Andrea to the couple under the banal pretext of needing to borrow a plumbing tool. Her recollection, years later, is indicative of the mutual respect and admiration that characterized their friendship:

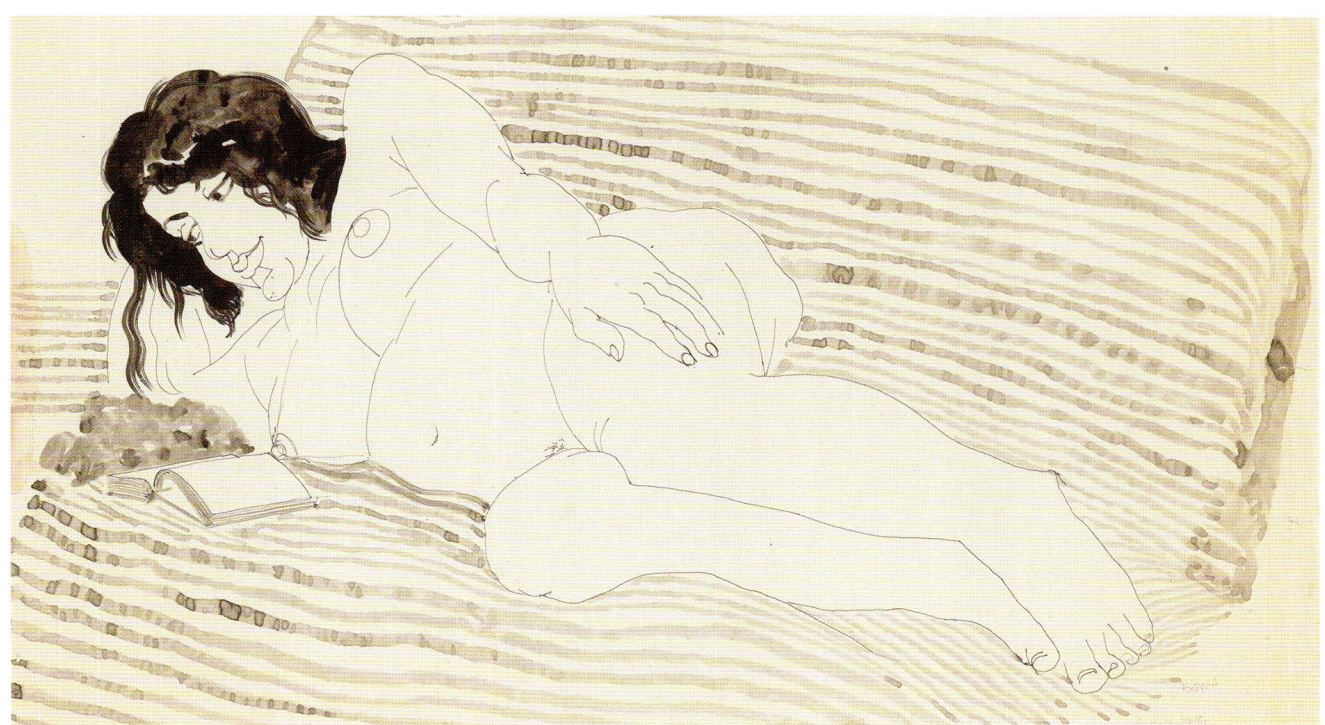

5.3 Ruth Asawa, *Untitled* (FF.685, Andrea Jepson Reclining Nude), c. 1965. Ink on paper, 14¼ × 25 in. Collection of Achenbach Foundation for Graphic Arts–Fine Arts Museums of San Francisco.

Albert was also involved in a plumbing problem, which he had solved with the discovery that someone had flushed an apple (whole) down the toilet. He asked who could have done such a thing and six faces ranging from about thirteen to three all managed to look properly innocent. At the time, I thought it very funny, but since then I have always cautioned my children and their friends not to throw apples down the toilet. So my first experience at their house was a lesson and I expect just about every visit since has also been to one extent or another.[14]

Andrea Jepson would go on to be a key figure in the establishment of the Alvarado School Arts Workshop, along with several other mothers from the neighborhood, and would become its earliest chronicler.

In early 1965, because of hypertension during Jepson's first pregnancy with her daughter Kiira, she had to remain bedridden, and Asawa would come over regularly to draw her (figs. 5.3, 5.5).[15] Often quickly executed and quite detailed, these drawings portray Jepson's domestic interior, her facial features, and growing midsection. As Jepson recalls, the drawing sessions became more frequent when Asawa received the invitation to spend two months as an artist in residence at the Tamarind Lithography Workshop in Los Angeles. Asawa suggested then that such drawings might be material she could use during her residency, and she did indeed use these drawings as the basis for two lithographs, both titled *Nude* (1965; TAM.1489 and TAM.1489-II). Though in part directed toward the residency in September and October 1965, the drawing sessions continued afterward. Jepson recalled: "Later, when Kiira was born, we talked about raising children (I think I did most of the talking). Ruth would sketch Kiira's chubby little hands and the curve of her baby cheek and soft little pursed lips."[16]

The drawing *Untitled* (FF.685) and the pair of lithographs titled *Nude* resulted from these drawing sessions, and can be seen as having been made in indirect preparation for *Andrea*; the title *Nude* is one of the few that Asawa gave to her work (the title *Andrea* is another such). In this drawing Jepson lies on her side on a couch, her head cradled in her bent arm, looking down at an open book. Ribbed fabric has been morphed into stripes of pooled ink, while Andrea's body is left almost blank, entirely delineated with pen-and-ink outline. Thin black lines mark the contours of her fleshy body, with distended ellipses describing the flush nipples and areola of the breast. The growing stomach is subtly indicated by discreet lines that allude to its expanding dimensions—a body not yet legible as "pregnant" unless one looks closely.

In a brilliant reading of Alice Neel's series of painted pregnant nudes, the art historian Pamela Allara has written of this genre's complexity as an art historical category. "If the ideal nude in Western culture has served both to contain and to regulate the female body," she writes, "then the pregnant body, by violating cultural norms of stability and unity, is 'an image of social deviation.'"[17] In their particularity—as pregnant portraits of individual women with bodies that do not conform to a transcendent ideal—Neel's paintings and Asawa's representation of Jepson's pregnancy refuse any essentialized and universalized picture of pregnancy. Both Neel and Asawa also dispense with the art historical convention that the female nude be offered up to the viewer as a sex object as well as the convention that, if not offered up as a sex object, that feminized body must then "masquerade as the Virgin Mary, the trope for pregnant women in our culture," states Allara.[18] Avoiding this binary, Neel and Asawa staked out a new terrain in American art in the 1960s for representations of the reproductive figure. Sex and reproduction came together in a new constellation that left critics like Halprin thoroughly bewildered.

As Allara and Isenberg have both pointed out, such representations of the pregnant body cannot be fully captured by the feminist movement, to which neither Asawa nor Neel laid claim, even if their work is now read as sympathetic to its politics. One of feminism's central issues was the mandated role of "nurturer-mother" as a source of oppression.[19] Motherhood thus became a topic generally avoided, if not outright critiqued, by feminist positions, such that even into the mid-1970s, Lucy Lippard could observe that in the so-called body art of that era, there were few (or no) representations of pregnancy and childbirth by women, even as men appropriated representations of the reproductive body toward violent and aggressive ends.[20] The pregnant body thus became a taboo both for feminist artists otherwise working to upend patriarchal taboos and for patriarchal positions themselves. Responding to a series of seven photographs that Imogen Cunningham took in 1959 of a pregnant Merry Renk, Cunningham's ex-husband, the printer Roi Partridge, described them as "com[ing] close to being repulsive" (see fig. II.3).[21] The pregnant body as transgressive of dominant pictorial norms in Western culture around purity and logic was a common refrain at the time, one also confirmed by a survey conducted by sociologist Pierre Bourdieu in 1963 using photographs depicting the pregnant belly, to which many respondents reacted with aversion.[22]

As a consequence, imagery of the pregnant nude from a masculinized, male perspective typically stages it in a natural environment and often includes a close cropping of the image, which sanitizes the pregnant body as rationalized geometry: taut spheres, elliptical lines, and a spectrum of light and shadow demarcating a curved surface. Like the feminized body, pregnancy thus becomes associated with the natural world, bodies of water, domesticated animals, and plants.[23] This naturalization strategy further intensified feminist ambivalence toward representations of pregnancy. It was, Allara writes, "the one subject that was an anathema to feminists, for it threatened to provide evidence for the charge—certain to send women back to their suburban prisons—that 'anatomy is destiny.'"[24]

By the 1960s, Allara argues, depictions of the pregnant nude thus constituted a "double taboo": the subject was both absent in the history of Western art and held a conflicted status among those working from a feminist perspective (and thus attempting to overturn that canonical history).[25] Asawa's drawings and prints of Jepson pregnant should be seen in a lineage of counterrepresentations of the female nude in the sense of this double taboo, a lineage that begins with Paula Modersohn-Becker's *Reclining Mother and Child Nude II* (1906), continues with Alice Neel's *Pregnant Maria* (1964; fig. 5.4), and culminates, at least with reference to Asawa's circle of artist-mothers, in

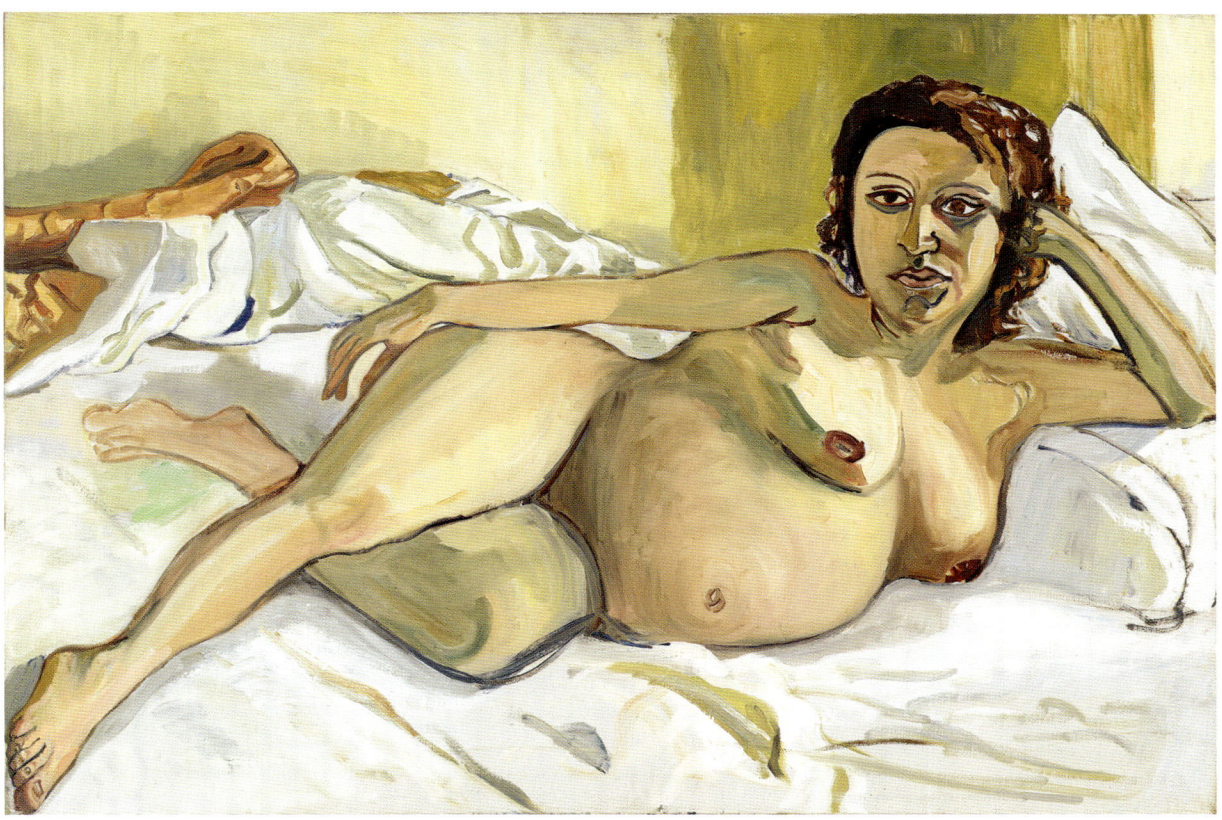

5.4 Alice Neel, *Pregnant Maria*, 1964. Oil on canvas, 32 × 47 in. Private collection.

Beth Van Hoesen's *Twins* (1987; fig. 5.6), an almost entirely black linocut depicting through the most minimal of lines her friend the photographer Diara Crane Citret pregnant with twins, likely during one of the weekly drawing sessions hosted by Van Hoesen and her husband, artist Mark Adams. These portrayals of the maternal nude, whether before the birth or postpartum, offer a vision of the human body that is in direct confrontation with the forces of life and death. They also reject classicizing ideals, such as the discreet covering of pubic hair, which had allowed the beholder to consume female sexuality in public without being subject to the charge of indecency. In the two lithograph prints based on *Untitled* (FF.685), for instance, Asawa registers this pubic hair plainly in sight, taking full advantage of the contrast of black and white to make the hair all the more conspicuous.

5.5 Ruth Asawa, *Andrea Jepson w Matthew* (FF.921, Andrea Jepson Pregnant with Matthew Jepson), c. 1967. Brown ink on technical paper, 24 × 18 in. Private collection.

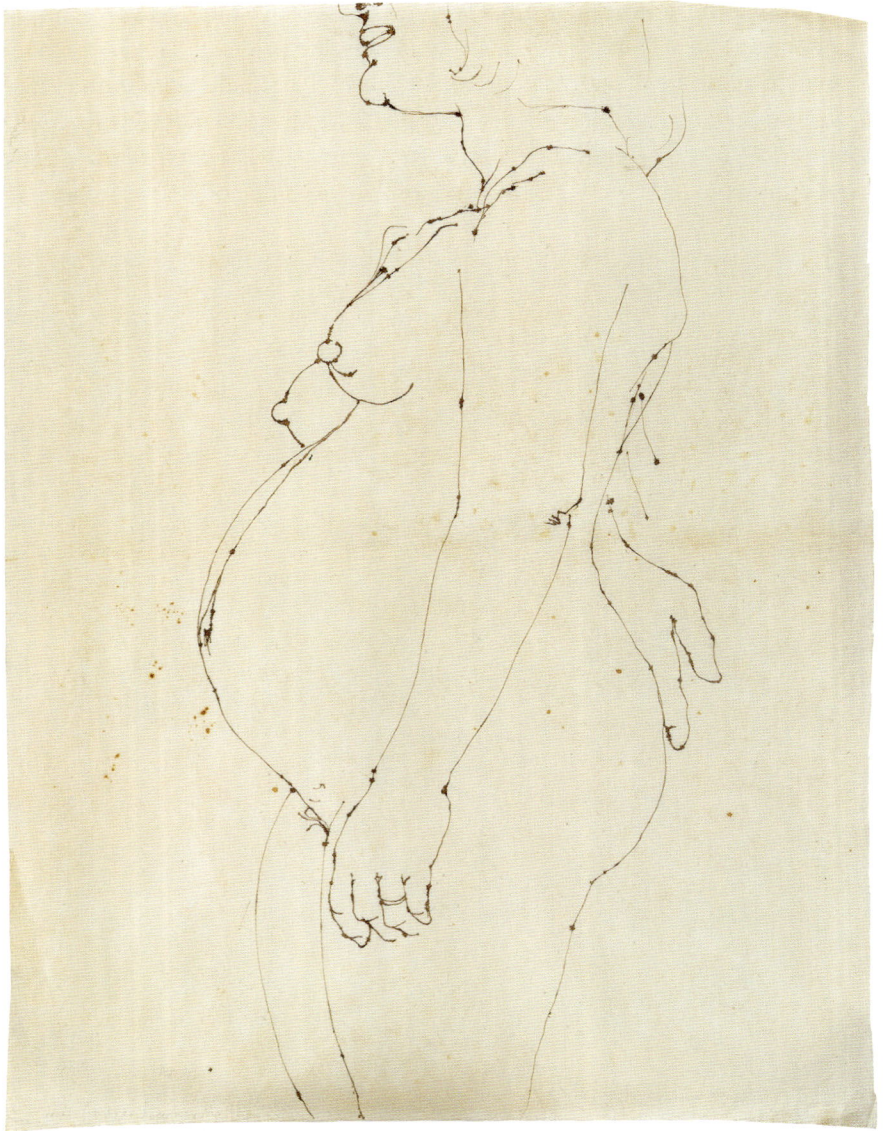

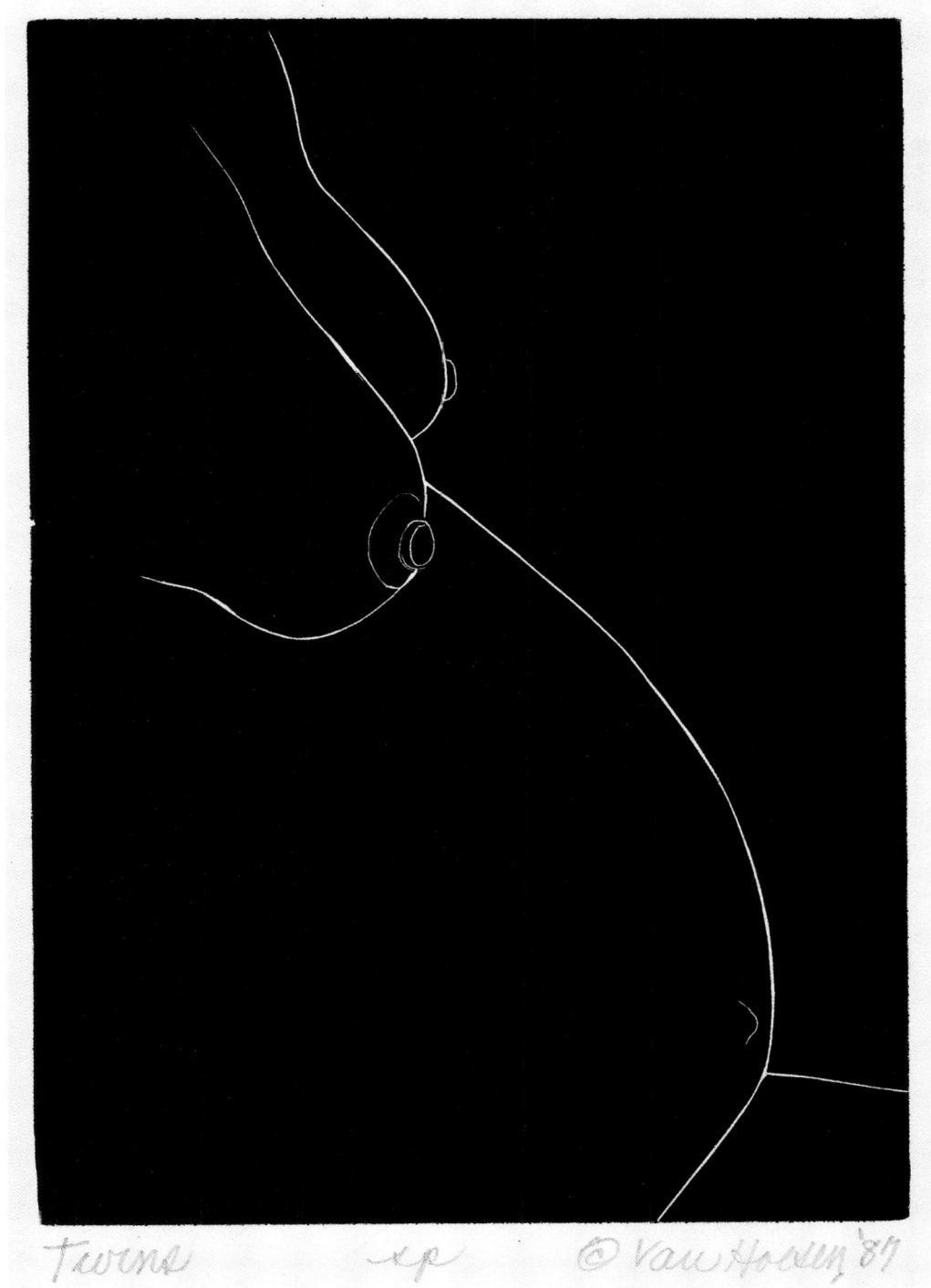

Twins   e.p.   © Van Hoesen '87

5.6 Beth Van Hoesen, *Twins*, 1987. Linocut: printer's ink on paper, 7 × 4⅞ in. Private collection. Photo: M. Lee Fatherree.

While Asawa was looking closely at the contours of the pregnant female body, Law-rence Halprin had begun the renovation of Ghirardelli Square at the directive of Wil-liam Roth, who with his mother had bought the property to spare it from being razed (fig. 5.7). A central challenge was how to preserve, as Halprin later put it, "the bal-ance between old 'victoriana' and newness in the square."[26] Built at the turn of the twentieth century to house the Ghirardelli Chocolate Factory, the buildings in the square were clad in brick and featured a clock tower along with other Victorian-era architectural features, such as wrought iron. Halprin's task was to maintain the his-toric character of the landmark while substantially renovating the square to create a pedestrian experience. A leading landscape architect who had studied with former Bauhaus luminaries at Harvard, including Walter Gropius, Halprin appeared to rep-resent the voice of a new generation, demanding a full-scale reevaluation of the pur-pose and function of the American city. In his conception of the landscape of cities, he advocated for preservation against the prevailing trend of razing whole city districts in the wake of white flight. Such cities "*are* retrievable and *can* be made enjoyable and exciting to be in and participate in, in addition to being economically viable . . . we need not destroy a city to have it rise like a phoenix from the ashes." He bemoaned the "sterile" aesthetic of much contemporary urban design and the turn away from the city toward the suburbs, the "new squares with no life in or around them, enormous new buildings which look better without the clutter of people, beautiful old buildings torn down to be replaced by characterless new facades or signs in shopping centers all done in extremely *good* taste."[27]

Halprin's plans for Ghirardelli Square recast the urban sphere as a "creative envi-ronment": "By creative, I mean a city which has great diversity and thus allows for freedom of choice; one which generates the maximum of interaction between people and their urban surroundings."[28] Creative living, for Halprin, was associated with "a rich and biologically satisfying life for all of the city's people." With the phrase "bio-logically satisfying," Halprin had in mind organic elements, including water features as well as "trees and growing things . . . [in order] to maintain, even in cities, that contact with nature which we should have the opportunity to enjoy."[29] A trained hor-ticulturalist, Halprin viewed the city as "a natural phenomenon as well as a work of art in the environment," and the role of the landscape architect as akin to a gardener who "does not give form to a preconceived idea" but rather "takes the elements and allows them to come together" as an evolving process of putting materials in dialogue with one another. As a participatory environment close to the natural world, in which the scale of civic art matched that of its inhabitants—rather than being monolithic and inhuman—civic art thus "becomes part of [the inhabitants] and they part of it in an act of *collective fantasy*."[30]

This invocation of fantasy was closely related to an encounter with nature. Marc Treib has argued that much of Halprin's output during the 1960s and 70s, including Ghirardelli Square, was "drawn from ideas first proposed and tested in his garden

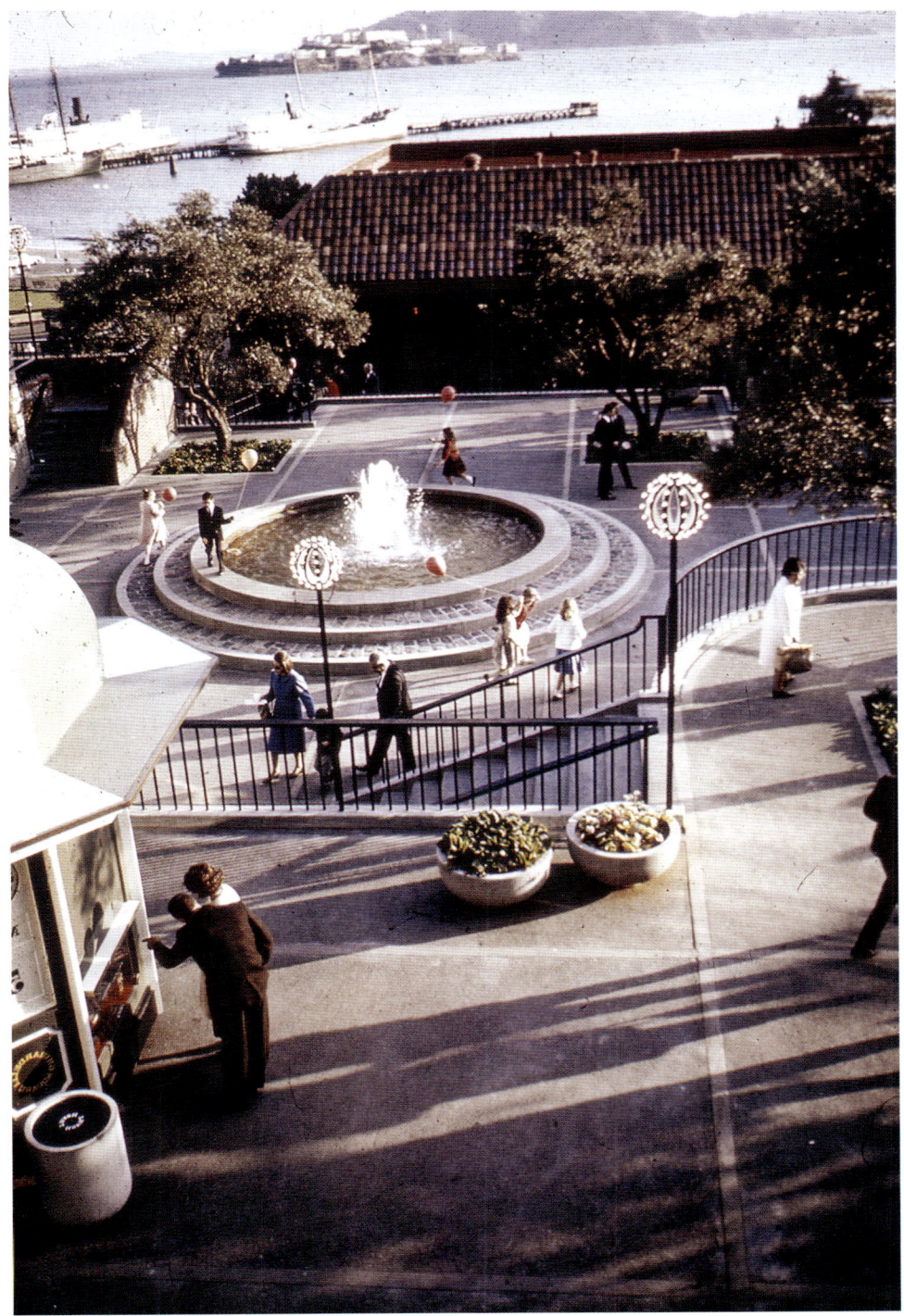

5.7 Ghirardelli Square after renovation by Lawrence
Halprin, c. 1965. Lawrence Halprin Collection,
Architectural Archives, University of Pennsylvania.

designs," particularly the notion of the design achieving "a theater for outdoor living."[31] This meant generating the conditions in which life could spill out into the outdoor spaces around the house in a rejection of the classical notion of the garden as a decorative space primarily to be looked upon. Typical characteristics of Halprin's early garden designs included establishing a connection between indoor and outdoor areas and selecting forms that seemed to be derived from the surrounding landscape. Such principles were continued in Halprin's landscape designs for plazas, including Ghirardelli Square's incorporation of outdoor seating areas, abundant trees, and subdued lighting features. Shops and restaurants were oriented around central terraces that themselves were terraced vertically so that pedestrians would be away from street noise and traffic, and a view of San Francisco Bay could be maintained.

Halprin had likely agreed to the idea of reaching out to Ruth Asawa for a fountain sculpture because her so-called biomorphic sculpture was seen to be compatible with these modernist design principles, a reception that I explore in chapters 1 and 4. A core tenet of such principles was, as Treib puts it, "a return to some form of naturalism, but to that word 'naturalism' we must add the word 'abstract.'"[32] And indeed, a monumental abstraction was exactly what Halprin had envisioned for the circular fountain that he had set aside for a major artwork. As early as 1963, he had written to Roth that they should pursue a solution similar to James FitzGerald's *Fountain of the Northwest*, a 5,500-pound bronze tangle of shards jutting upward in rhythm with vertical jets of water, which had been installed a year prior at the Seattle Center Playhouse. "[Halprin] apparently has in mind a rather massive piece of sculpture; he spoke of sculpture that would stand as high as the roof of the first level of the adjacent Giovanni restaurant," Ghirardelli President Warren Lemmon wrote to Asawa, who received the commission in early 1966. "Bill Roth commented Friday that he did not envision anything as monumental as that."[33] Although Halprin had unsuccessfully attempted to convince Roth that he be allowed to commission the sculpture himself, he was emphatic that it be abstract: every drawing of the plaza included some version of a FitzGerald-like form.[34] This style of abstraction embodied an approach to the human figure that saw it as sharing essential properties and universal needs. It was a discourse that extended to contemporary painting and often approached that of myth, evidenced not only in the evocation of the archaic and archetypal in titles used by the abstract expressionists, but also in Halprin's mobilization of "a primordial and pre-natal need shared by all":

Another example of a basic need is water . . . as it links us to our sources (erosion, wave actions, irrigation of crops, a multitude of interactions in nature, and from our common pre-natal experience of a nourishing liquid environment *in utero*). Water as part of the made landscape relates us in profound ways to the origins of our beginnings. Its sounds and shapes and feel in parks and plazas call up deep emotional responses in us. . . .

These needs to which we respond . . . belong to the human species. They are "of nature, innate, transpersonal, pre-rational and (when altered) compulsive."[35]

What is important here is Halprin's recourse to the embryonic stage of life as forming the basis for claims about humanity's collective nature. The figure of the mother, whether generic or individualized, plays no role; it is as if reproduction happens in a vacuum and the uterus were a liquid sac floating in space, as portrayed in the now-classic photographs by Lennart Nilsson in his book *A Child Is Born* (1965). In Halprin's formulation, it is significant that the emphasis he places on nature is raised to the level of mythology, with the last line of Halprin's gloss on uterine environments a citation of Joseph Campbell's *The Masks of God: Primitive Mythology*.

One way to understand Halprin's use of such archaicizing language is what Mary Daly calls "male motherhood" as a patriarchal cooptation of procreation. She defines this term in at least two ways: "1: the fundamental reversal characteristic of patriarchal myth, e.g., god the father creating the world, Adam giving birth to Eve, Zeus bringing forth Athena. 2: male attempts to possess the creative powers of women, resulting in berserk and destructive simulations of motherhood—exemplified in the activities of obstetricians and gynecologists."[36] Halprin's archaizing language about the uterine environment as our common origin obscures the figure of the mother. In fact, it equates the mother with nature, raising the former to a universalized status, as if beyond the particularities of time and place. Sculpture and urban design, by extension, thus become exercises in restaging that originary "event," to use his terminology—that is, pregnancy and birth are restaged outside of a maternal figure, indeed as a masculinized appropriation of it.

Instead of mythology, Asawa turned to the genre of fairy tales when approached by Roth to complete the fountain commission. Invoking the site's proximity to San Francisco Bay and its connection to the Pacific Ocean, Asawa explained her choice of design in approachable terms: it would be something that would remind viewers of this body of water and what may lie within it. It would also be a source of pleasure for adults and children alike, and a fond memory for those children who would later grow up and visit the site. She must have known exactly what these men expected from her—she and Halprin had visited the square together in early 1966 and continued to remain in discussion as her design developed, as Halprin recalled: "I have had long dialogues with the sculptor explaining my attitude and describing the intention of the spaces. I have explained that the square is for people to be in and move in, that the adventure of involvement would be demeaned by something so specific. It is too limiting," he wrote in reference to *Andrea*. "One gets hung up by the mermaids, the turtles, and the frogs. [But] the only answer [from her] has been, 'This is what I want to do.'"[37] Her concern was not with monumentality but with scale; she consistently adjusted the design so that the figures, both human and animal, were in proportion to the site and to one another. An early proposal, submitted in January 1967, portrays a figurative grouping of four pubescent mermaids, flat-chested and childless, each riding on a sea turtle, accompanied by frogs and "electroplated plants around the pool." Water would spray out from the tops of their heads, mimicking a veil, according to another early sketch. She later discarded this proposal out of a concern that the figures would be out of scale in relationship to the turtles, whose shell she had cast from life.[38]

In the course of 1967, the plan changed: Asawa, now joined by her friend and neighbor Mae Lee, shifted the work's iconography: instead of an androgynous young body, they opted for a work in dialogue with the maternal body of Andrea Jepson. It is unclear whether the intention was a portrait, in line with Alice Neel's approach to the pregnant body, or whether any maternal body would have sufficed. My suspicion, given Asawa's choice of title, is that the work was to be legible both as a portrait but also in the more generic terms of a nursing figure. At some point, Asawa approached Jepson, then expecting her second child, about casting her pregnant. "I wasn't up for that," Jepson said. "But she wanted to make a statement about nursing mothers. So, when I had Matt in 1967, she did a body sculpture," the source for *Andrea*.[39] That body sculpture became, as Jepson would later describe the work in an outline for a manuscript on the sculpture, a "motherhood statement." Written after 1988, the proposed book never materialized, but its sketched table of contents indicates the relevant coordinates, including "the case of modernity vs. romanticism—scientifically clean versus something with curves and private places."[40]

Part of the book would have relayed Jepson's own experience of being cast, a process which she later described as playing a significant role in Asawa's decision to pursue a figurative sculpture. The latter's request to Jepson came on the heels of her "mask period," in which Asawa made life casts of faces using plaster, which I return to in the introduction to part III. This process entailed working with an entirely new medium and in direct interaction with sitters—something which her tied- and looped-wire sculptures did not involve. Jepson recalls how it felt to sit for Asawa as the artist experimented for the first time with a full-body plaster cast, which unfolded over a period of months. Because Jepson had just given birth and was breastfeeding an infant, the physicality of that process was even more heightened than usual: "The baby would cry, the milk lets down, and I would be covered by Vaseline and milk. I had the most gorgeous skin—like Marie Antoinette. I am here to tell you she had a reason to bathe in milk."[41]

A sequence of photographs taken by Warner Jepson, Andrea's husband at the time, chronicles the making of *Andrea*. Notably, Jepson herself is entirely absent from this sequence (as is baby Matt). Instead of photographing the living model, Warner animates the cast figure and its rubber molds, staging the torso in positions as if it were alive: reclining in a chair or sitting upright on the edge of a workbench (fig. 5.8). Asawa and Lee make only a few appearances. Raking light lends the torso a roundness and fleshiness that further intensify the effect of an animate body. Numbering in the dozens and assembled into an album, the photographs lend another dimension of fantasy to *Andrea*; here we are to experience the sculpture as if engendered by a modern-day Pygmalion: a female figure, made by the hand of the artist, whose initially inert form is brought to life by the power of erotic desire.[42] At the same time, the photographs add a new dimension to Ovid's retelling of this classical myth, in that the feminized body at issue is not a generalized one but a maternal one, far from classicizing ideals. Warner's photographic interpretation suggests we understand the autonomy frequently associated with the modern artwork—an idea often traced to the Pygmalion myth—as bracketed by maternal reproduction. The artwork does not come into this world in a parthenogenetic act carried out by a romanticized genius, but is made over time, piece by piece.

Warner Jepson's sequence of images also portrays Asawa's unexpected incorporation of the abstract sculpture which had likely earned her the commission. The mermaids' tails were made of looped wire, which she had dipped in wax and cast in bronze (fig. 5.9). This was a lengthy process that involved experiments with casting test pieces. These test pieces brought her otherwise vertical, hanging looped-wire sculptures down to the ground, as such objects were later displayed as artworks in their own right, always without a base and sitting flush on a surface. Asawa included a photograph of this sculpture in a portfolio of her work, where it is accompanied by

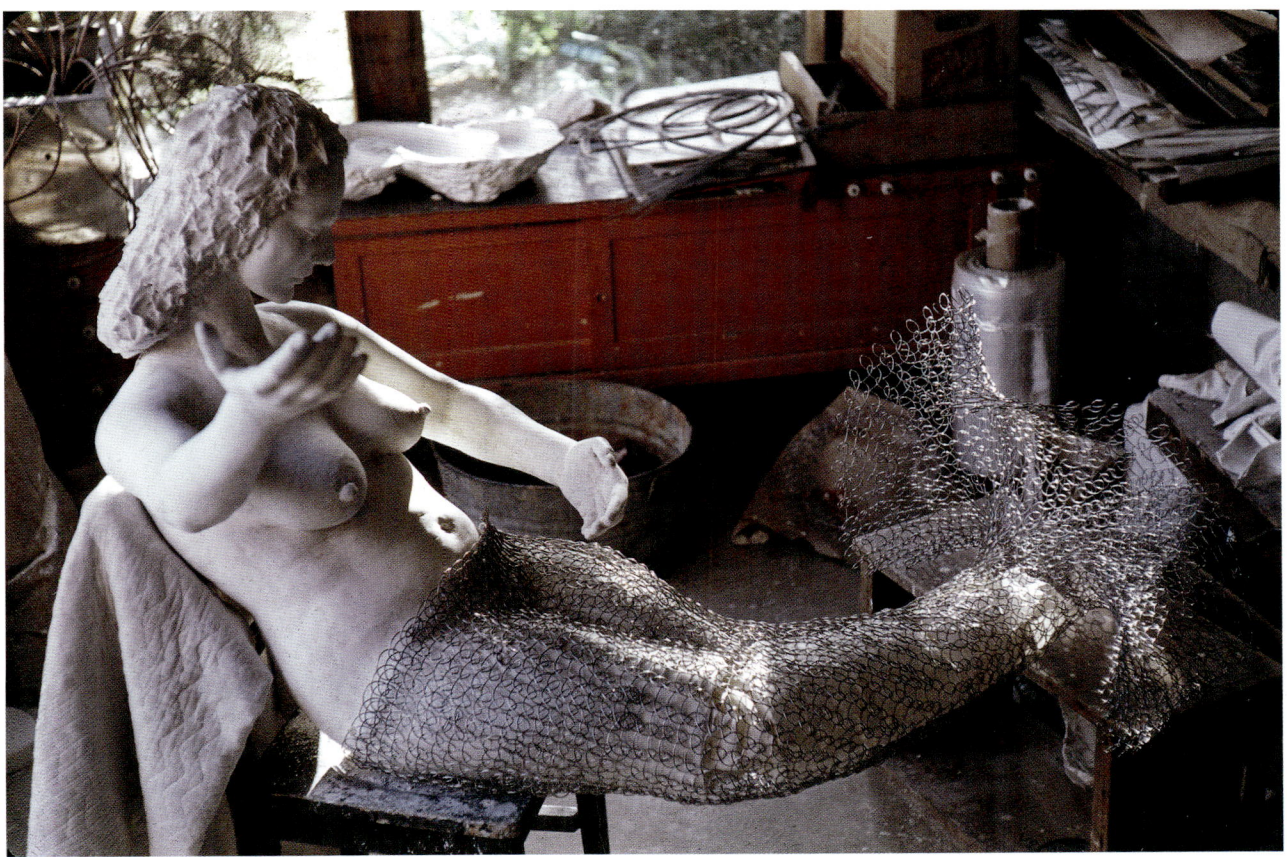

5.8 A plaster mold with looped-wire tail for Asawa's *Andrea* (PC.002), c. 1966. Photo: Warner Jepson.

the nondescript caption "cast bronze over wire," thus stripping the object of its figurative connotations and placing it back into the sphere of abstraction for which she was best known.[43] One could even propose that Asawa had indeed given Halprin what he wanted; it is just that no one could see it, the looped wire having been transformed into the tail of a mermaid.

As would become typical of the artist's public commissions, the entire fabrication was highly collaborative, involving a process of trial and error carried out by a group of people, particularly by Asawa and Lee but also the artists at the San Francisco Art Foundry, headed by Onno de Ruijter, which cast *Andrea* according to the lost-wax method. The process generated a multitude of other related works, including drawings and a life cast in bronze of the foundry artist Roi Brennan. Especially remarkable about the commission was the participation of Mae Lee and of Aiko, Asawa's eldest daughter. The three of them all figure in a photograph of the sculpture that was published in the local newspaper (fig. 5.10). Each of them, for instance, made frogs out of

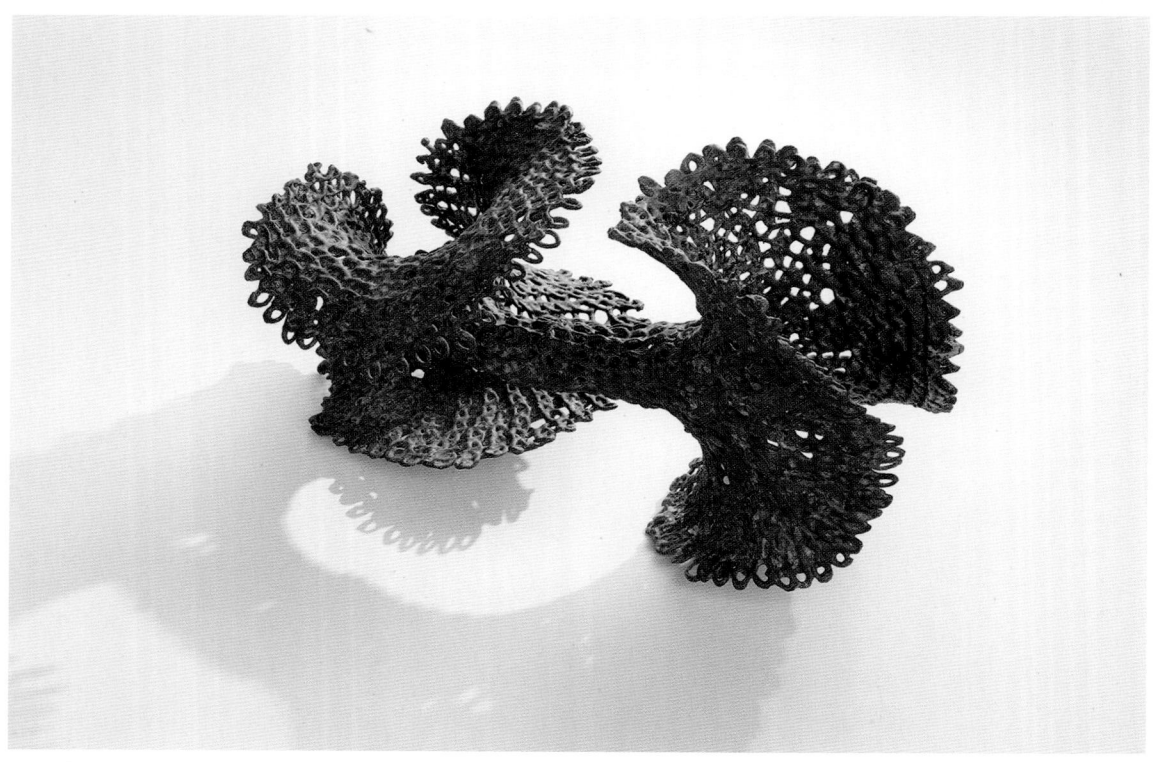

5.9 Ruth Asawa, *Study for Mermaid's Tail, Andrea, Ghirardelli Square Fountain* (S.218, Freestanding Reversible Undulating Form), c. 1967. Bronze, natural patina, 16½ × 29½ × 19 in. Private collection.

clay, which were then cast. Asawa had received an actual frog for Mother's Day, which she and Lee then observed; they also studied issues of *National Geographic*, enamored by the variety of different kinds of frogs and their movements as if "dancing," as the two women recalled, which accounts for the splayed limbs of several of the small amphibians in *Andrea* (fig. 5.11).[44] Strips of wax were used for the mermaids' hair (Asawa and Lee had considered initially using seaweed), and a baby doll provided the body of the infant, which also featured a small looped-wire tail dipped in wax and then cast. Once it was completed, the women decided to install the work under cover of night to avoid further publicity, given Halprin's stated opposition. The small affair was accompanied by champagne and congratulations, with one passerby—apparently inebriated, as Asawa and Lee recalled—claiming that it looked as if the sculpture had always been there.

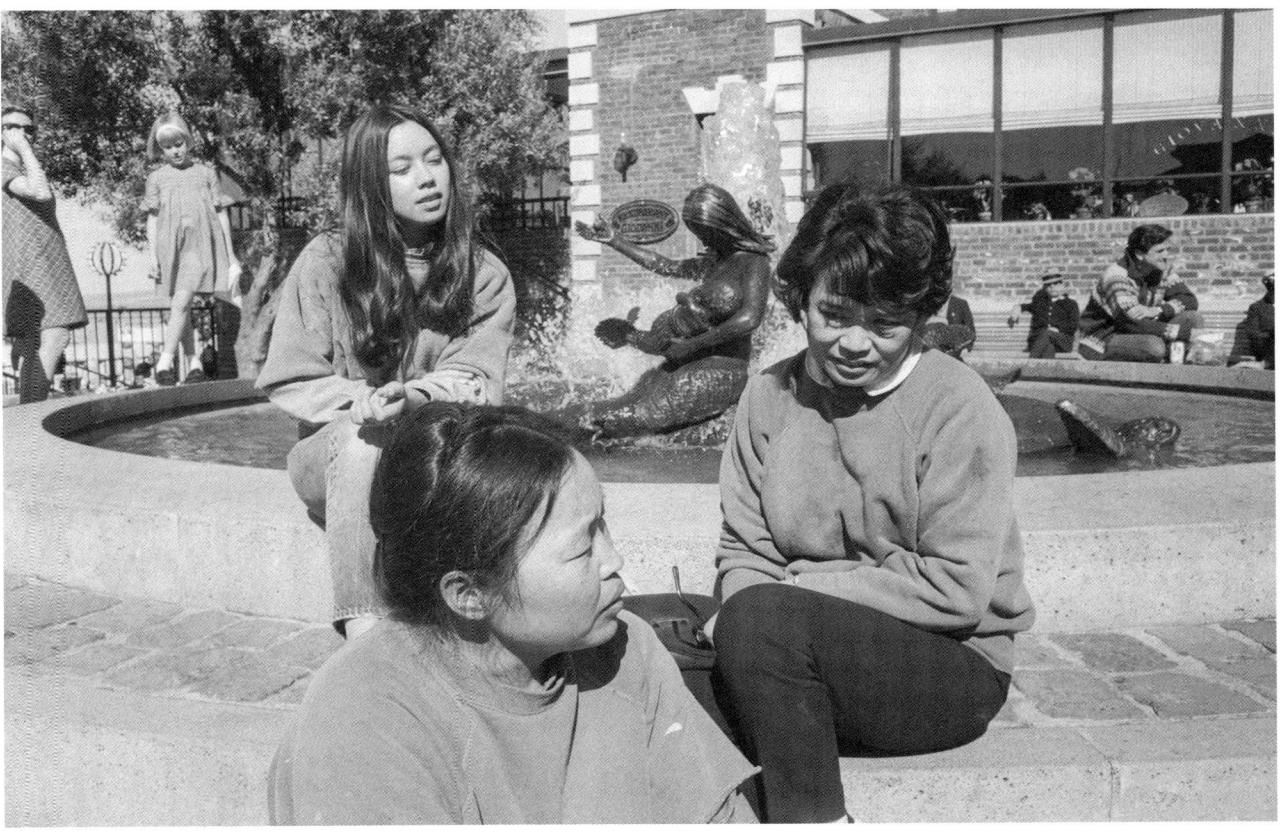

5.10 Ruth Asawa, Mae Lee, and Aiko Cuneo with *Andrea*, March 1968. Photo: Bill Nickols. Fang family *San Francisco Examiner* photograph archive negative files, BANC PIC 2006.029–NEG, The Bancroft Library, University of California, Berkeley.

Days after the sculpture's installation, Halprin circulated a two-page statement to colleagues and newspapers, stating his official position on the sculpture, as cited at the start of this chapter. In this "diatribe," as observers later called it, he attacked Asawa's choice of figurative imagery, dismissing the sculpture as sentimental and comparing it to lawn ornaments: "The cast iron deer, the little duck waddling on the lawn, now this sculpture are for other times, other places. The cuteness of Disneyland is appropriate for children—this is not meant to be only a playground for children."[45] Indeed, Ghirardelli was not necessarily meant to be a place for children at all, but rather for shopping, restaurants, and nightlife. The position he took was consistent with his opinion expressed a year before, when he explicitly called for cancellation of the commission: "I react to this as high camp on the same level as putting a cast iron deer in front of a modern house. It might work if *all* the buildings were very modern—as a fillip and contrast with tongue-in-cheek. But they aren't—they are old *and* new and the thing will just look cute in this context."[46]

Halprin's view of *Andrea* as "high camp" is extremely provocative, for it suggests a novel way of reading the work's appeal to a broad public as at once democratic and extremely sophisticated: that it could be a work of mass appeal at the same time as it could be read as tongue-in-cheek. To explore this hypothesis, we have to know more about what Halprin meant in comparing *Andrea* in Ghirardelli Square to a cast-iron deer placed in front a modern house—that is, the particular relationship to site that the sculpture invokes. As I have suggested already, Halprin envisioned a transcendent relationship to site as embodied in an abstract sculpture, an artwork that would engender "free play" of the viewer's imagination. The work of art should be inexhaustible, an ever-replenishing font of aesthetic experience. It should also be dynamic, "not formalized and constrained" or "static"—a sensibility finding articulation at virtually the same historical moment in the writings of art historian and critic Michael Fried, who in his 1967 essay "Art and Objecthood" defended the lyrical abstraction of modernist sculptors like Anthony Caro and David Smith against what he viewed as the mere everydayness of abstract minimalist sculpture, epitomized in the work of Tony Smith and Carl Andre. Halprin's complaints that representational sculpture fails to impact a viewer—that the figures "fix the design into an immutable, established shape which would inevitably have specific meaning"—parallel Fried's rejection of minimalist sculpture as reducing the artwork "to no more than a 'literal' object in the world."[47] For both Halprin and Fried, the enemy was precisely the "literal sculpture" that Asawa explicitly defended.

Halprin took this position while representing himself as the voice of a new generation. In the same month in which the *Andrea* controversy broke, he spoke to *San Francisco* magazine: "We are terribly hung-up on developing schemes for a generation that doesn't realize how outmoded it is. It has a certain set of values—making a nice place, making the world beautiful, making the family happy. And these values are being challenged right now to a degree most middle-aged people simply don't realize. As for me, I'd like to explore with young people what they want in the environment of the future."[48] This "future" for Halprin, especially in relation to Ghirardelli as a prominent preservationist project, meant achieving a "balance between the old 'victoriana' and newness in the Square," as I pointed to above. Ghirardelli was to be a model instance of this and was to be exemplary for future projects in other cities; it stood as testament "that the old can be preserved and put to use and be married to the new, to the mutual advantage of both."[49]

Some in the architectural community took issue with what Halprin had achieved in his design for Ghirardelli. Karl Kortum saw the designs as a "rebellion against everything that the Ghirardelli buildings stand for," with Halprin forcing the site to accept a kind of modern architecture he summed up as "world's-fair-hasty," defined by "a rigid grid of squares and rectangles," too much paving, "benches that appear to be derived from Charles Eames and the Herman Miller collection," hand-railings that are "gauche," and—perhaps most damning—the effect of a "warmed-over Brasilia"; the whole thing, Kortum wrote, reveals "the hollowness of any exhortation to 'be contemporary' in the Ghirardelli gardens."[50] The problem here was Halprin's drive to make the site "new," according to the injunction to be "creative," Kortum continued, an "ego-involvement" that ends up "rejecting everything that is good in the past in the process." Kortum's critique anticipated a broader response to Halprin's design, which Isenberg sums up as the insinuation that it was "standardized, cute, and tainted by an aura of the commercial amusement park," with one magazine calling the square a kind of "Disneyland for adults" and another comparing it to Tivoli Gardens, Copenhagen's Victorian-era amusement park, which Halprin had visited in 1965.[51] Several of Tivoli's architectural elements were incorporated into Ghirardelli Square, including the cast-iron streetlamps, illuminated buildings, "play sculpture," kiosks selling sweets, trees (willow and maple in Copenhagen, olive in Ghirardelli), and its "bubble fountain" in which pockets of air ascended through water captured in glass columns.

It is significant that Asawa was given the commission only after Halprin's renovations had been completed and people were using the square, with critiques like this circulating in the press. She was certainly aware of this reception. It is also significant that she repeatedly stressed her turn to figuration as resulting from her effort to create something in dialogue with the site. Years later, Asawa underscored the significance of context in her decision to go figurative: "I worked as an abstract artist. I knew that I could do that, I could please Larry [Halprin]. But I wanted something that fits the place. And I wanted to bring the ocean in. And because Ghirardelli is right near the water. So I wanted all that to be part of it. That's how I usually choose what I do. Not that I'm an abstract artist but what will fit the space."[52]

Isenberg has interpreted Asawa's dialogue with site in reference to the nearby topless bars of North Beach and the larger question of "the presence of women and female sexuality in public."[53] For some, *Andrea* represented a morally sound alternative to the topless club scene, while for others, it boldly flouted the prohibition against breastfeeding in public. One letter-writer interpreted the infant on the mermaid's chest as a "realistic" portrait of public breastfeeding: "With so many irresponsible abstractions claiming our time and attention today, it is refreshing to see a mermaid in the very real situation of nursing her young one," wrote one supporter, even sending a copy of her statement to La Leche International.[54] For others, the nudity invoked the obscene—but in both positive and negative ways. One viewer described her "shock at seeing in a family-frequented public place . . . one pair of frogs fornicating on a lily pad" and "another pair of frogs fornicating on another lily pad," adding how "each mermaid had clearly visible, at the end of her tail, a large open orifice completely unobstructed to the public's view."[55] Out of this "orifice" shot streams of high-pressured water, visible in a photograph by Laurence Cuneo. In contrast, other observers saw this explicit eroticism as part of the sculpture's success. As recently as 2003, the city's alternative *Bay Guardian* included *Andrea* in its "Best of" issue, describing the fountain as the city's "Best Public Orgy": even then, the debate was still present, prompting the paper to explain, "You see, the figures in her [Asawa's] mermaid fountain were breast-feeding, and that's still a touchy subject in public spaces in this country. But the lactating ladies are just a front for the fountain's truly scandalous feature. Bend down and take a good look at the lily pads—what the hell are those frogs doing together?"[56]

We should take seriously the strangeness of statements such as the one in which a fairy-tale character stands for the "very real situation" of public breastfeeding. This incongruence seems to be less the logical consequence of public debate around puritan morality in midcentury America than of an underlying uneasiness about sculpture's relationship to fantasy. As Naomi Wolf describes in her book *Promiscuities: The Secret Struggle for Womanhood*, *Andrea*'s explicit maternal iconography offers an alternative vision of female sexuality to that on offer in the urban context of downtown San Francisco in the 1960s, with its proliferation of topless bars:

My favorite was the scene in the bronze fountain at Ghirardelli Square, where two young mermaids played. They were surrounded by pond lilies, and on each lily pad was a welter of jolly toads. The scene was lewd: toads kissing, small toads jumped on the backs of big toads, and water spouted over it all. One mermaid held out her arms and toads leapt from her outstretched fingers. The mermaid bodies, though cast in metal, looked at once soft and strong. Each was a little pouchy in the belly and a little slack in the full breast. One mermaid cradled a merbaby in her arms.

The baby was laughing. The grown mermaids were naked in the most public of spaces—yet merry, confident, young and maternal.[57]

Wolf goes on to contrast this "imaginary" portrayal of motherhood to the "real" landscape of the city's nightclubs, though both were part of a context in which female nudity structured public space. Figures like Carol Doda, a well-known topless dancer in the city's North Beach district in the 1960s, as well as prevailing regulations around breastfeeding in public, formed the background against which Asawa's mermaids ignited a public conversation about gender in civic space, as Isenberg argues. "As I grew older," Wolf recalled, "the Carol Doda images proliferated and became active and three-dimensional, and the glimpses of what the mermaids represented grew rarer and quainter."

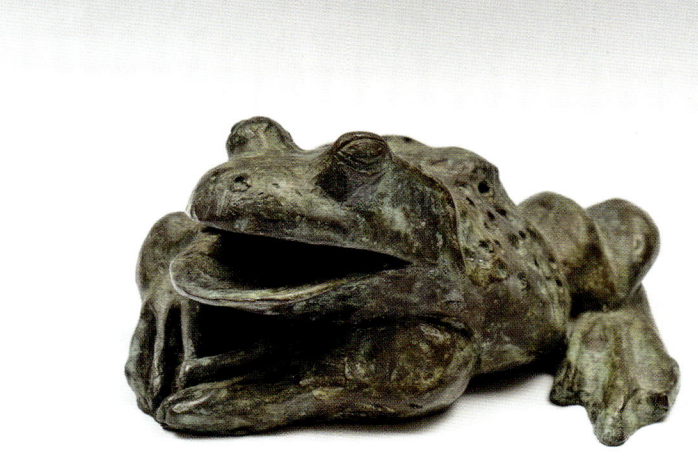

5.11 Ruth Asawa and Mae Lee, Ghirardelli Frog for *Andrea* (F.206, Cast Bronze Frog), 1968. Bronze, 3⅛ × 7¾ × 7 in. Private collection.

What the mermaids represented was deliberately left open by Asawa, available for the individual fantasy of each viewer. While Asawa remained largely silent on the debate (in inverse proportion to Halprin's verbosity on the issue), she did type up her "thoughts," which stayed in her own files (in distinction to Halprin's public "statement"). In this reflection, she emphasizes the sculpture's relationship to its environment beyond the plaza, especially its proximity to the sea: "I thought of all of the children and maybe even some adults who would stand by the seashore waiting for a turtle or a mermaid to appear." Here, wonderment is at issue: "As you look at the sculpture, you include rather than block out the ocean view which was saved for all of us, and you wonder what lies below that surface."[58] By contrast, Halprin would have this fantasy carefully orchestrated as an experience of the transcendent, with some unforeseen, revelatory insight into the relationship between Man and Nature. Halprin's colleague Fred Martin, director of the California School of Fine Arts, suggests as much when he wrote to Halprin after a Saturday afternoon visit to the fountain: "as you had suggested the fountain was actively debasing public taste by providing a diversion from the demands of art into the trivialities of anecdote." Apparently, this debasement took place in "parents saying to their children, 'Look at the turtle, darling, and see the cute little frogs.'"[59]

To suggest that *Andrea* is high camp is to see in her gesture a send-up of this position—of the absurdity that follows from patriarchy, based as it is on the incongruity between the sacred Mother and the profane Woman, to invoke again Esther Newton, but also the absurdity in such an egomaniacal conception of "the demands of art," in which the viewer must conform to the staged experience set out by the all-knowing artist-architect. And more concretely, it calls out the absurdity of a preservationist project that would seem to have inadvertently recycled commercialized, mass spectacle entertainment. We can read Asawa's reference to the plaza's "space" in terms of its proximity to the ocean, and thus explain the suitability of the mermaid as subject, but we can also read her invocation of site as a nod to the fact that *Andrea* merely made explicit contradictions that Halprin's own design for the plaza had already introduced. Instead of "violating" Halprin's original idea, as he had claimed in his public

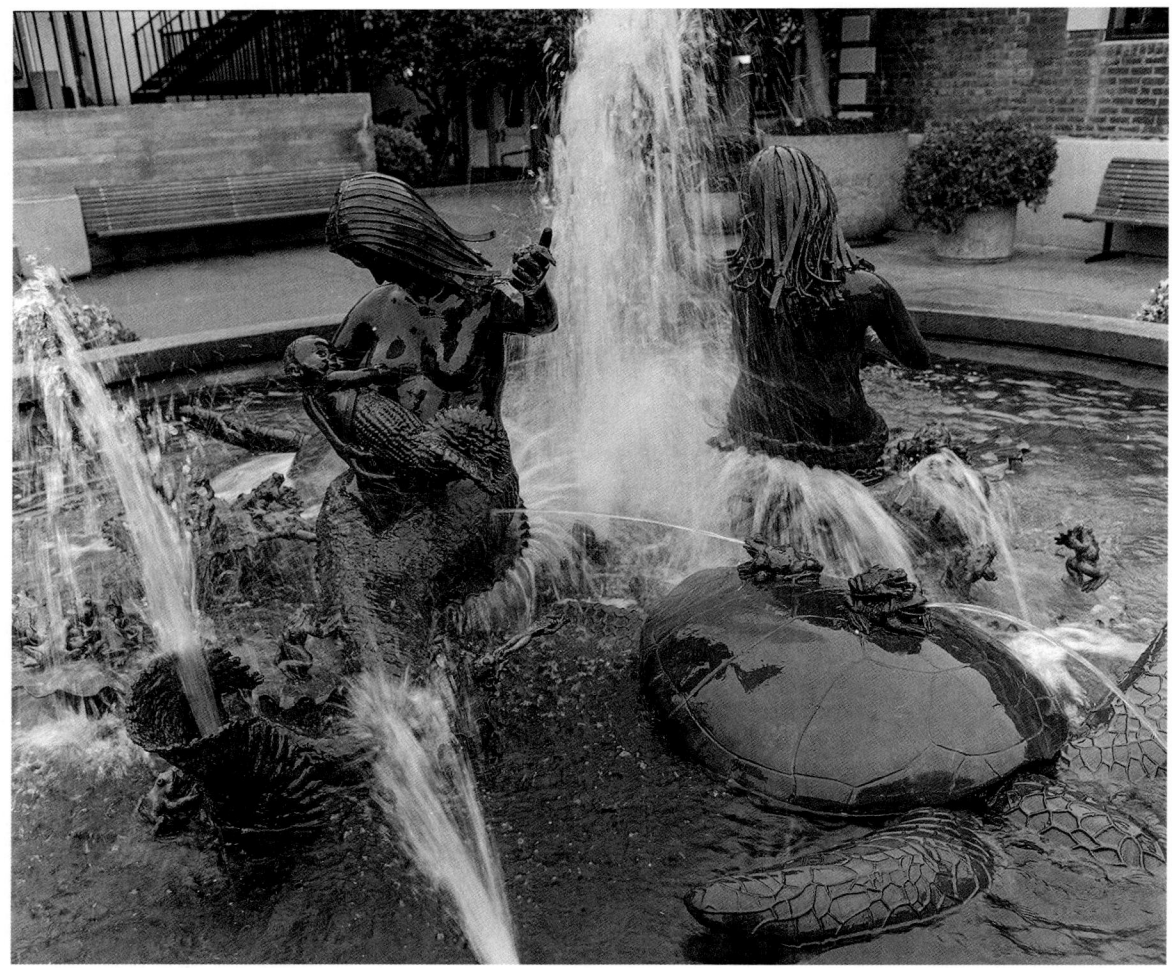

5.12 Ruth Asawa, *Andrea* (PC.002), detail, 1966–1968. Bronze, brown and green patina, 60 × 192 × 192 in. Photo: Laurence Cuneo.

statement, Asawa's mermaids outed his own suspicion that his design had failed to reconcile old and new, as he had wished: "I am also afraid," he tellingly wrote in 1967, "that [the sculpture] will tip the balance between Ghirardelli's 'atmosphere' into a Disneyland character with Victorian overtones."[60] Recalling the discussion earlier in this book of modernism in revolt against Victorian motherhood, Halprin's modernist credentials left him little prepared for a site dominated by this aesthetic and a central sculpture that would make his attempts at disavowal futile. The mermaid's iconography references Scandinavian Victoriana, both in terms of the Danish fairy tale published by Hans Christian Andersen in 1837, as part of a collection for children, and the *Little Mermaid* sculpture in Copenhagen by Edvard Eriksen—a prime example of what Halprin called, in making a hard distinction between "sculpture" versus "children's sculpture," one of those objects that "can become so identified with a city that its image is the city"—as has since become the case with *Andrea*.[61] In the case of Eriksen's sculpture, that identification was also evidenced by multiple acts of vandalism beginning in the 1960s, including its decapitation by a Danish member of the Situationist International in 1964—a year before Asawa was awarded the Ghirardelli commission. Asawa did indeed seem to upset Halprin's "balance between 'victoriana' and newness," tipping it "in the wrong direction."[62]

In an essay written at the same historical moment as the *Andrea* controversy, Susan Sontag famously defined "the sensibility—unmistakably modern, a variant of sophistication but hardly identical with it—that goes by the name of 'Camp.'"[63] Many of camp's central features are also characteristic of *Andrea* (keep in mind, too, that the circles of the two women overlapped in the early 1950s, as I discuss in chapter 1): the conversion of the "serious" into the "frivolous" and a "dethroning" of the serious; a sensibility that is overly "disengaged, depoliticized—or at least apolitical"; an explicit embrace of "the unnatural: of artifice and exaggeration"—"nothing in nature can be campy," Sontag writes—it is often decorative, at the expense of context; "the farthest extension, in sensibility, of the metaphor of life as theater." Importantly, Asawa and Mae Lee had planned to have a sound element, composed by Warner Jepson, in which croaking frogs would be heard through speakers placed in the surrounding olive trees. They had also proposed mechanically moving flippers on the sea turtles—both suggestions were never realized. Above all, Sontag writes, "Camp rests on innocence," which Asawa certainly brought to the table in her repeatedly self-effacing claims to have merely tried to make a sculpture that everyone could enjoy—a gesture that can only be read as camp, as either "completely naïve or else wholly conscious."

THE VIEWER'S SHARE

Such strategies were pervasive among Asawa and her colleagues. Sally Woodbridge created a campy version of the *Abduction of Europa* in ceramic. A self-satisfied Europa lounges dreamily on the back of Zeus-turned-white-bull. Her firm breasts with their target-like nipples and her long legs seem to have been modeled after the clichéd naked woman in heels leaning against a sports car. Barnacles ornament her flowing red locks, which become one with the red head and horns of the bull (fig. 5.13). This is hair, both human and animal, that seems to have been pressed through the same garlic presses that these women would use to make monumental sculptures from baker's clay, which I address in chapter 7. It is in line with a broader strategy of undoing patriarchal norms by embracing the language of its best-known narratives: as Esther Newton writes, one of the female impersonators she featured in her study "had a whole collection of these 'fairy tales,' which were his reworkings of traditional fairy tales to give them a homosexual dimension."[64] Woodbridge's *Europa and the Bull* and *Andrea* as hybrid woman-animal forms should be seen within a marginalized strand of critique investigating the foundations of what Dorothy Dinnerstein called our "sexual arrangements" from the perspective of "our continuities with, and our differences from, the earth's other animals," or put into more contemporary terminology, of our implication in a multispecies existence.[65]

Undoing the fairy tale as a method for undoing the myths of patriarchy would persist in work by younger artists, such as Ree Morton. Like Woodbridge and Asawa, Morton worked for years without a dedicated studio, constructing sculptures in suburban basements and behind washer-dryer units. "I still was not able to call myself an artist. I mean, I was a housewife, right?" she recalled in a 1974 interview. "I was a mother, I had children, I had a family to take care of. And [being an artist] was something I did in my extra time." She discussed how her teachers in art school would talk often about "being committed to your work." That word—"commitment"—had, as Morton said, "a lot of implications that I couldn't accept, the kind of lifestyle that I didn't think I wanted."[66] Her sketchbooks, maintained between 1968 and 1977, contain ideas for the papier-mâché sculptures that she would later make, as well as lines copied from Ludwig Wittgenstein and Victorian field guides. One widely reproduced entry lists, in two vertical columns, Morton's enthusiasms and antipathies. Her "likes" include Byzantine mosaics, Roman villa murals, Sumerian idols, and good liars; among her "hates" are abstract expressionism, Greek Hellenistic sculpture, Stephen Greene, and good taste.

One can read *Andrea* as mobilizing motherhood against itself, as a send-up of good taste and well-behaved public artists. If, as Helen Molesworth has read the work of Ree Morton, "the space of the sentimental" is the space of the maternal, then these works are instances of the maternal in drag—of seemingly sentimental gestures that, upon closer inspection, transform into an irreverent mockery, just as, to draw on Newton once more, "the camp is concerned with what might be called a philosophy of transformations and incongruity."[67] This is where it is important that Asawa had chosen the language of fairy tales and particularly the Little Mermaid. Marina Warner reads this tale in the version told by Hans Christian Andersen with an emphasis on the Little Mermaid's loss of her own voice, exchanging her ability to speak and sing for human form so she can be united with the beloved prince whom she saved from drowning. "The coupled image of voice and water," Warner argues, resonates with "the memory of the haven of the womb, and in the first sounds of the mother's voice, that acoustic mirror. Fairy tales attempt to restore its resonance; they pretend

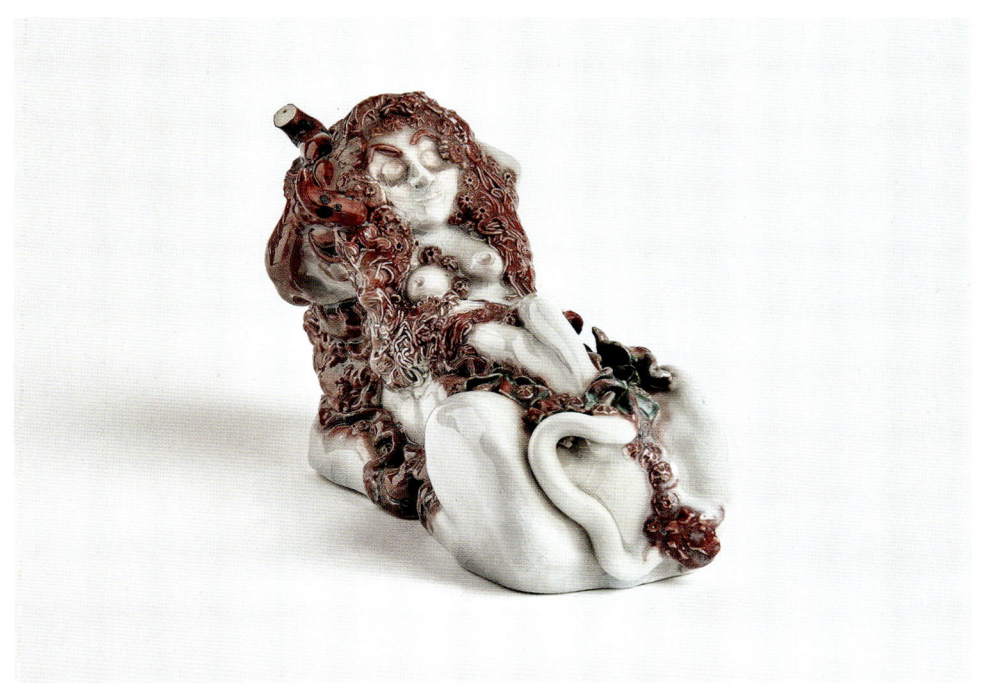

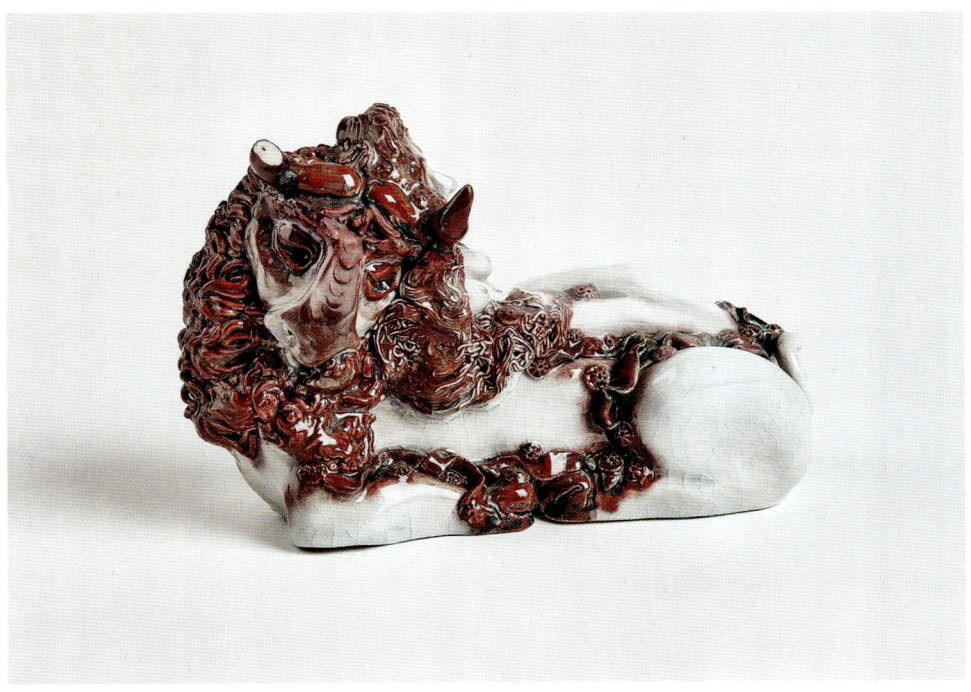

5.13 Sally Woodbridge, *Europa and the Bull*, c. 1970.
Ceramic, 6 × 9 × 4 in. Collection of Pamela Woodbridge.
Photos: James Paonessa.

to a world of nursery certainties. But they also often record that voice's obliteration, and never more so than in the tales of silenced mermaids."[68] Warner further points out that contemporary women writers have often turned to the figure of the "silent heroine." Looking back to the significance of this work, we should see *Andrea* in this lineage, with the figure of the silenced mermaid metaphorizing the silenced mother— whether or not Asawa herself would have made that claim (and she certainly did not). For works of art circulate and act on the world in an orbit that far exceeds the statements of their maker. If we learned nothing else from Andy Warhol, we learned to distrust the artist's claims and look closely at the work itself; without this lesson, we would be hard-pressed to see *Andrea* clearly.

In that sense, *Andrea* is best understood when we have a capacious understanding of motherhood, one that is closer to something like a queering of straight narratives of mastery and authenticity. Had Asawa been a man, such a provocation may have been entertained much earlier; no doubt her gender—and her identity as an Asian American woman—shaped a set of expectations in which this perceived naivete was welcomed—and believed. *Andrea* played to the equation Nature = Woman spelled out in the epigraph by Susan Griffin, while simultaneously deconstructing those terms by undercutting the universalizing claims made on their behalf. "Beyond the 'straight' public sense in which something can be taken, one has found a private zany experience of the thing," Sontag writes. She locates "a particular affinity" of camp with the marginalized position of "homosexual aestheticism and irony" as well as "Jewish moral seriousness." In both instances, "camp is a solvent of morality. It neutralizes moral indignation, sponsors playfulness."[69] We can even locate this queer undercurrent to *Andrea* in the ways in which the fairy tale itself is bound up with the homosexual desire of its author, having been read as an allegory of desire that could not be openly acknowledged.[70]

I end this chapter with one final consideration of *Andrea*'s reception, to be found in Halprin's archives at the University of Pennsylvania: a page torn from the *San Francisco Chronicle* on which an erect phallus has been drawn on top of a photograph of the fountain, complete with a tangle of pubic hair and two humps at its base (fig. 5.14). The drawing was apparently sent to Halprin by someone claiming to be "Art Kutecture"—a phonetical play on "architecture." From its red tip, four pronounced drops of liquid shoot out over the bay in the background. Delineated in blue, red, and yellow marker, as if gesturing to the primary colors, the phallus is accompanied by a measurement along its vertical axis: "about fifteen feet," it reads. The spurting phallus recalls the water spouting from the fountain's many copulating frogs—as well as the knowing laughter on the part of Asawa and Mae Lee as they looked back on this episode some thirty years later.[71]

5.14 Page from the *San Francisco Chronicle*, March 26, 1968, drawn upon by an anonymous person using the name "Art Kutecture." Lawrence Halprin Collection, Architectural Archives, University of Pennsylvania.

4 San Francisco Chronicle ☆ Tues., Mar. 26, 1968

Scorn for a New Sculpture

Ghirardelli Square Controversy

By George Draper

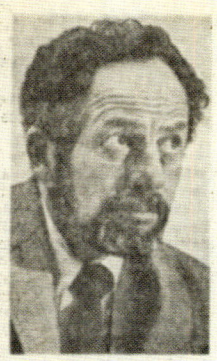

LAWRENCE HALPRIN
'The scale is wrong'

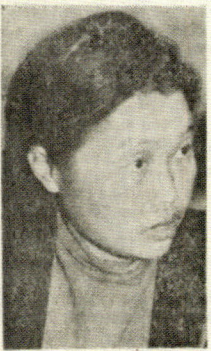

RUTH ASAWA
'A childhood fantasy'

A seemingly innocent and conventional piece of sculpture recently installed in the fountain at Ghirardelli Square was bitterly attacked yesterday by landscape architect Lawrence Halprin.

"This sculpture is out of character with the space it is in; it is at the wrong scale for the plaza; and in my view completely out of character with the design intent of Ghirardelli Square," Halprin wrote.

DESIGNERS

The two-page Halprin statement attacking the mermaids, turtles and frogs created by sculptress Ruth Asawa was widely distributed to newspapers and designers.

Halprin has been the landscape architect for Ghirardelli Square and was appointed by President Johnson last year to the newly formed Advisory Council on Historic Preservation.

Miss Asawa, wife of architect Albert Lanier, is the mother of six children and a new appointee to the San Francisco Art Commission.

She was commissioned by William Roth, owner of Ghirardelli Square, to design the fountain sculpture.

Contra Costa Residents Haul Garbage

Contra Costa county's striking garbagemen picketed emergency dumps yesterday, but did not stop residents from continuing to haul their own garbage.

Strikers complained that some of the do-it-yourself garbage dumpers actually were "strikebreakers" who were hauling the garbage of other residents for a fee.

Crowds of Contra Costa county householders made their way through the picket lines at the three dumps in

Warren Lemmon, president of Ghirardelli Square, said Roth approved Miss Asawa's concept although he had not seen the finished work.

Lemmon ordered the sculpture emplaced last week and he assumed it would remain where it is unless Roth has a change of mind.

CONCEPT

Lemmon said Halprin protested Miss Asawa's concept a year ago "and we listened carefully."

The sculpture is representational, depicting two mermaids seated more or less back-to-back on water lily

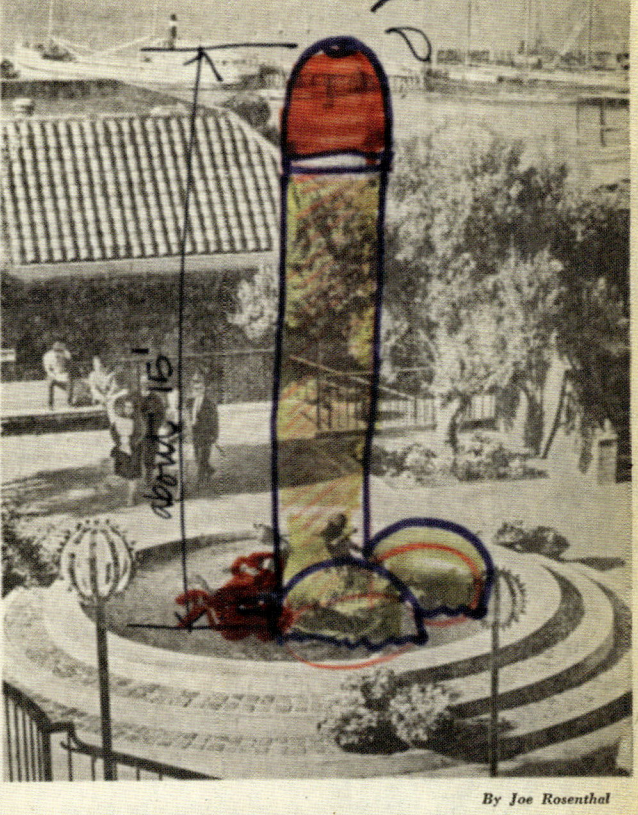

By Joe Rosenthal

This mermaid sculpture came under bitter attack

many frolicking frogs. The general mood expressed by the piece is one of serenity.

Miss Asawa, reached at her home, told The Chronicle she may not know as much about fountains as Halprin.

"But I think I know more than he about sculpture," she said.

Ultimately, she said, the sound of croaking frogs will be piped from the olive trees surrounding the fountain to make it all more realistic and amusing.

In defense of her work, Miss Asawa said:

WIND

thing for the young to remember when they are old."

Halprin, on the other hand, told The Chronicle he was thinking in terms of an abstraction for the fountain, a shaft of metal about 15 feet high.

Miss Asawa, however, said she was told by Ghirardelli Square officials that the fountain could not be over six feet high lest the wind blow the water all over the visitors.

"I did not want a sculpture in the fountain," Halprin said in his statement. "I wanted the fountain to be the sculp-

play of water and metal would give free play to the essential qualities of water — not formalized and constrained but organically evolved."

Halprin said there has been a battle in the development of Ghirardelli Square to preserve a balance between "Victoriana" and newness.

"There are, I believe, already too many Victorian overtones invading the Square."

The Halprin communique bravely concluded with: "Remove the bronze mermaids, the turtles, and the frogs."

The height measurement refers to Halprin's wish for a monumental public sculpture, delineated in the accompanying newspaper article. Halprin "told *The Chronicle* he was thinking in terms of an abstraction for the fountain, a shaft of metal about 15 feet high."[72] Apparently, the article elaborates, although this may have been Halprin's desire, it was far from that of Roth and the commissioning officials, who had told Asawa that the fountain could not be over six feet high or the wind would blow water all over the spectators. Telephoned at her home, Asawa responded to the media frenzy that ensued, saying that, although she might not know as much about fountains as Halprin, "I think I know more than he about sculpture." She also elaborated on her plan to include a recorded sound element, composed by Jepson: "croaking frogs will be piped from the olive trees surrounding the fountain to make it all more realistic and amusing"—thus circulating this element as an idea even if it did not end up being realized in the sculpture itself.

Once this "shaft" comment was printed and distributed, it unleashed another wave of anti-Halprin sentiment. One woman called his office to tell him that she wished "you would go take your fifteen-foot shaft of metal and go sit on it somewhere." Others described Halprin's complaints as the petulant whimpering of a small child. Another woman, writing to Asawa in a letter with the subject line "symbolic art," seemed to hit the nail on the head: "May I suggest that Mr. Halprin is offended more by the fact that a phallic symbol has been changed into a maternal one than by his logical objections to the mermaid piece in the Square? . . . I interpret your fantasy just as I please, but I still suspect Mr. Halprin's anger is based upon quite other motives than he is consciously aware of!"[73] These "other motives" are spelled out for us by art historian Griselda Pollock, who astutely observed that phallocentric culture "is premised on substitutions and repressions—particularly of the Mother."[74] In obscuring the mermaid sculpture with a gigantic phallus, the unnamed critic makes this equation of substitutions and repressions visible.

Thus the drawing makes explicit the erotic dimensions of a sculpture that almost everyone assumed to be "quaint" and "cute." This erotic dimension centers on the work's figural dimension—an invocation of eroticism that, Lucy Lippard had pointed out a year before, is much more difficult to attain "in figuration, where erotic subject matter rather than erotic effect tends to dominate the attention."[75] What is figured in *Andrea*, through Art Kutecture's reading, is a collision not between male and female, but between maternal and paternal paradigms—and particularly the way in which the mother under patriarchy, according to the logic of that power structure, must be supplanted. This is the psychoanalytic account of identity formation, in which "it is not the Female Nude but the Mother Nude that is the symbol of the castration threat, the absence of a penis, and the raising of the phallus-cum-child into the symbolic."[76] It is this logic that June Wayne, founder of the Tamarind Lithography Workshop and close colleague of Asawa, pinpointed as the source for common accounts of creativity as deriving from the woman artist who "substitute[s] making art for making babies as a pathological expression of penis envy, a view still voiced by male art teachers."[77]

Rather than dismiss *Andrea* as a work of sentimentality, I argue we need to include it in histories of 1960s sculpture and particularly in those histories that admit to the powerful place that the erotic held, whether explicitly acknowledged, as Lippard does, or acknowledged only in secret, as Christa Robbins has pointed out in her reading of Michael Fried's use of terms like "perversion" and "faggot sensibility" to describe minimalist sculpture's refusal to enact a "subversion of desire."[78] In her reading of Lippard's essay "Eros Presumptive," Anne Wagner reminds us that this was a moment in sculpture "when fantasy—even erotic fantasy—was one word for the viewer's share."[79] Whether one rejected figuration or embraced it, at stake was "the ability of the work of art to transcend atomized taste and enter into something like a community of meaning making," as Robbins points out.[80] This was a "plurality of responses to the questions of the erotic and gendered," according to David Getsy.[81] Just as recent art history has recovered modernism's debt to queering the work of art, its maker, and its beholder, offering an expansion of its meaning, so too does *Andrea*'s evocation of maternal camp revise the horizon of meaning offered by public sculpture at midcentury.

III CARETAKING IN PUBLIC

Entering through a wooden gate draped by wisteria, visitors to the Asawa-Lanier home in San Francisco's Noe Valley would have made their way along the winding stone path through the front garden to encounter a remarkable scene: a cedar-shingled wall of the house covered with hundreds of life-sized ceramic masks. Cast first in plaster from a living sitter, then in clay, and finally fired, the masks furnish a kind of informal guest book of those visiting. Those visitors included friends and family members, other artists, and important community members, but they also encompassed many schoolchildren who came on field trips to see the studio of a professional artist (fig. III.1). Displaying markers like "Room 12," corresponding to the student's class, several of the masks capture children involved in Asawa's work in the city's public school system as part of the Alvarado School Arts Workshop. Unnamed, the masks provide us with only the details of students' faces, which speak to the city's diverse population and gesture to its struggle to desegregate its schools, an effort that began in 1971, three years after Asawa became involved in its arts curriculum.

The initial inspiration for life casting came after Asawa read an article in *Life* magazine on Roman portraiture, and the verism of these casts—in which every detail has been recorded through the plaster mold once covering the sitter's skin—is one of the works' most remarkable features. It is as if hundreds of disembodied faces stare out from a living wall. This verism, however, stands in stark contrast to the masks' withholding of skin and hair color; although together they furnish a spectrum of clay tones, with the vast majority unpainted and unglazed and set off against the dark brown of the wooden shingles, none lay claim to resemblance. This is no physiognomic survey; each cast stands for nothing beyond the sitter from which it was pulled, and many bear remarkably detailed surfaces. Even the arrangement belies order: the array shown here, captured in a photograph taken by Asawa's son-in-law, was only one moment in its evolution over four decades, beginning in the mid-1960s, once

III.1 Ruth Asawa, *Untitled* [Unknown Young Adult(?)], detail of *Untitled* (LC.012, Wall of Masks), c. 1966–2000. Ceramic, bisque-fired clay, 8½ × 4⅜ × 2⅜ in. Cantor Arts Center at Stanford University; William Alden Campbell and Martha Campbell Art Acquisition Fund. Conservation made possible by the Robert Mondavi Family Fund at the Cantor Arts Center and the Asian American Art Initiative Fund.

III.2 Hundreds of bisque-fired life cast masks on the exterior of Ruth Asawa's Noe Valley home, San Francisco, CA, c. 2010. Photo: Laurence Cuneo.

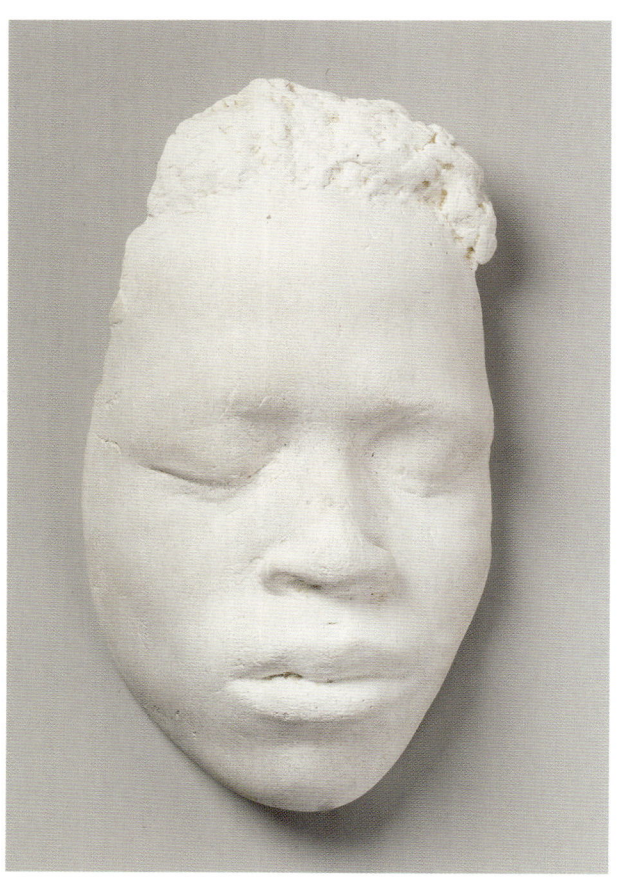

Asawa had learned the technique from a local schoolteacher (fig. III.2). Masks were added, exchanged, taken down, and replaced, with no rhyme or reason except for how the grouping appeared as a whole. At one point, Asawa conveyed to the curator Gerald Nordland that she intended to make ten thousand masks, guided by ceramicist Marguerite Wildenhain's insight that "history has never repeated a face."[1]

It is tempting to see this arrangement as resembling conceptual art's strict inventorying and seriality—Douglas Huebler's claim that he would photograph every person on earth comes to mind, as does Nicholas Nixon's forty-year-plus ritual of photographing his wife and her three sisters. But *Untitled* (LC.012, Wall of Masks), which comprises a work of 233 masks in its form as a single work in the collection of the Cantor Arts Center, is not exhaustive like these other examples. Rather, it plays, unsystematically, with sameness and difference: the faces conform to a set convention, with predictable edges marked by hairline and jawline, and devoid of emotional expression. And yet slight differences interrupt this repetition: an open pair of eyes or blank holes where we would expect the eyes to be. Taut, smooth skin betrays a youthful sitter, while etched grooves and sagging flesh evidence the presence of an aging body. Asawa described one mask made for a project supporting the VNA Hospice Foundation as "a drawing on clay."[2] It is singularity rather than systematicity that rules.

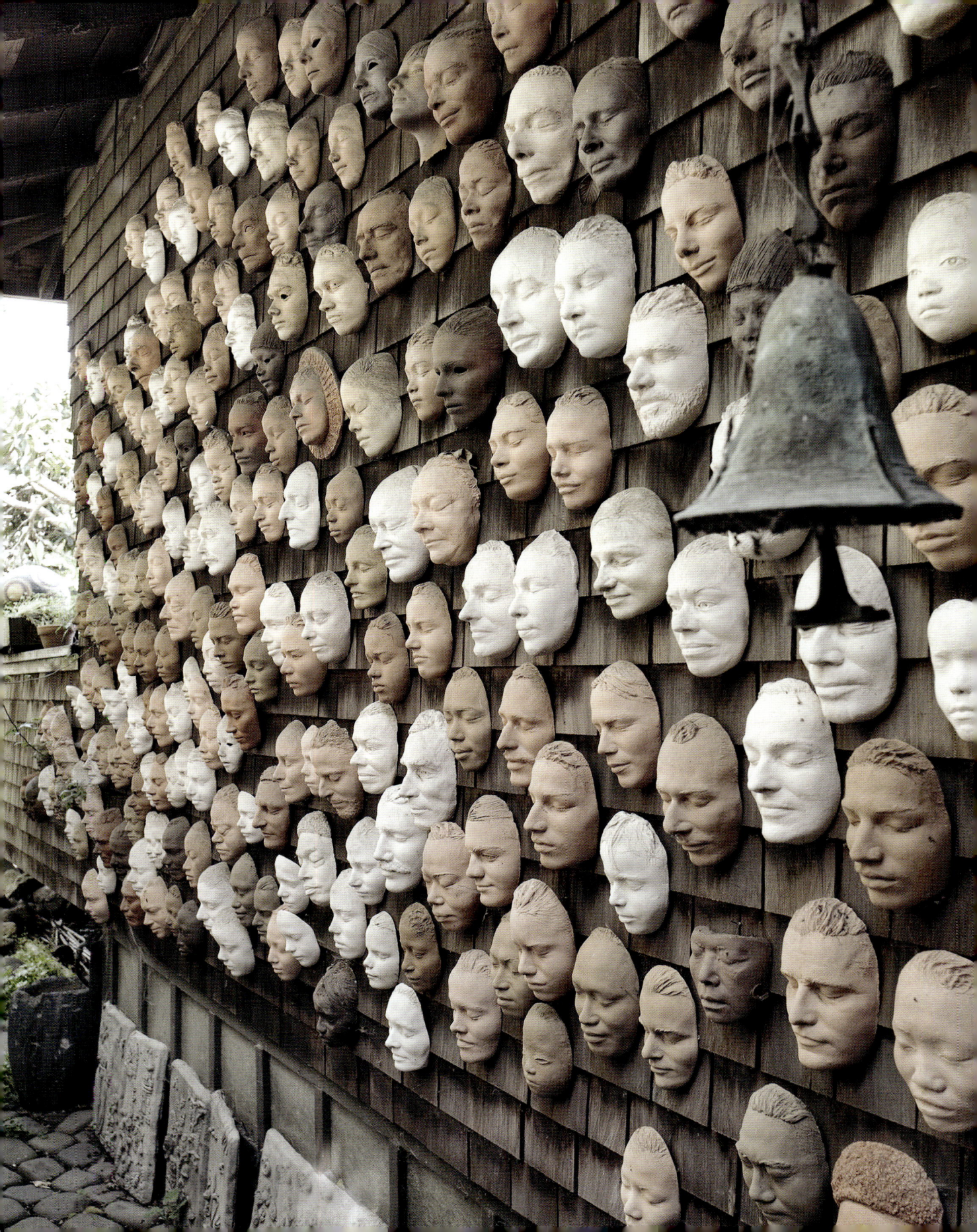

Although now canonized in Asawa's oeuvre, the work is less a "portrait" than an intense confrontation with time passing. It emerged from the profound grasp of temporality that one has when accompanying the growth of human life. As Asawa later recalled, "I like the idea of it lasting. So when I cast a face I know I'm just capturing a minute of a person. Or if I cast a foot of a baby I know that baby's foot will grow and grow and grow. But at the moment I like that. That moment that I caught in a way is what I like about casting faces. I don't care about making that a technique. But I like the idea of stopping the moment of a time. And it's going to disappear. I know it's going to go away but I like that, I like that moment."[3] This disappearance is the amnesia of mothering—that one truly forgets the younger version of the child or teenager or young adult, because one now knows that child or teenager or young adult as they are *now* and not as they were. It is the constant acceptance of loss that is an intrinsic part of raising another human, drawn to our attention by Albert Lanier in observing his own mother and writing his prescient observations to Asawa even before the two began having their own children: "Being a mother is hard ruth, there are so many deaths . . . the death of the baby, the death of the boy, the death of the collegiate son . . . and so much bewilderment."[4] Asawa's ritualistic practice of life casting over the decades in which her children were growing and had grown enabled her to come to terms with this monumental task of acceptance.

Poet and art critic John Yau has described *Untitled* as "a sculptural diary of the people in Asawa and her family's life, as well as a chronicle of a community's existence in time."[5] In addition to Asawa's children and family members, often cast repeatedly at multiple stages in their lives, many artist-mothers appear on the wall, including Merry Renk, Mae Lee, and Peggy Tolk-Watkins, as well as other women artists in Asawa's immediate circle of friends, including Beth Van Hoesen, Joan Pearson Watkins, and Trude Guermonprez. Other masks represent important figures in San Francisco's cultural landscape: Blanche Pastorino ran a legendary restaurant, while John Gutmann founded the photography department at San Francisco State University in 1946; Cyril Magnin, or "Mr. San Francisco," served as CEO and president of a luxury department store chain in the city, and Tommy Roberts, also known affectionately as the "puppet man," was a regular fixture in the Tenderloin and in the city's parks, entertaining children with his Asawa-created puppets. As evident in a drawing of the masks by Van Hoesen—who herself features in the grouping—these are better described as living "faces" rather than "masks" or "portraits" in their invocation of the ongoing temporality that is living (fig. III.3).

I open part III with *Untitled* (LC.012) because its arrest of snapshot-like individuality originated from Asawa's work with children in the public schools—the subject of the following two chapters. This encounter, which began in 1968 with the establishment of an arts program in the neighborhood's Alvarado Elementary School, gave rise to a vast spectrum of artistic creation, from mural-making to gardening to arts festivals which extended to several dozen schools across the city working in close collaboration with public offices like the Parks and Recreation Department. Some of this material culture has lasted, like the cast-bronze public sculpture *San Francisco Fountain* (1970–1973),

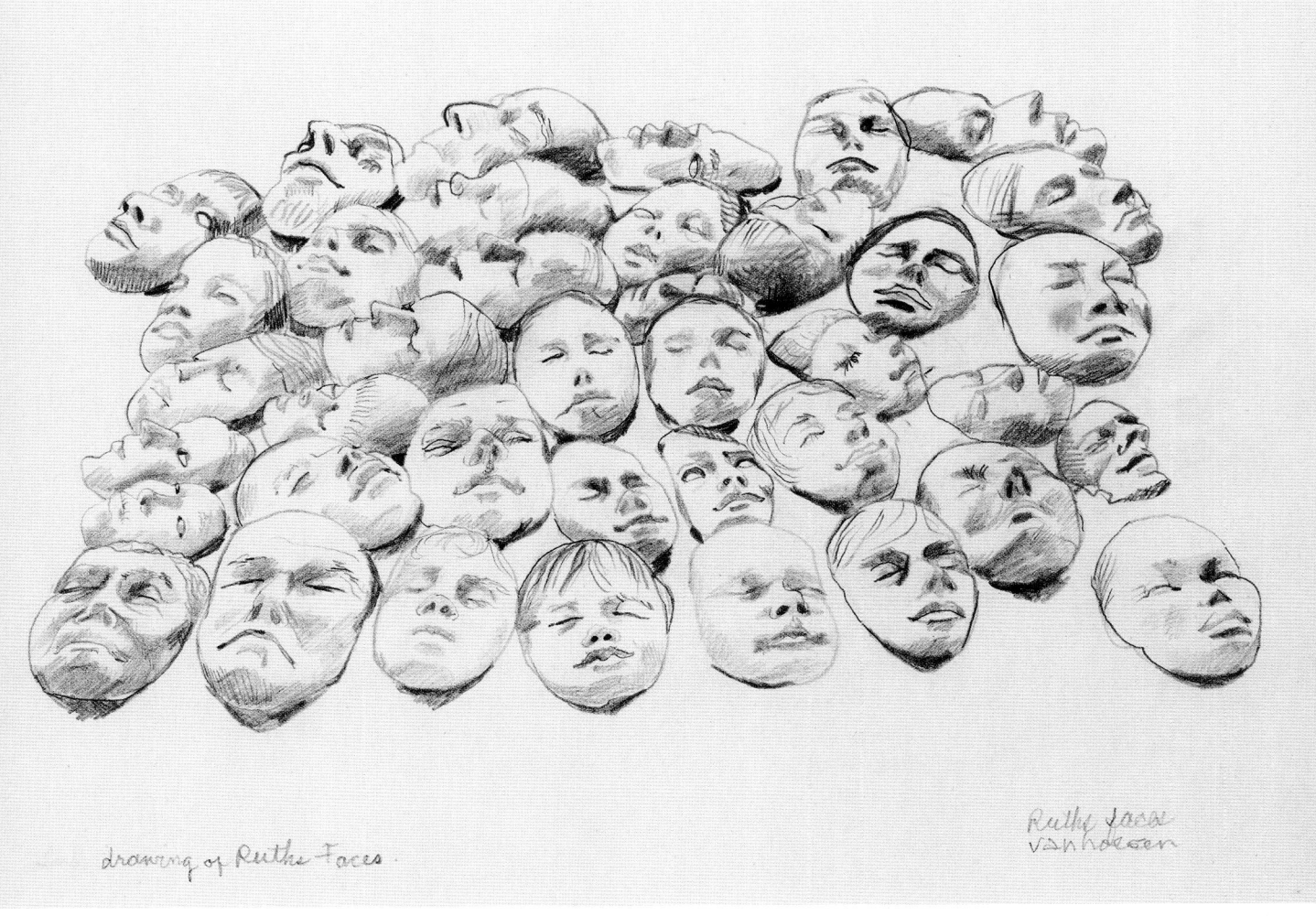

drawing of Ruths Faces.

*Ruths faces
Van Hoesen*

the subject of chapter 7, and has become part of Asawa's legacy as a fine artist. But most of it has now disappeared, never having been intended as permanent works of art. The goal, instead, was to use such everyday materials and techniques as life casting to bring children into closer contact with their immediate world. In the same way that "creativity, as it was theorized, studied, and sold in postwar America," writes Amy Ogata, "was inseparable from material objects," so too is a history of the Alvarado School Arts Workshop an attempt to introduce creative independence into an environment designed for standardization and conformity.[6] Such approaches included mobilizing the unlikely and humble everyday materials of dried beans, macaroni, birdseed, table knives, garlic presses, and "great globs of baker's dough"—to draw on just one workshop profiled by the journalist Nancy Faber in the progressive educational periodical *Learning: The Magazine for Creative Teaching*. Casting students' faces was just one in a spectrum of activities that, Faber pointed out, "may never become part of the permanent collections in the Louvre or any other museum."[7]

III.3 Beth Van Hoesen, *Ruth's Faces*, 1966. Graphite on paper, 9⅝ × 12¾ in. Private collection. Photo: M. Lee Fatherree.

It matters that Asawa was featured in a magazine like *Learning*. Browsing through a few adjacent issues, one encounters articles about the Teachers and Writers Collaborative, a New York City group placing artists and poets in the schools; the challenges of desegregating a Boston classroom; and exploring with "junk sculpture": "through this medium, Styrofoam packing materials, electronic gizmos, 35-mm film tins, fabric and wood scraps, old cardboard boxes, empty ice-cream containers—almost anything worthy of discard—become tools for creation. Here the medium dictates the message."[8] *Learning* communicated the pitfalls of a discipline-oriented classroom in biting, intelligent humor, including as one article title "Linda's Rewrite: How to Destroy a Child's Creative Imagery in 10 Easy-to-Follow Lessons" (August/September 1975). Articles railed against technocratic norms that equated standardization with education and testing with achievement. One of the most damning critiques involved the imbrication of the schools in the pharmaceutical industry. The educational reformer and author of *The Myth of the Hyperactive Kid: And Other Means of Child Control*, Diane Divoky, reported on studies that proved the uselessness of methylphenidate (better known as Ritalin) even as it continued to be prescribed widely to school-aged children perceived as "unruly." If "the great school movement of the 1960s" placed education in the national debate and forced congressional legislation to serve as a "major instrument for social change in a time of massive social turmoil," *Learning* was its megaphone.[9]

In was in this context that Faber's article elaborated the philosophy of the Alvarado School Arts Workshop. The goal was to make art a consistent and regular part of a child's experience in school, rather than being an afterthought and the first item to be cut when money is short. "When taught at all, art is often placed in the hands of people that know very little about it," Asawa argued.

"I am really concerned that in all education today, abstract learning is valued over real learning," says Ruth. "Words are abstract. Numbers are abstract. Evaluations are abstract. These have priority over learning by doing. And I believe you can only learn by doing.

"Parents and teachers unconsciously instill fear in children. School becomes a negative, failure-oriented experience. A child learns to regard a mistake as a failure. An artist is not afraid in this way. Out of his own experience, he respects and understands individual differences—the qualities that make a person unique. Mistakes to him are merely learning experiences."[10]

Faber observed how the Workshop demonstrated this principle of learning by doing even as it also revealed how early children's creative impulses are stifled; as she noticed during one workshop, many students looked around for instructions on what to do with the ball of dough on the table in front of them. Many in the school reform movement argued that it was institutionalized rigidity and banality in the classroom, epitomized by grades, standardized testing, and a workbook-based curriculum, that crippled a child's power of imagination. "I've seen twelve- and thirteen-year-olds so inhibited I could cry," said the librarian of McKinley School, who had invited Asawa to do a workshop there. "You wonder what happens to them between kindergarten and junior high."[11]

The next two chapters provide an introductory account of the Alvarado School Arts Workshop as a mother-led experiment in creative art education. I have written elsewhere of how this experiment took on a maternal countercultural form typically opposed to dominant expectations in this era around what a mother does and is—if drug use, bra-burning, and antiwar protest are what we think of as conventional markers of California counterculture, then the figure of the artist-mother working at home would seem to be a world away.[12] However, the artist-mother's involvement in the San Francisco schools radically expands what we now count as countercultural practices in this era. Rather than rehearse that argument here, I provide instead a more encompassing account of the Alvarado School Arts Workshop, given that this is a history still in the making. Chapter 6 focuses on the women who founded the Workshop. Many of these women were themselves involved in the arts, either as professionally trained artists or as self-taught practitioners, and many also had children in the public school system. Their involvement in the Workshop, primarily as volunteers, had far-reaching consequences for how they understood the value of their own labor, both as mothers and as cultural producers. Many of these women were writers, including Andrea Jepson, Sharon Litzky, and Sally Woodbridge, and they were also the first to provide a history of the Workshop, narrating their own achievement and setting the foundation for an alternative genealogy of arts education. In the same way that the Workshop sought to empower students to take control of their own education, the women who organized it emerged as subjects of agency in the eyes of second-wave feminism.

Chapter 7 extends this argument about the Workshop as a mother-led intervention to examine how Asawa's engagement in the schools fed directly into her public art. She had no reservations about drawing a direct connection between her labor as an artist and her labor as a mother: "Because I had the children, I chose to have my studio in my home. I wanted them to understand my work and learn how to work. If I hadn't spent all those years staying at home with my kids and experimenting with materials that children could use, I would never have done the Ghirardelli and Hyatt fountains."[13] While I discussed the Ghirardelli fountain, *Andrea*, in chapter 5, the *San Francisco Fountain*—often nicknamed the "Hyatt fountain" due to its proximity to the Grand Hyatt Hotel—has not yet been given its proper due. One of Asawa's lasting legacies—its popularity even defeating an attempt by Apple Inc. in 2013 to relocate the sculpture as part of plans to build a new retail store—the *San Francisco Fountain* was created from a flour-salt-and-water mixture, which she had initially begun using with her own children. Later introducing this medium into public school art workshops and into the permanent medium of bronze casting for public monuments, Asawa refigured the kitchen table as a site of civic world-making.

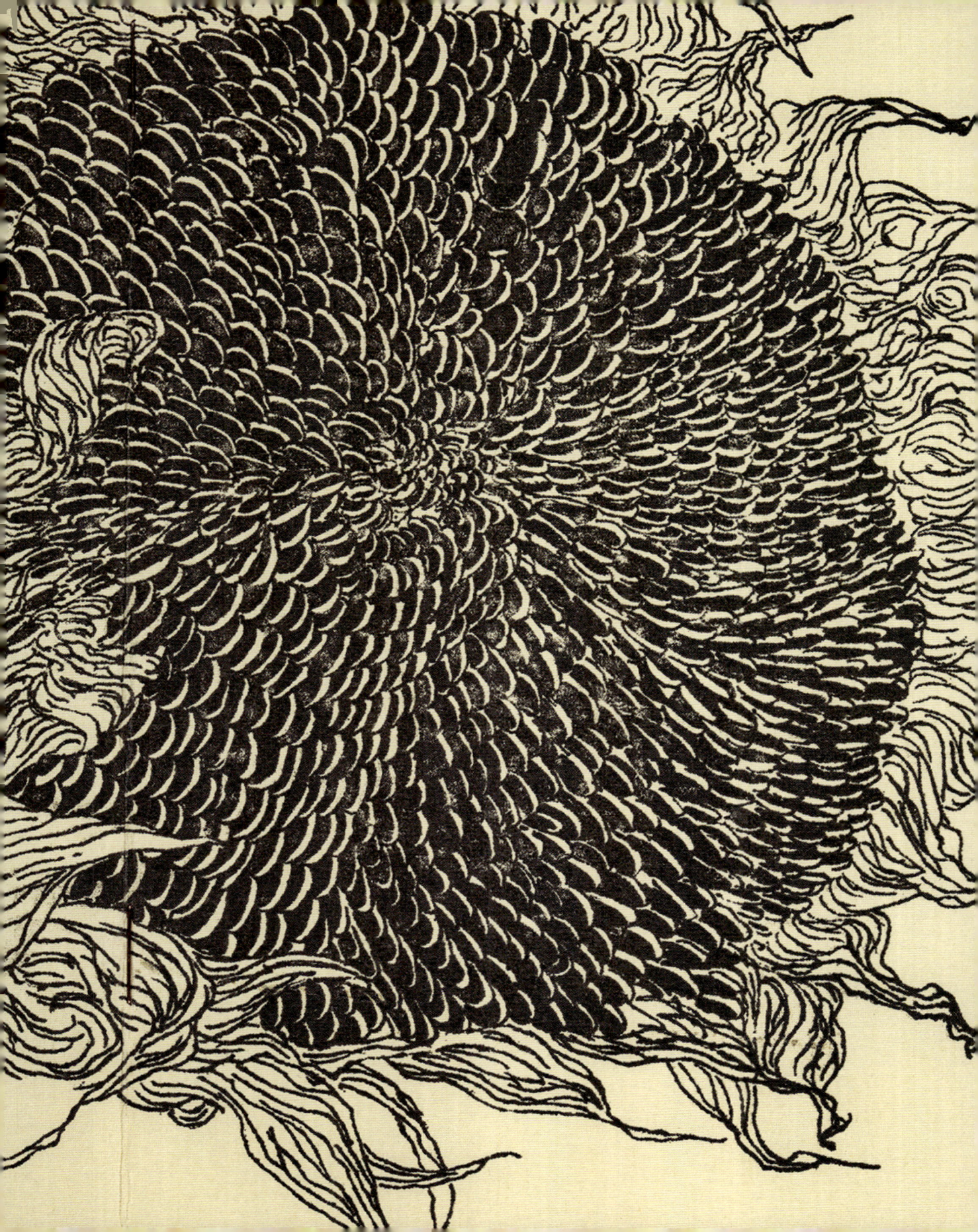

6 THE ALVARADO ART MOTHERS

It seems to me that coming of age is a coming to consciousness of one's own history and one's place in history (the future as well as the present and the past)—a difficult kind of consciousness to come by in a society that would erase history; in which we, especially as women, have to unearth our history before we can go on to understand it.
—Priscilla Barton[1]

"There was no official name for the venture, no sixty-page Master Plan, no budget. There were artists to act as teachers and resource people, enthusiasm, and a definite philosophical intent," wrote Andrea Jepson and Sharon Litzky in their book *The Alvarado Experience: Ten Years of a School-Community Art Program* (1978).[2] The "Alvarado" of their title refers to a local elementary school where the two, along with a dozen other women in the neighborhood, including Ruth Asawa and Sally Woodbridge, had established the nation's first artist-led curriculum in the public school system, the Alvarado School Arts Workshop. A photograph taken in the program's early years shows Litzky, one of these young mothers, with a child on her back as she works on assembling tiles for the *Alvarado Mosaic Mural* (1970; fig. 6.1). The mural, which the National Endowment for the Arts called "a major work of art," would become one of the program's earliest successes, with multiple grades taking part in its production alongside participating parents and teachers, all overseen by artist and mother Nancy Thompson.[3]

Referred to fondly as the "art mothers," as one teacher put it in a letter of thanks to Asawa, these women's identities as mothers were inextricable from their identities as artists.[4] Thompson had studied at the University of Chicago and earned her bachelor of fine arts at the Art Institute of Chicago. When the Workshop's pilot program began in summer 1968, she had two children attending Alvarado Elementary and, as Jepson and Litzky write, "was eager to join a group of parents who shared her belief that art should be part of the curriculum."[5] Other mothers included Andrea Jepson, whose postpartum body had served as the model for Asawa's *Andrea*, discussed in chapter 5, and Sharon Litzky, who later went on to found a cooperative art gallery (fig. 6.2). Jepson and Litzky wrote their history of the program at its tenth anniversary; Asawa had even arranged for a rented apartment nearby so that Jepson would have a room of her own to write in.[6] Asawa and Jepson were close; she drew Jepson often and especially

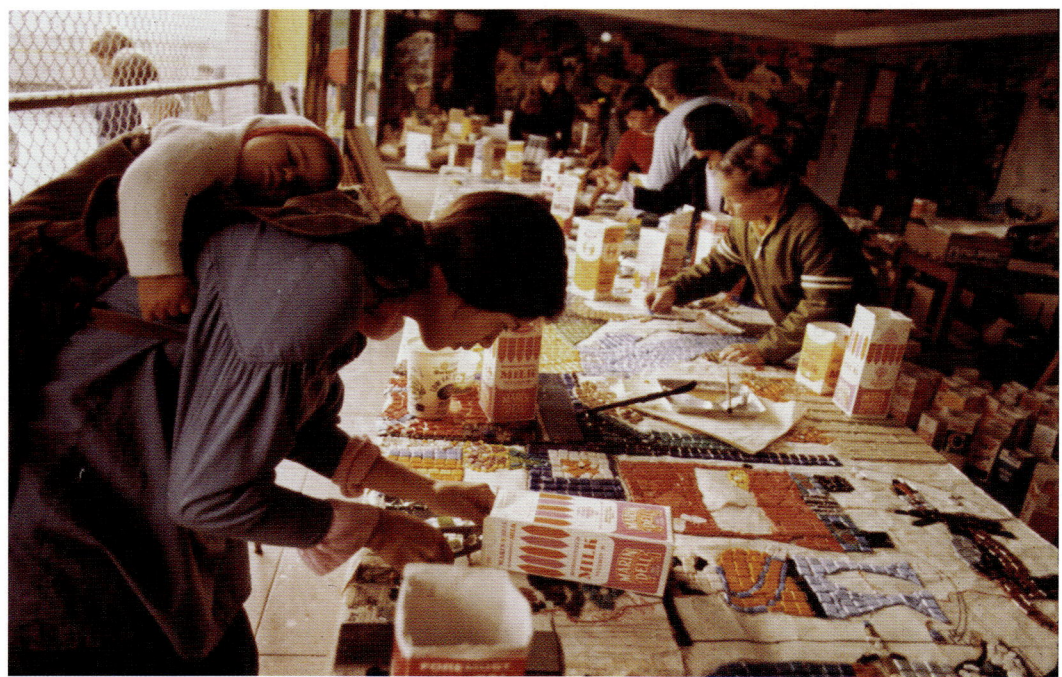

6.1 Sharon Litzky and students working on the *Alvarado Mosaic Mural*, Alvarado Elementary School, San Francisco, 1970. Photo: Michael Dixon. Special Collections, Stanford University.

during her pregnancies. Dottye Dean, Leah Forbes, Lois Link, Annette Clark, Anne Marie Theilen, and Charmalee Larkin were also involved, making a total of eleven key founding organizers. "When Ruth sent out the notice of the art workshop, it seemed to make sense, tied in with what we were doing remodeling an old Victorian," recalled Charmalee Larkin, who had four sons enrolled at Alvarado. "Crafts were just my bag, and I started concentrating on wood and wood carvings and wood collages."[7]

All of these women were neighbors, bound together by the shared experience of their children attending schools in the neighborhood. They were also all involved in the arts, understanding that the designation "art" meant not the production of a finished object, but the integration of aesthetic practice into everyday existence. While involved in more immediately recognizable artistic activities, like handicrafts and running galleries, these women also went on to own their own businesses and become active in politics as community organizers. This divergence from normative definitions of art explains why many understood themselves to be "more of a craftsman than an artist." Lois Link, whose four children took part in the Workshop, opened a French cheese and charcuterie shop in San Francisco after her involvement in the schools, citing "Asawa's philosophy" as fundamental to her self-understanding: "I like the way she puts it: 'Life is art.' I see good food, well done, beautifully served and presented as part of that kind of approach to life."[8] Similarly, Jepson recalled how

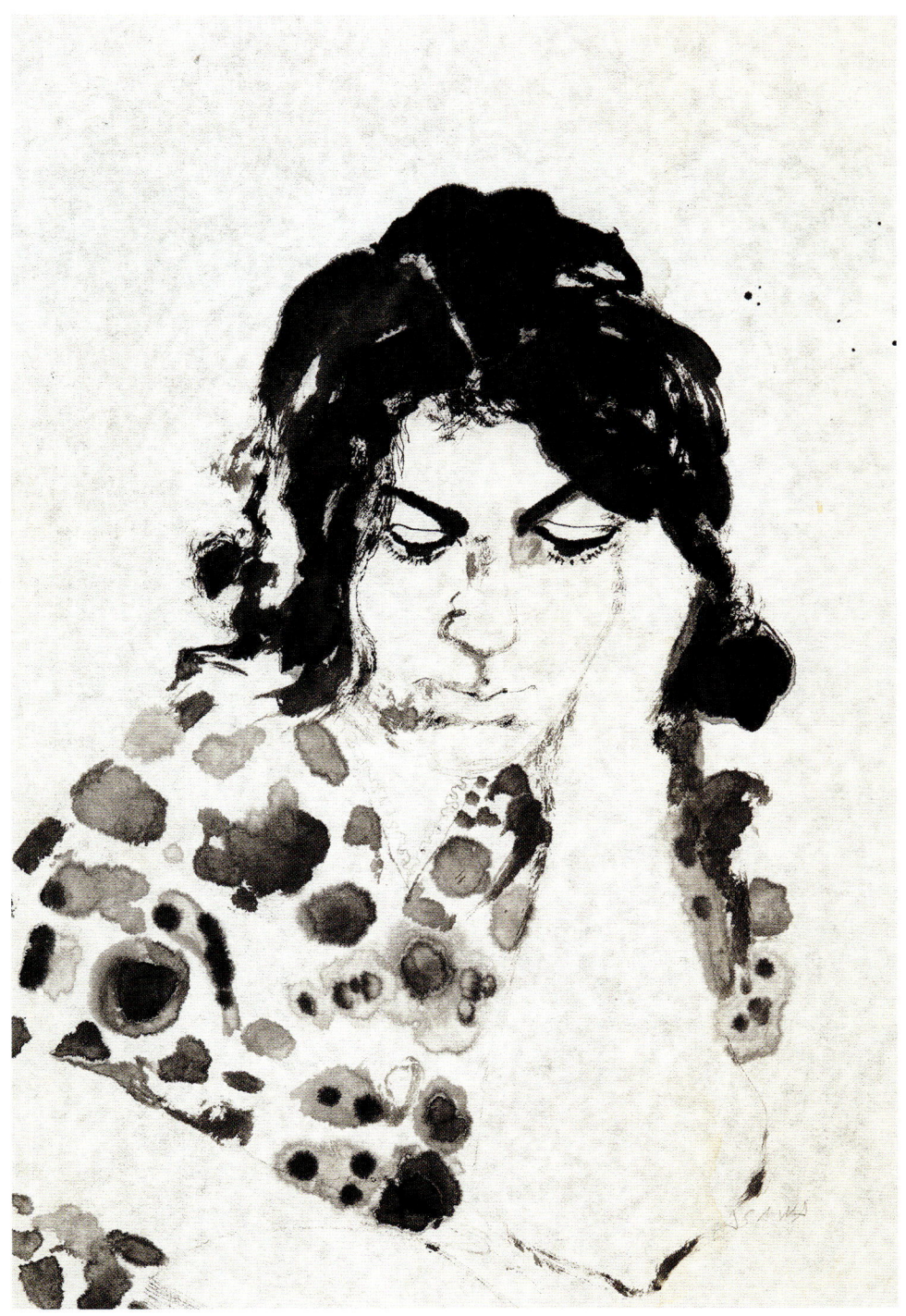

6.2 Ruth Asawa, *Untitled* (WC.112, Andrea Jepson), 1964.
Black ink on paper, 18 × 12 in. Fine Arts Museums of San
Francisco, Gift of the Artist.

important the lessons of the Workshop were to her own later career as a political organizer: "Ruth believed 'mistakes' were just part of the process; use what you learned when you didn't get the outcome [that you wanted], then go on to finish what you started. This was a hugely valuable lesson. [I] used it in every political campaign I directed and passed it on."[9]

By the late 1970s, the Workshop far exceeded its identity as a group of engaged artist-mothers in the schools. Recognized by the National Endowment for the Arts as the most vital school arts program in the country, it had grown into an ambitious undertaking, placing artists in 80 percent of San Francisco's public schools, employing hundreds of local artists, and impacting the lives of generations of students.[10] More a "method than a structure," the Workshop deemphasized its own identity as an organization; it owned few materials beyond a typewriter and a handful of tools, and it eschewed self-branding, even regarding its own letterhead as superfluous.[11] Instead, it focused its energies on content and people, bringing together artists and students, teachers and parents, school and public administrations in order to reimagine the role of arts education in the life of a city. As Asawa put it, the "Alvarado idea" was to integrate the artist back into the community as a whole, a seemingly simple idea that held the potential to "really change the social structure of our lives."[12]

A full history of the Workshop remains to be written; strangely, the program has been ignored by both art history and the history of art education. The few histories that do exist come from firsthand accounts of its organizers, such as *The Alvarado Experience*, with its cover bluntly illustrating the monochromatic concrete jungle of an urban schoolyard in contrast with the explosive color of the Workshop's contributions (fig. 6.3). In addition to *The Alvarado Experience*, Sally Woodbridge and Joan Abrahamson—a graduate student at the time, who later directed the Workshop beginning in 1978—wrote the first account of the program in the form of a five-year report, *The Alvarado School-Community Art Program*, and in 1975, the Education Program of the National Endowment for the Arts profiled the program's chronology and history of funding. Countless newspaper articles and contributions to progressive magazines like *Learning* and *Art Education* also detailed the Workshop's activities. Almost all of these materials are to be found in Asawa's own papers; given that the Workshop has no independent repository, this is its de facto archive. As a result, there is a tendency to conflate the Workshop, a collaborative venture, with Asawa herself. Much of the research now being done on the Workshop, for instance, is part of research on Asawa, making the distinction between Asawa as an individual and the Workshop as a group effort even more important to uphold.[13]

This chapter does not give a comprehensive history of the Workshop; rather, it argues for the program as a mother-led intervention into arts education. I suggest why this matters, particularly for art history's account of community-based arts, and how it distinguishes the Workshop from other art experiments in the schools during the late 1960s and 1970s. To do so I frame this argument in terms of the program's strategy of enabling self-portraiture by schoolchildren, which took form in a variety of materials, but especially in the public format of murals. As Asawa explained in

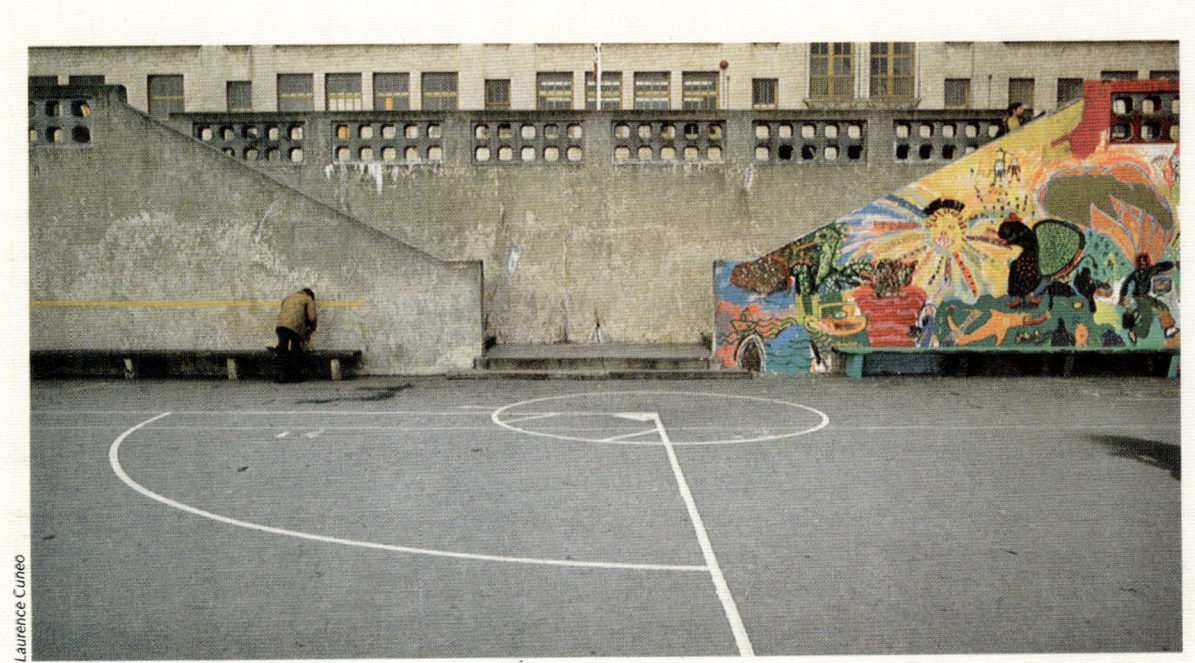

THE ALVARADO EXPERIENCE
Ten Years of a School-Community Art Program

by Andrea I. Jepson
Sharon S. Litzky

6.3 Cover of Andrea I. Jepson and Sharon S. Litzky, *The Alvarado Experience: Ten Years of a School-Community Art Program* (1978). Specia Collections, Stanford University.

footage taken by Robert Snyder for his filmic portrait of the artist, "children can learn that they have control over their own space and environment. By producing a mural on the wall, they are making history for themselves, and they begin to talk about what they've done rather than what somebody else has done."[14] Mural-making, and in particular the strategy of self-portraiture, empowered children to take ownership of their own education and, by extension, to become subjects of agency.

What if, as Asawa's daughter Addie Laurie once suggested to me, we understand this making of one's own history as taking place not only for the schoolchildren but for the mothers involved as well?[15] That it was as meaningful for them as it may have been for the children involved? In an extended profile on Asawa for the *San Francisco Examiner*, focused on her involvement in the Workshop, Jepson observes how the Workshop was the product of a particular historical moment: Asawa and Woodbridge "convinced the women in their neighborhood that the time for taking classes 'because the children were now in school all day' was over. That was a concept of the 1950s. Now was the time to go into the schools and provide the help that the schools needed."[16] The message here is that the Workshop benefited from the advances made by the women's movement of the 1960s, but it unfolded in the years before women expended their new agency in careers, when women would work long hours away from the home and thus be unable to take an active role in their children's education. None of the mothers involved in the Workshop necessarily described themselves as feminists or took part in feminist organizing—at least not during the years in which they were involved in the schools. As mothers and housewives, many of them even embodied an identity deeply contested within that movement: "the Mother as the Enemy," according to the writer Ursula K. Le Guin.[17] And yet, as I explore here, art education in the schools became an unlikely arena for a feminist politics unrecognized as such at the time.

COUNTERCULTURAL BEGINNINGS

The initial motivation for the Alvarado School Arts Workshop was a response to the sorry state of art education in the public schools. In the wake of a general shift in Cold War America toward funding for the sciences and technology-based curricula, the arts had become undervalued, with just one hour of art per week stipulated by the district curriculum and sixteen art teachers for a hundred elementary schools in San Francisco. According to Sally Woodbridge and Joan Abrahamson in 1973, part of this was due to a "conventional wisdom," which held "that art is an esoteric pursuit reserved for the talented few who are trained in specialized schools after completing elementary and secondary education"—a pursuit that had no place at the primary school level. As a consequence, few schools had a dedicated art teacher: "Instead the classroom teacher taught what art he or she could shoe-horn into the curriculum. Students, parents and teachers were mutually dissatisfied with the practice of getting out the crayons and construction paper or stenciled pictures to produce a take-home piece of evidence commemorating Thanksgiving or Columbus' discovery of

America."[18] Furthermore, as Woodbridge reflected decades later, "the participation of parents in changing school curricula to include the arts was not an acceptable idea, it was not even considered."[19] Asawa and the other Alvarado mothers understood this not as an aberration, but rather as the logical consequence of a system running as planned, "a system," to borrow from countercultural historians Peter Braunstein and Michael William Doyle, "geared up to perpetuate the new technocracy by educating young citizens, particularly white middle-class males, for compliantly assuming their rightful place in the corporate hierarchy."[20] The Workshop's goal was to transform that structure from the bottom up, beginning with a pilot program in the summer of 1968.

Earlier that year, in February, Asawa found herself newly appointed to the San Francisco Arts Commission. Established in 1932, amid a revival of public arts support, the commission reviewed funding requests for financial support from arts institutions and organizations. Though not the first municipal arts agency in the United States, it quickly became a leading force in defining art's civic role, "founded on the principle that a creative cultural environment is essential to the city's well-being."[21] While it had historically supported established arts institutions like the San Francisco Opera, this focus began to shift in the 1960s. The change was fueled by younger voices, like that of poet Kenneth Rexroth, who urged students at San Francisco State University to reject the "skyscraper cathedrals of culture" and move the cultural life of the city into the neighborhoods.[22] The commission thus became tasked with fostering a community-based cultural program, including "neighborhood arts facilities" and arts instruction across the city's entire school system, from primary levels to professional arts education.[23]

One of Asawa's first agenda items as a member of the commission was to review a request submitted by the recently created Neighborhood Arts Program (NAP). The NAP had been formed officially by residents in July 1967 after a year of lobbying the Board of Supervisors for support of grassroots arts initiatives. Their first big undertaking was in February 1968: an all-Black performing arts show of poetry, music, theater, and dance, which took place across five neighborhoods in the city. Now the NAP was asking the commission to fund a summer arts program to continue this work. In making their case, the NAP cited the urgency of such programs in light of the previous year's race riots—during one such riot, Asawa's eldest son had been knocked unconscious.[24] The NAP argued that such an investment at a grassroots level would help repair and restore community cohesion: "What the Neighborhood Arts Program is proposing is a means for giving young people and adults creative alternatives to the kinds of activities which could disrupt and destroy our city and our country."[25] The NAP succeeded and became a vital grassroots arts program that funded a range of decentralized cultural activities across the city's neighborhoods, with several ties to the Alvarado School Arts Workshop during the 1970s. In 1975, for instance, Anne Marie Theilen served as an administrative coordinator to both the Workshop and the NAP.

Witnessing the example of the NAP must have made an impression on Asawa as she mulled over what to do about the arts in the schools. The NAP's critical position toward protest set the tone for her work with the Workshop, for Asawa believed one could be more effective working in the schools than protesting on the streets. At the same time, she saw the limits to an approach that put the problem into the lap of bureaucrats: When she began pursuing the idea of an arts program in the public schools, Asawa had initially approached the San Francisco Arts Commission, but with no success. The commission saw itself as having nothing to do with the Board of Education and initially scoffed at Asawa's proposal that it tackle the question of the schools.[26] This setback illustrated for her how institutions for arts funding had become weighed down by red tape and technocracy, rarely working collaboratively. Asawa's solution was to bypass such channels and work directly in the schools with parents, teachers, administrators, and artists from the immediate community.

But how exactly did this work? First, it is important to understand the significance of the term "neighborhood" here, as designating the scale and conditions of the Workshop's intervention. After all, the fact that these women all shared a neighborhood—and a school to which those neighborhood children were sent—set out one significant condition for their involvement. Borrowing from Jane Jacobs, using the language of the era, this group could be described as a "community of interest": bound together not by ethnicity, race, or religion but by a common set of values, particularly around art education.[27] But even more specifically, this intervention in community was *sustainable*, in Miwon Kwon's use of the term, in that these women engaged a very specific group in which they were already embedded—as opposed to entering one from outside or creating one through an artwork—and thus were able to avoid many of the problems and contradictions attending community-based arts practices.[28] Asawa once projected that any significant change in the schools would take "a minimum of 5 to 10 years of daily work."[29]

Secondly, the economic situation of this area of San Francisco mattered: Asawa and Lanier had moved to the city in 1949 for its cheap rents and affordable living conditions. Given a certain racial and class background, a single income could support a large family, allowing one parent (often the mother) to engage in activities that were not paid, including child-raising, and—in the case of the Noe Valley neighborhood where these mothers lived—a spectrum of creative pursuits. These women largely fulfilled those conditions: many of them were white with husbands who performed well-paid, skilled labor outside the home, and, as a result, they were able to be involved in something for which they were not remunerated; they could afford not to work *for a wage* (for they surely did work). This dimension of class and race should not diminish the value of what the Workshop accomplished, but it should be stated explicitly, for when the Workshop expanded to other schools, in neighborhoods where the socioeconomic situation required that both parents work outside the home, the ability of parents to be involved in the classroom was significantly limited—a point to which I will return.

A third significant aspect is that the Workshop did not frame itself as a community-based arts practice nor as an artist's intervention in the schools, even though it was led by one of the city's most visible and successful artists. Its beginnings were far more self-effacing: Asawa and Woodbridge gathered together a group of other mothers and, gauging interest, pitched a summer program to Herbert Simon, head of the Department of Art Education; Verla Leonard, art supervisor of the San Francisco Unified School District; and the principal of Alvarado Elementary, who allowed the cafeteria to be used over the summer break in 1968. From the beginning, the emphasis was not on creating aesthetic objects but on a hands-on engagement with materials. "We weren't really interested in the art as such or in self-expression," Asawa relayed to a reporter. "That comes later, with maturity. What we wanted to give the children were simple, basic approaches to all kinds of materials with which they can effectively use their hands. Today's children are being robbed of such talents."[30] This pilot program was so successful that the school allowed it to continue, with spaces like the cafeteria and the schoolyard made available during the school year.

The structure of the Workshop depended on what it called "parent coordinators." In the beginning, Asawa and Woodbridge served as parent coordinators at Alvarado Elementary, while Anne Marie Theilen coordinated the program at Edison, a nearby elementary school. For the parent coordinators, tasks included gathering materials, arranging workshops with artists, and scheduling volunteer time with other community members, some of whom were part of the original parent planning group. At no point were the Workshop's activities part of the official curriculum; rather, the Workshop was treated as an expansion and enrichment of that structure, with the aim of involving the entire school. Entirely fueled by a volunteer structure (until 1972, when parent coordinators began to be paid $200 per month from school district funds), the Workshop had a collective and ad hoc decision-making process. Asawa's own power as a well-known local artist allowed her to funnel resources to the Workshop, including from donors like the Zellerbach Family Foundation and the prominent Bay Area businessman William Roth, Asawa's patron who had paid for *Andrea*. She also used this leverage to encourage professionally trained artists from the neighborhood, such as Nancy Thompson, to devote their time and energy.

The Workshop's most ambitious goal was to place a working, professional artist in every public school. No artist was perceived as being too successful or too serious to be involved: at one point, she had wanted Richard Diebenkorn to teach painting and Francis Ford Coppola to teach filmmaking.[31] As the Workshop grew to include more schools, it continued to follow this basic orientation and structure: a parent coordinator assigned to a school; a parent planning group of artists and non-artists; community volunteers; and professional artists from the neighborhood. While it eventually was able to draw federal funding from the National Endowment for the Arts' Artists-in-Schools program, one significant difference was that this NEA program never involved parents. By contrast, Asawa believed the involvement of parents was crucial to the Workshop's success; yet, "at the same time," she pointed out in an interview, "a parent program cannot do it alone. . . . It has to be a combination of artists and parents."[32]

These mothers were instrumental in setting the Workshop's orientation toward a process-based engagement intended to empower students. Instead of the acquisition of art historical facts or artistic techniques, the goal was to generate the conditions under which children would be exposed to a greater range of encounters than

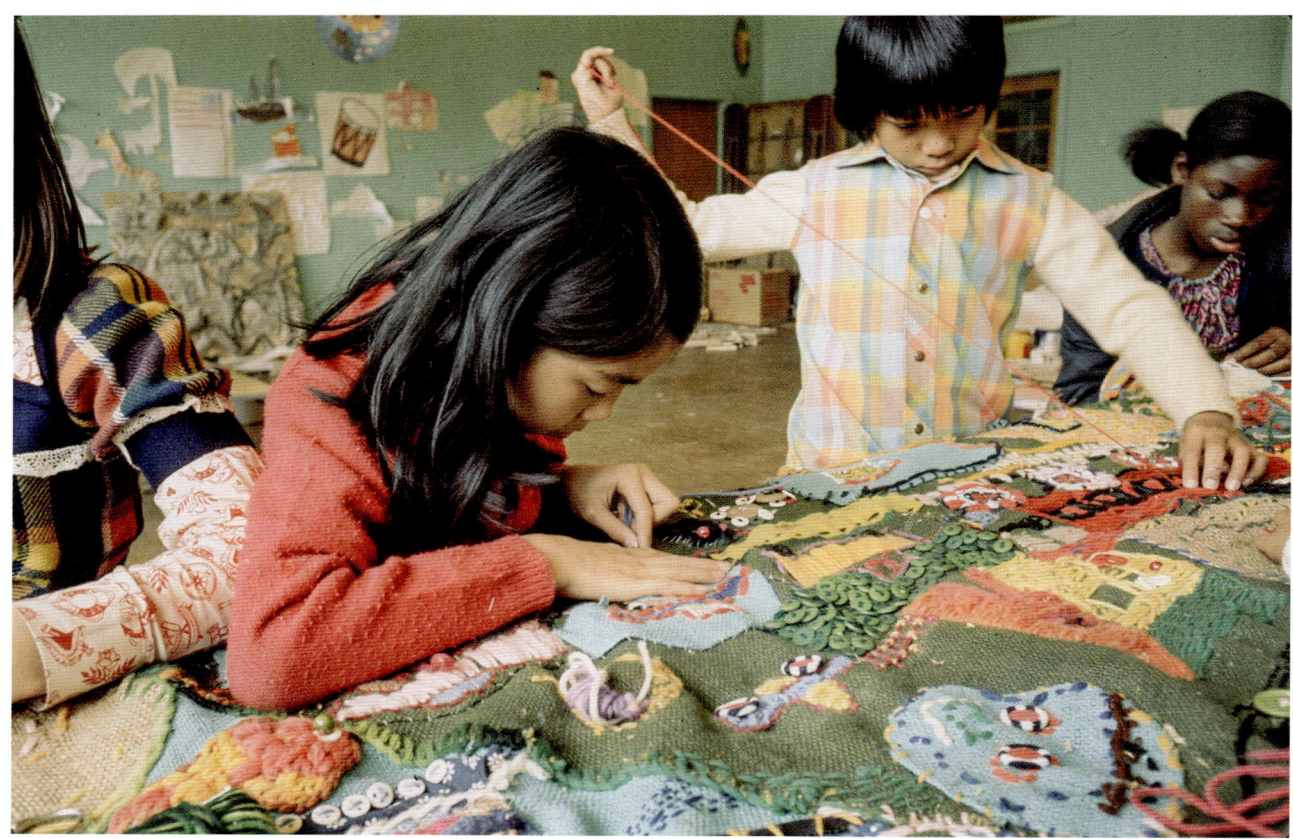

6.4 Students working on the *Stitchery Mural* at
Hillcrest Elementary School, San Francisco, led by
Nancy Thompson and Ruth Asawa as part of the
Alvarado School Arts Workshop, 1974. Special
Collections, Stanford University.

that offered to them by the society of consumption that had come to define postwar America, "the veritable cornucopia of consumer goods that seemed to materialize and dematerialize just out of reach," to cite historians of the counterculture.[33] For a concrete example of how that worked out in practice, Jepson and Litzky describe a typical planning meeting as follows:

The talk often centered on how best to work with children at school, how to transmit information without falling back on traditional authoritarian techniques, the value of encouraging rather than demanding, and the difficulties of accomplishing projects in classrooms filled with diverse personalities and widely ranging abilities.

It was at these times that the most far-flung fantasies came up for perusal and discussion: if conditions were ideal, what would we ask for? ". . . The children should see chickens and roosters everyday, have the chance to care for animals and see that eggs are not produced twelve at a time in the back of a supermarket. . . . Gardens, we need gardens. The lessons of nature are so important and observed so readily when a seed is planted. . . . What about bringing a sheep to school—shearing it and carding the wool and then weaving it so the kids could see the *whole* process? . . . Wouldn't it be great to have the high school kids come to Alvarado and work with our students in dance or drama or mime? It would set up a real connection between the schools. . . . My dream is to have an imaginative play structure in this barren school yard and real trees giving shade and maybe even sand for the very little children to tunnel in. . . . It would be so great to have a festival in the city that was just for kids with music and dance and art."[34]

Such proposals, which Jepson and Litzky point out "were just a few of the dreams, fantasies, and thoughts" that were in fact realized over the years, could be described in stronger terms as a maternal fantasy that sought to put the child in greater proximity to a range of life experiences. It was an effort to refigure social reproduction from the capitalist terms of the fetishized commodity, in which eggs would seem magically to materialize "in the back of a supermarket," to an intimate confrontation with cycles of birth, growth, life, aging, and death.

A common refrain, as one principal saw it, was that of "self-subsistence, where you become an independent organism in the sense that you can provide for yourself . . . as a community, you can organize your resources to do it."[35] Materials were often found or donated, with an emphasis not on technical mastery but on an engagement with "basic ideas, of putting things together: sewing, weaving, knitting, gluing, using materials that any child can find at home, such as egg cartons, cloth scraps, yarn, string, newspaper, paper bags, and flour paste" (fig. 6.4).[36] This emphasis on crafts, though, extended beyond small-scale handiwork to encompass a program that aimed at nothing less than the full-scale remaking of the educational environment, beginning with its physical contours, as students transformed previously barren public school spaces such as classrooms, hall corridors, cafeterias, libraries, and playgrounds. It also meant that the products of the Workshop were largely ephemeral and discarded over time, consistent with its overall rejection of the aesthetic as a privileged sphere of experience.

This was the reason Jepson and Litzky foreground the word "experience" in their book's title: here is an implicit argument for the Workshop as part of a broader landscape of craft as a critique of postwar consumption, materialism, and profit. In this respect, the Workshop can be seen as continuing a commitment to craft already evident in the early 1950s in the dialogue of Asawa and Renk with Pond Farm, as discussed in chapter 2. There Marguerite Wildenhain oversaw a pottery program (Asawa's youngest child, Paul Lanier, later studied with her). What was unique about this program was that students did not fire the pots they threw and thus generate finished ceramics. Instead, the emphasis was on the process of throwing—working the pottery wheel, dissecting the vessel's walls to assess thickness, and then smashing it all down in order to try again. Process, as Jenni Sorkin has written of Pond Farm, was central to the program's contemporaneity.[37] The Alvarado School Arts Workshop took on a similar orientation. As Jepson and Litzky wrote: "Given the time to explore the possibilities of their own creativity, children produced some wondrous art, only a fraction of which has remained permanently or semi-permanently in the school. Even on photographs and slides, it is impossible to keep record of the immense volume of work that has moved out of the schools and into the homes over the last ten years."[38] With this emphasis on child-driven process, the Workshop eschewed conventional definitions of art—as made by an artist or group of artists and of value to posterity—in favor of the ongoing generation of creative experience.

THE *ALVARADO MOSAIC MURAL*

In spring 1970, the Workshop embarked on what would become the most significant project of its early years: a mural, roughly twenty by forty feet, installed on a blank wall in the schoolyard of Alvarado Elementary. Part of the project's purpose was to "model" what Asawa described, following the ethos of Black Mountain College, as "a new physical environment" for learning.[39] That physical environment is conveyed in *Recess* by Beth Van Hoesen, a print that underscores the monochromatic blankness of asphalt and gridded windows of the Alvarado building (fig. 6.5). As Jepson and Litzky wrote, "With few exceptions, the city schools were bleak and institutional in character. San Quentin gray was rumored to be a color chip in the school painters' charts." The issue was not only aesthetic: Alvarado's "impersonal and unyielding" schoolyard had become "a massive symbol of authority."[40] A journalist drew an even stronger comparison between schools and state penitentiaries, describing Alvarado's grounds as "a typical big-city schoolyard—drab, uninspired, endless oceans of asphalt jungle behind an aging two-story building with a few painted lines for hopscotch, a handful of swings and the inevitable cyclone fence, like a prison—a prison for kids."[41] To transform these spaces into hospitable environments for learning and playing, the Workshop had begun experimenting with stained-glass "windows" made of recycled plastic, stitchery "murals" to cover endless corridors—both projects overseen by Thompson—as well as papier-mâché monsters that greeted students at school entrances and large pterodactyls and puffer fish that would sway over their heads.

After completing her mosaic mural *Growth* for the Bethany Senior Center, discussed in chapter 4, Asawa arranged to receive her design fee in the form of tiles. She

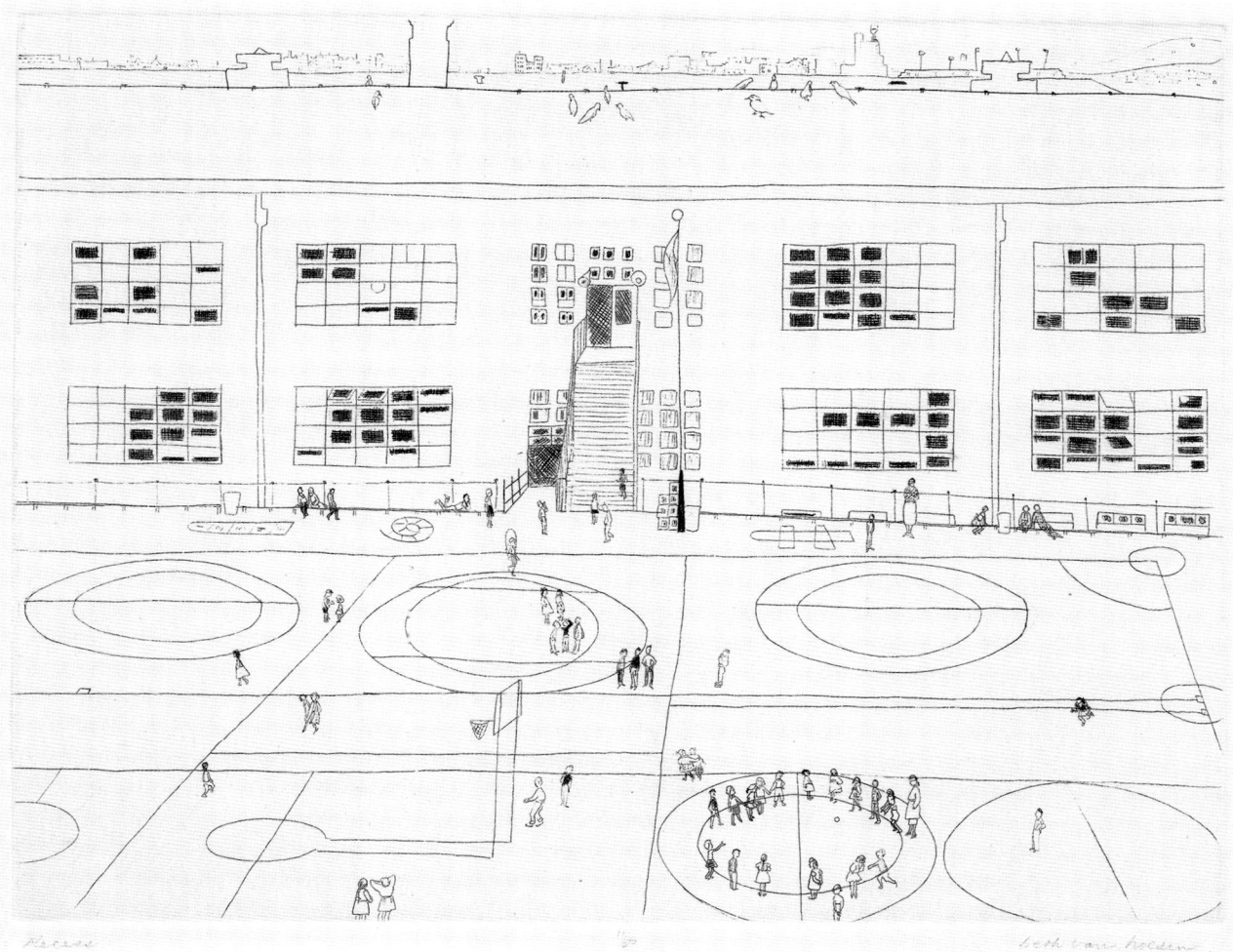

6.5 Beth Van Hoesen, *Recess*, 1959. Etching on moderately thick, moderately textured cream wove paper, 9½ × 12⅜ in. (image). Private collection. Photo: M. Lee Fatherree.

and Thompson decided to use the tiles to create a mural with the fourth-, fifth-, and sixth-graders at Alvarado Elementary School (figs. 6.6, 6.7). The visual theme was to be "a self-portrait of the neighborhood," including streets, houses, playgrounds, and shops, as well as the children themselves, whose faces were cast in plaster and the resulting ceramic masks affixed to the mosaic surface. Work on the mural began with field trips around the school's Noe Valley neighborhood. The older students drew their impressions from the field trips and then transferred these to special paper. These sheets occupied large tables in an area nicknamed "the cage" because of its drab gray walls on three sides and a cyclone fence on the fourth side. Over the course of several months and extending into the following school year, children placed the tiles where they saw fit. Thompson used a reverse method, so the tiles were positioned and glued face down onto the paper. As Dottye Dean recalled, "the process was akin to working in a darkened room, but it never seemed to faze any of the kids, who picked up this concept very easily."[42]

In addition to tiles, the mural comprised shells and other collected objects from the neighborhood. Integrated into the panorama of figures were also life casts of students' faces. The act of self-portraiture was meant to generate a sense of orientation and ownership in relationship to their place of learning. A parent volunteer who assisted Thompson in the year-long project observed:

You watch a class of eleven-year-olds making pariscraft masks on each other; measuring paper patterns first; learning about the properties of plaster as they apply the fast-setting bandages to foreheads and noses and chins; discussing the kinds of masks they want to end up with, whether monster or Japanese Noh. You observe traditional class adversaries patting Vaseline on each other's skin and then smoothing the bandages to make nice, even surfaces. You are fascinated by the interest and level of concentration. This process lends itself to a combined art, history, science, and math lesson. Yet many educators never see art in this capacity as a total learning experience.[43]

Photographs portray the face casts lined up along the edges of the mural, waiting to be fitted once it was installed. As a "total learning experience," this mural was the result of an environment in which students were given opportunities to make decisions so that "students . . . become teachers and teachers . . . become students" in a democratization of the learning process, Asawa explained.[44] When Alfonso Pardiñas of Byzantine Mosaics came to install the mural, "the kids sensed that it was like a birthing, and when the paper was pulled away from the tiles after they had been set in concrete and the mosaic revealed in its entirety, it was the most incredible feeling of joy and power and elation."[45]

An early instance of using life casting as a collective artistic practice, the *Alvarado Mosaic Mural* can be productively compared to John Ahearn's life casts of neighbors in his Bronx neighborhood in New York in the late 1970s and 1980s (fig. 6.8). Ahearn made these life casts on the street and in the display window of the interdisciplinary arts space Fashion Moda, in operation from 1978 to 1993. As in all life casts, but especially the casting of faces, the process entails a high degree of intimacy and trust between artist and sitter, given that sitters must remain very still and trust that they

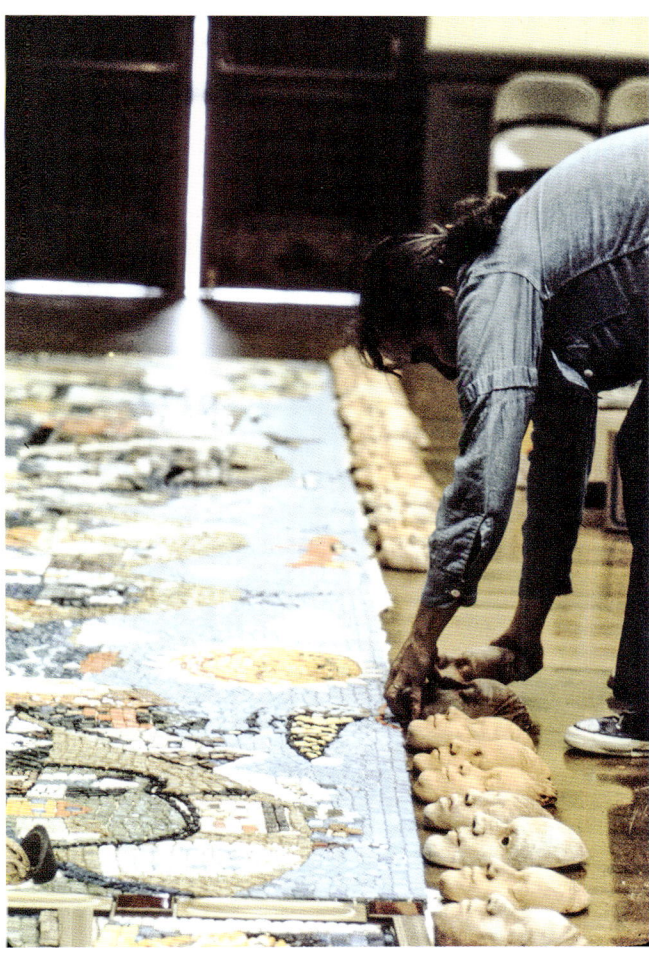

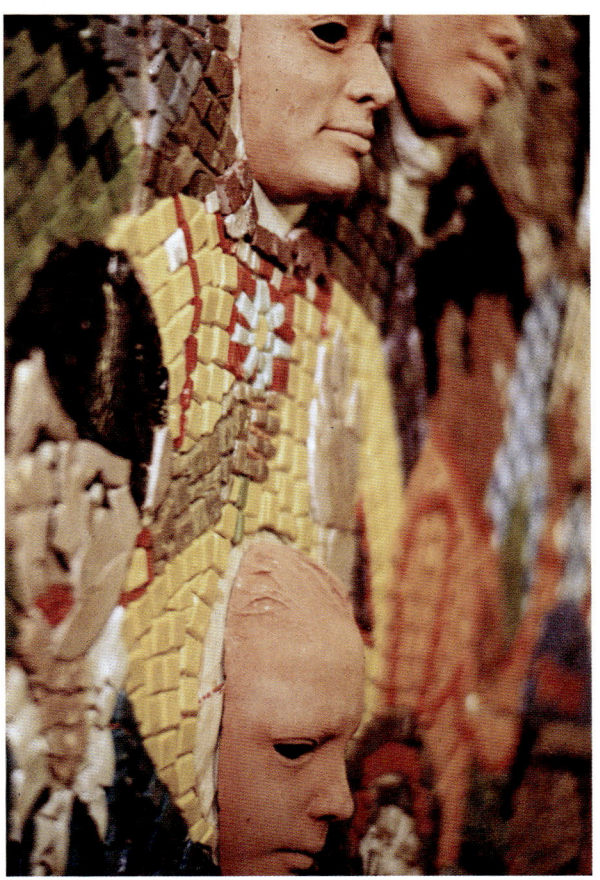

6.6 The *Alvarado Mosaic Mural* in progress, with Nancy Thompson, c. 1970. Photo: Nicholas King. Special Collections, Stanford University.

6.7 The *Alvarado Mosaic Mural* (detail), c. 1970. Photo: Michael Dixon. Special Collections, Stanford University.

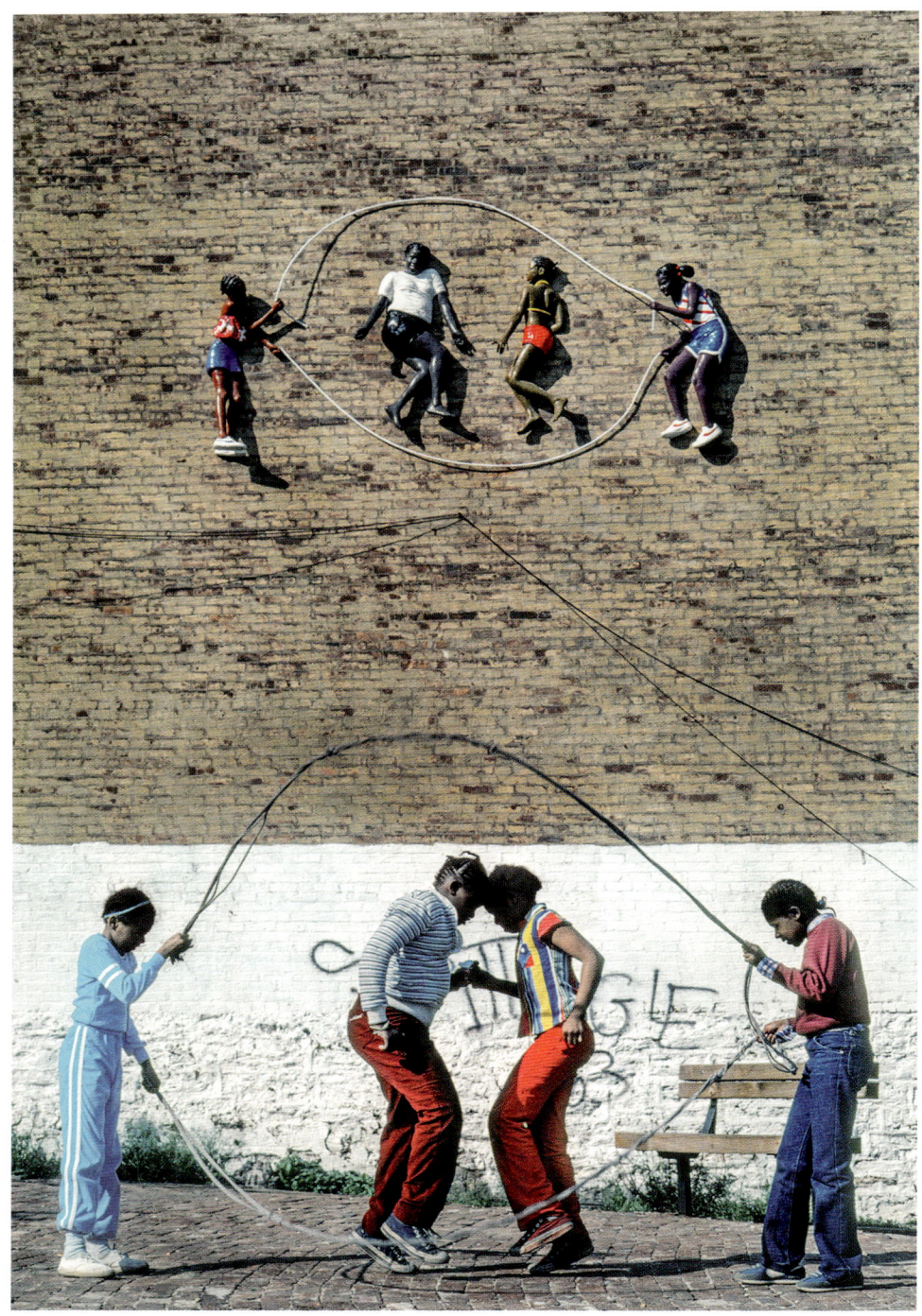

6.8 John Ahearn and Rigoberto Torres, *Banana Kelly Double Dutch*, The Bronx, New York City, 1982. Pictured: Freeda Mincey, Javette Potts, Tawana Brown, and Staice Seabrine. Photo: Martha Cooper.

will not suffocate. In addition to intimacy, the process entails immediacy: in its directness, Ahearn once compared it to taking Polaroids—a medium that Helen Molesworth also invoked in describing Asawa's life casts, comparing them to Andy Warhol's photographic portraits and screen tests.[46] In both instances, the direct temporality of the medium is what renders it well suited to engender community bonds. Ahearn valued this trust so much that he removed his own bronze public sculpture, based on such casts, five days after they had prompted critique from those same neighbors.

Miwon Kwon has identified Ahearn's art practice as a recent model of public art, one geared toward intervention and assimilation (as opposed to the confrontation and critique epitomized by Richard Serra's *Tilted Arc*). She identifies in this model a drive toward an "identificatory unity"—that the viewer of such works "is affirmed in his/her self-knowledge and world view through the art work's mechanisms of (self-) identification," thus making no demands on the viewer's existing sense of self.[47] This drive, in turn, she argues, is predicated on an ideal of unalienated collective labor in which the labor of the community and that of the artist are one and the same, an ideal that follows from a nineteenth-century conception of art as itself a form of unalienated labor. Kwon poses the challenge that labor play a role in the evaluation of such community-based practices, which it rarely does; and that is the point on which a productive distinction can be drawn between Ahearn's model and the Workshop's maternal paradigm: the latter successfully distributed ownership of the work among those who made it, thereby deflecting attention away from the artists involved to such a degree that the work has not been viewed as a work of art at all (but rather as "merely" a school art project or children's mural). In the same way that Ahearn produced work *with* and *for* his Bronx neighbors, the Alvarado mural constituted a co-production, with the children as much sitters as co-creators of their own self-image. But only the Workshop was able, to borrow again from Kwon, to generate the conditions in which "the community sees itself in 'the work' not through an iconic or mimetic identification but through the recognition of its own labor in the creation of, or becoming of, 'the work.'"[48]

To understand this dimension, we have to look more closely at the mural's making and reception. Phiz Mezey was one of several photographers to document the completed mural (fig. 6.9). Her photographs were taken after the ceramic life casts of the students' faces had been destroyed in acts of vandalism by high school students and the students had provisionally filled in the missing features. Mezey had been a neighbor of Merry Renk and Asawa when she lived on Saturn Street and had continued to photograph Asawa and her family well into the 1980s. She had become interested in the city's mural movement, documenting several examples in the Mission district. Her photograph of Michael Rios's mural at the Mini Park (at Twenty-Fourth and Bryant streets) had appeared on the cover of *California Living*; this same mural was mentioned in one of the Workshop's funding applications. Such murals celebrated the indigenous culture of the area's Chicanx residents and made this erased history newly visible. Timothy Dreschler argues that these murals, emerging in the 1960s in San Francisco, added "community" to the historical mural tradition, drawing a distinction between "community art" and "public art." Whereas New Deal-era murals tended to narrate a single master narrative of history, like Sargent Johnson's frieze of George Washington for the city's Washington High School, the mural movement of the 1960s and 70s was concerned with the complexities of multiple histories; in fact, the Washington frieze was replaced by a Black history panel in 1973 by one of the school's former students.[49] Giving voice to marginalized populations in the city, these mural movements "functioned as a challenge to the dominant myth of a coherent, centralized, white U.S. culture. Even if the images themselves were not openly oppositional, the mere fact that Black artists might paint large public statements celebrating Black culture was viewed as a provocation by conservatives," Dreschler argues.[50]

Mezey's photographs appeared in *Learning* in a feature, which she also authored, on the Workshop's mural program, attesting to her regular engagement with the Workshop.[51] This included a guide, written by Nancy Thompson, for other schools to do the same, with detailed instructions, material lists, and further resources, as well as information on how to estimate paint quantities, prepare the wall, and work with groups of various ages. Pointing to the wide spectrum of subject matter, from specific curriculum areas like social studies to "pure fantasy," Mezey underscores the ludic dimension of the mural program. This was an instance of children taking back their schoolyards and buildings, claiming for themselves a right to speak. In one photo, Mezey portrays a Black student with a silhouette of himself, the caption indicates, "made by having another student draw around his body as he lay on a sheet of paper. Once he outlines the silhouette on the wall, he'll have a self-portrait."

As a project aimed at bringing "realism into the school situation," the Workshop embraced unanticipated opportunities that arose from its activities, which nevertheless provided valuable lessons in responsibility and consequence.[52] For instance, vandalism, primarily by high schoolers, had been a problem that plagued many of the city's public schools. As Jepson and Litzky describe in their account:

The kids had always shot out the windows with BB guns but now, as the schoolyards were beautified, they began to direct their rage towards the planter boxes, which they ripped apart with crowbars, tearing out the flowers and vegetables and strewing them all over the yard. They lit fires in the polyhedron play structure that Alan Brooks' Design Class at City College had built for the kindergarten children. Still not content, they hurled beer bottles against the slide, scattering shards of glass all over the tanbark. They broke into the cage and poured yellow paint over George the rooster and Jessica the hen. They swung bats with perfect accuracy at the clay masks on the playground mosaic.

Photographs taken by Nicholas King show the masks in place; by the time Mezey arrived to document the mural, they had already been destroyed. Many photographs of the mural subsequently do not include these clay masks. Noting that "many people have avoided the task of environmental improvement" because they claimed such work would inevitably be undone, Jepson and Litzky added that vandalism was a topic of every PTA meeting, as parents proposed solutions like a "vigilante committee," a police detail, or more proactive neighbors who would "go out and stop the delinquents."

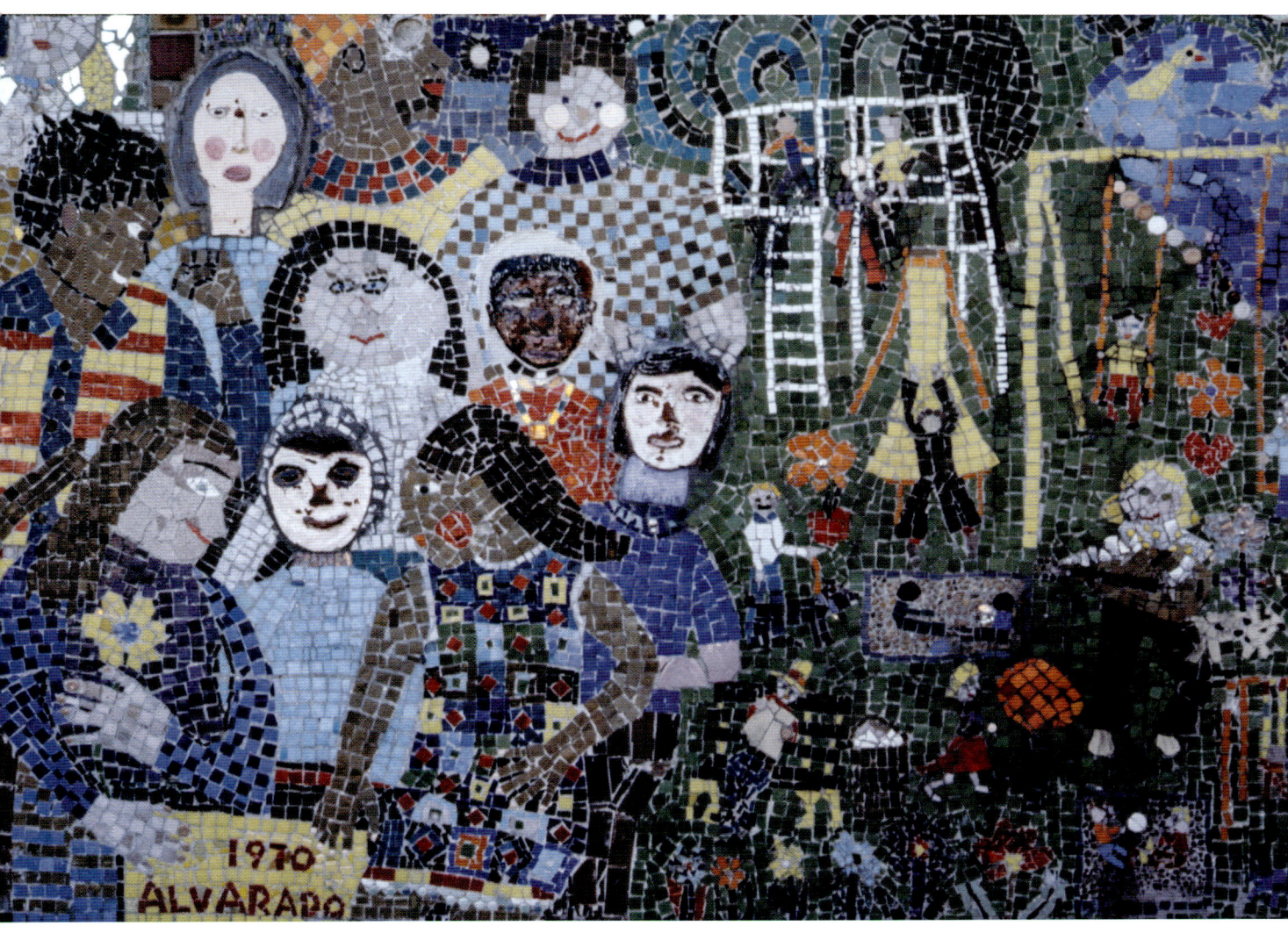

6.9 The *Alvarado Mosaic Mural* (detail), c. 1970.
Scanned color slide. Photo: Phiz Mezey. Phiz Mezey
Photographs and Papers, San Francisco History
Center, San Francisco Public Library.

For some reason, we never stopped planting or making plans to make the schoolyard a more attractive place. All of the vandalism took place during the program's early years. The Alvarado children would groan in outrage and dismay when they saw the fruits of their creative effort destroyed or damaged. They learned a hard but important object lesson. These children are now teenagers, and although someone takes an occasional potshot at the windows, the artwork is rarely harmed. The problems of anger and defiance still exist, but it seems that this latest group of teenagers has been reluctant to destroy or vandalize the products of its own decision-making and work.[53]

COMMUNITY AND COMMITMENT

Implicit in Jepson and Litzky's account of the Alvarado School Arts Workshop is an account of race and class in midcentury San Francisco—and the response of a group of mothers to this socioeconomic inequality. By the 1960s, the city's public school system had become one of the most segregated in the country. As Rand Quinn explores in his book *Class Action: Desegregation and Diversity in San Francisco Schools*, this racial imbalance has a long and complex history. Following World War II, during which San Francisco had grown economically as a strategic base for military personnel and weapons production, the city saw an influx of Black residents; following the 1965 passage of the Immigration and Nationality Act, there were also growing Chinese, Mexican, Filipino, and other communities with already long histories in the city. The racial imbalance in the public schools grew, and was exacerbated by unequal housing distribution. Given that the courts essentially tolerated segregated housing, Quinn explains, racial imbalance in the schools, which were tied to these neighborhoods, worsened; only segregation that was the result of direct discrimination in the schools could be litigated.[54]

By the late 1960s, the local NAACP chapter described the city as "behind such places as Mississippi and Texas in offering equal educational opportunity to Black students."[55] The art mothers saw this landscape firsthand and knew how closely race and class were intertwined in creating this situation. Early on in the Workshop, parent coordinator Anne Marie Theilen, who had studied art in France, led the program at Edison Elementary School, where a third of the families were on welfare assistance and almost every child was on the free lunch program.[56] Efforts to improve the situation led to a court-ordered desegregation of the San Francisco schools in 1971, beginning with the elementary grades. With this ruling, the city became the first large urban area to face court-ordered desegregation since *Brown v. Board of Education*. For the next three decades, paralleling the Workshop's efforts, the school district operated under court supervision. Busing students from one neighborhood to another was the primary way this court order was implemented. Desegregation went through multiple phases and was very contentious, with large portions of the population resistant to school assignments and busing across town. By the time court supervision of the school district's desegregation ended in 2005, the school district was more segregated than it had been since 1971.

Alvarado's most active years coincided with this court-ordered desegregation, and in many ways the program's reach—and success—was impacted by this legal structure. Asawa herself was skeptical of busing as a solution, feeling that its approach was superficial, failing to address deeper inequalities and pushing the problem onto the children. She would have agreed with bell hooks, who narrated the frustration of her own experience of being bused during the desegregation of her Kentucky high school:

I still remember my rage that we had to awaken an hour early so that we could be bussed to school before the white students arrived. We were made to sit in the gymnasium and wait. It was believed that this practice would prevent outbreaks of conflict and hostility since it removed the possibility of social contact before classes began. Yet, once again, the burden of this transition was placed on us. The white school was desegregated, but in the classroom, in the cafeteria, and in most social spaces racial apartheid prevailed.[57]

The Workshop recognized this perspective: the problem of school segregation was not simply a problem of enrollment numbers; it was a problem that ran deep in the social fabric of the city, encompassing housing, education, and the workplace. In this sense, the Workshop understood the issue as a structural problem, in contrast to the city's official legal and political response. Its systemic approach to the schools paralleled its rejection of art as an individualist and expressive pursuit. Projects continually sought to support children in situating themselves within larger socioeconomic forces—whose most concrete formulation was the city itself.

Asawa and the Alvarado art mothers did not allow busing to destroy the neighborhood-oriented approach of the Workshop, exploring how this development could productively expand the program. Jepson recalls that Asawa suggested, "if we get some seed money the parents in our program could take the program to the schools their children are being bused to because of the court order for integration."[58] With support from William Roth, the Zellerbach Family Foundation, and the Rosenberg Foundation, the Workshop implemented art programs in five additional schools, located in the Mission district, Chinatown, Hunters Point, and Potrero Hill. The expansion brought challenges. "Many parents worked full-time; others felt uncomfortable because their English was poor, or were intimidated by the word 'art' since they had never had any first-hand creative experience," according to Jepson and Litzky.[59] The Workshop also drew on federal funds, such as the Emergency School Aid Act, put in place in 1972 specifically "to deal with problems associated with minority-group isolation."[60] These additional funds compensated for the fact that volunteers and parent coordinators, so essential to the early success of the program, were not as readily available in poorer neighborhoods.

Addressing these inequalities was part of the program's efforts to reintegrate the arts into the schools and the schools into the community. The Workshop's three core approaches—urban gardening, the visual arts, and performing arts—drew on an ethos of overcoming separations, which Asawa had internalized during her studies at Black Mountain College in the late 1940s. As an education experiment and the first desegregated school in the American South, Black Mountain modeled the kind of integrated artistic experience that the Workshop attempted to realize in the primary and secondary schools of San Francisco with its goal of an artist in every school. This radical "decentralization of the artist," as Asawa put it, meant that education would be redefined "to work with the children where they live," and in "the space that's between the school and the home, which are the parks and empty lots, and the walk between the home and the school."[61] Overcoming a separation between home, work, and school would thus parallel the defeat of "separation, segregation" at other levels, as Asawa explained, including that between adults and children, between rich and poor, between Black and white.[62] Such racial divisions, Asawa argued, were not a matter of mere diversity; they were manifestations of a deeper division in modern life premised on the disposability and disenfranchisement of people.[63]

To take up the format of the self-portrait was to combat this disposability and disenfranchisement, and thus to address structural social inequality that registered in the public school demographics. Kwon has identified a central aim of community-based art as engendering an encounter in which community members "will see and recognize themselves in the work, not so much in the sense of being critically implicated but of being affirmatively pictured or validated."[64] In the case of the Workshop, that community was explicitly bureaucratic and thus demythologized; it derived from the zoning laws that determined which district schools served which neighborhood. There was no pretense of a unified, shared community vision (even if the Workshop may have had, as I mentioned at the outset of this chapter, a definite philosophical intent). And that in part explains the vandalism—that many other children in the neighborhood, who did not share in this decision-making, felt unrepresented by the work. "Community" for the Workshop was thus indivisible from a positioning of its members within larger socioeconomic structures that determined their lives. To create a self-portrait under these circumstances was not to fetishize some fantasy of expressive individualism on the part of middle schoolers; it was rather to create the conditions in which those subjects-in-formation could begin to think of themselves as sited within larger social forces.

On the point of responding to racial inequality, the Workshop can be compared to other countercultural efforts in which innovative pedagogical strategies were closely intertwined with school desegregation efforts. As Marta Gutman writes, such experiments were implemented in an effort to address situations in which a school may have achieved desegregation in terms of enrollment numbers but was still struggling to integrate classrooms.[65] The Berkeley Unified School District was an exemplary instance of this strategy. Voluntarily desegregating its fourteen elementary schools in 1968, the school district opened the door to programs implemented through appropriated spaces, either set up within existing schools (as the Alvarado School Arts Workshop did) or set up as alternative schools within existing buildings, such as churches, houses, warehouses, and storefronts, as Gutman writes. Artists and architects played a vital role in this process. Together with author and teacher Herbert Kohl, Allan Kaprow set up Project Other Ways in a Berkeley storefront in the fall of 1968, just as the Alvarado School Arts Workshop was getting under way. In a street that marked an unofficial boundary between the white and Black populations of Berkeley, the storefront's experimental art projects, including several Happenings, witnessed how race inflected the learning environment, with Kaprow later observing that the majority of participants were Black and Hispanic kids who had been discriminated against by the school system.[66]

The inability of Bay Area school districts to create equitable classrooms also plagued another artistic intervention in the schools that is worth comparing to the Alvarado School Arts Workshop, namely the involvement of Anna Halprin's Dancers' Workshop in the Sausalito School District. Halprin, like Asawa, had studied with practitioners of Bauhaus pedagogy as it had been transmitted into the postwar American educational context. Like Asawa, Halprin valued the artistic encounter as the engendering of experience, and her own artistic practice as a dancer was inextricably bound up with new models of education. In the late 1960s, several of her dancers were invited to work at Central School in Sausalito. Located directly north of San Francisco, the Sausalito School District also voted in 1965 to desegregate its schools, busing students from the predominantly Black neighborhoods of Mill Valley into Central School. As in Berkeley, a wide range of programs were implemented in order to foster integration.

In fall 1966, one hundred third- and fourth-graders met twice a week in small groups for forty minutes—the length of a class session—with Halprin's dancers. Together they investigated bodily movement, nonverbal communication, and emotional expression through creative dance. Photographs taken by Phiz Mezey, produced as part of her involvement in a teachers' training program at San Francisco State College and published in the book *Something That's Happening* (1968), capture this movement course (fig. 6.10). The photographs show dancers and children sometimes at ease with one another, while at other moments performing a direct confrontation punctuated by extreme emotions. In other photographs, adults and children kneel and lie on the floor, working with cloth bands and sheets of gauze in an exploration of counterbalanced bodily weight. One sequence captures students hitting one another with balloons and bouncing inflatable balls. Accompanied by poetry written by the students, the photographs and text together constitute a "portrait" of the Sausalito School District, published as such by the district in a dynamic and multidimensional portrayal of a situation far from straightforward.

Written reflections on the program elaborate how difficult this experiment was for many involved. With no experience in elementary schools, dancers were overwhelmed by the challenges of classroom management as well as the structural issues around power imbalances endemic to the school situation. Many of the dancers reported how ill-equipped they were for the discipline that was expected by the classroom teachers. Classroom teachers felt the dancers were underprepared, leading to boredom on the students' part, and suggested a more structured plan involving a warmup, a creative lesson, a period of relaxation and evaluation. On the other hand, the dancers' presence seemed to have encouraged the children to be more spontaneous, less inhibited, more confident, and better able to work in groups. Yet, as the principal observed, "all of us in the school recognize a rise in tensions, hostility, 'lack of respect.'"[67]

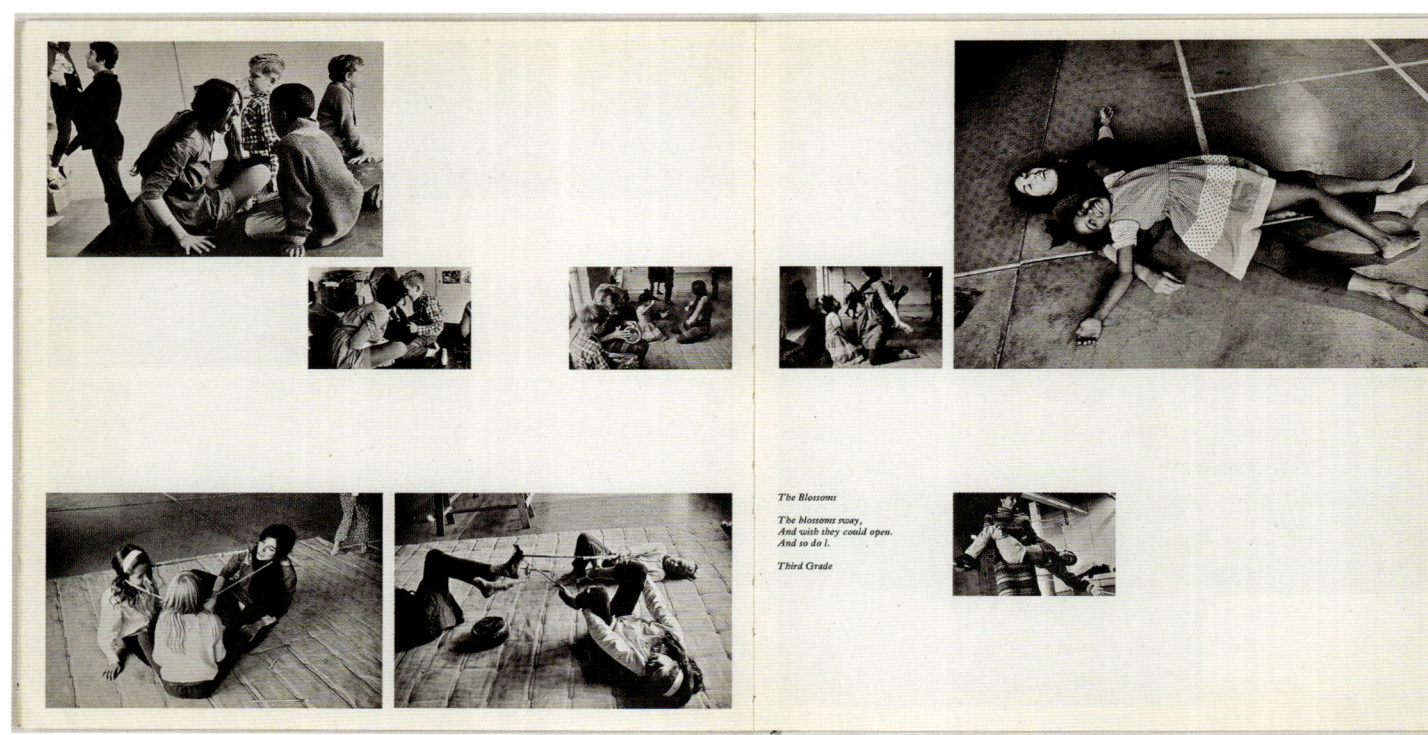

The Blossoms

The blossoms sway,
And wish they could open.
And so do I.

Third Grade

6.10 Photographs by Phiz Mezey in *Something That's Happening: A Portrait of the Sausalito School District* (1968). Phiz Mezey Photographs and Papers, San Francisco History Center, San Francisco Public Library.

In neither Berkeley nor Sausalito were parents, much less mothers, a structural component of these pedagogical experiments. Artists and educators attempted to work together without a systematic recruitment of parents and thus the children's home environment. Furthermore, these other interventions were all short-lived. Project Other Ways lasted mere months before Kaprow and Kohl suffered a falling-out, and its main accomplishment was an artwork added to Kaprow's oeuvre (*Six Ordinary Happenings*, staged in May 1969), thereby bolstering a mythologization of the artist, which the project arguably had set out to avoid. By contrast, the Alvarado School Arts Workshop strove for a *permanent* incorporation of artists and parents and purposely intervened into an existing institutional structure as the basis for its definition of community. Its long-term goal of enabling artists to have their studios on the school grounds, so that the students would be exposed on a regular basis to an active, professional artist at work, differentiated it substantially from the interventionist model pursued by Kaprow and by Halprin's dancers. Likewise, the Workshop engaged artists from the neighborhoods of the participating schools, artists who were already invested in that immediate environment; by contrast, the free-schools movement in Berkeley encompassed short-term interventions and had trouble finding a permanent home in the community.

A further point of differentiation can be found on the level of content: the Workshop fostered projects engaging the students' own experience of identity in transformation. Recruited to work with students from Everett Junior High as an artist in residence, Merry Renk oversaw the conception and execution of what she called the "metal mural experience" (figs. 6.11, 6.12). Volunteer parents and students from San Francisco State University and San Francisco City College provided support. Together they created a four-by-forty-foot mural made from salvaged metal cans and sheet metal. Its theme was "Ecology," portrayed by "using self-portraits in metamorphosis," with an emphasis on the four elements (earth, fire, water, air). In an Ovidian description of the mural's content, Renk wrote of it as "all animals and plants and dreams of living creatures expressing the sense of being one with the universe—through metamorphosis."[68] Students brought materials on their "metamorphic choice—for instance—if they choose to be a volcano—research—reaching and choosing and collecting sketches so that they can visually form the essence of the volcano to which they relate—a dragon—a tree—a cloud—phoenix—etc. etc."[69] In line with the Workshop's advocacy of the arts as a broad category, the *Metal Mural* engaged a range of subject fields: social studies (self-portraits), literature (mythology), math and geometry (calculating casting materials, enlarging drawings), chemistry (chemical coloring), and biology (plant life). These metaphors were combined with self-portraits made from plaster casts that were then electroplated with copper.

What is crucial to understand here is how much freedom students were given to pursue creativity; they were not asked to adapt to a preexisting aesthetic agenda (to enact a Happening), nor given too much unstructured time such that modern dance devolved into pummeling one another with balloons. Instead, children's creativity was funneled by the requirements of the materials, with Renk even bringing her own enameling kiln into the school, when she worked with students on metal pendants. Students were also held responsible for their accomplishments. Intended for the junior high's cafeteria, the mural was first on view to the public during the second annual Music, Art, Dance, Drama, and Science (MADDS) Festival, which took place in February 1974. Established as a way to share the Workshop's activities with the public, MADDS embodied the holistic concept of education—one well demonstrated by how the *Metal Mural* project spanned both the arts and sciences. At the same time, the festival sought to overcome divisions in how public space and resources were distributed by bringing multiple city agencies together, including the Art Department of the San Francisco United School District, the San Francisco Arts Commission, the Department of Parks and Recreation, the San Francisco Museum of Art, and the Exploratorium. Instead of offering conventional forms of evaluation, like report cards, such festivals, the Workshop argued, would demonstrate to the public the kinds of things the children were learning in school.[70] It was an opportunity, as Asawa pointed out in Snyder's film, for children to show each other and themselves what they had created; instead of talking about what someone else had made, they would begin to talk about what they themselves had accomplished.

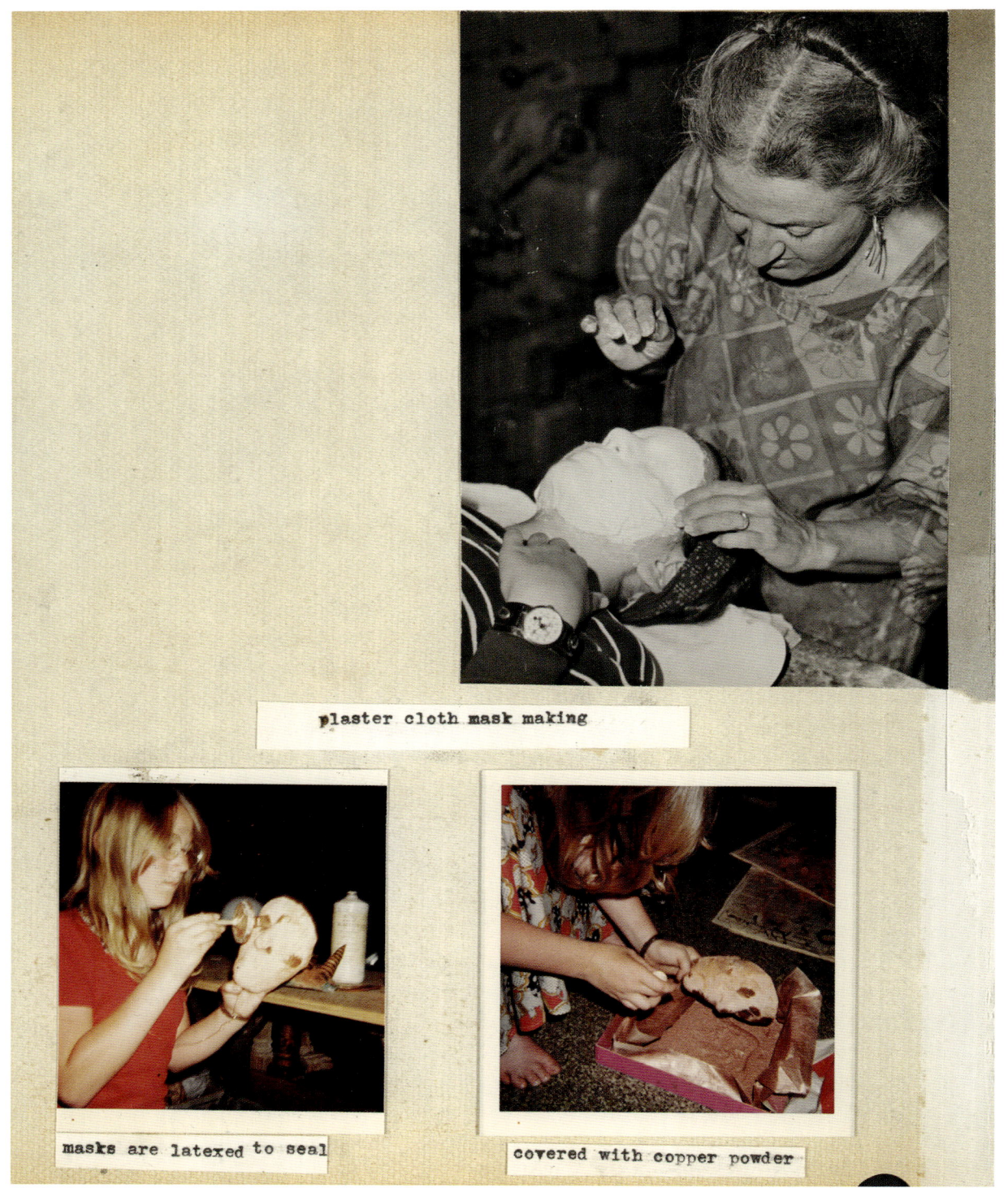

plaster cloth mask making

masks are latexed to seal

covered with copper powder

6.11 Merry Renk and students of Everett Junior
High, San Francisco, working on the *Metal Mural*,
1974. Special Collections, Stanford University.

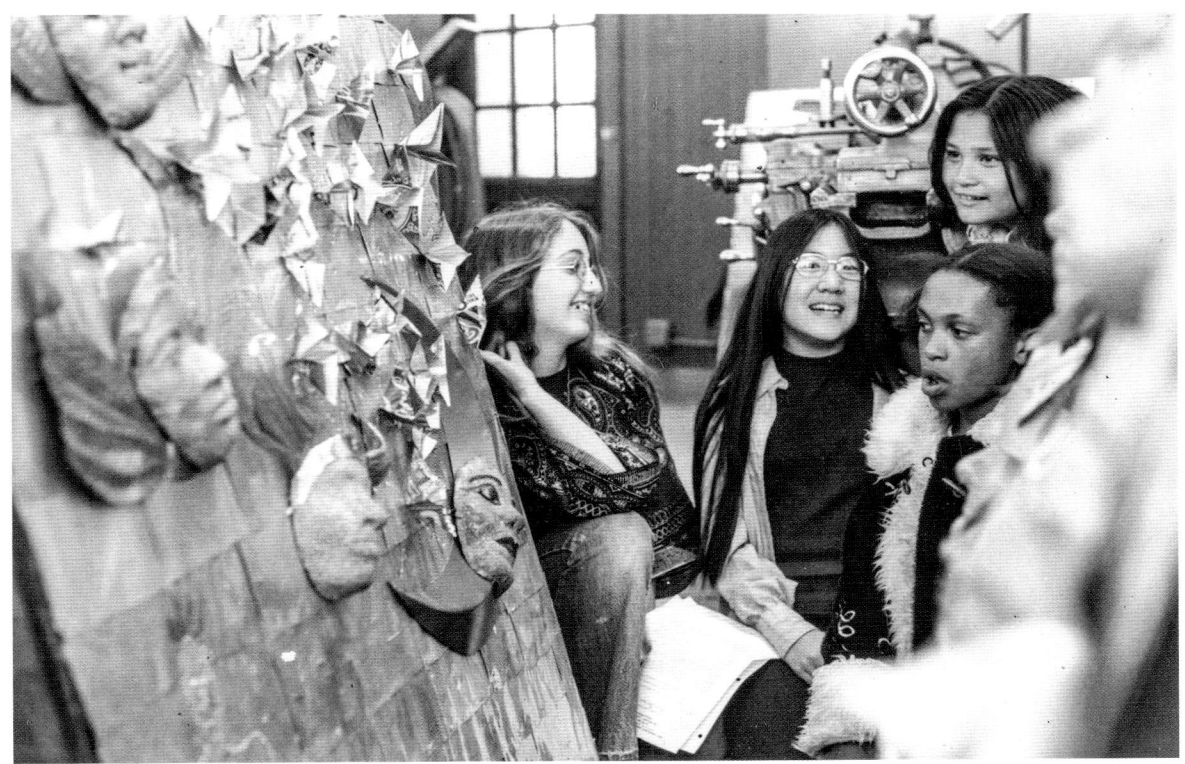

6.12 Students of Everett Junior High with the *Metal Mural*, 1974. Special Collections, Stanford University.

SELF-PORTRAITS IN METAMORPHOSIS

While the format of self-portraiture provided a tangible means for children to practice decision-making in the school environment, the art mothers, too, found in the Workshop a sphere in which to develop a sense of agency—to come into being as subjects defined by a multitude of social roles. As Sally Woodbridge reflected in an interview with a reporter in 1980, "The program in the early days, for all of us, had a cohesion that was more than a volunteer affair. It had a permanent impact on me. It was a compelling activity at the stage of life I was in, a way of self-identification. The strength of the idea was in its life-enhancing quality."[71] In the decade following the founding of the Workshop, Woodbridge enrolled as a doctoral student in architecture at the University of California, Berkeley, writing a dissertation on Julia Morgan, before going on to author three books on Bay Area architecture, among many other accomplishments as a prominent figure in her field.

The Workshop's lasting impact lies in how it valorized identity positions historically denied legitimacy. "Uncovering and reclaiming subjugated knowledge is one way to lay claims to alternative histories," knowledge, moreover, that must "be understood and defined pedagogically," feminist Chandra Mohanty has written.[72] The figure of the mother is a paradigmatic example of this phenomenon. The labor of caretaking has long been recognized by feminists as a sphere of activity historically coded as worthless and its agents as less than human. In contemporary America, those working in caretaking sectors—many of whom are themselves mothers, Angela Garbes points out—are three times as likely to live in poverty as those in other professions.[73] And yet this labor is indispensable, not only to the generation of wealth in a capitalist society but to the viability of future generations in general. As Garbes writes in her book exploring mothering as the labor of caretaking, "Mothers and caregivers are our first teachers."[74]

Although there is a tendency in Western culture to romanticize this identity, the reflections that emerged out of the Workshop, by the art mothers themselves, profoundly complicate this picture. Nancy Thompson kept a journal during these years, and excerpts speak to the challenges and rewards of this pedagogical experiment. On a woodworking project at Mission High School in the 1974–1975 school year, she wrote in November:

The students who are working with me come and go—and never seem to (to me) *finish* anything; or at least, they seem to not be able to take a thing to its conclusion without pressure from someone, and then would rather drop out than stick it out. I have been working with them on a few such pieces to show how the smallest bit more effort produces something that looks good instead of rough and disappointing to them. Some students then get on with it and are doing amazingly fine things—a real joy!—but a few will not make that kind of commitment to anything. They aren't used to really working at hard things . . . students don't really know that it's *good* to work!

[By the second week of March, the picture had changed considerably.]

March 10–15. Another very busy week with Friday being the busiest of all—Students in every period of the day—Nearly double the number of students that I had a month ago, and most of them putting in long hours—I'm going to have to get more and larger pieces of wood somehow—The last two figures on the totem pole are being carved—(Not all kids come to work—another tool has been stolen, a wood rasp, naturally the one we use the most. Actually, I've only had two tools go, probably a record for Mission, but I resent *any* being ripped off.) I'm going to have to be "closed" for a day a week to do my own work I think.[75]

Thompson is transparent about the tensions and complexities at play in the Workshop, and her own limits in this situation. She is honest about the ambivalence of these relationships—a foundational ambivalence in the relationship of caretaker to child, which, Rozsika Parker has argued, structurally defines maternal subjectivity. Such ambivalence should not be resolved; it is rather a constitutive feature of identity, in the same way that Miwon Kwon argues that the most effective examples of collective artistic practice involve a recognition of identity as continually in a state of negotiation.[76]

In addition to apathy and theft, the art mothers struggled against overtechnologized classrooms. A paradigmatic example was the trend toward computer-based education as opposed to art, which "exercises more mental skills than any other activity I can think of," Asawa stated to a journalist in 1984. "When I see children sitting down in those cubicles staring at computer screen terminals, I sense we are teaching these youngsters to be farther and farther away from people."[77] The overtechnologized classroom paralleled bureaucracy as another destructive force, what Thompson called

the "business" of school [that] seems to grind on regardless of anything else—I think the ground could open up and still meetings would be called, time sheets filled out, dittos run off, the same people would be exchanging memos—it would probably function better without any students!! Admittedly—this is looking at it from MY angle—but maybe schools as they are now aren't places where "real" work can be done and a "working artist" in such a place is a strange sight indeed. Everywhere I've been I find excellent teachers who have found a way to get *around* the machinery, to get real teaching done.[78]

Such encounters with the material world, as Thompson taught through stained glass and wood carving, reversed the tendency of the standard curriculum to be far too abstract, designed with an idealized child in mind, rather than with the reality of radically diverse learning capabilities. Through such abstraction, the Workshop argued, children lost a foundational orientation toward themselves, others, and their environment.

Because of their vantage point as mothers, the women involved in the Workshop recognized that artistic labor was also structurally underpaid and worked to redress this. In 1973, President Richard Nixon signed into law the Comprehensive Employment and Training Act (CETA), legislation that had been passed to address the country's rising unemployment. Its scope consisted of all critically underemployed sectors, not necessarily the arts. But in response to Asawa's proposal, San Francisco, through the efforts of John Kreidler, then an intern at the San Francisco Arts Commission, saw the potential of using these funds to hire artists.[79] The idea of the artist as a worker had not yet taken hold. By recoding artists' labor as labor worth remunerating, San Francisco's use of CETA funds continued efforts begun by organizations like the Art

Workers Coalition in New York. It provided a chance, as Asawa stated, "to demonstrate the social value of creative work," a task with even more urgency "as the economy gets worse and as work becomes more computerized and alienating."[80]

Leah Forbes, one of the founding mothers within the Workshop, became the first manager of CETA-funded artists in the city. With its successful request to fund twenty-four positions by December 1974, and then another ninety positions directly thereafter, given the overwhelming number of applications, the Arts Commission had tapped into an urgent need among artists. The Workshop received forty of these positions, designated for the visual and performing arts, and twenty more for a new gardening program that Asawa had devised. This program involved hiring master gardeners and was linked to the Workshop, but was also connected to existing initiatives around allotment gardens in the city. Virtually overnight, the city's successful CETA application tripled the Workshop's budget and allowed the number of schools in which it was active to grow at an exponential rate. A poster on the occasion of the program's fourteenth anniversary bears a verdant tree through which Thompson visualized the ever-growing reach of the Workshop's efforts (fig. 6.13).

The gardening program was especially successful (fig. 6.14). Distinctly different from what Lucy Lippard described as "1960s ecotopia" in her discussion of Bonnie Sherk's *Crossroads Community (The Farm)* in San Francisco's Potrero district, these did not constitute "a rural vision superimposed on a rundown urban industrial area," but rather provided an exercise in self-determination.[81] Gardener Robin Romanowski, for instance, worked with teachers and students of McAteer High School in several community gardens around the city. In an article that appeared in the *San Francisco Examiner* in 1976, Romanowski describes gardening as an equalizing force: "Gardening is still pretty foreign to these city kids, and it's hard work. But it offers them a great opportunity to design a project all their own and then see it through to a conclusion. In gardening, everyone starts out equal. No one is at a disadvantage. If a kid works honestly on his garden, and learns what he has to, it'll produce. If he goofs off and doesn't do this work, anyone can see. And he can't blame it on 'the system' or on anybody else, just himself."[82] The gardening program was an experimental space in which students could test the capabilities and limits of their agency—what they had control over and where that control ended. This was a concrete instance of how the Workshop motivated a child to consider how he or she was positioned within a field of determining forces and, through that recognition, to reflect upon identity as a function of positionality—rather than a matter of expression or individual transformation (thus Asawa's consistent and vocal dismissal of an abstract expressionist-derived notion of "creativity" as the goal of the Workshop). Such insights derived from a rigorous process of self-reflection on the part of the artist-mothers: Asawa herself, for example, had experienced systemic racism firsthand, having spent her late high school years incarcerated in a Japanese internment camp. She funneled this experience into pursuits like the Workshop that addressed racism on a structural level, starting with immediate, concrete interventions, like the gardening program, which could reach students right away, where they already were.

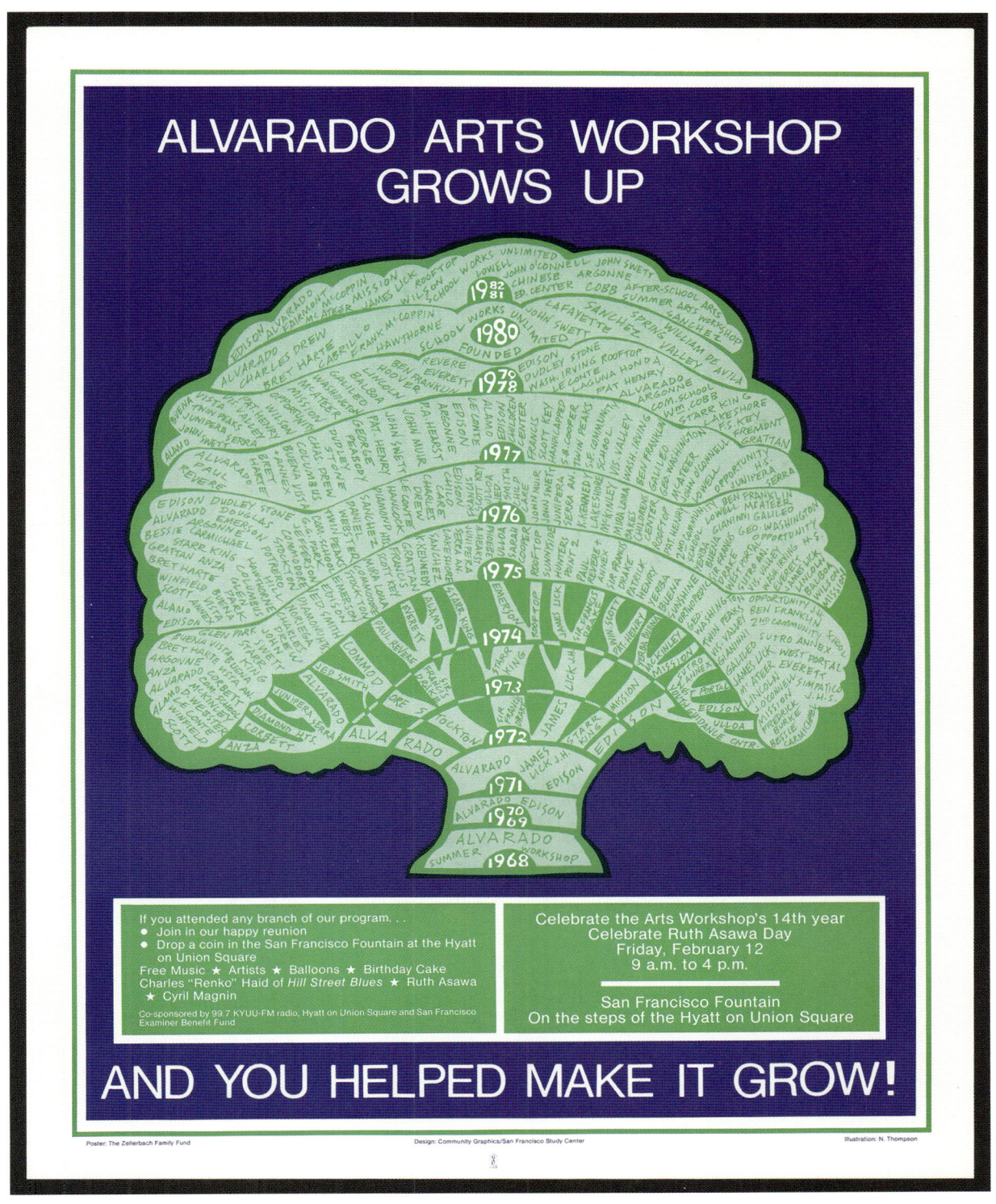

6.13 Poster for the Alvarado School Arts Workshop by Community Graphics/San Francisco Study Center with illustration by Nancy Thompson, 1982. Special Collections, Stanford University.

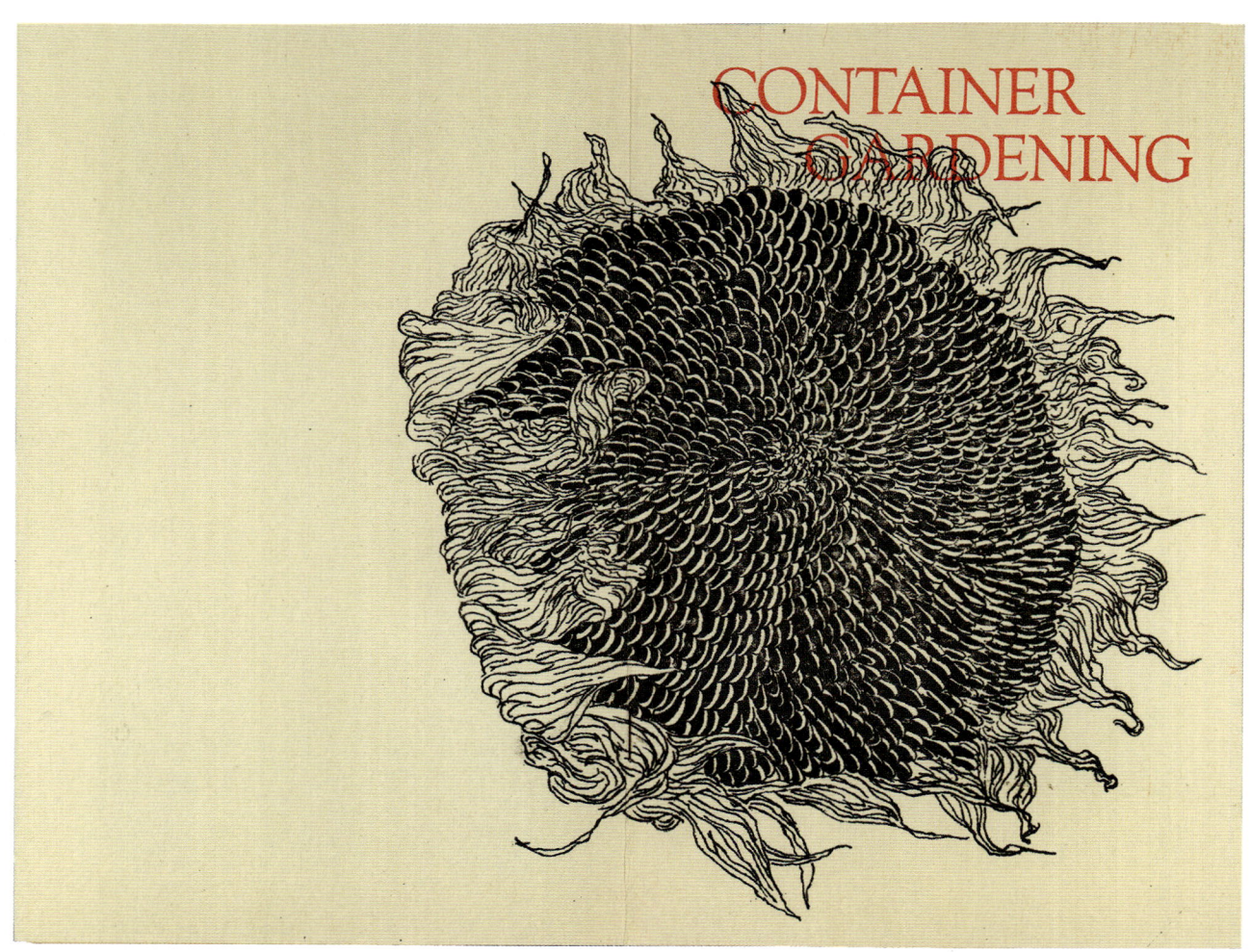

6.14 Cover of a brochure on container gardening produced by the Alvarado School Arts Workshop, with Ruth Asawa's drawing *Mai Arbegast's
Sunflower* (PF.277), c. 1976, Special Collections,
Stanford University.

The gardening project responded to an economic depression colliding with a rising environmental consciousness which sought "to make our lives fuller, less dependent on nonrenewable energy sources and on mass-produced gadgets that pollute our habitat and regularly self-destruct. Some of this work would fall under the heading of art; all would fall within CETA's broad definition of public service."[83] Workshops for local community members taught self-sufficiency, a "basic philosophy of the garden program."[84] In addition to lecturing on the topic "The Artist as Worker" at the Department of Labor's conference on the arts in 1979, Asawa also served on President Jimmy Carter's Commission for Mental Health, contributing to a subpanel addressing art's role in mental health—the first panel of its kind. Asawa was a strong voice in calling for "expanding the idea of 'creativity'": "In crowded urban neighborhoods," she stated, "gardening can provide a creative process through direct contact with soil, sun, and water by using one's own hands and energies to create both 'things' and relationships with neighbors. This can be a way of restoring identity and status to individuals as well as to communities."[85]

Silvia Federici has written of urban gardens as a significant tool in what she calls "the production of ourselves as a common subject."[86] Her conception of the commons is indivisible from community—an understanding of group cohesion founded not necessarily, or not only, on commonalities of religion or ethnicity, but on cooperation, including both "responsibility to each other and to the earth, the forests, the seas, the animals." Urban gardens, often established by immigrant communities, Federici points out, help to build and maintain this cohesion by providing control over one's food production, places of gathering and sociability, and a site of cultural exchange around farming and cooking practices (fig. 6.14). Community gardens thus provide a space in which subjectivity spans both individual and group identities. Asawa cited the artist as the figure who would be able to realize this goal, bringing together "children who are traditionally separated for various 'deficiencies' (mental, physical, emotional, language), in activities that make them aware of their individuality and ability as contributors of their community."[87]

With the Workshop's expansion through CETA funds, as John Kreidler recalls, "the days of being an organization run by inspired volunteer moms were over."[88] On the one hand, the CETA program was so successful that it became a model for similar efforts in other cities, including the Cultural Council Foundation (CCF) Artists Project in New York. As two artists from that program pointed out, CETA funds especially benefited African American, Latinx, Asian, and women artists, both as individuals and through the organizations in which they were often involved.[89] On the other hand, CETA was also the beginning of the end: with the passage of Proposition 13 in 1978, which significantly reduced California state revenues by lowering real estate taxes, many of the funding sources on which the Workshop relied dried up. By 1982, the program had been reduced to five schools, with art instruction largely falling to homeroom teachers instead of professional artists.[90] Thompson's poster from that year was created in large part to drum up funding, using the *San Francisco Fountain*, a massive bronze panorama of the city, which I address in the following chapter,

Scene/Arts

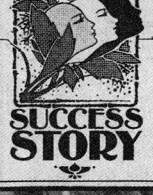

SUCCESS STORY

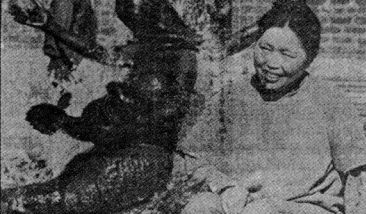

Sculptor Ruth Asawa, who started the Alvarado Art Workshop, by her mermaid fountain

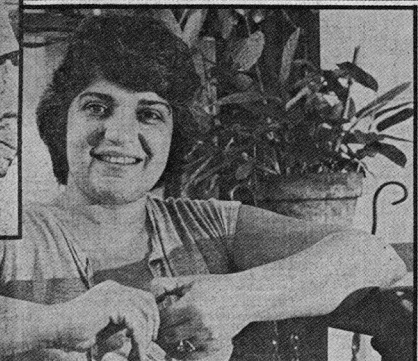

Andrea Jepson, who posed for Asawa's mermaid, and later joined the Alvarado mothers

Examiner/Bill Nichols

Examiner/Paul Glines

The careers that grew out of the arts project

By Mildred Hamilton

THIS IS THE STORY of 10 San Francisco women whose joint enterprise as neighbors and parents is influencing what they will do for the rest of their lives.

The women are mothers who, back in 1968, galvanized by an artistic gap in the public schools, set out as volunteers to help their children, and other children. Today their project has become the Alvarado Art Workshop, a national model for a school-community art program, enriching children's educations.

But what about the mothers?

No longer full-time homemakers, they have gone their separate ways, into a variety of mid-life careers and activities that were all seeded or stimulated by that cooperative effort.

"No one went into it with the idea of personal reward," said Dottye Dean, who recently sang one of the leads in a Marin production of "Amahl and the Night Visitors." "It was kind of an old-fashioned farm community idea, but the benefits just keep coming. I know the experience lit a fire in me. At age 41, I think: another frontier? It is reasonably hard to make major career changes at this point. Then I think: Why not?" Her smile radiated her confident anticipation.

Dean happened to be one of the neighbors and friends of San Francisco's living art treasure, Ruth Asawa, who was the originator and catalyst of the Alvarado program. The sculptor and her architect husband, Albert Lanier, had six children in the public schools and were distressed at the lack of attention to art and the creative process.

Asawa first mentioned her idea of parent intervention to her next-door neighbor, Sally Woodbridge, whose three children were also in Alvarado School. And then one, and another, and another mother were recruited.

"I remember that Sally called me," said Sharon Litzky, "and said, 'What do you think of an art program at Alvarado?' We had exchanged baby sitting and home chores, so we all went to a six-week summer organizing workshop." The program has grown from a budget of $50, mostly spent that summer for flour to learn to make Asawa's baker's clay, to today's multi-school, multi-fund enterprise reaching thousands of children and employing many artists and aides.

The women also have grown, as individuals.

Woodbridge, now an architectural historian and critic, said, "The program in the early days, for all of us, had a cohesion that was more than a volunteer affair. It had a permanent impact on me. It was a compelling activity at the stage of life I was in, a way of self-identification. The strength of the idea was in its life-enhancing quality."

Woodbridge's three children are now nearly grown. A son, 21, will be graduating from Amherst this year. A daughter, 19, in fine arts studies at UCLA, "was imprinted by the Alvarado program," and a second daughter in high school is interested in dance and dramatic arts.

"All our children were persuaded that the arts are important," said Woodbridge, who returned to school herself and is now a Ph.D. candidate in architectural history at UC, where she also teaches in the extension and summer school. One quarter each year she teaches a course at the University of Washington on the architectural history of the West Coast.

She also has been the co-author or editor, or both, of three books: the 1973 "Guide to Architecture in San Francisco and Northern California," the 1976 "Bay Area Houses," and the 1978 "Victorian Legacy: Guide to Victorians in San Francisco and the Bay Area."

Sharon Litzky and Andrea Jepson also became authors, among their other new activities, as a result of the art workshop. Last year they wrote its story, "The Alvarado Experience."

Litzky, a registered nurse, and her husband Lewis, an accountant, have four children, now 19, 17, 13 and 10. "I remember meetings in my kitchen or in Ruth's, scrounging materials, learning to work with baker's clay, in mosaics, paper mache, puppets. When busing started and our kids were moved to Commodore Stockton School, we started an art program there. When we moved to Muir Beach three years ago, I got involved with community artists."

She helped form a non-profit cooperative gallery to encourage developing and young artists. The Muir Beach Artisans Gallery opened at 39 Forrest St. in Mill Valley in September 1977. Litzky works there as a volunteer one day a week. She also had a one-woman baker's clay show there last fall.

"The art interest I had in childhood was reawakened by the Alvarado experience. Now I am thinking in terms of sculpture as I try many things in art. I also have established an after-school arts and crafts recreational program at Mill Valley's Homestead School. And I worked three months last year as a nurse. I am trying to decide whether to continue as an artist or a nurse."

Andrea Jepson is now doing research for another book, one on San Francisco, as well as looking forward to new community service. She got into the Alvarado program because she had been a model for Asawa. "Ruth did drawings of me when I was pregnant, and then as a nursing mother I was the model for the mermaid in her fountain in Ghirardelli Square. Soon I was taking my two little babies to Alvarado to help in the art program."

Her daughters, now 14 and 12 and active in that program, have gone into dramatics. Jepson, who has a B.A. in European history, did ceramics and painting as a parent leader. She administered the program for four years — "at one point we had 50 people there each week and geared our teaching through the arts. It was exciting."

She did tutoring, wrote a column for a weekly paper,

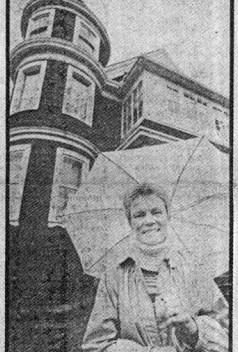
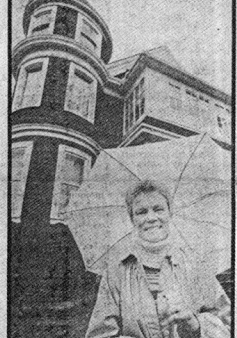

Examiner/Judith Calson Rausch

Sally Woodbridge is now a writer and lecturer

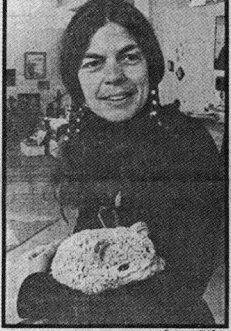

Examiner/Sid Tate

Sharon Litzky helped found a cooperative gallery

tion 13 wiped out her programs, "so I spent one year on my own things — murals, stained glass commissions, teaching in my studio. However, I like community work and I looked for other projects."

Now Thompson has another grant for art projects in the Hercules schools and community center. "Alvarado," she said, "opened up a lot of things in my head about how I wanted to do art work. It made so many more possibilities apparent to me. I can't say enough for the stimulation I received."

Another artist and parent volunteer at Alvarado, Anne-Marie Theilen, saw her three children, now 19, 17 and 11, drawn to the program, and her oldest, now in college, is a volunteer crafts teacher for 9- to 12-year-olds. Theilen became one of the artists in residence, moved into art administration and now heads the federally funded Comprehensive Education Training Act projects for the San Francisco Art Commission. "This never ends," she said. "It is like an art evolution." She can see the need for administration and community work. "That's why I have stayed with this so long, but it is always a struggle because I also want to get back to my personal painting."

Charmalee Larkin, whose four sons went to Alvarado School, credits what happened to her there developing into a livelihood. She had a social work degree, "but I didn't like that as a career. When Ruth sent out the notice of the art workshop, it seemed to make sense, tied in with what we were doing remodeling an old Victorian.

"Crafts were just my bag, and I started concentrating on wood and wood carvings and wood collages." When busing scattered the children, she went along to Commodore Stockton School, to help make life-size Chinese

— See Page 2, Col. 1

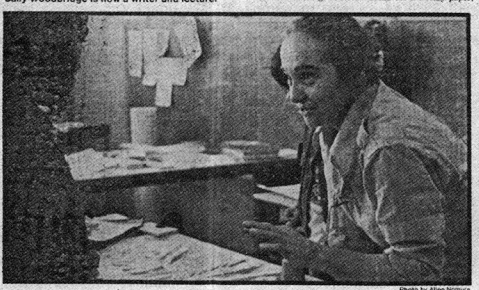

Photo by Allen Nomura

Alvarado's first artist-in-residence, Nancy Thompson, now heads community art programs in Hercules

worked in a bookstore and got back into politics. "I campaigned for district elections and for No on Proposition 13 I was administrative aide for Supervisor Harry Britt for nine months before I took a leave last fall to run his campaign. We won, and I just resigned my job for new activities."

The book, "The Alvarado Experience," started as a 10-year report on the project, as inquiries increased on how the program worked, the workshop published it.

"I learned an enormous lesson from the workshop and the wonderful people associated with it," she said. "You must not be afraid of making a mistake. You give your best shot, but if you make a mistake, you do it. Middle-class women are under pressure to be out there and to be perfect, with all eyes on you. What I learned is this: if you make a mistake, you correct it and you don't let it stop you.

"Ruth gave me a lot of lessons in finishing. Now I try to finish. A lot of people in the workshop were role models."

Nancy Thompson, who had earned a degree in art at the University of Chicago, was concentrating on rearing her two daughters, now 21 and 19, and doing some painting and stitchery at home when she was invited to join the workshop. Soon she was conducting a print class, working on a big mosaic at the school, "and then I moved into the job, with miniscule payment, as artist in residence."

As more art funds became available, she expanded her school work, directing art programs at five schools one year, operating with California Arts Council grants in the Eureka Valley Neighborhood Community Center. Proposi-

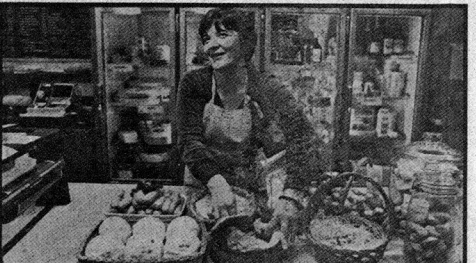

Examiner/John Gorman

Lois Link gained courage to enter the business world, and became a partner in a French food shop

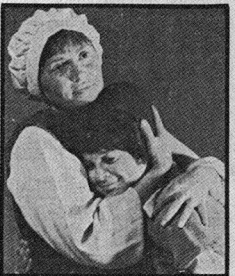

Dottye Dean in 'Amahl and the Night Visitors'

as a meeting point. The process-oriented approach gave way to the establishment of School Works, Unlimited, located in a downtown department store, which made the products of the Workshop available for sale. And several of the founding artist-mothers had gone on to other pursuits, opening businesses and galleries or doing community organizing, as profiled in the local paper. The radicality of the Workshop had given way to a distinctly mainstream brand of 1980s American feminism in which emancipation equated to working for a wage outside the home.

It would be a misreading to see the Alvarado School Arts Workshop as a project ancillary to Asawa's work as an artist; nor should it be seen as a program whose effect was exhausted by its impact on students. My argument here has been that it enacted a site in which a group of women could recognize their own agency within a structure they set out to change. The Workshop anticipated—and proposed a solution to—what Silvia Federici describes as "the main casualty of the neoliberal era of capitalism": "our recognition of history as a collective project."[91] To reduce this agency to the many careers these women led after their involvement in the Workshop is myopic. Certainly, it empowered them in an immediate way to go on and lead independent lives in the public sphere, pursuing careers of their own design, as Mildred Hamilton emphasized in her newspaper feature on the group of eleven founding mothers, writing that just as the program grew, the mothers themselves "have grown, as individuals" (fig. 6.15).[92] But this interpretation alone falls prey to what Andrea Garbes describes as a "mainstream white American feminism [that] has preached dignity and self-expression through career and work outside the home, a 'lean in' approach that values personal growth and gain. These women have had little interest in an inclusive feminism rooted in creating a better society for everyone." The art mothers may have represented a demographic that Garbes associates with Betty Friedan's *The Feminine Mystique*, "advocating for women to find fulfillment through work," but the work they did as part of the Workshop, under Asawa's guiding philosophy, was in line with intersectional efforts to strengthen solidarity—Garbes cites "the Black, Indigenous, and other leaders of the National Welfare Rights Organization [who] were developing a platform for a universal basic income that improved the lives of all Americans."[93]

A quilt given to Asawa on her forty-eighth birthday in 1974 is one of the few durable objects that emerged from the collective artistic labor brought into being by this group of artist-mothers (fig. 6.16). With each square sewn and assembled by parents, teachers, children, and artists associated with the Workshop, it is the closest that we come to a collective portrait of its members. There are squares by Sally Woodbridge and her two daughters, Diana and Pamela, a dragon by Nancy Thompson, hearts and hands by Merry Renk, a psychedelic sun from Warner Jepson, macramé by Judy Burns (whom Asawa had asked to learn the hippie craft and lead workshops), an example of

6.15 Mildred Hamilton, "The Careers That Grew Out of the Arts Project," *San Francisco Examiner*, January 27, 1980, 1–2. Special Collections, Stanford University.

a God's eye with two popsicle sticks, and a pair of hands that can be opened to reveal a dollar bill encased in clear vinyl. At the center is a red patch bearing the recipe for baker's clay—"4 cups flour, 1 cup salt, 1-1/2 cups water, 1 bunch kids"—a medium that I discuss in chapter 7. In a sequence from Robert Snyder's film portrait of Asawa, she sits on the quilt, spread out over a daybed in her home's sunroom, pointing to this square as unique: it's "what I think this entire program in the schools is all about."[94]

6.16 Quilt made for Ruth Asawa by parents, teachers, children, and artists involved in the Alvarado School Arts Workshop, c. 1974. Special Collections, Stanford University.

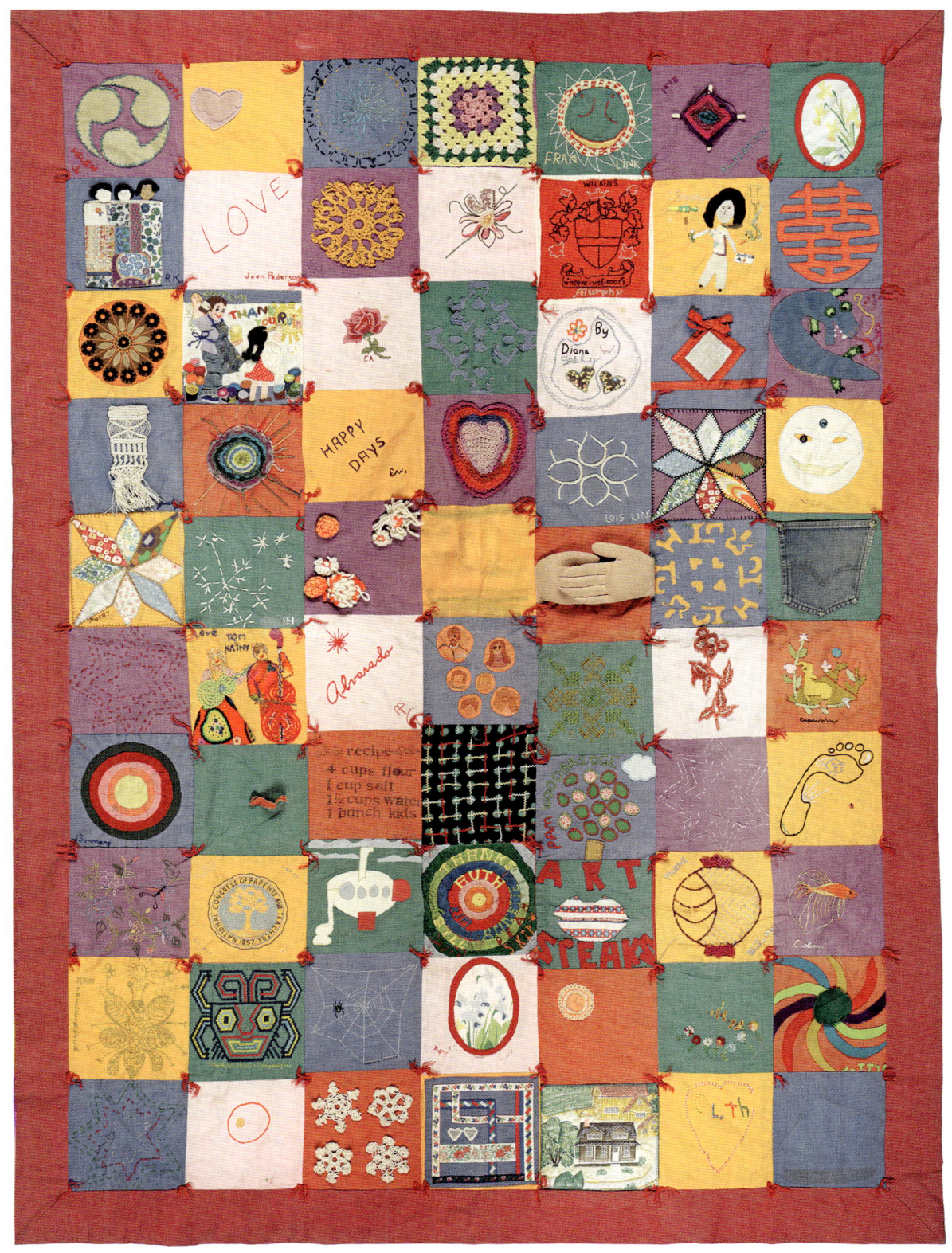

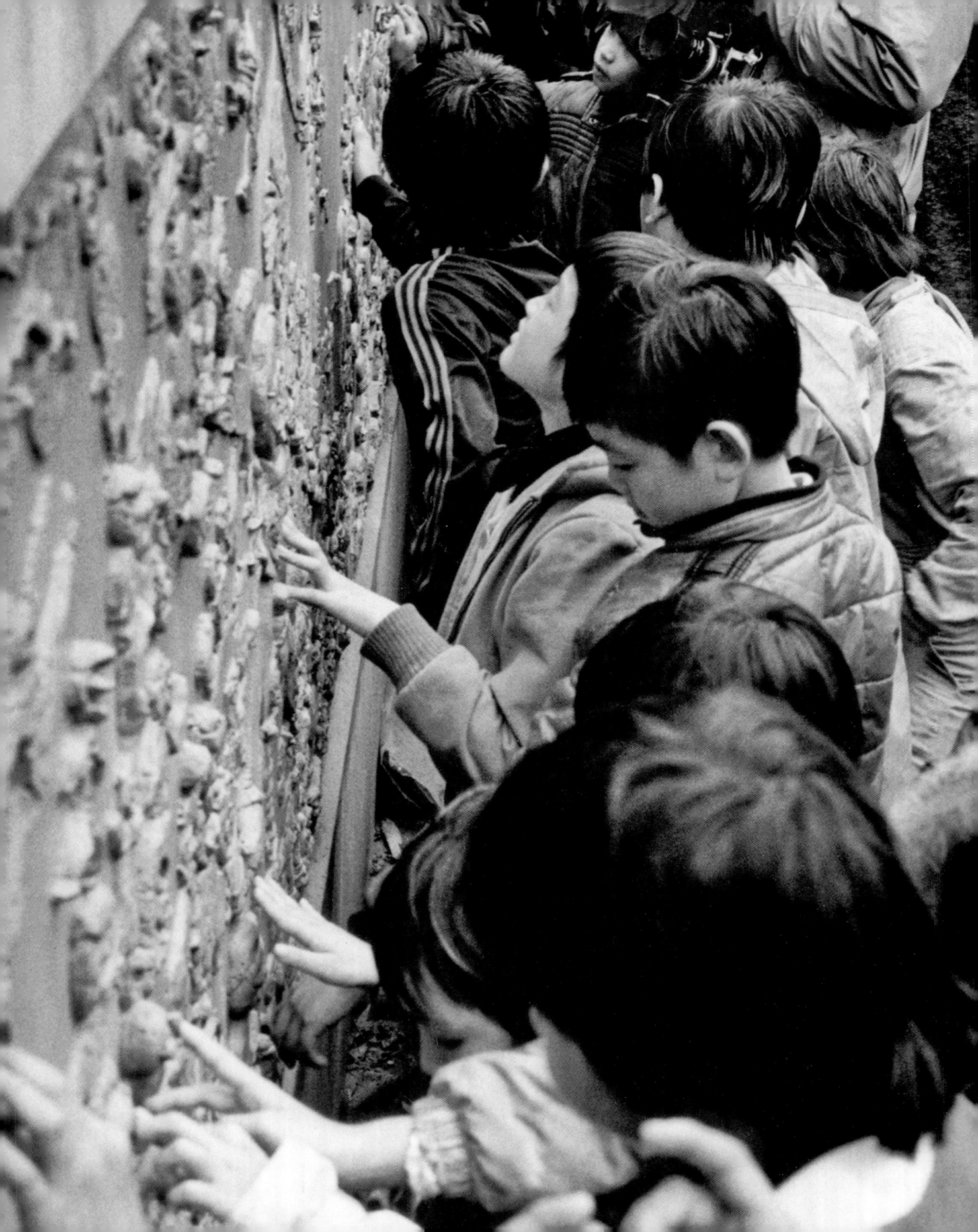

7 KITCHEN TABLE MONUMENTS

The maternal politics in Asawa's deployment of baker's clay—a mixture of household flour, salt, and water—can be introduced through a collectively made self-portrait installed in San Francisco's Tenderloin district (fig. 7.1). Historically home to cabarets, bars, brothels, and clubs, the Tenderloin, located downtown, witnessed a rapid population decline after World War II, with white, middle-class residents moving to the suburbs. By the 1970s, the district's reputation for open-air drug use and drinking prompted the local paper to describe it as a "low-life landscape."[1] While many people were living on the streets or in low-cost single-room-occupancy housing, the numerous empty apartment units came to house refugees from Southeast Asia who had fled the Vietnam War. These included ethnic Chinese from Vietnam, Khmer from Cambodia, and Hmong from Laos. As a consequence, the Tenderloin's population of children dramatically increased, introducing yet another vulnerable population into the district.

Because many of these families lived in crowded one-room apartments without yards, the city drafted plans to build a park and playground in the area. Given the city's recent experience with so-called Wino Park, a "disastrous example" of a park that had become "an open-air living room," officials promised residents that this new park would keep the unhoused at bay.[2] Its design became a classic instance of what artist Nils Norman calls "defense architecture"—now virtually the norm in the neoliberal city, whose increasingly privatized spaces deploy landscape architecture as a deterrent to those left behind by its gutting of social services.[3] Measures included a six-foot fence, portions of which were tipped by spikes and locked up at night with the park lights left on; a sprinkler system triggered at irregular intervals; park benches in wrought-iron Victorian style with metal dividers; and a pathway with no steps, to allow a police car to drive through. Even the landscaping was chosen with anti-homelessness in mind, with no low shrubs. "But perhaps the most effective deterrent of all," the local newspaper speculated, "will be the crowds of children, who are estimated to number between 2000 and 3000 in the Tenderloin."[4]

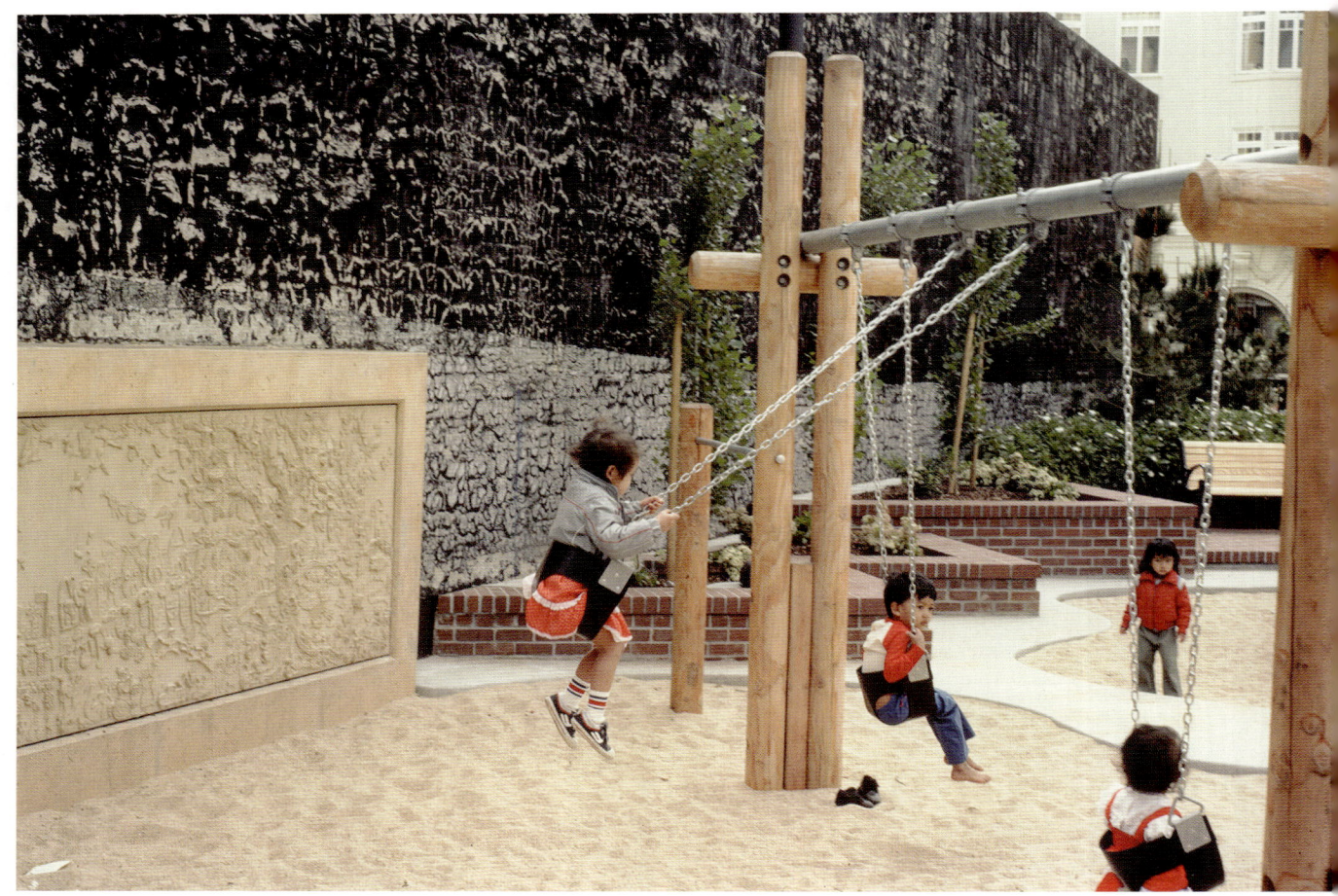

7.1 *Redding School, Self-Portrait* (detail, PC.007),
1984. Glass-fiber-reinforced concrete. Alfred E.
Boeddeker Park, San Francisco. Collection of the
City and County of San Francisco. Scanned color
slide. Special Collections, Stanford University.

Asawa responded to the call for proposals for a public artwork by suggesting she would do what she had been doing for some fifteen years: work with the area's local schoolchildren to create a sculptural panel out of baker's clay, which would then be cast and made permanent. The association with the kitchen was so strong that one observer called this homemade material "bread dough."[5] Her proposal was accepted, and in May 1984 she began working with Redding School, which served the Tenderloin as well as parts of Chinatown, recruiting three classes of third-, fourth- and fifth-graders, for a total of one hundred students participating in the project. Because the park was to be named after Father Alfred Boeddeker, who had established a free medical clinic and soup kitchen in the neighborhood, the panel's iconography represented a Saint Francis of Assisi–like monk, with outstretched arms, embracing self-portraits of the children, alongside a verdant tree of life teeming with animals. Before getting started, Asawa shared her previous work in baker's clay with the students and arranged for Boeddeker to come speak to the children. The modeling in baker's clay was done after a matter of several weeks, and the children—after Asawa petitioned the city's mayor for funding—were bused to the foundry, where the panels were cast in glass-fiber-reinforced concrete. In addition to a four-by-sixteen-foot bas-relief installed on one of the park's bounding walls alongside its playground, three individual panels were also cast and hung in each of the participating classrooms.

The resulting work was given the title *Redding School, Self-Portrait* (1984). What is especially remarkable about this public sculpture is that its title explicitly assigns authorship to the children who created it: the work is a *self*-portrait of the elementary school. During its making, the students worked with imagery of themselves, sometimes even the standardized school photos and other official forms of photo identification, understanding themselves in relationship to the structures to which they were asked to conform (fig. 7.2). How these children interacted with the panel once installed is a lesson in concentration: a photograph taken during the work's dedication depicts dozens of children touching a monument that they themselves had created. We look at the photographer, who looks at them carefully inspecting the results of their labor with a wonderment approximating an incredulous Saint Thomas touching the wounds of Christ (fig. 7.3). The project must have been an experience that stayed with them for years, for by the mid-1980s, to be a child in urban San Francisco was to inhabit a vulnerable demographic: the park's plan included the planting of two trees that would commemorate a little boy recently crushed to death in a building elevator and a young girl from Redding School who had been brutally murdered just weeks before the children commenced their work.

Redding School, Self-Portrait can be seen as a retort to the city's attempt to solve the problems of the Tenderloin by "shooing the children into parks and playgrounds," as Jane Jacobs wrote in *The Death and Life of Great American Cities* (1961), a pseudo-solution that is "worse than useless."[6] Jacobs railed against the expectation that parks alone can address structural deficiencies in the neighborhood itself; far more important, she wrote, is how "the neighborhood acts upon them."[7] Asawa's assignment of authorship to the children of the Tenderloin marks an attempt to validate this population as an agent of its own urban environment. It is significant that she did so using an everyday medium—composed of flour, water, and salt, which can be modeled like clay and "fired" in an oven—indelibly associated with reproductive labor. What constitutes public space and its participants thus became a question about what constitutes caretaking. *Redding School, Self-Portrait* is a moment, like so many of Asawa's collectively produced public sculptures, in which the elision between mothering and artmaking takes on a civic dimension, as I will argue in this chapter. Caretaking thus acquires a dignity otherwise absent in public perception, and the monumental business of public art is brought down low, with one reporter observing, "The mother made up batches of baker's clay (4 parts flour, 1 part salt, 1-1/2 parts water) for her children; the artist turned the children's plaything into an 'adult' art form, after being told that working with clay was a craft, not an art."[8]

7.2 Students of Redding School, San Francisco, making baker's clay self-portraits for *Redding School, Self-Portrait* (PC.007; 1984). Photo: Allen Nomura. Special Collections, Stanford University.

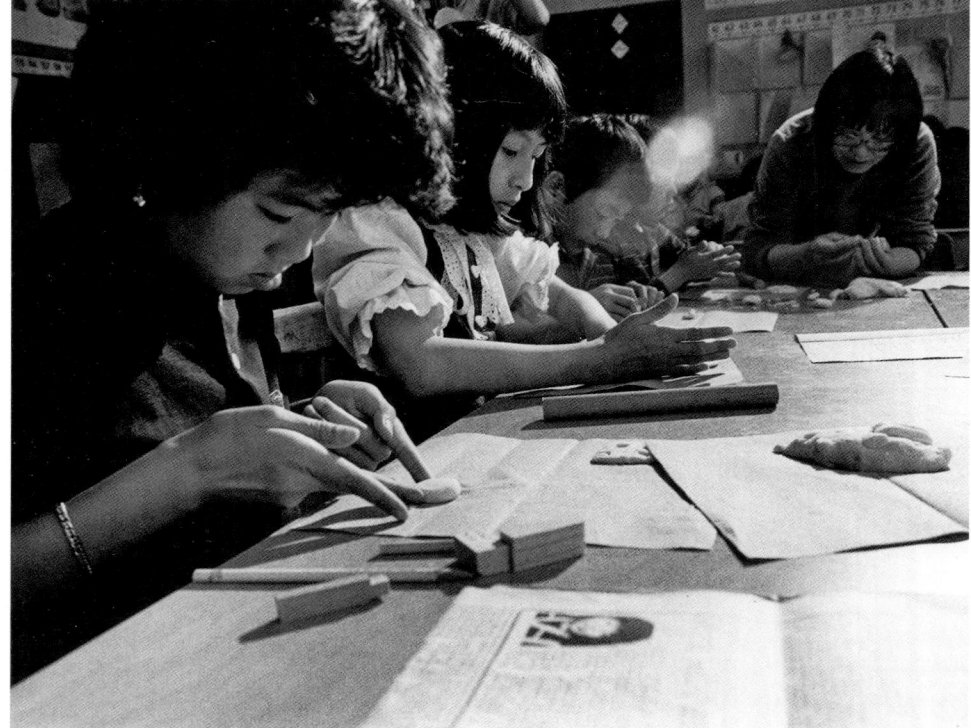

I explore this ambiguity of baker's dough—as both an anti-aesthetic, "craft" medium and the material for what Sally Woodbridge called a "folk monument"—as a new medium introduced into the history of art by the artist-mother. And I do so by focusing on the most visible of these collective public commissions, the *San Francisco Fountain* (1970–1973; often nicknamed the Hyatt fountain, given its location in front of the Grand Hyatt in downtown San Francisco).[9] Comprising over forty-one panels made from 1,400 pounds of flour that were then cast in bronze using the lost-wax method, the *Fountain* is a monumental achievement. It is also a collective accomplishment, with over 250 neighbors, ranging in age from three to eighty-eight, contributing to its realization. Its iconography is equally ambitious: local art critic Alfred Frankenstein likened its panorama of the city to a mixture of "ancient Hittite reliefs with the puppets they show on *Sesame Street*."[10] Although twentieth-century art's dialogue with folk art, ancient monoliths, "primitive" art, and other catchall terms opposing fine art is by now well established, the position of the artist-mother in this field has not yet been acknowledged, even as that figure squarely opposed the normative definitions of the artist. In what follows, I suggest that the *San Francisco Fountain* can be productively read in these terms, exploring how a feminized, domestic material became a mobilizing force in a new approach to public art that claimed the child as an agent of civic engagement.

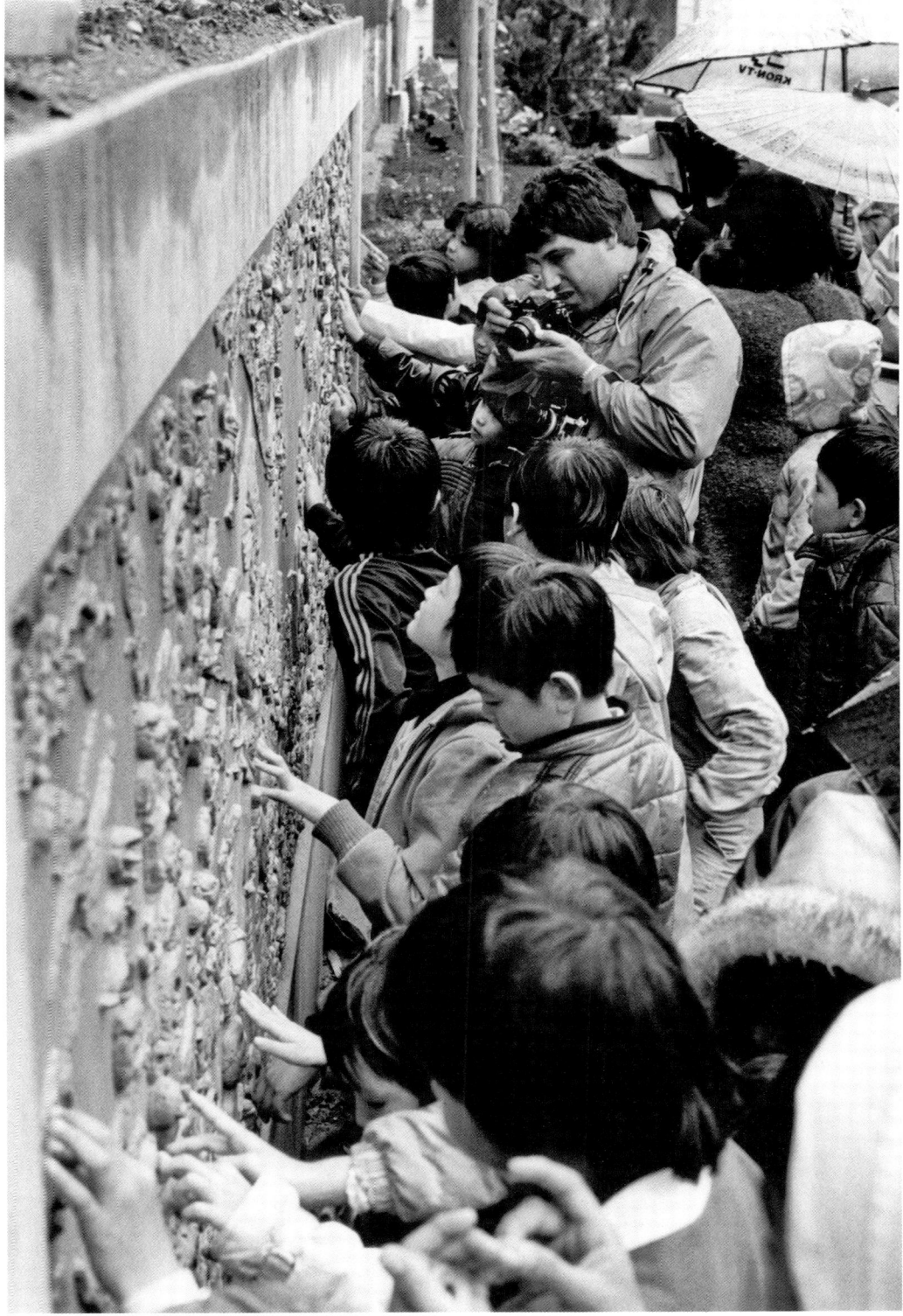

7.3 Students of Redding School, San Francisco, inspecting *Redding School, Self-Portrait* (PC.007; 1984) during its dedication on May 1, 1985. Photo: Clarence Towers. Special Collections, Stanford University.

"BREAD-DOUGH" SCULPTURE

In her book *Silences*, based on lectures first given in the early 1960s, Tillie Olsen quotes Harriet Beecher Stowe, at age twenty-seven, "making light" of her attempt to write with three young children underfoot. The dialogue that Stowe imagines between herself and Mina unfolds in the kitchen, with the two women struggling to put pen to paper amid a barrage of interruptions. It is a drama that centers around the kitchen table, "a table with flour, rolling pin, ginger, and lard on one side, a dresser with eggs, pork, and beans, and various cooking utensils on the other, near her an oven heating"—the same table used as a surface for composing. The one woman is instructed to "take your seat at the kitchen table, with your writing weapons," to "write a few minutes till it is time to mould up the bread," while the other dictates. A misplaced inkstand is found finally on top of the teakettle, while further "interruptions" throw one woman into doubt: "Come, come, you see how it is. . . . We must give up writing for today." "No, no; you can dictate as easily as you can write. Come, I can set the baby in this clothes-basket and give him some mischief or other to keep him quiet; you shall dictate and I will write. Now . . . what shall I write next?"[11]

Stowe was writing in the mid-nineteenth century, but Olsen recognizes the timeliness in her irony. Just as literary criticism was for Olsen, art history is virtually silent on the role that the kitchen table has played in the production of art. The few exceptions prove the rule. Art historian Tara McDowell, for instance, points to poet Robert Duncan's "preference for the kitchen table" when writing, even though he had an office on the third floor of their San Francisco Victorian, and mentions philosopher Sara Ahmed's apt comments on the kitchen table as providing "the kind of surface on which women tend to work. To use the table that supports domestic work to do political work (including the work that makes explicit the politics of domestic work) is a reorientation device."[12] Such a device upends the idea that serious works are made on an easel, in a foundry, at a workbench—not on a surface intended for rolling out dough.

I would venture to claim that no other artist has made as much of the kitchen table as a reorienting device as Asawa. The piece of furniture, "always filled with pens and paper and teacups," Andrea Jepson recalled, figures perennially in newspaper and magazine articles reporting on her artistic activities.[13] By 1963, the *San Francisco Chronicle* ran an article with the headline "Her Ingenious Way with Dough," which reported on how Asawa began "painting pictures of dough" by adapting "a concoction common to kindergartens."[14] Journalists, photographers, and other artists visiting Asawa's home featured the table in their accounts. In a photograph by the ceramicist Joan Pearson Watkins, Asawa works surrounded by her children, bags of flour, and rolling pins at the long wooden table that her husband Albert had built, a table "at least two inches thick and 12 [feet] long, right beside the stove," Diana Merritt describes in her article "Ruth Asawa: Artist and Mother" (fig. 7.4). It is a common theme in this reception that sculpture and kitchen utensils, clay and bread dough, are interchangeable: "In the kitchen there were no wire sculptures above our heads," as there were in the living room, Merritt relays during a visit to Asawa's home,

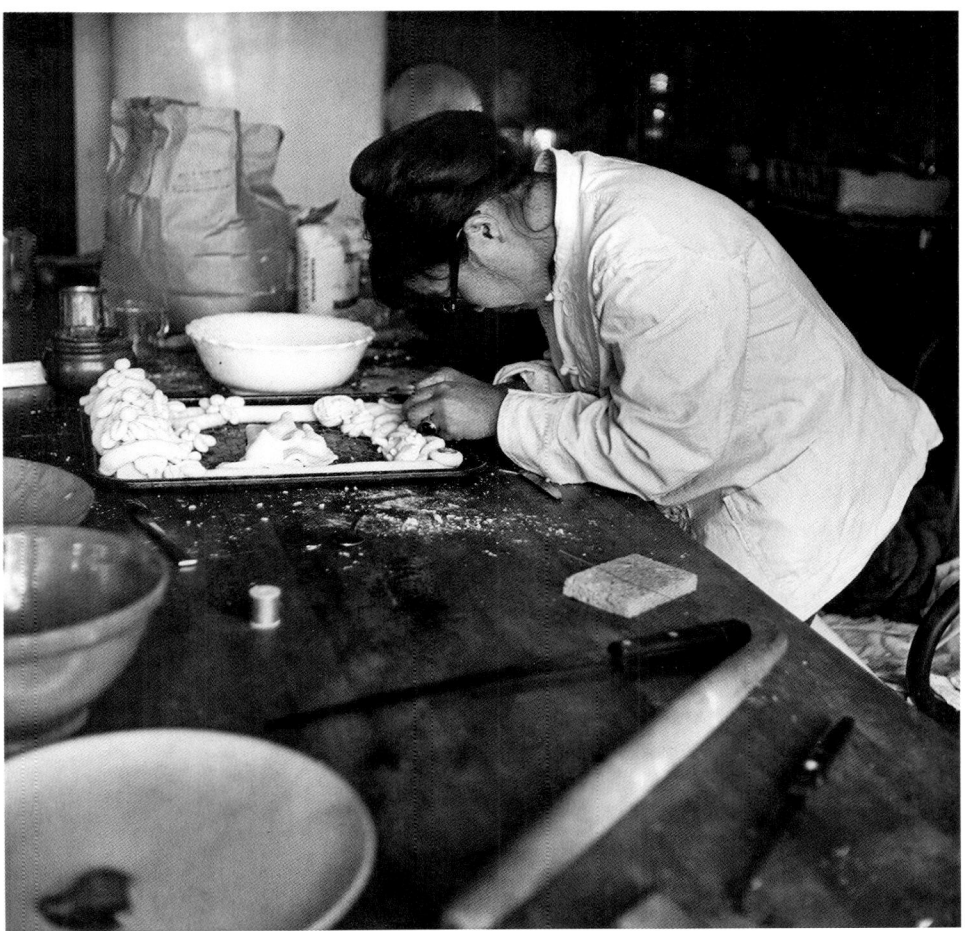

7.4 Joan Pearson Watkins, *Untitled* (Ruth Asawa working on baker's clay crèche in the kitchen of her Noe Valley home, San Francisco), c. 1965. Gelatin silver print, 10 × 8 in. Private collection.

"but instead, French pans of heavy copper hung from the ceiling."[15] Sometimes this collision was literal, as when Asawa's son Paul Lanier narrated an encounter with a gooey waffle iron that attested to Asawa's tendency to store bags of plaster of Paris and flour next to each other in the kitchen.[16] In that same kitchen hung a panel depicting "a Safeway in high relief and high colors—ads, bins of fruit and vegetables, women pushing carts loaded with enough food for a trip to Alaska." Calling it "bread-dough sculpture," Asawa elaborated, with reference to the grape strike led by the United Farm Workers under Cesar Chavez: "[The children] put in that big sign: 'Boycott Grapes.' I doubt if the Safeway would approve!"[17]

Asawa was attracted to using baker's clay, a recipe that she had originally found in a children's cookbook, because it was simple to make. Its name apparently came from none other than the *Ladies' Home Journal*. Sally Woodbridge had arranged for the magazine to come visit the Asawa-Lanier home (and the negatives from the photo session are still with Woodbridge's daughter, who also features in the scene; fig. 7.5). The magazine profiled Asawa, her six children, and neighborhood children including Pamela Woodbridge, in its December 1964 issue on the family's annual "Christmas claybake": "From a simple mixture of salt, flour and water (we call it baker's clay), Ruth, her architect husband, Albert, their six children, ranging from 5 to 14, and occasional guests of all ages make, bake and paint (or leave untouched in the burnished, oven-baked bisque color) delightful Christmas decorations."[18] Its ingredients were cheap and easy to find, and the results could also be hardened in the kitchen oven, rather than in a kiln. The dough could be molded by hand or with household tools, "serrated joining nails, ridged coin edges, toothbrush bristles"; "squeezing a lump of dough through a garlic press gives fine hair strands or a grass skirt. Slender limbs can be stiffened with wire or toothpicks," explained *Sunset Magazine*, reporting on Asawa's subject, San Francisco, "sitting" for a new portrait— what would later become the *San Francisco Fountain*.[19] At once a how-to guide for creating your own baker's clay figures at home and reportage of an emerging public monument, *Sunset*'s feature encapsulates the politicized domesticity of this everyday material.

Asawa's turn to baker's clay began as a pastime with her own children in the early 1960s, producing ornaments and figures for the Christmas Festival exhibition at the San Francisco Museum of Art. She quickly saw the potential for bringing this material into the schools, where it became a staple of the Alvarado School Arts Workshop (fig. 7.7). It featured regularly in public workshops, such as at the Los Angeles County Fair, where in 1969 Asawa and her children did demonstrations each day of the festival. Invited to Hawaii by an Episcopal minister to do workshops at several schools, Asawa and her daughter Aiko were also recruited to create a gigantic penny, ten inches in diameter, out of baker's clay—she did the Lincoln side, Aiko did the tail side—for a local bank, as a way to discourage hoarding and bring pennies back into circulation. Such events included even a "Dough-In" during the opening of her retrospective at the San Francisco Museum of Art in 1973, which was attended by over a thousand children—far more than expected, causing the flour to run out during the first hour.[20] The results of the Dough-In were also displayed in Asawa's exhibition and then returned to the children when the show closed. Such events were wildly successful with the general public, tapping into a desire for participation in the arts that was going largely unheeded at institutions of fine art.

Bringing baker's clay into the context of the San Francisco Museum of Art was a gesture in line with a postwar shift in museums toward supporting creativity by young audiences. In her book *Designing the Creative Child*, Amy Ogata chronicles this development, examining how "the creative child was therefore constructed and embodied in the aims of public museums that encouraged autonomous exploration through play."[21] Although Ogata's focus is on the emergence of children's museums, she describes how these institutions are indebted to the progressive educational programs of museums geared toward adults, such as the Museum of Modern Art in New York, which hosted an annual children's festival in dialogue with modern art beginning in 1942, and the Exploratorium in San Francisco, which organized their adult programming around the conviction that play and experimentation were the best approach to science and technology, arguing that "a childlike experience of wonder and play could make natural phenomena and human perception accessible to the general public."[22] Asawa was one of several artists in residence at the Exploratorium beginning in the mid-1970s, hosting workshops with both adults and children using recycled milk cartons, while the poet Muriel Rukeyser developed interactive exhibits about perception using graphic materials.

To have included panels of baker's clay—some thirty could be seen in Asawa's retrospective, all done with children, and positioned next to her and Imogen Cunningham's *Hair Skirt*—was to argue that fine art and craft should be seen alongside one another (fig. 7.6). In 1966, Asawa had contributed baker's clay figures to the exhibition *Cookies and Bread: The Baker's Art*, organized by Paul J. Smith for the Museum of Contemporary Crafts in New York. The show introduced a "radical change" in public engagement: "as over-the-top as it was and 'why is a museum doing such a show?' it turned out to be a great success," Smith observed decades later, "by attracting a totally new audience of young people and an audience that may never come to the museum."[23] Smith also immediately saw the parallels between baker's clay and traditional clay: "when you look at the process of kneading bread, for example, it's not unlike working with clay. Bread needs to be baked, and ceramics get fired in a higher heat. So there were analogies that were not so farfetched about the hand skills of a material. So I felt the exhibition had a serious focus and certainly broke the mold for reaching out to new audiences, and its success offered encouragement for us to do some more." Even the ceramicist Marguerite Wildenhain, who typically worked with clay, made "holiday bread-dough figures" in the mid-1970s—perhaps as a consequence of Asawa's turn to the medium, given that the two were in regular communication during these decades.

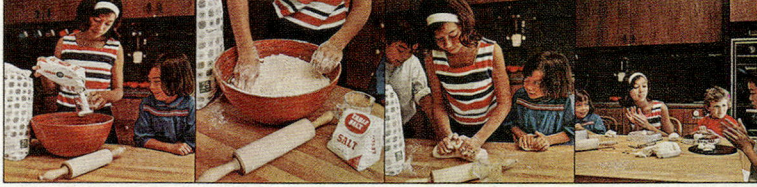

To begin, Aiko, 14, measures out ingredients for baker's clay: 4 cups unsifted flour, 1 cup salt, 1½ cups water. Recipe should not be doubled or halved.

Aiko mixes the clay with her fingers. Aiko knows from experience that if the clay is too stiff she should add a bit more water. It must be used up within four hours, or it gets too dry.

When baker's clay is thoroughly mixed, Aiko takes it out of the bowl and kneads it for four to five minutes. Sister Laurie, 6, helps with a small piece. Brother Hudson, 12, watches.

Laurie, Aiko and Pam, a visiting friend, begin to work on inverted pie pans. One recipe makes eight to ten angels. Cookie . . .

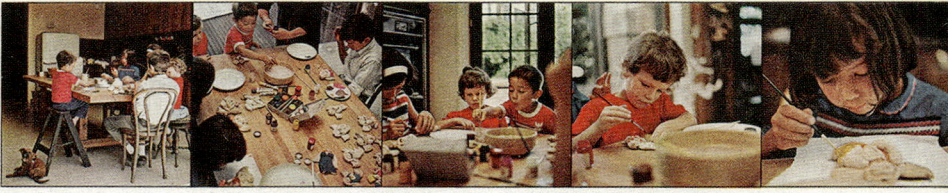

Paul, 5, Hudson, Pam, Aiko and Laurie start painting baked figures. That's the children's dog, Henry-Clyde.

The Laniers usually work at this ten-foot-long butcher-block kitchen table. To color figures, they use poster paints and Magic Markers.

While Aiko concentrates, Paul shows Pam his latest color scheme.

Pam applies red paint to an angel while her next figure bakes in the oven.

Laurie has decided to try bright yellow on an angel. Baked figures are sturdy and handle easily.

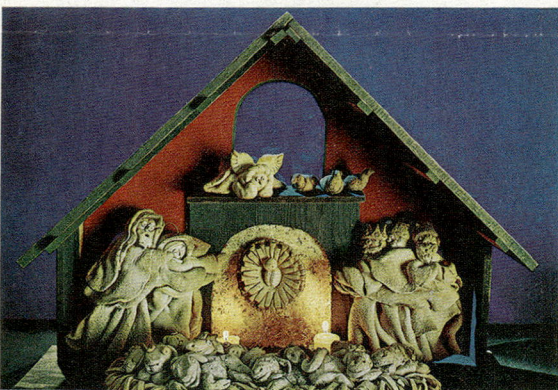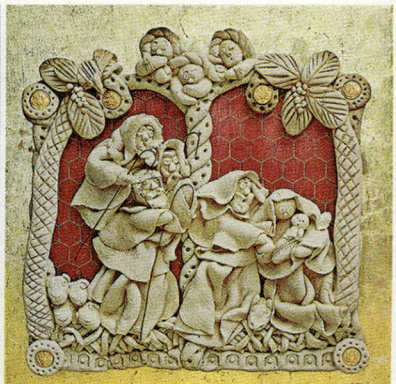

A CHRISTMAS CLAYBAKE CAN COVER WIDE RANGE OF PROJECTS, FROM AN INTRICATE CHRISTMAS CRÈCHE AND A NATIVITY SCENE,

7.5 Margaret White, "Christmas Claybake,"
Ladies' Home Journal, December 1964, 58–59.
Special Collections, Stanford University.

. . . sheets are also good to work on. Metal buttons make marvelous decorations, are baked right into the figures.

All kinds of kitchen utensils come in handy for shaping and imprinting figures.

Hudson puts an angel into the oven. He bakes figures on the same tin he worked on. Figures should bake for at least an hour at 350 degrees.

Hooks for hanging finished figures are made of hairpins, wire or paper clips, and should be inserted in figures before they are baked.

Children make up ideas for angel personalities as they work. Aiko and Hudson are expert angel makers. Simple objects, like medallions, are made by the younger children.

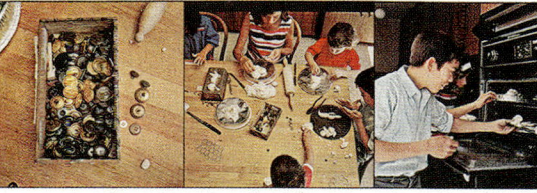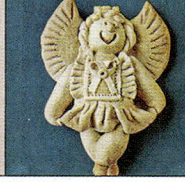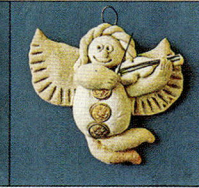

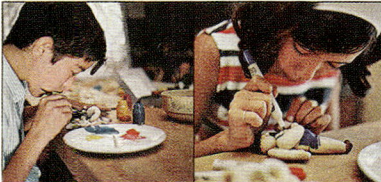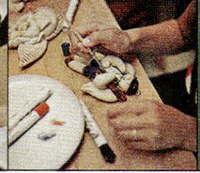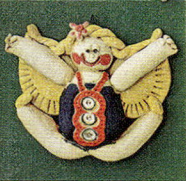

Hudson chooses a palette of blue, yellow and red to partially paint an angel. The children usually leave some areas unpainted in the natural, bisque finish.

Aiko colors an angel fisherman with Magic Marker. After painting, figures can be sprayed with a clear fixative to make them more durable.

This amusing creation of Aiko's is a baseball-player angel.

A completed, brightly painted angel, dancing. For complete details on baker's clay and planning your own claybake, turn to page 115.

PHOTOGRAPHS BY FRED LYON

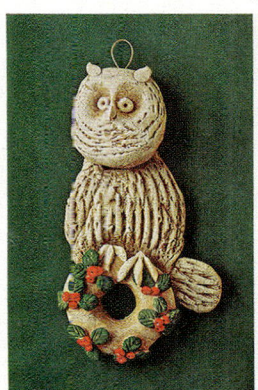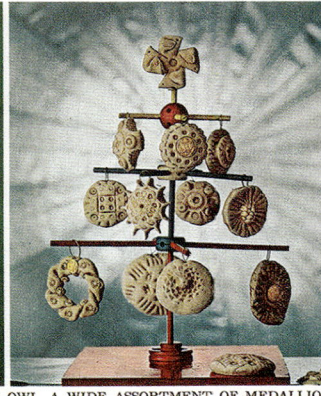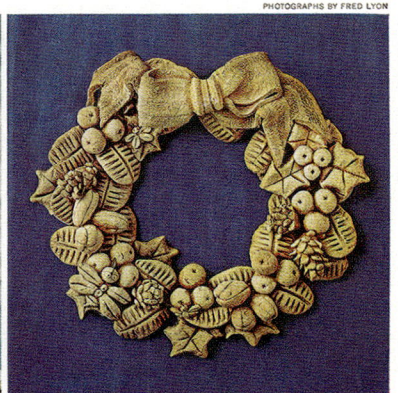

WHICH RUTH CREATED, TO AN OWL, A WIDE ASSORTMENT OF MEDALLIONS HUNG ON A TINKER-TOY TREE AND A WREATH.

59

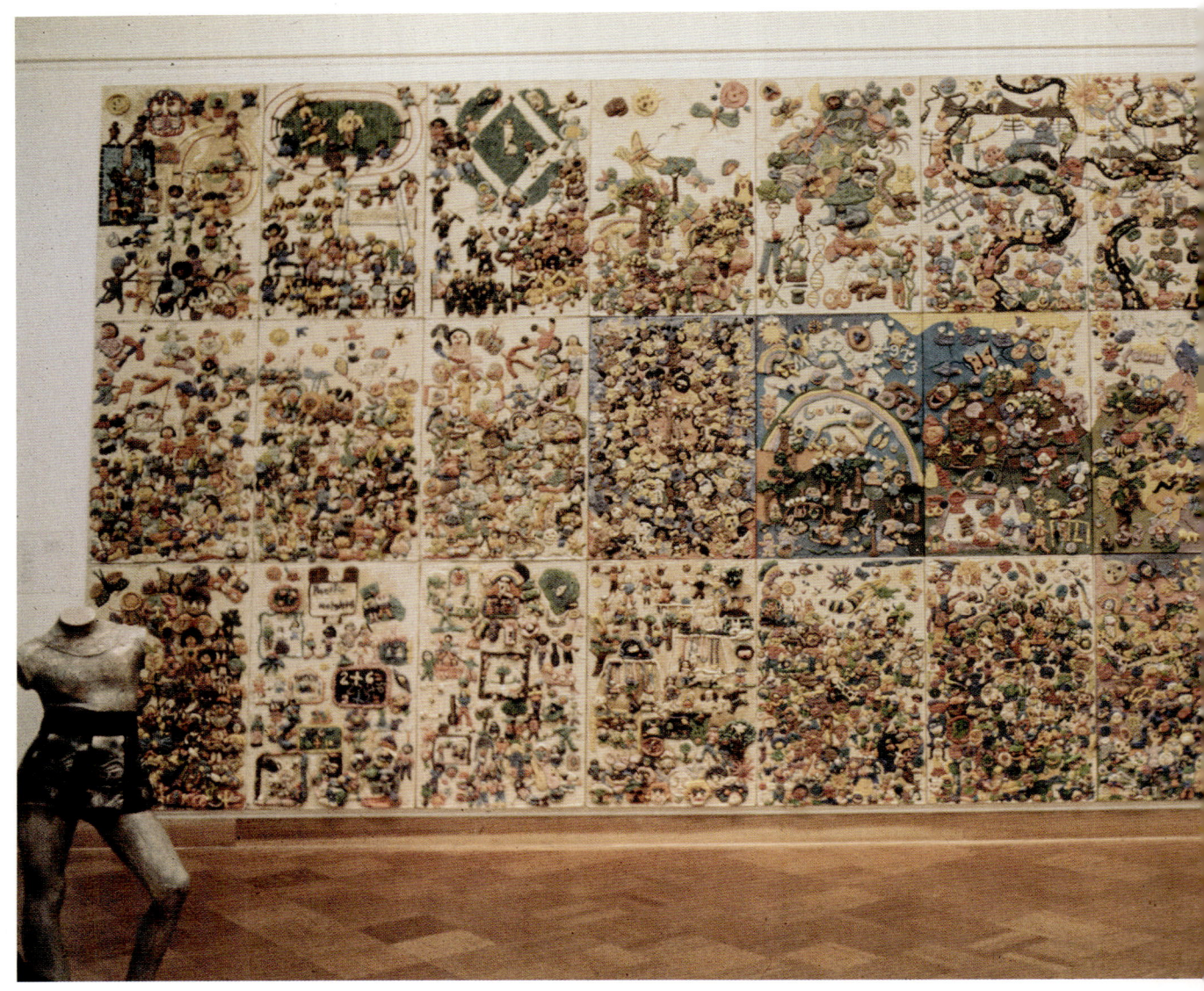

7.6 Panels of baker's clay self-portraits made by school-children of the Alvarado School Arts Workshop, in Ruth Asawa's retrospective at the San Francisco Museum of Art, June 1973. Special Collections, Stanford University.

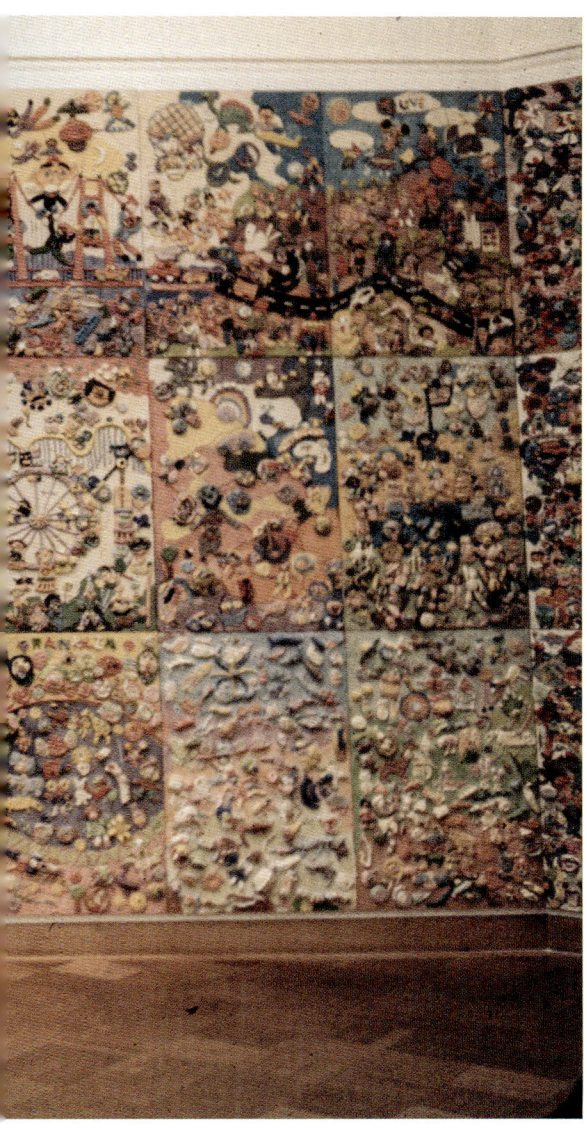

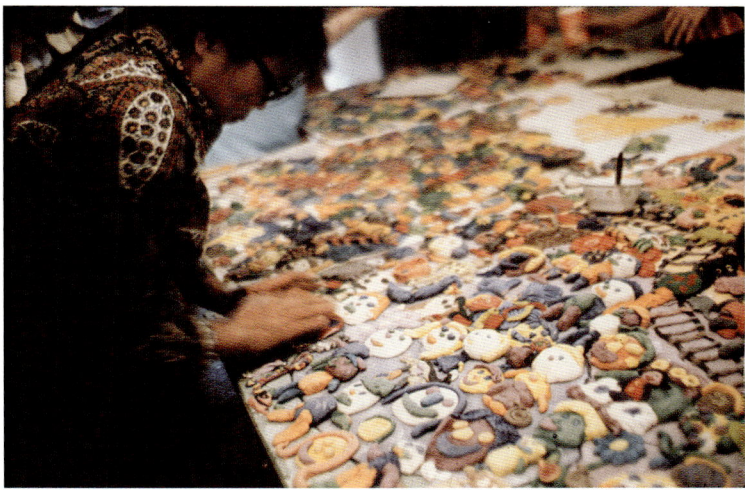

7.7 Ruth Asawa with baker's clay figures, made by schoolchildren of the Alvarado School Arts Workshop, on wooden panels, c. 1975. Special Collections, Stanford University.

FEMINIST FOLK ART

Part of the challenge of the *San Francisco Fountain* is to give an account of its medium—baker's clay—within a broader field of cultural production; to resist dismissing it, in other words, as a quirky, idiosyncratic, one-off foray into modeling by other means. A direction for reclaiming its contribution to public art is provided by Asawa herself when she compares baker's clay to folk art: "I see bread-dough sculpture as an attempt to revive American Folk Art in a medium available to everyone," Asawa explained in 1969.[24] What Asawa may have had in mind when invoking "American Folk Art" is unclear; certainly generational peers like the ceramicist Susan Peterson, whose pottery drew from what she later called "faux folk art," admitted that the category was notoriously vague, especially in the 1950s and 60s: "Neither I nor my colleagues [at Chouinard Art Institute in Los Angeles] knew what folk art was except perhaps early American weather vanes."[25]

In her chapter on Susan Peterson's pottery lessons, televised from a studio kitchen, the art historian Jenni Sorkin locates Peterson's introduction to clay in the rituals of bread making of the Mennonite community in which she grew up. In such communities, preparing Communion bread each Sunday morning amounted to "an individual kitchen task transposed to a public forum."[26] Sorkin describes this ritual as a tactile experience: balls of dough pass through each woman's kneading hands for a set amount of time, while nonverbal cues indicate pace and turn-taking. "In this way," Sorkin writes, "bread making becomes the epitome of a collective material that prefigures Peterson's own introduction to clay."[27] Rituals like these, in such a tradition-laden and religious context as the Mennonite community, may have served as one point of reference for Asawa's invocation of folk art in the United States.

However, it is more likely that what she had in mind was more generalized. By the 1960s, the category of folk art emerged as a critique of the heroic and individualist rhetoric of painting and sculpture. Art historian Lynne Cooke argues that artists were newly receptive to discarded traditions like quilt making because such practices could investigate "the reassessment of normative notions of quality, finish, and process. Concurrently, the folklife field was established, galvanizing an explosion of related disciplinary studies in which a preoccupation with the past gave way to issues relating to place: attachments based in rootedness, cultural particularism, and local, ethnic, and kinship ties were now privileged."[28] Although American folk art is as diverse as the country's demographics, it is this imagination of collectivity, tied to place, that has permeated both its cultural function in the communities in which it is made and its reception further afield. The turn to folk art in the 1960s is not unlike the popularity of folk art in the 1930s, as art historian Thomas Crow argues in his account of the "long march" of pop art's history: "the salience of folkloric authenticity," Crow maintains, served "as a constituent part of the belief system that established a viable avant-garde for the visual arts in America."[29] Crow chronicles several exhibitions at the Museum of Modern Art in New York that placed this diverse spectrum on view in the context of a modernist discourse, everything from the anonymous *fraktur* paintings by Germans in Pennsylvania to self-taught artists like Joseph Pickett and Ann Mary Robertson "Grandma" Moses.

Women artists in the 1960s and 1970s were especially receptive to anonymous folk art practices as distinguished from a broader interest in craft, discussed in chapter 2 of this book. This interest in folk as the moment when craft becomes collective and anonymous is largely why textiles and ceramics became the preferred reference points, rather than the paintings of someone like Grandma Moses, whose mainstream reception "as a simple farmwife" marked such commercialized forms of folk art as woefully essentializing and iterative of the artist as mythic genius.[30] As Judith Stein points out in her essay reevaluating Grandma Moses from a feminist perspective, artists informed by feminism thus had little to say on prominent women folk practitioners like Moses, turning instead to traditions whose authorship was more difficult to pin down. Artists like Faith Ringgold turned to masks, quilts, and dolls in her thangka paintings, composed of acrylic paint and embroidered fabric, as a way to break down distinctions between high and low materials and, in doing so, to reevaluate the category of private experience. Folk art provided a vehicle for circumventing the mythic figure of the artist, and artists informed by feminism saw themselves as having been erased just as folk artists were assigned to "the obscurity of their grass-roots authenticity," writes Judith Friedlander in a special issue of the feminist journal *Heresies*. She names a nascent "feminist folk culture" in which women artists—and Asawa can be included here too—were increasingly receptive to forgotten or vernacular traditions and incorporated them into their work as artists.[31]

Asawa, importantly, never claimed a feminist politics. And yet, as this book has attempted to demonstrate, her choice of materials, her decision to work at home, and her willingness to be identified as a mother at a time when such a move equated to self-erasure attest to a feminist orientation in her practice as an artist. We can even understand her identification as an artist-mother as an embrace of feminist folk in that the artist-mother at midcentury stood in opposition to so-called avant-garde production; she was the ultimate figure of conservatism and tradition, from the perspective of the dominant, patriarchal art world. This allowed for an iconography to emerge that bears a similarity to Andy Warhol's pop art as another oblique reception of folk art: consider, for instance, that both he and artist-mother Aiko Cuneo (Asawa's eldest daughter) appropriated Botticelli's *The Birth of Venus* from the fifteenth century (fig. 7.8). Botticelli's Venus is a portrait of "the one Great Mother Goddess who is the origin of all things," Anne Baring and Jules Cashford write in their magisterial *The Myth of the Goddess*.[32] Drawing on Erich Neumann's argument in *The Great Mother* (1955) that patriarchal culture recodes her image to signify sexualized femininity, Baring and Cashford restore Aphrodite/Venus's original significance as a personification of creation, marking the separation of Heaven and Earth. Deflating this eroticism through the puffy, round features of Cuneo's relief in baker's clay, her homemade rendition of Aphrodite/Venus takes up exactly what is already overwrought in dominant culture, while utterly emptying it of authority. It furthermore upends an icon of high,

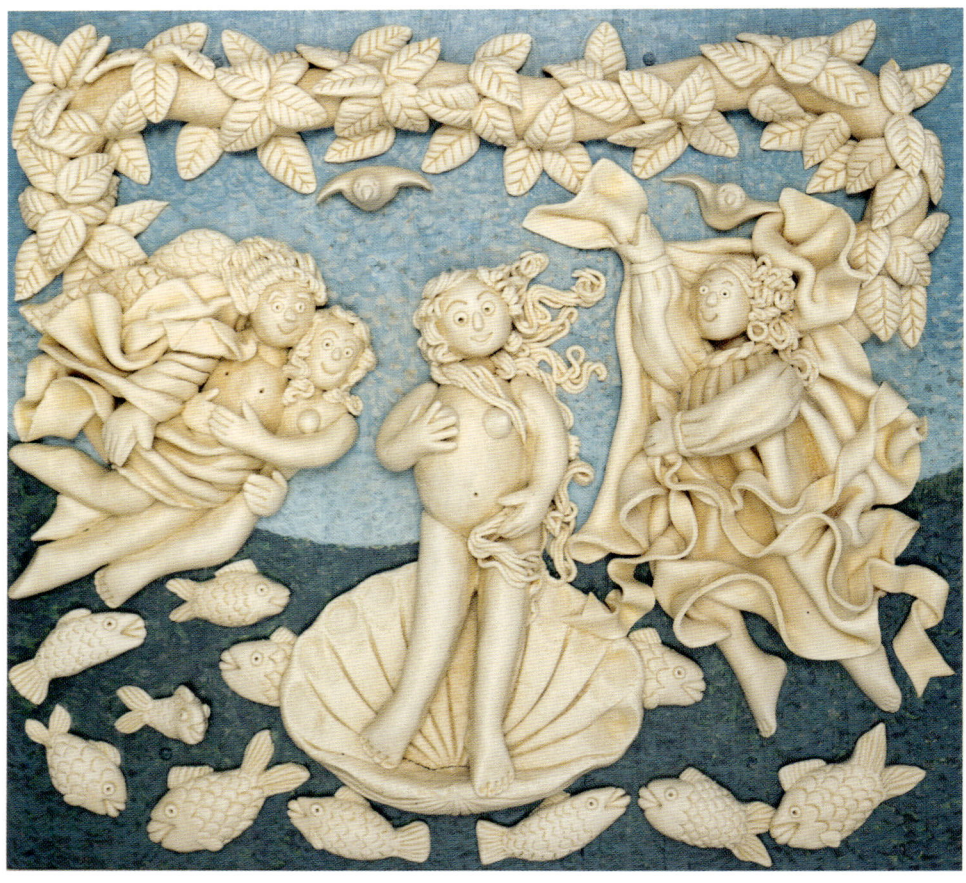

7.8 Aiko Cuneo, *Botticelli's Birth of Venus*, 1991. Baker's clay in frame, 19 × 20 × 3.5 in. Private collection.

elevated art in the low, domesticated material of dough, while also draining Botticelli's claim on a sensuous female nude offered up for visual consumption.

Julia Bryan-Wilson has pointed to the specific reception of feminist folk in California, which "aligned handmaking with countercultural worldmaking—as an individualist practice of differentiation but also within a larger, if somewhat inchoate, communalist project."[33] She speaks specifically of the book *Native Funk and Flash* (1974) by the northern California artist Alexandra Jacopetti Hart (fig. 7.9). Famous for her "macramé playground," built in the early 1970s in Bolinas, California, Hart was a generation younger than Asawa, but the two overlapped in terms of creating for (and with) children. (Macramé was also widely used in the Alvarado School Arts Workshop.) In her book, Hart chronicles "contemporary folk art" of the San Francisco Bay Area, homing in on "bread dough" as a more affordable alternative to ceramics and well suited to groovy stuff like homemade Christmas tree ornaments. Baker's clay in this context sits comfortably alongside other crafts recruited for the Bay Area counterculture, including embroidery and wood carving in the format of doors—Asawa had also carved a set of wooden doors with her children. While the imagery in

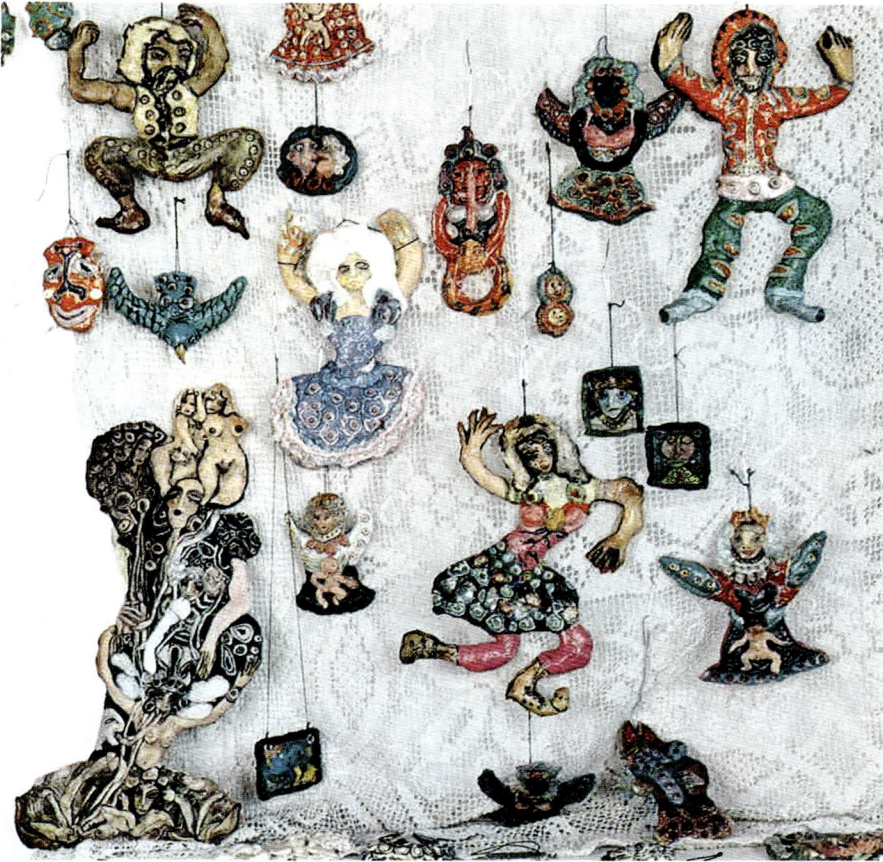

7.9 Baker's clay figures illustrated in Alexandra Jacopetti Hart's book *Native Funk and Flash* (1974).

the book opens up onto unconventional gender constellations—including a sequined mandala phallus and drag queens—Hart herself, writing in the first person, couches her own turn to craft in the rigid terms of housewifery, the consequence of her husband's returning from a trip with a torn pair of Levi's: "'Fix them,' he said plaintively."[34]

POSTERITY'S HANDS

Asawa fell into neither the category of the hippie housewife nor that of the self-taught artist, and I do not set out to claim her as either. Rather, the point here is the permeability of such categories and to suggest that we see such ambivalence as an artistic strategy, though not necessarily an explicit one. Asawa was an artist of ambition and commitment, yet she was not interested in having a "career"; she was intensely preoccupied by questions of form and materials, yet worked for years with bread dough. In the same vein, she was a remarkably intelligent person, yet made statements that could be described in the same terms as the evasive Warholian gesture, in which the artist continually sidesteps and deflects—the same naivete used to characterize folk artists. What reads as flat-footedness in her description of turning to bronze casting is a case in point: "Friends said to me, 'This is child's play. You should do serious, permanent things.' So I began making bronzes by means of dough models instead of traditional clay. People agree that even an artist's sketchy drawings on flimsy paper can be permanent. So can dough."[35]

Although this material originally "had no professional significance," as Woodbridge relays, Asawa quickly developed it into highly elaborate and detailed figural representations.[36] She came to know its properties intimately: you first mixed the flour, salt—and dried pigment if you were using color—and then the water, kneading for three to five minutes. Because of the flour, the material has a spring to it that clay does not. "If you want to make a standing figure, you have to make it in the same way that you would draw it on a piece of paper. You'd have to draw it flat."[37] Figures made in baker's clay bear similarities to figures in Moses's paintings: they are minimally described, separated from one another at equal intervals, and situated within a pictorial space that sometimes recedes into the distance, following perspectival conventions, but at other moments—such as the winding Lombard Street made by Aiko Cuneo in the *San Francisco Fountain*—has the figures sitting atop the ground, as if viewed from above. After modeling, pieces were often glued to boards and then left to dry (or baked in the oven); cracks would then be repaired and, lastly, the whole thing coated with Varathane or polyester resin.

Asawa's first attempt at bronze casting from baker's clay resulted in a small mermaid figure, referencing her sculpture *Andrea* in Ghirardelli Square. It was on view in an exhibition in the lobby of the California Redwood Association in downtown San Francisco alongside other baker's clay works, including panels that students from Alvarado Elementary had created as a collective self-portrait. All of the work on view was "inspired by or done with the children," according to journalist Mildred Hamilton, who reported on the exhibition (Hamilton's article is pasted into an album below the photograph by Joan Pearson Watkins of Asawa bent over her kitchen table with a mixing bowl and baking sheets laid out before her; see fig. 7.4).[38] In spring 1969, Chuck Bassett, partner in the architecture firm in charge of the design for a new Hyatt hotel building in downtown San Francisco, saw Asawa's exhibition at the California Redwood Association; he then commissioned her to come up with a design for the drum-shaped fountain that would stand at the top of wide stairs leading up to an outdoor plaza. Once she had received the commission from Bassett, they finalized the subject matter. As Woodbridge recalls in her small book on the fountain, Asawa wanted to work on "something involving fantasy," to which Bassett responded that there was more fantasy in the reality of a city like San Francisco than in most products of the imagination.[39]

The panorama that resulted, according to art writer Sarah Archer, resembles nothing less than "a monochromatic, sculptural Brueghel painting touched with the relentless energy of Richard Scarry's *Busytown*: jolly, stylized, and densely packed with detail" (fig. 7.10). Scenes ranged from a peace march in Golden Gate Park protesting the Vietnam War, with signs reading "Pull out, Dick," to rows of Victorian houses in

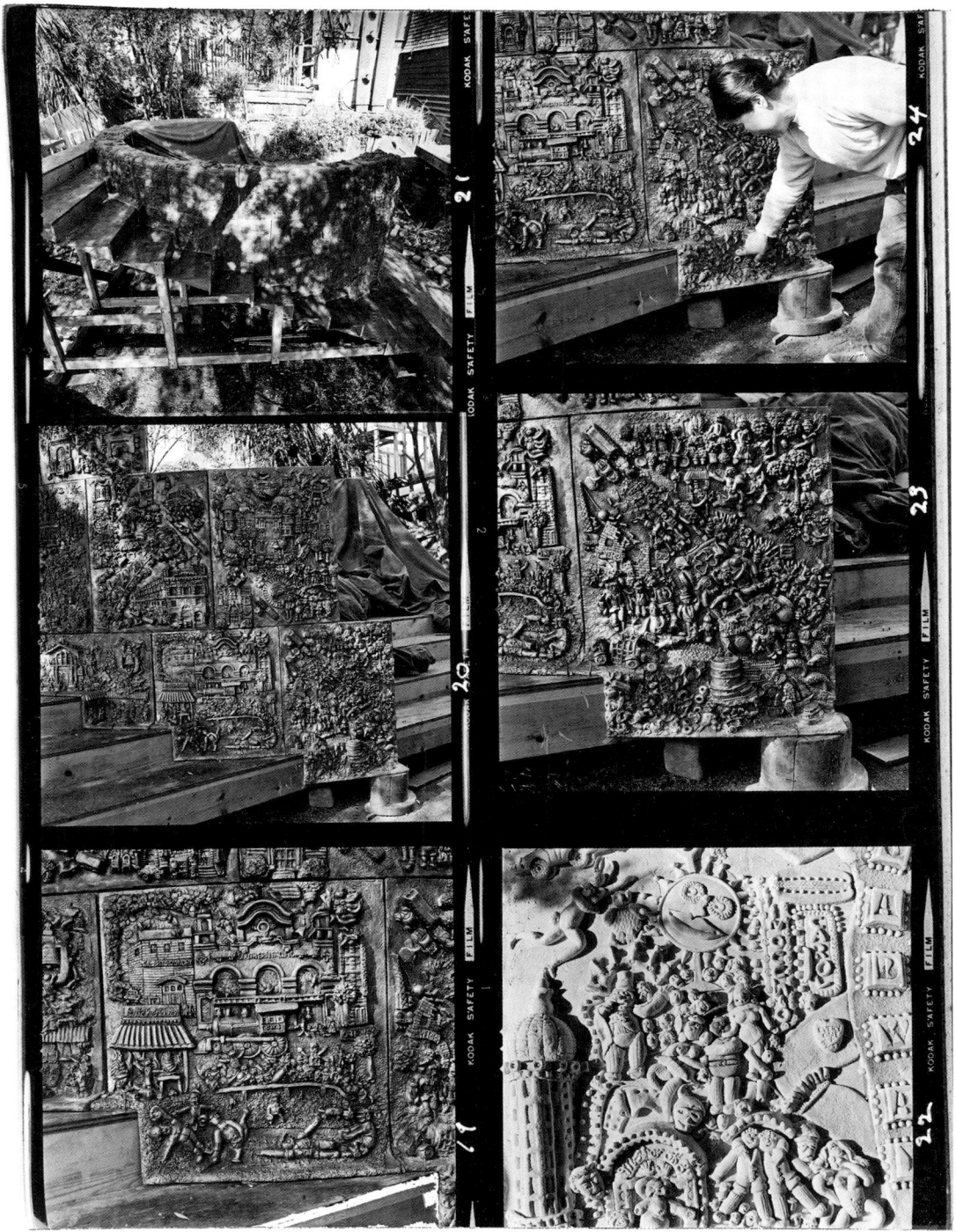

7.10 Details of *San Francisco Fountain* (PC.004) in Asawa's Noe Valley backyard, c. 1972. Collage of contact prints in loose album, 10 × 8 in. Photo: Rondal Partridge. Special Collections, Stanford University.

Haight-Ashbury modeled after Woodbridge's photographs (fig. 7.11). Woodbridge was not only instrumental in the architectural detail on the fountain; she also framed the work for the public, describing many of its features, from "the denizens of skid row" to "the buildings of the Yerba Buena neighborhood [which] fall before urban redevelopment's wrecking ball."[41] Fleischhacker Pool, once the largest saltwater pool in the world, closed for lack of maintenance funds, is revived. Seiji Ozawa directs the symphony orchestra, while the two Hs in the fountain's center panels (standing for "Hyatt Hotel") bear not only a banner reading "You are Here" (that is, at the corner of Post and Stockton Streets, where the fountain is located) but also a panoply of references to people and events associated with the location now known as Union Square: "The Monument to Admiral Dewey, Birdwhistle Armstrong . . ."[42] Well-known locations like the Powell Street Cable Car turnabout and Japantown exist alongside the city dump, Aiko Lanier's wedding, the Zip Code Man, the Vedanta Society, and Hell's Angels motorcyclists, in addition to a multitude of unique neighborhoods in the city and better-known buildings. Culture both high and low makes an appearance, from Snoopy sitting on a cloud "blessing" the peace marchers below to Rodin's *The Thinker* perched atop the Palace of the Legion of Honor.

The composition emerged from a dialogue with the city and its contemporary events, which Asawa culled from the news (including the recent deaths of Gaye Spiegelman and three of her children; Spiegelman had been a club dancer known in the city's North Beach nightlife as the "Topless Mother of Eight").[43] Asawa also consulted city institutions like the Fire Department and the California Historical Society, incorporated material from books, and polled friends, neighbors, and colleagues. Hundreds of photographs, many of which she took, served as source material; Woodbridge's vast knowledge of Bay region and Victorian architecture lent an incredible amount of detail to the houses and city buildings. A drawing reveals that an earlier version of the composition included perspectival views in which one had the sense of the picture receding into the distance (fig. 7.12). This conventional mode of rendering landscape, however, dropped out, as the composition was allowed to become fuller, denser, and bubbling over with surface detail. Ornament and decoration abound. When she presented the design to Donald Pritzker, who owned the Hyatt Hotel, he worried that it might turn out looking like a cookie, to which Asawa responded, "That's what I want it to look like."[44]

One especially remarkable aspect of the fountain is how its pictorial content relates to the surrounding city. The composition is structured according to the four cardinal directions: when viewers stand in front of it, at the base of the stairs, they face west, toward the hotel in direct proximity, and see in the center of the sculpture two Hs, standing for Hyatt Hotel—with Imogen Cunningham standing prominently alongside one of the letters. Everything to the viewers' left on the sculpture is geographically located south, which for viewers is physically also on their left side; by the same logic, the sculptural depiction located on the viewers' right side is geographically north, which is also physically located for viewers on their right side. Similarly, Market Street, a huge artery running through the city, bolts at a diagonal on the fountain

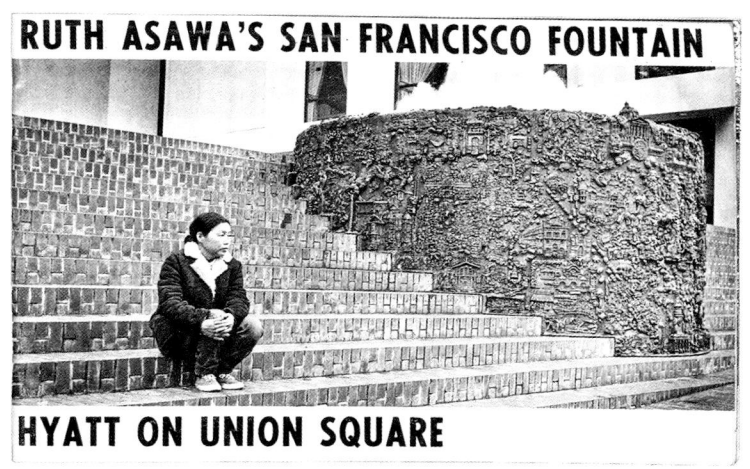

RUTH ASAWA'S SAN FRANCISCO FOUNTAIN

HYATT ON UNION SQUARE

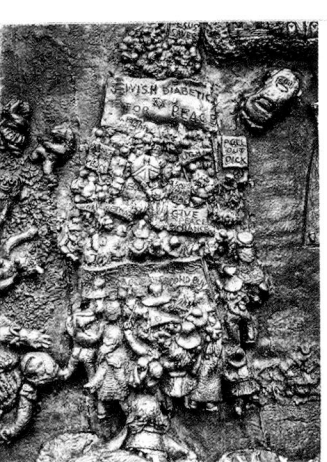

A peace march passes the park's sun worshippers on its way to the polo field. The scene commemorates the marches that took place to protest the Vietnam war. The marchers are blessed by the presence of the American Eagle below and Snoopy sitting on a cloud to his right.

The march is passing through the Haight-Ashbury district of the Western Addition, an area of the city largely built up during a real estate boom of the 1880's and '90's. Its stand of Victorian houses is still one of the best in the city. Those shown in the photo to the right and on the following page were made from photos taken in the area. Above, the houses grow smaller, change character, and march like ticky-tacky boxes up the lower slopes of Twin Peaks, located on the rim.

The scene to the right was created by the children of the Alvarado Elementary School at 22nd and Douglass Streets in San Francisco. In 1968 Ruth and Sally Woodbridge organized an arts and crafts program in the school with the help of a group of parents and the cooperation of school administrators and teachers. The goals were to invest the energies of the neighborhood in the school and provide a way for professional artists to work in the curriculum. The program has now spread to schools throughout the city. As explained in the introduction, one of its early

8

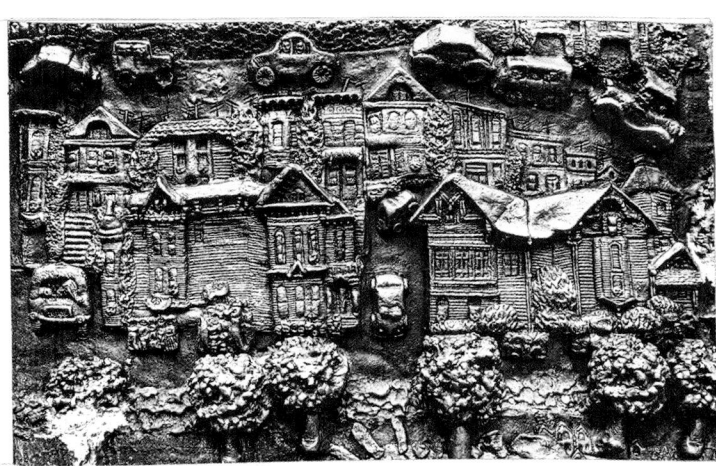

7.11 Cover and interior pages of Sally B. Woodbridge, *Ruth Asawa's San Francisco Fountain: Hyatt on Union Square* (1973).

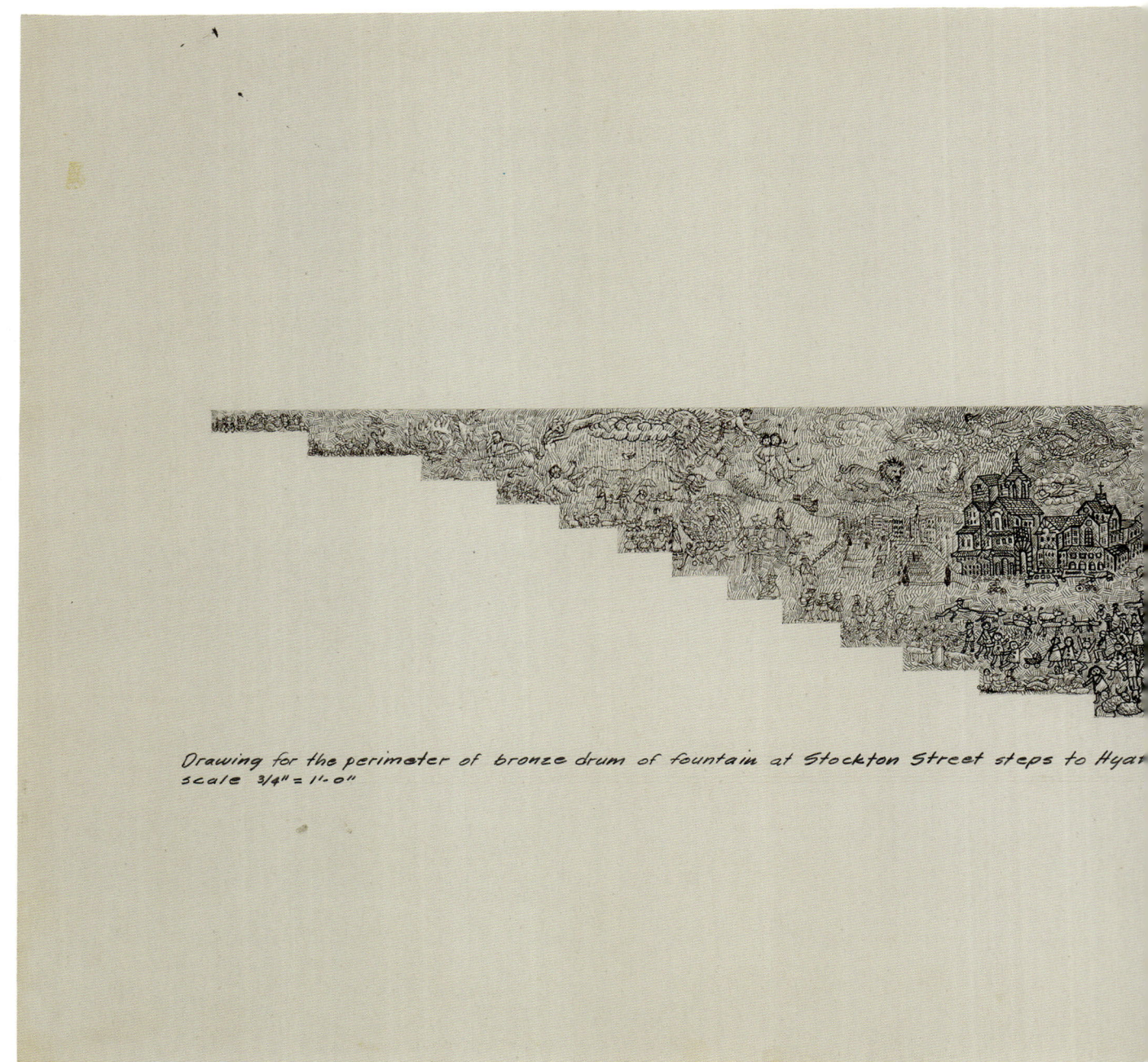

Drawing for the perimeter of bronze drum of fountain at Stockton Street steps to Hya~
scale 3/4" = 1'-0"

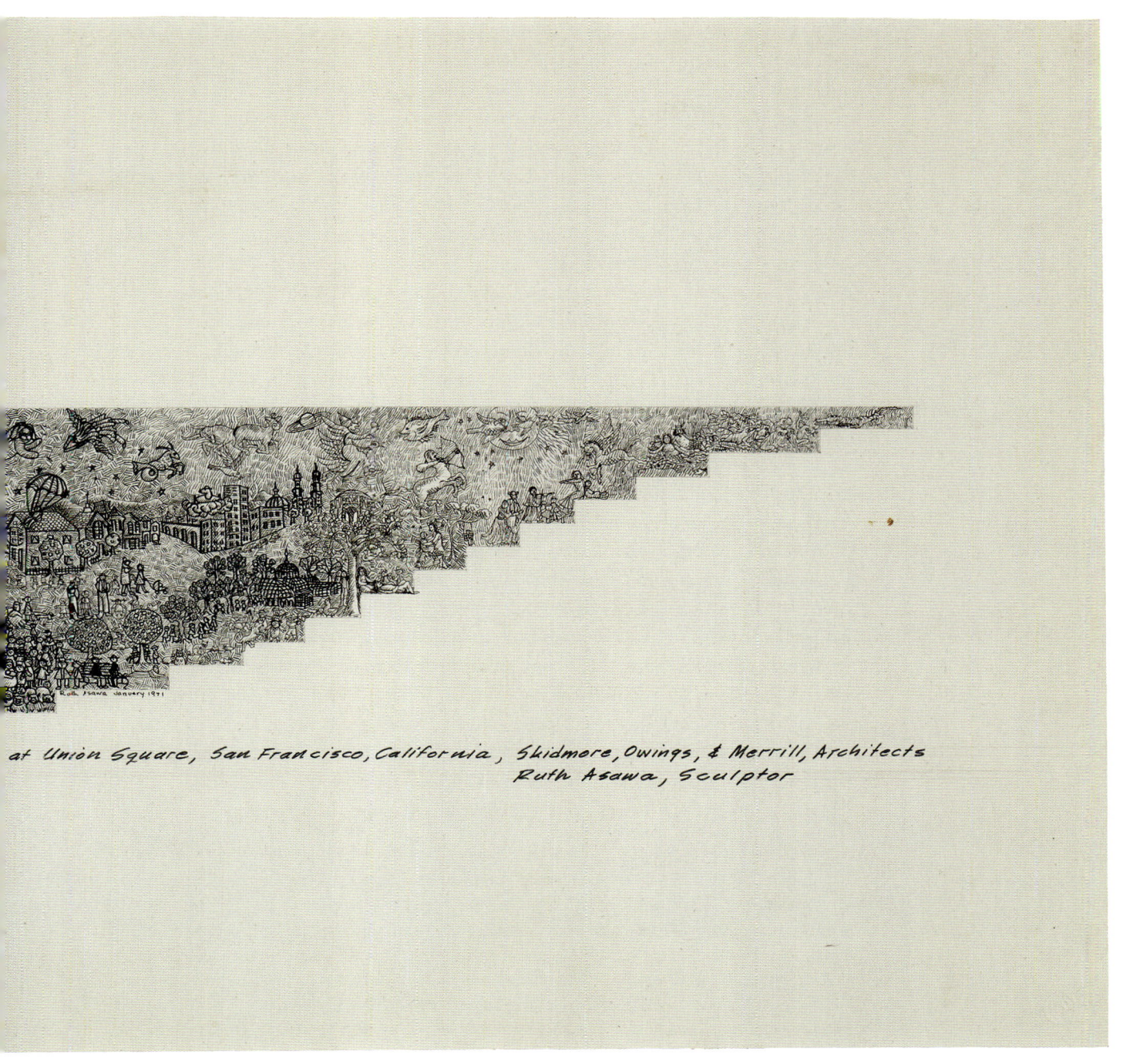

at Union Square, San Francisco, California, Skidmore, Owings, & Merrill, Architects
Ruth Asawa, Sculptor

7.12 Ruth Asawa, *Untitled* (SD.201A, Preliminary Sculpture Drawing for *San Francisco Fountain* [PC.004]), January 1971. Black ink on paper, 18½ × 40 in. Private collection.

and further follows this spatial orientation, with everything to the left of Market Street located to the south: one comes upon the Court House, for instance, and then even further south, we read on the index of sites, "the San Francisco Giants"—the former Candlestick Stadium, once home to the baseball team. What we have, in other words, is the layering of multiple spatial orientations: the fountain is at once a map of the city, as a bird's-eye abstraction, and a landscape that recedes away from us, with buildings depicted not from above but frontally, as if we were standing before them. At the same time, the fountain is site-specific in that the orientation of each geographic location depicted correlates to the actual geographic location of these sites in real space and in relationship to the standing beholder.

Asawa was able to conceptualize this vast undertaking through a full-size model of the drum on which the panels would be placed. Built by her husband, the architect Albert Lanier, and the pattern maker Hector Villaneuva, this model drum was placed on a mock-up of the stairs (fig. 7.13). As the number of panels grew, they spilled out into the house and occupied much of the garden. The drum measured fourteen feet in diameter and up to seven feet high at its highest point. Each of the panels (except for those at the top of the stairs) measured twenty-six by thirty-two inches, dimensions determined by the foundry's casting requirements.

"Because of Ruth's desire to show what many hands working together could do," neighbors and visitors to the Asawa home were encouraged to add to the collage.[45] The process of making the panorama was a collaboration, with many "participatory artists" including dozens of schoolchildren and neighborhood residents who helped make the figures. Key contributors included Sally Woodbridge; Mae Lee and her daughter Mei Mei; all of the Asawa children and especially Aiko, who spent her summer break from university working on it; and Haru Asawa, Ruth's mother. "The youngest person to contribute was three-year-old Mary Bylin from across the street; the oldest was the eighty-eight-year-old photographer, Imogen Cunningham," who contributed palm trees and who herself also appears in the fountain.[46] Woodbridge's slim book on the fountain stressed the collaborative nature of the work:

Most artists, having received a commission, proceed to shut themselves up in their studio devoting long, lonely hours to the process of creation. Ruth had a different approach. Years of working in groups with family and friends gave her a new philosophy:

"Since we have no real folk art or craft tradition any more in the country, this kind of activity has to be recreated to bring families and communities together. No one feels he has to be an artist to work in dough with kitchen utensils. When we started a community art program with parents, teachers, and children working together in school it was natural to use dough sculpture on large panels which everyone could work on. When the fountain came along I thought it was a great opportunity to show how group skills could be used to make something that people usually think of as high art—one product from one person's mind and hands. We have this egocentric idea that the artist has to do his own thing alone. Because of this I think art has become weaker in many ways and less able to satisfy us. There have always been great individuals in art, but great art has also been produced by skilled people working together. It is the idea of bringing skills together that interests me. We see this in science, in the space program, but we have lost it in art."[47]

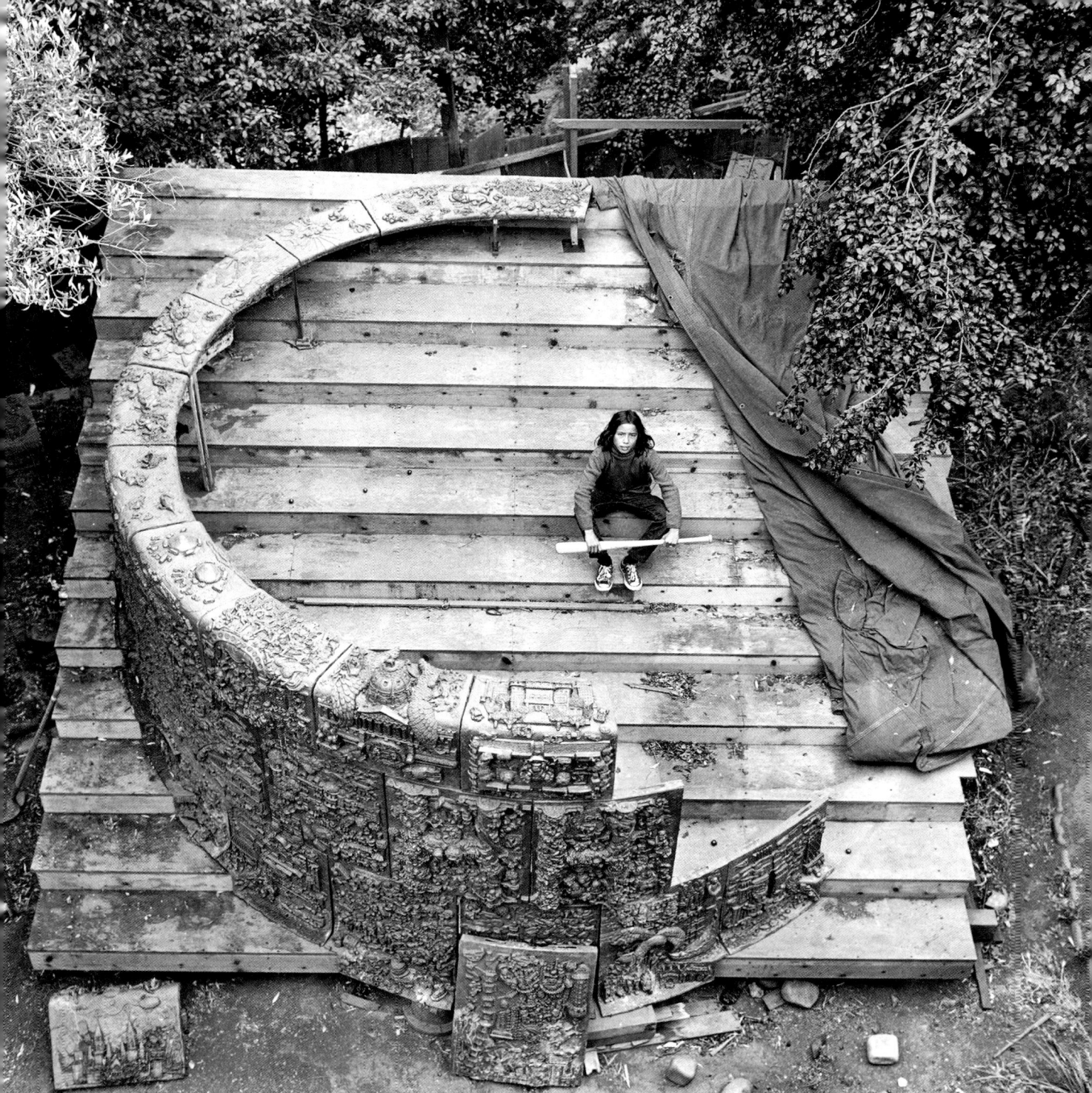

7.13 Ruth Asawa's son Paul Lanier with the partially assembled *San Francisco Fountain* (PC.004) in the garden of Asawa's Noe Valley home, San Francisco, CA, c. 1972. Photo: Laurence Cuneo. Special Collections, Stanford University.

The press at the time conveyed the collective aspect of the commission, with *Sunset Magazine* calling it "a participatory sculpture": "To honor her many helpers (the youngest was 3, the oldest 88), the sculptor has left the new work unsigned."[48] This is in large part why art history has been at a loss to embrace this work, for, as Sarah Archer points out, "Asawa's role in the creation of the fountain (which did come to be well-loved by San Franciscans) seems to align much more strongly with her role as educator and artistically inclined mother. The work itself is not hers per se; rather, it is the result of her art direction and community organizing."[49]

The *San Francisco Fountain* helps us to see how malleable feminist folk art could be in the 1970s, mobilized in both the presence and absence of an explicit feminist agenda. One of the most prominent examples of the former is Judy Chicago's *The Dinner Party* (1974–1979), a room-sized installation of banners, embroidered place settings, and porcelain plates in which key thinkers, writers, artists, and political figures are each given their place at a triangular banquet table. In terms that evoke Asawa's call "to recapture the times when cathedrals were built and the whole village worked together," Chicago compared this collective endeavor to medieval guild production: "the artist needs more resources than can be achieved working alone. . . . *The Dinner Party* is really a throwback to the Middle Ages."[50] And like the *San Francisco Fountain*, this was a collaborative project, involving over four hundred ceramicists, weavers, and textile fabricators. Differing in their relationship to feminist politics, both Chicago and Asawa advocated for a meaningful engagement with making, one in which the artist-as-genius would be dislodged from its typical central position and replaced by a revaluation of collective artistic practice.

Buckminster Fuller described the fountain as an "amazing sculptural and social accomplishment. It epitomizes the great twentieth-century art of San Francisco's 1960s activists out of whose graffiti-epitaphed, socio-economic cultural burial of build-alike, non-entity-style dress-shirt-front real estate row house plowing-under has emerged the first Ruth-Asawa-cultivated progress of a just-now-aborning planetary democracy era."[51] Asawa's portrayal of the city depicts its resistance to mainstream white suburban America—its embrace of protest culture, Victoriana, and the Summer of Love, all of which have since become part of the city's appeal. A journalist writing in 2003 described the work as attracting "gaggles of tourists, who, Herb Caen once joked, were always scrutinizing its sculptural face for the rumored 'couple making love inside the Victorian house.'"[52] Bucking public sculpture's tendency to speak in lofty generalizations, Asawa chose idiosyncratic detail—to such an extreme that many parts of the fountain are illegible to anyone unfamiliar with the city. But then again, its sitedness as a composition in direct dialogue with its immediate surroundings asks exactly that engagement from the viewer, whatever his or her previous encounter with the city might have been.

Created a decade before calls for the removal of Richard Serra's abstract slab of steel from Federal Plaza in New York City galvanized a debate on public sculpture in America, the *San Francisco Fountain* staked a claim on site specificity—and, in doing so, on sculpture's right to be something other than a "mobile, marketable product," to borrow from Serra.[53] This is an artwork that calls into being an oft-ignored public. It appeals to the uninitiated, to those who feel left behind by the universalizing claims of monumental abstraction, to those seeking "intimate, amusing, sometimes irreverent detail" in their public art.[54] In hoping that the public would touch the work, Asawa and Bassett compared it to the popular *Il Porcellino* in Florence, Italy, a Baroque-era bronze replica of a Hellenistic marble piglet, whose polished snout, touched by the hands of countless viewers, attests to its beloved status as a fixture for the city. The touchability of the *San Francisco Fountain* expands sculpture's audience: in 1998, it featured in field trips by students from the Rose Resnick Lighthouse for the Blind and Visually Disabled, which pointed to the fountain as one of the few sculptures in San Francisco that could be experienced through touch.[55]

At issue in the *San Francisco Fountain* is a mode of making and beholding that lends itself to the popular in ways that do not comply with art history's usual categories: it does not invoke the commodity culture of pop art, nor does it recycle folk art's hackneyed landscapes of regional America, nor does it proselytize the moralizing messages of a Norman Rockwell painting. Its subject matter is much too specific and its composition too reliant on an immediate geographic context. In the late 1960s, it became imperative for a group of artist-mothers to picture that geographic context, and in doing so they sited their marginalized status as cultural producers and as caretakers in relationship to the civic horizons of childhood. The work calls into being a public that does not properly exist as such, given the legal exclusion of children from the purportedly mature rationality of the public sphere. As a work of "posterity's hands," to quote again the reporter Mildred Hamilton, the sculpture orients itself so radically away from reigning norms of artistic production that we can hardly see it as such, blinded as we are by unspoken prohibitions against baker's clay as an artistic medium, children as makers and viewers of art, and the mother as a committed cultural producer.[56]

CODA: "FOR SIX CHILDREN AND SCULPTURE"

I end this chapter where I began the book: with a consideration of the domestic sphere, so long identified as the site of motherhood, as in fact a deeply public space in that it hosts ambivalence and permanent negotiation. We see that in a photograph of Asawa's cedar-paneled sunroom which houses the varied modality of her artistic engagement, from the hanging looped-wire sculptures, to the presence of schoolchildren on a field trip to the house, to a baker's clay panel from the *San Francisco Fountain* depicting a self-portrait of children from the Alvarado Elementary School (fig. 7.14). As part of the Alvarado School Arts Workshop, children regularly visited the artist and her garden, transforming Asawa's own home into a classroom and the classroom into a place of social reproduction.

Asawa's "baked sculpture" figured prominently in an article published in 1967 in the design and architecture journal *Interiors*.[57] Predating the *San Francisco Fountain* by three years, the article remarks on the potential of the artist's unusual choice of

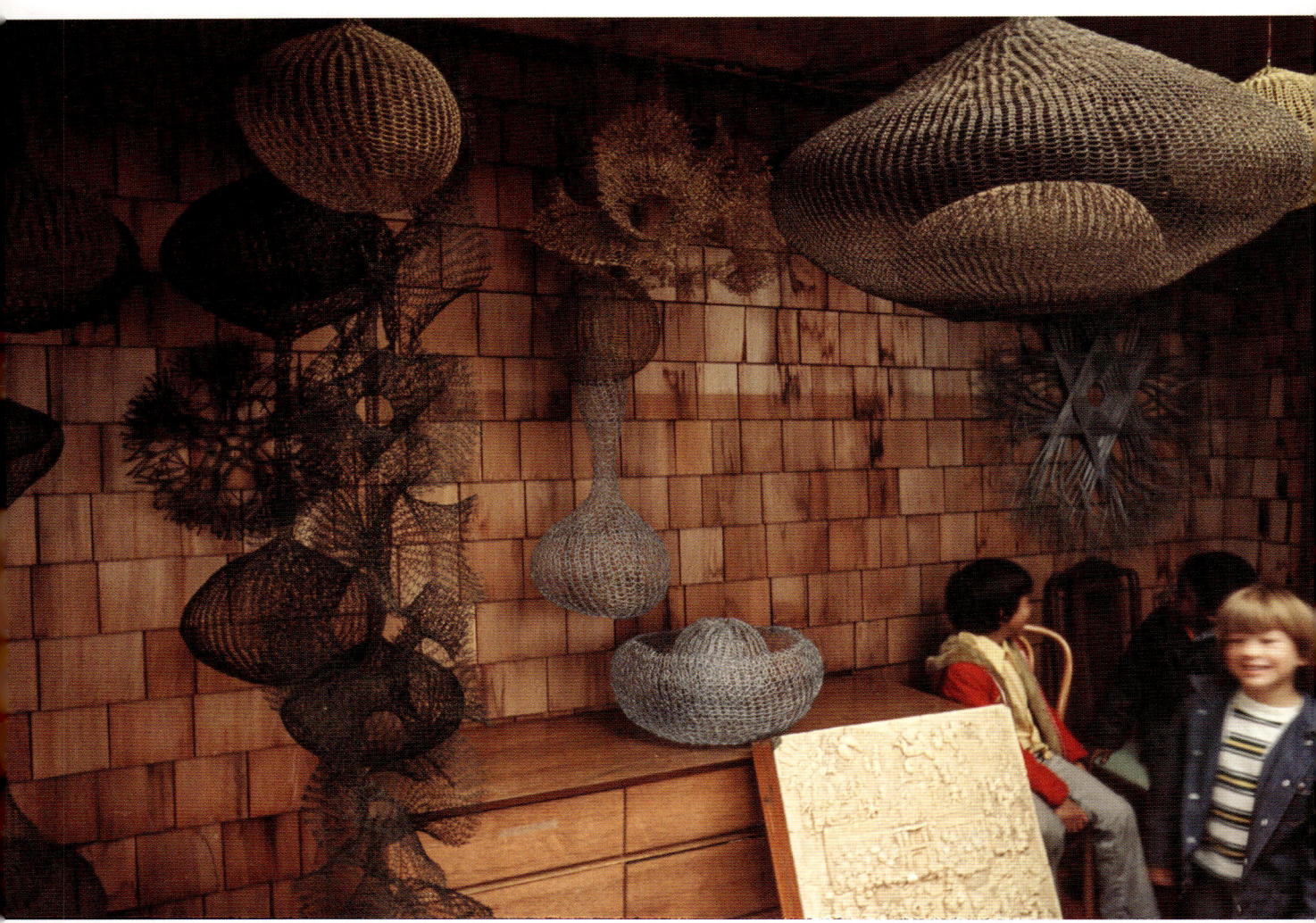

7.14 Children with sculptures and a baker's
clay panel in the sunroom of Ruth Asawa's
Noe Valley home, San Francisco, CA, c. 1976.
Photo: Laurence Cuneo.

materials, reading their significance in direct relationship to the domestic environment, especially the kitchen: here "Mrs. Lanier not only cooks for her family and for an endless stream of casual guests, but also produces bread dolls and other baked sculpture," the magazine's editor Olga Gueft writes. Photographs, taken by Gueft, underscore this point. In one, Asawa glances up at the camera, hands busy with spatula and brush, which we mistake at first for kitchen utensils. But this confusion—between cooking and sculpting, homemaking and artmaking—is precisely the point. In another view, small figures made of baker's clay adorn the kitchen's shallow alcove. "Some of our readers," Gueft points out, "may remember examples from the Museum of Contemporary Craft's December 1965 exhibition called *The Baker's Art*—first chilling the flour-and-salt dough in the large refrigerator, and finally popping them (not edible) into the oven."

With the title "For Six Children and Sculpture," the article encapsulates the extent to which these two integers—craft and clay, art and family—became intertwined with one another. An encounter with Asawa's work was an encounter with her home—or rather the *house*, for at stake in this joining was as much architecture as it was domesticity. The article foregrounds a house that is lived-in, chock-full of objects and projects in various stages of completion. In close proximity to the baked-dough objects, Asawa's horn-rimmed spectacles lie front and center on the table, figuring the artist whose absence permeates the home. Geodesic globe lamps populate a table in the background, while tied-wire sculptures hover above them. On the next page of the article, we see a well-fed husband lunching in a Mies van der Rohe chair at the kitchen table that he had designed, a simple solution devised from sturdy planks; in other images, paintings by Peggy Tolk-Watkins, a friend and former Black Mountain student who lived in nearby Sausalito, ornament the walls, including one below a ladder on which stand two of the Lanier daughters, posing for Gueft's camera, echoing the photograph with which I began this book.

Part of Gueft's interest in the residence—presumably an interest her readers share—is what the couple had made of the turn-of-the-century structure in San Francisco's Noe Valley. The house had originally been built in 1908 by the Bay Area architects Walter H. Ratcliff and Alfred Henry Jacobs. Designed in the style typical of so-called Bay region architecture, it combined elements of the English arts and crafts tradition with an openness to natural light and mixed-use spaces typical of International Style modernism. It was one of the first houses built by Ratcliff, who had emigrated from England with his family as a young boy and first gained experience in the architectural firm of John Galen Howard, where he helped with Howard's buildings for the University of California in Berkeley. Ratcliff would have been familiar with Howard's "enthusiasm for the landscape of the Sierra and the redwood forests of the coast," as well as the generous living-room ceilings of his own house in Berkeley, as Sally Woodbridge emphasizes in her monograph on Howard.[58] For the house in Noe Valley, Ratcliff had been contracted by a newly married attorney, Alfred Scaiffe, whose bride played the organ. The vaulted ceilings, one of the house's most distinctive features, were meant to accommodate the instrument and its acoustics. The living room alone convinced Asawa and Lanier to buy the house when it came up for sale in 1960, after Scaiffe's death.[59] In later decades, Asawa's sculptures would hang by the dozens from these ceilings, creating an underwater-like environment of floating forms, while her ground-floor studio would spill out into the garden.

The house was a work in progress, just as, in the process of its making, the *San Francisco Fountain* permeated Asawa's home, transforming the kitchen into a space of aesthetic production and the sunroom into an ad hoc classroom. If, for Virginia Woolf, "the kitchen table represents not what the modernist artist must discard but what she must transform into the basis of her work," Asawa fits the bill.[60] Motherhood was for her "both a familial and a civic act," to borrow from Rebecca Jo Plant's study of how the mother in Victorian-era America was as much a public figure as she was a consequence of family structures—a public dimension that may later have been replaced by "a more narrow, psychological, and biological conception," but continued to be "simultaneously outmoded and still pervasive."[61] This is the maternal genealogy of modernism, punctuated by both continuity and rupture, by a total commitment to artistic making, as Asawa often stressed, but also by a complete devotion to art as a means of education. "The schools are only one step away from the family," she wrote in 1974.[62]

We should thus understand Asawa's now-iconic wire sculpture and her public art, her drawings of sleeping children and the Alvarado School Arts Workshop, as constituting a single artistic project—the work of the artist-mother. Although one was abstract and the other representative, one inhabited museums and galleries while the other populated classrooms and abandoned city lots, these varying manifestations encompassed a common goal: to demonstrate that artmaking and mothering at mid-century were compatible endeavors. The one remade the other; the mother had a pursuit of her own apart from and beyond her children, while the artist was a caretaker, a citizen responsible to a broader community and committed to the viability of future generations.

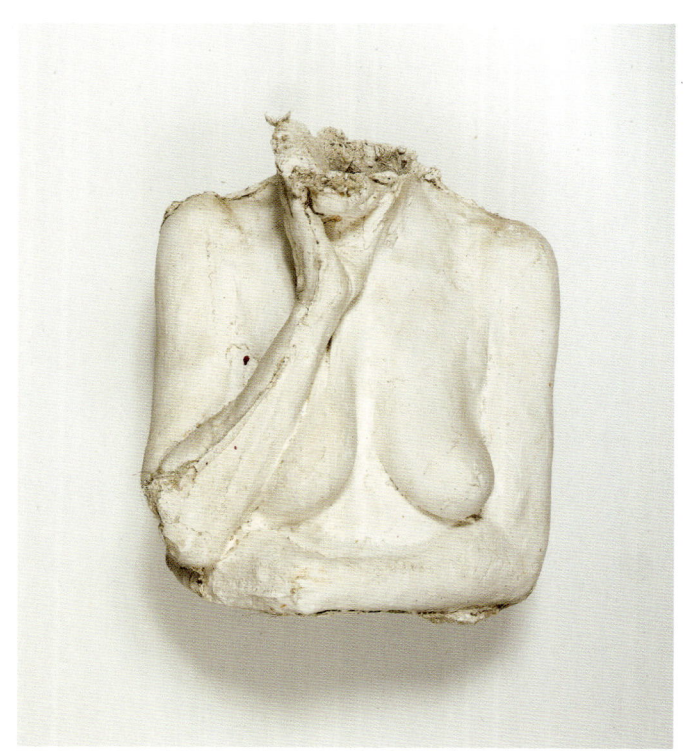

CONCLUSION: ART HISTORY'S BLIND SPOT

This book has argued for the difference that motherhood made to midcentury modern art. The figure of the artist-mother encodes that difference inasmuch as this figure's labor challenged many of modernism's aesthetic tenets, including autonomy, medium specificity, and originality. The artist-mother is thus above all a discursive figure—a subject constituted out of the suppression of the maternal in telling and retelling what art could (and could not) be at midcentury, a figure that profoundly questions the tacit modernist agreement that "the greatest contribution to the world of art that could be made by a woman was to be the mother of a genius."[1] The artist-mother continually rejected being reduced to her role as parent and caretaker, and proposed a countermodel to artistic genius in the making of art as a recursive and relational dialogue. As Ruth Asawa wrote to Albert Lanier in 1949, "There is no genius in my hands."[2]

I end this book with a reflection on how, for so long, art history as a discipline could not speak of this figure, even though other disciplines, like literary studies, had begun to do so. This silence was not simply a matter of gender bias, for second-wave feminists writing on art had as much difficulty with the prospect of the artist-mother as did male-dominated discourses at midcentury. What is the relationship of the artist-mother at midcentury to the artist-mothers in the 1970s, who began to address their own motherhood explicitly in their work? How do we square Asawa's patent refusal of feminist protest with a life that clearly lived principles of equality and reproductive justice? To stay with the figure of the kitchen evoked at the end of the preceding chapter: how do the baker's clay projects led by the Alvarado art mothers compare, for instance, to Ree Morton's *Bake Sale* (1974), a makeshift stand of "fake" bows and cakes and cookies invoking, as Helen Molesworth observed, "the language of PTA (Parent Teacher Association) meetings, Hallmark card notions of sentimentality, and motherhood," all mobilized to "take the sting out of her work in a 'women's faculty show' at the Philadelphia College of Art"?[3]

The figure of the artist-mother embodied by Asawa and women in her circle at midcentury was a very different proposition from the artist-mothers who followed. Morton belongs to a generation of women artists who, emboldened by second-wave feminism of the 1970s and third-wave feminism of the 1990s and beyond, made motherhood the subject of their critique. This is already well-trodden terrain; Andrea Liss lays out this arc of work, which has fearlessly engaged themes of the maternal in a variety of materials and artistic strategies.[4] Writing in 1972, Tillie Olsen observed the sea change, with more and more women "assuming as their right fullness of work *and* family life. Their emergence is evidence of changing circumstances making possible for them what (with rarest exception) was not possible in the generations of women before."[5] It was at this moment—in the 1970s—that the mother gradually became a legitimate author, not merely enabled to make work that would be recognized *as work* (rather than hobby art) but to make work whose subject matter addressed that very experience.

I write at a historical moment in which that transformation has now been normalized. Contemporary artists addressing motherhood have proliferated in recent decades, such that the litany of thematic exhibitions and group shows, documentary films and works of literary fiction, manifestos and handbooks—including *How Not to Exclude Artist Mothers (and Other Parents)* by Hettie Judah—have become a veritable cottage industry in both the arts and literature. "Why All the Books about Motherhood?" read a recent contribution to the *Paris Review*, remarking on how such a genre is still often treated as "a niche concern" instead of "the serious, pressing, and universal subject that it is."[6] In the arts, the exhibition surveys now typically follow a predictable chronology: pointing out the difference between this work and the pervasive Virgin Mary figure in Western art, they foreground the emergent actual mothers critically reflecting on the continuum between the personal and the political, between care and maintenance, between the viability of life and ecological futurity, between indigenous kinship and state structures that have long abandoned mothers. There are now major figures and artworks in this subcanon, from Mierle Laderman Ukeles's *Manifesto for Maintenance Art* (1969) and Mary Kelly's *Post-Partum Document* (1973–1979) to *Womanhouse* (1972) and Judy Chicago's *The Birth Project* (1980–1985), to Catherine Opie's *Self-Portrait/Nursing* (2004), LaToya Ruby Frazier's *Flint Is Family in Three Acts* (2016–2022), Andrea Chung's *Midwives* series (2017), and Titus Kaphar's *Analogous Colors* (2020).

Asawa and her circle, however, broached these themes in ways that are not always recognizable on the surface of the work: the iconography of motherhood sometimes appears, but more often it is invoked as a method of embracing interruption, or as a deliberately collaborative exchange that rejects individual authorship, or as a radical pedagogy in the public schools. In relation to this revisionist history, Asawa and her circle of artist-mothers mark the possibility of rewriting this genealogy as one that extends beyond iconography and encompasses questions of process, identification, institutional critique—ultimately one that approaches mothering less as a noun and more as a verb, acting on the world, as I discussed in the introduction. This could fulfill Adrienne Rich's injunction that we see motherhood as part of a range of experiences, experiences that go beyond stable gender identities or traditional family structures.

But most importantly, the artist-mother demonstrates a paradigm of working as a woman who does not consciously make art in reference to her own identity. Asawa and her circle most obviously marked their distance from this generation informed by feminism through the fact that they rarely made motherhood an explicit subject of their work. Except for *Andrea*, one is hard-pressed to find overt references to motherhood in Asawa's work, as we find in Ree Morton's *I'll Only Read You the Good Parts* (1975), for instance, a title that evokes the nightly ritual of reading to one's child and the fear and anxiety that often accompany bedtime (or, as the experts call it, "independent sleep"). Morton and her generation still valued originality and invocation: her engagement with Raymond Roussel's *Impressions of Africa* and her discovery of the unusual textile-mummifying material *celastic* mark her avant-garde credentials. What's more, Morton lived apart from her three children beginning in 1972, four years after her separation from her husband, and saw them only during the summers; it was also the year art historians often identify as a turning point in her work.[7] Even when making work explicitly about motherhood, one could still be caught in the modernist prohibition against the artist-mother.

Instead of innovation, Asawa embraced replication and repetition, bringing art down to the level of routine: "Art is doing and that's all there is," she often stated. Motherhood became a method to undo modernism's matricide by replacing the modernist artist's autonomy with relations of dependency; narratives of the heroic genius gave way to all-night dialogues over folding and branching; and domestic routine was viewed not as oppressive but as constructive—all of this allowed these women modernists to continue being mothers. In doing so, they made motherhood into a medium.

At times, Asawa's practice willingly embraces the all-too-familiar to such a degree that those responding to the work grasp for the moment of innovation; this is largely why the looped-wire pieces, with their unusual technique, have become the best-known of her work, while more familiar artistic strategies, such as representative bas-relief, are tacitly viewed as "retrograde" in the resounding silence with which they are met (at least in art historical discourse). Her *Japanese American Internment Memorial* is a case in point. It is a bas-relief bronze sculpture whose iconography was drawn from Asawa's own experience of being incarcerated for sixteen months during World War II at Santa Anita, California, and in Rohwer, Arkansas, as well as from the oral histories of Santa Clara County residents affected by Executive Order no. 9066. The work would seem unremarkable were it not for its photographic afterlife. In the 1990s, her son-in-law photographed Asawa posing next to the work (fig. 8.1). On her lap sits one of her ten grandchildren, Emma. Barefoot and at ease in close proximity to Asawa's body, Emma twists toward the memorial, touching its metal surface. Here is, once more, an image of the artist-(grand)mother putting her identity as caretaker in direct dialogue with her identity as artist. For the work that she has just completed is as much a statement against war, racism, and violence—a statement against that "society hostile to life," to quote again from Tillie Olsen—as it is an intricate visual panorama with a complex compositional structure.

In the United States after World War II, the available frameworks for art production failed to account for an entire spectrum of aesthetic making that I have gathered under the term "artist-mother." Similarly, such practices do not resemble those more familiar feminist engagements with the maternal at the level of the work's iconography. I have borrowed from literature to show this blind spot, finding it useful to define the figure of the artist-mother in the terms that figures from Tillie Olsen to Susan Rubin Suleiman use to describe the "writing mother." Suleiman surveys a body of literature, ranging from fiction to memoir to the psychoanalytic-informed essays of French feminism, written by mothers. Her point is to show "the limitations of Western culture's traditional discourses about motherhood."[8] That traditional discourse has posed motherhood as an either/or distinction: "to write the book and deny the child (not the child we were but the child we have, or might have) or love the child and postpone/renounce the book" is, as we have seen, a familiar opposition in Western thought.[9]

Suleiman points to how this distinction excludes a whole modality of being in the world—not only of mothering and caretaking but of interdependency itself, the "not-me" that exists in the space between mother and child. And that is a powerful model of art, given that "artistic creation, indeed all cultural experience, belongs to the realm of transitional phenomena. Successful creation, like all creative living, depends on the trust and self-confidence first developed in the child's earliest relationship to the mother."[10] We need to restore that entire body of knowledge that comes out of this transitional existence of simultaneous autonomy and dependence. And above all, we need to recognize, as Julia Kristeva asks us to do, that any effective feminist practice "will not be possible until we have elucidated motherhood, feminine creation, and the relationship between them."[11] It is then, finally, the terms of creativity that are at issue—who, and whose *labor*, is recognized as creative. Long excluded as a creative subject, the artist-mother has been confined to procreativity. Lisa Baraitser argues that this is how maternity is itself in turn reinvented through the creative act: "through a displacement or entanglement of the creative act that involves both 'child' and 'artwork,'" the artist "brings creativity, generation and intergeneration into view, even as such creative practices produce maternity itself. The practice of motherhood, then, can make for a different kind of making, one imbued with an ethical concern for the other."[12]

To return to Cuneo's photograph of Asawa with her grandchild foregrounded against a scene of twentieth-century atrocity: what we see here may not qualify as artistic innovation, but it offers a radical destabilization of the received narrative of what an artist does: *he* offers a moment of original and individual self-expression; *she* proposes that we envision anew our relationships to one another, to our natural

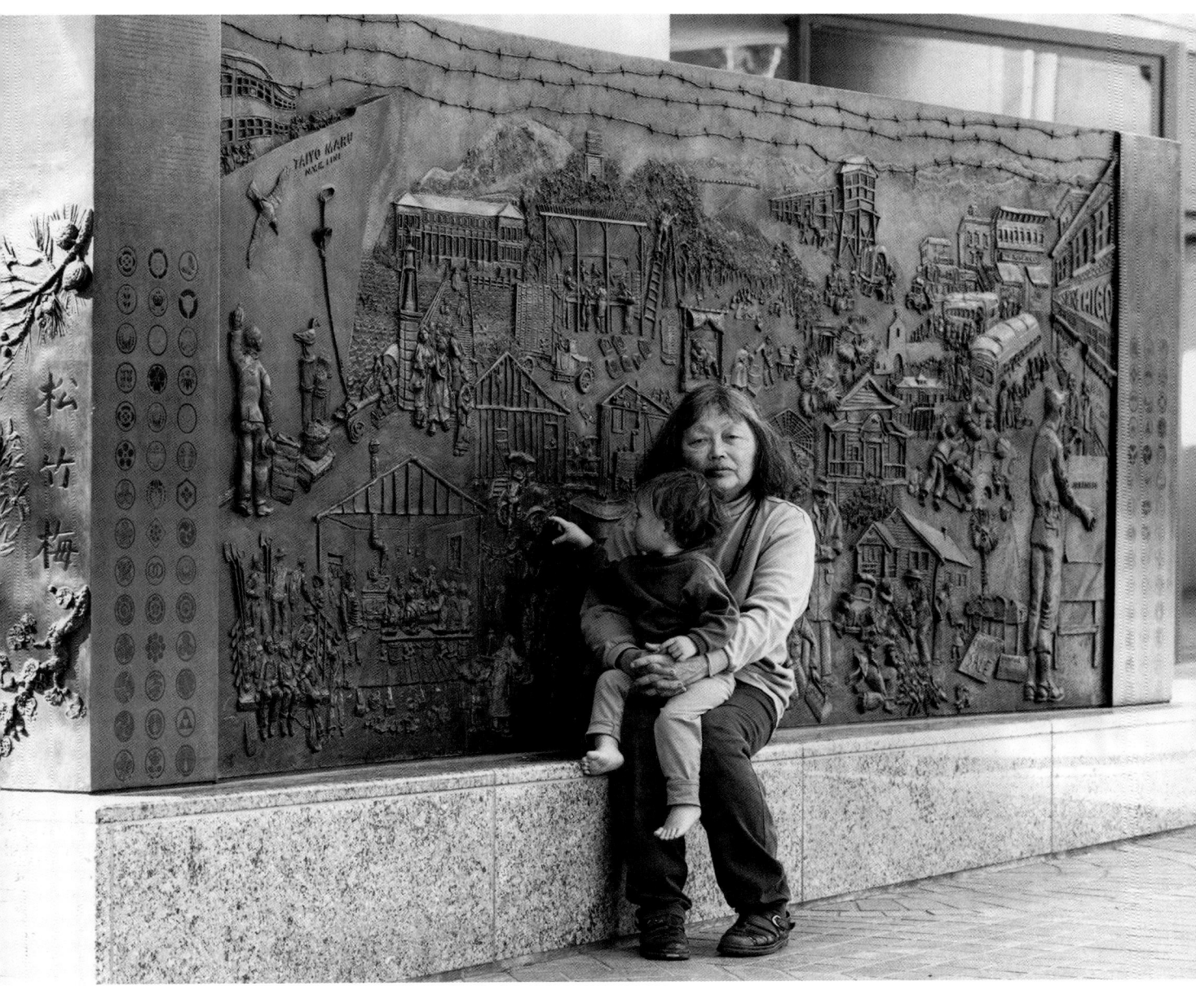

8.1 Ruth Asawa and granddaughter Emma Lanier sitting in front of Asawa's *Japanese American Internment Memorial* (PC.011, bas-relief in bronze, 60 × 172 × 18 in., 300 South First Street, San Jose, 1990–1994), c. 1996. Photo: Laurence Cuneo.

environment, and to posterity. For, as Jacqueline Rose observes in her book *Mothers*, Hannah Arendt proposes that "every new birth is the supreme anti-totalitarian moment," the moment in which the world can be created anew.[13] What we glimpse in the archives, in the photograph staging Asawa with Emma, is the possibility that art and motherhood generate that anti-totalitarian moment—the retort to the scene of terror at hand. To be an artist and a mother at midcentury was to practice that possibility, however briefly.

ACKNOWLEDGMENTS

I am grateful to the families, and particularly to the daughters and granddaughters, of the women in this book, for all that they have done over the years to preserve the legacies of their mothers' work. Without that labor, this book could not have been written. Special thanks go to Baunnie Sea, Pamela Woodbridge, Judi Mozesson, Rachel Mozesson, Meg Partridge, Aiko Cuneo, and Addie Laurie Lanier. Asawa's grandson Henry Weverka took over the management of his grandmother's estate at a crucial point and helped usher this manuscript to completion through endless support and assistance, joined by the tireless efforts of Vivian Tong, whose keen eye spotted photographs that enriched the book's illustrations. Further thanks are due to Marc Aronson, Marina Budhos, Laurence Cuneo, Andrea Jepson, Paul Lanier, Terry Lanier, Hudson Lanier, Emma Lanier, Lisa Lee Peterson, Clifford Peterson, and Susan Stauter for speaking with me on various occasions.

While conducting research for this book, I had the privilege of working with incredibly competent archivists and librarians, who made available materials that changed the direction of the manuscript. These include Jeff Gunderson, of the San Francisco Art Institute Legacy and Archives Foundation; Tim Noakes at Special Collections, Stanford University; Christina Moretta, Photo Archivist at the San Francisco Public Library; Heather Isbell Schumacher, Archivist, University of Pennsylvania Architectural Archives; Sharon Seymour, Collections Manager of the Sausalito Historical Society; and Peggy Tran-Le, Archivist of the San Francisco Museum of Modern Art.

A semester at the University of California, Berkeley, under the mentorship of Lauren Kroiz, enabled discussions with colleagues, including Gregory Levine, Aglaya K. Glebova, Elizabeth Fair, and Tausif Noor, which enriched my understanding of the work at hand. A residency at the Cape Cod Modern House Trust, at the invitation of Elizabeth Otto, gave me precious time to write and stimulating exchange, and set in motion the process that led to this book finding a home at the MIT Press. I am also grateful to audiences at the Menil Collection and at the Courtauld Institute of Art, where some of these ideas met with helpful suggestions. Further support came from the University of Graz in Austria, and the Freie Universität in Berlin, where a postdoc in the research group "Normativity, Critique, Change," under the guidance of Karin Gludovatz and Georg Bertram, expanded my thinking on this topic. More recently, colleagues at Leuphana Universität Lüneburg facilitated the space and resources necessary to bring this manuscript to completion. A special acknowledgment goes to Beate Söntgen, who believed in this project long before I knew where it could lead and made possible a successful grant application to the VolkswagenStiftung's Freigeist Fellowship, which contributed to the book's production and funded a broader research context for this publication. Additional financial support came from the Terra Foundation for the Arts, the Henry Moore Foundation, and, most generously, the Andy Warhol Foundation Arts Writers Grant, which made the last stages of research and writing possible.

Further thanks go to the colleagues and friends whose support and discussions shaped this manuscript: especially Susan Dackerman, Antje Engelmann, Ruth Erickson, Robert Felfe, David Getsy, Aglaya K. Glebova, Johanna Gosse, Maria Gough, Sarah Hamill, Chelsea Knoren, Edouard Kopp, Sabine Kriebel, Jenelle Porter, Susie Quillinan, Jeffrey Saletnik, and Caroline Lillian Schopp. The many conversations spent planning the symposium "Surrogates: Embodied History of Sculpture in the Short Twentieth Century" at Yale University with Joanna Fiduccia vastly improved the scope of this book's questions. I am furthermore grateful to all of the participants for the enlivening discussions during that event. One of the conference keynote speakers, Anne M. Wagner, may not think she did much to shape this book, but her example, both as a scholar and a feminist—and her mentorship early on—emboldened me to take on what seemed for so long unsayable.

Rachel Kravetz gave the manuscript a careful read at a crucial point in its development and strengthened it tremendously. I am also grateful to the team at MIT Press, including Matthew Abbate, Gabriela Bueno Gibbs, and Yasuyo Iguchi. My editor, Victoria Hindley, believed in this project from the start and provided encouragement and feedback on an earlier draft, which helped shepherd the book to completion. The suggestions from several anonymous readers of the manuscript further improved the book's structure and content.

Finally, I wish to thank my parents, Mark and Julie Troeller, for their unfailing confidence, as well as for the many hours of childcare they provided over the years which enabled research trips and writing. Thanks go additionally to my grandmother, Bettye Troeller. This book first germinated in the year following the birth of my first child, Bruno; his presence, soon joined by Ramona and Jack, enabled me to see questions in the history of art that previously had been invisible to me. Ruby pushed my thinking on motherhood outside of biological ties. To them, this book is dedicated, as well as to Immanuel, whose strength as a caretaker daily models for me motherhood as a genderless category.

NOTES

INTRODUCTION

1. Ruth Asawa, "Report to the San Francisco Foundation," June 1974, Folder 5, Box 135, Ruth Asawa Papers (M1585), Department of Special Collections and University Archives, Stanford University Libraries, Stanford, California (hereafter Asawa Papers).

2. Lucy Lippard, "Household Images in Art," *Ms.* 1, no. 9 (1973), repr. in Lippard, *From the Center: Feminist Essays on Women's Art* (New York: E. P. Dutton, 1976), 57.

3. Ursula K. Le Guin, "The Fisherwoman's Daughter" (1988), repr. in *Mother Reader: Essential Writings on Motherhood*, ed. Moyra Davey (New York: Seven Stories Press, 2001), 171. I take Le Guin's neologism "Canoneers" to refer to those writing histories that have become canonical.

4. Ruth Asawa discusses her decision to remain at home in "Art, Competence, and Citywide Cooperation for San Francisco," an oral history conducted in 1974 and 1976 by Harriet Nathan, Regional Oral History Office, The Bancroft Library, University of California, Berkeley, 1980, 37–38.

5. Ruth Asawa to Brenda Danilowitz, July 28, 2001, Josef and Anni Albers Foundation, Bethany, CT.

6. Whitney Davis, *Replications: Archaeology, Art History, Psychoanalysis* (University Park: Pennsylvania State University Press, 1996), 2 and 134.

7. Linda Nochlin, "Why Have There Been No Great Women Artists?" (1971), in Nochlin, *Women, Art, and Power* (New York: Harper & Row, 1988), 158.

8. An exception is Aleesa Pitchamarn Alexander, "Drawn Together: Ruth Asawa and Community," in *Ruth Asawa: Through Line*, ed. Kim Conaty and Edouard Kopp, exh. cat. (Houston: Menil Collection; New York: Whitney Museum of American Art, 2023), 31–35.

9. Ruth Asawa, statement in the brochure *Ruth Asawa: Completing the Circle*, produced on the occasion of the eponymous exhibition at the Fresno Art Museum and Oakland Museum of California in 2001–2002, n.p.

10. Gerald Nordland, *Ruth Asawa: A Retrospective View*, exh. cat. (San Francisco: San Francisco Museum of Art, 1973), n.p.

11. Meredith A. Brown, "'I'll Show Everybody': An Artist-Mother at Home," in *Alice Neel: People Come First*, ed. Kelly Baum and Randall Griffey, exh. cat. (New York: Metropolitan Museum of Art, 2021), 67.

12. See, for instance, Allan Kaprow, "The Education of the Un-Artist, Part I (1972)," in *Essays on the Blurring of Art and Life*, ed. Jeff Kelley (Berkeley: University of California Press, 1993), 97–109.

13. Tillie Olsen, *Silences* (1978; repr., New York: Feminist Press, 2003), 32.

14. Julie Phillips, *The Baby on the Fire Escape: Creativity, Motherhood, and the Mind-Baby Problem* (New York: W. W. Norton, 2022), 3.

15. Angela Garbes, *Essential Labor: Mothering as Social Change* (New York: HarperCollins, 2022), 9.

16. Garbes, *Essential Labor*, 9. Here Garbes cites Alexis Pauline Gumbs, China Martens, and Mai'a Williams, ed., *Revolutionary Mothering: Love on the Front Lines* (Oakland, CA: PM Press, 2016). See also Sarah Knott, *Mother Is a Verb: An Unconventional History* (New York: Farrar, Straus and Giroux, 2019), for another example of how a historian has made methodological use of this shift in discourse.

17. Yasmine Ergas, Jane Jenson, and Sonya Michel, "Negotiating 'Mother' in the Twenty-First Century," in *Reassembling Motherhood: Procreation and Care in a Globalized World*, ed. Yasmine Ergas, Jane Jenson, and Sonya Michel (New York: Columbia University Press, 2017), 1.

18. Helen Molesworth, "'San Francisco Housewife and Mother,'" in *Ruth Asawa: Life's Work*, ed. Tamara H. Schenkenberg, exh. cat. (St. Louis: Pulitzer Arts Foundation, 2019), 35–36.

19. Merry Renk and Earle Curtis in an unpublished interview, June 17, 2004, Ruth Asawa Lanier, Inc.

20. Joan Pearson Watkins, "Opulent and Organic: The Jewelry of Merry Renk," *American Craft* 41, no. 2 (April/May 1981): 33.

21. Ruth Asawa to Mr. and Mrs. Lanier, n.d. (postmarked October 21, 1965), Ruth Asawa Lanier, Inc.

22. See Rebecca Jo Plant, *Mom: The Transformation of Motherhood in America* (Chicago: University of Chicago Press, 2010).

23. Norma Broude and Mary D. Garrard, "Introduction: Feminism and Art in the Twentieth Century," in *The Power of Feminist Art: The American Movement of the 1970s, History and Impact*, ed. Norma Broude and Mary D. Garrard (New York: Harry N. Abrams, 1994), 17. See also Andrea Liss, *Feminist Art and the Maternal* (Minneapolis: University of Minnesota Press, 2009).

24. Adrienne Rich, *Of Woman Born: Motherhood as Experience and Institution* (1976; repr., New York: W. W. Norton, 1995), 13; italics in original.

25. Alice Neel, cited in Patricia Hills, *Alice Neel* (New York: Harry N. Abrams, 1983), 29.

26. Mary Gabriel, *Ninth Street Women* (New York: Little, Brown, 2018), 10.

27. Alexander Nemerov, *Fierce Poise: Helen Frankenthaler and 1950s New York* (New York: Penguin, 2021), 196, 194.

28. Emily Mason, interviewed by Cathy Curtis in 2015 and cited in Curtis, *A Generous Vision: The Creative Life of Elaine de Kooning* (New York: Oxford University Press, 2017), 31.

29. Louise Bourgeois, "Interview with Marie-Laure Bernadac" (1995), in Louise Bourgeois, *Destruction of the Father, Reconstruction of the Father: Writings and Interviews, 1923–1997*, ed. Marie-Laure Bernadac and Hans Ulrich Obrist (London: Violette, 1998), 295–296.

30. Olsen, *Silences*, 30. She cites Anaïs Nin, *The Diary of Anaïs Nin*, vol. III, 1939–1944.

31. Reg Butler (1962), repr. in *New Society* 31 (August 1978): 433; cited in Rozsika Parker and Griselda Pollock, *Old Mistresses: Women, Art, and Ideology* (London: Routledge, 1981), 6–7.

32. Susan Rubin Suleiman, "Writing and Motherhood," in Davey, *Mother Reader*, 119; first published in *The (M)other Tongue: Essays in Feminist Psychoanalytic Interpretation*, ed. Shirley Nelson Garner, Claire Kahane, and Madelon Sprengnether (Ithaca: Cornell University Press, 1985).

33. Suleiman, "Writing and Motherhood," 118.

34. Parker and Pollock, *Old Mistresses*, 8; emphasis added.

35. Sarah Kofman, *The Childhood of Art: An Interpretation of Freud's Aesthetics*, trans. Winifred Woodhull (New York: Columbia University Press, 1988), 95.

36. Honoré de Balzac, cited in Olsen, *Silences*, 12.

37. Roxanne Guerrero, "A Maternal Art," *Life* 37, no. 23 (December 6, 1954): 101.

38. Guerrero, "A Maternal Art," 102.

39. Roland Barthes, "Novels and Children," in *Mythologies* (1957), trans. Annette Lavers (New York: Farrar, Straus and Giroux, 1991), 50.

40. Barthes, "Novels and Children," 51.

41. Alicia Ostriker, *Writing Like a Woman* (Ann Arbor: University of Michigan Press, 1983), 126.

42. Jill Johnston, *Mother Bound* (New York: Alfred A. Knopf, 1983), 116.

43. Johnston, *Mother Bound*, 115 (this and the preceding quote).

44. Johnston, *Mother Bound*, 125, 116, 130 (all quotations in this paragraph).

45. Shelley M. Park, "Adoptive Maternal Bodies: A Queer Paradigm for Rethinking Mothering?," *Hypatia* 21, no. 1 (Winter 2006): 202.

46. Margaret F. Gibson, introduction to *Queering Motherhood in Narrative, Theory, and the Everyday*, ed. Margaret F. Gibson (Branford, ON: Demeter Press, 2014), 6.

47. Jean Rochin to Ruth Asawa, November 24, 1966, Folder 3, Box 28, Asawa Papers.

48. Shelley M. Park, *Mothering Queerly, Queering Motherhood* (Albany: State University of New York Press, 2013), 12.

49. Laurence Cuneo in conversation with the author, March 25, 2022.

50. See Asawa in Nathan, "Art, Competence, and Citywide Cooperation for San Francisco," 119.

51. Ann Douglas, *Terrible Honesty: Mongrel Manhattan in the 1920s* (New York: Farrar, Straus and Giroux, 1995), 217.

52. Douglas, *Terrible Honesty*, 230.

53. See David Getsy's discussion of David Smith in *Abstract Bodies: Sixties Sculpture in the Expanded Field of Gender* (Chicago: University of Chicago Press, 2015), esp. 54–57.

54. Ruth Asawa, statement in the brochure *Ruth Asawa: Honor Award Show* produced on the occasion of the eponymous exhibition at the San Francisco Art Commission Gallery, Capricorn Asunder, 1976, n.p. (all quotations in this paragraph), Ruth Asawa Ephemeral File, San Francisco History Center, San Francisco Public Library.

55. Daniel Belasco, *Women Artists in Midcentury America: A History in Ten Exhibitions* (London: Reaktion Books, 2024), 138–139.

56. Tara McDowell, *The Householders: Robert Duncan and Jess* (Cambridge, MA: MIT Press, 2019), 11.

57. Robert Duncan, cited in McDowell, *The Householders*, 195n58 and 11.

58. Asawa, statement in the brochure *Ruth Asawa: Completing the Circle*, n.p.

59. Mildred Hamilton, "A Tour of Ruth Asawa's San Francisco," *San Francisco Examiner*, September 19, 1976, Arts Section, 1.

60. Asawa, statement in *Ruth Asawa: Completing the Circle*, n.p.

61. See Jonathan Fineberg, *The Innocent Eye: Children's Art and the Modern Artist* (Princeton, NJ: Princeton University Press, 1997), and Jonathan Fineberg, ed., *Discovering Child Art: Essays on Childhood, Primitivism, and Modernism* (Princeton, NJ: Princeton University Press, 1998).

62. See Jonathan Marsden, *Victoria and Albert: Art and Love* (London: Royal Collection, 2010), 76–77. My thanks to Rachel Kravetz for this reference. For a discussion of these casts as part of the popular practice of taking casts from babies, see Marcia Pointon, "Casts, Imprints, and the Deathliness of Things: Artefacts at the Edge," *Art Bulletin* 96, no. 2 (June 2014): 187.

63. Helen Molesworth, "Drawing after Dinner," in *Ruth Asawa: All Is Possible*, ed. Helen Molesworth, exh. cat. (New York: David Zwirner, 2022), 12.

64. Katherine Fein, "'The Sense of Nearness': Harriet Hosmer's Clasped Hands and the Materials and Bodies of Nineteenth Century Life Casting," *British Art Studies*, no. 14 (November 2019), https://doi.org/10.17658/issn.2058-5462/issue-14/kfein.

65. Percy Bysshe Shelley, cited in Anne M. Wagner, *Mother Stone: The Vitality of Modern British Sculpture* (New Haven: Yale University Press, 2005), 72.

66. Lauren Elkin, "Why All the Books about Motherhood?," *The Paris Review Blog*, July 17, 2018, https://www.theparisreview.org/blog/2018/07/17/why-all-the-books-about-motherhood/. Elkin cites Judith Newman writing in the *New York Times Book Review* on Mother's Day in 2012.

67. Rich, *Of Woman Born*, 33.

68. Suleiman, "Writing and Motherhood," 117; italics in original.

69. Jordan Troeller, "The Maternal in Drag: Towards a Mother-Driven Theory of Artistic Creation," *kritische berichte* 50, no. 2 (2022): 45–52.

PART I

1. Nancy Gray, "World of Wire: Sculpture Comes from Crocheting," *San Francisco Examiner*, May 12, 1957, 4.

2. Meredith A. Brown, "'I'll Show Everybody': An Artist-Mother at Home," in *Alice Neel: People Come First*, ed. Kelly Baum and Randall Griffey, exh. cat. (New York: Metropolitan Museum of Art, 2021), 67–79.

3. Gerald Nordland, *Ruth Asawa: A Retrospective View*, exh. cat. (San Francisco: San Francisco Museum of Art, 1973), n.p. Another example from the catalogue: "In just ten years from terminating her studies at Black Mountain Ruth Asawa had established a national reputation as an artist of high originality, intelligence and quality, while becoming the mother of and caring for six children."

4. See, for instance, Ann Reynolds, "Lessons in Transparency: Ruth Asawa in Mexico," in *In a Cloud, in a Wall, in a Chair: Six Modernists in Mexico at Midcentury*, ed. Zoë Ryan, exh. cat. (Chicago: Art Institute of Chicago, 2019), 173–179; Cora Chalaby, "The Immateriality of Materiality: Ruth Asawa's Looped Wire Sculpture," *Immediations*, no. 18 (2021): 64–83.

5. Eleanor C. Munro, "Globe within a Cup within a Sphere," *Art News* 55 (April 1956): 26; cited in Emily K. Doman Jennings, "Critiquing the Critique: Ruth Asawa's Early Reception," in *The Sculpture of Ruth Asawa: Contours in the Air*, ed. Daniell Cornell and Timothy Anglin Burgard, rev. ed. (San Francisco: Fine Arts Museums of San Francisco; Berkeley: University of California Press, 2020), 159.

6. Jennings, "Critiquing the Critique," 165; see also Zach Hatfield, "Ruth Asawa: Tending the Metal Garden," *New York Review of Books*, September 21, 2017.

7. Aruna D'Souza, "Transparency and Its Other," in *Ruth Asawa: Life's Work*, ed. Tamara H. Schenkenberg, exh. cat. (St. Louis: Pulitzer Arts Foundation, 2019), 45–52.

8. Helen Molesworth, "'San Francisco Housewife and Mother,'" in Schenkenberg, *Ruth Asawa: Life's Work*, 42.

9. Rozsika Parker, "Portrait of the Artist as Housewife," *Spare Rib*, no. 60 (1977): 5–8; repr. in *Framing Feminism: Art and the Women's Movement 1970–85*, ed. Rozsika Parker and Griselda Pollock (New York: Pandora, 1987), 207.

10. Sarah Archer, "From Maker to Market: Ruth Asawa Reappraised," *Journal of Modern Craft* 8, no. 2 (November 2015): 141–154.

11. For this reading, see Jennings, "Critiquing the Critique," 131.

12. Mary Frazer, "Making an Art of Living," *San Francisco Examiner*, December 18, 1960, 8.

13. See for instance Ernst Beadle's photographs of Asawa, her children, and the chalkboard in Margaret White, "Art, Creativity, and the Home Fires," *Ladies' Home Journal*, June 1964, 66–68. On the phrase "housewife market," see Susan Rubin Suleiman, "Writing and Motherhood," in *Mother Reader: Essential Writings on Motherhood*, ed. Moyra Davey (New York: Seven Stories Press, 2001), 121.

14. Ursula K. Le Guin, "The Fisherwoman's Daughter" (1988), repr. in Davey, *Mother Reader*, 167.

15. Sally B. Woodbridge, preface to *Bay Area Houses*, ed. Woodbridge, rev. ed. (1976; repr., Salt Lake City: Peregrine Smith, 1988), v.

16. Lucy Lippard, "Household Images in Art," *Ms.* 1, no. 9 (March 1973), repr. in Lippard, *From the Center: Feminist Essays on Women's Art* (New York: E. P. Dutton, 1976), 57.

CHAPTER 1

1. Ruth Asawa to Celia Sieverts, August 11, 1954, Ruth Asawa Lanier, Inc. Unless otherwise indicated, personal correspondence is from this repository.

2. Ruth Asawa to Mr. and Mrs. W. H. Lanier, March 21, 1950.

3. Tara McDowell, *The Householders: Robert Duncan and Jess* (Cambridge, MA: MIT Press, 2019), 25 and 18.

4. Sally B. Woodbridge, "Arcadia Revisited," in *Bay Area Houses*, ed. Woodbridge, rev. ed. (1976; Salt Lake City: Peregrine Smith, 1988), 313.

5. McDowell, *The Householders*, 5.

6. Richard Cándida Smith, "Utopia and the Private Realm," in *Utopia and Dissent: Art, Poetry, and Politics in California* (Berkeley: University of California Press, 1995), 212–268.

7. Elizabeth Ferrell, *About "The Rose": Creation and Community in Jay DeFeo's Circle* (New Haven: Yale University Press, 2022), 80.

8. McDowell, *The Householders*, 5.

9. Michael McClure, cited in McDowell, *The Householders*, 25.

10. On the racial prejudices that Asawa and Lanier encountered, see Marilyn Chase, *Everything She Touched: The Life of Ruth Asawa* (San Francisco: Chronicle Books, 2020), 71.

11. "Correspondence between Ray Johnson and May Wilson some years ago when May Wilson was a little old lady in Maryland," in *Ray Johnson Ray Johnson*, ed. William S. Wilson (New York: Between Books, 1977), n.p. My thanks to Johanna Gosse for bringing this to my attention. Sally B. Woodbridge, "The California House," in Woodbridge, *Bay Area Houses*, 84, 90.

12. Albert Lanier to Ruth Asawa, January 7, 1949.

13. On the Tin Angel in the context of the city's queer histories, see Nan Alamilla Boyd, "Lesbian Space, Lesbian Territory," in *Wide-Open Town: A History of Queer San Francisco to 1965* (Berkeley: University of California Press, 2002).

14. Joan Ockman, "Mirror Images: Technology, Consumption, and the Representation of Gender in American Architecture since World War II," in *The Sex of Architecture*, ed. Diana Agrest, Patricia Conway, and Leslie Kanes Weisman (New York: Harry N. Abrams, 1996), 201.

15. Ruth Asawa to Albert Lanier, September 17, 1948.

16. On Asawa at Black Mountain College, see Mary Emma Harris, "Black Mountain College," in *The Sculpture of Ruth Asawa: Contours in the Air*, ed. Daniell Cornell and Timothy Anglin Burgard, rev. ed. (San Francisco: Fine Arts Museums of San Francisco; Berkeley: University of California Press, 2020), 64–88; and Helen Molesworth with Ruth Erickson, *Leap before You Look: Black Mountain College, 1933–1957*, exh. cat. (New Haven: Yale University Press, 2015).

17. Ruth Asawa, interviewed by Paul Karlstrom, June 21, 2002, Archives of American Art, Smithsonian Institution.

18. Paul Williams to Ruth Asawa and Albert Lanier, March 9, 1950.

19. Albert Lanier to his parents, January 11, 1949.

20. Albert Lanier to Ruth Asawa, September 13, 1948.

21. Albert Lanier to Ruth Asawa, September 13, 1948.

22. Peggy Tolk-Watkins to Ruth Asawa, January 28, 1949; Asawa describes her idea in a letter to Albert Lanier, February 2, 1949.

23. Robert Krauskopf, "Peggy Tolk-Watkins Paints for Kids and Adults," *S.F. Progress* [1961], clipping 2020.19.8.7, Sausalito Historical Society.

24. Alexander Fried, "Women a World Apart: Contrasting a Parisian with a Sausalitan," *San Francisco Examiner*, January 1, 1961, clipping 2020.19.8.10, Sausalito Historical Society.

25. The book is mentioned in Stephen R. Duncan, *The Rebel Café: Sex, Race, and Politics in Cold War America's Nightclub Underground* (Baltimore: Johns Hopkins University Press, 2018), 212. A second edition, published in a run of 100 copies, was illustrated by the sculptor and mixed-media artist Brio Burgess. When Burgess became pregnant in 1971, Tolk-Watkins asked her to illustrate the new edition, which she did "while hanging out in bed trying to carry the baby," and, like Asawa, she mailed the drawings to Tolk-Watkins; see Brio Burgess, *Wail! An American Journey* (Tempe, AZ: Jacobs Ladder Press, 2002), 50.

26. Peggy Tolk-Watkins to Ruth Asawa, January 28, 1949.

27. Ruth Asawa to Peggy Tolk-Watkins, January [day unknown], 1949.

28. Duncan, *The Rebel Café*, 216; Albert Lanier to Mrs. W. H. Lanier [his mother], February 1, 1949.

29. Susan Sontag, "Notebook #21," Sontag Papers, cited in Duncan, *The Rebel Café*, 217. Duncan adds in his footnote that "Peggy Tolk-Watkins" can be found in the original notebook but was omitted from the journal's publication as *Reborn*.

30. Julie Phillips, *The Baby on the Fire Escape: Creativity, Motherhood, and the Mind-Baby Problem* (New York: W. W. Norton, 2022), 196.

31. Albert Lanier to Ruth Asawa, January 5, 1949.

32. Ralph Gleason, cited in Duncan, *The Rebel Café*, 212.

33. Ralph Gleason, cited in Duncan, *The Rebel Café*, 212. Rafael Marin, "Marin Musings," *Daily Independent Journal*, June 2, 1949, 1.

34. Albert Lanier to unknown recipient, February 13, 1949; Albert Lanier to Ruth Asawa, February 12, 1949.

35. Duncan, *The Rebel Café*, 212.

36. Wally Hedrick, cited in Ferrell, *About "The Rose,"* 104–105.

37. Ferrell, *About "The Rose,"* 111.

38. Sally B. Woodbridge, "From the Large-Small House to the Large-Large House," in Woodbridge, *Bay Area Houses*, 183.

39. Albert Lanier cites the September 1948 issue of *Progressive Architecture* in a letter to Ruth Asawa, January 11, 1949.

40. Alan Hess, *Forgotten Modern: California Houses, 1940–1970* (Layton, UT: Gibbs Smith, 2007), 82.

41. Albert Lanier to Ruth Asawa, January 5, 1949.

42. Albert Lanier to Mrs. W. H. Lanier, December 11, 1948.

43. Albert Lanier to Mrs. W. H. Lanier, February 1, 1949; Albert Lanier to Ruth Asawa, January 29, 1949. See also "Minimum House, a Student Project—Black Mountain College," *Arts and Architecture* (April 1949): 30–31. The article is unattributed, but correspondence indicates it was written by Lanier, who drew on Hazel Archer's photographs. John Entenza had reached out to Lanier and Asawa about publishing the article about Minimum House on the recommendation of Anni and Josef Albers.

44. Albert Lanier to Ruth Asawa, January 11, 1949, and February 25, 1949.

45. Albert Lanier to Ruth Asawa, April 18, 1949.

46. Albert Lanier to Ruth Asawa, January 7, 1949.

47. Albert Lanier, "Albert's Stories" (2003), 21, manuscript, Ruth Asawa Lanier, Inc.

48. Lanier, "Albert's Stories" (2003), 22.

49. R. Buckminster Fuller, cited in Ruth Asawa to Albert Lanier, December 29, 1948.

50. Ruth Asawa to Mr. and Mrs. Lanier, July 19, 1949.

51. Ferrell, *About "The Rose,"* 81.

52. Ferrell, *About "The Rose,"* 103.

53. Susan Griffin, "Feminism and Motherhood" (1974), repr. in *Mother Reader: Essential Writings on Motherhood*, ed. Moyra Davey (New York: Seven Stories Press, 2001), 37.

54. Ferrell, *About "The Rose,"* 105–106.

55. Phillips, *The Baby on the Fire Escape*, 149–150.

56. Mignon Nixon, *Fantastic Reality: Louise Bourgeois and a Story of Modern Art* (Cambridge, MA: MIT Press, 2005), 3.

57. Rebecca Jo Plant, *Mom: The Transformation of Motherhood in Modern America* (Chicago: University of Chicago Press, 2010), 3.

58. Ruth Asawa to Mr. and Mrs. Lanier, August 24, 1950.

59. Prudence Martin, "Twin Peaks: The Gradual Taming of a Downtown Slope," *San Francisco Examiner*, February 12, 1961.

60. Michael E. Bry and Harold Gilliam, *Our San Francisco* (San Francisco: Diablo Press, 1964).

61. Lisa Lee Peterson and Clifford Peterson in conversation with the author, March 15, 2022.

62. Merry Renk and Earle Curtis in an unpublished interview, June 17, 2004, Ruth Asawa Lanier, Inc.

63. Sally B. Woodbridge and Judith Lynch Waldhorn, *Victoria's Legacy: Tours of San Francisco Bay Area Architecture* (San Francisco: 101 Productions, 1978), 7.

64. Cited in Randolph Delehanty, *In the Victorian Style* (San Francisco Chronicle Books, 1991), 153.

65. Delehanty, *In the Victorian Style*, 153.

66. Thomas Aidala, *The Great Houses of San Francisco* (New York: Knopf, 1974), 197. See, too, Wesley D. Vail, *San Francisco Victorians: An Account of Domestic Architecture in Victorian San Francisco, 1870–1890* (1964).

67. Kate Millett, "The Debate over Women: Ruskin and Mill," in *Suffer and Be Still: Women in the Victorian Age*, ed. Martha Vicinus (Bloomington: Indiana University Press, 1972), 121–139.

68. This firehouse might have easily belonged to Asawa and Lanier: both Lanier and Adams had been at the auction when it was up for sale, but once Lanier saw that Adams was also there, he refrained from making a bid. Renk's husband Earle Curtis, incidentally, helped with the minimal interior renovations, including installing a circular staircase. Hudson Lanier in conversation with the author, April 13, 2022.

69. Jim Duggins, "Out in the Castro: Creating a Gay Subculture, 1947–1969," in *Out in the Castro: Desire, Promise, Activism*, ed. Winston Leyland (San Francisco: Leyland Publications, 2002), 22.

70. McDowell, *The Householders*, 12 (this and the preceding quotation); italics in original.

71. Asawa observed of her neighborhood on Saturn Street that "it has all the qualities of North Beach but none of the involvement." Asawa, cited in Martin, "Twin Peaks."

72. Sally B. Woodbridge, *Ruth Asawa's San Francisco Fountain: Hyatt on Union Square* (San Francisco: self-published, 1973), 42.

73. Renk and Curtis, unpublished interview, June 17, 2004.

74. On "separate spheres" as one of the "fundamental organizing categories, if not the organizing category of modern British women's history," see Amanda Vickery, "Golden Age to Separate Spheres? A Review of the Categories and Chronology of English Women's History," *Historical Journal* 36 (1993): 389.

75. Albert Lanier to Ruth Asawa, January 29, 1949.

76. Albert Lanier to Ruth Asawa, April 20, 1949.

77. Albert Lanier to Ruth Asawa, April 18, 1949.

78. Albert Lanier to Ruth Asawa, April 20, 1949.

79. Albert Lanier to Ruth Asawa, January 7, 1949; Lanier cites Asawa in this letter.

80. Ruth Asawa to Albert Lanier, February 2, 1949.

81. Renk and Curtis, unpublished interview, June 17, 2004.

82. Lisa Lee Peterson and Clifford Peterson in conversation with the author, March 15, 2022.

83. Renk and Curtis, unpublished interview, June 17, 2004.

84. Caroline A. Jones, *Machine in the Studio: Constructing the Postwar American Artist* (Chicago: University of Chicago, 1996), 40–41.

85. Anne M. Wagner, *Mother Stone: The Vitality of Modern British Sculpture* (New Haven: Yale University Press, 2005), 137–138.

86. Bailey Doogan's contribution to the forum "On Motherhood, Art, and Apple Pie" (1992), in *M/E/A/N/I/N/G: An Anthology of Artists' Writings, Theory, and Criticism*, ed. Susan Bee and Mira Shor (Durham: Duke University Press, 2000), 265.

87. Lucy Lippard, "Changing since *Changing* (1976)," in *The Pink Glass Swan: Selected Essays on Feminist Art: 1970–1993* (New York: New Press, 1995), 33.

88. Lucy Lippard, *Eva Hesse* (New York: New York University Press, 1976), 105, 112.

89. Bernice Stevens Decker, "Artist 'Crochets' Sculptural Forms," *Christian Science Monitor*, July 28, 1959, 6 (this and the preceding quote).

90. Mary Waldon, "Artist Creates amid Marvelous Mess," *Indianapolis Star*, March 14, 1967.

91. Wagner, *Mother Stone*, 138.

92. Gertrude Stein, *Four Saints in Three Acts*, cited in Sally B. Woodbridge, *California Architecture* (San Francisco: Chronicle Books, 1988), 103.

93. Asawa, cited in Helen Molesworth, "'San Francisco Housewife and Mother,'" in *Ruth Asawa: Life's Work*, ed. Tamara Schenkenberg, exh. cat. (St. Louis: Pulitzer Arts Foundation, 2019), 35.

94. Daniel Belasco, *Women Artists in Midcentury America: A History in Ten Exhibitions* (London: Reaktion Books, 2024), 149.

95. Albert Lanier, interview with Alison Isenberg, 2005, Folder 6, Box 117, Asawa Papers.

96. Daniell Cornell, "The Art of Space," in Cornell and Burgard, *The Sculpture of Ruth Asawa: Contours in the Air*, 150, 153.

97. Molesworth, "'San Francisco Housewife and Mother,'" 38.

98. Adrienne Rich, *Of Woman Born: Motherhood as Experience and Institution* (1976; repr., New York: W. W. Norton, 1995), 195, 194.

99. Kenneth L. Ames, *Death in the Dining Room and Other Tales of Victorian Culture* (Philadelphia: Temple University Press, 1992), 236.

CHAPTER 2

1. Norman Brown, *Love's Body* (1966; repr., Berkeley: University of California Press, 1990), 74. The original source for the cited text is unclear. Brown cites William Blake, *The Gates of Paradise*, 771; Heinrich Zimmer, *The King and the Corpse*, 240; and Algernon Charles Swinburne, "Mater Triumphalis." It is likely in reference to the Blake poem he includes: "Thou'rt my Mother from the Womb, / Wife, Sister, Daughter, to the Tomb, / Weaving to Dreams the Sexual strife / And weeping over the Web of Life."

2. Albert Lanier to Erwine Laverne, January 18, 1952 ("wire stuff"); Asawa, draft of a letter to Erwine Laverne, undated (c. 1952), Folder 7, Box 100, Asawa Papers.

3. Alfred Frankenstein, "Some Roses and Some Barbs for the Art Commission's Exhibit," *San Francisco Chronicle*, April 11, 1954, 22.

4. "San Francisco Sculptor Ruth Asawa Lanier Holding One-Man Show at New York Gallery, Learned Her Art Basis from Mexico Kiddies," *Hokubei Mainichi*, undated [1954], Folder 2, Box 243, Asawa Papers.

5. Nancy Gray, "World of Wire: Sculpture Comes from Crocheting," *San Francisco Examiner*, May 12, 1957, 4.

6. Ann Reynolds, "Lessons in Transparency: Ruth Asawa in Mexico," in *In a Cloud, in a Wall, in a Chair: Six Modernists in Mexico at Midcentury*, ed. Zoë Ryan, exh. cat. (Chicago: Art Institute of Chicago, 2019), 177.

7. Emily K. Doman Jennings, "Critiquing the Critique: Early Reception," in *The Sculpture of Ruth Asawa: Contours in the Air*, ed. Daniell Cornell and Timothy Anglin Burgard, rev. ed. (San Francisco: Fine Arts Museums of San Francisco; Berkeley: University of California Press, 2020), 161.

8. Elissa Auther, *String, Felt, Thread: The Hierarchy of Art and Craft in American Art* (Minneapolis: University of Minnesota Press, 2010), 22.

9. Lucy Lippard, "Household Images in Art," *Ms.* 1, no. 9 (March 1973), repr. in Lippard, *From the Center: Feminist Essays on Women's Art* (New York: E. P. Dutton, 1976), 57.

10. Rozsika Parker, *The Subversive Stitch: Embroidery and the Making of the Feminine* (New York: Routledge, 1989), 17 and 2.

11. Janet Koplos and Bruce Metcalf, *Makers: A History of American Studio Craft* (Chapel Hill: University of North Carolina Press, 2010), 238.

12. Helen Molesworth, "Drawing after Dinner," in *Ruth Asawa: All Is Possible,* ed. Helen Molesworth, exh. cat. (New York: David Zwirner, 2022), 9.

13. Marilyn Chase, *Everything She Touched: The Life of Ruth Asawa* (San Francisco: Chronicle Books, 2020), 75.

14. For an overview of these categories, see Aiko Cuneo, Addie Lanier, and Tamara H. Schenkenberg, "Evolution of Forms," in *Ruth Asawa: Life's Work*, ed. Tamara H. Schenkenberg, exh. cat. (St. Louis: Pulitzer Arts Foundation, 2019), 130–144.

15. *The Oakland Art Museum California Sculptors' Annual Exhibition for 1959*, exhibition brochure with text by Paul Mills, Folder 4, Box 110, Asawa Papers.

16. Asawa, cited in Ruth Miller, "Her Ingenious Way with Dough," *San Francisco Chronicle*, December 26, 1963, 26.

17. Ruth Asawa, application to the Guggenheim Foundation, 1955, Folder 2, Box 129, Asawa Papers.

18. See my "Drawing Lessons: Ruth Asawa's Early Work on Paper," in *Object Lessons: The Bauhaus and Harvard*, ed. Laura Muir, exh. cat. (Cambridge, MA: Harvard University Art Museums, 2021), 163.

19. The first quote comes from the exhibition brochure *The Oakland Art Museum California Sculptors' Annual Exhibition for 1959*, while the second comes from a Design Research Inc. brochure, Folder 2, Box 110, Asawa Papers.

20. See the letter from Ray Johnson to Ruth Asawa (RJ.027), c. 1952, private collection. The quote in the previous sentence is from Erwine Laverne to Albert Lanier, January 2, 1952, Folder 7, Box 100, Asawa Papers.

21. Ruth Asawa to Jack Miller, September 17, 1952, Folder 8, Box 100, Asawa Papers.

22. Albert Lanier to Erwine Laverne, January 18, 1952, Folder 8, Box 100, Asawa Papers.

23. See Box 275, Asawa Papers.

24. Ruth Asawa in Katie Simon, "A Conversation with Ruth Asawa, Artist," in Schenkenberg, *Ruth Asawa: Life's Work*, 16. Another account of the episode is given in Ruth Asawa to Celia Sieverts, January 31, 1950.

25. Cited in Daniel Belasco, *Women Artists in Midcentury America: A History in Ten Exhibitions* (London: Reaktion Books, 2024), 133.

26. Ruth Asawa to Chester LeMaistre, undated [1953], Folder 10, Box 100, Asawa Papers.

27. "April, 1965, Invoice #4," in *Ray Johnson Ray Johnson*, ed. William S. Wilson (New York: Between Books, 1977), n.p. My thanks to Johanna Gosse for bringing this to my attention.

28. Elizabeth Wayland Barber, *Women's Work: The First 20,000 Years: Women, Cloth, and Society in Early Times* (New York: W. W. Norton, 1994), 29. See also Lisa Baraitser, *Maternal Encounters: The Ethics of Interruption* (New York: Routledge, 2008).

29. Barber, *Women's Work*, 30.

30. "Asawa," *Domus*, August 1952, 34 (translation sent to Asawa by a colleague in New York), Folder 2, Box 243, Asawa Papers. See also "Interno di una sala d'esposizione a New York: Estelle e Erwine Laverne," *Domus*, August 1952, 35–37.

31. Erwine Laverne to Ruth Asawa, September 18, 1953, Folder 7, Box 100, Asawa Papers. He also suggested introducing color, which she apparently did by painting the pieces and probably also through the incorporation of colored wire. See the letters between Albert Lanier and Erwine Laverne, February 4 and February 12, 1952, Folder 7, Box 100, Asawa Papers.

32. See Belasco, *Women Artists in Midcentury America*, 135 and 143.

33. Toni Greenbaum, "Constructivism and American Studio Jewelry, 1940 to the Present," *Studies in the Decorative Arts* 6, no. 1 (Fall-Winter 1998–1999): 77.

34. Merry Renk, "Design Autobiography," *Goldsmith's Journal* 6, no. 3 (Summer 1980): 28.

35. Merry Renk, "Brancusi as Oracle," 2, Renk Papers, Archives of American Art, Smithsonian Institution.

36. Renk, "Design Autobiography," 28.

37. Margaret De Patta, "De Patta," *Design Quarterly*, no. 33 (1955): 6, Renk Papers (this and the next quotation).

38. Renk, "Design Autobiography," 28.

39. Sarah Knott, *Mother Is a Verb: An Unconventional History* (New York: Farrar, Straus and Giroux, 2019).

40. Bernice Stevens Decker, "Couple Make Sculptured Jewelry," *Christian Science Monitor*, November 24, 1958, 10.

41. De Patta quickly corrected the mistake, writing to Decker that it was Ruth Asawa who had made the hanging wire object; see the file "Miscellaneous Correspondence" in the De Patta Papers, Archives of American Art. The correction led Decker to write a feature on Asawa: Bernice Stevens Decker, "Artist 'Crochets' Sculptural Forms," *Christian Science Monitor*, July 28, 1959, 6. And after Asawa pointed out to Decker the importance of Cunningham's photographs, Decker wrote a piece on Cunningham, too: "Years Add Camera Skill," *Christian Science Monitor*, October 1, 1959, 16. See also Asawa to Bernice Decker, February 26, 1959, Folder 1, Box 6, Asawa Papers.

42. Ruth Asawa, in "Art, Competence, and Citywide Cooperation for San Francisco," an oral history conducted in 1974 and 1976 by Harriet Nathan, Regional Oral History Office, The Bancroft Library, University of California, Berkeley, 1980. 36.

43. See Isabel Bird, "Doubled Abstraction: Ruth Asawa's Stamp and Its Afterlife," *Art History* 46, no. 3 (June 2023): 568–596.

44. John Potvin, "The Materials of Shame: Decoration, Masculinity, and the Birth of Modern Interior Design," *Art Bulletin* 106, no. 1 (March 2024): 17.

45. The quotation comes from an exhibition brochure of the Ross Widen Gallery in Cleveland, Ohio, Folder 4, Box 110, Asawa Papers.

46. Edgar Kaufmann, *What Is Modern Design?* (New York: Museum of Modern Art, 1951), 8.

47. John Entenza to Albert Lanier, February 20, 1952; see also Erwine Laverne to Albert Lanier, September 14, 1951, Folder 7, Box 100, Asawa Papers. Correspondence from September 1951 indicates that Laverne had inquired after someone who could design his new exhibition space in San Francisco. At the time, Laverne also asked about Asawa's textile designs.

48. Joy F. Ross, "The Levities of Laverne: New 57th Street Headquarters," *Interiors* 111, no. 8 (March 1952), reprinted in a brochure published by Laverne Originals Inc., Folder 1, Box 243, Asawa Papers (this and following quotations).

49. Richard Petterson, "A Climate for Craft Art," *Craft Horizons* 16, no. 5 (September-October 1956): 11.

50. Dorothy Giles, "The Craftsman in America," brochure published on the occasion of the exhibition *Designer Craftsmen U.S.A. 1953*, 11, Renk Papers, Archives of American Art.

51. Lucy R. Lippard, "Making Something from Nothing (Towards a Definition of Women's Hobby Art)," *Heresies: A Feminist Publication on Art and Politics* 1, no. 4 (Winter 1978): 63.

52. Petterson, "A Climate for Craft Art," 11.

53. See for instance "A House Divided," *Arts and Architecture* 66 (January 1949): 27–30.

54. Sally B. Woodbridge, "The California House," in *Bay Area Houses*, ed. Woodbridge, rev. ed. (1976; Salt Lake City: Peregrine Smith, 1988), 83.

55. "San Francisco Houses," *Life*, September 5, 1949, 51, 44, 45.

56. Jenelle Porter, correspondence with the author, October 9, 2020. Christensen taught the Alexander and Feldenkrais methods for residents in retirement homes, according to Christensen's daughter in conversation with Porter.

57. Jenelle Porter, "Sculpture for a Dancer," in *Making Strange: The Chara Schreyer Collection*, ed. Douglas Fogle and Hanneke Skerath (New York: DelMonico Books, 2021), 145.

58. Louis Pollock to Ruth Asawa, April 18, 1961, Folder 11, Box 101, Asawa Papers.

59. Albert Lanier to John Entenza, May 5, 1952, Folder 8, Box 100, Asawa Papers.

60. See a receipt dated August 29, 1960, Folder 10, Box 101, Asawa Papers.

61. "Checklist from first jurying of Designer Craftsman Competition 1953," Box 42, Folder 19, San Francisco Museum of Modern Art Archives. Asawa's submission was accepted to the first jurying, but the results of this first competition were so dismal that Morley called for a second jurying, and Renk and Asawa did not resubmit. See also Belasco, *Women Artists in Midcentury America*, 138–139, on Morley's support of craft and design.

62. See the list of entries in the exhibition files at the San Francisco Museum of Modern Art Archives, Folder 8, Box 32.

63. Albert Lanier to Grace L. McCann Morley, September 15, 1953, Folder 11, Box 100, Asawa Papers.

64. Grace L. McCann Morely to Albert Lanier, September 21, 1953, Folder 11, Box 100, Asawa Papers.

65. Marguerite Wildenhain to Albert Lanier, August 17, 1953, Folder 11, Box 100, Asawa Papers.

66. Albert Lanier to Mrs. W. H. Lanier, April 7, 1949. He gifted a vase to his cousin, who responded, "my pond-farm-piece is wonderful. I fear I'll never put flowers in it—it is too beautiful without them"; see Laurie Pearson to Albert Lanier, April 30, 1949.

67. Wildenhain's house was originally built by her and Gordon Herr in 1942; she lived there until her death in 1985. It was a single-room cabin, twelve by twenty feet, with two rooms added in 1948. In 1962, Albert Lanier designed and built a guest house for the property, a symmetrical one-story building in a squat T-shape in close proximity to the barn and with a low-pitched gable roof with a windowed shed-roofed monitor on the front of the house for additional light. Built-in cabinets were later added. See Pond Farm Pottery Historic District, National Register of Historic Places Registration Form, 2014, https://www.nps.gov/nr/feature/places/pdfs/14000307.pdf.

68. Lippard, "Making Something from Nothing," 65.

69. Anni Albers, "Conversations with Artists" (1961), in *On Designing* (Middletown, CT: Wesleyan University Press, 1962), 62.

70. Ruth Asawa, application to the Guggenheim Foundation, 1959, Folder 5, Box 129, Asawa Papers.

71. Kay Sekimachi, "The Weaver's Weaver: Explorations in Multiple Layers and Three-Dimensional Fiber Art," an oral history conducted in 1993 by Harriet Nathan, Regional Oral History Office, The Bancroft Library, University of California, Berkeley, 1996, 13.

72. Ruth Asawa to Peggy Tolk-Watkins, January 1949, on "understanding Trudi [sic] G. more and more . . . her longings are not only for one, but hundreds of things, necessary and unnecessary things."

73. Undated letter from Trude Guermonprez, Aronson-Jalowetz family collection, New Jersey.

74. Yoshiko Uchida, "Trude Guermonprez," *Craft Horizons* 19, no. 2 (March/April 1959): 30.

75. Guermonprez, cited in Uchida, "Trude Guermonprez," 30.

76. A. James Speyer, "Art News from Chicago," *ArtNews* (January 1957): 52, 62, cited in Gerald Nordland, *Ruth Asawa: A Retrospective View* (San Francisco: San Francisco Museum of Art, 1973), n.p.

77. Merry Renk, "Folded Silver Hairband, 1954," Renk Papers, Archives of American Art.

78. John Entenza wanted to publish material on the San Francisco Laverne showroom in *Arts and Architecture*, writing: "incidentally, there are great stories about Ruth's folded papers, whatever they are." See John Entenza to Ruth and Albert Lanier, February 20, 1952, Folder 8, Box 100, Asawa Papers.

79. Renk, "Folded Silver Hairband, 1954" (this and the preceding quote). See also the oral history interview with Merry Renk conducted by Arline M. Fisch for the Archives of American Art, Smithsonian Institution, January 18–19, 2001.

80. Jeffrey Saletnik, *Josef Albers, Late Modernism, and Pedagogic Form* (Chicago: University of Chicago Press, 2022), 108.

81. Asawa, cited in Nordland, *Ruth Asawa*, n.p.

82. Saletnik, *Josef Albers, Late Modernism, and Pedagogic Form*, 100.

83. Judith Butler, *Bodies That Matter: On the Discursive Limits of Sex* (New York: Routledge, 1993), 31.

84. See Renk, interview with Fisch, Archives of American Art.

85. Merry Renk, cited in *Craft Horizons*, special issue on California (September-October 1956): 28.

86. "'Media Explored 1967' Theme: Work of 112 Artists from Across Country on Display," *Daily Pilot, Orange Coast Weekender* (April 7, 1967), 6. One of Asawa's tied-wire star sculptures was included in the show, organized by "artist-craftsman" Dextra Frankel for the Laguna Beach Art Association.

87. Dextra Frankel and Bernard Kester, *The Intersection of Line*, exh. cat. (Fullerton: California State Fullerton, 1968), n.p.

88. Correspondence between the author and Debra Winters, Visual Resources Specialist, California State University Fullerton, March 9, 2020.

89. Auther, *String, Felt, Thread*, 40. See also Mildred Constantine and Jack Lenor Larsen, *Beyond Craft: The Art Fabric* (New York: Van Nostrand, 1972).

90. Constantine and Larsen, *Beyond Craft*, 31.

91. Lippard, "Making Something from Nothing," 64, 65. See also Auther's discussion in *String, Felt, Thread* of the housewife "as a key figure in critical considerations of fiber art, where she functions as a signifier for amateurism and lack of creativity" (23).

92. Xavier Lanier, interviewed by Marilyn Chase, August 2, 2017; cited in Chase, *Everything She Touched*, 78.

93. Christopher Reed, introduction to *Not at Home: The Suppression of Domesticity in Modern Art and Architecture*, ed. Christopher Reed (London: Thames and Hudson, 1996), 15.

94. Albert Lanier to Erwine Laverne, January 18, 1952 ("wire stuff"); Ruth Asawa, draft of a letter to Erwine Laverne, undated (c. 1952), Folder 7, Box 100, Asawa Papers.

95. See the dossier of letters in Joan Pearson Watkins, Artist File, 1951–1957, San Francisco Art Institute Legacy Foundation and Archives.

96. Margaret White, "Art, Creativity, and the Home Fires," *Ladies' Home Journal*, June 1964, 66.

PART II

1. This quotation is from Käthe Kollwitz's diaries, as published in *Life in Art*, ed. and trans. Mina C. Klein and H. Arthur Klein (New York: Holt, Rinehart and Winston, 1972); it is transcribed here as it appears in Tillie Olsen's *Silences* (1978; repr., New York: Feminist Press, 2003), 211.

2. Anne M. Wagner, *Mother Stone. The Vitality of Modern British Sculpture* (New Haven: Yale University Press, 2005), 59.

3. Wagner, *Mother Stone*, 52. Wagner relies on Eugenia Herbert and S. Toulmin and J. Goodfield, *The Architecture of Matter* (1962).

4. For this argument, see David Summers, "Form and Gender," *New Literary History* 24, no. 2 (1993): 245–247.

5. Summers, "Form and Gender," 249

6. Wagner, *Mother Stone*, 72.

7. Honoré de Balzac, cited in Olsen, *Silences*, 12.

8. Henry James, cited in Olsen, *Silences*, 12.

9. Susan Stanford Friedman, "Creativity and the Childbirth Metaphor: Gender Difference in Literary Discourse," *Feminist Studies* 13, no. 1 (Spring 1987): 49.

10. Helen Molesworth, "Drawing after Dinner," in *Ruth Asawa: All Is Possible*, ed. Helen Molesworth, exh. cat. (New York: David Zwirner, 2022), 10. See also Molesworth's invocation of "allusions to cells, embryos, fetuses, and whole human bodies" in her "'San Francisco Housewife and Mother,'" in *Ruth Asawa: Life's Work*, ed. Tamara H. Schenkenberg, exh. cat. (St. Louis: Pulitzer Arts Foundation, 2019), 41.

11. Friedman lays out feminist positions for and against the childbirth metaphor, including specific references to Cixous, de Beauvoir, and Nina Auerbach, among several others; see Friedman, "Creativity and the Childbirth Metaphor," 50.

12. Quoted in "Josef Albers, Artist and Teacher, Dies," *New York Times*, March 26, 1976, cited in Marilyn Chase, *Everything She Touched: The Life of Ruth Asawa* (San Francisco: Chronicle Books, 2020), 127.

13. Ruth Asawa, interviewed by Paul Karlstrom, June 21, 2002, Archives of American Art, Smithsonian Institution.

CHAPTER 3

1. Adrienne Rich, cited in Susan Griffin, *Woman and Nature: The Roaring Inside Her* (New York: Harper & Row, 1978), 200.

2. Sally B. Woodbridge diary, February 21, 1961, Woodbridge Family Archive.

3. Imogen Cunningham, *After Ninety* (Seattle: University of Washington Press, 1977).

4. Susan Ehrens, "'Making It Mine as Well as Hers': Ruth Asawa and Imogen Cunningham," in *The Sculpture of Ruth Asawa: Contours in the Air*, ed. Daniell Cornell and Timothy Anglin Burgard, rev. ed. (San Francisco: Fine Arts Museums of San Francisco; Berkeley: University of California Press, 2020), 171.

5. Whitney Chadwick and Isabelle de Courtivron, eds., *Significant Others: Creativity and Intimate Partnership* (London: Thames and Hudson, 1993), 7.

6. Ruth Perry and Martine Watson Brownley, eds., *Mothering the Mind: Twelve Studies of Writers and Their Silent Partners* (New York: Holmes and Meier, 1984); cited in Chadwick and de Courtivron, *Significant Others*, 8.

7. Lisa Tickner, "Mediating Generation: The Mother-Daughter Plot," in *Women Artists at the Millennium*, ed. Carol Armstrong and Catherine de Zegher (Cambridge, MA: MIT Press, 2006), 87.

8. Jonathan Fineberg, *The Innocent Eye: Children's Art and the Modern Artist* (Princeton: Princeton University Press, 1997), 209. For a summation of this trope, see especially the first chapter in Fineberg, *The Innocent Eye*, 2–27. On childhood as a broad topic for modern artists, see Juliet Kinchin and Aiden O'Connor, eds., *Century of the Child: Growing by Design, 1900–2000*, exh. cat. (New York: Museum of Modern Art, 2012); and Ruth Erickson, ed., *To Begin Again: Artists and Childhood* (Boston: Institute of Contemporary Art, 2022).

9. Imogen Cunningham to Elizabeth Broun, November 25, 1973, Imogen Cunningham Papers, Archives of American Art, Smithsonian Institution.

10. Imogen Cunningham, in "Imogen Cunningham: Portraits, Ideas, and Design," an interview conducted by Edna Tartaul Daniel in June 1959, University of California, Berkeley, Regional Cultural History Project, 1961, 18–19.

11. Carol Armstrong, "From Clementina to Käsebier: The Photographic Attainment of the 'Lady Amateur,'" *October* 91 (Winter 2000): 132.

12. Judith Fryer Davidov, *Women's Camera Work: Self/Body/Other in American Visual Culture* (Durham: Duke University Press, 1998), 332.

13. Imogen Cunningham to Roi Partridge, August 11, 1916; cited in Richard Lorenz, *Imogen Cunningham: Ideas without End* (San Francisco: Chronicle Books, 1993), 21.

14. Unpublished lecture by Cunningham, cited in Lorenz, *Imogen Cunningham: Ideas without End*, 24.

15. Consuelo Kanaga, interview by Margaretta K. Mitchell, *Recollections: Ten Women of Photography* (New York: Viking, 1979), 159; cited in Davidov, *Women's Camera Work*, 467n78.

16. Imogen Cunningham to Roi Partridge, August 18, 1916, cited in Lorenz, *Imogen Cunningham: Ideas without End*, 21.

17. Carol Armstrong, "Cupid's Pencil of Light: Julia Margaret Cameron and the Maternalization of Photography," *October* 76 (Spring 1996): 115; on the Narcissus myth, see also Tickner, "Mediating Generation," 91.

18. Margery Mann, introduction to *Imogen Cunningham: Photographs* (Seattle: University of Washington Press, 1970), n.p.

19. Davidov, *Women's Camera Work*, 331–332.

20. Armstrong, "Cupid's Pencil of Light," 117.

21. Alan Simms Lee to Imogen Cunningham, October 17, 1920, cited in Lorenz, *Imogen Cunningham: Ideas without End*, 24.

22. Imogen Cunningham, "Photography as a Profession for Women" (1913), in *Imogen Cunningham: Selected Texts and Bibliography*, ed. Amy Rule (Boston: G. K. Hall, 1992), 49.

23. Meg Cunningham, correspondence with the author, June 6, 2024.

24. Imogen Cunningham to Ruth Asawa and Albert Lanier, August 17, 1951, Folder 1, Box 6, Asawa Papers.

25. Pamela Woodbridge, in conversation with the author, April 14, 2022. See also Marina Warner, *From the Beast to the Blond: On Fairy Tales and Their Tellers* (London: Vintage, 1994), 211.

26. See Armstrong, "From Clementina to Käsebier," 103, and especially footnote 4 in which Armstrong traces this identification of the mother with the amateur family photographer to turn-of-the-century advertisements for mass-market Kodak cameras.

27. Ruth Asawa, application to the Guggenheim Foundation, 1952, 3, Folder 1, Box 129, Asawa Papers.

28. See Makeda Best's discussion of these shared formal interests in her essay "Spaces of Relation," in *Ruth Asawa: All Is Possible*, ed. Helen Molesworth, exh. cat. (New York: David Zwirner, 2022), 95.

29. Catherine de Zegher, "The Inside Is the Outside," in Armstrong and de Zegher, *Women Artists at the Millennium*, 216.

30. De Zegher, "The Inside Is the Outside," 215.

31. The ERC-funded research project "Better Understanding the Metaphysics of Pregnancy" (2016–2022), led by Elselijn Kingma at the University of Southampton and King's College London, explores the philosophical problems that pregnancy presents, including questions around the nature of the relationship between the fetus and the maternal body, and the exact point at which one person or organism becomes two entities.

32. Adrienne Rich, *Of Woman Born: Motherhood as Experience and Institution* (1976; repr., New York: W. W. Norton, 1995), 64; italics in original. Rich here has in mind Freud's essay "On Negation," in which he lays out that "fundamental split" which "divides the 'inner' from the 'outer,'" generating the individual.

33. Diana Fuss, "Inside/Out," in *Inside/Out: Lesbian Theories, Gay Theories*, ed. Diana Fuss (New York: Routledge, 1991), 2.

34. Kenneth L. Ames, *Death in the Dining Room and Other Tales of Victorian Culture* (Philadelphia: Temple University Press, 1992), 216 (previous sentence) and 217.

35. Lorenz, *Imogen Cunningham: Ideas without End*, 50 (this and the following quotation).

36. Ruth Erickson, "Wide-Awake," in Molesworth, *Ruth Asawa: All Is Possible*, 32.

37. Erickson, "Wide-Awake," 34.

38. Rich, *Of Woman Born*, 31.

39. Tille Olsen, *Silences* (1978; repr., New York: Feminist Press, 2003), 18–19.

40. Sarah Knott, *Mother Is a Verb: An Unconventional History* (New York: Farrar, Straus and Giroux, 2019), 119.

41. Knott, *Mother Is a Verb*, 116.

42. Thomas Albright, "'USA in Your Heart' Show," *San Francisco Chronicle*, July 24, 1969; also "The Summer Art Scene," *San Francisco Chronicle*, July 23, 1969.

43. Albright, "'USA in Your Heart' Show." See Erin O'Toole's mention of *Hair Skirt* in the context of this transformation of photography: O'Toole, "Delightful Anxiety: Photography in California circa 1970," in *The Photographic Object 1970*, ed. Mary Statzer (Berkeley: University of California Press, 2016), 98–99.

44. Marcia Pointon, "Casts, Imprints, and the Deathliness of Things: Artefacts at the Edge," *Art Bulletin* 96, no. 2 (June 2014): 177. On Krauss, referenced in the following sentence, see Pointon's discussion on this page.

45. "Famed Photographer, Octogenarian, Has Poetic Approach with Camera," *The Arrow of Pi Beta Phi*, 1970, 9. Imogen Cunningham File, San Francisco Art Institute Legacy Foundation and Archive.

46. Rich, *Of Woman Born*, 25.

47. Albert Lanier to Erwine Laverne, December 30, 1951, Folder 7, Box 100, Asawa Papers.

48. Ruth Asawa to Bernice Stevens Decker, February 26, 1959, Folder 1, Box 6, Asawa Papers.

49. Margaretta Mitchell, introduction to Cunningham, *After Ninety*, 9.

50. Mann, introduction to *Imogen Cunningham: Photographs*, n.p.

51. Ruth Asawa and Albert Lanier in conversation with Susan Ehrens, January 1, 1983; see also Aiko Cuneo and Addie Lanier in conversation with Ehrens, August 24, 2018, cited in Ehrens, "'Making It Mine as Well as Hers,'" 309n13.

52. Imogen Cunningham to Ansel Adams, February 9, 1967; cited in Davidov, *Women's Camera Work*, 325. Davidov comments here in a note about the gendered reception of Cunningham, noting that "women—critics and theorists, curators, collectors, other photographers—are overwhelmingly positive in their responses to her work, often taking her 'as a kind of lodestar,' whereas many men (though by no means all)—especially other photographers—criticize her technique (Brett Weston, Ansel Adams, Morley Baer) or find that 'her photographs don't do for me what those of some other photographers do,' as Stephen Goldstine expresses it" (Davidov, *Women's Camera Work*, 463n56). Minor White would be one of the exceptions. Asawa's comment about cataloging her work can be found in Ruth Asawa to Brenda Danilowitz, July 28, 2001, Josef and Anni Albers Foundation, Bethany, CT.

53. Lorenz, *Imogen Cunningham: Ideas without End*, 9; he cites a 1970 *New York Times* review.

54. Imogen Cunningham to John Granville, June 7, 1973, Imogen Cunningham Papers, Archives of American Art, cited in Davidov, *Women's Camera Work*, 385.

55. Ruth Asawa, untitled Older Woman's Speech, November 9, 1989, Ruth Asawa Lanier, Inc.

56. Imogen Cunningham, letter to John Simon Guggenheim Foundation, November 3, 1956; cited in Ehrens, "'Making It Mine as Well as Hers,'" 171 (this and the preceding quotation).

57. Asawa, untitled Older Woman's Speech, November 9, 1989.

58. Gertrude Stein, "Many Many Women," in *The Gertrude Stein Reader*, ed. Richard Kostelanetz (New York: Cooper Square Press, 2002), 213.

59. Richard Kostelanetz, introduction to *The Gertrude Stein Reader*, xxv.

60. Kostelanetz, introduction, xxxiv; Barbaralee Diamonstein, *Open Secrets* (New York: Viking Press, 1972), 79. In her interview with Diamonstein, Cunningham cites Asawa as one of the women whom she most respects.

61. Mignon Nixon, *Fantastic Reality: Louise Bourgeois and a Story of Modern Art* (Cambridge, MA: MIT Press, 2005), 43–44.

62. Tickner, "Mediating Generation," 88, 91.

63. Tickner, "Mediating Generation," 91.

CHAPTER 4

1. Ruth Asawa, in Robert Snyder (dir.), *Ruth Asawa: Of Forms and Growth* (Santa Barbara, CA: Masters and Masterworks, 1978), video, 30 min.

2. Ruth Asawa, in "Art, Competence, and Citywide Cooperation for San Francisco," an oral history conducted in 1974 and 1976 by Harriet Nathan, Regional Oral History Office, The Bancroft Library, University of California, Berkeley, 1980, 35.

3. Adrienne Rich, *Of Woman Born: Motherhood as Experience and Institution* (1976; repr., New York: W. W. Norton, 1995), xxxiv.

4. Prospectus for *Ruth Asawa: Of Forms and Growth*, Folder 3, Box 5, Asawa Papers. The feminist critique of the identification of woman with nature is too vast to cite here, but an exemplary instance can be found in Susan Griffin, *Woman and Nature: The Roaring inside Her* (New York: Harper & Row, 1978).

5. Robert Snyder to Buckminster Fuller, January 29, 1974, Folder 3, Box 5, Asawa Papers.

6. Ruth Asawa to John Hoare Kerr (National Endowment for the Arts), August 6, 1974, Folder 3, Box 5, Asawa Papers.

7. Ruth Asawa, application to the Guggenheim Foundation, 1952, Folder 1, Box 129, Asawa Papers. "The work is one which dictates a way of growing and the more one learns about this way of growing the more possibilities are opened up for the creating of sculpture peculiar to the process."

8. Heather MacDonald, "Information and Illusion: Botany and Painting at the Turn of the Nineteenth Century," in *Working among Flowers: Floral Still-Life Painting in Nineteenth-Century France*, exh. cat. (Dallas: Dallas Museum of Art, 2014), 7.

9. Paul Taylor, *Dutch Flower Painting, 1600–1720* (New Haven: Yale University Press, 1995), 47.

10. Annette Scott, "Floral Femininity: A Pictorial Definition," *American Art* 6, no. 2 (Spring 1992): 60–77.

11. Albert Lanier to Olga Gueft, May 21, 1967, Folder 1, Box 127, Asawa Papers.

12. Karen Higa, "What Is an Asian American Woman Artist?," in *Art/Women/California, 1950–2000: Parallels and Intersections*, ed. Diana Burgess Fuller and Daniela Salvioni (Berkeley: University of California Press, 2002), 81–94.

13. Helen Molesworth, "Drawing after Dinner," in *Ruth Asawa: All Is Possible*, ed. Helen Molesworth, exh. cat. (New York: David Zwirner, 2022), 14.

14. Baunnie Sea, email communication with the author, January 3, 2024.

15. Josef Albers, cited in Marilyn Chase, *Everything She Touched: The Life of Ruth Asawa* (San Francisco: Chronicle Books, 2020), 68.

16. Anne M. Wagner, *Three Artists (Three Women): Modernism and the Art of Hesse, Krasner, and O'Keeffe* (Berkeley: University of California Press, 1996), 60.

17. Imogen Cunningham, interviewed by Barnaby Conrad III, "Photography: An Interview with Imogen Cunningham," *Art in America* (May/June 1977): 47.

18. Imogen Cunningham to Ansel Adams, June 15, 1970, Imogen Cunningham Papers, roll 1639; cited in Richard Lorenz, *Imogen Cunningham: Ideas without End* (San Francisco: Chronicle Books, 1993), 57.

19. Mai K. Arbegast, cited in Judy Dater, *Imogen Cunningham* (Boston: New York Graphic Society, 1979), 50–51.

20. Arbegast, cited in Dater, *Imogen Cunningham*, 49.

21. Ruth Asawa, presentation at Tamarind Lithography Workshop, audio recording, August 29, 1965, Tamarind Institute Records (MSS 574, Box 31, CD 20), Center for Southwest Research, University Libraries, University of New Mexico, Albuquerque.

22. Ruth Asawa to Josef Albers, April 26, 1963, Folder 3, Box 1, Asawa Papers.

23. Ruth Asawa interviewed in Snyder (dir.), *Ruth Asawa: Of Forms and Growth*.

24. Gerald Nordland, *Ruth Asawa: A Retrospective View,* exh. cat. (San Francisco: San Francisco Museum of Art, 1973), n.p.

25. Joan Pearson Watkins, "Opulent and Organic: The Jewelry of Merry Renk," *American Craft* 41, no. 2 (April/May 1981): 33.

26. Watkins, "Opulent and Organic," 35.

27. This document is in the Merry Renk Papers, Archives of American Art, Smithsonian Institution.

28. See Nordland, *Ruth Asawa*; and Gerald Nordland, "Ruth Asawa: Ankrum Gallery," *Artforum* 1, no. 1 (June 1962): 8.

29. Norman Bryson, "Still Life and 'Feminine' Space," in *Looking at the Overlooked: Four Essays on Still Life Painting* (Cambridge, MA: Harvard University Press, 1990), 136.

30. Bryson, "Still Life," 172; italics in original.

31. Bryson, "Still Life," 173.

32. Alexander Fried, "Drawings by Ruth Asawa: Sculptor's Other Talent," 1969, clipping in Folder 5, Box 244, Asawa Papers.

33. Martica Sawin, "Fortnight in Review," *Arts Digest,* December 15, 1954, 22; cited in Nordland, *Ruth Asawa*, n.p. The previous quotation from Nordland also appears here.

34. Joseph Goldyne, "Committed to the Line: Prints and Drawings by Beth Van Hoesen," in *Beth Van Hoesen: The Observant Eye* (Fresno: Fresno Art Museum, 2009), 17.

35. Jack Burnham, *Beyond Modern Sculpture* (New York: G. Braziller, 1968), 68.

36. Burnham, *Beyond Modern Sculpture*, 80–81.

37. Burnham, *Beyond Modern Sculpture*, 126, quoting Albert E. Elsen, *Rodin* (New York: Museum of Modern Art, 1963).

38. Clement Greenberg, "The New Sculpture" (1949), in *The Collected Essays and Criticism*, ed. John O'Brian (Chicago: University of Chicago Press, 1986–1993), 2:318.

39. Greenberg, "The New Sculpture," 318.

40. Millie Robbins, "This Sculpture Is for the Birds," *San Francisco Chronicle*, May 18, 1960; italics in original.

41. Stephen Beck, cited in *California Video: Artists and Histories*, ed. Glenn Phillips (Los Angeles: Getty Research Institute, 2008), 43.

42. Anne M. Wagner, *Mother Stone: The Vitality of Modern British Sculpture* (New Haven: Yale University Press, 2005), 155.

43. Burnham, *Beyond Modern Sculpture*, 68.

44. Nordland, *Ruth Asawa*, n.p.

45. Nordland, *Ruth Asawa*, n.p.

46. Jennifer L. Roberts, "The Mimeograph and the Chrysanthemum," in Molesworth, *Ruth Asawa: All Is Possible*, 144, 146.

47. Jason Vartikar, "Ruth Asawa's Early Wire Sculpture and a Biology of Equality," *American Art* 34, no. 1 (Spring 2020): 3, 6.

48. John Yau, "Ruth Asawa: Shifting the Terms of Sculpture," in *Ruth Asawa: Objects and Apparitions* (New York: Christie's, 2013), 19.

49. Clement Greenberg, "David Smith," *Art in America* (Winter 1956–1957), reprinted in *The Collected Essays and Criticism*, 3:276.

50. Rosalind E. Krauss, *Passages in Modern Sculpture* (1977; repr., Cambridge, MA: MIT Press, 1981), 33.

51. Natania Meeker and Antónia Szabari, *Radical Botany: Plants and Speculative Fiction* (New York: Fordham University Press, 2020), 182.

CHAPTER 5

1. Susan Griffin, *Woman and Nature: The Roaring inside Her* (New York: Harper & Row, 1978), 1.

2. Albert Morch, "'Best Tressed' Women Named," *San Francisco Examiner*, January 9, 1969, 15.

3. David Sawyer to Ruth Asawa, January 20, 1969, Folder 5, Box 117; cited in Alison Isenberg, *Designing San Francisco* (Princeton, NJ: Princeton University Press, 2017), 102.

4. Isenberg, *Designing San Francisco*, 110.

5. Ruth Asawa, "My Thoughts on the Ghirardelli Square Fountain Sculpture," Folder 117, Box 8, Asawa Papers. Asawa had initially planned a child to be the figurative element and toyed with the idea of four figures based on her eldest daughter Aiko, evidenced by a 1966 drawing.

6. Lawrence Halprin, "Statement on the New Sculpture in the Fountain at Ghirardelli Square," March 22, 1968, Halprin Papers, Architectural Archives, University of Pennsylvania. This and the following quotation are from the statement. Halprin's reference to camp is from his letter to William M. Roth, November 27, 1967, Folder 12, Carton 1, Ghirardelli Square Architectural Records, The Bancroft Library, University of California, Berkeley (hereafter GSAR).

7. Halprin, "Statement on the New Sculpture in the Fountain at Ghirardelli Square."

8. Christa Robbins, "The Sensibility of Michael Fried," *Criticism* 60, no. 4 (Fall 2018): 433. As Robbins points out, James Meyer describes 1966, the year after Asawa received the commission, as "the season of the minimal," with multiple exhibitions on view and several essays legitimizing this formal language; see Meyer, *Minimalism: Art and Polemics in the Sixties* (New Haven: Yale University Press, 2001), 154.

9. When Asawa expressed doubt about the progress of the commission, Roth encouraged her to continue, reassuring her that if the casting processes did not work, he would buy the sculpture himself; William Roth to Ruth Asawa, July 31, 1967, Folder 4, Box 117, Asawa Papers.

10. Ruth Asawa, in "Art, Competence, and Citywide Cooperation for San Francisco," an oral history conducted in 1974 and 1976 by Harriet Nathan, Regional Oral History Office, The Bancroft Library, University of California, Berkeley, 1980, 85 (this quote) and 87 (for the reference in the following sentence).

11. Mrs. Ingram to President, Ghirardelli Square, March 27, 1968; Mrs. Gordon Grannis to San Francisco Art Commission, March 26, 1968. Folder 12, Carton 1, GSAR.

12. Isenberg, *Designing San Francisco*, 110.

13. Esther Newton, "Note to the Reader," in *Mother Camp: Female Impersonators in America* (Chicago: University of Chicago Press, 1972).

14. Andrea Jepson, "In Praise of Ruth Asawa," *California Living Magazine*, 7, published as part of the *San Francisco Examiner*, May 11, 1975.

15. Andrea Jepson, telephone interview with the author, December 15, 2020.

16. Jepson, "In Praise of Ruth Asawa," 7.

17. Pamela Allara, "'Mater' of Fact: Alice Neel's Pregnant Nudes," *American Art* 8, no. 2 (Spring 1994): 11.

18. Allara, "'Mater' of Fact," 17.

19. Allara, "'Mater' of Fact," 8. For a full account of how Neel's pregnant portraits and Asawa's *Andrea* stand within a broader field of feminist social history, see Allara, "'Mater' of Fact," and chapter 3 of Isenberg, *Designing San Francisco*.

20. Lucy Lippard, "The Pains and Pleasures of Rebirth: European-American Women's Body Art," repr. in Lippard, *From the Center: Feminist Essays on Women's Art* (New York: E. P. Dutton, 1976), 138.

21. Roi Partridge, quoted in Judith Fryer Davidov, *Women's Camera Work: Self/Body/Other in American Visual Culture* (Durham: Duke University Press, 1998), 466n71.

22. See Sandra Matthews and Laura Wexler's discussion of this study in their *Pregnant Pictures* (New York: Routledge, 2000), 19.

23. Matthews and Wexler, *Pregnant Pictures*, 98.

24. Allara, "'Mater' of Fact," 10.

25. Allara, "'Mater' of Fact," 10.

26. Halprin, "Statement on the New Sculpture in the Fountain at Ghirardelli Square."

27. Lawrence Halprin, *Cities* (1963; repr., Cambridge, MA: MIT Press, 1972), 221 and 9; italics in original.

28. Halprin, *Cities*, 7 (this and the following quotation).

29. Halprin, *Cities*, 9.

30. Halprin, *Cities*, 221; italics in original; 220 (quotation in previous sentence).

31. Marc Treib, "From the Garden: Lawrence Halprin and the Modern Landscape," *Landscape Journal* 31, no. 1/2 (2012): 22, 17.

32. Treib, "From the Garden," 22.

33. Warren M. Lemmon to Ruth Asawa, June 27, 1966, Folder 12, Carton 1, GSAR.

34. Halprin's suggestion to Roth as well as his request to select the commissioned artist can be found in Folder 12, Carton 1, GSAR; Halprin's drawings are housed at the Halprin Collection, Architectural Archives, University of Pennsylvania.

35. Lawrence Halprin, "Nature into Landscape into Art" (1988); cited in Alison B. Hirsch, *City Choreographer: Lawrence Halprin in Urban Renewal America* (Minneapolis: University of Minnesota Press, 2014), 68–69.

36. Mary Daly and Jane Caputi, *Websters' First New Intergalactic Wickedary of the English Language* (Boston: Beacon Press, 1987), 210.

37. Halprin, "Statement on the New Sculpture in the Fountain at Ghirardelli Square."

38. See Asawa's summary of the sculpture's realization, which included life drawing sessions of turtles at the California Academy of Sciences: Ruth Asawa to Warren Lemmon, March 18, 1968, Folder 12, Carton 1, GSAR. See also the pencil sketch in Folder 4, Box 78, Asawa Papers.

39. Andrea Jepson, cited in Marilyn Chase, *Everything She Touched: The Life of Ruth Asawa* (San Francisco: Chronicle Books, 2020), 117.

40. Untitled typed outline in Folder 8, Box 117, Asawa Papers. Asawa herself had an idea for a book on the sculpture, which also never materialized: a collection of the drawings made by a junior high school class when they sketched the fountain, which was especially meaningful for Asawa in the contrast between the drawn work and the students' written descriptions of *Andrea*. The drawings also establish a direct relationship between the sculpture and her work with the Alvarado School Arts Workshop, in which she continually emphasized "why art is such an essential part of understanding an individual, not just for self-expression and all of that that people go into now, but that it also is a part of the development of a person." See Nathan, "Art, Competence, and Citywide Cooperation for San Francisco," 85.

41. Jepson, cited in Chase, *Everything She Touched*, 117.

42. In this respect, *Andrea* could have been one of the case studies included in Victor I. Stoichita, *The Pygmalion Effect: From Ovid to Hitchcock*, trans. Alison Anderson (Chicago: University of Chicago Press, 2008), which provides an account of the relationship between this myth and the modern idea of the work of art as existing independently of its creator.

43. See Box 99, Asawa Papers.

44. Ruth Asawa and Mae Lee in a recorded interview on the mermaid fountain at Ghirardelli Square, audiocassette, April 4, 1997, Folder 10. Box 41, Asawa Papers.

45. Lawrence Halprin, draft circulated March 21, 1968, 014.IA.6221, Halprin Collection, Architectural Archives, University of Pennsylvania, cited in Isenberg, *Designing San Francisco*, 99 (this and the following reference).

46. Lawrence Halprin to Mr. William M. Roth, November 27, 1967, Folder 12, Carton 1, GSAR.

47. Halprin, "Statement on the New Sculpture in the Fountain at Ghirardelli Square"; Robbins, "The Sensibility of Michael Fried," 435.

48. Halprin, cited in Isenberg, *Designing San Francisco*, 112–113.

49. Halprin, "Statement on the New Sculpture in the Fountain at Ghirardelli Square."

50. Karl Kortum to Mr. William M. Roth, August 22, 1963, GSAR.

51. Isenberg, *Designing San Francisco*, 100. See also Halprin, *Cities*, 91.

52. Ruth Asawa, interviewed by Alison Isenberg, March 31, 2005, Folder 6, Box 117, Asawa Papers.

53. Isenberg, *Designing San Francisco*, 98.

54. Mrs. Samuel H. Coxe III to Roth, April 4, 1968; cited in Isenberg, *Designing San Francisco*, 101.

55. Marion Conrad to Temp, April 2, 1968, 0.14.IA.6221, Halprin Collection, Architectural Archives, University of Pennsylvania, cited in Isenberg, *Designing San Francisco*, 104.

56. "Best Public Orgy," *Bay Guardian*, July or August 2003, cited in Isenberg, *Designing San Francisco*, 104.

57. Naomi Wolf, *Promiscuities: The Secret Struggle for Womanhood* (New York: Random House, 1997), 38–39, cited in Isenberg, *Designing San Francisco*, 109 (this and the following quotations).

58. Asawa, "My Thoughts on the Ghirardelli Square Fountain Sculpture."

59. Fred Martin to Lawrence Halprin, March 26, 1968, Halprin Papers, Architectural Archives, University of Pennsylvania.

60. Lawrence Halprin to William M. Roth, November 27, 1967, GSAR.

61. Halprin, *Cities*, 87. In the 1990s, Asawa and Lee spoke about *Andrea*'s iconicity in the recorded interview on the mermaid fountain in the Asawa Papers.

62. Halprin, "Statement on the New Sculpture in the Fountain at Ghirardelli Square."

63. Susan Sontag, "Notes on 'Camp'" (1964), in *Against Interpretation, and Other Essays* (New York: Farrar, Straus and Giroux, 1966), 275 (this and the following quotes).

64. Newton, *Mother Camp*, 75.

65. Dorothy Dinnerstein, *The Mermaid and the Minotaur: Sexual Arrangements and Human Malaise* (New York: Harper & Row, 1976), 2.

66. Ree Morton, in Kate Horsfield and Lyn Blumental, "Ree Morton: An Interview" (1974), Video Data Bank, School of the Art Institute of Chicago, cited in *Ree Morton: Works 1971–1977*, ed. Sabine Folie (Vienna: Generali Foundation, 2009), 180.

67. Helen Molesworth, "Sentiment and Sentimentality: Ree Morton and Installation Art," in Folie, *Ree Morton: Works 1971–1977*, 20; Newton, *Mother Camp*, 105.

68. Marina Warner, *From the Beast to the Blond: On Fairy Tales and Their Tellers* (London: Vintage, 1994), 407.

69. Sontag, "Notes on 'Camp,'" 281, 290.

70. See Hans Christian Andersen's letters in *My Dear Boy: Gay Love Letters through the Centuries*, ed. Rictor Norton (San Francisco: Leyland Publications, 1998), as well as Gabrielle Bellot, "Dear Internet: The Little Mermaid Also Happens to Be Queer Allegory," *Literary Hub*, July 12, 2019, https://lithub.com/dear-internet-the-little-mermaid-also-happens-to-be-queer-allegory/.

71. Ruth Asawa and Mae Lee in a recorded interview on the mermaid fountain in the Asawa Papers.

72. Asawa, cited in George Draper, "Scorn for a New Sculpture," *San Francisco Chronicle*, March 26, 1968 (all quotations in this paragraph).

73. "Office phone messages," March 26, 1968, 014.IA.6221, Halprin Collection, Architectural Archives, University of Pennsylvania; Jeanne Fahey Crother to Asawa, March 26, 1968, Folder 5, Box 117, Asawa Papers.

74. Griselda Pollock, *Differencing the Canon: Feminist Desire and the Writing of Art's Histories* (London: Routledge, 1999), 18.

75. Lucy Lippard, "Eros Presumptive," *Hudson Review* 20, no. 1 (Spring 1967): 95.

76. J. Diane Radycki, *Paula Modersohn-Becker: The First Modern Woman Artist* (New Haven: Yale University Press, 2013), 173.

77. June Wayne, "The Creative Process: Artists, Carpenters, and the Flat Earth Society," *Craft Horizons* 36, no. 6 (October 1976): 31.

78. Robbins, "The Sensibility of Michael Fried," 447.

79. Anne M. Wagner, "Reading Minimal Art," in *Minimal Art: A Critical Anthology*, ed. Gregory Battcock (Berkeley: University of California Press, 1995), 13.

80. Robbins, "The Sensibility of Michael Fried," 432.

81. David Getsy, *Abstract Bodies: Sixties Sculpture in the Expanded Field of Gender* (Chicago: University of Chicago Press, 2023), 14.

PART III

1. Gerald Nordland, *Ruth Asawa: A Retrospective View*, exh. cat. (San Francisco: San Francisco Museum of Art, 1973), n.p.

2. See Asawa's handwritten notes on the form "The Mask Project," Folder 1, Box 168, Asawa Papers.

3. Ruth Asawa, interviewed by Paul Karlstrom, June 21, 2002, Archives of American Art, Smithsonian Institution.

4. Albert Lanier to Ruth Asawa, April 20, 1949, Ruth Asawa Lanier, Inc.

5. John Yau, "Ruth Asawa's Life Masks," in *Ruth Asawa: All Is Possible*, ed. Helen Molesworth, exh. cat. (New York: David Zwirner, 2022), 58.

6. Amy F. Ogata, *Designing the Creative Child: Playthings and Places in Midcentury America* (Minneapolis: University of Minnesota Press, 2013), xx.

7. Nancy Faber, "Ruth Asawa: Sculptor with a Mission," *Learning: The Magazine for Creative Teaching* (December 1973), 17.

8. Bruce Raskin, "Sculpturing with Junk," *Learning* (May/June 1974), 66; see also Diane Divoky, "Art Is a Many Splendored Thing," *Learning* (December 1973); and Kim Marshall, "The Desegregation of a Boston Classroom," *Learning* (September 1975).

9. Diane Divoky, "Where Are You Now? Charles Silberman," *Learning* (August/September 1975), 17.

10. Ruth Asawa, cited in Faber, "Ruth Asawa," 18.

11. Deloras Viñal, cited in Faber, "Ruth Asawa," 19.

12. Jordan Troeller, "Milk-Carton Sculpture: Ruth Asawa, Geodesic Geometry, and the Maternal Counterculture of the Alvarado School Arts Workshop," *Art Bulletin* 106, no. 3 (September 2024): 64–90.

13. "Interview with Sculptor Ruth Asawa," *Noe Valley Voice* 13, no. 10 (December 1989/January 1990): 20.

CHAPTER 6

1. Priscilla Barton, editorial in *Heresies* 6, no. 3, "Coming of Age" (1988): 2.

2. Andrea Jepson and Sharon Litzky, *The Alvarado Experience: Ten Years of a School-Community Art Program* (San Francisco: Alvarado School Arts Workshop, 1978), 5.

3. National Endowment for the Arts, Education Program, *Profile: The Alvarado School Art Workshop* (Washington, DC: National Endowment for the Arts, 1975), 3.

4. Shirley Dindjelis (?) to Ruth Asawa, June 1, 1970, Folder 5, Box 134, Asawa Papers.

5. Jepson and Litzky, *The Alvarado Experience*, 34.

6. Andrea Jepson, telephone interview with the author, December 15, 2020.

7. Charmalee Larkin, cited in Mildred Hamilton, "The Careers That Grew Out of the Arts Project," *San Francisco Examiner*, January 27, 1980, 123.

8. Lois Link, cited in Hamilton, "The Careers That Grew Out of the Arts Project," 123.

9. Andrea Jepson, correspondence with the author, February 16, 2022.

10. The statistic comes from a 1982–1983 calendar produced by the Workshop; Folder 2, Box 158, Asawa Papers.

11. Ruth Asawa, in "Art, Competence, and Citywide Cooperation for San Francisco," an oral history conducted in 1974 and 1976 by Harriet Nathan, Regional Oral History Office, The Bancroft Library, University of California, Berkeley, 1980, 177.

12. Ruth Asawa, in Nathan, "Art, Competence, and Citywide Cooperation for San Francisco," 171.

13. The examples include Emily Pringle, "The Artist as Lifelong Learner: Ruth Asawa and Education," in *Ruth Asawa: Citizen of the Universe*, ed. Emma Ridgway and Vibece Salthe (London: Thames and Hudson, 2022), 136–148. See also Woodbridge's essay published on the occasion of Asawa's retrospective at the de Young Museum in 2006: Sally B. Woodbridge, "The Alvarado Art Workshop," in *The Sculpture of Ruth Asawa: Contours in the Air*, ed. Daniell Cornell and Timothy Anglin Burgard, rev. ed. (San Francisco: Fine Arts Museums of San Francisco; Berkeley: University of California Press, 2020), 258–263.

14. Ruth Asawa in Robert Snyder (dir.), *Ruth Asawa: Of Forms and Growth* (Santa Barbara, CA: Masters and Masterworks, 1978), video, 30 min.

15. Addie Lanier, correspondence with the author, August 1, 2023.

16. Andrea Jepson, "In Praise of Ruth Asawa," *San Francisco Examiner and Chronicle*, May 11, 1975, 7.

17. Ursula K. Le Guin, "A Woman Writing, or The Fisherman's Daughter" (1987), cited in Shelley Fisher Fishkin, introduction to Tillie Olsen, *Silences* (1978; repr., New York: Feminist Press, 2003), xxiii.

18. Joan Abrahamson and Sally B. Woodbridge, *The Alvarado School-Community Art Program*, a self-published report conducted on the occasion of the program's five-year anniversary (1973), 9, Folder 2, Box 135, Asawa Papers (this and the preceding quotation).

19. Woodbridge, "The Alvarado Art Workshop," 258–259.

20. Peter Braunstein and Michael William Doyle, introduction to *Imagine Nation: The American Counterculture of the 1960s and '70s* (New York: Routledge, 2002), 9.

21. Susan Wels, *San Francisco: Arts for the City* (Berkeley: Hayday, 2013), 9.

22. Kenneth Rexroth, cited in Wels, *San Francisco*, 77.

23. Wels, *San Francisco*, 73.

24. Jean Rochin to Ruth Asawa, undated, Folder 3, Box 28, Asawa Papers.

25. "Request for Funds for Special Summer 1968 Arts Program," Folder 5, Box 84, Asawa Papers.

26. See Nathan, "Art, Competence, and Citywide Cooperation for San Francisco," 56.

27. Jane Jacobs, *The Death and Life of Great American Cities* (1961; New York: Vintage Books, 1992), 119.

28. Miwon Kwon, *One Place after Another: Site-Specific Art and Locational Identity* (Cambridge, MA: MIT Press, 2004), 132–134.

29. Ruth Asawa, "Report to the San Francisco Foundation," June 1974, 3, Folder 5, Box 135, Asawa Papers.

30. Asawa, quoted in Margene Morris, "Exhibit of Egg Crate Art," *San Francisco Examiner*, September 18, 1968, 22.

31. Paul Lanier, in "Interview with the Asawa Family," in Ridgway and Salthe, *Ruth Asawa: Citizen of the Universe*, 177.

32. Asawa, in Nathan, "Art, Competence, and Citywide Cooperation for San Francisco," 58.

33. Braunstein and Doyle, introduction to *Imagine Nation*, 9.

34. Jepson and Litzky, *The Alvarado Experience*, 9.

35. Interview with Theodore Scoarkes, principal, Mission High School, December 1974, cited in National Endowment for the Arts, *Profile: Alvarado School Art Workshop*, 6.

36. Asawa to Dr. Galant, principal of James Lick Junior High, November 23, 1968, Folder 3, Box 134, Asawa Papers.

37. Jenni Sorkin, *Live Form: Women, Ceramics, and Community* (Chicago: University of Chicago Press, 2016), 57.

38. Jepson and Litzky, *The Alvarado Experience*, 10.

39. Asawa, cited in Jepson and Litzky, *The Alvarado Experience*, 11.

40. Jepson and Litzky, *The Alvarado Experience*, 11. This and the previous quotation.

41. Walter Blum, "Greening the Schoolyards," *California Living Magazine*, published as part of the *San Francisco Examiner and Chronicle*, March 16, 1975, 7.

42. Dottye Dean, cited in Jepson and Litzky, *The Alvarado Experience*, 75.

43. Barbara Purcell, cited in Jepson and Litzky, *The Alvarado Experience*, 74.

44. Asawa, cited in Snyder (dir.), *Ruth Asawa: Of Forms and Growth*; see also Abrahamson and Woodbridge, *The Alvarado School-Community Art Program*, 67–68.

45. Dean, cited in Jepson and Litzky, *The Alvarado Experience*, 75.

46. See John Ahearn in Veronica Esposito, "'Over Time You Become Family': The Intimacy of Lifecasting," *The Guardian*, October 26, 2022. Molesworth's comparison can be found in *Ruth Asawa: All Is Possible*, ed. Helen Molesworth, exh. cat. (New York: David Zwirner, 2022), 12.

47. Kwon, *One Place after Another*, 97.

48. Kwon, *One Place after Another*, 96–97.

49. On the mural by Dewey Crumpler, a Black artist responding to student demands for more relevant sociopolitical content on their walls, see Yoko Clark, Chizu Hama, and Marshall Gordon, *California Murals* (Berkeley: Lancaster-Miller, 1979), 8.

50. Timothy Dreschler, "Street Subversion," in *Reclaiming San Francisco: History, Politics, Culture*, ed. James Brook, Chris Carlsson, and Nancy J. Peters (San Francisco: City Lights Books, 1998), 234.

51. See Phiz Mezey, "Mural Making," and Nancy Thompson, "Make Way for Murals," *Learning* (May/June 1976): 12–17. The quotations in this paragraph are from Mezey.

52. National Endowment for the Arts, *Profile: Alvarado School Art Workshop*, 2

53. Jepson and Litzky, *The Alvarado Experience*, 11–12 (this and the previous quotes in the paragraph).

54. Rand Quinn, *Class Action: Desegregation and Diversity in San Francisco Schools* (Minneapolis: University of Minnesota, 2020), 4. My summary account here relies on Quinn's study.

55. Cited in Quinn, *Class Action*, 2–3.

56. Abrahamson and Woodbridge, *The Alvarado School-Community Art Program*, 22, 26.

57. bell hooks, *Teaching to Transgress: Education as the Practice of Freedom* (New York: Routledge, 1994), 24.

58. Asawa, cited in Jepson, "In Praise of Ruth Asawa," 6.

59. Jepson and Litzky, *The Alvarado Experience*, 18.

60. John E. Coulson, "The First Year of Emergency School Aid Act (ESAA) Implementation, Preliminary Analysis," Office of Education, Washington DC, September 1975, xi, https://files.eric.ed.gov/fulltext/ED117229.pdf.

61. Asawa, in Nathan, "Art, Competence, and Citywide Cooperation for San Francisco," 166.

62. Asawa, in Nathan, "Art, Competence, and Citywide Cooperation for San Francisco," 180.

63. Asawa, in Nathan, "Art, Competence, and Citywide Cooperation for San Francisco," 191.

64. Kwon, *One Place after Another*, 95.

65. Marta Gutman, "Children of the Revolution: The Odessey School Experiment in Berkeley," in *Design Radicals: Spaces of Bay Area Counterculture*, ed. Greg Castillo and Lee Stickells (Minneapolis: University of Minnesota Press, forthcoming).

66. My summary of Project Other Ways relies on Chay Allen, "Allan Kaprow's Radical Pedagogy," *Performance Research* 21, no. 6 (2016): 7–12; Catherine Spencer, "Allan Kaprow's Lesson Plans," in *Beyond the Happening* (Manchester, UK: Manchester University Press, 2020), 31–80; and Allan Kaprow, "Success and Failure When Art Changes," in *Mapping the Terrain*, ed. Suzanne Lacey (Port Townsend, WA: Bay Press, 1995), 152–159. For a reading of these Happenings as more explicitly engaging this politicized context than has been previously argued, see Laura Routledge, "Reconsidering 'Art' and 'Life': The Multiple Entanglements of Allan Kaprow's Happenings," *Journal of Avant-Garde Studies* 1, no. 2 (August 2022): 243–268.

67. "November 3, 1966: Reactions, Perceptions to Movement Classes," Folder 6, Box 5, Anna Halprin Papers, Museum of Performance and Design, San Francisco.

68. Merry Renk, "Everett Project—Interior Metal Mural," Folder 1, Box 159, Asawa Papers.

69. Renk, "Everett Project—Interior Metal Mural."

70. Asawa, in Nathan, "Art, Competence, and Citywide Cooperation for San Francisco," 74.

71. Sally Woodbridge, cited in Hamilton, "The Careers That Grew Out of the Arts Project," 1.

72. Chandra Mohanty, "On Race and Voice: Challenges for Liberation Education in the 1990s," cited in hooks, *Teaching to Transgress*, 22.

73. Angela Garbes, *Essential Labor: Mothering as Social Change* (New York: HarperCollins, 2022), 38. Garbes cites research published by the Economic Policy Institute in 2020.

74. Garbes, *Essential Labor*, 11.

75. Nancy Thompson, cited in Jepson and Litzky, *The Alvarado Experience*, 34–35; italics in original.

76. Kwon, *One Place after Another*, 142; see also Rozsika Parker, *Torn in Two: The Experience of Maternal Ambivalence* (London: Virago, 1995).

77. Dan Borsuk, "Sculptor Sees Too Much Computer Education, Not Enough Art," *S.F. Progress*, October 10, 1984, A3.

78. Thompson, cited in Jepson and Litzky, *The Alvarado Experience*, 36; italics in original.

79. See John Kreidler, "The CETA Years, 1975–1980," in Cornell and Burgard, *The Sculpture of Ruth Asawa: Contours in the Air*, 264–267.

80. Asawa, cited in Peter Barnes, "Bringing Back the WPA," *New Republic*, March 15, 1975, 21

81. Lucy Lippard, "Foreword: Memory as Model," in *West of Center: Art and Counterculture Experiment in America, 1965–1977*, ed. Elissa Auther and Adam Lerner (Minneapolis: University of Minnesota Press, 2011), xi.

82. Robin Romanowski, cited in Kreidler, "The CETA Years," 266.

83. Barnes, "Bringing Back the WPA," 21.

84. See the report by the San Francisco Art Commission, "Neighborhood Arts Program and Alvarado Art Workshop: Documentation: Manpower Employees under CETA, March-May 1975," 3, Folder 7, Box 87, Asawa Papers.

85. First draft of the "Final Report: Task Panel on the Role of the Arts in Mental Health," submitted as part of The President's Commission on Mental Health, January 9, 1978, Folder 5, Box 90, Asawa Papers.

86. Silvia Federici, "Feminism and the Politics of the Commons in an Era of Primitive Accumulation," in *Re-enchanting the World: Feminism and the Politics of the Commons* (Oakland: PM Press, 2019), 110. This and the following quotation.

87. Asawa, draft statement to the task force assigned to The Role of the Artist in Mental Health, September 28, 1977, Folder 4, Box 90, Asawa Papers.

88. Kreidler, "The CETA Years," 265.

89. Virginia Maksymowicz and Blaise Tobia, "The Forgotten Federally Employed Artists," *Hyperallergic*, December 25, 2020, https://hyperallergic.com/610071/the-forgotten-federally-employed-artists/.

90. Judith Anderson, "A Life Immersed in Art and Affection," *San Francisco Chronicle*, February 8, 1982, 18.

91. Federici, "Feminism and the Politics of the Commons," 110.

92. Hamilton, "The Careers That Grew Out of the Arts Project," 1.

93. Garbes, *Essential Labor*, 37.

94. Asawa, in Snyder (dir.), *Ruth Asawa: Of Forms and Growth*.

CHAPTER 7

1. Marshall Kilduff, "Officials Promise Winos Won't Rule New Tenderloin Park," *San Francisco Chronicle*, April 23, 1985, 2.

2. Kilduff, "Officials Promise Winos Won't Rule New Tenderloin Park," 2.

3. Nils Norman, *The Contemporary Picturesque* (London: Book Works, 2000).

4. Kilduff, "Officials Promise Winos Won't Rule New Tenderloin Park," 2.

5. Alexander Fried, "Stop, Look and Pat It," *San Francisco Examiner*, February 4, 1973, 14.

6. Jane Jacobs, *The Death and Life of Great American Cities* (1961; repr., New York: Vintage Books, 1992), 87.

7. Jacobs, *The Death and Life of Great American Cities*, 95.

8. Judith Anderson, "A Life Immersed in Art and Affection," *San Francisco Chronicle*, February 8, 1982, 16.

9. Sally B. Woodbridge, *Ruth Asawa's San Francisco Fountain: Hyatt on Union Square* (San Francisco: self-published, 1973), 44.

10. Alfred Frankenstein, "Ruth Asawa's Valentine to the City," *San Francisco Chronicle*, February 14, 1973, San Francisco Examiner Archive, Asawa and Lanier File, San Francisco History Center, San Francisco Public Library.

11. Harriet Beecher Stowe, cited in Tillie Olsen, *Silences* (1978; repr., New York: Feminist Press, 2003), 204.

12. Tara McDowell, *The Householders: Robert Duncan and Jess* (Cambridge, MA: MIT Press, 2019), 37; Sara Ahmed, *Queer Phenomenology* (Durham: Duke University Press, 2006), 61.

13. Andrea Jepson, "In Praise of Ruth Asawa," *California Living Magazine*, 7, published as part of the *San Francisco Examiner*, May 11, 1975.

14. Ruth Miller, "Her Ingenious Way with Dough," *San Francisco Chronicle*, December 26, 1963, 26.

15. Diana L. Merritt, "Ruth Asawa: Artist and Mother" [unknown publication], c. 1969, Folder 4, Box 244, Asawa Papers.

16. See Annie Nakao, "Asawa Has Helped Mold Cultural Life of City," *San Francisco Chronicle*, April 29, 2003, newspaper clipping, Ephemera Collection, Ruth Asawa File, San Francisco Public Library.

17. Asawa, cited in Merritt, "Ruth Asawa: Artist and Mother."

18. Margaret White, "Christmas Claybake," *Ladies' Home Journal*, December 1964, 56–57.

19. "San Francisco Sits for a New Portrait . . . ," *Sunset Magazine*, October 1972, 99.

20. Ken Wong, "Kids Pat, Mold, and Shape at Dough-In," *San Francisco Examiner*, June 30, 1973, clipping in San Francisco Examiner Archive, Asawa and Lanier File, San Francisco Public Library.

21. Amy F. Ogata, *Designing the Creative Child: Places and Playthings in Midcentury America* (Minneapolis: University of Minnesota Press, 2013), 173.

22. Ogata, *Designing the Creative Child*, 177.

23. Paul J. Smith, oral history interview, April 19–20, 2010, unpaginated, Archives of American Art, Smithsonian Institution (this and the following quotation).

24. Asawa, cited in Merritt, "Ruth Asawa: Artist and Mother."

25. Susan Peterson, "Faux or Real Folk Art: The Story of Mingei," transcript of Dorothy Wilson Perkins Lecture, International Museum of Ceramic Art, Alfred University, October 26, 1999; cited in Jenni Sorkin, *Live Form: Women, Ceramics, and Community* (Chicago: University of Chicago Press, 2016), 205.

26. Sorkin, *Live Form*, 217.

27. Sorkin, *Live Form*, 218.

28. Lynne Cooke, "Boundary Trouble: Navigating Margin and Mainstream," in *Outliers and American Vanguard Art*, exh. cat. (Washington, DC: National Gallery of Art, 2018), 13. Cooke references here C. Lasch, "Mass Culture Reconsidered," *Democracy* 1, no. 4 (October 1981): 7–22.

29. Thomas Crow, *The Long March of Pop: Art, Music, and Design, 1930–1995* (New Haven: Yale University Press, 2014), 3.

30. Judith E. Stein, "A White-Haired Girl: A Feminist Reading," in *Grandma Moses in the 21st Century*, ed. Jane Kallir (New Haven: Yale University Press, 2001), 53–54.

31. Judith Friedlander, "Traditional Arts of Women in Mexico," *Heresies* (1978), cited in Elissa Auther, *String, Felt, Thread: The Hierarchy of Art and Craft in American Art* (Minneapolis: University of Minnesota Press, 2010), 101.

32. Anne Baring and Jules Cashford, *The Myth of the Goddess: Evolution of an Image* (London: Viking, 1991), 353.

33. Julia Bryan-Wilson, *Fray: Art and Textile Politics* (Chicago: University of Chicago Press, 2017), 45.

34. Alexandra Jacopetti, *Native Funk and Flash: An Emerging Folk Art* (San Francisco: Scrimshaw Press, 1974), 5.

35. Asawa, cited in "Ruth Asawa: Fountainhead," *San Francisco Examiner and Chronicle,* May 9, 1971, Folder 6, Box 118, Asawa Papers; cited in Marilyn Chase, *Everything She Touched: The Life of Ruth Asawa* (San Francisco: Chronicle Books, 2020), 121–122.

36. Woodbridge, *Ruth Asawa's San Francisco Fountain*, 3.

37. Ruth Asawa, in "Art, Competence, and Citywide Cooperation for San Francisco," an oral history conducted in 1974 and 1976 by Harriet Nathan, Regional Oral History Office, The Bancroft Library, University of California, Berkeley, 1980, 86.

38. Quoted in Mildred Hamilton, *San Francisco Examiner*, May 14, 1969, newspaper clipping, San Francisco Examiner Archive, Asawa and Lanier File, San Francisco Public Library. The album is in Box 99, Asawa Papers.

39. Woodbridge, *Ruth Asawa's San Francisco Fountain*, 4.

40. Sarah Archer, "From Maker to Market: Ruth Asawa Reappraised," *Journal of Modern Craft* 8, no. 2 (July 2015): 149–150.

41. Woodbridge, *Ruth Asawa's San Francisco Fountain*, 17.

42. Woodbridge, *Ruth Asawa's San Francisco Fountain*, 23.

43. Mildred Hamilton, "Posterity's Little Hands," *San Francisco Examiner*, September 19, 1972, 21, San Francisco Examiner Archive, Asawa and Lanier File, San Francisco Public Library.

44. Jacqueline Hoefer, "A Working Life," in *The Sculpture of Ruth Asawa: Contours in the Air*, ed. Daniell Cornell and Timothy Anglin Burgard, rev. ed. (San Francisco: Fine Arts Museums of San Francisco; Berkeley: University of California Press, 2020), 26.

45. Woodbridge, *Ruth Asawa's San Francisco Fountain*, 43.

46. Woodbridge, *Ruth Asawa's San Francisco Fountain*, 44.

47. Woodbridge, *Ruth Asawa's San Francisco Fountain*, 5.

48. "San Francisco Sits for a New Portrait . . . ," 98–99.

49. Archer, "From Maker to Market," 150.

50. Asawa, cited in Judith Anderson, "A Life Immersed in Art and Affection," *San Francisco Chronicle*, February 8, 1982, 16. Judy Chicago, cited in Elaine Levine, "Clay: Judy Chicago's Dinner Party," *Craft Horizons* (April 1979): 54; cited in Bryan-Wilson, *Fray*, 16.

51. R. Buckminster Fuller, typed sheet, "Ruth Asawa," January 18, 1982, Folder 1, Box 4, Asawa Papers.

52. Herb Caen, cited in Nakao, "Asawa Has Helped Mold Cultural Life of City."

53. Richard Serra, introduction to *The Destruction of Tilted Arc: Documents*, ed. Clara Weyergraf-Serra and Martha Buskirk (Cambridge, MA: MIT Press, 1991), 5.

54. "New San Francisco Fountain Is Succeeding as a People Pleaser," *Sunset Magazine* (August 1973), Box 132, Asawa Papers.

55. "Celebrating a City to Be Touched," *San Francisco Examiner*, May 3, 1998, Folder 2, Box 78, Asawa Papers.

56. Hamilton, "Posterity's Little Hands," 21.

57. Olga Gueft, "For Six Children and Sculpture," *Interiors* (July 1967), 96–99.

58. Sally Byrne Woodbridge, *John Galen Howard and the University of California: The Design of a Great Public University Campus* (Berkeley: University of California Press, 2002), 73.

59. Cathleen Rountree, "Ruth Asawa," in *On Women Turning 70: Honoring the Voices of Wisdom* (San Francisco: Jossey-Bass Publishers, 1999), 86.

60. Victoria Rosner, *Modernism and the Architecture of Private Life* (New York: Columbia University Press, 2005), 4.

61. Rebecca Jo Plant, *Mom: The Transformation of Motherhood in Modern America* (Chicago: University of Chicago Press, 2010), 7, 13, and 5 respectively.

62. Ruth Asawa, "Report to the San Francisco Foundation," June 1974, Folder 5, Box 135, Asawa Papers.

CONCLUSION

1. Albert Ten Eyck Gardner, "A Century of Women" (1948), cited in Daniel Belasco, *Women Artists in Midcentury America: A History in Ten Exhibitions* (London: Reaktion Books, 2024), 190.

2. Ruth Asawa to Albert Lanier, January 6, 1949, Ruth Asawa Lanier, Inc.

3. Helen Molesworth, "Sentiment and Sentimentality: Ree Morton and Installation Art," in *Ree Morton: Works 1971–1977*, ed. Sabine Folie (Vienna: Generali Foundation, 2009), 17.

4. For an overview of this movement, see Andrea Liss, *Feminist Art and the Maternal* (Minneapolis: University of Minnesota Press, 2009).

5. Tillie Olsen, *Silences* (1978; repr., New York: Feminist Press, 2003), 32; italics in original.

6. Lauren Elkin, "Why All the Books about Motherhood?," *Paris Review*, July 17, 2018, https://www.theparisreview.org/blog/2018/07/17/why-all-the-books-about-motherhood/. See also Hettie Judah, *How Not to Exclude Artist Mothers (and Other Parents)* (London: Lund Humphries, 2022).

7. See the artist's chronology in Folie, *Ree Morton: Works 1971–1977*, 182.

8. Susan Rubin Suleiman, "Writing and Motherhood," in *Mother Reader: Essential Writings on Motherhood*, ed. Moyra Davey (New York: Seven Stories Press, 2001), 128.

9 Suleiman, "Writing and Motherhood," 120.

10. Suleiman, "Writing and Motherhood," 117.

11. Julia Kristeva, "Un nouveau type d'intellectuel: Le dissident," *Tel Quel*, no. 74 (Winter 1977): 7; cited in Suleiman, "Writing and Motherhood," 120.

12. Lisa Baraitser, "Foreword," in *The Maternal in Creative Work*, ed. Elena Marchevska and Valerie Walkerdine (London: Routledge, 2021), xx.

13 Jacqueline Rose, *Mothers: An Essay on Love and Cruelty* (London: Faber and Faber, 2018), 79.

ILLUSTRATION CREDITS

Courtesy Altman-Siegel Gallery, San Francisco, CA, and The E. Mark Adams and Beth Van Hoesen Adams Trust. © 2025 Estate of Beth Van Hoesen/Artists Rights Society (ARS), New York: figures 0.4, 1.9, 4.3, 5.6, III.3, 6.5, page 192

Courtesy Architectural Archives, University of Pennsylvania: figure 5.7

Artwork © Aronson-Jalowetz Collection: figures 2.9, 5.14

Courtesy Ruth Asawa Lanier, Inc.: figures 0.2, 0.6, I.2, 1.2, 1.3, 1.11, 2.4, 2.13, 3.1, 4.14, 5.1, 5.8, 6.1, 6.3, 6.4, 6.6, 6.7, 6.11, 6.12, 6.13, 6.14, 6.15, 6.16, 7.1, 7.2, 7.3, 7.4, 7.5, 7.6, 7.7, 7.8, 7.13, pages 232, 270

Artwork © 2025 Ruth Asawa Lanier, Inc./Artists Rights Society, New York. Courtesy David Zwirner: figures 0.1, 0.3, 0.8, 0.9, 0.10, 0.11, 0.12, I.1, I.2, I.3, 1.1, 1.5, 1.6, 1.11, 1.12, 1.13, 1.14, 2.1, 2.2, 2.4, 2.5, 2.6, 2.7, 2.10, 2.12, 2.14, II.1, II.2, II.4, II.5, 3.8, 3.9, 3.11, 3.12, 3.13, 3.17, 3.18, 3.19, 3.20, 3.21, 4.1, 4.2, 4.5, 4.6, 4.9, 4.12, 4.13, 4.14, 4.15, 4.16, 4.17, 5.1, 5.2, 5.3, 5.5, 5.8, 5.9, 5.10, 5.11, 5.12, III.1, III.2, 6.2, 6.14, 7.10, 7.11, 7.12, 7.13, 7.14, 8.1, pages vi, viii, 42, 76, 160, 232, 302

Artwork © Isabel Case Borgatta: figure 0.7

Artwork © 2025 Aiko Cuneo: figure 7.8

Photo © Hudson Cuneo: figure 2.10

Photo © Laurence Cuneo: figures 0.8, 2.12, 4.12, 5.12, III.2, 7.11, 7.13, 7.14, 8.1, page viii

Photo © 2025 Imogen Cunningham Trust/www.ImogenCunningham.com: figures 0.5, 1.7, 1.13, 1.14, II.3, II.4, II.5, 3.3, 3.5, 3.6, 3.7, 3.8, 3.10, 3.15, 3.18, 3.19, 3.21, 3.22, 3.23, 4.4, 4.9, page 120

Photos © Imogen Cunningham Trust and Rondal Partridge Archive. Courtesy Aiko and Laurence Cuneo: figure 3.16

Photo © Nat Farbman/The LIFE Picture Collection/Shutterstock: figure 1.5

Photo © Andreas Feininger/The LIFE Picture Collection/Shutterstock: figure 0.7

Photo © 2025 Estate of Paul Hassel: figures I.1, I.2, 1.11, 4.14

Courtesy Matt Jepson: figure 4.13

Photo © Estate of Warner Jepson: figures 5.1, 5.8

Courtesy The Estate of Alice Neel and David Zwirner. © The Estate of Alice Neel: figures 3.4, 5.4

Photo © Rondal Partridge Archive: figure 7.10

Photo © Joan Pearson Watkins Trust: figure 0.11

Courtesy Baunnie Sea: figures 2.3, 4.10

Photo © Joan Pearson Watkins Trust: figure 7.4

Courtesy Ragland Watkins and Ruth Asawa Lanier, Inc.: figure 1.4

CAPTIONS TO THE OPENING IMAGES

page vi: Ruth Asawa, *Untitled* (Mae Lee), detail of *Untitled* (LC.012, Wall of Masks), c. 1966–2000. Ceramic, bisque-fired clay, 4⅞ × 4⅞ × 2¾ in. Cantor Arts Center at Stanford University; William Alden Campbell and Martha Campbell Art Acquisition Fund. Conservation made possible by the Robert Mondavi Family Fund at the Cantor Arts Center and the Asian American Art Initiative Fund.

page viii: Ruth Asawa's son Paul Lanier with the partially assembled *San Francisco Fountain* (PC.004) in the garden of Asawa's Noe Valley home, San Francisco, CA, c. 1972 (detail). Photo: Laurence Cuneo. Special Collections, Stanford University.

page 42: Ruth Asawa, *Untitled* (MI.107, Cityscape), c. 1958 (detail). Black ink on newsprint, 9 × 30 in. Private collection.

page 76: Ruth Asawa, *Untitled* (S.784), c. 1948–1949 (detail). Copper wire, 14 × 20 × 2½ in. The Josef and Anni Albers Foundation, 1976.30.3. Photo: Tim Nighswander / Imaging4Art.

page 120: Imogen Cunningham, *Child in Landscape*, 1966 (detail). Gelatin silver print mounted in album, 8½ × 8½ in. Collection of Pamela Woodbridge.

page 160: Ruth Asawa, *Laurie Happy Birthday* (WC.282, Four Red Opium Poppies and Pods), 1991 (detail). Watercolor paint on coated paper, 12 × 10½ in. Private collection.

page 192: Beth Van Hoesen, *Twins*, 1987 (detail). Linocut: printer's ink on paper, 7 × 4⅞ in. Private collection. Photo: M. Lee Fatherree.

page 232: Cover of a brochure on container gardening produced by the Alvarado School Arts Workshop, with Ruth Asawa's drawing *Mai Arbegast's Sunflower* (PF.277), c. 1976 (detail). Special Collections, Stanford University.

page 270: Students of Redding School, San Francisco, inspecting *Redding School, Self-Portrait* (PC.007; 1984) during its dedication on May 1, 1985 (detail). Photo: Clarence Towers. Special Collections, Stanford University.

page 302: Ruth Asawa, *Untitled* (LC.031, Female Torso), no date. Cast plaster, 17 × 14½ × 12 in. Private collection.

INDEX

Page numbers in *italics* refer to illustrations.

Bauhaus, 11, 86, 96, 183, 204, 255. *See also* Institute of Design

Bay Guardian, 214

Beat movement, 60, 62

Beauvoir, Simone de, 116, 324n11

Benderson, Nanny, 92

Berkeley, 44, 254–256, 299. *See also* University of California, Berkeley

Bethany Senior Center, 189, 244

Biała, Janice, 14

Bielawski, Eugene, 88

Bill, Max, 134

biomorphism, 185, 186, 206

Black Mountain College, 46–53, 57, 92, 94, 96, 317n43
    RA at, 1, 2, 19–20, 46–47, 52–53, 79, 82, 88, 92, 96, 168, 171, 186, 244, 253–254, 299, 314n3

Bloom, Harold, 158

body art, 200

Boeddeker, Alfred, 272–273

bohemianism, 17, 44, 46, 50–55, 69, 71
    Beat, 60, 62
    motherhood and children antithetical to, 44, 52, 55, 65

Borgatta, Isabel Case, 15–17, *16*

Botticelli, Sandro, 285–286

Bourdieu, Pierre, 200

Bourgeois, Louise, 13, 14, 54–55, 158

bourgeois domesticity and normativity, 44, 52

Brancusi, Constantin, 86, 121

Braque, Georges, 28, 158

Braunstein, Peter, 239

breastfeeding, 85, 137–138, 304
    Andrea and, 193–195, 198, 208, 213–214

Brennan, Roi, 210

bronze, 305

bronze casting, 3, 6, 25–28, 101, 231, 249, 288. *See also Andrea*; *San Francisco Fountain*

Broude, Norma, 11

Brown, Joan, 2

Brown, Judith, 85

Brown, Meredith A., 6, 33

Brown, Trisha, 18

Brownley, Martine, 122

Bryan-Wilson, Julia, 286

Bryson, Norman, 176

Buller, Rachel Epp, 7

Burchard, Jerry, 142

Burgess, Brio, 316n25

Burnham, Jack, 180–182, 185

Burns, Judy, 268

Butler, Judith, 100

Butler, Reg, 14–15, 186

Bylin, Mary, 294

Caen, Herb, 296

Calder, Alexander, 82, 85–86

California College of Arts and Crafts, 106

California Redwood Association, 288

California School of Fine Arts, 26, 215

California State University, Fullerton, 106

Cameron, Julia Margaret, 129, 130

camp, 51, 89, 212–218, 220
    Andrea as, 119, 196, 198, 212–217, 223

Campbell, Joseph, 207

Capricorn Asunder Gallery, 3, 25, 103

Caro, Anthony, 212

Carter, Jimmy, 265

Cashford, Jules, 285

Cassatt, Mary, 127

casting. *See* bronze casting; concrete; life casts; plaster

ceramics, 10, *12*, 13, 22, 25, 40, 77, 217–218, 244, 284–286, 296. *See also* Watkins, Joan Pearson
    Alvarado Mosaic Mural, 246–249
    "bread dough" as alternative to, 279, 286
    masks, 225–226, 246

Chadwick, Whitney, 122–123

chalkboard, *34*, 35, 37, 107, 191, 315n13

Chardin, Jean Siméon, 69

Chicago, Judy, 79, 296, 304

childbirth, 113–114, 116, 200, 324n11

childcare, 3, 10, 37, 64, 85

childhood, 26, 28, 37, 133, 142, 149, 195, 297
    depictions of, 26, 28, 116, 123, 130, 149

childrearing, 28, 35, 185

children's art, 35, 66, 116, 123, 297

Christensen, June Lane, 92–94, *93*, 321n56

Christian Science Monitor, 88, 149–152, 321n41

Chung, Andrea, 304

Citret, Diara Crane, 202

Cixous, Hélène, 116, 324n11

Clark, Annette, 234

Clark, Larry, 142

Clark, Lygia, 134

clutter, 28, 66

Coe, Gertrude Walsh, 146

collaboration, 3, 122–123, 146, 240. *See also Andrea*; Asawa, Ruth, children; Cunningham, Imogen; Lanier, Albert; *San Francisco Fountain*; Tolk-Watkins, Peggy
    Alvarado School Arts Workshop and, 228, 236
    artist-mother and, 22, 30, 158, 304

Comprehensive Employment and Training Act (CETA) (1973), 261–262, 265

concrete, life casts in, 3, 28, 157, 246, 273

National Highway Act (1956), 60
Neel, Alice, 6, 7, 13–14, 17, 18, 30, 35
    Pregnant Maria, 201, *201*
    pregnant nudes, 200, 201, 208
    Richard in High Chair, 123, *126*
Neighborhood Arts Program, 239–240
Nelson, Maggie, 30
neo-concrete movement, 134
Neumann, Erich, 285
Newton, Esther, 198, 216, 218
New Woman, 163
New York, 3, 13, 18, 51, 246, *248*, 265
    art world, 3, 25, 38, 46, 65
New York Times, 14, 30, 38
Nilsson, Lennart, 207
Nin, Anaïs, 14
Nixon, Mignon, 54–55, 158
Nixon, Nicholas, 226
Nixon, Richard M., 261, 288
Nochlin, Linda, 4, 54
non-art and non-artist, 3, 6, 79, 96, 109, 241
Nordland, Gerald, 100, 173, 175, 180, 226, 314n3
Norman, Nils, 271
Nude (RA), 200
nudes, 133, 286
    Andrea and, 193–195, 214, 217, 222
    children, 128–129, 131–133, 158
    pregnant, 198–202, 208
nursing. *See* breastfeeding

Oakland Art Museum, 80
Ockman, Joan, 46
Ogata, Amy, 229, 279
O'Keeffe, Georgia, 168
Olsen, Tillie, 7, 14, 15, 19, 25, 113, 141, 276, 304, 306
Onslow Ford, Gordon, 52
Opie, Catherine, 304
O'Reilly, Andrea, 7
origami, 22, 50
originality, 28, 38, 89, 303, 305, 314n3
    casting and, 4, 145
Ostriker, Alicia, 17
Ovid (Publius Ovidius Naso), 208, 257
Ozawa, Seiji, 290

paperfolding, 3, 4, 10, 25, 28, 83, 100–101, 103, *104*, 322n78
Pardiñas, Alfonso, 246
Paris Review, 304
Park, Shelley, 19
Parker, Rozsika, 37, 79, 261
Partridge, Gryffyd, 127–129

Partridge, Meg, 131
Partridge, Roi, 13, 133, 200
Partridge, Rondal, 131, 145, 146, *147*, *289*
Pastorino, Blanche, 228
patriarchy, 74, 161, 198, 200, 207, 216, 218, 222, 285
pattern, 80–83, 136, 139, *140*, 141, *141*, 176, 183, 294
Paxton, Steve, 18
Peridot Gallery, New York, 13, 35, 94, 186
permutations, 28, 80, 156–157, 172–173
Perry, Ruth, 122
Peterson, Susan, 284
Phillips, Julie, 7, 50, 54
photography, 88, 142–146, 228. *See also* Asawa, Ruth: photographs of, and related to; baby albums; Cunningham, Imogen; family: snapshots and albums; pictorialism; straight photography
Picasso, Pablo, 28, 158
Pickett, Joseph, 285
pictorialism, 11, 121, 127, 129, 136, 146
Plant, Rebecca Jo, 11, 55, 300
plants and trees
    Andrea and, 195, 207
    artist-mothers' depictions of, 162, 168, 193
    botanical illustration, 163–164, 186, 187
    branching, 2, 170–171, 173–174, 189, 305
    Cunningham's knowledge and depictions of, 25, 130, 131, 168–169, 294
    Ghirardelli Square, Halprin's and RA's interventions, 204, 206, 213, 217, 222
    Metal Mural and, 257
    RA's depictions of, 10, 25, 77, 119, 162, 163, 168, 173, 176
plaster, life casts in, 3, 28, 111, *112*, 142, 193, *194*, 195, 208, 225, 246, 257
play of light, 35, 149
Pliny the Elder (Gaius Plinius Secundus), 163
Pointon, Marcia, 145
Pollock, Griselda, 222
Pollock, Jackson, 8
Pond Farm, 46, 94–96, 99, 106, 244, 322nn66–67
pop art, 284–285, 297
Poppy (RA), 169
Porset, Clara, 79
Porter, Jenelle, 94
Potvin, John, 88–89
pregnancy, 11, 14, 18, 109, 207, 316n25
    Cunningham's photograph of RA during, 136–138, *137*
    Cunningham's photographs of Renk during, 114, *115*, 116